Microsoft® Office 365™
ACCESS® 2016

COMPREHENSIVE

Philip J. Pratt
Mary Z. Last

CENGAGE

SHELLY CASHMAN SERIES®

Australia • Brazil • Mexico • Singapore • United Kingdom • United States

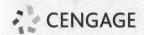

Microsoft® Access® 2016: Comprehensive
Philip J. Pratt and Mary Z. Last

SVP, General Manager: Balraj S. Kalsi

Product Director: Kathleen McMahon

Senior Product Team Manager: Lauren Murphy

Product Team Manager: Andrea Topping

Senior Director, Development: Julia Caballero

Product Development Manager: Leigh Hefferon

Managing Content Developer: Emma F. Newsom

Developmental Editor: Amanda Brodkin

Product Assistant: Erica Chapman

Manuscript Quality Assurance: Jeffrey Schwartz, John Freitas, Serge Palladino, Susan Pedicini, Danielle Shaw, Chris Scriver

Production Director: Patty Stephan

Senior Content Project Manager: Stacey Lamodi

Manufacturing Planner: Julio Esperas

Designer: Diana Graham

Text Designer: Joel Sadagursky

Cover Template Designer: Diana Graham

Cover image(s): karawan/Shutterstock.com; Click Bestsellers/Shutterstock.com

Compositor: Lumina Datamatics, Inc.

Vice President, Marketing: Brian Joyner

Marketing Director: Michele McTighe

Marketing Manager: Stephanie Albracht

Microsoft and the Office logo are either registered trademarks or trademarks of Microsoft Corporation in the United States and/ or other countries. Cengage Learning is an independent entity from the Microsoft Corporation, and not affiliated with Microsoft in any manner.

The material in this book was written using Microsoft Office 2016 and was Quality Assurance tested before the publication date. As Microsoft continually updates Office 2016 and Office 365, your software experience may vary slightly from what is seen in the printed text.

Mac users: If you're working through this product using a Mac, some of the steps may vary. Additional information for Mac users is included with the data files for this product.

For product information and technology assistance, contact us at
**Cengage Customer & Sales Support, 1-800-354-9706
or support.cengage.com.**

For permission to use material from this text or product, submit all
requests online at **www.cengage.com/permissions.**

Library of Congress Control Number: 2016943178

Soft-cover Edition ISBN: 978-1-305-87063-5

Loose-leaf Edition ISBN: 978-1-337-25107-5

Cengage
20 Channel Street
Boston, MA 02210
USA

Cengage is a leading provider of customized learning solutions with employees residing in nearly 40 different countries and sales in more than 125 countries around the world. Find your local representative at: **www.cengage.com.**

Cengage products are represented in Canada by Nelson Education, Ltd.

To learn more about Cengage platforms and services, register or access your online learning solution, or purchase materials for your course, visit **www.cengage.com.**

Printed at CLDPC, USA, 06-18

Microsoft® Office 365™
ACCESS® 2016

COMPREHENSIVE

Contents

Productivity Apps for School and Work

OneNote
Sway
Office Mix
Edge

Corinne Hoisington

Lochlan keeps track of his class notes, football plays, and internship meetings with OneNote.

Zoe is using the annotation features of Microsoft Edge to take and save web notes for her research paper.

Nori is creating a Sway site to highlight this year's activities for the Student Government Association.

Hunter is adding interactive videos and screen recordings to his PowerPoint resume.

© Rawpixel/Shutterstock.com

Being computer literate no longer means mastery of only Word, Excel, PowerPoint, Outlook, and Access. To become technology power users, Hunter, Nori, Zoe, and Lochlan are exploring Microsoft OneNote, Sway, Mix, and Edge in Office 2016 and Windows 10.

In this Module

Learn to use productivity apps!
Links to companion **Sways**, featuring **videos** with hands-on instructions, are located on www.cengage.com.

Introduction to OneNote 2016

notebook | section tab | To Do tag | screen clipping | note | template | Microsoft OneNote Mobile app | sync | drawing canvas | inked handwriting | Ink to Text

Bottom Line
- OneNote is a note-taking app for your academic and professional life.
- Use OneNote to get organized by gathering your ideas, sketches, webpages, photos, videos, and notes in one place.

As you glance around any classroom, you invariably see paper notebooks and notepads on each desk. Because deciphering and sharing handwritten notes can be a challenge, Microsoft OneNote 2016 replaces physical notebooks, binders, and paper notes with a searchable, digital notebook. OneNote captures your ideas and schoolwork on any device so you can stay organized, share notes, and work with others on projects. Whether you are a student taking class notes as shown in Figure 1 or an employee taking notes in company meetings, OneNote is the one place to keep notes for all of your projects.

Figure 1: OneNote 2016 notebook

Each **notebook** is divided into sections, also called **section tabs**, by subject or topic.

Use **To Do tags**, icons that help you keep track of your assignments and other tasks.

Type on a page to add a **note**, a small window that contains text or other types of information.

Personalize a page with a **template**, or stationery.

Write or draw directly on the page using drawing tools.

Pages can include pictures such as **screen clippings**, images from any part of a computer screen.

Attach files and enter equations so you have everything you need in one place.

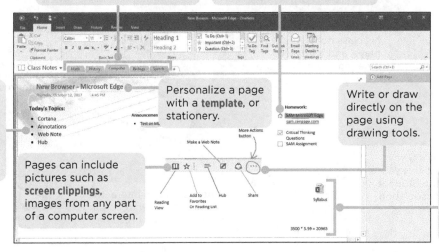

Creating a OneNote Notebook

OneNote is divided into sections similar to those in a spiral-bound notebook. Each OneNote notebook contains sections, pages, and other notebooks. You can use One-Note for school, business, and personal projects. Store information for each type of project in different notebooks to keep your tasks separate, or use any other organization that suits you. OneNote is flexible enough to adapt to the way you want to work.

When you create a notebook, it contains a blank page with a plain white background by default, though you can use templates, or stationery, to apply designs in categories such as Academic, Business, Decorative, and Planners. Start typing or use the buttons on the Insert tab to insert notes, which are small resizable windows that can contain text, equations, tables, on-screen writing, images, audio and video recordings, to-do lists, file attachments, and file printouts. Add as many notes as you need to each page.

Syncing a Notebook to the Cloud

OneNote saves your notes every time you make a change in a notebook. To make sure you can access your notebooks with a laptop, tablet, or smartphone wherever you are, OneNote uses cloud-based storage, such as OneDrive or SharePoint. **Microsoft OneNote Mobile app**, a lightweight version of OneNote 2016 shown in Figure 2, is available for free in the Windows Store, Google Play for Android devices, and the AppStore for iOS devices.

If you have a Microsoft account, OneNote saves your notes on OneDrive automatically for all your mobile devices and computers, which is called **syncing**. For example, you can use OneNote to take notes on your laptop during class, and then

Learn to use OneNote!
Links to companion **Sways**, featuring **videos** with hands-on instructions, are located on www.cengage.com.

open OneNote on your phone to study later. To use a notebook stored on your computer with your OneNote Mobile app, move the notebook to OneDrive. You can quickly share notebook content with other people using OneDrive.

Figure 2: Microsoft OneNote Mobile app

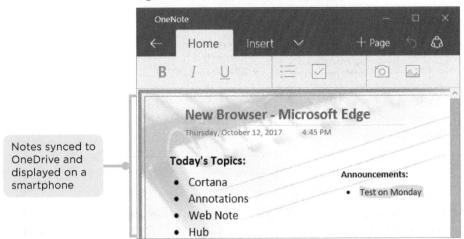

Notes synced to OneDrive and displayed on a smartphone

Taking Notes

Use OneNote pages to organize your notes by class and topic or lecture. Beyond simple typed notes, OneNote stores drawings, converts handwriting to searchable text and mathematical sketches to equations, and records audio and video.

OneNote includes drawing tools that let you sketch freehand drawings such as biological cell diagrams and financial supply-and-demand charts. As shown in Figure 3, the Draw tab on the ribbon provides these drawing tools along with shapes so you can insert diagrams and other illustrations to represent your ideas. When you draw on a page, OneNote creates a **drawing canvas**, which is a container for shapes and lines.

On the Job Now

OneNote is ideal for taking notes during meetings, whether you are recording minutes, documenting a discussion, sketching product diagrams, or listing follow-up items. Use a meeting template to add pages with content appropriate for meetings.

Figure 3: Tools on the Draw tab

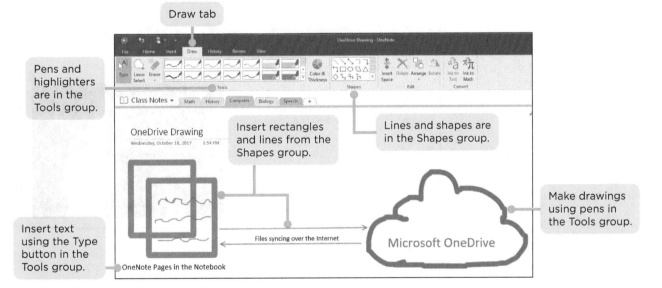

Draw tab

Pens and highlighters are in the Tools group.

Insert rectangles and lines from the Shapes group.

Lines and shapes are in the Shapes group.

Make drawings using pens in the Tools group.

Insert text using the Type button in the Tools group.

Files syncing over the Internet

Microsoft OneDrive

OneNote Pages in the Notebook

Converting Handwriting to Text

When you use a pen tool to write on a notebook page, the text you enter is called **inked handwriting**. OneNote can convert inked handwriting to typed text when you use the **Ink to Text** button in the Convert group on the Draw tab, as shown in Figure 4. After OneNote converts the handwriting to text, you can use the Search box to find terms in the converted text or any other note in your notebooks.

Figure 4: Converting handwriting to text

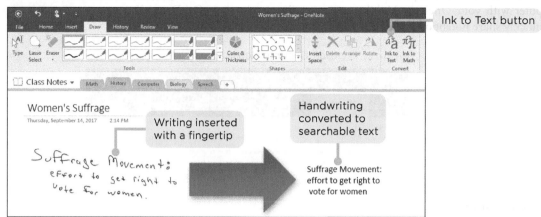

Ink to Text button

Writing inserted with a fingertip

Handwriting converted to searchable text

Suffrage Movement: effort to get right to vote for women

Recording a Lecture

If your computer or mobile device has a microphone or camera, OneNote can record the audio or video from a lecture or business meeting as shown in **Figure 5**. When you record a lecture (with your instructor's permission), you can follow along, take regular notes at your own pace, and review the video recording later. You can control the start, pause, and stop motions of the recording when you play back the recording of your notes.

Figure 5: Video inserted in a notebook

Record Video button

Audio & Video Recording tab

Video recording

Math Lecture video file

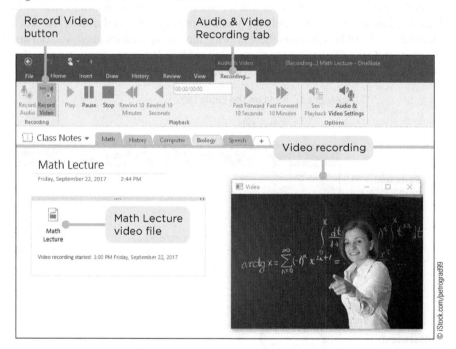

© iStock.com/petrograd99

Try This Now

Learn to use OneNote!
Links to companion **Sways**, featuring **videos** with hands-on instructions, are located on www.cengage.com.

1: Taking Notes for a Week

As a student, you can get organized by using OneNote to take detailed notes in your classes. Perform the following tasks:

    a. Create a new OneNote notebook on your Microsoft OneDrive account (the default location for new notebooks). Name the notebook with your first name followed by "Notes," as in **Caleb Notes**.

    b. Create four section tabs, each with a different class name.

    c. Take detailed notes in those classes for one week. Be sure to include notes, drawings, and other types of content.

    d. Sync your notes with your OneDrive. Submit your assignment in the format specified by your instructor.

2: Using OneNote to Organize a Research Paper

You have a research paper due on the topic of three habits of successful students. Use OneNote to organize your research. Perform the following tasks:

    a. Create a new OneNote notebook on your Microsoft OneDrive account. Name the notebook **Success Research**.

    b. Create three section tabs with the following names:

- **Take Detailed Notes**
- **Be Respectful in Class**
- **Come to Class Prepared**

    c. On the web, research the topics and find three sources for each section. Copy a sentence from each source and paste the sentence into the appropriate section. When you paste the sentence, OneNote inserts it in a note with a link to the source.

    d. Sync your notes with your OneDrive. Submit your assignment in the format specified by your instructor.

3: Planning Your Career

Note: This activity requires a webcam or built-in video camera on any type of device.

Consider an occupation that interests you. Using OneNote, examine the responsibilities, education requirements, potential salary, and employment outlook of a specific career. Perform the following tasks:

    a. Create a new OneNote notebook on your Microsoft OneDrive account. Name the notebook with your first name followed by a career title, such as **Kara - App Developer**.

    b. Create four section tabs with the names **Responsibilities, Education Requirements, Median Salary**, and **Employment Outlook**.

    c. Research the responsibilities of your career path. Using OneNote, record a short video (approximately 30 seconds) of yourself explaining the responsibilities of your career path. Place the video in the Responsibilities section.

    d. On the web, research the educational requirements for your career path and find two appropriate sources. Copy a paragraph from each source and paste them into the appropriate section. When you paste a paragraph, OneNote inserts it in a note with a link to the source.

    e. Research the median salary for a single year for this career. Create a mathematical equation in the Median Salary section that multiplies the amount of the median salary times 20 years to calculate how much you will possibly earn.

    f. For the Employment Outlook section, research the outlook for your career path. Take at least four notes about what you find when researching the topic.

    g. Sync your notes with your OneDrive. Submit your assignment in the format specified by your instructor.

Introduction to Sway

Sway site | responsive design | Storyline | card | Creative Commons license | animation emphasis effects | Docs.com

Expressing your ideas in a presentation typically means creating PowerPoint slides or a Word document. Microsoft Sway gives you another way to engage an audience. Sway is a free Microsoft tool available at Sway.com or as an app in Office 365. Using Sway, you can combine text, images, videos, and social media in a website called a **Sway site** that you can share and display on any device. To get started, you create a digital story on a web-based canvas without borders, slides, cells, or page breaks. A Sway site organizes the text, images, and video into a **responsive design**, which means your content adapts perfectly to any screen size as shown in **Figure 6**. You store a Sway site in the cloud on OneDrive using a free Microsoft account.

Figure 6: Sway site with responsive design

You can display a Sway presentation in a web browser.

Sway uses responsive design to make sure pages fit perfectly on any device.

© iStock.com/marinello, © iStock.com/marekuliasz

Creating a Sway Presentation

You can use Sway to build a digital flyer, a club newsletter, a vacation blog, an informational site, a digital art portfolio, or a new product rollout. After you select your topic and sign into Sway with your Microsoft account, a **Storyline** opens, providing tools and a work area for composing your digital story. See **Figure 7**. Each story can include text, images, and videos. You create a Sway by adding text and media content into a Storyline section, or **card**. To add pictures, videos, or documents, select a card in the left pane and then select the Insert Content button. The first card in a Sway presentation contains a title and background image.

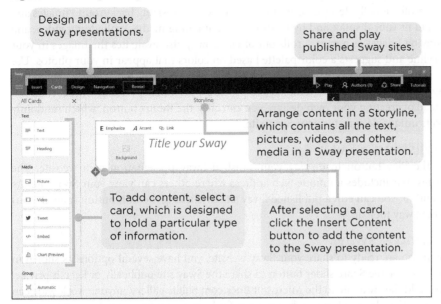

Design and create Sway presentations.

Share and play published Sway sites.

Arrange content in a Storyline, which contains all the text, pictures, videos, and other media in a Sway presentation.

To add content, select a card, which is designed to hold a particular type of information.

After selecting a card, click the Insert Content button to add the content to the Sway presentation.

Adding Content to Build a Story

As you work, Sway searches the Internet to help you find relevant images, videos, tweets, and other content from online sources such as Bing, YouTube, Twitter, and Facebook. You can drag content from the search results right into the Storyline. In addition, you can upload your own images and videos directly in the presentation. For example, if you are creating a Sway presentation about the market for commercial drones, Sway suggests content to incorporate into the presentation by displaying it in the left pane as search results. The search results include drone images tagged with a **Creative Commons license** at online sources as shown in Figure 8. A Creative Commons license is a public copyright license that allows the free distribution of an otherwise copyrighted work. In addition, you can specify the source of the media. For example, you can add your own Facebook or OneNote pictures and videos in Sway without leaving the app.

On the Job Now

If you have a Microsoft Word document containing an outline of your business content, drag the outline into Sway to create a card for each topic.

Figure 8: Images in Sway search results

Select the source of media objects

Information about Creative Commons licenses

Storyline title

The Market for Commercial Drones

Drag an image to the picture placeholder box

Suggested images in the search results

On the Job Now

If your project team wants to collaborate on a Sway presentation, click the Authors button on the navigation bar to invite others to edit the presentation.

Designing a Sway

Sway professionally designs your Storyline content by resizing background images and fonts to fit your display, and by floating text, animating media, embedding video, and removing images as a page scrolls out of view. Sway also evaluates the images in your Storyline and suggests a color palette based on colors that appear in your photos. Use the Design button to display tools including color palettes, font choices, **animation emphasis effects**, and style templates to provide a personality for a Sway presentation. Instead of creating your own design, you can click the Remix button, which randomly selects unique designs for your Sway site.

Publishing a Sway

Use the Play button to display your finished Sway presentation as a website. The Address bar includes a unique web address where others can view your Sway site. As the author, you can edit a published Sway site by clicking the Edit button (pencil icon) on the Sway toolbar.

Sharing a Sway

When you are ready to share your Sway website, you have several options as shown in Figure 9. Use the Share slider button to share the Sway site publically or keep it private. If you add the Sway site to the Microsoft **Docs.com** public gallery, anyone worldwide can use Bing, Google, or other search engines to find, view, and share your Sway site. You can also share your Sway site using Facebook, Twitter, Google+, Yammer, and other social media sites. Link your presentation to any webpage or email the link to your audience. Sway can also generate a code for embedding the link within another webpage.

Figure 9: Sharing a Sway site

Share button

▷ Play   ⌖ Authors (1)   ⌬ Share

Share ⬤◯ Just me

Drag the slider button to Just me to keep the Sway site private

Share with the world

Ⓓ Docs.com - Your public gallery

Post the Sway site on Docs.com

Share with friends

Ⓕ Ⓨ Ⓖ⁺ Ⓨ⁼ ⬤ •••

Options differ depending on your Microsoft account

Send friends a link to the Sway site

https://sway.com/JQDFrUaxmg4IEbbk

◢ More options

☑ Viewers can duplicate this Sway

Stop sharing

Try This Now

Learn to use Sway!
Links to companion **Sways**, featuring **videos** with hands-on instructions, are located on www.cengage.com.

1: Creating a Sway Resume

Sway is a digital storytelling app. Create a Sway resume to share the skills, job experiences, and achievements you have that match the requirements of a future job interest. Perform the following tasks:

   a. Create a new presentation in Sway to use as a digital resume. Title the Sway Storyline with your full name and then select a background image.
   b. Create three separate sections titled **Academic Background, Work Experience**, and **Skills**, and insert text, a picture, and a paragraph or bulleted points in each section. Be sure to include your own picture.
   c. Add a fourth section that includes a video about your school that you find online.
   d. Customize the design of your presentation.
   e. Submit your assignment link in the format specified by your instructor.

2: Creating an Online Sway Newsletter

Newsletters are designed to capture the attention of their target audience. Using Sway, create a newsletter for a club, organization, or your favorite music group. Perform the following tasks:

   a. Create a new presentation in Sway to use as a digital newsletter for a club, organization, or your favorite music group. Provide a title for the Sway Storyline and select an appropriate background image.
   b. Select three separate sections with appropriate titles, such as Upcoming Events. In each section, insert text, a picture, and a paragraph or bulleted points.
   c. Add a fourth section that includes a video about your selected topic.
   d. Customize the design of your presentation.
   e. Submit your assignment link in the format specified by your instructor.

3: Creating and Sharing a Technology Presentation

To place a Sway presentation in the hands of your entire audience, you can share a link to the Sway presentation. Create a Sway presentation on a new technology and share it with your class. Perform the following tasks:

   a. Create a new presentation in Sway about a cutting-edge technology topic. Provide a title for the Sway Storyline and select a background image.
   b. Create four separate sections about your topic, and include text, a picture, and a paragraph in each section.
   c. Add a fifth section that includes a video about your topic.
   d. Customize the design of your presentation.
   e. Share the link to your Sway with your classmates and submit your assignment link in the format specified by your instructor.

Introduction to Office Mix

add-in | clip | slide recording | Slide Notes | screen recording | free-response quiz

Bottom Line

- Office Mix is a free PowerPoint add-in from Microsoft that adds features to PowerPoint.
- The Mix tab on the PowerPoint ribbon provides tools for creating screen recordings, videos, interactive quizzes, and live webpages.

To enliven business meetings and lectures, Microsoft adds a new dimension to presentations with a powerful toolset called Office Mix, a free add-in for PowerPoint. (An **add-in** is software that works with an installed app to extend its features.) Using Office Mix, you can record yourself on video, capture still and moving images on your desktop, and insert interactive elements such as quizzes and live webpages directly into PowerPoint slides. When you post the finished presentation to OneDrive, Office Mix provides a link you can share with friends and colleagues. Anyone with an Internet connection and a web browser can watch a published Office Mix presentation, such as the one in Figure 10, on a computer or mobile device.

Figure 10: Office Mix presentation

Adding Office Mix to PowerPoint

Learn to use Office Mix!

Links to companion **Sways**, featuring **videos** with hands-on instructions, are located on www.cengage.com.

To get started, you create an Office Mix account at the website mix.office.com using an email address or a Facebook or Google account. Next, you download and install the Office Mix add-in (see Figure 11). Office Mix appears as a new tab named Mix on the PowerPoint ribbon in versions of Office 2013 and Office 2016 running on personal computers (PCs).

Figure 11: Getting started with Office Mix

Capturing Video Clips

A **clip** is a short segment of audio, such as music, or video. After finishing the content on a PowerPoint slide, you can use Office Mix to add a video clip to animate or illustrate the content. Office Mix creates video clips in two ways: by recording live action on a webcam and by capturing screen images and movements. If your computer has a webcam, you can record yourself and annotate the slide to create a **slide recording** as shown in Figure 12.

On the Job Now

Companies are using Office Mix to train employees about new products, to explain benefit packages to new workers, and to educate interns about office procedures.

Figure 12: Making a slide recording

Record your voice; also record video if your computer has a camera.

Use the Slide Notes button to display notes for your narration.

For best results, look directly at your webcam while recording video.

Choose a video and audio device to record images and sound.

Use inking tools to write and draw on the slide as you record.

When you are making a slide recording, you can record your spoken narration at the same time. The **Slide Notes** feature works like a teleprompter to help you focus on your presentation content instead of memorizing your narration. Use the Inking tools to make annotations or add highlighting using different pen types and colors. After finishing a recording, edit the video in PowerPoint to trim the length or set playback options.

The second way to create a video is to capture on-screen images and actions with or without a voiceover. This method is ideal if you want to show how to use your favorite website or demonstrate an app such as OneNote. To share your screen with an audience, select the part of the screen you want to show in the video. Office Mix captures everything that happens in that area to create a **screen recording**, as shown in Figure 13. Office Mix inserts the screen recording as a video in the slide.

On the Job Now

To make your video recordings accessible to people with hearing impairments, use the Office Mix closed-captioning tools. You can also use closed captions to supplement audio that is difficult to understand and to provide an aid for those learning to read.

Figure 13: Making a screen recording

Record the action on the screen within the red dashed outline.

Record audio while capturing your on-screen actions.

Select Area button

Inserting Quizzes, Live Webpages, and Apps

To enhance and assess audience understanding, make your slides interactive by adding quizzes, live webpages, and apps. Quizzes give immediate feedback to the user as shown in Figure 14. Office Mix supports several quiz formats, including a **free-response quiz** similar to a short answer quiz, and true/false, multiple-choice, and multiple-response formats.

Figure 14: Creating an interactive quiz

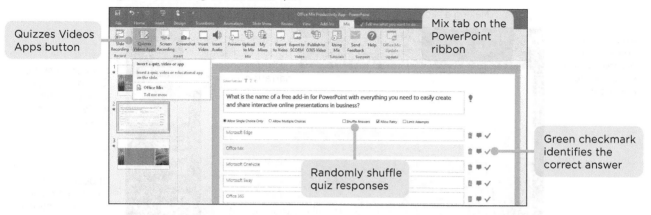

Quizzes Videos Apps button

Mix tab on the PowerPoint ribbon

Randomly shuffle quiz responses

Green checkmark identifies the correct answer

Sharing an Office Mix Presentation

When you complete your work with Office Mix, upload the presentation to your personal Office Mix dashboard as shown in Figure 15. Users of PCs, Macs, iOS devices, and Android devices can access and play Office Mix presentations. The Office Mix dashboard displays built-in analytics that include the quiz results and how much time viewers spent on each slide. You can play completed Office Mix presentations online or download them as movies.

Figure 15: Sharing an Office Mix presentation

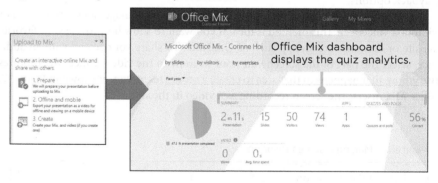

Office Mix dashboard displays the quiz analytics.

Try This Now

1: Creating an Office Mix Tutorial for OneNote

Note: This activity requires a microphone on your computer.

Office Mix makes it easy to record screens and their contents. Create PowerPoint slides with an Office Mix screen recording to show OneNote 2016 features. Perform the following tasks:

a. Create a PowerPoint presentation with the Ion Boardroom template. Create an opening slide with the title **My Favorite OneNote Features** and enter your name in the subtitle.
b. Create three additional slides, each titled with a new feature of OneNote. Open OneNote and use the Mix tab in PowerPoint to capture three separate screen recordings that teach your favorite features.
c. Add a fifth slide that quizzes the user with a multiple-choice question about OneNote and includes four responses. Be sure to insert a checkmark indicating the correct response.
d. Upload the completed presentation to your Office Mix dashboard and share the link with your instructor.
e. Submit your assignment link in the format specified by your instructor.

2: Teaching Augmented Reality with Office Mix

Note: This activity requires a webcam or built-in video camera on your computer.

A local elementary school has asked you to teach augmented reality to its students using Office Mix. Perform the following tasks:

a. Research augmented reality using your favorite online search tools.
b. Create a PowerPoint presentation with the Frame template. Create an opening slide with the title **Augmented Reality** and enter your name in the subtitle.
c. Create a slide with four bullets summarizing your research of augmented reality. Create a 20-second slide recording of yourself providing a quick overview of augmented reality.
d. Create another slide with a 30-second screen recording of a video about augmented reality from a site such as YouTube or another video-sharing site.
e. Add a final slide that quizzes the user with a true/false question about augmented reality. Be sure to insert a checkmark indicating the correct response.
f. Upload the completed presentation to your Office Mix dashboard and share the link with your instructor.
g. Submit your assignment link in the format specified by your instructor.

3: Marketing a Travel Destination with Office Mix

Note: This activity requires a webcam or built-in video camera on your computer.

To convince your audience to travel to a particular city, create a slide presentation marketing any city in the world using a slide recording, screen recording, and a quiz. Perform the following tasks:

a. Create a PowerPoint presentation with any template. Create an opening slide with the title of the city you are marketing as a travel destination and your name in the subtitle.
b. Create a slide with four bullets about the featured city. Create a 30-second slide recording of yourself explaining why this city is the perfect vacation destination.
c. Create another slide with a 20-second screen recording of a travel video about the city from a site such as YouTube or another video-sharing site.
d. Add a final slide that quizzes the user with a multiple-choice question about the featured city with five responses. Be sure to include a checkmark indicating the correct response.
e. Upload the completed presentation to your Office Mix dashboard and share your link with your instructor.
f. Submit your assignment link in the format specified by your instructor.

Introduction to Microsoft Edge

Reading view | Hub | Cortana | Web Note | Inking | sandbox

Bottom Line

- Microsoft Edge is the name of the new web browser built into Windows 10.
- Microsoft Edge allows you to search the web faster, take web notes, read webpages without distractions, and get instant assistance from Cortana.

Microsoft Edge is the default web browser developed for the Windows 10 operating system as a replacement for Internet Explorer. Unlike its predecessor, Edge lets you write on webpages, read webpages without advertisements and other distractions, and search for information using a virtual personal assistant. The Edge interface is clean and basic, as shown in Figure 16, meaning you can pay more attention to the webpage content.

Figure 16: Microsoft Edge tools

Forward button — New tab button — Web address in the Address bar — Add to favorites or reading list button — Back button — Reading view button — More button — Refresh (F5) button — Hub (Favorites, reading list, history, and downloads) button — Share Web Note button — Make a Web Note button

Learn to use Edge!

Links to companion **Sways**, featuring **videos** with hands-on instructions, are located on www.cengage.com.

On the Job Now

Businesses started adopting Internet Explorer more than 20 years ago simply to view webpages. Today, Microsoft Edge has a different purpose: to promote interaction with the web and share its contents with colleagues.

Browsing the Web with Microsoft Edge

One of the fastest browsers available, Edge allows you to type search text directly in the Address bar. As you view the resulting webpage, you can switch to **Reading view**, which is available for most news and research sites, to eliminate distracting advertisements. For example, if you are catching up on technology news online, the webpage might be difficult to read due to a busy layout cluttered with ads. Switch to Reading view to refresh the page and remove the original page formatting, ads, and menu sidebars to read the article distraction-free.

Consider the **Hub** in Microsoft Edge as providing one-stop access to all the things you collect on the web, such as your favorite websites, reading list, surfing history, and downloaded files.

Locating Information with Cortana

Cortana, the Windows 10 virtual assistant, plays an important role in Microsoft Edge. After you turn on Cortana, it appears as an animated circle in the Address bar when you might need assistance, as shown in the restaurant website in Figure 17. When you click the Cortana icon, a pane slides in from the right of the browser window to display detailed information about the restaurant, including maps and reviews. Cortana can also assist you in defining words, finding the weather, suggesting coupons for shopping, updating stock market information, and calculating math.

Figure 17: Cortana providing restaurant information

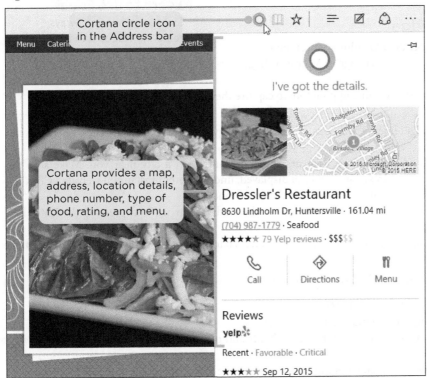

Cortana circle icon in the Address bar

Cortana provides a map, address, location details, phone number, type of food, rating, and menu.

I've got the details.

Dressler's Restaurant
8630 Lindholm Dr, Huntersville · 161.04 mi
(704) 987-1779 · Seafood
★★★★☆ 79 Yelp reviews · $$$$$

Call   Directions   Menu

Reviews
yelp
Recent · Favorable · Critical
★★★☆☆ Sep 12, 2015

Annotating Webpages

One of the most impressive Microsoft Edge features are the **Web Note** tools, which you use to write on a webpage or to highlight text. When you click the Make a Web Note button, an **Inking** toolbar appears, as shown in **Figure 18**, that provides writing and drawing tools. These tools include an eraser, a pen, and a highlighter with different colors. You can also insert a typed note and copy a screen image (called a screen clipping). You can draw with a pointing device, fingertip, or stylus using different pen colors. Whether you add notes to a recipe, annotate sources for a research paper, or select a product while shopping online, the Web Note tools can enhance your productivity. After you complete your notes, click the Save button to save the annotations to OneNote, your Favorites list, or your Reading list. You can share the inked page with others using the Share Web Note button.

On the Job Now

To enhance security, Microsoft Edge runs in a partial sandbox, an arrangement that prevents attackers from gaining control of your computer. Browsing within the **sandbox** protects computer resources and information from hackers.

Figure 18: Web Note tools in Microsoft Edge

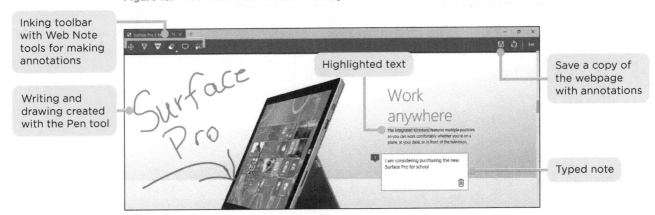

Inking toolbar with Web Note tools for making annotations

Writing and drawing created with the Pen tool

Highlighted text

Save a copy of the webpage with annotations

Typed note

Try This Now

Learn to use Edge!
Links to companion **Sways**, featuring **videos** with hands-on instructions, are located on www.cengage.com.

1: Using Cortana in Microsoft Edge

Note: This activity requires using Microsoft Edge on a Windows 10 computer.

Cortana can assist you in finding information on a webpage in Microsoft Edge. Perform the following tasks:

a. Create a Word document using the Word Screen Clipping tool to capture the following screenshots.

   • Screenshot A—Using Microsoft Edge, open a webpage with a technology news article. Right-click a term in the article and ask Cortana to define it.
   • Screenshot B—Using Microsoft Edge, open the website of a fancy restaurant in a city near you. Make sure the Cortana circle icon is displayed in the Address bar. (If it's not displayed, find a different restaurant website.) Click the Cortana circle icon to display a pane with information about the restaurant.
   • Screenshot C—Using Microsoft Edge, type **10 USD to Euros** in the Address bar without pressing the Enter key. Cortana converts the U.S. dollars to Euros.
   • Screenshot D—Using Microsoft Edge, type **Apple stock** in the Address bar without pressing the Enter key. Cortana displays the current stock quote.

b. Submit your assignment in the format specified by your instructor.

2: Viewing Online News with Reading View

Note: This activity requires using Microsoft Edge on a Windows 10 computer.

Reading view in Microsoft Edge can make a webpage less cluttered with ads and other distractions. Perform the following tasks:

a. Create a Word document using the Word Screen Clipping tool to capture the following screenshots.

   • Screenshot A—Using Microsoft Edge, open the website **mashable.com**. Open a technology article. Click the Reading view button to display an ad-free page that uses only basic text formatting.
   • Screenshot B—Using Microsoft Edge, open the website **bbc.com**. Open any news article. Click the Reading view button to display an ad-free page that uses only basic text formatting.
   • Screenshot C—Make three types of annotations (Pen, Highlighter, and Add a typed note) on the BBC article page displayed in Reading view.

b. Submit your assignment in the format specified by your instructor.

3: Inking with Microsoft Edge

Note: This activity requires using Microsoft Edge on a Windows 10 computer.

Microsoft Edge provides many annotation options to record your ideas. Perform the following tasks:

a. Open the website **wolframalpha.com** in the Microsoft Edge browser. Wolfram Alpha is a well-respected academic search engine. Type **US$100 1965 dollars in 2015** in the Wolfram Alpha search text box and press the Enter key.

b. Click the Make a Web Note button to display the Web Note tools. Using the Pen tool, draw a circle around the result on the webpage. Save the page to OneNote.

c. In the Wolfram Alpha search text box, type the name of the city closest to where you live and press the Enter key. Using the Highlighter tool, highlight at least three interesting results. Add a note and then type a sentence about what you learned about this city. Save the page to OneNote. Share your OneNote notebook with your instructor.

d. Submit your assignment link in the format specified by your instructor.

Office 2016 and Windows 10: Essential Concepts and Skills

Objectives

You will have mastered the material in this module when you can:

- Use a touch screen
- Perform basic mouse operations
- Start Windows and sign in to an account
- Identify the objects in the Windows 10 desktop
- Identify the apps in and versions of Microsoft Office 2016
- Run an app

- Identify the components of the Microsoft Office ribbon
- Create folders
- Save files
- Change screen resolution
- Perform basic tasks in Microsoft Office apps
- Manage files
- Use Microsoft Office Help and Windows Help

This introductory module covers features and functions common to Office 2016 apps, as well as the basics of Windows 10.

Roadmap

In this module, you will learn how to perform basic tasks in Windows and the Office apps. The following roadmap identifies general activities you will perform as you progress through this module:

1. SIGN IN to an account
2. USE WINDOWS
3. USE Office APPS
4. FILE and Folder MANAGEMENT
5. SWITCH between APPS
6. SAVE and Manage FILES

7. CHANGE SCREEN RESOLUTION
8. EXIT Office APPS
9. USE Office and Windows HELP

At the beginning of the step instructions throughout each module, you will see an abbreviated form of this roadmap. The abbreviated roadmap uses colors to indicate module progress: gray means the module is beyond that activity, blue means the task being shown is covered in that activity, and black means that activity is yet to be covered. For example, the following abbreviated roadmap indicates the module would be showing a task in the Use Apps activity.

1 SIGN IN | 2 USE WINDOWS | 3 USE APPS | 4 FILE MANAGEMENT | 5 SWITCH APPS
6 SAVE FILES | 7 CHANGE SCREEN RESOLUTION | 8 EXIT APPS | 9 USE HELP

Use the abbreviated roadmap as a progress guide while you read or step through the instructions in this module.

Introduction to the Windows 10 Operating System

Windows 10 is the newest version of Microsoft Windows, which is a popular and widely used operating system (Figure 1). An **operating system (OS)** is a set of programs that coordinate all the activities among computer or mobile device hardware.

Figure 1

The Windows operating system simplifies the process of working with documents and apps by organizing the manner in which you interact with the computer. Windows is used to run apps. An application, or **app**, consists of programs designed to make users more productive and/or assist them with personal tasks, such as word processing or browsing the web.

Using a Touch Screen and a Mouse

Windows users who have computers or devices with touch screen capability can interact with the screen using gestures. A **gesture** is a motion you make on a touch screen with the tip of one or more fingers or your hand. Touch screens are convenient because they do not require a separate device for input. Table 1 presents common ways to interact with a touch screen.

If you are using your finger on a touch screen and are having difficulty completing the steps in this module, consider using a stylus. Many people find it easier to be precise with a stylus than with a finger. In addition, with a stylus you see the pointer. If you still are having trouble completing the steps with a stylus, try using a mouse.

CONSIDER THIS

Will your screen look different if you are using a touch screen?
The Windows and Microsoft Office interface varies slightly if you are using a touch screen. For this reason, you might notice that your screen looks slightly different from the screens in the module.

Table 1 Touch Screen Gestures

Motion	Description	Common Uses	Equivalent Mouse Operation
Tap	Quickly touch and release one finger one time.	Activate a link (built-in connection). Press a button. Run a program or an app.	Click
Double-tap	Quickly touch and release one finger two times.	Run a program or an app. Zoom in (show a smaller area on the screen, so that contents appear larger) at the location of the double-tap.	Double-click
Press and hold	Press and hold one finger to cause an action to occur, or until an action occurs.	Display a shortcut menu (immediate access to allowable actions). Activate a mode enabling you to move an item with one finger to a new location.	Right-click
Drag or slide	Press and hold one finger on an object and then move the finger to the new location.	Move an item around the screen Scroll.	Drag
Swipe	Press and hold one finger and then move the finger horizontally or vertically on the screen.	Select an object. Swipe from edge to display a bar such as the Action Center, Apps bar, and Navigation bar.	Drag
Stretch	Move two fingers apart.	Zoom in (show a smaller area on the screen, so that contents appear larger).	None
Pinch	Move two fingers together.	Zoom out (show a larger area on the screen, so that contents appear smaller).	None

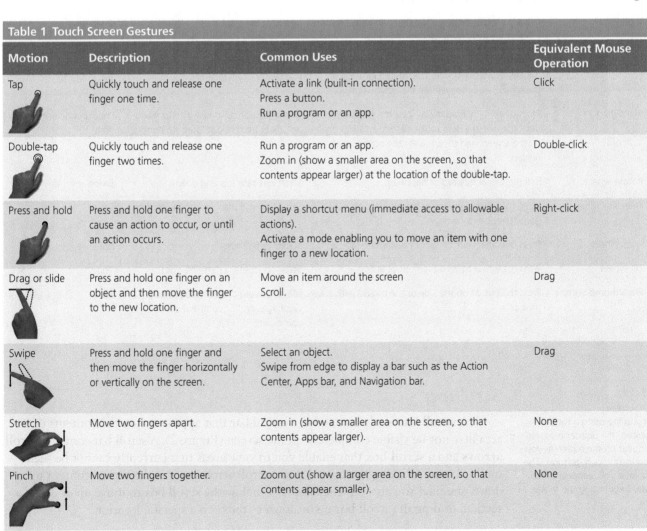

Windows users who do not have touch screen capabilities typically work with a mouse that has at least two buttons. For a right-handed user, the left button usually is the primary mouse button, and the right mouse button is the secondary mouse button. Left-handed people, however, can reverse the function of these buttons.

Table 2 explains how to perform a variety of mouse operations. Some apps also use keys in combination with the mouse to perform certain actions. For example, when you hold down the CTRL key while rolling the mouse wheel, text on the screen may become larger or smaller based on the direction you roll the wheel. The function of the mouse buttons and the wheel varies depending on the app.

Table 2 Mouse Operations

Operation	Mouse Action	Example	Equivalent Touch Gesture
Point	Move the mouse until the pointer on the desktop is positioned on the item of choice.	Position the pointer on the screen.	None
Click	Press and release the primary mouse button, which usually is the left mouse button.	Select or deselect items on the screen or run an app or app feature.	Tap
Right-click	Press and release the secondary mouse button, which usually is the right mouse button.	Display a shortcut menu.	Press and hold
Double-click	Quickly press and release the primary mouse button twice without moving the mouse.	Run an app or app feature.	Double-tap
Triple-click	Quickly press and release the primary mouse button three times without moving the mouse.	Select a paragraph.	Triple-tap
Drag	Point to an item, hold down the primary mouse button, move the item to the desired location on the screen, and then release the mouse button.	Move an object from one location to another or draw pictures.	Drag or slide
Right-drag	Point to an item, hold down the right mouse button, move the item to the desired location on the screen, and then release the right mouse button.	Display a shortcut menu after moving an object from one location to another.	Press and hold, then drag
Rotate wheel	Roll the wheel forward or backward.	Scroll vertically (up and down).	Swipe
Free-spin wheel	Whirl the wheel forward or backward so that it spins freely on its own.	Scroll through many pages in seconds.	Swipe
Press wheel	Press the wheel button while moving the mouse.	Scroll continuously.	None
Tilt wheel	Press the wheel toward the right or left.	Scroll horizontally (left and right).	None
Press thumb button	Press the button on the side of the mouse with your thumb.	Move forward or backward through webpages and/or control media, games, etc.	None

BTW
Pointer
If you are using a touch screen, the pointer may not appear on the screen as you perform touch gestures. The pointer will reappear when you begin using the mouse.

Scrolling

A **scroll bar** is a horizontal or vertical bar that appears when the contents of an area may not be visible completely on the screen (Figure 2). A scroll bar contains **scroll arrows** and a **scroll box** that enable you to view areas that currently cannot be seen on the screen. Clicking the up and down scroll arrows moves the screen content up or down one line. You also can click above or below the scroll box to move up or down a section, or drag the scroll box up or down to move to a specific location.

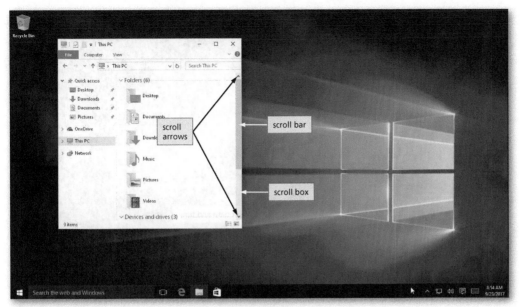

Figure 2

Keyboard Shortcuts

In many cases, you can use the keyboard instead of the mouse to accomplish a task. To perform tasks using the keyboard, you press one or more keyboard keys, sometimes identified as a **keyboard shortcut**. Some keyboard shortcuts consist of a single key, such as the F1 key. For example, to obtain help in many apps, you can press the F1 key. Other keyboard shortcuts consist of multiple keys, in which case a plus sign separates the key names, such as CTRL+ESC. This notation means to press and hold down the first key listed, press one or more additional keys, and then release all keys. For example, to display the Start menu, press CTRL+ESC, that is, hold down the CTRL key, press the ESC key, and then release both keys.

Starting Windows

It is not unusual for multiple people to use the same computer in a work, educational, recreational, or home setting. Windows enables each user to establish a **user account**, which identifies to Windows the resources, such as apps and storage locations, a user can access when working with the computer.

Each user account has a user name and may have a password and an icon, as well. A **user name** is a unique combination of letters or numbers that identifies a specific user to Windows. A **password** is a private combination of letters, numbers, and special characters associated with the user name that allows access to a user's account resources. An icon is a small image that represents an object; thus, a **user icon** is a picture associated with a user name.

When you turn on a computer, Windows starts and displays a **lock screen** consisting of the time and date (Figure 3). To unlock the screen, swipe up or click the lock screen. Depending on your computer's settings, Windows might display a sign-in screen that shows the user names and user icons for users who have accounts on the computer. This **sign-in screen** enables you to sign in to your user account and makes the computer available for use. Clicking the user icon begins the process of signing in, also called logging on, to your user account.

BTW

Minimize Wrist Injury
Computer users frequently switch between the keyboard and the mouse during an Access session; such switching strains the wrist. To help prevent wrist injury, minimize switching. For instance, if your fingers already are on the keyboard, use keyboard keys to scroll. If your hand already is on the mouse, use the mouse to scroll. If your hand is on the touch screen, use touch gestures to scroll.

Figure 3

At the bottom of the sign-in screen (Figure 4) is the 'Connect to Internet' button, 'Ease of access' button, and a Shut down button. Clicking the 'Connect to Internet' button displays a list of each network connection and its status. You also can connect to or disconnect from a network. Clicking the 'Ease of access' button displays the Ease of access menu, which provides tools to optimize a computer to accommodate the needs of the mobility, hearing, and vision-impaired users. Clicking the Shut down button displays a menu containing commands related to putting the computer or mobile device in a low-power state, shutting it down, and restarting the computer or mobile device. The commands available on your computer or mobile device may differ.

- The Sleep command saves your work, turns off the computer fans and hard drive, and places the computer in a lower-power state. To wake the computer from sleep mode, press the power button or lift a laptop's cover, and sign in to your account.
- The Shut down command exits running apps, shuts down Windows, and then turns off the computer.
- The Restart command exits running apps, shuts down Windows, and then restarts Windows.

To Sign In to an Account

1 SIGN IN | 2 USE WINDOWS | 3 USE APPS | 4 FILE MANAGEMENT | 5 SWITCH APPS
6 SAVE FILES | 7 CHANGE SCREEN RESOLUTION | 8 EXIT APPS | 9 USE HELP

The following steps, which use SCSeries as the user name, sign in to an account based on a typical Windows installation. **Why?** *After starting Windows, you might be required to sign in to an account to access the computer or mobile device's resources.* You may need to ask your instructor how to sign in to your account.

- Click the lock screen (shown in Figure 3) to display a sign-in screen.
- Click the user icon (for SCSeries, in this case) on the sign-in screen, which depending on settings, either will display a second sign-in screen that contains a Password text box (Figure 4) or will display the Windows desktop (Figure 5).

Q&A

Why do I not see a user icon?
Your computer may require you to type a user name instead of clicking an icon.

What is a text box?
A text box is a rectangular box in which you type text.

Why does my screen not show a Password text box?
Your account does not require a password.

- If Windows displays a sign-in screen with a Password text box, type your password in the text box.

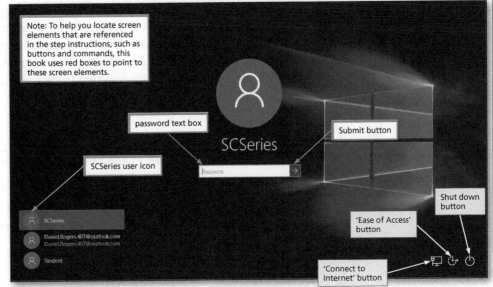

Figure 4

2
- Click the Submit button (shown in Figure 4) to sign in to your account and display the Windows desktop (Figure 5).

Q&A

Why does my desktop look different from the one in Figure 5?
The Windows desktop is customizable, and your school or employer may have modified the desktop to meet its needs. Also, your screen resolution, which affects the size of the elements on the screen, may differ from the screen resolution used in this book. Later in this module, you learn how to change screen resolution.

How do I type if my tablet has no keyboard?
You can use your fingers to press keys on a keyboard that appears on the screen, called an on-screen keyboard, or you can purchase a separate physical keyboard that attaches to or wirelessly communicates with the tablet.

The Windows Desktop

The Windows 10 desktop (Figure 5) and the objects on the desktop emulate a work area in an office. Think of the Windows desktop as an electronic version of the top of your desk. You can perform tasks such as placing objects on the desktop, moving the objects around the desktop, and removing items from the desktop.

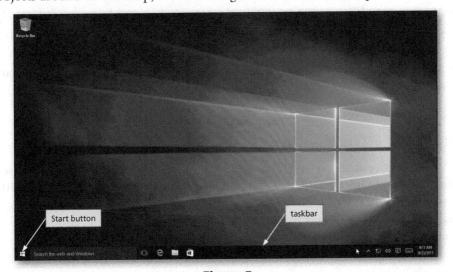

Figure 5

When you run a program or app in Windows 10, it appears on the desktop. Some icons also may be displayed on the desktop. For instance, the icon for the **Recycle Bin**, the location of files that have been deleted, appears on the desktop by default. A **file** is a named unit of storage. Files can contain text, images, audio, and video. You can customize your desktop so that icons representing programs and files you use often appear on your desktop.

Introduction to Microsoft Office 2016

Microsoft Office 2016 is the newest version of Microsoft Office, offering features that provide users with better functionality and easier ways to work with the various files they create. This version of office also is designed to work more optimally on mobile devices and online.

Microsoft Office 2016 Apps

Microsoft Office 2016 includes a wide variety of apps, such as Word, PowerPoint, Excel, Access, Outlook, Publisher, and OneNote:

- **Microsoft Word 2016**, or Word, is a full-featured word processing app that allows you to create professional-looking documents and revise them easily.

- **Microsoft PowerPoint 2016**, or PowerPoint, is a complete presentation app that enables you to produce professional-looking presentations and then deliver them to an audience.

- **Microsoft Excel 2016**, or Excel, is a powerful spreadsheet app that allows you to organize data, complete calculations, make decisions, graph data, develop professional-looking reports, publish organized data to the web, and access real-time data from websites.

- **Microsoft Access 2016**, or Access, is a database management system that enables you to create a database; add, change, and delete data in the database; ask questions concerning the data in the database; and create forms and reports using the data in the database.

- **Microsoft Outlook 2016**, or Outlook, is a communications and scheduling app that allows you to manage email accounts, calendars, contacts, and access to other Internet content.

- **Microsoft Publisher 2016**, or Publisher, is a desktop publishing app that helps you create professional-quality publications and marketing materials that can be shared easily.

- **Microsoft OneNote 2016**, or OneNote, is a note-taking app that allows you to store and share information in notebooks with other people.

Microsoft Office 2016 Suites

A **suite** is a collection of individual apps available together as a unit. Microsoft offers a variety of Office suites, including a stand-alone desktop app, Microsoft Office 365, and Microsoft Office Online. **Microsoft Office 365**, or Office 365, provides plans that allow organizations to use Office in a mobile setting while also being able to communicate and share files, depending upon the type of plan selected by the organization. **Microsoft Office Online** includes apps that allow you to edit and share files on the web using the familiar Office interface.

During the Office 365 installation, you select a plan, and depending on your plan, you receive different apps and services. Office Online apps do not require a local installation and can be accessed through OneDrive and your browser. **OneDrive** is a cloud storage service that provides storage and other services, such as Office Online, to computer users.

How do you sign up for a OneDrive account?

• Use your browser to navigate to onedrive.live.com.

• Create a Microsoft account by clicking the Sign up button and then entering your information to create the account.

• Sign in to OneDrive using your new account or use it in Office to save your files on OneDrive.

Apps in a suite, such as Microsoft Office, typically use a similar interface and share features. Once you are comfortable working with the elements and the interface and performing tasks in one app, the similarity can help you apply the knowledge and skills you have learned to another app(s) in the suite. For example, the process for saving a file in Word is the same in PowerPoint, Excel, and the other Office apps.

Running and Using An App

To use an app, you must instruct the operating system to run the app. Windows provides many different ways to run an app, one of which is presented in this section (other ways to run an app are presented throughout this module). After an app is running, you can use it to perform a variety of tasks. The following pages use Access to discuss some elements of the Office interface and to perform tasks.

Access

The term **database** describes a collection of data organized in a manner that allows access, retrieval, and use of that data. **Access** is a database management system. A **database management system** is software that allows you to use a computer to create a database; add, change, and delete data in the database; create queries that allow you to ask questions concerning the data in the database; and create forms and reports using the data in the database.

To Run Access Using the Start Menu

1 SIGN IN | 2 USE WINDOWS | 3 USE APPS | 4 FILE MANAGEMENT | 5 SWITCH APPS
6 SAVE FILES | 7 CHANGE SCREEN RESOLUTION | 8 EXIT APPS | 9 USE HELP

Across the bottom of the Windows 10 desktop is the taskbar. The taskbar contains the **Start button**, which you use to access apps, files, folders, and settings. A **folder** is a named location on a storage medium that usually contains related documents.

Clicking the Start button displays the **Start menu**. The Start menu allows you to access programs, folders, and files on the computer or mobile device and contains commands that allow you to start programs, store and search for documents, customize the computer or mobile device, and sign out of a user account or shut down the computer or mobile device. A **menu** is a list of related items, including folders, programs, and commands. Each **command** on a menu performs a specific action, such as saving a file or obtaining help. *Why? When you install an app, for example, tiles are added to the Start menu for the various Office apps included in the suite.*

The following steps, which assume Windows is running, use the Start menu to run Access based on a typical installation. You may need to ask your instructor how to run an Office app on your computer. Although the steps illustrate running the Access app, the steps to run any Office app are similar.

- Click the Start button on the Windows 10 taskbar to display the Start menu (Figure 6).

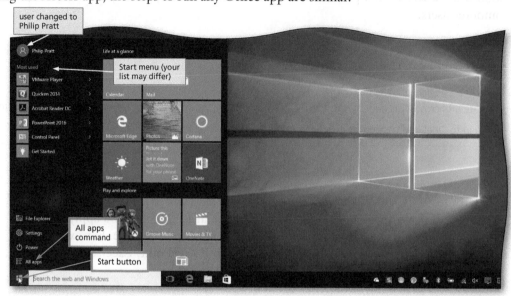

Figure 6

- Click All apps at the bottom of the left pane of the Start menu to display a list of apps installed on the computer or mobile device (Figure 7).

Figure 7

- If the app you want to run is located in a folder, click or scroll to and then click the folder in the All apps list to display a list of the folder's contents.
- Click, or scroll to and then click, the program name (Microsoft Access 2016, in this case) in the list to run the selected program (Figure 8).

Q&A What happens when you run an app?

The app appears in a window. A **window** is a rectangular area that displays data and information. The top of a window has a **title bar**, which is a horizontal space that contains the window's name.

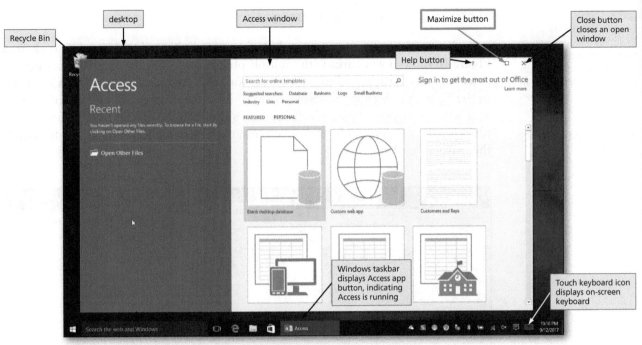

Figure 8

Other Ways

1. Type app name in search box, click app name in results list

2. Double-click file created in app you want to run

To Maximize a Window

1 SIGN IN | 2 USE WINDOWS | 3 USE APPS | 4 FILE MANAGEMENT | 5 SWITCH APPS
6 SAVE FILES | 7 CHANGE SCREEN RESOLUTION | 8 EXIT APPS | 9 USE HELP

Sometimes content is not visible completely in a window. One method of displaying the entire contents of a window is to **maximize** it, or enlarge the window so that it fills the entire screen. The following step maximizes the Access window; however, any Office app's window can be maximized using this step. *Why? A maximized window provides the most space available for using the app.*

1

- If the app window is not maximized already, click the Maximize button (shown in Figure 8 to the left of the Close button on the window's title bar (the Access window title bar, in this case) to maximize the window (Figure 9).

Q&A

What happened to the Maximize button?
It changed to a Restore Down button, which you can use to return a window to its size and location before you maximized it.

How do I know whether a window is maximized?
A window is maximized if it fills the entire display area and the Restore Down button is displayed on the title bar.

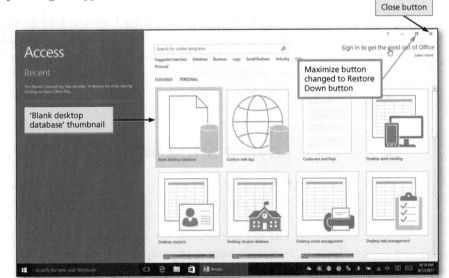

Figure 9

Other Ways

1. Double-click title bar

2. Drag title bar to top of screen

BTW

Touch Keyboard
To display the on-screen
touch keyboard, click the
Touch Keyboard button on
the Windows taskbar (shown
in Figure 8). When finished
using the touch keyboard,
click the X button on the
touch keyboard to close the
keyboard.

Access Unique Elements

You work on objects such as tables, forms, and reports in the **Access work area**. Figure 10 shows a work area with multiple objects open. **Object tabs** for the open objects appear at the top of the work area. You select an open object by clicking its tab. In the figure, the Account Manager Form is the selected object. To the left of the work area is the Navigation Pane, which contains a list of all the objects in the database. You use this pane to open an object. You also can customize the way objects are displayed in the Navigation Pane.

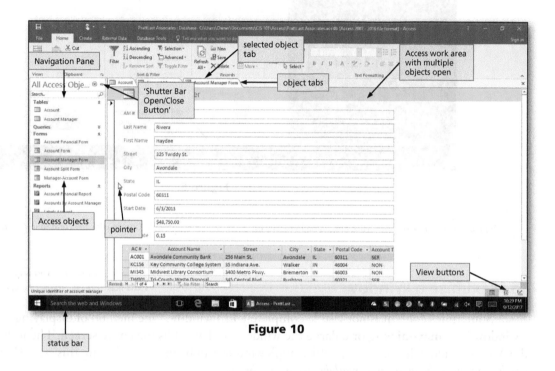

Figure 10

Because the Navigation Pane can take up space in the window, you might not have as much open space for working as you would with Word or Excel. You can use the 'Shutter Bar Open/Close Button' to minimize the Navigation Pane when you are not using it, which allows more space to work with tables, forms, reports, and other database elements.

Saving and Organizing Files

Before starting to work in Access, you must either create a new database or open an existing database. When you create a database, the computer places it on a storage medium such as a hard disk, solid state drive (SSD), USB flash drive, or optical disc. The storage medium can be permanent in your computer, can be portable where you remove it from your computer, or can be on a web server you access through a network or the Internet.

A database or other saved document is referred to as a file. A **file name** is the name assigned to a file when it is saved. When saving files, you should organize them so that you easily can find them later. Windows provides tools to help you organize files.

Organizing Files and Folders

You should organize and store databases and other files in folders to help you find the databases or other files quickly.

If you are taking an introductory computer class (CIS 101, for example), you may want to design a series of folders for the different subjects covered in the class. To accomplish this, you can arrange the folders in a hierarchy for the class, as shown in Figure 11.

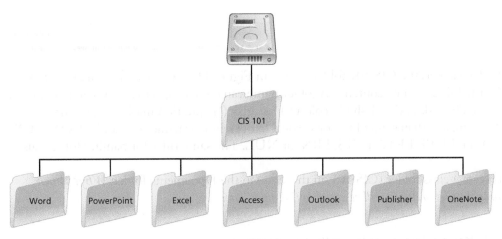

Figure 11

The hierarchy contains three levels. The first level contains the storage medium, such as a hard disk. The second level contains the class folder (CIS 101, in this case), and the third level contains seven folders, one each for a different Office app that will be covered in the class (Word, PowerPoint, Excel, Access, Outlook, Publisher, and OneNote).

When the hierarchy in Figure 11 is created, the storage medium is said to contain the CIS 101 folder, and the CIS 101 folder is said to contain the separate Office folders (i.e., Word, PowerPoint, Excel, etc.). In addition, this hierarchy easily can be expanded to include folders from other classes taken during additional semesters.

The vertical and horizontal lines in Figure 11 form a pathway that allows you to navigate to a drive or folder on a computer or network. A **path** consists of a drive letter (preceded by a drive name when necessary) and colon, to identify the storage device, and one or more folder names. A hard disk typically has a drive letter of C. Each drive or folder in the hierarchy has a corresponding path.

By default, Windows saves documents in the Documents library, music in the Music library, photos in the Pictures library, and videos in the Videos library. A **library** helps you manage multiple folders stored in various locations on a computer and devices. It does not store the folder contents; rather, it keeps track of their locations so that you can access the folders and their contents quickly. For example, you can save pictures from a digital camera in any folder on any storage location on a computer. Normally, this would make organizing the different folders difficult. If you add the folders to a library, however, you can access all the pictures from one location regardless of where they are stored.

The following pages illustrate the steps to organize the folders for this class and create a database in one of those folders:

1. Create the folder identifying your class.
2. Create the Access folder in the folder identifying your class.
3. Create the remaining folders in the folder identifying your class.
4. Create a database in the Access folder.

To Create a Folder

1 SIGN IN | 2 USE WINDOWS | 3 USE APPS | 4 FILE MANAGEMENT | 5 SWITCH APPS
6 SAVE FILES | 7 CHANGE SCREEN RESOLUTION | 8 EXIT APPS | 9 USE HELP

When you create a folder, such as the CIS 101 folder shown in Figure 11, you must name the folder. A folder name should describe the folder and its contents. A folder name can contain spaces and any uppercase or lowercase characters, except a backslash (\), slash (/), colon (:), asterisk (*), question mark (?), quotation marks ("), less than symbol (<), greater than symbol (>), or vertical bar (|). Folder names cannot be CON, AUX, COM1, COM2, COM3, COM4, LPT1, LPT2, LPT3, PRN, or NUL. The same rules for naming folders also apply to naming files.

The following steps create a class folder (CIS 101, in this case) in the Documents folder. *Why? When storing files, you should organize the files so that it will be easier to find them later.*

- Click the File Explorer app button on the taskbar to run the File Explorer.
- If necessary, double-click This PC in the navigation pane to expand the contents of your computer.
- Click the Documents folder in the navigation pane to display the contents of the Documents folder in the file list (Figure 12).

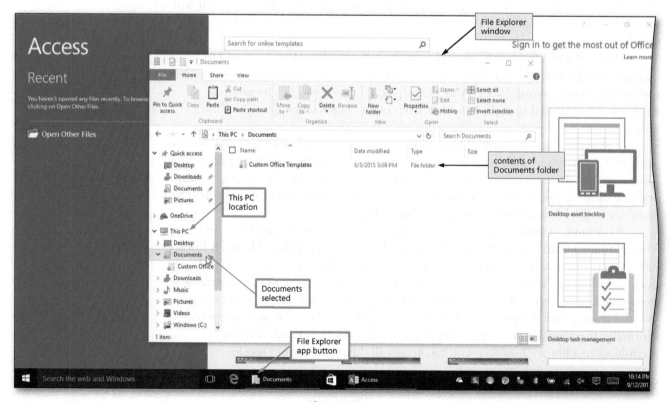

Figure 12

2

- Click the New folder button on the Quick Access Toolbar to create a new folder with the name, New folder, selected in a text box (Figure 13).

Q&A Why is the folder icon displayed differently on my computer or mobile device?
Windows might be configured to display contents differently on your computer or mobile device.

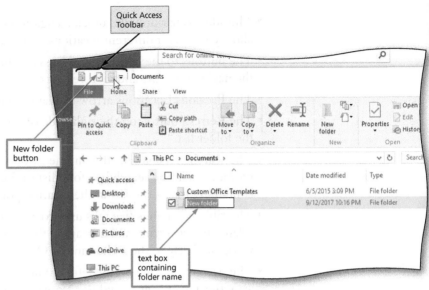

Figure 13

3

- Type **CIS 101** (or your class code) in the text box as the new folder name.

- If requested by your instructor, add your last name to the end of the folder name.

- Press the ENTER key to change the folder name from New folder to a folder name identifying your class (Figure 14).

Q&A What happens when I press the ENTER key?
The class folder (CIS 101, in this case) is displayed in the file list, which contains the folder name, date modified, type, and size.

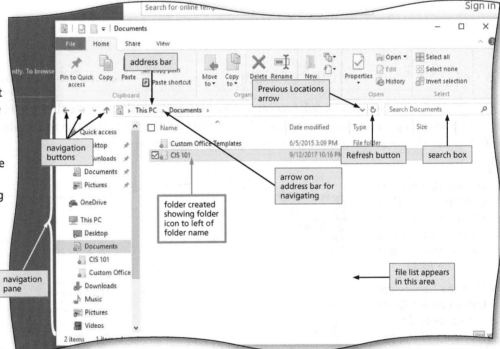

Figure 14

Other Ways

1. Press CTRL+SHIFT+N	2. Click the New folder button (Home tab | New group)

Folder Windows

The File Explorer window (shown in Figure 14) is called a folder window. Recall that a folder is a specific named location on a storage medium that contains related files. Most users rely on **folder windows** for finding, viewing, and managing information on their computers. Folder windows have common design elements, including the following (shown in Figure 14).

- The address bar provides quick navigation options. The arrows on the address bar allow you to visit different locations on the computer or mobile device.

- The buttons to the left of the address bar allow you to navigate the contents of the navigation pane and view recent pages.

- The Previous Locations arrow displays the locations you have visited.

- The Refresh button on the right side of the address bar refreshes the contents of the folder list.

- The search box contains the dimmed words, Search Documents. You can type a term in the search box for a list of files, folders, shortcuts, and elements containing that term within the location you are searching.

- The ribbon contains five tabs used to accomplish various tasks on the computer related to organizing and managing the contents of the open window. This ribbon works similarly to the ribbon in the Office apps.

- The navigation pane on the left contains the Quick access area, the OneDrive area, the This PC area, and the Network area.

- The Quick Access area shows locations you access frequently. By default, this list contains links only to your Desktop, Downloads, Documents, and Pictures.

To Create a Folder within a Folder

1 SIGN IN | 2 USE WINDOWS | 3 USE APPS | 4 FILE MANAGEMENT | **5 SWITCH APPS**
6 SAVE FILES | 7 CHANGE SCREEN RESOLUTION | 8 EXIT APPS | 9 USE HELP

With the class folder created, you can create folders that will store the files you create using each Office app. The following step creates an Access folder in the CIS 101 folder (or the folder identifying your class). *Why? To be able to organize your files, you should create a folder structure.*

- Double-click the icon or folder name for the CIS 101 folder (or the folder identifying your class) in the file list to open the folder.

- Click the New folder button on the Quick Access Toolbar to create a new folder with the name, New folder, selected in a text box folder.

- Type **Access** in the text box as the new folder name.

- Press the ENTER key to rename the folder (Figure 15).

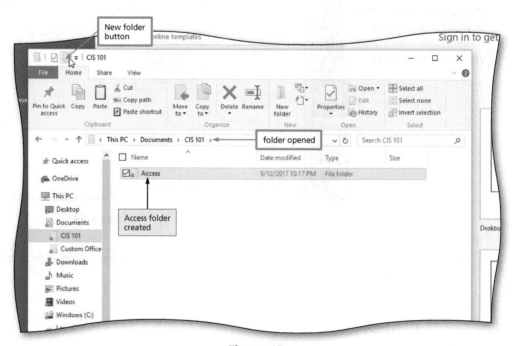

Figure 15

Other Ways

Other Ways	
1. Press CTRL+SHIFT+N	2. Click New folder button (Home tab | New group)

To Create the Remaining Folders

The following steps create the remaining folders in the folder identifying your class (in this case, CIS 101).

1 Click the New folder button on the Quick Access Toolbar to create a new folder with the name, New folder, selected in a text box.

2 Type **Excel** in the text box as the new folder name.

3 Press the ENTER key to rename the folder.

4 Repeat Steps 1 through 3 to create each of the remaining folders, using OneNote, Outlook, PowerPoint, Publisher, and Word as the folder names (Figure 16).

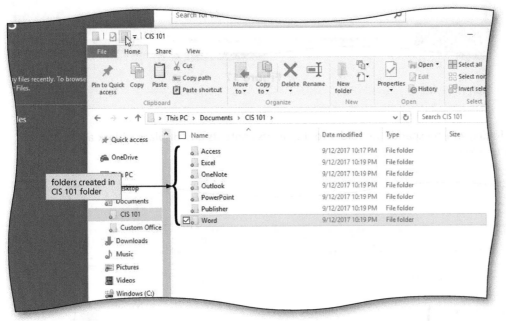

Figure 16

To Expand a Folder, Scroll through Folder Contents, and Collapse a Folder

1 SIGN IN | 2 USE WINDOWS | 3 USE APPS | 4 FILE MANAGEMENT | 5 SWITCH APPS
6 SAVE FILES | 7 CHANGE SCREEN RESOLUTION | 8 EXIT APPS | 9 USE HELP

Folder windows display the hierarchy of items and the contents of drives and folders in the file list. You might want to expand a folder in the navigation pane to view its contents, slide or scroll through its contents, and collapse it when you are finished viewing its contents. *Why? When a folder is expanded, you can see all the folders it contains. By contrast, a collapsed folder hides the folders it contains.* The following steps expand, slide or scroll through, and then collapse the folder identifying your class (CIS 101, in this case).

1

- Double-click the Documents folder in the This PC area of the navigation pane, which expands the folder to display its contents and displays a black arrow to the left of the Documents folder icon (Figure 17).

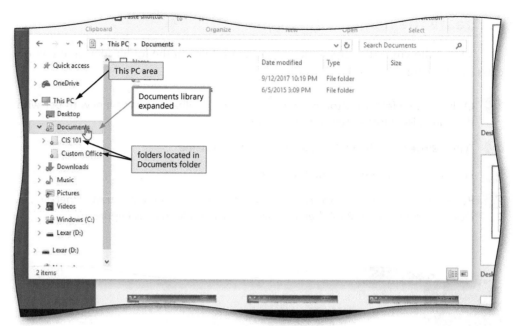

Figure 17

2

- Double-click the CIS 101 folder, which expands the folder to display its contents and displays a black arrow to the left of the folder icon (Figure 18).

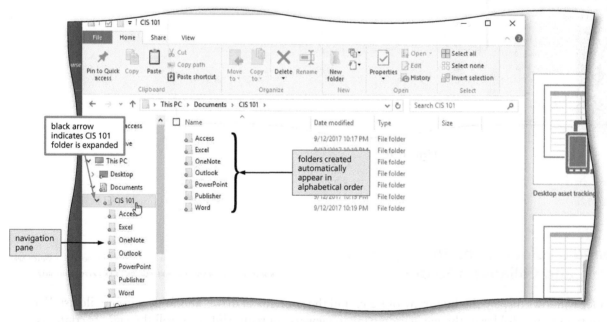

Figure 18

 Experiment

- Drag the scroll bar down or click the down scroll arrow on the vertical scroll bar to display additional folders at the bottom of the navigation pane. Drag the scroll bar up or click the scroll bar above the scroll box to move the scroll box to the top of the navigation pane. Drag the scroll box down the scroll bar until the scroll box is halfway down the scroll bar.

3

- Double-click the folder identifying your class (CIS 101, in this case) to collapse the folder (Figure 19).

Q&A Why are some folders indented below others?
A folder contains the indented folders below it.

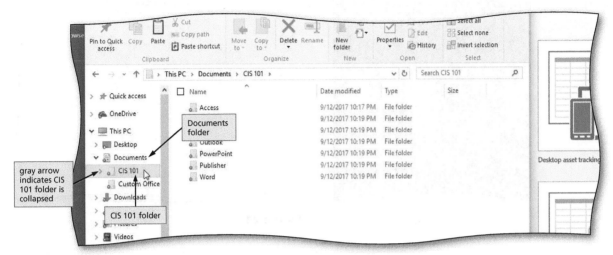

Figure 19

To Switch from One App to Another

1 SIGN IN | 2 USE WINDOWS | 3 USE APPS | 4 FILE MANAGEMENT | **5 SWITCH APPS**
6 SAVE FILES | 7 CHANGE SCREEN RESOLUTION | 8 EXIT APPS | 9 USE HELP

The next step is to create the Access database. Access, however, currently is not the active window. You can use the button on the taskbar and live preview to switch to Access and then use Access to create the database. *Why? By clicking the appropriate app button on the taskbar, you can switch to the open app you want to use.* The steps below switch to the Access window; however, the steps are the same for any active Office app currently displayed as a button on the taskbar.

1

- Point to the Access app button on the taskbar (Figure 20).

Q&A What if I am using a touch screen?
If you are using a touch screen and do not have a mouse, proceed to Step 2.

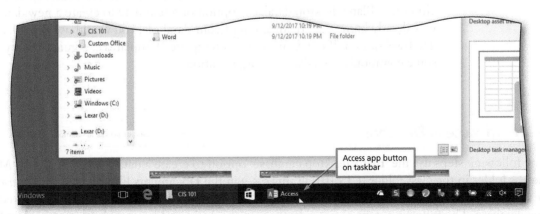

Figure 20

②
● Click the button to make the app associated with the app button the active window (Figure 21).

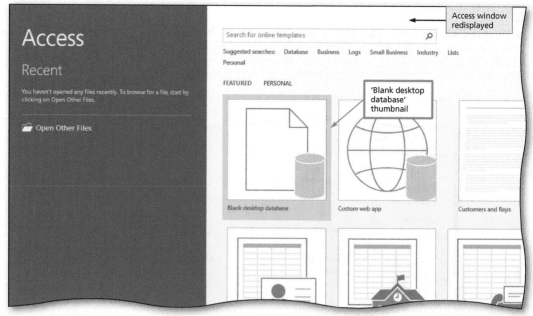

Figure 21

Other Ways

1. Press ALT+TAB until app you want to display is selected

Break Point: If you wish to take a break, this is a good place to do so. To resume at a later time, continue to follow the steps from this location forward.

Creating an Access Database

Unlike the other Office apps, Access saves a database when you first create it. When working in Access, you will add data to an Access database. As you add data to a database, Access automatically saves your changes rather than waiting until you manually save the database or exit Access. In other apps, you first enter data and then save it.

Because Access automatically saves the database as you add and change data, you do not always have to click the Save button on the Quick Access Toolbar. Instead, the Save button in Access is used for saving the objects (including tables, queries, forms, reports, and other database objects that you create) a database contains. You can use either the 'Blank desktop database' option or a template to create a new database. If you already know the organization of your database, you would use the 'Blank desktop database' option. If not, you can use a template. Templates can guide you by suggesting some commonly used database organizations.

To Create an Access Database

1 SIGN IN | 2 USE WINDOWS | 3 USE APPS | 4 FILE MANAGEMENT | 5 SWITCH APPS
6 SAVE FILES | 7 CHANGE SCREEN RESOLUTION | 8 EXIT APPS | 9 USE HELP

The following steps use the 'Blank desktop database' option to create a database named MZL Marketing in the Access folder in the class folder (CIS 101, in this case) in the Documents library. *Why? If you want to maintain data for a company, a database is perfect for the job.* With the folders for storing your files created, you can create the database. The following steps create a database in the Access folder contained in your class folder (CIS 101, in this case) using the file name, MZL Marketing.

1

- Click the 'Blank desktop database' thumbnail (shown in Figure 21) to select the database type (Figure 22).

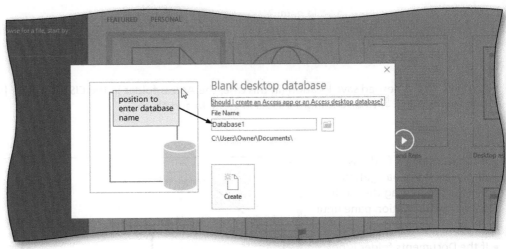

Figure 22

2

- Type **MZL Marketing** in the File Name text box to enter the new file name. Do not press the ENTER key after typing the file name because you do not want to create the database yet (Figure 23).

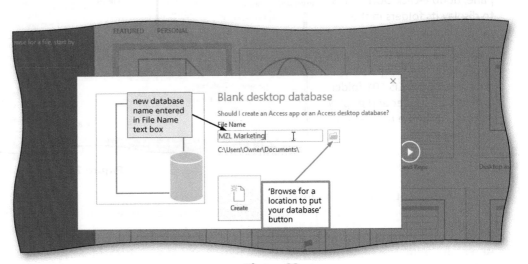

Figure 23

3

- Click the 'Browse for a location to put your database' button to display the File New Database dialog box (Figure 24).

Q&A

How do I close the Backstage view?
Click the Back button in the upper-left corner of the Backstage view to return to the app window.

Why does a file name already appear in the File name box?
You already entered the name of the Access database.

Why does the 'Save as type' box say Microsoft Access 2007–2016 Databases?
Microsoft Access database formats change with some new versions of Microsoft Access. The most recent format is the Microsoft Access 2007–2016 Databases format.

Figure 24

Q&A What characters can I use in a file name?

The only invalid characters are the backslash (\), slash (/), colon (:), asterisk (*), question mark (?), quotation mark ("), less than symbol (<), greater than symbol (>), and vertical bar (|).

4

- Navigate to the desired save location (in this case, the Access folder in the CIS 101 folder [or your class folder] in the Documents folder) by performing the tasks in Steps 4a and 4b.

4a

- If the Documents folder is not displayed in the navigation pane, scroll or drag the scroll bar in the navigation pane until Documents appears.

- If the Documents folder is not expanded in the navigation pane, double-click Documents to display its folders in the navigation pane.

- If your class folder (CIS 101, in this case) is not expanded, double-click the CIS 101 folder to select the folder and display its contents in the navigation pane (Figure 25).

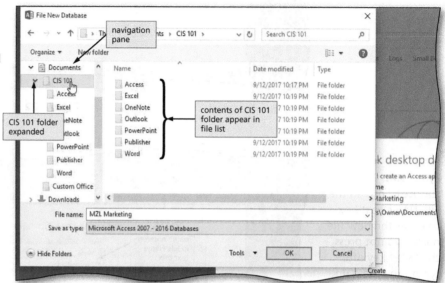

Figure 25

Q&A What if I wanted to save on OneDrive instead?

You would click OneDrive. Saving on OneDrive is discussed in a later section in this module.

What if I do not want to save in a folder?

Although storing files in folders is an effective technique for organizing files, some users prefer not to store files in folders. If you prefer not to save this file in a folder, select the storage device on which you wish to save the file and then proceed to Step 5.

4b

- Click the Access folder in the navigation pane to select it as the new save location and display its contents in the file list (Figure 26).

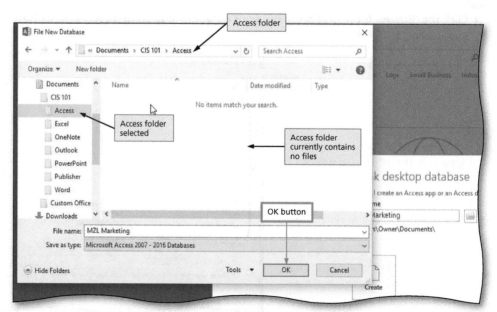

Figure 26

5

- Click the OK button (File New Database dialog box) to select the Access folder as the location for the database and close the dialog box.

- Click the Create button to create the database on the selected drive in the selected folder with the file name, MZL Marketing (Figure 27).

Q&A | How do I know that the MZL Marketing database is created?
The file name of the database appears on the title bar.

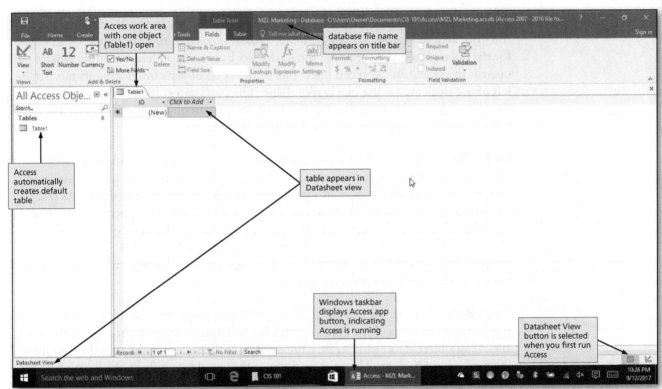

Figure 27

Navigating in Dialog Boxes

Navigating is the process of finding a location on a storage device. While creating the MZL Marketing database, for example, Steps 4a and 4b in the previous set of steps navigated to the Access folder located in the CIS 101 folder in the Documents folder. When performing certain functions in Windows apps, such as saving a file, opening a file, or inserting a picture in a database object, you most likely will have to navigate to the location where you want to save the file or to the folder containing the file you want to open or insert. Most dialog boxes in Windows apps requiring navigation follow a similar procedure; that is, the way you navigate to a folder in one dialog box, such as the Save As dialog box, is similar to how you might navigate in another dialog box, such as the Open dialog box. If you chose to navigate to a specific location in a dialog box, you would follow the instructions in Steps 4a and 4b.

The Access Window

The Access window consists of a variety of components to make your work more efficient. These include the Navigation Pane, Access work area, ribbon, shortcut menus, and Quick Access Toolbar. Some of these components are common to other Office apps; others are unique to Access.

Navigation Pane and Access Work Area

You work on objects such as tables, forms, and reports in the Access work area. In the work area in Figure 27, a single table, Table1, is open in the work area. Object tabs for the open objects appear at the top of the work area. If you have multiple objects open at the same time, you can select one of the open objects by clicking its tab. To the left of the work area is the Navigation Pane. The Navigation Pane contains a list of all the objects in the database. You use this pane to open an object. You also can customize the way objects are displayed in the Navigation Pane.

Status Bar   The status bar, located at the bottom of the Access window, presents information about the database object, the progress of current tasks, and the status of certain commands and keys; it also provides controls for viewing the object. As you enter data or perform certain commands, various indicators may appear on the status bar. The left edge of the status bar in Figure 27 shows that the table object is open in Datasheet view. In Datasheet view, the table is represented as a collection of rows and columns called a datasheet. Toward the right edge are View buttons, which you can use to change the view that currently appears.

Scroll Bars   You use a scroll bar to display different portions of an object. If an object is too long to fit vertically, a vertical scroll bar will appear at the right edge of the work area. If an object is too wide to fit, a horizontal scroll bar also appears at the bottom of the work area. On a scroll bar, the position of the scroll box reflects the location of the portion of the object that is displayed in the work area.

Ribbon   The ribbon, located near the top of the window below the title bar, is the control center in Access and other Office apps (Figure 28). The ribbon provides easy, central access to the tasks you perform while creating a database. The ribbon consists of tabs, groups, and commands. Each tab contains a collection of groups, and each group contains related functions. When you run an Office app, such as Access, it initially displays several main tabs, also called default or top-level tabs. All Office apps have a Home tab, which contains the more frequently used commands.

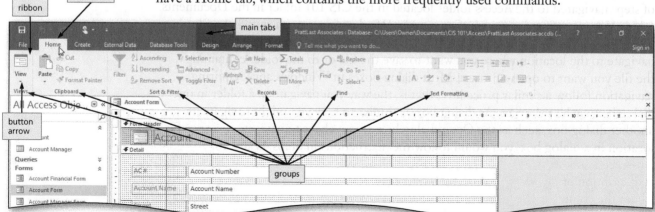

Figure 28

In addition to the main tabs, the Office apps display tool tabs, also called contextual tabs (Figure 29), when you perform certain tasks or work with objects such as pictures or tables. If you modify the design of a form, for example, the Form Design Tools tab and its related subordinate Design tab appear, collectively referred to as the Form Design Tools Design tab. When you are finished working with the form, the Form Design Tools Design tab disappears from the ribbon. Access and other Office apps determine when tool tabs should appear and disappear based on tasks you perform.

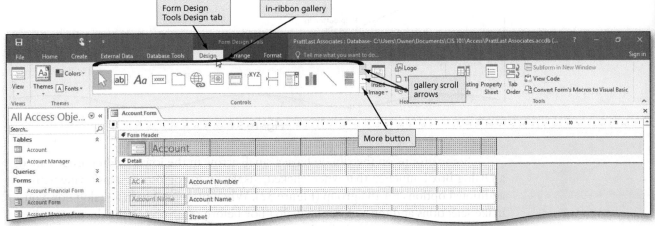

Figure 29

Items on the ribbon include buttons, boxes, and galleries (shown in Figure 29). A **gallery** is a set of choices, often graphical, arranged in a grid or in a list. You can scroll through choices in an in-ribbon gallery by clicking the gallery's scroll arrows. Or, you can click a gallery's More button to view more gallery options on the screen at a time.

Some buttons and boxes have arrows that, when clicked, also display a gallery; others always cause a gallery to be displayed when clicked (Figure 30).

BTW

Touch Mode
The Office and Windows interfaces may vary if you are using touch mode. For this reason, you might notice that the function or appearance of your touch screen differs slightly from this module's presentation.

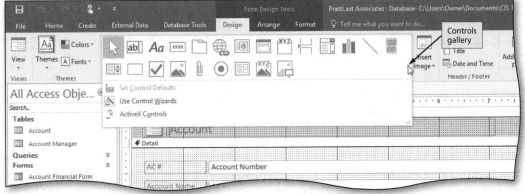

Figure 30

Some commands on the ribbon display an image to help you remember their function. When you point to a command on the ribbon, all or part of the command glows in a shade of blue, and a ScreenTip appears on the screen. A ScreenTip is an on-screen note that provides the name of the command, available keyboard shortcut(s), a description of the command, and sometimes instructions for how to obtain help about the command (Figure 31).

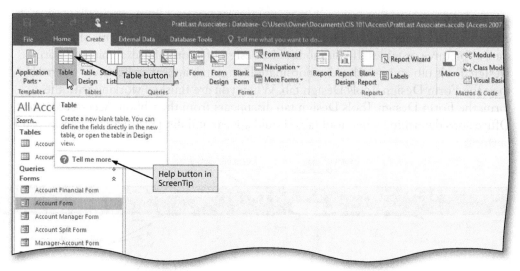

Figure 31

Some groups on the ribbon have a small arrow in the lower-right corner, called a Dialog Box Launcher, that when clicked, displays a dialog box or a task pane with additional options for the group (Figure 32). When presented with a dialog box, you make selections and must close the dialog box before returning to the document. A **task pane**, in contrast to a dialog box, is a window that can remain open and visible while you work in the document.

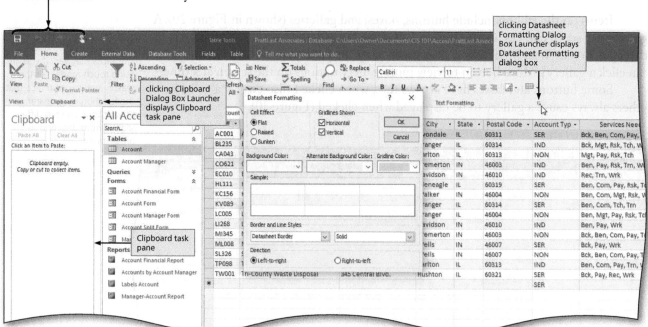

Figure 32

Quick Access Toolbar The Quick Access Toolbar, located initially (by default) above the ribbon at the left edge of the title bar, provides convenient, one-click access to frequently used commands (shown in Figure 32). The commands on the Quick Access Toolbar always are available, regardless of the task you are performing. The Touch/Mouse Mode button on the Quick Access Toolbar allows you to switch between Touch mode and Mouse mode. If you primarily use touch gestures, Touch mode will add more space between commands on menus and on the ribbon so that they are easier to tap. While touch gestures are convenient ways to interact with Office apps, not all features are supported when you are using Touch mode. If you are using a mouse,

Mouse mode will not add the extra space between buttons and commands. The Quick Access Toolbar is discussed in more depth later in the module.

KeyTips If you prefer using the keyboard instead of the mouse, you can press the ALT key on the keyboard to display KeyTips, or keyboard code icons, for certain commands (Figure 33). To select a command using the keyboard, press the letter or number displayed in the KeyTip, which may cause additional KeyTips related to the selected command to appear. To remove KeyTips from the screen, press the ALT key or the ESC key until all KeyTips disappear, or click anywhere in the app window.

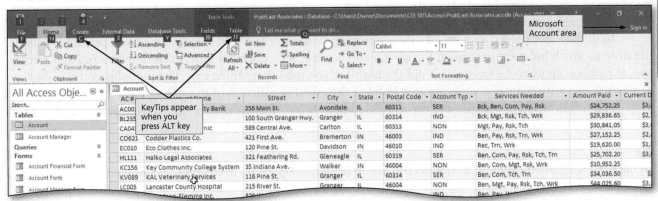

Figure 33

Microsoft Account Area In this area, you can use the Sign in link to sign in to your Microsoft account. Once signed in, you will see your account information as well as a picture if you have included one in your Microsoft account.

To Display a Different Tab on the Ribbon

1 SIGN IN | 2 USE WINDOWS | 3 USE APPS | 4 FILE MANAGEMENT | 5 SWITCH APPS
6 SAVE FILES | 7 CHANGE SCREEN RESOLUTION | 8 EXIT APPS | 9 USE HELP

When you run Access, the ribbon displays five main tabs: File, Home, Create, External Data, and Database Tools. The tab currently displayed is called the **active tab**.

The following step displays the Create tab, that is, makes it the active tab. *Why? When working with an Office app, you may need to switch tabs to access other options for working with a database.*

• Click Create on the ribbon to display the Create tab (Figure 34).

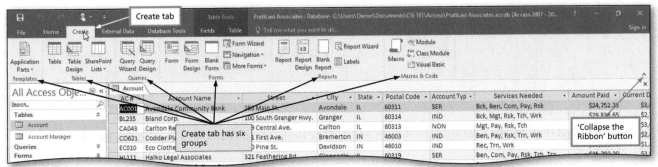

Figure 34

(🔍) **Experiment**

- Click the other tabs on the ribbon to view their contents. When you are finished, click Create on the ribbon to redisplay the Create tab.

Q&A If I am working in a different Office app, such as PowerPoint or Word, how do I display a different tab on the ribbon?

Follow this same procedure; that is, click the desired tab on the ribbon.

To Collapse and Expand the Ribbon

1 SIGN IN | 2 USE WINDOWS | 3 USE APPS | 4 FILE MANAGEMENT | 5 SWITCH APPS
6 SAVE FILES | 7 CHANGE SCREEN RESOLUTION | 8 EXIT APPS | 9 USE HELP

To display more of a document or other item in the window of an Office app, some users prefer to collapse the ribbon, which hides the groups on the ribbon and displays only the main tabs. Each time you run an Office app, the ribbon appears the same way it did the last time you used that Office app. The modules in this book, however, begin with the ribbon appearing as it did at the initial installation of the software.

The following steps collapse and expand the ribbon. *Why? If you need more space on the screen to work with your document, you may consider collapsing the ribbon to gain additional workspace.*

1

- Click the 'Collapse the Ribbon' button on the ribbon (shown in Figure 34) to collapse the ribbon (Figure 35).

Q&A What happened to the 'Collapse the Ribbon' button?

The 'Pin the ribbon' button replaces the 'Collapse the Ribbon' button when the ribbon is collapsed. You will see the 'Pin the ribbon' button only when you expand a ribbon by clicking a tab.

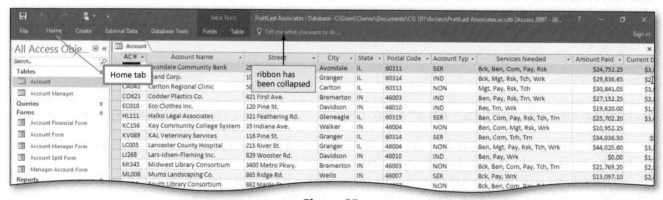

Figure 35

2

- Click Home on the ribbon to expand the Home tab (Figure 36).

Q&A Why would I click the Home tab?

If you want to use a command on a collapsed ribbon, click the main tab to display the groups for that tab. After you select a command on the ribbon and resume working in the document, the groups will be collapsed once again. If you decide not to use a command on the ribbon, you can collapse the groups by clicking the same main tab or clicking in the app window.

(🔍) **Experiment**

- Click Home on the ribbon to collapse the groups again. Click Home on the ribbon to expand the Home tab.

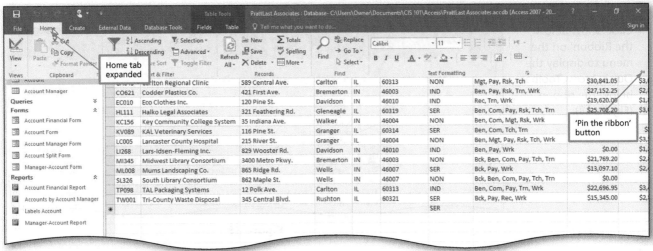

Figure 36

3

- Click the 'Pin the ribbon' button on the expanded Home tab to restore the ribbon (see Figure 34).

Other Ways	
1. Double-click a main tab on the ribbon	2. Press CTRL+F1

To Relocate the Quick Access Toolbar

1 SIGN IN | 2 USE WINDOWS | 3 USE APPS | 4 FILE MANAGEMENT | 5 SWITCH APPS
6 SAVE FILES | 7 CHANGE SCREEN RESOLUTION | 8 EXIT APPS | 9 USE HELP

When you click the 'Customize Quick Access Toolbar' button, you will see a list of commands you can use to customize the Quick Access Toolbar. One of the commands allows you to relocate the Quick Access Toolbar below the ribbon. **Why?** *You might prefer this location.* The following steps use the 'Customize Quick Access Toolbar' button to move the Quick Access Toolbar, which by default is located on the title bar.

1

- Click the 'Customize Quick Access Toolbar' button to display a menu of commands related to the Quick Access Toolbar (Figure 37).

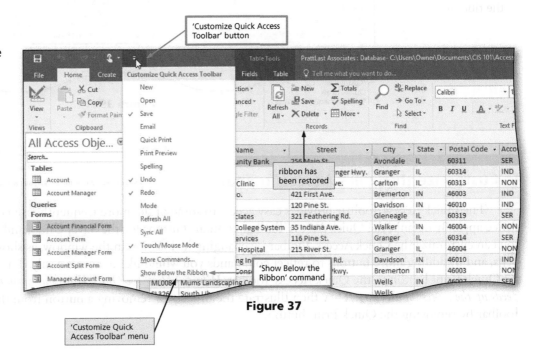

Figure 37

- Click 'Show Below the Ribbon' on the menu to display the Quick Access Toolbar below the ribbon (Figure 38).

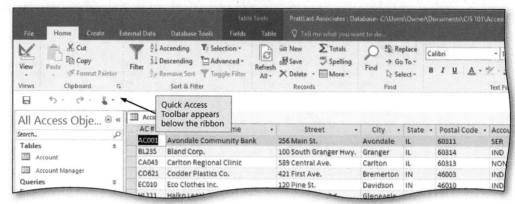

Figure 38

- Click the 'Customize Quick Access Toolbar' button, now located below the ribbon, to display a menu of commands related to the Quick Access Toolbar (Figure 39).

- Click 'Show Above the Ribbon' on the menu to once again display the Quick Access Toolbar above the ribbon.

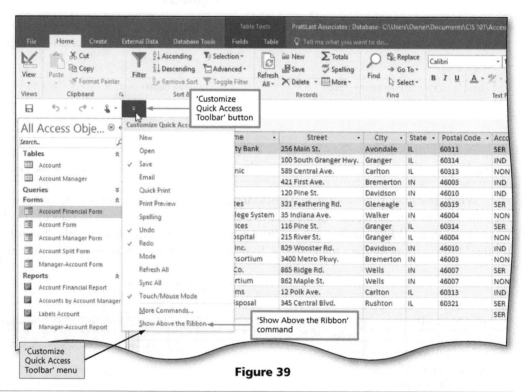

Figure 39

To Customize the Quick Access Toolbar

1 SIGN IN | 2 USE WINDOWS | 3 USE APPS | 4 FILE MANAGEMENT | 5 SWITCH APPS
6 SAVE FILES | 7 CHANGE SCREEN RESOLUTION | 8 EXIT APPS | 9 USE HELP

The Quick Access Toolbar provides easy access to some of the more frequently used commands in the Office apps. By default, the Quick Access Toolbar contains buttons for the Save, Undo, and Redo commands. You can customize the Quick Access Toolbar by changing its location in the window, as shown in the previous steps, and by adding more buttons to reflect commands you would like to access easily. The following steps add the Quick Print button to the Quick Access Toolbar. *Why? Adding the Quick Print button to the Quick Access Toolbar speeds up the process of printing.* They then Illustrate the process of removing a button from the Quick Access Toolbar by removing the Quick Print button.

1

- Click the 'Customize Quick Access Toolbar' button to display the Customize Quick Access Toolbar menu (Figure 40).

Q&A
Which commands are listed on the Customize Quick Access Toolbar menu?
It lists commands that commonly are added to the Quick Access Toolbar.

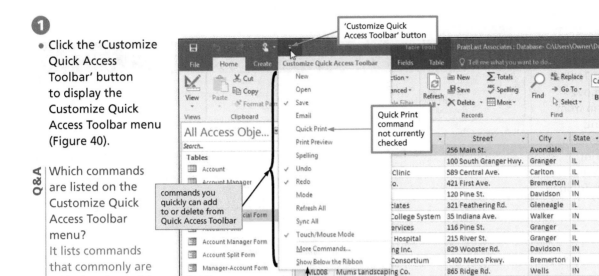

Figure 40

2

- Click Quick Print on the Customize Quick Access Toolbar menu to add the Quick Print button to the Quick Access Toolbar (Figure 41).

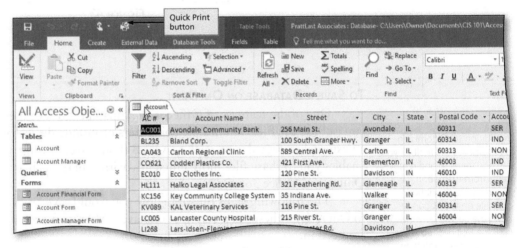

Figure 41

3

- Click the 'Customize Quick Access Toolbar' button to display the Customize Quick Access Toolbar menu (Figure 42).

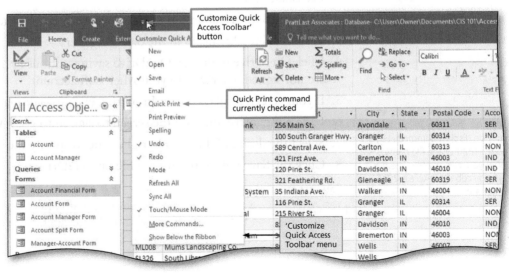

Figure 42

4

- Click Quick Print on the Customize Quick Access Toolbar menu to remove check mark in front of Quick Print, which will remove the Quick Print button from the Quick Access Toolbar (Figure 43).

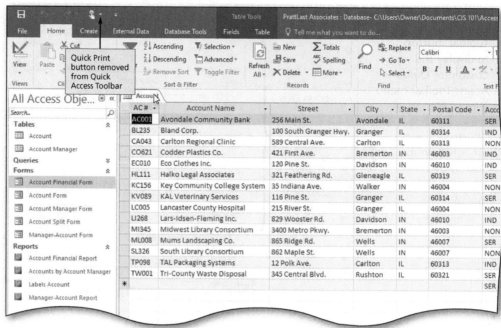

Figure 43

BTW

Customizing the Ribbon

In addition to customizing the Quick Access Toolbar, you can add items to and remove items from the ribbon. To customize the ribbon, click File on the ribbon to open the Backstage view, click the Options tab in the Backstage view, and then click Customize Ribbon in the left pane of the Options dialog box.

BTW

File Type

Depending on your Windows settings, the file type .accdb may be displayed immediately to the right of the file name after you save the file. The file type .accdb is an Access 2016 database.

To Save a Database on OneDrive

One of the features of Office is the capability to save files on OneDrive so that you can use the files on multiple computers or mobile devices without having to use an external storage device, such as a USB flash drive. Storing files on OneDrive also enables you to share files more efficiently with others, such as when using Office Online and Office 365.

The following steps illustrate how you would save an existing Access database to OneDrive. These steps require you have a Microsoft account and an Internet connection.

1. With the database to be saved open, click File on the ribbon to open the Backstage view.
2. Click the Save As tab in the Backstage view to display the Save As gallery.
3. Click the Save As button in the Save As gallery.
4. Click OneDrive to display OneDrive saving options or a Sign In button, if you are not signed in already to your Microsoft account.
5. If your screen displays a Sign In button, click it to display the Sign in dialog box.
6. Follow the instructions on the screen to sign in to your Microsoft account.
7. Select the desired folder in the right pane to specify the save location
8. Click the Save button to save the file on OneDrive.

Q&A

Can I create a database on OneDrive?

Yes. After "browsing for a location to put your database," select OneDrive for the location. You can then select the desired folder within OneDrive.

To Copy a Folder to OneDrive

To back up your files or easily make them available on another computer or mobile device, you can copy them to OneDrive. To do so, you would use the following steps.

1. Click the File Explorer button on the taskbar to make the folder window the active window.
2. Navigate to the folder to be copied. For example, to navigate to the folder called CIS 101, you could click Documents in the This PC area of the navigation pane to display the CIS 101 folder in the file list, and then click the CIS 101 folder in the file list to select it.
3. Click Home on the ribbon to display the Home tab.
4. Click the Copy to button (Home tab | Organize group) to display the Copy to menu.
5. Click Choose location on the Copy to menu to display the Copy Items dialog box.
6. Click OneDrive (Copy Items dialog box) to select it.
7. Click the Copy button (Copy Items dialog box) to copy the selected folder to OneDrive.
8. Click OneDrive in the navigation pane to verify the CIS 101 folder is displayed in the file list.

To Unlink a OneDrive Account

If you are using a public computer and are not signed in to Windows with a Microsoft account, you should unlink your OneDrive account so that other users cannot access it. To do so, you would use the following steps, which begin with clicking the 'Show hidden icons' button on the Windows taskbar to show a menu of hidden icons, including the OneDrive icon (Figure 44).

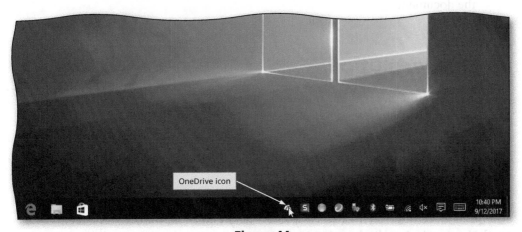

OneDrive icon

Figure 44

1. Click the 'Show hidden icons' button on the Windows taskbar to display a menu of hidden icons.
2. Right-click the OneDrive icon to display a shortcut menu, and then click Settings on the shortcut menu to display the Microsoft OneDrive dialog box.

3. Click the Unlink OneDrive button (Microsoft OneDrive dialog box) to unlink the OneDrive account.

4. When the Microsoft OneDrive dialog box appears with a Welcome to OneDrive message, click the Close button.

To Sign Out of a Microsoft Account

If you are using a public computer or otherwise wish to sign out of your Microsoft account, you should sign out of the account from the Account gallery in the Backstage view. Signing out of the account is the safest way to make sure that nobody else can access online files or settings stored in your Microsoft account.

To sign out of a Microsoft account from Access, you would use the following steps.

1. Click File on the ribbon to open the Backstage view.

2 Click the Account tab to display the Account gallery.

3. Click the Sign out link, which displays the Remove Account dialog box. If a Can't remove Windows accounts dialog box appears instead of the Remove Account dialog box, click the OK button and skip the remaining steps.

Q&A Why does a Can't remove Windows accounts dialog box appear?
If you signed in to Windows using your Microsoft account, then you also must sign out from Windows, rather than signing out from within Access. When you are finished using Windows, be sure to sign out at that time.

4. Click the Yes button (Remove Account dialog box) to sign out of your Microsoft account on this computer.

Q&A Should I sign out of Windows after removing my Microsoft account?
When you are finished using the computer, you should sign out of Windows for maximum security.

5. Click the Back button in the upper-left corner of the Backstage view to return to the document.

Screen Resolution

Screen resolution indicates the number of pixels (dots) that the computer uses to display the letters, numbers, graphics, and background you see on the screen. When you increase the screen resolution, Windows displays more information on the screen, but the information decreases in size. The reverse also is true: as you decrease the screen resolution, Windows displays less information on the screen, but the information increases in size.

Screen resolution usually is stated as the product of two numbers, such as 1366 × 768 (pronounced "thirteen sixty-six by seven sixty-eight"). A 1366 × 768 screen resolution results in a display of 1366 distinct pixels on each of 768 lines, or about 1,050,624 pixels. Changing the screen resolution affects how the ribbon appears in Office apps and some Windows dialog boxes. Figure 45 shows the Access ribbon at screen resolutions of 1366 × 768 and 1024 × 768. All of the same commands are available regardless of screen resolution. The app (Access, in this case), however, makes changes to the groups and the buttons within the groups to accommodate the various screen resolutions. The result is that certain commands may need to be accessed differently depending on the resolution chosen. A command that is visible on the ribbon and available by clicking a button at one resolution may not be visible and may need to be accessed using its Dialog Box Launcher at a different resolution.

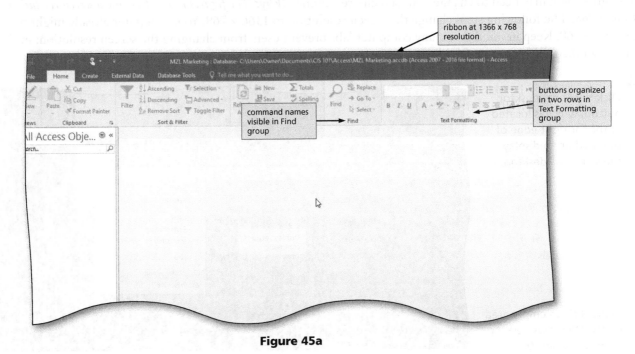

Figure 45a

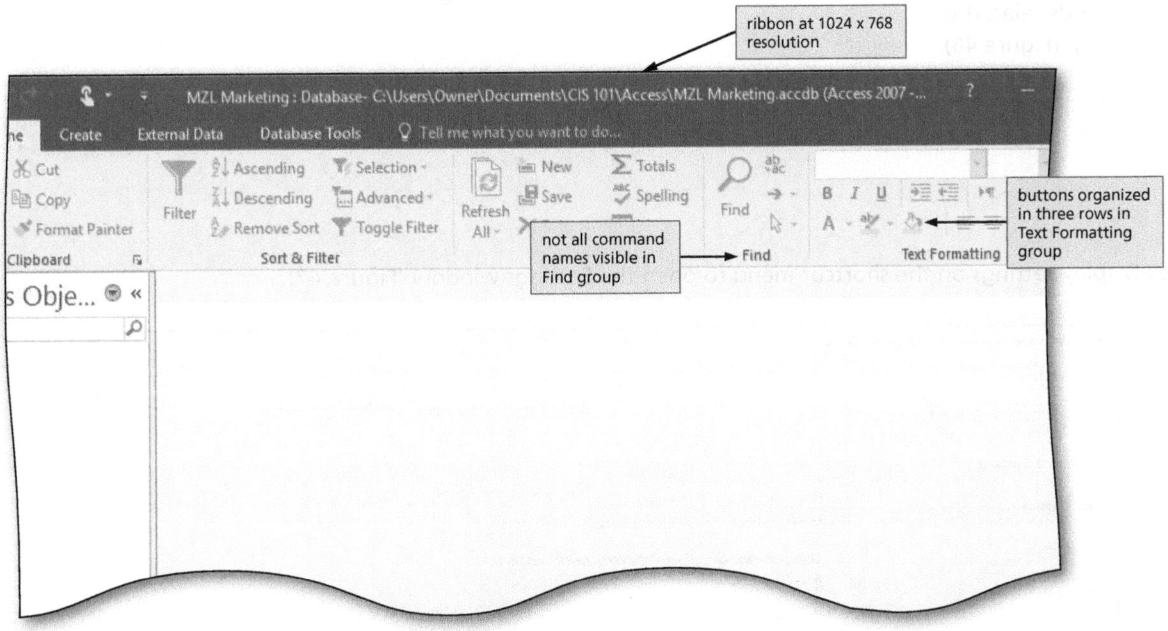

Figure 45b

Comparing the two ribbons in Figure 45, notice the changes in content and layout of the groups and galleries. In some cases, the content of a group is the same in each resolution, but the layout of the group differs. For example, the same gallery and buttons appear in the Text Formatting groups in the two resolutions, but the layouts differ. In other cases, the content and layout are the same across the resolution, but the level of detail differs with the resolution.

OFF 36   Office 2016 and Windows 10 Module   Essential Concepts and Skills

1 SIGN IN | 2 USE WINDOWS | 3 USE APPS | 4 FILE MANAGEMENT | 5 SWITCH APPS
6 SAVE FILES | 7 CHANGE SCREEN RESOLUTION | 8 EXIT APPS | 9 USE HELP

To Change the Screen Resolution

If you are using a computer to step through the modules in this book and you want your screen to match the figures, you may need to change your screen's resolution. *Why? The figures in this book use a screen resolution of 1366 × 768.* The following steps change the screen resolution to 1366 × 768. Your computer already might be set to 1366 × 768. Keep in mind that many computer labs prevent users from changing the screen resolution; in that case, read the following steps for illustration purposes.

1

- Click the Show desktop button, which is located at the far-right edge of the taskbar, to display the Windows desktop.

Q&A | I cannot see the Show desktop button. Why not? When you point to the far-right edge of the taskbar, a small outline appears to mark the Show desktop button.

- Right-click an empty area on the Windows desktop to display a shortcut menu that contains a list of commands related to the desktop (Figure 46).

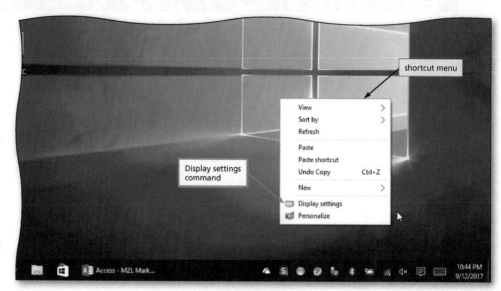

Figure 46

Q&A | Why does my shortcut menu display different commands?
Depending on your computer's hardware and configuration, different commands might appear on the shortcut menu.

2

- Click Display settings on the shortcut menu to open the Settings window (Figure 47).

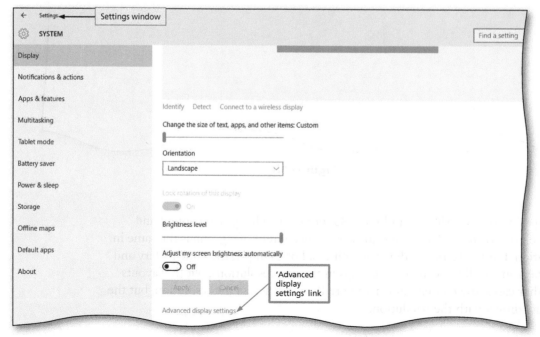

Figure 47

- Scroll down, if necessary, so that 'Advanced display settings' appears, and then click 'Advanced display settings' in the Settings window to display the advanced display settings.

- If necessary, scroll to display the Resolution box (Figure 48).

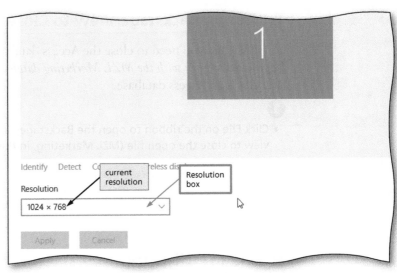

Figure 48

- Click the Resolution box to display a list of available screen resolutions (Figure 49).

- If necessary, scroll to and then click 1366 × 768 to select the screen resolution.

Q&A What if my computer does not support the 1366 × 768 resolution?
Some computers do not support the 1366 × 768 resolution. In this case, select a resolution that is close to the 1366 × 768 resolution.

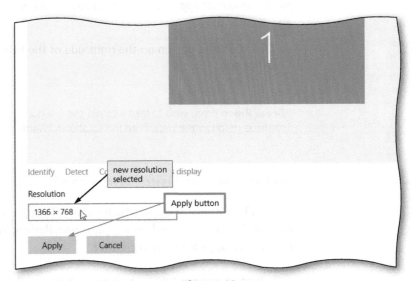

Figure 49

- Click the Apply button (Advanced Display Settings window) to change the screen resolution and display a confirmation message (Figure 50).

- Click the Keep changes button to accept the new screen resolution.

- Click the Close button to close the Settings window.

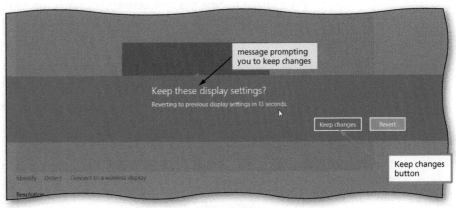

Figure 50

Other Ways

1. Click Start button, click Settings, click System, click Display, click 'Advanced display settings,' select desired resolution in Resolution box, click Apply button, click Keep changes button

2. Type `screen resolution` in search box, click 'Change the screen resolution,' select desired resolution in Resolution box, click Apply, click Keep changes

To Use the Backstage View to Close a Database

Assume you need to close the Access database and return to it later. *Why? You no longer need to work with the MZL Marketing database, so you may close it.* The following step closes an Access database.

- Click File on the ribbon to open the Backstage view and then click Close in the Backstage view to close the open file (MZL Marketing, in this case) without exiting Access.

Q&A Why is Access still on the screen?
When you close a database, the app remains running.

To Exit an Office App

You are finished using Access. The following step exits Access. *Why? It is good practice to exit an app when you are finished using it.*

- Click the Close button on the right side of the title bar to close the file and exit the Office app.

Break Point: If you wish to take a break, this is a good place to do so. To resume at a later time, continue to follow the steps from this location forward.

To Run Access Using the Search Box

The following steps, which assume Windows is running, use the search box to run the Access app based on a typical installation. You may need to ask your instructor how to run apps for your computer.

1 Type **Access 2016** as the search text in the Search box and watch the search results appear in the search results.

Q&A Do I need to type the complete app name or use correct capitalization?
No, you need to type just enough characters of the app name for it to appear in the Apps list. For example, you may be able to type Access or access, instead of Access 2016.

2 Click the app name, Access 2016 in this case, in the search results to run Access.

3 If the app window is not maximized, click the Maximize button on its title bar to maximize the window (Figure 51).

Q&A Do I have to run Access using these steps?
No. You can use whichever method you prefer to run Access.

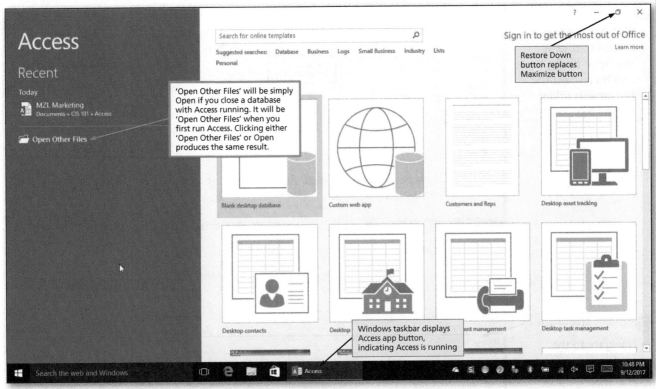

Figure 51

To Open an Existing Database

To work on an existing database, that is, a database you previously created, you must open the database. To do so, you will use the Backstage view. The following step opens an existing database, specifically the MZL Marketing database. *Why? Because the database has been created already, you just need to open it.*

1

- If you have just run Access, click 'Open Other Files' to display the Open gallery in the Backstage view. If not, click File on the ribbon to open the Backstage view and then click Open in the Backstage view to display the Open gallery (Figure 52).

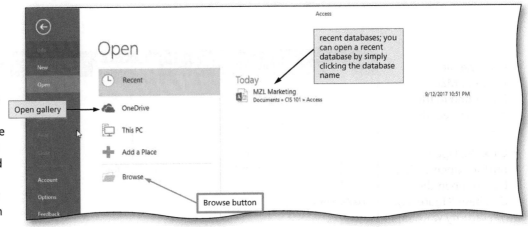

Figure 52

Q&A I see the name of the database I want to open in the Recent list in Backstage view. Can I just click the name to open the file?

Yes. That is an alternative way to open a database, provided the name of the database is included in the Recent list.

- Click the Browse button to display the Open dialog box and then select the Documents folder (Figure 53).

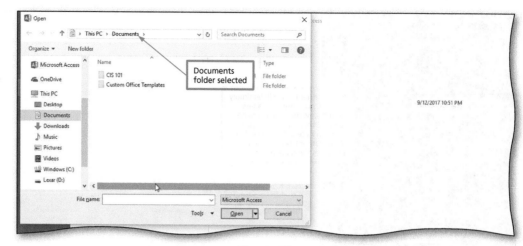

Figure 53

- Navigate to the folder containing the file to open (for example, the Access folder) in the CIS 101 folder (Figure 54).

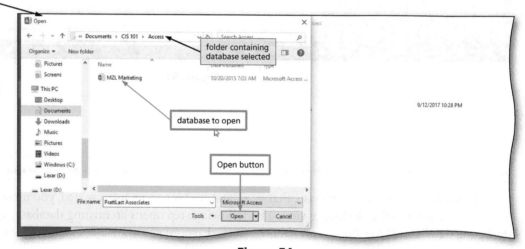

Figure 54

- Click the file to open, MZL Marketing in this case, to select the file.

- Click the Open button (Open dialog box) to open the database (Figure 55). If a security warning appears, click the Enable Content button.

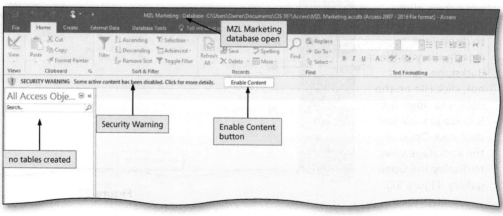

Figure 55

Q&A | Why might a Security Warning appear?
A Security Warning appears when you open a database that might contain harmful content. The files you create in this chapter are not harmful, but you should be cautious when opening files from other people.

Other Ways	
1. Press CTRL+O	2. Navigate to File Explorer window, double-click file

To Exit Access

You are finished using Access. The following step exits Access.

 Click the Close button on the right side of the title bar to close the file and exit Access.

TO CREATE A NEW ACCESS DATABASE FROM FILE EXPLORER

File Explorer provides a means to create an Access database without running an Office app. To do so, you would use the following steps.

1. Double-click the File Explorer app button on the taskbar to make the folder window the active window, and then navigate to the folder in which you want to create the database.

2. Double-click the folder in which you wish to create the database.

3. Right-click an open area in the file list to display a shortcut menu, and then point to New on the shortcut menu to display the New submenu.

4. Click 'Microsoft Access Database' on the New submenu to display an icon and text box for a new file in the current folder window with the file name, New Microsoft Access Database, selected.

5. Type the desired name in the text box and then press the ENTER key to create the database in the desired folder.

TO RUN ACCESS FROM FILE EXPLORER AND OPEN A DATABASE

Previously, you learned how to run Access using the Start screen and the Search bar. You can also run it from File Explorer. To do so, you would use the following steps.

1. If necessary, display the database to open in the folder window in File Explorer.

2. Right-click the file icon or database name to display a shortcut menu, and then click Open on the shortcut menu to open the selected database in Access. If a security warning appears, click the Enable Content button.

Renaming, Moving, and Deleting Files

Earlier in this module, you learned how to organize files in folders, which is part of a process known as **file management**. The following sections cover additional file management topics including renaming, moving, and deleting files.

TO RENAME A FILE

In some circumstances, you may want to change the name of, or rename, a file or a folder. To do so, you would use the following steps.

1. If necessary, click the File Explorer button on the taskbar to make the folder window the active window, and then navigate to the location of the file to be renamed.

2. Right-click the icon or file name of the file to be renamed to display a shortcut menu that presents a list of commands related to files.

3. Click Rename on the shortcut menu to place the current file name in a text box, type the new name, and then press the ENTER key.

Q&A
Are any risks involved in renaming files that are located on a hard drive?
If you inadvertently rename a file that is associated with certain apps, the apps might not be able to find the file and, therefore, might not run properly. Always use caution when renaming files.

Can I rename a file when it is open?
No, a file must be closed to change its name.

TO MOVE A FILE

When you move a file, it no longer appears in the original folder. If the destination and the source folders are on the same media, you can move a file by dragging it. If the folders are on different media, then you will need to right-click the file, and then click Cut on the shortcut menu. In the destination folder, you will need to right-click and then click Paste on the shortcut menu. To do so, you would use the following steps.

1. If necessary, click the File Explorer button on the taskbar to make the folder window the active window, and then navigate to the location of the file to be moved.

2. Right-click the icon or file name of the file to be moved to display a shortcut menu that presents a list of commands related to files.

3. Click Cut on the shortcut menu to cut the current file to the clipboard, and then navigate to the folder to which you wish to move the file.

4. Click any open area in the folder, and then click Paste on the shortcut menu to paste the file.

TO DELETE A FILE

A final task you may want to perform is to delete a file. Exercise extreme caution when deleting a file or files. When you delete a file from a hard drive, the deleted file is stored in the Recycle Bin where you can recover it until you empty the Recycle Bin. If you delete a file from removable media, such as a USB flash drive, the file is deleted permanently. To delete a file, you would use the following steps.

1. If necessary, click the File Explorer button on the taskbar to make the folder window the active window, and then navigate to the location of the file to be deleted.

2. Right-click the icon or file name of the file to be deleted to display a shortcut menu that presents a list of commands related to files.

3. Click Delete on the shortcut menu to delete the file, and then click the Yes button to confirm the deletion.

Q&A

Can I use this same technique to delete a folder?

Yes. Right-click the folder and then click Delete on the shortcut menu. When you delete a folder, all of the files and folders contained in the folder you are deleting, together with any files and folders on lower hierarchical levels, are deleted as well. For example, if you delete the CIS 101 folder, you will delete all folders and files inside the CIS 101 folder.

Microsoft Office and Windows Help

At any time while you are using one of the Office apps, you can use Office Help to display information about all topics associated with the app. To illustrate the use of Office Help, this section uses Access. Help in other Office apps operates in a similar fashion.

In Office, Help is presented in a window that has browser-style navigation buttons. Each Office app has its own Help home page, which is the starting Help page that is displayed in the Help window. If your computer is connected to the Internet, the contents of the Help page reflect both the local help files installed on the computer and material from Microsoft's website.

To Open the Help Window in an Office App

1 SIGN IN | 2 USE WINDOWS | 3 USE APPS | 4 FILE MANAGEMENT | 5 SWITCH APPS
6 SAVE FILES | 7 CHANGE SCREEN RESOLUTION | 8 EXIT APPS | **9 USE HELP**

The following step opens the Access Help window. **Why?** *You might not understand how certain commands or operations work in Access, so you can obtain the necessary information using help.*

1

- Run an Office app, in this case Access.

- Click the MZL Marketing database in the Recent list to open the MZL Marketing database.

- Press F1 to open the app's Help window (Figure 56).

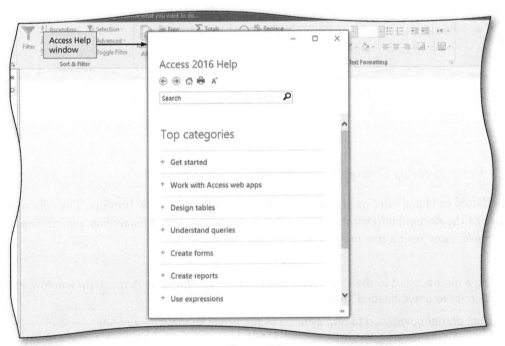

Figure 56

Moving and Resizing Windows

At times, it is useful, or even necessary, to have more than one window open and visible on the screen at the same time. You can resize and move these open windows so that you can view different areas of and elements in the window. In the case of the Help window, for example, it could be covering database objects in the Access window that you need to see.

To Move a Window by Dragging

1 SIGN IN | 2 USE WINDOWS | 3 USE APPS | 4 FILE MANAGEMENT | 5 SWITCH APPS
6 SAVE FILES | 7 CHANGE SCREEN RESOLUTION | 8 EXIT APPS | 9 USE HELP

You can move any open window that is not maximized to another location on the desktop by dragging the title bar of the window. **Why?** *You might want to have a better view of what is behind the window or just want to move the window so that you can see it better.* The following step drags the Access Help window to the upper-left corner of the desktop.

- Drag the window title bar (the Access Help window title bar, in this case) so that the window moves to the upper-left corner of the desktop, as shown in Figure 57.

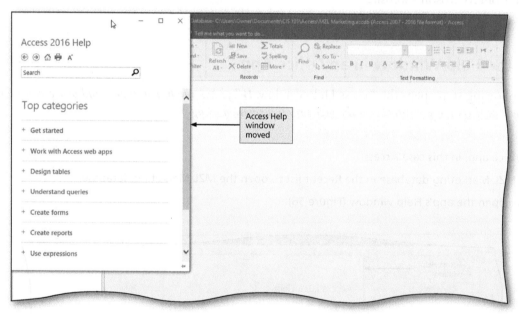

Figure 57

To Resize a Window by Dragging

1 SIGN IN | 2 USE WINDOWS | 3 USE APPS | 4 FILE MANAGEMENT | 5 SWITCH APPS
6 SAVE FILES | 7 CHANGE SCREEN RESOLUTION | 8 EXIT APPS | 9 USE HELP

A method used to change the size of the window is to drag the window borders. The following step changes the size of the Access Help window by dragging its borders. **Why?** *Sometimes, information is not visible completely in a window, and you want to increase the size of the window.*

- If you are using a mouse, point to the lower-right corner of the window (the Access Help window, in this case) until the pointer changes to a two-headed arrow.

- Drag the bottom border downward to display more of the active window (Figure 58).

Q&A
Can I drag other borders on the window to enlarge or shrink the window?
Yes, you can drag the left, right, and top borders and any window corner to resize a window.

Will Windows remember the new size of the window after I close it?
Yes. When you reopen the window, Windows will display it at the same size it was when you closed it.

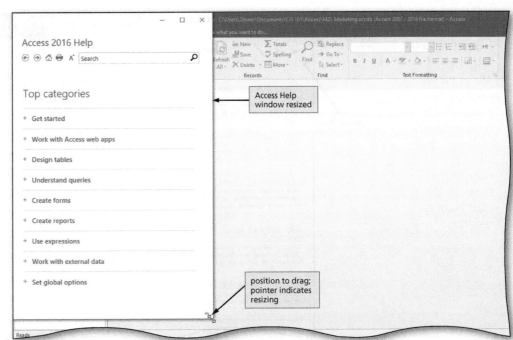

Figure 58

Using Office Help

Once an Office app's Help window is open, several methods exist for navigating Help. You can search for help by using any of the three following methods from the Help window:

1. Enter search text in the Search text box.
2. Click the links in the Help window.
3. Use the Table of Contents.

To Obtain Help Using the Search Text Box

1 SIGN IN | 2 USE WINDOWS | 3 USE APPS | 4 FILE MANAGEMENT | 5 SWITCH APPS
6 SAVE FILES | 7 CHANGE SCREEN RESOLUTION | 8 EXIT APPS | 9 USE HELP

Assume for the following example that you want to know more about forms. The following steps use the 'Search online help' text box to obtain useful information about forms by entering the word, forms, as search text. *Why? You may not know the exact help topic you are looking to find, so using keywords can help narrow your search.*

- Type **forms** in the Search text box at the top of the Access Help window to enter the search text.
- Press the ENTER key to display the search results (Figure 59).

Q&A Why do my search results differ?
If you do not have an Internet connection, your results will reflect only the content of the Help files on your computer. When searching for help online, results also can change as material is added, deleted, and updated on the online Help webpages maintained by Microsoft.

Q&A

Why were my search results not very helpful?
When initiating a search, be sure to check the spelling of the search text; also, keep your search specific to return the most accurate results.

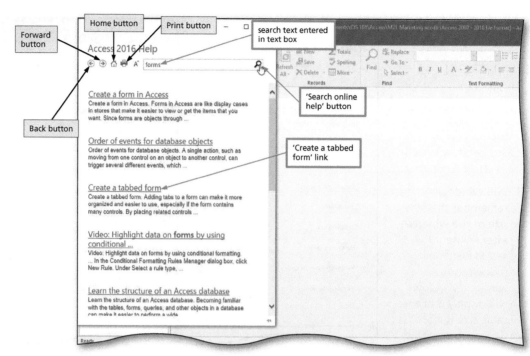

Figure 59

2

- Click the 'Create a tabbed form' link to display the Help information associated with the selected topic (Figure 60).

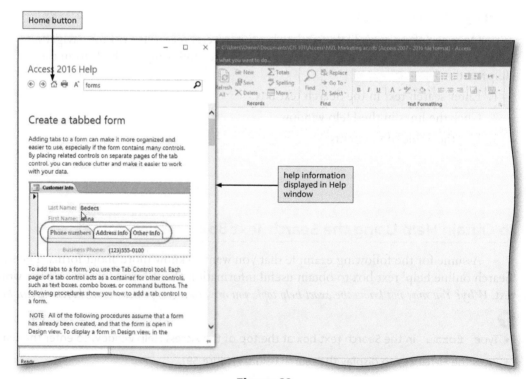

Figure 60

③

- Click the Home button in the Help window to clear the search results and redisplay the Help home page (Figure 61).

- Click the Close button in the Access 2016 Help window to close the window.

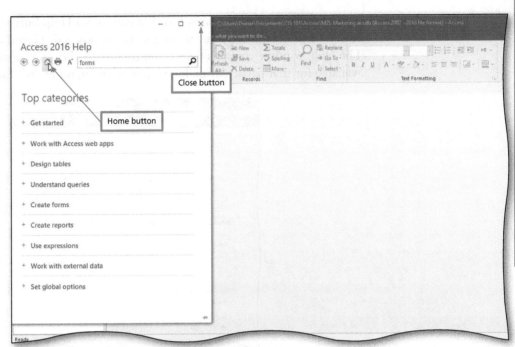

Figure 61

Obtaining Help while Working in an Office App

Help in the Office apps provides you with the ability to obtain help directly, without opening the Help window and initiating a search. For example, you may be unsure about how a particular command works, or you may be presented with a dialog box that you are not sure how to use.

Figure 62 shows one option for obtaining help while working in an Office app. If you want to learn more about a command, point to its button and wait for the ScreenTip to appear. If the Help icon and 'Tell me more' link appear in the ScreenTip, click the 'Tell me more' link or press the F1 key while pointing to the button to open the Help window associated with that command.

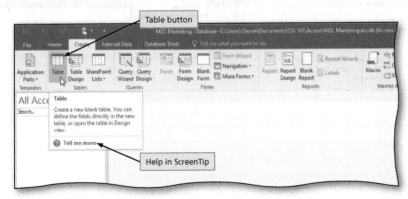

Figure 62

Figure 63 shows a dialog box that contains a Help button. Clicking the Help button or pressing the F1 key while the dialog box is displayed opens a Help window. The Help window contains help about that dialog box, if available. If no help file is available for that particular dialog box, then the main Help window opens.

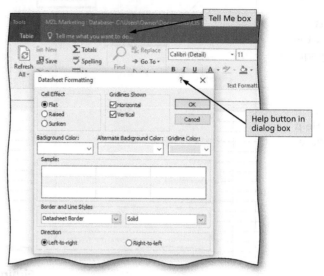

Figure 63

The Tell Me box is available in most Office apps and can perform a variety of functions. One of these functions is to provide easy access to commands by typing a description of the command.

To Obtain Help Using the Tell Me Box

1 SIGN IN | 2 USE WINDOWS | 3 USE APPS | 4 FILE MANAGEMENT | 5 SWITCH APPS
6 SAVE FILES | 7 CHANGE SCREEN RESOLUTION | 8 EXIT APPS | 9 USE HELP

If you are having trouble finding a command in an Office app, you can use the Tell Me box to search for the function you are trying to perform. As you type, the Tell Me box will suggest commands that match the search text you are entering. *Why? You can use the Tell Me box to quickly access commands you otherwise may be unable to find on the ribbon.* The following step finds information about forms.

- Type **forms** in the Tell Me box and watch the search results appear.

- Point to Client Forms to display a submenu displaying the various types of forms (Figure 64).

- Click an empty area of the document window to close the search results.

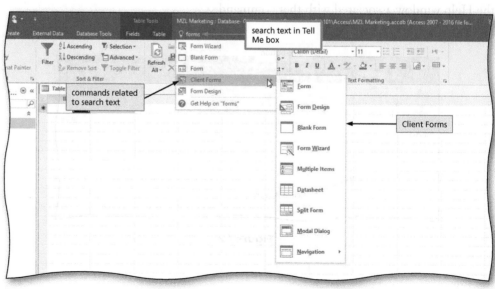

②

- Exit Microsoft Access.

Figure 64

Using the Windows Search Box

One of the more powerful Windows features is the Windows search box. The search box is a central location from where you can type search text and quickly access related Windows commands or web search results. In addition, **Cortana** is a new search tool in Windows that you can access using the search box. It can act as a personal assistant by performing functions such as providing ideas; searching for apps, files, and folders; and setting reminders. In addition to typing search text in the search box, you also can use your computer or mobile device's microphone to give verbal commands.

To Use the Windows Search Box

1 SIGN IN | 2 USE WINDOWS | 3 USE APPS | 4 FILE MANAGEMENT | 5 SWITCH APPS
6 SAVE FILES | 7 CHANGE SCREEN RESOLUTION | 8 EXIT APPS | 9 USE HELP

The following step uses the Windows search box to search for a Windows command. *Why? Using the search box to locate apps, settings, folders, and files can be faster than navigating windows and dialog boxes to search for the desired content.*

- Type **notification** in the search box to display the search results. The search results include related Windows settings, Windows Store apps, and web search results (Figure 65).

- Click an empty area of the desktop to close the search results.

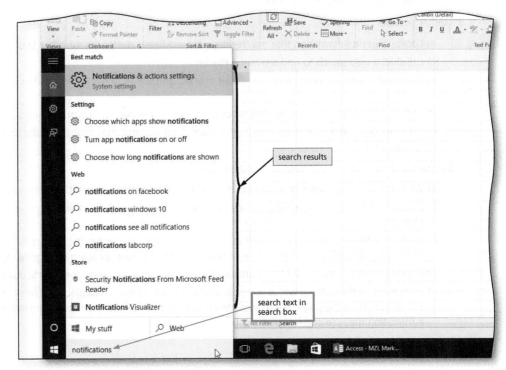

Figure 65

Summary

In this module, you learned how to use the Windows interface, several touch screen and mouse operations, file and folder management, some basic features of Microsoft Access, and discovered the common elements that exist among the different Office apps. Topics covered included signing in, using Windows, using apps, file management, switching between apps, saving files, changing screen resolution, exiting apps, and using help.

What guidelines should you follow to plan your projects?

The process of communicating specific information is a learned, rational skill. Computers and software, especially Microsoft Office 2016, can help you develop ideas and present detailed information to a particular audience and minimize much of the laborious work of drafting and revising projects. No matter what method you use to plan a project, it is beneficial to follow some specific guidelines from the onset to arrive at a final product that is informative, relevant, and effective. Use some aspects of these guidelines every time you undertake a project, and others as needed in specific instances.

1. Determine the project's purpose.

   a) Clearly define why you are undertaking this assignment.

   b) Begin to draft ideas of how best to communicate information by handwriting ideas on paper; composing directly on a laptop, tablet, or mobile device; or developing a strategy that fits your particular thinking and writing style.

2. Analyze your audience.

   a) Learn about the people who will read, analyze, or view your work.

   b) Determine their interests and needs so that you can present the information they need to know and omit the information they already possess.

   c) Form a mental picture of these people or find photos of people who fit this profile so that you can develop a project with the audience in mind.

3. Gather possible content.

   a) Locate existing information that may reside in spreadsheets, databases, or other files.

   b) Conduct a web search to find relevant websites.

   c) Read pamphlets, magazine and newspaper articles, and books to gain insights of how others have approached your topic.

   d) Conduct personal interviews to obtain perspectives not available by any other means.

   e) Consider video and audio clips as potential sources for material that might complement or support the factual data you uncover.

4. Determine what content to present to your audience.

   a) Write three or four major ideas you want an audience member to remember after reading or viewing your project.

   b) Envision your project's endpoint, the key fact you wish to emphasize, so that all project elements lead to this final element.

   c) Determine relevant time factors, such as the length of time to develop the project, how long readers will spend reviewing your project, or the amount of time allocated for your speaking engagement.

   d) Decide whether a graph, photo, or artistic element can express or enhance a particular concept.

   e) Be mindful of the order in which you plan to present the content, and place the most important material at the top or bottom of the page, because readers and audience members generally remember the first and last pieces of information they see and hear.

How should you submit solutions to questions in the assignments identified with a ✳ symbol?

Every assignment in this book contains one or more questions with a ✳ symbol. These questions require you to think beyond the assigned file. Present your solutions to the question in the format required by your instructor. Possible formats may include one or more of these options: write the answer; create a document that contains the answer; present your answer to the class; discuss your answer in a group; record the answer as audio or video using a webcam, smartphone, or portable media player; or post answers on a blog, wiki, or website.

Apply Your Knowledge

Reinforce the skills and apply the concepts you learned in this module.

Creating a Folder and a Database

Instructions: You will create an Access Assignments folder and then create an Access database and save it in the folder.

Perform the following tasks:

1. Open the File Explorer window and then double-click to open the Documents folder.
2. Click the New folder button on the Quick Access Toolbar to display a new folder icon and text box for the folder name.
3. Type `Access Assignments` in the text box to name the folder. Press the ENTER key to create the folder in the Documents folder.
4. Run Access.
5. Use the 'Blank desktop database' option to create a database with the name AYK 1. Do not press the ENTER key after typing the file name.
6. If requested by your instructor, name the database AYK 1 Lastname where Lastname is your last name.
7. Click the 'Browse for a location to put your database' button and navigate to the Access Assignments folder in the Documents library. Click the OK button to select the Access Assignments folder as the location for the database and close the dialog box. Click the Create button to create the database.
8. If your Quick Access Toolbar does not show the Quick Print button, add the Quick Print button to the Quick Access Toolbar.
9. Exit Access.
10. Open the File Explorer window, open the Documents library, and then open the Access Assignments folder you created.
11. Double-click the AYK 1 database to run Access and open the AYK 1 database.
12. Remove the Quick Print button from the Quick Access Toolbar.
13. Submit the database in the format specified by your instructor.
14. ✷ What other commands might you find useful to include on the Quick Access Toolbar?

Extend Your Knowledge

Extend the skills you learned in this module and experiment with new skills. You will use Help to complete the assignment.

Using Help

Instructions: Use Access Help to perform the following tasks.

Perform the following tasks:

1. Run Access.
2. Click the Microsoft Access Help button to open the Access Help window (see Figure 56).
3. Search Access Help to answer the following questions.

   a. What shortcut keys are available for entering data in Datasheet or Form view?
   b. What is the AutoCorrect feature?

Continued >

Extend Your Knowledge *continued*

    c. What is the purpose of the Navigation Pane?

    d. How do you back up a database?

    e. What are data types?

    f. What is a query?

    g. What is a template?

    h. What is the purpose of compacting and repairing a database?

4. Exit Access.

5. Type the answers from your searches in a new blank Word document.

6. If requested to do so by your instructor, enter your name in the Word document.

7. Save the document with a new file name and then submit it in the format specified by your instructor.

8. Exit Word.

9. ✳ What search text did you use to perform the searches above? Did it take multiple attempts to search and locate the exact information for which you were searching?

Expand Your World

Create a solution that uses cloud or web technologies by learning and investigating on your own from general guidance.

Instructions: Create the folders shown in Figure 66. Then, using the respective Office Online app, create a small file to save in each folder (i.e., create a Word document to save in the Word folder, a PowerPoint presentation to save in the PowerPoint folder, and so on).

Perform the following tasks:

1. Sign in to OneDrive in your browser.

2. Use the New button to create the folder structure shown in Figure 66.

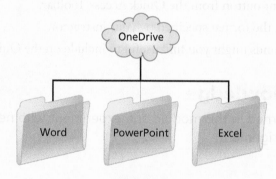

Figure 66

3. In the Word folder, use the New button to create a Word document with the file name, Reminders, and containing the text, Lunch with Laura on Tuesday.

4. Save the document and then exit the app.

5. Navigate to the PowerPoint folder.

6. Create a PowerPoint presentation called Database Sales with one slide containing the title text, Online Presentation, and then exit the app.

7. Navigate to the Excel folder.

8. Create an Excel spreadsheet called Database Sales Analysis containing the text, Sales Cost Analysis, in cell A1, and then exit the app.

9. Submit the assignment in the format specified by your instructor.

10. ✳ Based on your current knowledge of OneDrive, do you think you will use it? What about the Office Online apps?

In the Labs

Design, create, modify, and/or use files following the guidelines, concepts, and skills presented in this module. Labs 1 and 2, which increase in difficulty, require you to create solutions based on what you learned in the module; Lab 3 requires you to apply your creative thinking and problem-solving skills to design and implement a solution.

Lab 1: Creating Folders for a Bookstore

Problem: Your friend works for a local bookstore. He would like to organize his files in relation to the types of books available in the store. He has seven main categories: fiction, biography, children, humor, social science, nonfiction, and medical. You are to create a folder structure similar to the one in Figure 67.

Perform the following tasks:

1. Click the File Explorer button on the taskbar and display the contents of the Documents folder.

2. In the Documents folder, create the main folder and name it Book Categories.

3. Navigate to the Book Categories folder.

4. Within the Book Categories folder, create a folder for each of the following: Fiction, Biography, Children, Humor, Social Science, Nonfiction, and Medical.

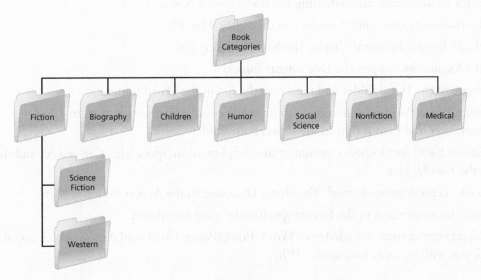

Figure 67

Continued >

In the Labs *continued*

5. Within the Fiction folder, create two additional folders, one for Science Fiction and the second for Western.

6. Submit the assignment in the format specified by your instructor.

7. Think about how you use your computer for various tasks (consider personal, professional, and academic reasons). What folders do you think will be required on your computer to store the files you save?

Lab 2: **Saving Files in Folders**

Problem: You are taking a class that requires you to create Word, PowerPoint, Excel, and Access files. You will save these files to folders named for four different Office apps (Figure 68).

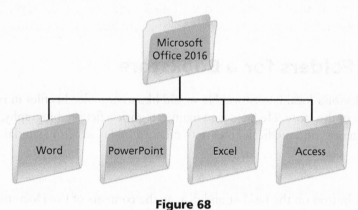

Figure 68

Perform the following tasks:

1. Create the folders shown in Figure 68.

2. Create a Word document containing the text, Week 1 Notes.

3. In the Backstage view, click Save As and then click This PC.

4. Click the Browse button to display the Save As dialog box.

5. Click Documents to open the Documents folder.

6. Navigate to the Word folder and then save the file in the Word folder.

7. Create a PowerPoint presentation with one slide containing the title text, In-Class Presentation, and then save it in the PowerPoint folder.

8. Create an Excel spreadsheet containing the text, Financial Spreadsheet, in cell A1 and then save it in the Excel folder.

9. Save an Access database named, My Movie Database, in the Access folder.

10. Submit the assignment in the format specified by your instructor.

11. Based on your current knowledge of Word, PowerPoint, Excel, and Access, which app do you think you will use most frequently? Why?

Lab 3: **Consider This: Your Turn**

Performing Research about Malware

Problem: You have just installed a new computer with the Windows operating system. Because you want to be sure that it is protected from the threat of malware, you decide to research malware, malware protection, and removing malware.

Part 1:   Research the following three topics: malware, malware protection, and removing malware. Use the concepts and techniques presented in this module to use the search box to find information regarding these topics. Create a Word or OneNote document that contains steps to properly safeguard a computer from malware, ways to prevent malware, as well as the different ways to remove malware or a virus should your computer become infected. Submit your assignment in the format specified by your instructor.

Part 2:   You made several decisions while searching for this assignment. What decisions did you make? What was the rationale behind these decisions? How did you locate the required information about malware?

1 Databases and Database Objects: An Introduction

Objectives

You will have mastered the material in this module when you can:

- Describe the features of the Access window
- Create a database
- Create tables in Datasheet and Design views
- Add records to a table
- Close a database
- Open a database
- Print the contents of a table

- Import data
- Create and use a query
- Create and use a form
- Create and print custom reports
- Modify a report in Layout view
- Perform special database operations
- Design a database to satisfy a collection of requirements

Introduction

The term **database** describes a collection of data organized in a manner that allows access, retrieval, and use of that data. Microsoft Access 2016, usually referred to as simply Access, is a database management system. A **database management system** is software that allows you to use a computer to create a database; add, change, and delete data in the database; ask and answer questions concerning the data; and create forms and reports using the data.

Project — Database Creation

PrattLast Associates is a human resources outsourcing company that provides HR services, such as payroll, hiring, training, and employee benefits management to small and medium-size businesses in the Midwest. Organizations might outsource only one function, such as payroll, or might outsource several functions. While there are many different ways to charge customers, PrattLast charges a set amount per employee per month. The amount varies based on number and type of functions outsourced.

Account managers serve their respective client companies by providing HR solutions and understanding the businesses for which they are responsible. The PrattLast account managers can earn bonuses if their client companies elect to outsource additional HR functions. For example, if the business currently outsources only payroll but is convinced by the account manager to add hiring to the outsourced functions, the account manager receives a bonus.

To ensure that operations run smoothly, PrattLast organizes data on its accounts and account managers in a database managed by Access. In this way, PrattLast keeps its data current and accurate and can analyze it for trends; PrattLast can also create a variety of useful reports.

In a **relational database** such as those maintained by Access, a database consists of a collection of tables, each of which contains information on a specific subject. Figure 1–1 shows the database for PrattLast Associates. It consists of two tables: the Account table (Figure 1–1a) contains information about PrattLast accounts, and the Account Manager table (Figure 1–1b) contains information about the account managers to whom these accounts are assigned.

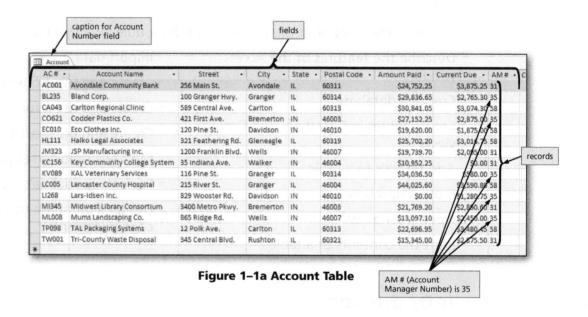

Figure 1–1a Account Table

AM # (Account Manager Number) is 35

Figure 1–1b Account Manager Table

AM # (Account Manager Number) for Mark Simson is 35

The rows in the tables are called **records**. A record contains information about a given person, product, or event. A row in the Account table, for example, contains information about a specific account, such as the account's name, address information, and other data.

The columns in the tables are called fields. A **field** contains a specific piece of information within a record. In the Account table, for example, the fourth field, City, contains the name of the city where the account is located.

The first field in the Account table is AC #, which is an abbreviation for Account Number. PrattLast Associates assigns each account a number; the PrattLast account numbers consist of two uppercase letters followed by a three-digit number.

The account numbers are unique; that is, no two accounts have the same number. Such a field is a **unique identifier**. A unique identifier, as its name suggests, is a way of uniquely identifying each record in the database. A given account number will appear only in a single record in the table. Only one record exists, for example, in which the account number is JM323. A unique identifier is also called a **primary key**. Thus, the Account Number field is the primary key for the Account table. This means the Account Number field can be used to uniquely identify a record in the table. No two records can have the same value in the Account Number field.

The next seven fields in the Account table are Account Name, Street, City, State, Postal Code, Amount Paid, and Current Due. The Amount Paid column contains the amount that the account has paid PrattLast Associates year to date (YTD) prior to the current period. The Current Due column contains the amount due to PrattLast for the current period. For example, account JM323 is JSP Manufacturing Inc. The address is 1200 Franklin Blvd., in Wells, Indiana. The postal code is 46007. The amount paid is $19,739.70 and the current due amount is $2,095.00.

PrattLast assigns a single account manager to work with each account. The last column in the Account table, AM # (an abbreviation for Account Manager Number) gives the number of the account's account manager. The account manager number for JSP Manufacturing is 31.

The first field in the Account Manager table is also AM #, for Account Manager Number. The account manager numbers are unique, so the Account Manager Number field is the primary key of the Account Manager table.

The other fields in the Account Manager table are Last Name, First Name, Street, City, State, Postal Code, Start Date, Salary, and Bonus Rate. The Start Date field gives the date the account manager began working for PrattLast. The Salary field gives the salary paid to the account manager thus far this year. The Bonus Rate gives the potential bonus percentage based on personal performance. The bonus rate applies when the account manager either brings in new business or recommends productivity improvements. For example, account manager 31 is Haydee Rivera. Her address is 325 Twiddy St., in Avondale, Illinois. Her postal code is 60311. Haydee started working for PrattLast on June 3, 2013. So far this year, she has been paid $48,750.00 in salary. Her bonus rate is 0.15 (15%).

The account manager number appears in both the Account table and the Account Manager table, and relates accounts and account managers. Account manager 42, Peter Lu, was recently promoted to account manager and has not yet been assigned any accounts. His account manager number, therefore, does not appear on any row in the Account table.

BTW
Naming Fields
Access 2016 has a number of reserved words, words that have a special meaning to Access. You cannot use these reserved words as field names. For example, Name is a reserved word and could not be used in the Account table to describe an account's name. For a complete list of reserved words in Access 2016, consult Access Help.

How would you find the name of the account manager for Midwest Library Consortium?
In the Account table, you see that the account manager number for account Midwest Library Consortium is 31. To find the name of this account manager, look for the row in the Account Manager table that contains 31 in the AM # column. After you have found it, you know that the account manager for Midwest Library Consortium is Haydee Rivera.

CONSIDER THIS

CONSIDER THIS

How would you find all the accounts assigned to Haydee Rivera?
First, look in the Account Manager table to find that her number is 31. You would then look through the Account table for all the accounts that contain 31 in the AM # column. Haydee's accounts are AC001 (Avondale Community Bank), JM323 (JSP Manufacturing Inc.), KC156 (Key Community College System), MI345 (Midwest Library Consortium), and TW001 (Tri-County Waste Disposal).

For an introduction to Windows and instructions about how to perform basic Windows tasks, read the Office and Windows module at the beginning of this book, where you can learn how to resize windows, change screen resolution, create folders, move and rename files, use Windows Help, and much more.

In this module, you will learn how to create and use the database shown in Figure 1–1. The following roadmap identifies general activities you will perform as you progress through this module:

1. CREATE the FIRST TABLE, Account Manager, using Datasheet view.
2. ADD RECORDS to the Account Manager table.
3. PRINT the CONTENTS of the Account Manager table.
4. IMPORT RECORDS into the second table, Account.
5. MODIFY the SECOND TABLE using Design view.
6. CREATE a QUERY for the Account table.
7. CREATE a FORM for the Account table.
8. CREATE a REPORT for the Account table.

Creating a Database

For an introduction to Office and instructions about how to perform basic tasks in Office apps, read the Office and Windows module at the beginning of this book, where you can learn how to run an application, use the ribbon, save a file, open a file, print a file, exit an application, use Help, and much more.

In Access, all the tables, reports, forms, and queries that you create are stored in a single file called a database. A database is a structure that can store information about multiple types of objects, the properties of those objects, and the relationships among the objects. The first step is to create the database that will hold your tables, reports, forms, and queries. You can use either the Blank desktop database option or a template to create a new database. If you already know the tables and fields you want in your database, you would use the Blank desktop database option. If not, you can use a template. Templates can guide you by suggesting some commonly used databases.

To Create a Database

Because you already know the tables and fields you want in the PrattLast Associates database, you would use the Blank desktop database option rather than using a template. The following steps create the database.

 Run Access.

② Using the steps in the "To Create an Access Database" section in the Office and Windows module, create the database on your hard disk, OneDrive, or other storage location using PrattLast Associates as the file name (Figure 1–2).

Q&A The title bar for my Navigation Pane contains All Tables rather than All Access Objects, as in the figure. Is that a problem?
It is not a problem. The title bar indicates how the Navigation Pane is organized. You can carry out the steps in the text with either organization. To make your screens match the ones in the text, click the Navigation Pane arrow and then click Object Type.

I do not have the Search bar that appears in the figure. Is that a problem?
It is not a problem. If your Navigation Pane does not display a Search bar and you want your screens to match the ones in the text, right-click the Navigation Pane title bar arrow to display a shortcut menu, and then click Search Bar.

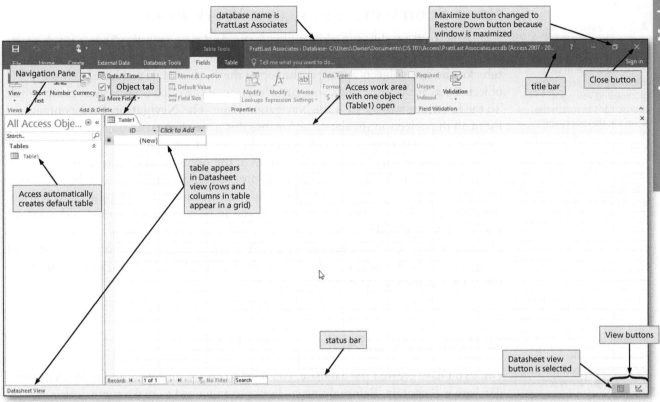

Figure 1–2

To Create a Database Using a Template

Ideally, you will design your own database, create a blank database, and then create the tables you have determined that your database should contain. If you are not sure what database design you will need, you could use a template. Templates can guide you by suggesting some commonly used databases. To create a database using a template, you would use the following steps.

1. If you have another database open, close it without exiting Access by clicking File on the ribbon to open the Backstage view and then clicking Close.

2. If you do not see a template that you want, you can search Microsoft Office online for additional templates.

3. Click the template you want to use. Be sure you have selected one that indicates it is for a desktop database.

4. Enter a file name and select a location for the database.

5. Click the Create button to create the database.

The Access Window

The Access window consists of a variety of components to make your work more efficient. These include the Navigation Pane, Access work area, ribbon, shortcut menus, and Quick Access Toolbar. Some of these components are common to other Microsoft Office apps; others are unique to Access.

BTW
Available Templates
The templates gallery includes both desktop and web-based templates. If you are creating an Access database for your own use, select a desktop template. Web-based templates allow you to create databases that you can publish to a SharePoint server.

BTW
Organizing Files and Folders
You should organize and store files in folders so that you easily can find the files later. For example, if you are taking an introductory computer class called CIS 101, a good practice would be to save all Access files in an Access folder in a CIS 101 folder. For a discussion of folders and detailed examples of creating folders, refer to the Office and Windows module at the beginning of this book.

BTW
Access Screen Resolution
If you are using a computer or mobile device to step through the project in this module and you want your screens to match the figures in this book, you should change your screen's resolution to 1366 x 768. For information about how to change a computer's resolution, refer to the Office and Windows module at the beginning of this book.

Navigation Pane and Access Work Area

You work on objects such as tables, forms, and reports in the **Access work area**. In the work area in Figure 1–2, a single table, Table1, is open in the work area. **Object tabs** for the open objects appear at the top of the work area. If you have multiple objects open at the same time, you can select one of the open objects by clicking its tab. To the left of the work area is the Navigation Pane. The **Navigation Pane** contains a list of all the objects in the database. You use this pane to open an object. You can also customize the way objects are displayed in the Navigation Pane.

The **status bar**, located at the bottom of the Access window, presents information about the database object, the progress of current tasks, and the status of certain commands and keys; it also provides controls for viewing the object. As you type text or perform certain commands, various indicators might appear on the status bar. The left edge of the status bar in Figure 1–2 shows that the table object is open in **Datasheet view**. In Datasheet view, the table is represented as a collection of rows and columns called a **datasheet**. Toward the right edge are View buttons, which you can use to change the view that currently appears.

Determining Tables and Fields

Once you have created the database, you need to create the tables and fields that your database will contain. Before doing so, however, you need to make some decisions regarding the tables and fields.

BTW
Naming Tables
Database users typically have their own guidelines for naming tables. Some use the singular version of the object being described while others use the prefix tbl with a table name. This book uses the singular version of the object (Account, Account Manager).

Naming Tables and Fields

In creating your database, you must name tables, fields, and other objects. Before beginning the design process, you must understand the rules Access applies to table and field names. These rules are:

1. Names can be up to 64 characters in length.
2. Names can contain letters, digits, and spaces, as well as most of the punctuation symbols.
3. Names cannot contain periods (.), exclamation points (!), accent graves (`), or square brackets ([ ]).
4. Each field in a table must have a unique name.

BTW
Multiple-Word Names
There are several ways to handle multiple word names. You can omit the space (AccountNumber) or use an underscore in place of the space (Account_Number). Another option is to use an underscore in place of a space, but use the same case for all letters (ACCOUNT_NUMBER or account_number).

The approach to naming tables and fields used in this text is to begin the names with an uppercase letter and to use lowercase for the other letters. In multiple-word names, each word begins with an uppercase letter, and there is a space between words (for example, Account Number).

Determining the Primary Key

For each table, you need to determine the primary key, the unique identifier. In many cases, you will have obvious choices, such as Account Number or Account Manager Number. If you do not have an obvious choice, you can use the primary key that Access creates automatically. It is a field called ID. It is an **autonumber field**, which means that Access will assign the value 1 to the first record, 2 to the second record, and so on.

Determining Data Types for the Fields

For each field in your database, you must determine the field's **data type**, that is, the type of data that can be stored in the field. Four of the most commonly used data types in Access are:

1. **Short Text** — The field can contain any characters. A maximum number of 255 characters is allowed in a field whose data type is Short Text.

2. **Number** — The field can contain only numbers. The numbers can be either positive or negative. Fields assigned this type can be used in arithmetic operations. You usually assign fields that contain numbers but will not be used for arithmetic operations (such as postal codes) a data type of Short Text.

3. **Currency** — The field can contain only monetary data. The values will appear with currency symbols, such as dollar signs, commas, and decimal points, and with two digits following the decimal point. Like numeric fields, you can use currency fields in arithmetic operations. Access assigns a size to currency fields automatically.

4. **Date & Time** — The field can contain dates and/or times.

Table 1–1 shows the other data types that are available in Access.

Table 1-1 Additional Data Types	
Data Type	**Description**
Long Text	Field can store a variable amount of text or combinations of text and numbers where the total number of characters may exceed 255.
AutoNumber	Field can store a unique sequential number that Access assigns to a record. Access will increment the number by 1 as each new record is added.
Yes/No	Field can store only one of two values. The choices are Yes/No, True/False, or On/Off.
OLE Object	Field can store an OLE object, which is an object linked to or embedded in the table.
Hyperlink	Field can store text that can be used as a hyperlink address.
Attachment	Field can contain an attached file. Images, spreadsheets, documents, charts, and other elements can be attached to this field in a record in the database. You can view and edit the attached file.
Calculated	Field specified as a calculation based on other fields. The value is not actually stored.

In the Account table, because the Account Number, Account Name, Street, City, and State can all contain letters, their data types should be Short Text. The data type for Postal Code is Short Text instead of Number because you typically do not use postal codes in arithmetic operations; you do not add postal codes or find an average postal code, for example. The Amount Paid and Current Due fields contain monetary data, so their data types should be Currency. The Account Manager Number field contains numbers, but you will not use these numbers in arithmetic operations, so its data type should be Short Text.

Similarly, in the Account Manager table, the data type for the Account Manager Number, Last Name, First Name, Street, City, State, and Postal Code fields should all be Short Text. The Start Date field should have a data type of Date & Time. The Salary field contains monetary amounts, so its data type should be Currency. The Bonus Rate field contains numbers that are not dollar amounts, so its data type should be Number.

For fields whose data type is Short Text, you can change the field size, that is, the maximum number of characters that can be entered in the field. If you set the field size

BTW
Data Types
Different database management systems have different available data types. Even data types that are essentially the same can have different names. The Currency data type in Access, for example, is referred to as Money in SQL Server.

BTW
AutoNumber Fields
AutoNumber fields also are called AutoIncrement fields. In Design view, the New Values field property allows you to increment the field sequentially (Sequential) or randomly (Random). The default is sequential.

BTW
Currency Symbols
To show the symbol for the Euro (€) instead of the dollar sign, change the Format property for the field whose data type is currency. To change the default symbols for currency, change the settings in Windows.

for the State field to 2, for example, Access will not allow the user to enter more than two characters in the field. On the other hand, fields whose data type is Number often require you to change the field size, which is the storage space assigned to the field by Access. Table 1–2 shows the possible field sizes for Number fields.

Table 1-2 Field Sizes for Number Fields	
Field Size	**Description**
Byte	Integer value in the range of 0 to 255
Integer	Integer value in the range of -32,768 to 32,767
Long Integer	Integer value in the range of -2,147,483,648 to 2,147,483,647
Single	Numeric values with decimal places to seven significant digits—requires 4 bytes of storage
Double	Numeric values with decimal places to more accuracy than Single—requires 8 bytes of storage
Replication ID	Special identifier required for replication
Decimal	Numeric values with decimal places to more accuracy than Single or Double—requires 12 bytes of storage.

CONSIDER THIS

What is the appropriate size for the Bonus Rate field?
If the size were Byte, Integer, or Long Integer, only integers could be stored. If you try to store a value that has decimal places, such as 0.18, in fields of these sizes, the portion to the right of the decimal point would be removed, giving a result of 0. To address this problem, the bonus rate should have a size of Single, Double, or Decimal. With such small numbers involved, Single, which requires the least storage of the three, is the appropriate choice.

BTW
Naming Files
The following characters cannot be used in a file name: question mark (?), quotation mark ("), slash (/), backslash (\ ), colon (:), asterisk (*), vertical bar (|), greater than symbol (>), and less than symbol (<).

Creating a Table

To create a table in Access, you must define its structure. That is, you must define all the fields that make up the table and their characteristics. You must also indicate the primary key.

In Access, you can use two different views to create a table: Datasheet view and Design view. In **Datasheet view**, the data in the table is presented in rows and columns, similar to a spreadsheet. Although the main reason to use Datasheet view is to add or update records in a table, you can also use it to create a table or to later modify its structure. The other view, **Design view**, is only used to create a table or to modify the structure of a table.

As you might expect, Design view has more functionality for creating a table than Datasheet view. That is, there are certain actions that can only be performed in Design view. One such action is assigning Single as the field size for the Bonus Rate field. In this module, you will create the first table, the Account Manager table, in Datasheet view. Once you have created the table in Datasheet view, you will use Design view to change the field size.

Whichever view you choose to use, before creating the table, you need to know the names and data types of the fields that will make up the table. You can also decide to enter a description for a particular field to explain important details about the field. When you select this field, this description will appear on the status bar. You might also choose to assign a **caption** to a particular field. If you assign a caption, Access will display the value you assign, rather than the field name, in datasheets and in forms. If you do not assign a caption, Access will display the field name.

When would you want to use a caption?
You would use a caption whenever you want something other than the field name displayed. One common example is when the field name is relatively long and the data in the field is relatively short. In the Account Manager table, the name of the first field is Account Manager Number, but the field contains data that is only two characters long. You will change the caption for this field to AM #, which is much shorter than Account Manager Number yet still describes the field. Doing so will enable you to greatly reduce the width of the column.

The results of these decisions for the fields in the Account Manager table are shown in Table 1–3. The table also shows the data types and field sizes of the fields as well as any special properties that need to be changed. The Account Manager Number field has a caption of AM #, enabling the width of the Account Manager Number column to be reduced in the datasheet.

Table 1-3 Structure of Account Manager Table			
Field Name	**Data Type**	**Field Size**	**Description**
Account Manager Number	Short Text	2	Primary Key **Description:** Unique identifier of account manager **Caption:** AM #
Last Name	Short Text	15	
First Name	Short Text	15	
Street	Short Text	20	
City	Short Text	20	
State	Short Text	2	
Postal Code	Short Text	5	
Start Date	Date/Time	(This appears as Date & Time on the menu of available data types)	
Salary	Currency		
Bonus Rate	Number	Single	Format: Fixed Decimal Places: 2

How do you determine the field size?
You need to determine the maximum number of characters that can be entered in the field. In some cases, it is obvious. Field sizes of 2 for the State field and 5 for the Postal Code field are certainly the appropriate choices. In other cases, you need to determine how many characters you want to allow. In the list shown in Table 1–3, PrattLast decided allowing 15 characters was sufficient for last names. This field size can be changed later if it proves to be insufficient.

What is the purpose of the Format and Decimal Places properties?
The format guarantees that bonus rates will be displayed with a fixed number of decimal places. Setting the decimal places property to 2 guarantees that the rates will be displayed with precisely two decimal places. Thus, a bonus rate of 0.2 will be displayed as 0.20.

To Modify the Primary Key

When you first create your database, Access automatically creates a table for you. You can immediately begin defining the fields. If, for any reason, you do not have this table or inadvertently delete it, you can create the table by clicking Create on the ribbon and then clicking the Table button (Create tab | Tables group). In either case, you are ready to define the fields.

The following steps change the name, data type, and other properties of the first field to match the Account Manager Number field in Table 1–3, which is the primary key. *Why? Access has already created the first field as the primary key field, which it has named ID. Account Manager Number is a more appropriate choice.*

1

- Right-click the column heading for the ID field to display a shortcut menu (Figure 1–3).

Q&A Why does my shortcut menu look different?
You displayed a shortcut menu for the column instead of the column heading. Be sure you right-click the column heading.

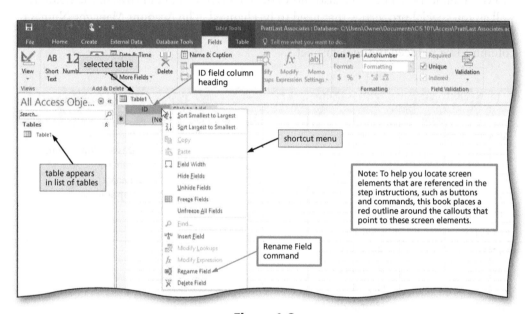

Figure 1–3

2

- Click Rename Field on the shortcut menu to highlight the current name.

- Type `Account Manager Number` to assign a name to the new field.

- Click the white space immediately below the field name to complete the addition of the field (Figure 1–4).

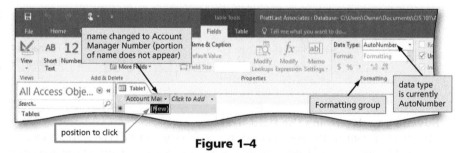

Figure 1–4

Q&A Why does the full name of the field not appear?
The default column size is not large enough for Account Manager Number to be displayed in its entirety. You will address this issue in later steps.

3

- Because the data type needs to be changed from AutoNumber to Short Text, click the Data Type arrow (Table Tools Fields tab | Formatting group) to display a menu of available data types (Figure 1–5).

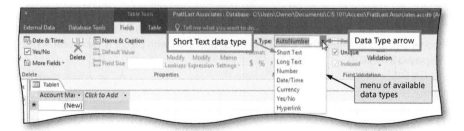

Figure 1–5

4

- Click Short Text to select the data type for the field (Figure 1–6).

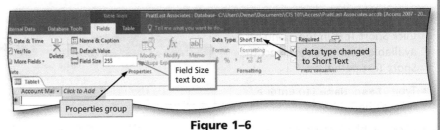

Figure 1–6

5

- Click the Field Size text box (Table Tools Fields tab | Properties group) to select the current field size, use either the DELETE or BACKSPACE keys to erase the current field size, if necessary, and then type 2 as the new field size.

- Click the Name & Caption button (Table Tools Fields tab | Properties group) to display the Enter Field Properties dialog box.

- Click the Caption text box (Enter Field Properties dialog box), and then type **AM #** as the caption.

- Click the Description text box, and then type **Unique identifier of account manager** as the description (Figure 1–7).

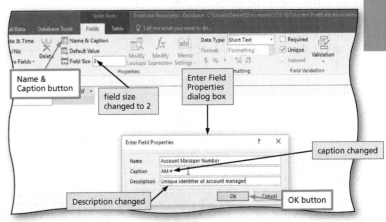

Figure 1–7

6

- Click the OK button (Enter Field Properties dialog box) to change the caption and description (Figure 1–8).

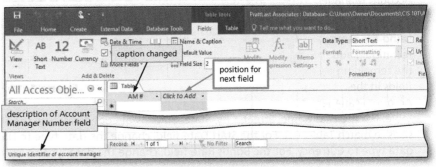

Figure 1–8

To Define the Remaining Fields in a Table

1 CREATE FIRST TABLE | 2 ADD RECORDS | 3 PRINT CONTENTS | 4 IMPORT RECORDS
5 MODIFY SECOND TABLE | 6 CREATE QUERY | 7 CREATE FORM | 8 CREATE REPORT

To define an additional field, you click the 'Click to Add' column heading, select the data type, and then type the field name. This is different from the process you used to modify the ID field. The following steps define the remaining fields shown in Table 1–3. These steps do not change the field size of the Bonus Rate field, however. **Why?** *You can only change the field size of a Number field in Design view. Later, you will use Design view to change this field size and change the format and number of decimal places.*

1

- Click the 'Click to Add' column heading to display a menu of available data types (Figure 1–9).

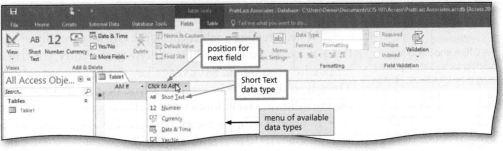

Figure 1–9

2

- Click Short Text in the menu of available data types to select the Short Text data type.

- Type **Last Name** to enter a field name.

- Click the blank space below the field name to complete the change of the name. Click the blank space a second time to select the field (Figure 1–10).

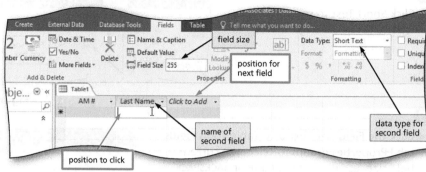

Figure 1–10

 After entering the field name, I realized that I selected the wrong data type. How can I correct it?
Click the Data Type arrow, and then select the correct type.

I inadvertently clicked the blank space before entering the field name. How can I correct the name?
Right-click the field name, click Rename Field on the shortcut menu, and then type the new name.

3

- Change the field size to 15 just as you changed the field size of the Account Manager Number field.

- Using the same technique, add the remaining fields in the Account Manager

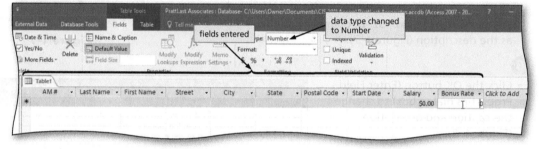

Figure 1–11

table. For the First Name, Street, City, State, and Postal Code fields, use the Short Text data type, but change the field sizes to match Table 1–3. For the Start Date field, change the data type to Date/Time. For the Salary field, change the data type to Currency. For the Bonus Rate field, change the data type to Number (Figure 1–11).

 I have an extra row between the row containing the field names and the row that begins with the asterisk. What happened? Is this a problem? If so, how do I fix it?
You inadvertently added a record to the table by pressing a key. Even pressing the SPACEBAR would add a record. You now have an unwanted record. To fix it, press the ESC key or click the Undo button to undo the action. You may need to do this more than once.

When I try to move on to specify another field, I get an error message indicating that the primary key cannot contain a null value. How do I correct this?
First, click the OK button to remove the error message. Next, press the ESC key or click the Undo button to undo the action. You may need to do this more than once.

Making Changes to the Structure

When creating a table, check the entries carefully to ensure they are correct. If you discover a mistake while still typing the entry, you can correct the error by repeatedly pressing the BACKSPACE key until the incorrect characters are removed. Then, type the correct characters. If you do not discover a mistake until later, you can use the following techniques to make the necessary changes to the structure:

- To undo your most recent change, click the Undo button on the Quick Access Toolbar. If there is nothing that Access can undo, this button will be dim, and clicking it will have no effect.

- To delete a field, right-click the column heading for the field (the position containing the field name), and then click Delete Field on the shortcut menu.

- To change the name of a field, right-click the column heading for the field, click Rename Field on the shortcut menu, and then type the desired field name.

- To insert a field as the last field, click the 'Click to Add' column heading, click the appropriate data type on the menu of available data types, type the desired field name, and, if necessary, change the field size.

- To insert a field between existing fields, right-click the column heading for the field that will follow the new field, and then click Insert Field on the shortcut menu. Right-click the column heading for the field, click Rename Field on the shortcut menu, and then type the desired field name.

- To move a field, click the column heading for the field to be moved to select the field, and then drag the field to the desired position.

As an alternative to these steps, you might want to start over. To do so, click the Close button for the table, and then click the No button in the Microsoft Access dialog box. Click Create on the ribbon, and then click the Table button to create a table. You then can repeat the process you used earlier to define the fields in the table.

To Save a Table

1 CREATE FIRST TABLE | 2 ADD RECORDS | 3 PRINT CONTENTS | 4 IMPORT RECORDS
5 MODIFY SECOND TABLE | 6 CREATE QUERY | 7 CREATE FORM | 8 CREATE REPORT

The Account Manager table structure is complete. The final step is to save the table within the database. As part of the process, you will give the table a name. The following steps save the table, giving it the name Account Manager. **Why?** *PrattLast has decided that Account Manager is an appropriate name for the table.*

- Click the **Save** button on the Quick Access Toolbar to display the Save As dialog box (Figure 1–12).

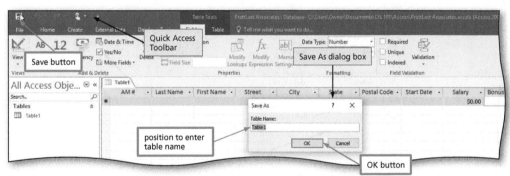

Figure 1–12

- Type **Account Manager** to change the name assigned to the table.

- Click the OK button (Save As dialog box) to save the table (Figure 1–13).

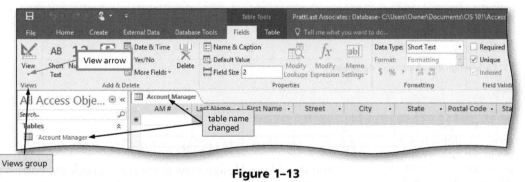

Figure 1–13

Other Ways

1. Click File on the ribbon, click Save in the Backstage view
2. Right-click tab for table, click Save on shortcut menu
3. Press **CTRL+S**

To View the Table in Design View

Even when creating a table in Datasheet view, Design view can be helpful. *Why? You easily can view the fields, data types, and properties to ensure you have entered them correctly. It is also easier to determine the primary key in Design view.* The following steps display the structure of the Account Manager table in Design view so that you can verify the design is correct.

1

- Click the View arrow (Table Tools Fields tab | Views group) to display the View menu (Figure 1–14).

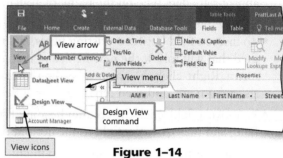

Q&A

Could I just click the View button rather than the arrow?
Yes. Clicking the button is equivalent to clicking the command represented by the icon currently appearing on the button. Because the icon on the button in Figure 1–14 is for Design view, clicking the button would display the table in Design view. If you are uncertain, you can always click the arrow and select from the menu.

Figure 1–14

2

- Click Design View on the View menu to view the table in Design view (Figure 1–15).

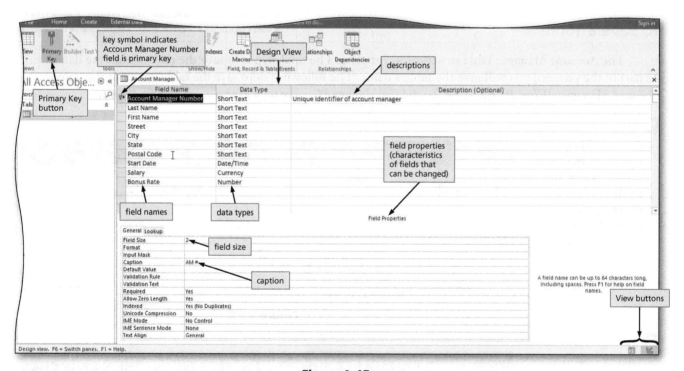

Figure 1–15

Other Ways

1. Click Design View button on status bar

Checking the Structure in Design View

You should use Design view to carefully check the entries you have made. In Figure 1–15, for example, you can see that the Account Manager Number field is the primary key of the Account Manager table by the key symbol in front of the field name. If your table does not have a key symbol, you can click the Primary Key button (Table Tools Design tab | Tools group) to designate a field as the primary key. You can also check that the data type, description, field size, and caption are all correct.

For the other fields, you can see the field name, data type, and description without taking any special action. To see the field size and/or caption for a field, click the field's **row selector**, the small box to the left of the field. Clicking the row selector for the Last Name field, for example, displays the properties for that field. You then can check to see that the field size is correct. In addition, if the field has a caption, you can check to see if that is correct. If you find any mistakes, you can make the necessary corrections on this screen. When you have finished, click the Save button to save your changes.

To Change a Field Size in Design View

1 CREATE FIRST TABLE | 2 ADD RECORDS | 3 PRINT CONTENTS | 4 IMPORT RECORDS
5 MODIFY SECOND TABLE | 6 CREATE QUERY | 7 CREATE FORM | 8 CREATE REPORT

Most field size changes can be made in either Datasheet view or Design view. However, changing the field size for Number fields, such as the Bonus Rate field, can only be done in Design view. Because the values in the Bonus Rate field have decimal places, only Single, Double, or Decimal are possible choices for the field size. The difference between these choices concerns the amount of accuracy, that is, the number of decimal places to which the number is accurate. Double is more accurate than Single, for example, but requires more storage space. Because the rates are only two decimal places, Single is an acceptable choice.

The following steps change the field size of the Bonus Rate field to Single, the format to Fixed, and the number of decimal places to 2. *Why change the format and number of decimal places? Changing the format and number ensures that each value will appear with precisely two decimal places.*

1

- If necessary, click the vertical scroll bar to display the Bonus Rate field. Click the row selector for the Bonus Rate field to select the field (Figure 1–16).

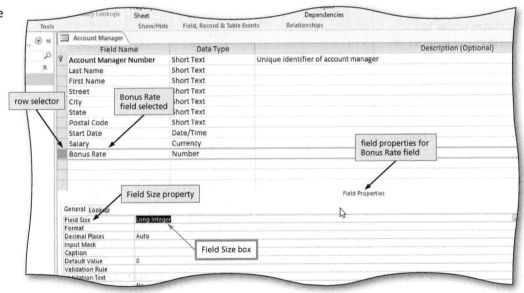

Figure 1–16

2

- Click the Field Size box to display the Field Size arrow.

- Click the Field Size arrow to display the Field Size menu (Figure 1–17).

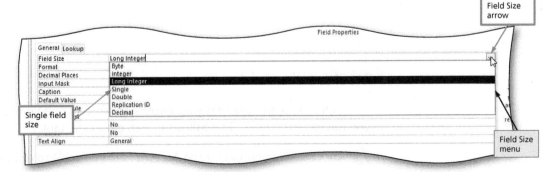

Figure 1–17

 Q&A What would happen if I left the field size set to Long Integer?

If the field size is Long Integer, Integer, or Byte, no decimal places can be stored. For example, a value of .10 would be stored as 0. If you enter rates and the values all appear as 0, chances are you did not change the field size property.

3

- Click Single to select single precision as the field size.

- Click the Format box to display the Format arrow (Figure 1-18).

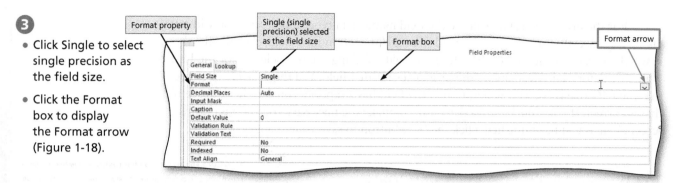

Figure 1–18

4

- Click the Format arrow to display the Format menu.

- Click Fixed to select fixed as the format.

- Click the Decimal Places box to display the Decimal Places arrow.

- Click the Decimal Places arrow to enter the number of decimal places.

- Click 2 to assign the number of decimal places.

- Click the Save button to save your changes (Figure 1–19).

Q&A Why did the 'Property Update Options' button appear?
You changed the number of decimal places. The 'Property Update Options' button offers a quick way of making the same change everywhere Bonus Rate appears. So far, you have not added any data or created any forms or reports that use the Bonus Rate field, so no such changes are necessary.

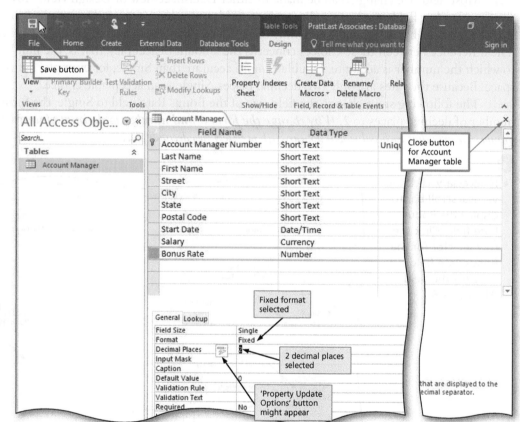

Figure 1–19

To Close the Table

Once you are sure that your entries are correct and you have saved your changes, you can close the table. The following step closes the table.

1 Click the Close button for the Account Manager table to close the table.

Other Ways

1. Right-click tab for table, click Close on shortcut menu

To Add Records to a Table

Creating a table by building the structure and saving the table is the first step in the two-step process of using a table in a database. The second step is to add records to the table. To add records to a table, the table must be open. When making changes to tables, you work in Datasheet view.

You often add records in phases. *Why? You might not have enough time to add all the records in one session, or you might not have all the records currently available.* The following steps open the Account Manager table in Datasheet view and then add the first two records in the Account Manager table (Figure 1–20).

AM #	Last Name	First Name	Street	City	State	Postal Code	Start Date	Salary	Bonus Rate
42	Lu	Peter	5624 Murray Ave.	Davidson	IN	46007	8/3/2015	$36,750.00	0.09
31	Rivera	Haydee	325 Twiddy St.	Avondale	IL	60311	6/3/2013	$48,750.00	0.15

Figure 1–20

1
- Right-click the Account Manager table in the Navigation Pane to display the shortcut menu (Figure 1–21).

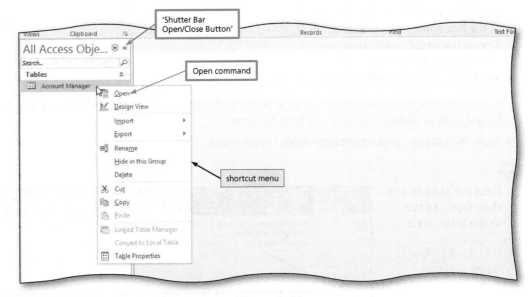

Figure 1–21

2
- Click Open on the shortcut menu to open the table in Datasheet view.
- Click the 'Shutter Bar Open/Close Button' to close the Navigation Pane (Figure 1–22).

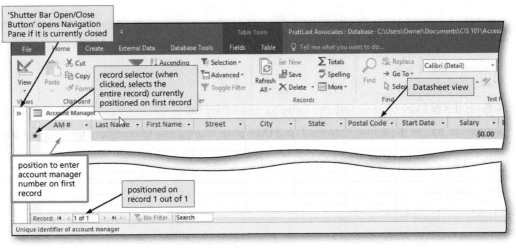

Figure 1–22

- Click the first row in the AM # field if necessary to display an insertion point, and type 42 to enter the first account manager number (Figure 1–23).

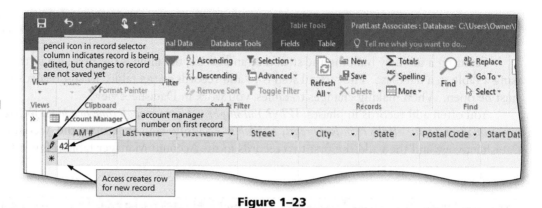

Figure 1–23

❹

- Press the TAB key to move to the next field.

- Enter the last name, first name, street, city, state, and postal code by typing the following entries, pressing the TAB key after each one: Lu as the last name, Peter as the first name, 5624 Murray Ave. as the street, Davidson as the city, IN as the state, and 46007 as the postal code.

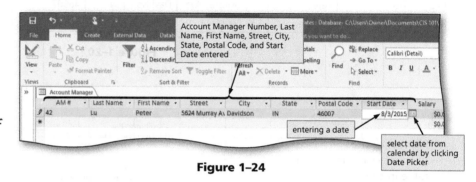

Figure 1–24

- If requested by your instructor, enter your address instead of 5624 Murray Ave. as the street. If your address is longer than 20 characters, enter the first 20 characters.

- Type 8/3/2015 in the Start Date field (Figure 1–24).

❺

- Press the TAB key and then type 36750 in the Salary field.

Q&A
Do I need to type a dollar sign?
You do not need to type dollar signs or commas. In addition, because the digits to the right of the decimal point are both zeros, you do not need to type either the decimal point or the zeros.

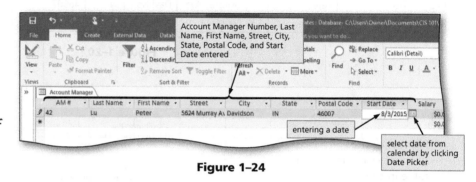

Figure 1–25

- Press the TAB key to complete the entry for the Salary field.

- Type 0.09 in the Bonus Rate field, and then press the TAB key to complete the entry of the first record (Figure 1–25).

Q&A
Do I need to type the leading zero for the Bonus Rate?
Typing the leading zero is not necessary. You could type .09 if you prefer. In addition, you would not have to type any final zeros. For example, if you needed to enter 0.20, you could simply type .2 as your entry.

How and when do I save the record?
As soon as you have entered or modified a record and moved to another record, Access saves the original record. This is different from other applications. The rows entered in an Excel worksheet, for example, are not saved until the entire worksheet is saved.

6

- Use the techniques shown in Steps 3 through 5 to enter the data for the second record (Figure 1–26).

Q&A Does it matter that I entered account manager 31 after I entered account manager 42? Should the account manager numbers be in order?

The order in which you enter the records is not important. When you close and later reopen the table, the records will be in account manager number order, because the Account Manager Number field is the primary key.

Experiment

- Click the Salary field on either of the records. Be sure the Table Tools Fields tab is selected. Click the Format arrow, and then click each of the formats in the Format box menu to see the effect on the values in the Salary field. When finished, click Currency in the Format box menu.

Q&A I made a mistake in entering the data. When should I fix it?

It is a good idea to fix it now, although you can fix it later as well. In any case, the following section gives you the techniques you can use to make any necessary corrections. If you want to fix it now, read that section and make your corrections before proceeding to the next step.

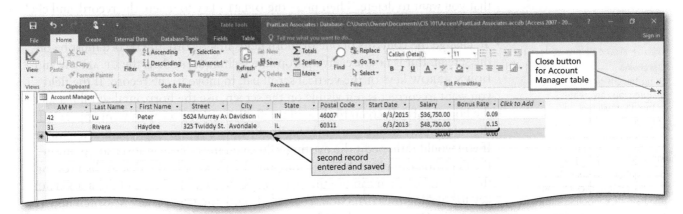

Figure 1–26

7

- Click the Close button for the Account Manager table, shown in Figure 1–26, to close the table (Figure 1–27).

- Exit Access.

Q&A Is it necessary for me to exit Access at this point?

No. The step is here for two reasons.

First, you will often not be able to add all the records you need to add in one sitting. In such a case, you will add some records, and then exit Access. When you are ready to resume adding the records, you will run Access, open the table, and then continue the addition process. Second, there is a break point coming up in the module. If you want to take advantage of that break, you need to first exit Access.

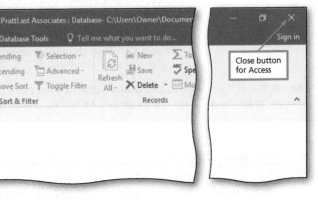

Figure 1–27

Making Changes to the Data

As you enter data, check your entries carefully to ensure they are correct. If you make a mistake and discover it before you press the TAB key, correct it by pressing the BACKSPACE key until the incorrect characters are removed, and then type the correct characters. If you do not discover a mistake until later, you can use the following techniques to make the necessary corrections to the data:

• To undo your most recent change, click the Undo button on the Quick Access Toolbar. If there is nothing that Access can undo, this button will be dimmed, and clicking it will have no effect.

• To add a record, click the 'New (blank) record' button, click the position for the Account Manager Number field on the first open record, and then add the record. Do not worry about it being in the correct position in the table. Access will reposition the record based on the primary key, in this case, the Account Manager Number.

• To delete a record, click the record selector, shown in Figure 1–22, for the record that you want to delete. Then press the DELETE key to delete the record, and click the Yes button when Access asks you to verify that you want to delete the record.

• To change the contents of one or more fields in a record, the record must be on the screen. If it is not, use any appropriate technique, such as the UP ARROW and DOWN ARROW keys or the vertical scroll bar, to move to the record. If the field you want to correct is not visible on the screen, use the horizontal scroll bar along the bottom of the screen to shift all the fields until the one you want appears. If the value in the field is currently highlighted, you can simply type the new value. If you would rather edit the existing value, you must have an insertion point in the field. You can place the insertion point by clicking in the field or by pressing the F2 key. You then can use the arrow keys, the DELETE key, and the BACKSPACE key for making the correction. You can also use the INSERT key to switch between Insert and Overtype mode. When you have made the change, press the TAB key to move to the next field.

If you cannot determine how to correct the data, you may find that you are "stuck" on the record, in which case Access neither allows you to move to another record nor allows you to close the table until you have made the correction. If you encounter this situation, simply press the ESC key. Pressing the ESC key will remove from the screen the record you are trying to add. You then can move to any other record, close the table, or take any other action you desire.

BTW
AutoCorrect Feature
The AutoCorrect feature of Access corrects common data entry errors. AutoCorrect corrects two capital letters by changing the second letter to lowercase and capitalizes the first letter in the names of days. It also corrects more than 400 commonly misspelled words.

BTW
Other AutoCorrect Options
Using the Office AutoCorrect feature, you can create entries that will replace abbreviations with spelled-out names and phrases automatically. To specify AutoCorrect rules, click File on the ribbon to open the Backstage view, click Options, and then click Proofing in the Access Options dialog box.

Break Point: If you wish to take a break, this is a good place to do so. You can exit Access now. To resume at a later time, run Access, open the database called PrattLast Associates, and continue following the steps from this location forward.

To Add Records to a Table that Contains Data

1 CREATE FIRST TABLE | 2 ADD RECORDS | 3 PRINT CONTENTS | 4 IMPORT RECORDS
5 MODIFY SECOND TABLE | 6 CREATE QUERY | 7 CREATE FORM | 8 CREATE REPORT

You can add records to a table that already contains data using a process almost identical to that used to add records to an empty table. The only difference is that you place the insertion point after the last record before you enter the additional data. To position the insertion point after the last record, you can use the **Navigation buttons,** which are buttons used to move within a table, found near the lower-left corner of the screen when a table is open. *Why not just click the Account Manager Number (AM #) on the first open record? You could click the first open record, but it is a good habit to use the 'New (blank) record' button. Once a table contains more records than will fit on the screen, it is easier to click the 'New (blank) record' button.* The purpose of each Navigation button is described in Table 1–4.

Table 1–4 Navigation Buttons in Datasheet View	
Button	**Purpose**
First record	Moves to the first record in the table
Previous record	Moves to the previous record
Next record	Moves to the next record
Last record	Moves to the last record in the table
New (blank) record	Moves to the end of the table to a position for entering a new record

BTW
Enabling Content
If the database is one that you created, or if it comes from a trusted source, you can enable the content. You should disable the content of a database if you suspect that your database might contain harmful content or damaging macros.

The following steps add the remaining records (Figure 1–28) to the Account Manager table.

AM #	Last Name	First Name	Street	City	State	Postal Code	Start Date	Salary	Bonus Rate
58	Murowski	Karen	168 Truesdale Dr.	Carlton	IL	60313	11/9/2016	$24,000.00	0.08
35	Simson	Mark	1467 Hartwell St.	Walker	IN	46004	5/19/2014	$40,500.00	0.12

Figure 1–28

- Run Access, unless it is already running.
- Open the PrattLast Associates database from your hard disk, OneDrive, or other storage location (Figure 1-29).
- If a Security Warning appears, click the Enable Content button.

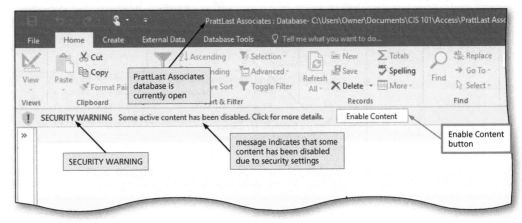

Figure 1–29

- If the Navigation Pane is closed, click the 'Shutter Bar Open/Close Button', shown in Figure 1–27, to open the Navigation Pane (Figure 1–30).

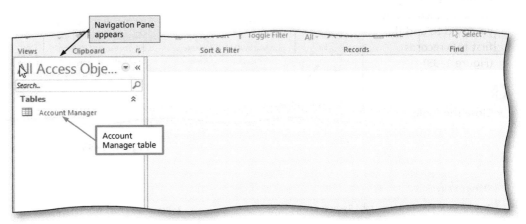

Figure 1–30

- Right-click the Account Manager table in the Navigation Pane to display a shortcut menu.

- Click Open on the shortcut menu to open the table in Datasheet view.

Q&A Why do the records appear in a different order than the order in which I entered them?
When you open the table, they are sorted in the order of the primary key. In this case, that means they will appear in Account Manager Number order.

- Close the Navigation Pane by clicking the 'Shutter Bar Open/ Close Button' (Figure 1–31).

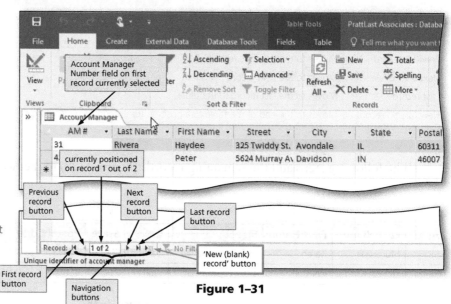

Figure 1–31

- Click the 'New (blank) record' button to move to a position to enter a new record (Figure 1–32).

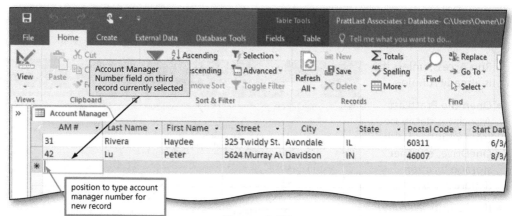

Figure 1–32

- Add the records shown in Figure 1–28 using the same techniques you used to add the first two records (Figure 1–33).

- Close the table.

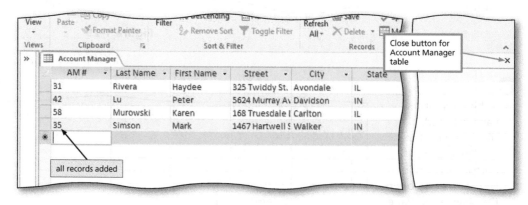

Figure 1–33

Other Ways

1. Click New button (Home tab | Records group)   2. Press CTRL+PLUS SIGN (+)

1 CREATE FIRST TABLE | 2 ADD RECORDS | 3 PRINT CONTENTS | 4 IMPORT RECORDS
5 MODIFY SECOND TABLE | 6 CREATE QUERY | 7 CREATE FORM | 8 CREATE REPORT

To Resize Columns in a Datasheet

Access assigns default column sizes, which do not always provide space to display all the data in the field. In some cases, the data might appear but the entire field name will not. You can correct this problem by resizing the column (changing its size) in the datasheet. In some instances, you may want to reduce the size of a column. *Why? Some fields, such as the State field, are short enough that they do not require all the space on the screen that is allotted to them.* Changing a column width changes the layout, or design, of a table. The following steps resize the columns in the Account Manager table and save the changes to the layout.

1
- Open the Navigation Pane if it is not already open.

- Open the Account Manager table and then close the Navigation Pane.

- Point to the right boundary of the field selector for the Account Manager Number (AM #) field (Figure 1–34) so that the pointer becomes a two-headed arrow.

Q&A
I am using touch and I cannot see the pointer. Is this a problem?
It is not a problem. Remember that if you are using your finger on a touch screen, you will not see the pointer.

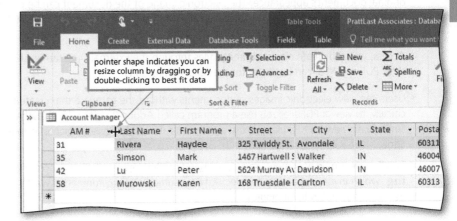

Figure 1–34

2
- Double-click the right boundary of the field selector to resize the field so that it best fits the data.

- Use the same technique to resize all the other fields to best fit the data.

- Save the changes to the layout by clicking the Save button on the Quick Access Toolbar (Figure 1–35).

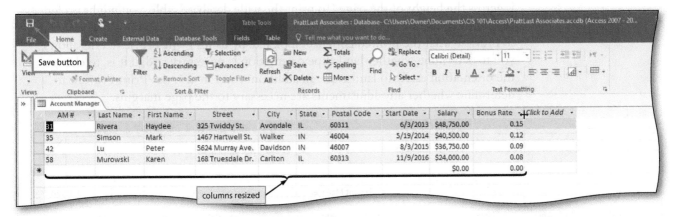

Figure 1–35

3
- Click the table's Close button (shown in Figure 1–33) to close the table.

Q&A
What if I closed the table without saving the layout changes?
You would be asked if you want to save the changes.

Other Ways

1. Right-click field name, click Field Width

What is the best method for distributing database objects?

The traditional method of distributing database objects such as tables, reports, and forms uses a printer to produce a hard copy. A hard copy or printout is information that exists on a physical medium such as paper. Hard copies can be useful for the following reasons:

• Some people prefer proofreading a hard copy of a document rather than viewing it on the screen to check for errors and readability.

• Hard copies can serve as a backup reference if your storage medium is lost or becomes corrupted and you need to recreate the document. Instead of distributing a hard copy, users can distribute the document as an electronic image that mirrors the original document's appearance. The electronic image of the document can be emailed, posted on a website, or copied to a portable storage medium such as a USB flash drive. Two popular electronic image formats, sometimes called fixed formats, are PDF by Adobe Systems and XPS by Microsoft.

In Access, you can create electronic image files through the External Data tab on the ribbon. Electronic images of documents, such as PDF and XPS, can be useful for the following reasons:

• Users can view electronic images of documents without the software that created the original document (e.g., Access). Specifically, to view a PDF file, you use a program called Adobe Reader, which can be downloaded free from Adobe's website. Similarly, to view an XPS file, you use a program called XPS Viewer, which is included in the latest versions of Windows and Edge.

• Sending electronic documents saves paper and printer supplies. Society encourages users to contribute to **green computing**, which involves reducing the electricity consumed and environmental waste generated when using computers, mobile devices, and related technologies.

Previewing and Printing the Contents of a Table

When working with a database, you will often need to print a copy of the table contents. Figure 1–36 shows a printed copy of the contents of the Account Manager table. (Yours might look slightly different, depending on your printer.) Because the Account Manager table is substantially wider than the screen, it will also be wider than the normal printed page in portrait orientation. **Portrait orientation** means the printout is across the width of the page. **Landscape orientation** means the printout is across the height of the page. To print the wide database table, you might prefer to use landscape orientation. A convenient way to change to landscape orientation is to preview what the printed copy will look like by using Print Preview. This allows you to determine whether landscape orientation is necessary and, if it is, to change the orientation easily to landscape. In addition, you can also use Print Preview to determine whether any adjustments are necessary to the page margins.

Account Manager   9/12/2017

AM #	Last Name	First Name	Street	City	State	Postal Code	Start Date	Salary	Bonus Rate
31	Rivera	Haydee	325 Twiddy St.	Avondale	IL	60311	6/3/2013	$48,750.00	0.15
35	Simson	Mark	1467 Hartwell St.	Walker	IN	46004	5/19/2014	$40,500.00	0.12
42	Lu	Peter	5624 Murray Ave.	Davidson	IN	46007	8/3/2015	$36,750.00	0.09
58	Murowski	Karen	168 Truesdale Dr.	Carlton	IL	60313	11/9/2016	$24,000.00	0.08

Figure 1–36

To Preview and Print the Contents of a Table

The following steps use Print Preview to preview and then print the contents of the Account Manager table. **Why?** *By previewing the contents of the table in Print Preview, you can make any necessary adjustments to the orientation or to the margins before printing the contents.*

1

- If the Navigation Pane is closed, open the Navigation Pane by clicking the 'Shutter Bar Open/ Close Button'.

- Be sure the Account Manager table is selected.

Q&A Why do I have to be sure the Account Manager table is selected? It is the only object in the database.
When the database contains only one object, you do not have to worry about selecting the object. Ensuring that the correct object is selected is a good habit to form, however, to make sure that the object you print is the one you want.

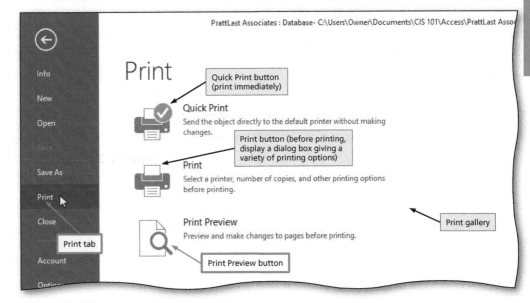

Figure 1–37

- Click File on the ribbon to open the Backstage view.

- Click the Print tab in the Backstage view to display the Print gallery (Figure 1–37).

2

- Click the Print Preview button in the Print gallery to display a preview of what the table will look like when printed (Figure 1–38).

Q&A I cannot read the table. Can I magnify a portion of the table?
Yes. Point the pointer, whose shape will change to a magnifying glass, at the portion of the table that you want to magnify, and then click. You can return to the original view of the table by clicking a second time.

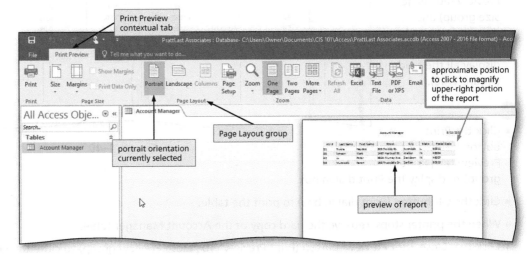

Figure 1–38

3

- Click the pointer in the position shown in Figure 1–38 to magnify the upper-right section of the table (Figure 1–39).

Q&A

My table was already magnified in a different area. How can I see the area shown in the figure? One way is to use the scroll bars to move to the desired portion of the table. You can also click the pointer anywhere in the table to produce a screen like the one shown in Figure 1–38, and then click in the location shown in the figure.

When I magnify the upper-right section, my table moves to the right of the screen and there is a lot of white space. Is that a problem?
No, use the horizontal scroll bar to move the table to the left and reduce the size of the white space.

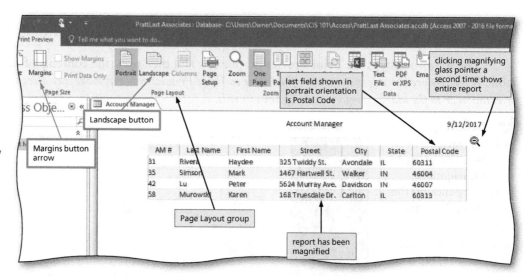

Figure 1–39

4

- Click the Landscape button (Print Preview tab | Page Layout group) to change to landscape orientation.

- Click the Margins button arrow (Print Preview tab | Page Size group) and then click Normal, if necessary, to display all the fields (Figure 1–40).

5

- Click the Print button (Print Preview tab | Print group) to display the Print dialog box.

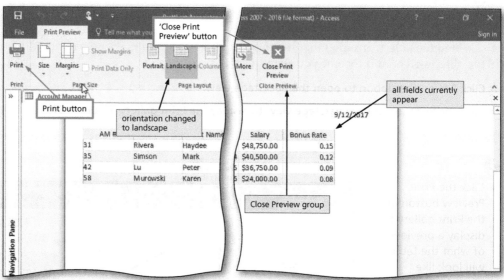

Figure 1–40

- Click the OK button (Print dialog box) to print the table.

- When the printer stops, retrieve the hard copy of the Account Manager table.

- Click the 'Close Print Preview' button (Print Preview tab | Close Preview group) to close the Print Preview window.

Q&A

Do I have to select Print Preview before printing the table?
No. If you want to print without previewing, you would select either Print or Quick Print rather than Print Preview.

Other Ways

1. Press CTRL+P, click OK button in Print dialog box

Importing or Linking Data From Other Applications to Access

If your data for a table is stored in an Excel worksheet, you can **import** the data, which means to make a copy of the data as a table in the Access database. In this case, any changes to the data made in Access would not be reflected in the Excel worksheet.

Figure 1–41, which contains the Account data, is an example of the type of worksheet that can be imported. In this type of worksheet, the data is stored as a **list**, that is, a collection of rows and columns in which all the entries in a column represent the same type of data. In this type of list, the first row contains **column headings**, that is, descriptions of the contents of the column, rather than data. In the worksheet in Figure 1–41, for example, the entry in the first column of the first row is Account Number. This indicates that all the other values in this column are account numbers. The fact that the entry in the second column of the first row is Account Name indicates that all the other values in the second column are account names.

BTW
Linking Versus Importing
When you link to the data in the worksheet, the data appears as a table in the Access database but it is maintained in its original form in Excel. Any changes to the Excel data are reflected when the linked table is viewed in Access. In this arrangement, Access would typically be used as a vehicle for querying and presenting the data, with actual updates being made in Excel.

BTW
Importing Data in Other Formats
You can import data into a table from Excel workbooks, Access databases, XML files, ODBC databases such as SQL Server, text files, HTML documents, Outlook folders, and SharePoint lists.

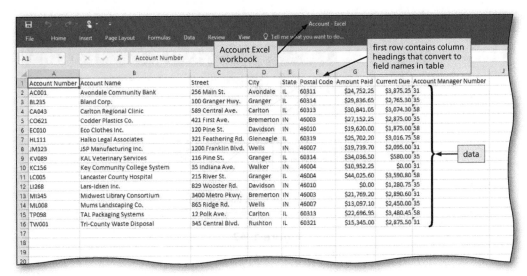

Figure 1–41

Does it matter how the data in the Excel workbook is formatted? If so, how can you be sure the Excel data is formatted in such a way that you can import it?

The format of data in an Excel workbook is important when you want to import it into Access. To ensure the data is in an appropriate format:

1. Make sure the data is in the form of a list; a collection of rows and columns in which all the entries in a column represent the same type of data.

2. Make sure there are no blank rows within the list. If there are, remove them prior to importing or linking.

3. Make sure there are no blank columns within the list. If there are, remove them prior to importing or linking.

4. Determine whether the first row contains column headings that will make appropriate field names in the resulting table. If not, you should consider adding such a row. In general, the process is simpler if the first row in the worksheet contains appropriate column headings.

CONSIDER THIS

The Import process will create a table. In this table, the column headings in the first row of the worksheet become the field names. The rows of the worksheet, other than the first row, become the records in the table. In the process, each field will be assigned the data type that seems the most reasonable, given the data currently in the worksheet. When the Import process is finished, you can use Datasheet view or Design view to modify these data types or to make any other changes to the structure you feel are necessary.

To Import an Excel Worksheet

1 CREATE FIRST TABLE | 2 ADD RECORDS | 3 PRINT CONTENTS | 4 IMPORT RECORDS
5 MODIFY SECOND TABLE | 6 CREATE QUERY | 7 CREATE FORM | 8 CREATE REPORT

You import a worksheet by using the Import Spreadsheet Wizard. In the process, you will indicate that the first row in the worksheet contains the column headings. *Why? You are indicating that Access is to use those column headings as the field names in the Access table.* In addition, you will indicate the primary key for the table. As part of the process, you could, if appropriate, choose not to include all the fields from the worksheet in the resulting table.

The following steps import the Account worksheet.

1

- Click External Data on the ribbon to display the External Data tab (Figure 1–42).

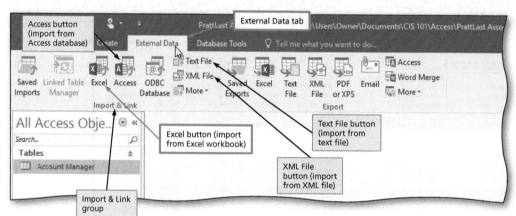

Figure 1–42

2

- Click the Excel button (External Data tab | Import & Link group) to display the Get External Data - Excel Spreadsheet dialog box.

- Click the Browse button in the Get External Data - Excel Spreadsheet dialog box.

- Navigate to the location containing the workbook (for example, the Access folder in the CIS 101 folder). For a detailed example of this procedure, refer to the Office and Windows module at the beginning of this book.

- Click the Account workbook, and then click the Open button to select the workbook (Figure 1–43).

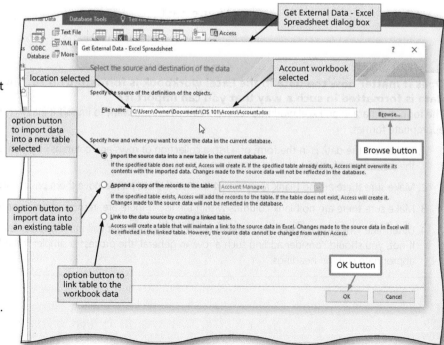

Figure 1–43

3

- With the option button to import the source data to a new table selected, click the OK button to display the Import Spreadsheet Wizard dialog box (Figure 1–44).

Q&A What happens if I select the option button to append records to an existing table?
Instead of the records being placed in a new table, they will be added to an existing table that you specify, provided the value in the primary key field does not duplicate that of an existing record.

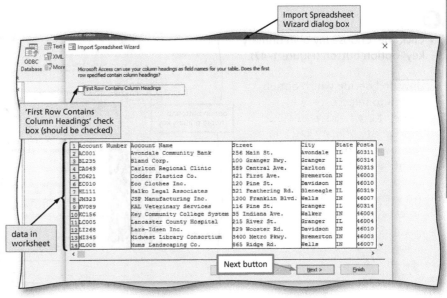

Figure 1–44

4

- Be sure the 'First Row Contains Column Headings' check box is selected. If it is not, click the 'First Row Contains Column Headings' check box to select it.

- Click the Next button (Figure 1–45).

Q&A When would I use the Field Options on the Import Spreadsheet Wizard?
You would use these options if you wanted to change properties for one or more fields. You can change the name, the data type, and whether the field is indexed. You can also indicate that some fields should not be imported.

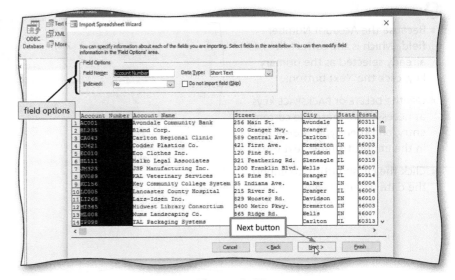

Figure 1–45

5

- Because the Field Options need not be specified, click the Next button (Figure 1–46).

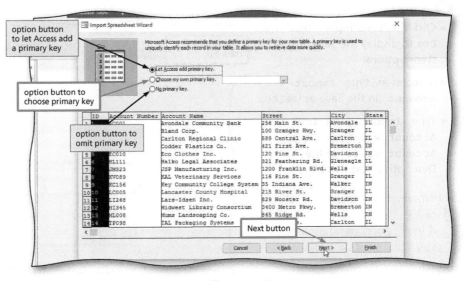

Figure 1–46

6

- Click the 'Choose my own primary key' option button (Figure 1–47).

Q&A How do I decide which option button to select?

If one of the fields is an appropriate primary key, choose your own primary key from the list of fields. If you are sure you do not want a primary key, choose 'No primary key'. Otherwise, let Access add the primary key.

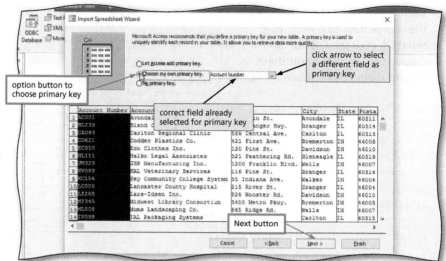

Figure 1–47

7

- Because the Account Number field, which is the correct field, is already selected as the primary key, click the Next button.

- Use the DELETE or BACKSPACE keys as necessary to erase the current entry, and then type **Account** in the Import to Table text box.

- Click the Finish button to import the data (Figure 1–48).

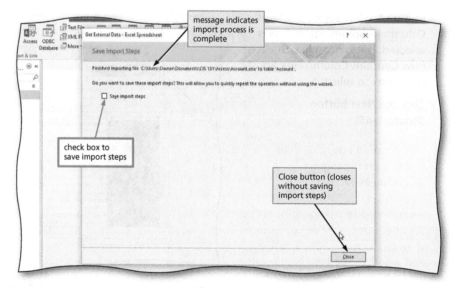

Figure 1–48

8

- Click the 'Save import steps' check box to display the Save import steps options.

- If necessary, type **Import-Account** in the Save as text box.

- Type **Import data from Account workbook into Account table** in the Description text box (Figure 1–49).

Q&A When would I create an Outlook task?

If the import operation is one you will repeat on a regular basis, you can create and schedule the import process just as you can schedule any other Outlook task.

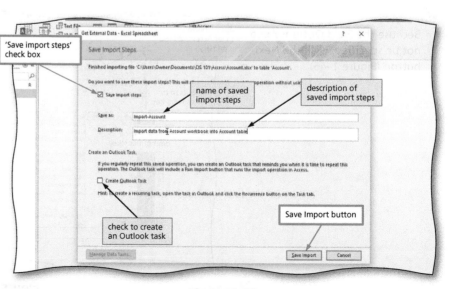

Figure 1–49

9
- Click the Save Import button to save the import steps (Figure 1–50).

I saved the table as Account Data. How can I change the name? Right-click the table name in the Navigation Pane. Click Rename on the shortcut menu and change the table name to Account.

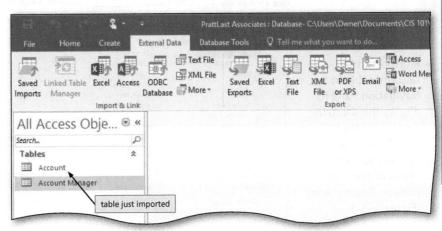

Figure 1–50

Modifying the Table

The import process has created the Account table. The table has the correct fields and records. There are some details the process cannot handle, however. These include field sizes, descriptions, and captions. You will use Design view to make the necessary changes. The information you need is shown in Table 1–5.

Table 1–5 Structure of Account Table			
Field Name	**Data Type**	**Field Size**	**Notes**
Account Number	Short Text	5	Primary Key **Description:** Account Number (two uppercase letters followed by 3-digit number) **Caption:** AC #
Account Name	Short Text	30	
Street	Short Text	20	
City	Short Text	20	
State	Short Text	2	
Postal Code	Short Text	5	
Amount Paid	Currency		
Current Due	Currency		
Account Manager Number	Short Text	2	**Description:** Account Manager Number (number of account manager for account) **Caption:** AM #

BTW

Creating a Table in Design View
To create a table in Design view, display the Create tab, and then click the Table Design button (Create tab | Tables group). You will then see the same screen as in Figure 1–51, except that there will be no entries. Make all the necessary entries for the fields in your table, save the table, and assign the table a name.

To Modify a Table in Design View

You will usually need to modify the design of a table created during the import process. *Why? Some properties of a table are not specified during the import process, such as descriptions, captions, and field sizes. You might also need to change a data type.* The following steps make the necessary modifications to the design of the Account table.

1

- Open the Navigation Pane, if necessary.

- Right-click the Account table in the Navigation Pane to display the shortcut menu, and then click Design View on the shortcut menu to open the table in Design view (Figure 1–51).

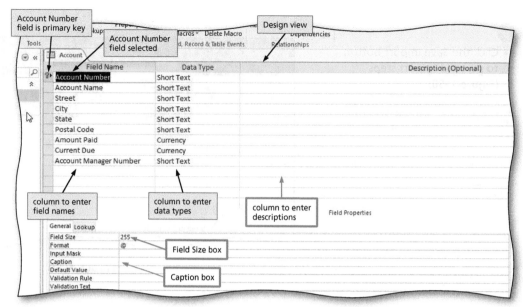

Figure 1–51

2

- Click the Description (Optional) box for the Account Number field, and then type **Account Number (two uppercase letters followed by a 3-digit number)** as the description.

- With the Account Number field selected, click the Field Size box, erase the current field size, and type **5** as the new field size.

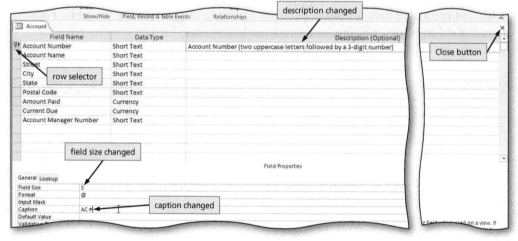

Figure 1–52

- Click the Caption box, and type **AC #** as the caption (Figure 1–52).

Q&A | What does the @ symbol represent in the Format box?
| The @ symbol is a default format added by Access when the table was imported from Excel.

3

- Make the other changes shown in Table 1–5. To select a field to be changed, click the field's row selector. For most fields, you only need to change the field size. For the Account Manager Number field, you also need to change the description and caption.

- Click the Save button on the Quick Access Toolbar to save your changes.

- Because you know the data will satisfy the new field sizes, click the Yes button when given a message about the possibility of data loss.

Other Ways

1. Press F6 to move between upper and lower panes in Table Design window

Correcting Errors in the Structure

Whenever you create or modify a table in Design view, you should check the entries carefully to ensure they are correct. If you make a mistake and discover it before you press the TAB key, you can correct the error by repeatedly pressing the BACKSPACE key until the incorrect characters are removed. Then, type the correct characters. If you do not discover a mistake until later, you can click the entry, type the correct value, and then press the ENTER key. You can use the following techniques to make changes to the structure:

- If you accidentally add an extra field to the structure, select the field by clicking the row selector (the leftmost column on the row that contains the field to be deleted). Once you have selected the field, press the DELETE key. This will remove the field from the structure.

- If you forget to include a field, select the field that will follow the one you want to add by clicking the row selector, and then press the INSERT key. The remaining fields move down one row, making room for the missing field. Make the entries for the new field in the usual manner.

- If you made the wrong field a primary key field, click the correct primary key entry for the field and then click the Primary Key button (Table Tools Design tab | Tools group).

- To move a field, click the row selector for the field to be moved to select the field, and then drag the field to the desired position.

As an alternative to these steps, you might want to start over. To do so, click the Close button for the window containing the table, and then click the No button in the Microsoft Access dialog box. You then can repeat the process you used earlier to define the fields in the table.

BTW
Importing Data to an Existing Table
When you create a new table in Design view, you can import data from other sources into the table using the External Data tab.

To Close the Table

Now that you have completed and saved the Account table, you can close it. The following step closes the table.

1 Click the Close button for the Account table (see Figure 1–52) to close the table.

To Resize Columns in a Datasheet

You can resize the columns in the datasheet for the Account table just as you resized the columns in the datasheet for the Account Manager table. The following steps resize the columns in the Account table to best fit the data.

1 Open the Account table in Datasheet view.

2 Double-click the right boundary of the field selectors of each of the fields to resize the columns so that they best fit the data.

3 Save the changes to the layout by clicking the Save button on the Quick Access Toolbar.

4 Close the table.

BTW
Resizing Columns
To resize all columns in a datasheet to best fit simultaneously, select the column heading for the first column, hold down the SHIFT key and select the last column in the datasheet. Then, double-click the right boundary of any field selector.

Break Point: If you wish to take a break, this is a good place to do so. You can exit Access now. To resume at a later time, run Access, open the database called PrattLast Associates, and continue following the steps from this location forward.

Additional Database Objects

A database contains many types of objects. Tables are the objects you use to store and manipulate data. Access supports other important types of objects as well; each object has a specific purpose that helps maximize the benefits of a database. Through queries (questions), Access makes it possible to ask complex questions concerning the data in the database and then receive instant answers. Access also allows the user to produce attractive and useful forms for viewing and updating data. Additionally, Access includes report creation tools that make it easy to produce sophisticated reports for presenting data.

BTW
Creating Queries
Although the Simple Query Wizard is a convenient way to create straightforward queries, you will find that many of the queries you create require more control than the wizard provides. In Module 2, you will use Design view to create customized queries.

Creating Queries

Queries are simply questions, the answers to which are in the database. Access contains a powerful query feature that helps you find the answers to a wide variety of questions. Once you have examined the question you want to ask to determine the fields involved in the question, you can begin creating the query. If the query involves no special sort order, restrictions, or calculations, you can use the Simple Query Wizard.

To Use the Simple Query Wizard to Create a Query

1 CREATE FIRST TABLE | 2 ADD RECORDS | 3 PRINT CONTENTS | 4 IMPORT RECORDS
5 MODIFY SECOND TABLE | 6 CREATE QUERY | 7 CREATE FORM | 8 CREATE REPORT

The following steps use the Simple Query Wizard to create a query that PrattLast Associates might use to obtain financial information on its accounts. **Why?** *The Simple Query Wizard is the quickest and easiest way to create a query.* This query displays the number, name, amount paid, current due, and account manager number of all accounts.

- If the Navigation Pane is closed, click the 'Shutter Bar Open/Close Button' to open the Navigation Pane.

- Be sure the Account table is selected.

- Click Create on the ribbon to display the Create tab.

- Click the Query Wizard button (Create tab | Queries group) to display the New Query dialog box (Figure 1–53).

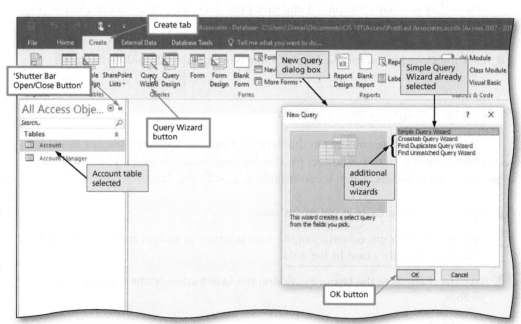

Figure 1–53

2

- Be sure Simple Query Wizard is selected, and then click the OK button (New Query dialog box) to display the Simple Query Wizard dialog box (Figure 1–54).

Q&A What would happen if the Account Manager table were selected instead of the Account table?
The list of available fields would contain fields from the Account Manager table rather than the Account table.

If the list contained Account Manager table fields, how could I make it contain Account table fields?
Click the arrow in the Tables/Queries box, and then click the Account table in the list that appears.

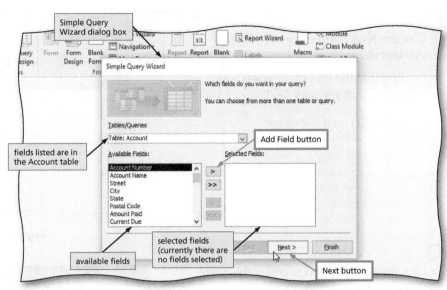

Figure 1–54

3

- With the Account Number field selected, click the Add Field button to add the field to the query.

- With the Account Name field selected, click the Add Field button a second time to add the field.

- Click the Amount Paid field, and then click the Add Field button to add the field.

- In a similar fashion, add the Current Due and Account Manager Number fields (Figure 1–55).

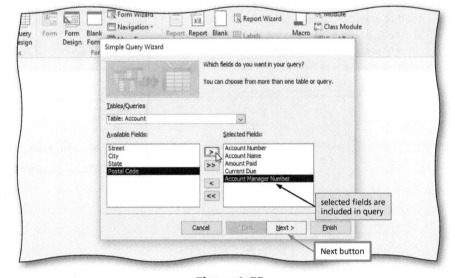

Figure 1–55

4

- Click the Next button to move to the next screen.

- Ensure that the 'Detail (shows every field of every record)' option button is selected (Figure 1–56).

Q&A What is the difference between Detail and Summary?
Detail shows all the records and fields. Summary only shows computations (for example, the total amount paid).

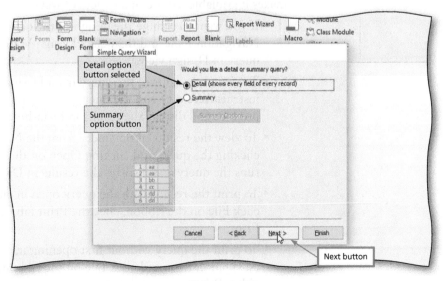

Figure 1–56

⑤

• Click the Next button to move to the next screen.

• Confirm that the title of the query is Account Query (Figure 1–57).

Q&A What should I do if the title is incorrect?
Click the box containing the title to produce an insertion point. Erase the current title and then type Account Query.

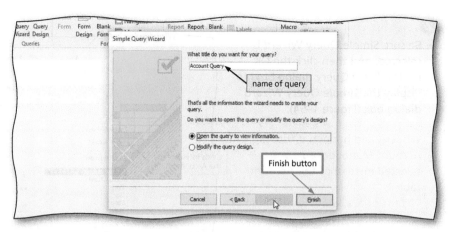

Figure 1–57

⑥

• Click the Finish button to create the query (Figure 1–58).

• Click the Close button for the Account Query to remove the query results from the screen.

Q&A If I want to use this query in the future, do I need to save the query?
Normally you would. The one exception is a query created by the wizard. The wizard automatically saves the query it creates.

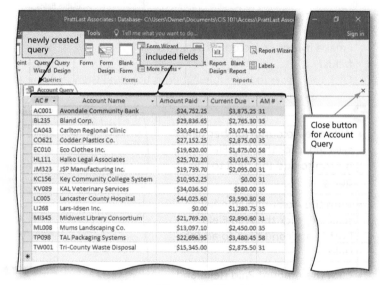

Figure 1–58

Using Queries

After you have created and saved a query, Access stores it as a database object and makes it available for use in a variety of ways:

• If you want to change the design of the query, right-click the query in the Navigation Pane and then click Design View on the shortcut menu to open the query in Design view.

• To view the results of the query from Design view, click the Run button to instruct Access to **run** the query, that is, to perform the necessary actions to produce and display the results in Datasheet view.

• To view the results of the query from the Navigation Pane, open it by right-clicking the query and clicking Open on the shortcut menu. Access automatically runs the query and displays the results in Datasheet view.

• To print the results with the query open in either Design view or Datasheet view, click File on the ribbon, click the Print tab, and then click either Print or Quick Print.

• To print the query without first opening it, be sure the query is selected in the Navigation Pane and click File on the ribbon, click the Print tab, and then click either Print or Quick Print.

You can switch between views of a query using the View button (Home tab | Views group). Clicking the arrow in the bottom of the button produces the View button menu. You then click the desired view in the menu. The two query views you will use in this module are Datasheet view (which displays the query results) and Design view (for changing the query design). You can also click the top part of the View button, in which case you will switch to the view identified by the icon on the button. For the most part, the icon on the button represents the view you want, so you can usually simply click the button.

To Use a Criterion in a Query

1 CREATE FIRST TABLE | 2 ADD RECORDS | 3 PRINT CONTENTS | 4 IMPORT RECORDS
5 MODIFY SECOND TABLE | 6 CREATE QUERY | 7 CREATE FORM | 8 CREATE REPORT

After you have determined the fields to be included in a query, you will determine whether you need to further restrict the results of the query. For example, you might want to include only those accounts managed by account manager 35, Mark Simson. In such a case, you need to enter the number 35 as a criterion for the account manager field. *Why? A criterion is a condition that the records must satisfy in order to be included in the query results.* To do so, you will open the query in Design view, enter the criterion below the appropriate field, and then view the results of the query. The following steps enter a criterion to include only the accounts of account manager 35 and then view the query results.

- Right-click the Account Query in the Navigation Pane to produce a shortcut menu (Figure 1–59).

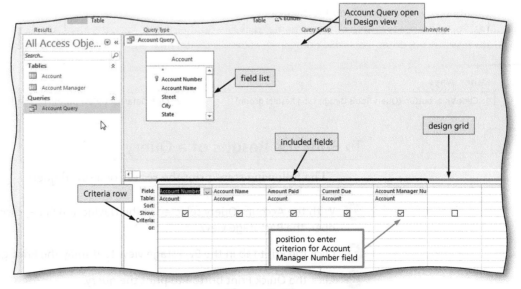

Figure 1–59

- Click Design View on the shortcut menu to open the query in Design view (Figure 1–60).

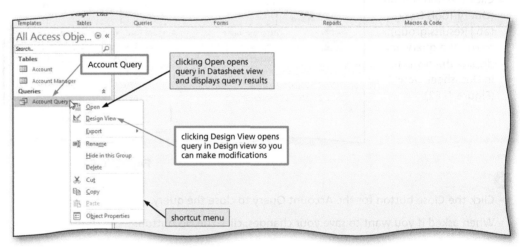

Figure 1–60

3

- Click the Criteria row in the Account Manager Number column of the grid, and then type 35 as the criterion (Figure 1–61).

Q&A The Account Manager Number field is a text field. Do I need to enclose the value for a text field in quotation marks?
You could, but it is not necessary because Access inserts the quotation marks for you automatically.

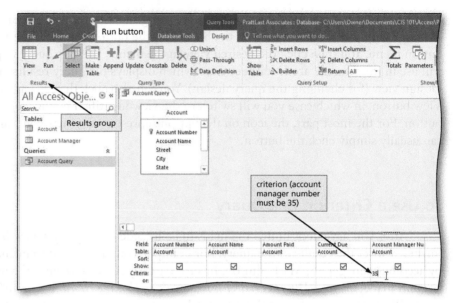

Figure 1–61

4

- Click the Run button (Query Tools Design tab | Results group) to run the query and display the results in Datasheet view (Figure 1–62).

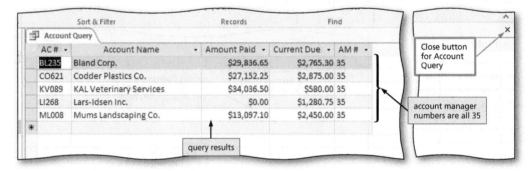

Figure 1–62

5

- Click the Close button for the Account Query to close the query.
- When asked if you want to save your changes, click the No button.

Q&A If I saved the query, what would happen the next time I ran the query?
You would see only accounts of account manager 35.

Could I save a query with another name?
Yes. To save a query with a different name, click File on the ribbon, click the Save As tab, click Save Object As, click the Save As button, enter a new file name in the Save As dialog box, and then click the OK button (Save As dialog box).

Other Ways

1. Click View button (Query Tools Design tab | Results group)   2. Click Datasheet View button on status bar

---

To Print the Results of a Query

The following steps print the results of a saved query.

1 With the Account Query selected in the Navigation Pane, click File on the ribbon to open the Backstage view.

2 Click the Print tab in the Backstage view to display the Print gallery.

3 Click the Quick Print button to print the query.

Creating Forms

In Datasheet view, you can view many records at once. If there are many fields, however, only some of the fields in each record might be visible at a time. In **Form view**, where data is displayed in a form on the screen, you can usually see all the fields, but only for one record.

To Create a Form

1 CREATE FIRST TABLE | 2 ADD RECORDS | 3 PRINT CONTENTS | 4 IMPORT RECORDS
5 MODIFY SECOND TABLE | 6 CREATE QUERY | 7 **CREATE FORM** | 8 **CREATE REPORT**

Like a paper form, a **form** in a database is a formatted document with fields that contain data. Forms allow you to view and maintain data. Forms can also be used to print data, but reports are more commonly used for that purpose. The simplest type of form in Access is one that includes all the fields in a table stacked one above the other. The following steps use the Form button to create a form. *Why? Using the Form button is the simplest way to create this type of form. The steps use the form to view records and then save the form.*

1

- Select the Account table in the Navigation Pane.

- If necessary, click Create on the ribbon to display the Create tab (Figure 1–63).

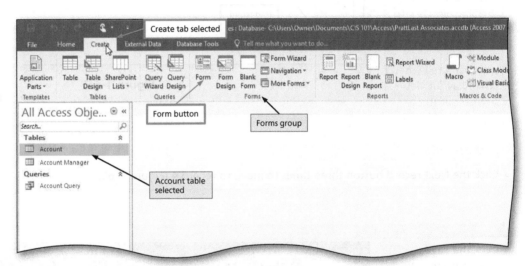

Figure 1–63

2

- Click the Form button (Create tab | Forms group) to create a simple form (Figure 1–64).

Q&A A Field list appeared on my screen. What should I do?
Click the 'Add Existing Fields' button (Form Layout Tools Design tab | Tools group) to remove the Field list from the screen.

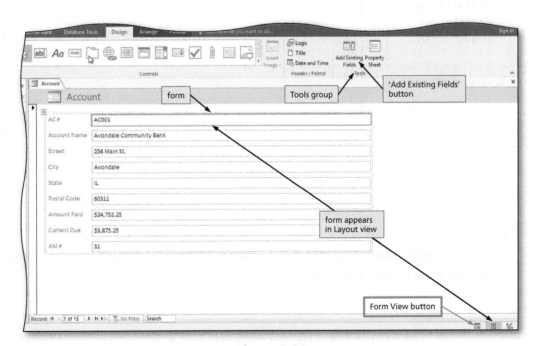

Figure 1–64

• Click the Form View button on the Access status bar to display the form in Form view rather than Layout view.

What is the difference between Layout view and Form view?
Layout view allows you to make changes to the look of the form. Form view is the view you use to examine or make changes to the data.

How can I tell when I am in Layout view?
Access identifies Layout view in three ways. The left side of the status bar will contain the words, Layout View; shading will appear around the outside of the selected field in the form; and the Layout View button will be selected on the right side of the status bar.

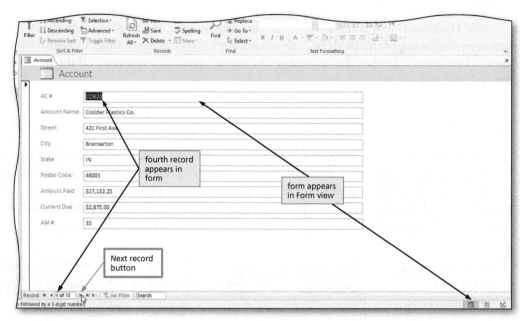

Figure 1–65

• Click the Next record button three times to move to record 4 (Figure 1–65).

• Click the Save button on the Quick Access Toolbar to display the Save As dialog box (Figure 1–66).

Do I have to click the Next record button before saving?
No. The only reason you were asked to click the button was so that you could experience navigation within the form.

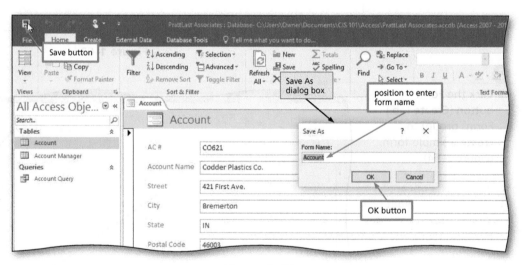

Figure 1–66

• Type **Account Form** as the form name, and then click the OK button to save the form.

• Click the Close button for the form to close the form.

Other Ways

1. Click View button (Form Layout Tools Design tab | Views group)

Using a Form

After you have saved a form, you can use it at any time by right-clicking the form in the Navigation Pane and then clicking Open on the shortcut menu. In addition to viewing data in the form, you can also use it to enter or update data, a process that is very similar to updating data using a datasheet. If you plan to use the form to enter or revise data, you must ensure you are viewing the form in Form view.

Break Point: If you wish to take a break, this is a good place to do so. You can exit Access now. To resume at a later time, run Access, open the database called PrattLast Associates, and continue following the steps from this location forward.

Creating and Printing Reports

PrattLast Associates wants to be able to present account financial data in a useful format. To do so, they will create the Account Financial Report shown in Figure 1–67. To create this report, you will first create a simple report containing all records. Then, you will modify the report to match the one shown in Figure 1–67.

Account Number	Account Name	Amount Paid	Current Due	Account Manager Number
	Account Financial Report		Tuesday, September 12, 2017 7:54:24 PM	
AC001	Avondale Community Bank	$24,752.25	$3,875.25	31
BL235	Bland Corp.	$29,836.65	$2,765.30	35
CA043	Carlton Regional Clinic	$30,841.05	$3,074.30	58
CO621	Codder Plastics Co.	$27,152.25	$2,875.00	35
EC010	Eco Clothes Inc.	$19,620.00	$1,875.00	58
HL111	Halko Legal Associates	$25,702.20	$3,016.75	58
JM323	JSP Manufacturing Inc.	$19,739.70	$2,095.00	31
KV089	KAL Veterinary Services	$34,036.50	$580.00	35
KC156	Key Community College System	$10,952.25	$0.00	31
LC005	Lancaster County Hospital	$44,025.60	$3,590.80	58
LI268	Lars-Idsen Inc.	$0.00	$1,280.75	35
MI345	Midwest Library Consortium	$21,769.20	$2,890.60	31
ML008	Mums Landscaping Co.	$13,097.10	$2,450.00	35
TP098	TAL Packaging Systems	$22,696.95	$3,480.45	58
TW001	Tri-County Waste Disposal	$15,345.00	$2,875.50	31
		$339,566.70	$36,724.70	

Figure 1–67

1 CREATE FIRST TABLE | 2 ADD RECORDS | 3 PRINT CONTENTS | 4 IMPORT RECORDS
5 MODIFY SECOND TABLE | 6 CREATE QUERY | 7 CREATE FORM | **8 CREATE REPORT**

To Create a Report

You will first create a report containing all fields. *Why? It is easiest to create a report with all the fields and then delete the fields you do not want.* The following steps create and save the initial report. They also modify the report title.

1

- Be sure the Account table is selected in the Navigation Pane.

- Click Create on the ribbon to display the Create tab (Figure 1–68).

Q&A Do I need to select the Account table prior to clicking Create on the ribbon?
You do not need to select the table at that point. You do need to select a table prior to clicking the Report button, because Access will include all the fields in whichever table or query is currently selected.

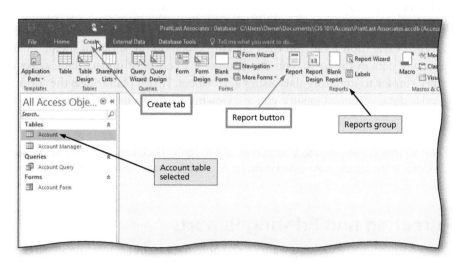

Figure 1–68

2

- Click the Report button (Create tab | Reports group) to create the report (Figure 1–69).

Q&A Why is the report title Account?
Access automatically assigns the name of the table or query as the title of the report. It also automatically includes the date and time. You can change either of these later.

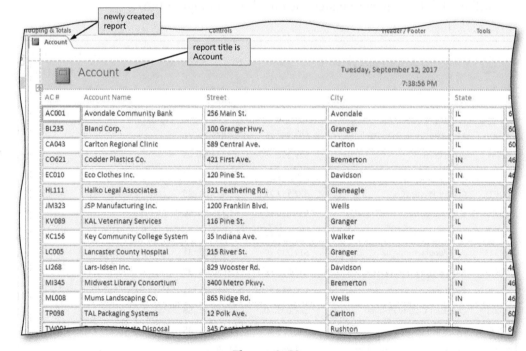

Figure 1–69

3

- Click the Save button on the Quick Access Toolbar to display the Save As dialog box, and then type Account Financial Report as the name of the report (Figure 1–70).

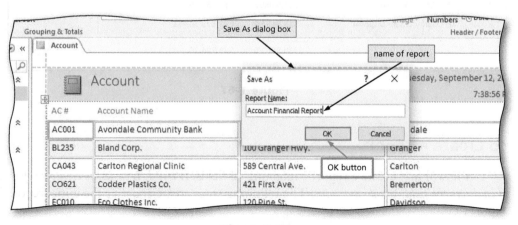

Figure 1–70

- Click the OK button (Save As dialog box) to save the report (Figure 1–71).

Q&A The name of the report changed. Why did the report title not change?

The report title is assigned the same name as the report by default. Changing the name of the report does not change the report title. You can change the title at any time to anything you like.

Figure 1–71

- Close the report by clicking its Close button.

Using Layout View in a Report

Access has four different ways to view reports: Report view, Print Preview, Layout view, and Design view. Report view shows the report on the screen. Print Preview shows the report as it will appear when printed. Layout view is similar to Report view in that it shows the report on the screen, but it also allows you to make changes to the report. Layout view is usually the easiest way to make such changes. Design view also allows you to make changes, but does not show you the actual report. Design view is most useful when the changes you need to make are especially complex. In this module, you will use Layout view to modify the report.

BTW

Report Navigation
When previewing a report, you can use the Navigation buttons on the status bar to move from one page to another.

To Modify Report Column Headings and Resize Columns

1 CREATE FIRST TABLE | 2 ADD RECORDS | 3 PRINT CONTENTS | 4 IMPORT RECORDS

5 MODIFY SECOND TABLE | 6 CREATE QUERY | 7 CREATE FORM | **8 CREATE REPORT**

To make the report match the one shown in Figure 1–67, you need to change the title, remove some columns, modify the column headings, and also resize the columns. The following steps use Layout view to make the necessary modifications to the report. *Why? Working in Layout view gives you all the tools you need to make the desired modifications. You can view the results of the modifications immediately.*

1

- Right-click Account Financial Report in the Navigation Pane, and then click Layout View on the shortcut menu to open the report in Layout view.

- If a Field list appears, click the 'Add Existing Fields' button (Report Layout Tools Design tab | Tools group) to remove the Field list from the screen.

- Close the Navigation Pane.

- Click the report title once to select it.

- Click the report title a second time to produce an insertion point (Figure 1–72).

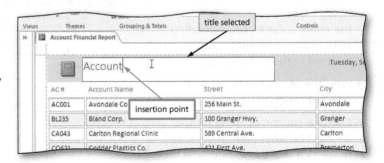

Figure 1–72

Q&A My insertion point is in the middle of Account. How do I produce an insertion point at the position shown in the figure?

You can use the RIGHT ARROW key to move the insertion point to the position in the figure, or you can click the desired position.

2

- Press the SPACEBAR to insert a space, and then type `Financial Report` to complete the title.

- Click the column heading for the Street field to select it.

- Press and hold the CTRL key and then click the column headings for the City, State, and Postal Code fields to select multiple column headings.

Q&A What happens if I do not hold down the CTRL key?

When you click another column heading, it will be the only one that is selected. To select multiple objects, you need to hold the CTRL key down for every object after the first selection.

I selected the wrong collection of objects. What should I do?

You can click somewhere else on the report so that the objects you want are not selected, and then begin the process again. Alternatively, you can repeatedly click the Undo button on the Quick Access Toolbar to undo your selections. Once you have done so, you can select the objects you want.

- Click Arrange on the ribbon to display the Report Layout Tools Arrange tab (Figure 1–73).

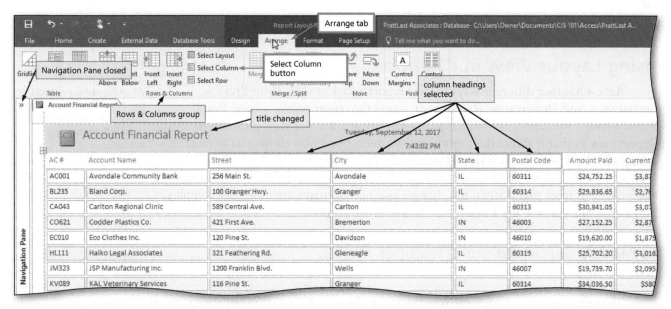

Figure 1–73

3

- Click the Select Column button (Report Layout Tools Arrange tab | Rows & Columns group) to select the entire columns corresponding to the column headings you selected in the previous step.

- Press the DELETE key to delete the selected columns.

- Click the column heading for the Account Number field twice, once to select it and the second time to produce an insertion point (Figure 1–74).

Q&A I selected the wrong field. What should I do?

Click somewhere outside the various fields to deselect the one you have selected. Then, click the Account Number field twice.

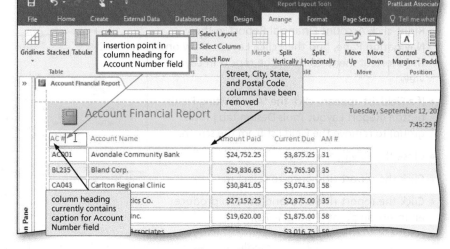

Figure 1–74

4

- Use the DELETE or BACKSPACE keys as necessary to erase the current entry, and then type `Account Number` as the new entry.

- Click the heading for the Account Manager Number field twice, erase the current entry, and then type `Account Manager Number` as the new entry.

- Click the Account Number field heading to select it, point to the lower boundary of the heading for the Account Number field so that the pointer changes to a two-headed arrow, and then drag the

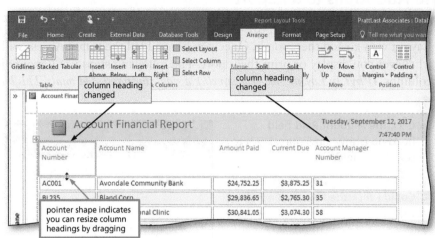

Figure 1–75

lower boundary to the approximate position shown in Figure 1–75 to expand the column headings.

Q&A   I did something wrong when I dragged and now my report looks strange. What should I do?
Click the Undo button on the Quick Access Toolbar to undo the change. Depending on the specific action you took, you might need to click it more than once.

My screen displays Account Manager Number on one line, not two. Is this a problem?
No. You will adjust the column heading in a later step.

5

- Point to the right boundary of the heading for the Account Number field so that the pointer changes to a two-headed arrow, and then drag the right boundary to the approximate position shown in Figure 1–76 to reduce the width of the column.

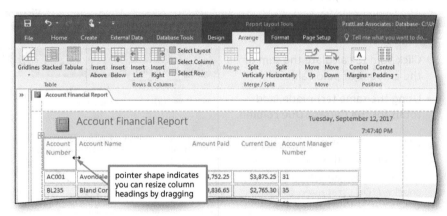

Figure 1–76

6

- Using the same technique, resize the other columns to the sizes shown in Figure 1–77.

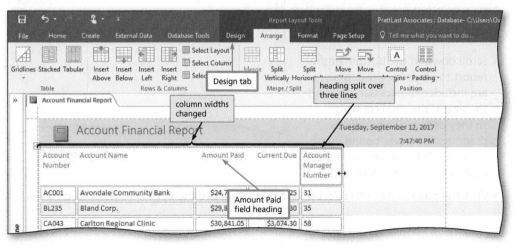

Figure 1–77

To Add Totals to a Report

The report in Figure 1–67 contains totals for the Amount Paid and Current Due columns. You can use Layout view to add these totals. Once you have added the totals, Access will calculate the appropriate values whenever you display or print the report. The following steps use Layout view to include totals for these three columns. **Why?** *In Layout view you can click a single button to add totals. This button sums all the values in the field.*

1

- Click the Amount Paid field heading (shown in Figure 1–77) to select the field.

Q&A Do I have to click the heading? Could I click the field on one of the records?
You do not have to click the heading. You also could click the Amount Paid field on any record.

- Click Design on the ribbon to display the Design tab.

- Click the Totals button (Report Layout Tools Design tab | Grouping & Totals group) to display the Totals menu containing a list of available calculations (Figure 1–78).

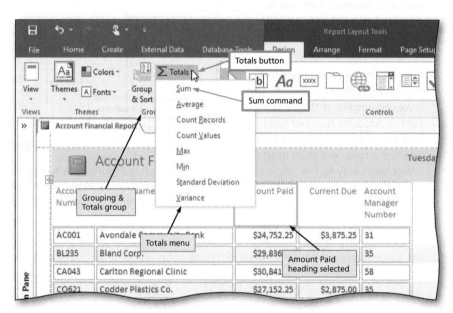

Figure 1–78

2

- Click Sum to calculate the sum of the amount of paid values.

- Using the same technique, add totals for the Current Due column.

Q&A When I clicked the Totals button after selecting the Current Due field heading, Sum was already checked. Do I still need to click Sum?
No. In fact, if you do click it, you will remove the check mark, which will remove the total from the column.

- Scroll down to the bottom of the report to verify that the totals are included. If necessary, expand the size of the total controls so they appear completely by dragging the lower boundary of the controls to the approximate position shown in Figure 1–79.

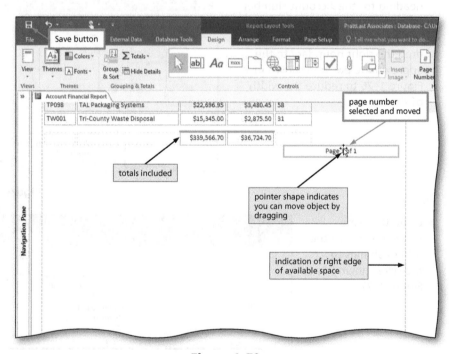

Figure 1–79

- Click the page number to select it, and then drag it to the approximate position shown in Figure 1–79.

Q&A Why did I need to move the page number?
The dotted line near the right-hand edge of the screen indicates the right-hand border of the available space on the printed page, based on whatever margins and orientation are currently selected. A portion of the page number extends beyond this border. By moving the page number, it no longer extends beyond the border.

3
- Click the Save button on the Quick Access Toolbar to save your changes to the report layout.
- Close the report.

To Print a Report

The following steps print the report.

1 Open the Navigation Pane, if necessary, confirm that the Account Financial Report is selected, and then click File on the ribbon to open the Backstage view.

2 Click the Print tab in the Backstage view to display the Print gallery.

3 Click the Quick Print button to print the report.

Q&A When I print the report, I have pound signs (####) rather than numbers where the totals should be for the Amount Paid and Current Due columns. The report looked fine on the screen. How can I correct it?

The columns are not wide enough to display the complete number. Open the report in Layout view and slightly increase the width of the Amount Paid and Current Due columns by dragging the right boundary of the column headings.

How can I print multiple copies of my report?

Click File on the ribbon to open the Backstage view. Click the Print tab, click Print in the Print gallery to display the Print dialog box, increase the number in the Number of Copies box, and then click the OK button .

How can I print a range of pages rather than printing the whole report?

Click File on the ribbon to open the Backstage view. Click the Print tab, click Print in the Print gallery to display the Print dialog box, click the Pages option button in the Print Range area, enter the desired page range, and then click the OK button (Print dialog box).

Database Properties

Access helps you organize and identify your databases by using **database properties**, which are the details about a file. Database properties, also known as **metadata**, can include such information as the project author, title, or subject. **Keywords** are words or phrases that further describe the database. For example, a class name or database topic can describe the file's purpose or content.

Five different types of database properties exist, but the more common ones used in this book are standard and automatically updated properties. **Standard properties** are associated with all Microsoft Office documents and include author, title, and subject. **Automatically updated properties** include file system properties, such as the date you create or change a file, and statistics, such as the file size.

Why would you want to assign database properties to a database?
Database properties are valuable for a variety of reasons:

- Users can save time locating a particular file because they can view a file's database properties without opening the database.

- By creating consistent properties for files having similar content, users can better organize their databases.

- Some organizations require Access users to add database properties so that other employees can view details about these files.

CONSIDER THIS

To Change Database Properties

To change database properties, you would follow these steps.

1 Click File on the ribbon to open the Backstage view and then, if necessary, click the Info tab in the Backstage view to display the Info gallery.

2 Click the 'View and edit database properties' link in the right pane of the Info gallery to display the PrattLast Associates Properties dialog box.

Q&A Why are some of the database properties already filled in?
The person who installed Office 2016 on your computer or network might have set or customized the properties.

3 If the property you want to change is displayed in the Properties dialog box, click the text box for the property and make the desired change. Skip the remaining steps.

4 If the property you want to change is not displayed in the Properties dialog box, click the appropriate tab so the property is displayed and then make the desired change.

5 Click the OK button in the Properties dialog box to save your changes and remove the dialog box from the screen.

BTW
Tabbed Documents Versus Overlapping Windows
By default, Access 2016 displays database objects in tabbed documents instead of in overlapping windows. If your database is in overlapping windows mode, click File on the ribbon, click Options in the Backstage view, click Current Database in the Access Options dialog box, and select the 'Display Document Tabs' check box and the Tabbed Documents option button.

Special Database Operations

Additional operations involved in maintaining a database are backup, recovery, compacting, and repairing.

Backup and Recovery

It is possible to damage or destroy a database. Users can enter data that is incorrect; programs that are updating the database can end abnormally during an update; a hardware problem can occur; and so on. After any such event has occurred, the database may contain invalid data or it might be totally destroyed.

Obviously, you cannot allow a situation in which data has been damaged or destroyed to go uncorrected. You must somehow return the database to a correct state. This process is called recovery; that is, you **recover** the database.

The simplest approach to recovery involves periodically making a copy of the database (called a **backup copy** or a **save copy**). This is referred to as **backing up** the database. If a problem occurs, you correct the problem by overwriting the actual database — often referred to as the **live database** — with the backup copy.

To back up the database that is currently open, you use the Back Up Database command on the Save As tab in the Backstage view. In the process, Access suggests a name that is a combination of the database name and the current date. For example, if you back up the PrattLast Associates database on October 20, 2017, Access will suggest the name, PrattLast Associates_2017-10-20. You can change this name if you desire, although it is a good idea to use this name. By doing so, it will be easy to distinguish between all the backup copies you have made to determine which is the most recent. In addition, if you discover that a critical problem occurred on October 18, 2017, you may want to go back to the most recent backup before October 18. If, for example, the database was not backed up on October 17 but was backed up on October 16, you would use PrattLast Associates_2017-10-16.

TO BACK UP A DATABASE

You would use the following steps to back up a database to a file on a hard disk, high-capacity removable disk, or other storage location.

1. Open the database to be backed up.
2. Click File on the ribbon to open the Backstage view, and then click the Save As tab.
3. With Save Database As selected in the File Types area, click 'Back Up Database' in the Save Database As area, and then click the Save As button.
4. Navigate to the desired location in the Save As box. If you do not want the name Access has suggested, enter the desired name in the File name text box.
5. Click the Save button to back up the database.

Access creates a backup copy with the desired name in the desired location. Should you ever need to recover the database using this backup copy, you can simply copy it over the live version.

Compacting and Repairing a Database

As you add more data to a database, it naturally grows larger. When you delete an object (records, tables, forms, or queries), the space previously occupied by the object does not become available for additional objects. Instead, the additional objects are given new space; that is, space that was not already allocated. To remove this empty space from the database, you must **compact** the database. The same option that compacts the database also repairs problems that might have occurred in the database.

TO COMPACT AND REPAIR A DATABASE

You would use the following steps to compact and repair a database.

1. Open the database to be compacted.
2. Click File on the ribbon to open the Backstage view, and then, if necessary, select the Info tab.
3. Click the 'Compact & Repair Database' button in the Info gallery to compact and repair the database.

The database now is the compacted form of the original.

Additional Operations

Additional special operations include opening another database, closing a database without exiting Access, and saving a database with another name. They also include deleting a table (or other object) as well as renaming an object.

When you are working in a database and you open another database, Access will automatically close the database that was previously open. Before deleting or renaming an object, you should ensure that the object has no dependent objects; that is, other objects that depend on the object you want to delete.

TO CLOSE A DATABASE WITHOUT EXITING ACCESS

You would use the following steps to close a database without exiting Access.

1. Click File on the ribbon to open the Backstage view.
2. Click Close.

TO SAVE A DATABASE WITH ANOTHER NAME

To save a database with another name, you would use the following steps.

1. Click File on the ribbon to open the Backstage view, and then select the Save As tab.
2. With Save Database As selected in the File Types area and Access Database selected in the Save Database As area, click the Save As button.
3. Enter a name and select a location for the new version.
4. Click the Save button.

If you want to make a backup, could you just save the database with another name?
You could certainly do that. Using the backup procedure discussed earlier is useful because doing so automatically includes the current database name and the date in the name of the file it creates.

TO DELETE A TABLE OR OTHER OBJECT IN THE DATABASE

You would use the following steps to delete a database object.

1. Right-click the object in the Navigation Pane.
2. Click Delete on the shortcut menu.
3. Click the Yes button in the Microsoft Access dialog box.

TO RENAME AN OBJECT IN THE DATABASE

You would use the following steps to rename a database object.

1. Right-click the object in the Navigation Pane.
2. Click Rename on the shortcut menu.
3. Type the new name and press the ENTER key.

To Exit Access

All the steps in this module are now complete.

1 If desired, sign out of your Microsoft account.

2 Exit Access.

BTW

Access Help
At any time while using Access, you can find answers to questions and display information about various topics through Access Help. Used properly, this form of assistance can increase your productivity and reduce your frustrations by minimizing the time you spend learning how to use Access. For instructions about Access Help and exercises that will help you gain confidence in using it, read the Office and Windows module at the beginning of this book.

BTW

Determining Database Requirements
The determination of database requirements is part of a process known as systems analysis. A systems analyst examines existing and proposed documents, and examines organizational policies to determine exactly the type of data needs the database must support.

Database Design

This section illustrates the **database design** process, that is, the process of determining the tables and fields that make up the database. It does so by showing how you would design the database for PrattLast Associates from a set of requirements. In this section, you will use commonly accepted shorthand to represent the tables and fields that make up the database as well as the primary keys for the tables. For each table, you give the name of the table followed by a set of parentheses. Within the parentheses is a list of the fields in the table separated by commas. You underline the primary key. For example,

Product (<u>Product Code</u>, Description, On Hand, Price)

represents a table called Product. The Product table contains four fields: Product Code, Description, On Hand, and Price. The Product Code field is the primary key.

Database Requirements

The PrattLast Associates database must maintain information on both accounts and account managers. The business currently keeps this data in two Word tables and two Excel workbooks, as shown in Figure 1–80. They use Word tables for address information and Excel workbooks for financial information.

- For accounts, PrattLast needs to maintain address data. It currently keeps this data in a Word table (Figure 1–80a).
- PrattLast also maintains financial data for each account. This includes the amount paid and current amount due for the account. It keeps these amounts, along with the account name and number, in the Excel worksheet shown in Figure 1–80b.
- PrattLast keeps account manager address data in a Word table, as shown in Figure 1–80c.
- Just as with accounts, it keeps financial data for account managers, including their start date, salary, and bonus rate, in a separate Excel worksheet, as shown in Figure 1–80d.

Finally, PrattLast keeps track of which accounts are assigned to which account managers. Each account is assigned to a single account manager, but each account manager might be assigned many accounts. Currently, for example, accounts AC001 (Avondale Community Bank), JM323 (JSP Manufacturing Inc.), KC156 (Key Community College System), MI345 (Midwest Library Consortium), and TW001 (Tri-County Waste Disposal) are assigned to account manager 31 (Haydee Rivera). Accounts BL235 (Bland Corp.), CO621 (Codder Plastics Co.), KV089 (KAL Veterinary Services), LI268 (Lars-Idsen Inc.), and ML008 (Mums Landscaping Co.) are assigned to account manager 35 (Mark Simson). Accounts CA043 (Carlton Regional Clinic), EC010 (Eco Clothes Inc.), HL111 (Halko Legal Associates), LC005 (Lancaster County Hospital), and TP098 (TAL Packaging Systems) are assigned to account manager 58 (Karen Murowski). PrattLast has an additional account manager, Peter Lu, whose number has been assigned as 42, but who has not yet been assigned any accounts.

BTW
Additional Data for PrattLast Associates
PrattLast could include other types of data in the database. The Account table could include data on a contact person at each organization, such as name, telephone number, and email address. The Account Manager table could include the mobile telephone number, email address, and emergency contact information for the account manager.

Account Number	Account Name	Street	City	State	Postal Code
AC001	Avondale Community Bank	256 Main St.	Avondale	IL	60311
BL235	Bland Corp.	100 Granger Hwy.	Granger	IL	60314
CA043	Carlton Regional Clinic	589 Central Ave.	Carlton	IL	60313
CO621	Codder Plastics Co.	421 First Ave.	Bremerton	IN	46003
EC010	Eco Clothes Inc.	120 Pine St.	Davidson	IN	46010
HL111	Halko Legal Associates	321 Feathering Rd.	Gleneagle	IL	60319
JM323	JSP Manufacturing Inc.	1200 Franklin Blvd.	Wells	IN	46007
KC156	Key Community College System	35 Indiana Ave.	Walker	IN	46004
KV089	KAL Veterinary Services	116 Pine St.	Granger	IL	60314
LC005	Lancaster County Hospital	215 River St.	Granger	IL	46004
LI268	Lars-Idsen Inc.	829 Wooster Rd.	Davidson	IN	46010
MI345	Midwest Library Consortium	3400 Metro Pkwy.	Bremerton	IN	46003
ML008	Mums Landscaping Co.	865 Ridge Rd.	Wells	IN	46007
TP098	TAL Packaging Systems	12 Polk Ave.	Carlton	IL	60313
TW001	Tri-County Waste Disposal	345 Central Blvd.	Rushton	IL	60321

Figure 1–80a Account Addresses

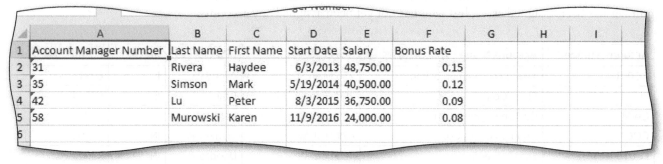

A1	▾	:	✕	✓	fx	Account Number						

	A	B	C	D	E	F	G	H	I	J
1	Account Number	Account Name	Amount Paid	Current Due						
2	AC001	Avondale Community Bank	24,752.25	3,875.25						
3	BL235	Bland Corp.	29,836.65	2,765.30						
4	CA043	Carlton Regional Clinic	30,841.05	3,074.30						
5	CO621	Codder Plastics Co.	27,152.25	2,875.00						
6	EC010	Eco Clothes Inc.	19,620.00	1,875.00						
7	HL111	Halko Legal Associates	25,702.20	3,016.75						
8	JM323	JSP Manufacturing Inc.	19,739.70	2,095.00						
9	KV089	KAL Veterinary Services	34,036.50	580.00						
10	KC156	Key Community College System	10,952.25	0.00						
11	LC005	Lancaster County Hospital	44,025.60	3,590.80						
12	LI268	Lars-Idsen Inc.	0.00	1,280.75						
13	MI345	Midwest Library Consortium	21,769.20	2,890.60						
14	ML008	Mums Landscaping Co.	13,097.10	2,450.00						
15	TP098	TAL Packaging Systems	22,696.95	3,480.45						
16	TW001	Tri-County Waste Disposal	15,345.00	2,875.50						

Figure 1–80b Account Financial Data

Account Manager Number	Last Name	First Name	Street	City	State	Postal Code
31	Rivera	Haydee	325 Twiddy St.	Avondale	IL	60311
35	Simson	Mark	1467 Hartwell St.	Walker	IN	46004
42	Lu	Peter	5624 Murray Ave.	Davidson	IN	46007
58	Murowski	Karen	168 Truesdale Dr.	Carlton	IL	60313

Figure 1–80c Account Manager Addresses

	A	B	C	D	E	F	G	H	I
1	Account Manager Number	Last Name	First Name	Start Date	Salary	Bonus Rate			
2	31	Rivera	Haydee	6/3/2013	48,750.00	0.15			
3	35	Simson	Mark	5/19/2014	40,500.00	0.12			
4	42	Lu	Peter	8/3/2015	36,750.00	0.09			
5	58	Murowski	Karen	11/9/2016	24,000.00	0.08			
6									

Figure 1–80d Account Manager Financial Data

Database Design Process

The database design process involves several steps.

CONSIDER THIS

What is the first step in the process?
Identify the tables. Examine the requirements for the database to identify the main objects that are involved. There will be a table for each object you identify.

In a database for one organization, for example, the main objects might be departments and employees. This would require two tables: one for departments and the other for employees. In the database for another organization, the main objects might be accounts and account managers. In this case, there also would be two tables: one for accounts and the other for account managers. In still another organization's database, the main objects might be books, publishers, and authors. This database would require three tables: one for books, a second for publishers, and a third for authors.

Identifying the Tables

For the PrattLast Associates database, the main objects are accounts and account managers. This leads to two tables, which you must name. Reasonable names for these two tables are:

Account

Account Manager

After identifying the tables, what is the second step in the database design process?

Determine the primary keys. Recall that the primary key is the unique identifier for records in the table. For each table, determine the unique identifier. In a Department table, for example, the unique identifier might be the Department Code. For a Book table, the unique identifier might be the ISBN (International Standard Book Number).

Determining the Primary Keys

The next step is to identify the fields that will be the unique identifiers, or primary keys. Account numbers uniquely identify accounts, and account manager numbers uniquely identify account managers. Thus, the primary key for the Account table is the account number, and the primary key for the Account Manager table is the account manager number. Reasonable names for these fields would be Account Number and Account Manager Number, respectively. Adding these primary keys to the tables gives:

Account (<u>Account Number</u>)

Account Manager (<u>Account Manager Number</u>)

What is the third step in the database design process after determining the primary keys?

Determine the additional fields. The primary key will be a field or combination of fields in a table. A table will typically contain many additional fields, each of which contains a type of data. Examine the project requirements to determine these additional fields. For example, in an Employee table, additional fields might include Employee Name, Street Address, City, State, Postal Code, Date Hired, and Salary.

Determining Additional Fields

After identifying the primary keys, you need to determine and name the additional fields. In addition to the account number, the Account Address Information shown in Figure 1–80a contains the account name, street, city, state, and postal code. These would be fields in the Account table. The Account Financial Information shown in Figure 1–80b also contains the account number and account name, which are already included in the Account table. The financial information also contains the amount paid and current due. Adding the amount paid and current due fields to those already identified in the Account table and assigning reasonable names gives:

Account (<u>Account Number</u>, Account Name, Street, City, State, Postal Code, Amount Paid, Current Due)

Similarly, examining the Account Manager Address Information in Figure 1–80c adds the last name, first name, street, city, state, and postal code fields to the Account Manager table. In addition to the account manager number, last name, and first name, the Account Manager Financial Information in Figure 1–80d would add the start date, salary, and bonus rate. Adding these fields to the Account Manager table and assigning reasonable names gives:

Account Manager (<u>Account Manager Number</u>, Last Name, First Name, Street, City, State, Postal Code, Start Date, Salary, Bonus Rate)

BTW
Database Design Language (DBDL)
Database Design Language (DBDL) is a commonly accepted shorthand representation for showing the structure of a relational database. You write the name of the table and then within parentheses you list all the columns in the table. If the columns continue beyond one line, indent the subsequent lines.

What happens as the fourth step, after determining additional fields?
Determine relationships between the tables. A relationship is an association between objects. In a database containing information about departments and employees, there is an association between the departments and the employees. A department is associated with all the employees in the department, and an employee is associated with the department to which he or she is assigned. Technically, you say that a department is related to all the employees in the department, and an employee is related to his or her department.

The relationship between department and employees is an example of a **one-to-many relationship** because one employee is associated with one department, but each department can be associated with many employees. The Department table would be the "one" table in the relationship. The Employee table would be the "many" table in the relationship.

When you have determined that two tables are related, follow these general guidelines:

• Identify the "one" table.

• Identify the "many" table.

• Include the primary key from the "one" table as a field in the "many" table.

Determining and Implementing Relationships between the Tables

According to the requirements, each account has one account manager, but each account manager can have many accounts. Thus, the Account Manager table is the "one" table, and the Account table is the "many" table. To implement this one-to-many relationship between account managers and accounts, add the Account Manager Number field (the primary key of the Account Manager table) to the Account table. This produces:

Account (<u>Account Number</u>, Account Name, Street, City, State, Postal Code, Amount Paid, Current Due, Account Manager Number)

Account Manager (<u>Account Manager Number</u>, Last Name, First Name, Street, City, State, Postal Code, Start Date, Salary, Bonus Rate)

After creating relationships between tables, what is the fifth step in the database design process?
Determine data types for the fields, that is, the type of data that can be stored in the field.

Assigning Data Types to the Fields

See the earlier section Determining Data Types for the Fields for a discussion of the available data types and their use in the PrattLast Associates database. That section also discusses other properties that can be assigned, such as captions, field size, and the number of decimal places.

BTW
Postal Codes
Some organizations with accounts throughout the country have a separate table of postal codes, cities, and states. When placing an order, you typically are asked for your postal code (or ZIP code), rather than city, state, and postal code. You then are asked to confirm that the city and state correspond to that postal code.

Identifying and Removing Redundancy

Redundancy means storing the same fact in more than one place. It usually results from placing too many fields in a table — fields that really belong in separate tables — and often causes serious problems. If you had not realized there were two objects, such as accounts and account managers, you might have placed all the data in a single Account table. Figure 1–81 shows an example of a table that includes both account and account manager information. Notice that the data for a given account manager (number, name, address, and so on) occurs on more than one record. The data for rep 35, Mark Simson, is repeated in the figure. Storing this data on multiple records is an example of redundancy.

Account table

Account Number	Account Name	Street	...	Account Manager Number	Last Name	First Name
AC001	Avondale Community Bank	256 Main St.	...	31	Rivera	Haydee
BL235	Bland Corp.	100 Granger Hwy.	...	35	Simson	Mark
CA043	Carlton Regional Clinic	589 Central Ave.	...	58	Murowski	Karen
CO621	Codder Plastics Co.	421 First Ave.	...	35	Simson	Mark
EC010	Eco Clothes Inc.	120 Pine St.	...	58	Murowski	Karen
...	...	Account Manager numbers are 35	...	...	...	...
...	...	...	...	...	...	name of Account Manager 35 appears more than once

Figure 1–81

What problems does this redundancy cause?

Redundancy results in several problems, including:

1. Wasted storage space. The name of account manager 35, Mark Simson, for example, should be stored only once. Storing this information several times is wasteful.

2. More complex database updates. If, for example, Mark Simson's name is spelled incorrectly and needs to be changed in the database, his name would need to be changed in several different places.

3. Possible inconsistent data. Nothing prohibits the account manager's last name from being Simson on account BL235's record and Stimson on account CO621's record. The data would be inconsistent. In both cases, the account manager number is 35, but the last names are different.

How do you eliminate redundancy?

The solution to the problem is to place the redundant data in a separate table, one in which the data will no longer be redundant. If, for example, you place the data for account managers in a separate table (Figure 1–82), the data for each account manager will appear only once.

Account table

Account Number	Account Name	Street	...	Account Manager Number
AC001	Avondale Community Bank	256 Main St.	...	31
BL235	Bland Corp.	100 Granger Hwy.	...	35
CA043	Carlton Regional Clinic	589 Central Ave.	...	58
CO621	Codder Plastics Co.	421 First Ave.	...	35
EC010	Eco Clothes Inc.	120 Pine St.	...	58
...	...	...	...	...
...	...	...	...	...

Account Manager numbers are 35

Account Manager Table

Account Manager Number	Last Name	First Name	...
31	Rivera	Haydee	...
35	Simson	Mark	...
42	Lu	Peter	...
58	Murowski	Karen	...

name of Account Manager 35 appears only once

Figure 1–82

CONSIDER THIS

CONSIDER THIS

Notice that you need to have the account manager number in both tables. Without it, there would be no way to tell which account manager is associated with which account. The remaining account manager data, however, was removed from the Account table and placed in the Account Manager table. This new arrangement corrects the problems of redundancy in the following ways:

- Because the data for each account manager is stored only once, space is not wasted.

- Changing the name of an account manager is easy. You need to change only one row in the Account Manager table.

- Because the data for an account manager is stored only once, inconsistent data cannot occur.

Designing to omit redundancy will help you to produce good and valid database designs. You should always examine your design to see if it contains redundancy. If it does, you should decide whether you need to remove the redundancy by creating a separate table.

If you examine your design, you will see that there is one area of redundancy (see the data in Figure 1–1). Cities and states are both repeated. Every account whose postal code is 60314, for example, has Granger as the city and IL as the state. To remove this redundancy, you would create a table with the primary key Postal Code and City and State as additional fields. City and State would be removed from the Account table. Having City, State, and Postal Code in a table is very common, however, and usually you would not take such action. No other redundancy exists in your tables.

Summary

In this module you have learned to create an Access database, create tables and add records to a database, print the contents of tables, import data, create queries, create forms, create reports, and change database properties. You have also learned how to design a database.

What decisions will you need to make when creating your next database?
Use these guidelines as you complete the assignments in this module and create your own databases outside of this class.

1. Identify the tables that will be included in the database.

2. Determine the primary keys for each of the tables.

3. Determine the additional fields that should be included in each of the tables.

4. Determine relationships between the tables.

 a) Identify the "one" table.

 b) Identify the "many" table.

 c) Include the primary key of the "one" table as a field in the "many" table.

5. Determine data types for the fields in the tables.

6. Determine additional properties for fields.

 a) Determine if a caption is warranted.

 b) Determine if a description of the field is warranted.

 c) Determine field sizes.

 d) Determine formats.

7. Identify and remove any unwanted redundancy.

8. Determine a storage location for the database.

9. Determine the best method for distributing the database objects.

CONSIDER THIS

How should you submit solutions to questions in the assignments identified with a symbol?
Every assignment in this book contains one or more questions identified with a symbol. These questions require you to think beyond the assigned database. Present your solutions to the questions in the format required by your instructor. Possible formats may include one or more of these options: write the answer; create a document that contains the answer; present your answer to the class; discuss your answer in a group; record the answer as audio or video using a webcam, smartphone, or portable media player; or post answers on a blog, wiki, or website.

Apply Your Knowledge

Reinforce the skills and apply the concepts you learned in this module.

Adding a Caption, Changing a Data Type, and Creating a Query, Form, and Report

Note: To complete this assignment, you will be required to use the Data Files. Please contact your instructor for information about accessing the Data Files.

Instructions: Friendly Janitorial Services provides janitorial services to local businesses. The company uses a team-based approach and each team has a team leader or supervisor. Friendly Janitorial Services has a database that keeps track of its supervisors and its clients. Each client is assigned to a single supervisor; each supervisor may be assigned many clients. The database has two tables. The Client table contains data on the clients who use Friendly Janitorial Services. The Supervisor table contains data on the supervisors. You will add a caption, change a data type, and create a query, a form, and a report, as shown in Figure 1–83.

Perform the following tasks:

1. Run Access, open the Apply Friendly Janitorial Services database from the Data Files, and enable the content.

2. Open the Supervisor table in Datasheet view, add SU # as the caption for the Supervisor Number field, and resize all columns to best fit the data. Save the changes to the layout of the table and close the table.

3. Open the Client table in Design view and change the data type for the Supervisor Number field to Short Text. Change the field size for the field to 3 and add SU # as the caption for the Supervisor Number field. Save the changes to the table and close the table. Then, open the Client table in Datasheet view and resize all columns to best fit the data. Save the changes to the layout of the table and close the table.

4. Use the Simple Query Wizard to create a query for the Client table that contains the Client Number, Client Name, Amount Paid, Current Due, and Supervisor Number. The query is a detail query. Use the name Client Query for the query and close the query.

5. Create a simple form for the Supervisor table. Save the form and use the name Supervisor for the form. Close the form.

6. Create the report shown in Figure 1–83 for the Client table. The report includes totals for both the Amount Paid and Current Due fields. Be sure the totals appear completely. You might need to expand the size of the total controls. Move the page number so that it is within the margins. Save the report as Client Financial Report.

7. If requested by your instructor, add your last name to the title of the report, that is, change the title to Client Financial Report LastName where LastName is your actual last name.

8. Compact and repair the database.

9. Submit the revised database in the format specified by your instructor.

10. ✳ How would you change the field name of the Street field in the Client table to Address?

Continued >

Apply Your Knowledge *continued*

| Client Financial Report | | | Tuesday, September 12, 2017 |
| | | | 6:19:45 PM |

Client Number	Client Name	Amount Paid	Current Due	Supervisor Number
AT13	Atlas Repair	$5,400.00	$600.00	103
AZ01	AZ Auto	$9,250.00	$975.00	110
BB35	Babbage Bookkeeping	$8,820.00	$980.00	110
BL24	Blanton Shoes	$1,850.75	$210.25	120
MM01	Moss Manufacturing	$10,456.25	$1,125.00	114
PL03	Prime Legal Associates	$19,905.00	$2,245.00	110
PS67	PRIM Staffing	$4,500.00	$500.00	114
TE15	Telton-Edwards	$0.00	$700.00	120
		$129,979.20	$14,542.55	

Figure 1–83

Extend Your Knowledge

Extend the skills you learned in this module and experiment with new skills. You may need to use Help to complete the assignment.

Using a Database Template to Create an Events Database

Instructions: Access includes both desktop database templates and web-based templates. You can use a template to create a beginning database that can be modified to meet your specific needs. You will use a template to create an Events database. The database template includes sample tables, queries, forms, and reports. You will modify the database and create the Events Query shown in Figure 1–84.

Perform the following tasks:

1. Run Access.
2. Select the Desktop event management template in the template gallery and create a new database with the file name Extend Events.
3. Enable the content and close the Event List form.
4. Open the Navigation Pane and change the organization to Object Type.
5. Open the Events table in Datasheet view and delete the Attachments field in the table. The Attachments field has a paperclip as the column heading.
6. Add the Event Type field to the end of the table. Assign the Short Text data type with a field size of 15.
7. Save the changes to the Events table and close the table.
8. Use the Simple Query Wizard to create the Events Query shown in Figure 1–84. Close the query.

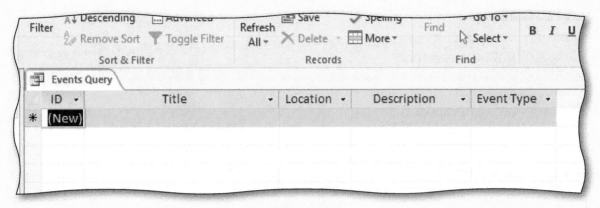

Figure 1–84

9. Open the Current Events report in Layout view. Delete the controls containing the current date and current time in the upper-right corner of the report. Change the title of the report to Current Events List.

10. Save the changes to the report.

11. If requested to do so by your instructor, add your first and last names to the end of the title and save the changes to the report.

12. Submit the revised database in the format specified by your instructor.

13. ✹ a.   Why would you use a template instead of creating a database from scratch with just the fields you need?

    b.   The Attachment data type allows you to attach files to a database record. If you were using this database to keep track of events for a 4th of July celebration in a small town, what specific documents might you attach to an Events record?

Expand Your World

Create a solution, which uses cloud and web technologies, by learning and investigating on your own from general guidance.

Problem: You and two friends recently started a business that provides temporary non-medical help to individuals and families in need of assistance. You want to be able to share query results and reports, so you have decided to store the items in the cloud. You are still learning Access, so you are going to create a sample query and the report shown in Figure 1–85, export the results, and save to a cloud storage location, such as Microsoft OneDrive, Dropbox, or Google Drive.

Note: To complete this assignment, you will be required to use the Data Files. Please contact your instructor for information about accessing the Data Files.

Instructions:

1. Open the Expand Temporary Help database from the Data Files and enable the content.

2. Use the Simple Query Wizard to create a query that includes the Client Number, First Name, Last Name, Balance, and Helper Number. Save the query as Client Query.

3. Export the Client Query as an XPS document to a cloud-based storage location of your choice.

4. Create the report shown in Figure 1–85. Save the report as Client Status Report.

Continued >

Expand Your World *continued*

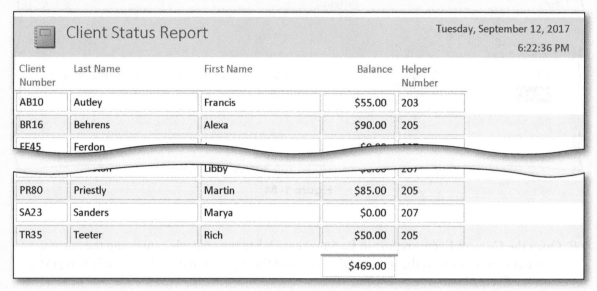

Client Status Report				Tuesday, September 12, 2017 6:22:36 PM
Client Number	Last Name	First Name	Balance	Helper Number
AB10	Autley	Francis	$55.00	203
BR16	Behrens	Alexa	$90.00	205
FE45	Ferdon			
		Libby		207
PR80	Priestly	Martin	$85.00	205
SA23	Sanders	Marya	$0.00	207
TR35	Teeter	Rich	$50.00	205
			$469.00	

Figure 1–85

5. Export the Client Status Report as a PDF document to a cloud-based storage location of your choice. You do not need to change any optimization or export settings. Do not save the export steps.

6. If requested to do so by your instructor, open the Helper table and change the last name and first name for helper 203 to your last name and your first name.

7. Submit the assignment in the format specified by your instructor.

8. ✳ Which cloud-based storage location did you use for this assignment? Why?

In the Labs

Design, create, modify, and/or use a database following the guidelines, concepts, and skills presented in this module. Labs are listed in order of increasing difficulty. Labs 1 and 2, which increase in difficulty, require you to create solutions based on what you learned in the module; Lab 3 requires you to apply your creative thinking and problem-solving skills to design and implement a solution.

Lab 1: Creating Objects for the Garden Naturally Database

Problem: Garden Naturally is a company that provides products for the organic gardening community. Sales representatives are responsible for selling to distributors, nurseries, and retail stores. The company recently decided to store its customer and sales rep data in a database. Each customer is assigned to a single sales rep, but each sales rep may be assigned many customers. The database and the Sales Rep table have been created, but the Salary YTD field needs to be added to the table. The records shown in Table 1–6 must be added to the Sales Rep table. The company plans to import the Customer table from the Excel worksheet shown in Figure 1–86. Garden Naturally would like to finish storing this data in a database and has asked you to help.

Note: To complete this assignment, you will be required to use the Data Files. Please contact your instructor for information about accessing the Data Files.

Instructions: Perform the following tasks:

1. Run Access, open the Lab 1 Garden Naturally database from the Data Files, and enable the content.
2. Open the Sales Rep table in Datasheet view and add the Salary YTD field to the end of the table. The field has the Currency data type. Assign the caption SR # to the Sales Rep Number field.
3. Add the records shown in Table 1–6.

Table 1–6 Data for Sales Rep Table

Sales Rep Number	Last Name	First Name	Street	City	State	Postal Code	Start Date	Commission Rate	Salary YTD
32	Ortiz	Gloria	982 Victoria Ln.	Chesnee	NJ	07053	9/12/2015	.05	$32,555.65
35	Sinson	Mike	45 Elm St.	Quaker	DE	19719	8/28/2017	.04	$1,500.00
29	Gupta	Rufus	678 Hillcrest Rd.	Gossett	PA	19157	6/1/2015	.06	$35,075.30
26	Jones	Pat	43 Third St.	Greer	PA	19158	5/16/2016	.05	$33,100.50

4. Resize the columns to best fit the data. Save the changes to the layout of the table.
5. Import the Lab 1–1 Customer workbook shown in Figure 1–86 into the database. The first row of the workbook contains the column headings. Customer Number is the primary key for the new table. Assign the name Customer to the table. Save the Import steps, and assign the name Import-Customer Workbook to the steps. Assign Import Customer Workbook as the description.

	A	B	C	D	E	F	G	H	I
1	Customer Number	Customer Name	Address	City	State	Postal Code	Amount Paid	Balance Due	Sales Rep Number
2	AA30	All About Gardens	47 Berton St.	Greer	PA	19158	$1,190.00	$365.00	26
3	CT02	Christmas Tree Farm	483 Cantor Rd.	Pleasantburg	NJ	07025	$2,285.50	$825.35	29
4	GG01	Garden Gnome	10 Main St.	Gossett	PA	19157	$1,300.00	$297.50	29
5	GT34	Green Thumb Growers	26 Jefferson Hwy.	Pleasantburg	NJ	07025	$3,325.45	$865.50	32
6	LH15	Lawn & Home Store	33 Maple St.	Chambers	NJ	07037	$895.00	$515.00	26
7	ML25	Mum's Landscaping	196 Lincoln Ave.	Quaker	DE	19719	$0.00	$1,805.00	29
8	OA45	Outside Architects	234 Magnolia Rd.	Gaston	DE	19723	$4,205.50	$945.00	32
9	PL10	Pat's Landscaping	22 Main St.	Chesnee	NJ	07053	$1,165.00	$180.00	26
10	PN18	Pyke Nurseries	10 Grant Blvd.	Adelphia	PA	19159	$2,465.00	$530.00	32
11	SL25	Summit Lawn Service	345 Oaktree Rd.	Chesnee	NJ	07053	$3,225.45	$675.50	26
12	TG38	TriState Growers	24 Main St.	Gaston	DE	19723	$1,075.00	$0.00	29
13	TW34	TAL Wholesalers	234 Cantor Rd.	Pleasantburg	NJ	07025	$4,125.00	$350.00	26
14	TY03	TLC Yard Care	24 Berton St.	Greer	PA	19158	$1,845.00	$689.45	29
15	YS04	Yard Shoppe	124 Elm St.	Quaker	DE	19719	$445.00	$575.00	32
16	YW01	Young's Wholesalers	5239 Lancaster Hwy.	Adelphia	PA	19156	$1,785.50	$345.60	32
17									
18									
19									
20									
21									

Figure 1–86

Continued >

In the Labs *continued*

6. Open the Customer table in Design view and make the following changes:

   a. Change the field size for the Customer Number field to 4. Change the field size for the Customer Name field to 30. Change the field size for the Address field to 25 and the field size for the City field to 20. Change the field size for the State field to 2 and the field size for the Postal Code field to 5. Change the field size for the Sales Rep Number field to 2.

   b. Add the caption CU # to the Customer Number field.

   c. Add the caption SR # to the Sales Rep Number field.

7. Save the changes to the Customer table. If a Microsoft Access dialog box appears with the 'Some data may be lost' message, click the Yes button.

8. Open the Customer table in Datasheet view and resize all columns to best fit the data. Save the changes to the layout of the table.

9. Create a query using the Simple Query Wizard for the Customer table that displays the Customer Number, Customer Name, Amount Paid, Balance Due, and Sales Rep Number. Save the query as Customer Query.

Customer Financial Report

Tuesday, September 12, 2017
6:25:09 PM

Customer Number	Customer Name	Amount Paid	Balance Due	Sales Rep Number
AA30	All About Gardens	$1,190.00	$365.00	26
CT02	Christmas Tree Farm	$2,285.50	$825.35	29
TG38	TriState Growers	$1,075.00	$0.00	29
TW34	TAL Wholesalers	$4,125.00	$350.00	26
TY03	TLC Yard Care	$1,845.00	$689.45	29
YS04	Yard Shoppe	$445.00	$575.00	32
YW01	Young's Wholesalers	$1,785.50	$345.60	32
		$29,332.40	$8,963.90	

Figure 1–87

10. Create the report shown in Figure 1–87 for the Customer table. The report should include the Customer Number, Customer Name, Amount Paid, Balance Due, and Sales Rep Number fields. Include totals for the Amount Paid and Balance Due fields. Be sure to change the column headings to those shown in Figure 1–87. Save the report as Customer Financial Report.

11. If requested to do so by your instructor, change the address for Pat Jones in the Sales Rep table to your address. If your address is longer than 20 characters, simply enter as much as you can.

12. Submit the revised database in the format specified by your instructor.

13. ✷ The Commission Rate field has a field size of Single. If you changed the field size to Integer, what values would appear in the Commission Rate column? Why?

Lab 2: **Creating the Museum Gift Shop Database**

Problem: The local science museum operates a gift shop that sells science-related items. The gift shop purchases the items from vendors that deal in science-related games, toys, and other merchandise. Currently, the information about the items and the vendors is stored in two Excel workbooks. Each item is assigned to a single vendor, but each vendor may be assigned many items. You are to create a database that will store the item and vendor information. You have already determined that you need two tables, a Vendor table and an Item table, in which to store the information.

Note: To complete this assignment, you will be required to use the Data Files. Please contact your instructor for information about accessing the Data Files.

Instructions: Perform the following tasks:

1. Use the Blank desktop database option to create a new database in which to store all objects related to the items for sale. Call the database Lab 2 Museum Gift Shop.

2. Import the Lab 1–2 Vendor Data Excel workbook into the database. The first row of the workbook contains the column headings. Vendor Code is the primary key for the new table. Assign the name Vendor to the table. Do not save the Import steps.

3. Open the Vendor table in Datasheet view. Change the field size for the Vendor Code field to 2; the field size for the Vendor Name field to 25; and the field size for the Telephone Number field to 12. Assign the caption VC to the Vendor Code field.

4. Import the Lab 1–2 Item Data Excel workbook into the database. The first row of the workbook contains the column headings. Item Number is the primary key for this table. Assign the name Item to the table. Do not save the Import steps.

5. Open the Item table in Design view. Change the field size for the Item Number field to 4. Change the field size for the Description field to 28. Add the caption Wholesale for the Wholesale Cost field, the caption Retail for the Retail Price field, and the caption VC for the vendor code. The On Hand field should be an Integer field. Be sure that the field size for the Vendor Code in the Item table is identical to the field size for the Vendor Code in the Vendor table. Save the changes to the table and close the table.

6. Open the Item table in Datasheet view and resize the columns to best fit the data. Save the changes to the layout of the table and close the table.

7. Create a query for the Item table. Include the Item Number, Description, Wholesale Cost, Retail Price, and Vendor Code. Save the query as Item Query.

8. Create a simple form for the Item table. Use the name Item for the form.

9. Create the report shown in Figure 1–88 for the Item table. Do not add any totals. Save the report as Item Status Report.

Item Status Report

Tuesday, September 12, 2017
6:26:31 PM

Item Number	Description	On Hand	Wholesale Price
3663	Agate Bookends	4	$16.25
3673	Amazing Science Fun	8	$13.50
4553	Cosmos Uncovered	9	$8.95
4573	Crystal Growing Kit	7	$6.75
4583	Dinosaur Egg Ornament	12	$7.50

Figure 1–88

Continued >

In the Labs *continued*

10. If requested to do so by your instructor, change the telephone number for Atherton Wholesalers to your telephone number.

11. Submit the database in the format specified by your instructor.

12. ✸ If you had designed this database, could you have used the field name, Name, for the Vendor Name field name? If not, why not?

Lab 3: **Consider This: Your Turn**

Apply your creative thinking and problem solving skills to design and implement a solution.

Creating the Camshay Marketing Database

Note: To complete this assignment, you will be required to use the Data Files. Please contact your instructor for information about accessing the Data Files.

Part 1:   Camshay Marketing Associates is a small company that specializes in data mining for marketing research and analysis. The company focuses on the service, nonprofit, and retail sectors. Camshay uses marketing analysts to work collaboratively with clients. Marketing analysts are paid a base salary and can earn incentive pay for maintaining and expanding client relationships. Based on the information in the Lab 1–3 Camshay Marketing workbook, use the concepts and techniques presented in this module to design and create a database to store the Camshay Marketing data. Change data types and field sizes as necessary. Add captions where appropriate. Create a form for the Client table and a report for the Client table similar to the Account Financial Report shown in Figure 1-67. Use the simple query wizard to create a query for the Client table that includes the Client Number, Client Name, Current Due and Marketing Analyst Number. Open the query and add a criterion to the query results to find only those clients whose amount due is $0.00 and save this modified query with a different name. Submit your assignment in the format specified by your instructor.

Part 2:   You made several decisions while determining the table structures and adding data to the tables in this assignment. What method did you use to add the data to each table? Are there any other methods that would also have worked?

2 | Querying a Database

Objectives

You will have mastered the material in this module when you can:

- Create queries using Design view
- Include fields in the design grid
- Use text and numeric data in criteria
- Save a query and use the saved query
- Create and use parameter queries
- Use compound criteria in queries
- Sort data in queries

- Join tables in queries
- Create a report and a form from a query
- Export data from a query to another application
- Perform calculations and calculate statistics in queries
- Create crosstab queries
- Customize the Navigation Pane

Introduction

One of the primary benefits of using a database management system such as Access is having the ability to find answers to questions related to data stored in the database. When you pose a question to Access, or any other database management system, the question is called a query. A **query** is simply a question presented in a way that Access can process.

To find the answer to a question, you first create a corresponding query using the techniques illustrated in this module. After you have created the query, you instruct Access to run the query, that is, to perform the steps necessary to obtain the answer. Access then displays the answer in Datasheet view.

For an introduction to Windows and instructions about how to perform basic Windows tasks, read the Office and Windows module at the beginning of this book, where you can learn how to resize windows, change screen resolution, create folders, move and rename files, use Windows Help, and much more

Project — Querying a Database

Examples of questions related to the data in the PrattLast Associates database are shown in Figure 2–1.

In addition to these questions, PrattLast managers need to find information about accounts located in a specific city, but they want to enter a different city each time they ask the question. The company can use a parameter query to accomplish this task. PrattLast managers also want to summarize data in a specific way, which might involve performing calculations, and they can use a crosstab query to present the data in the desired form.

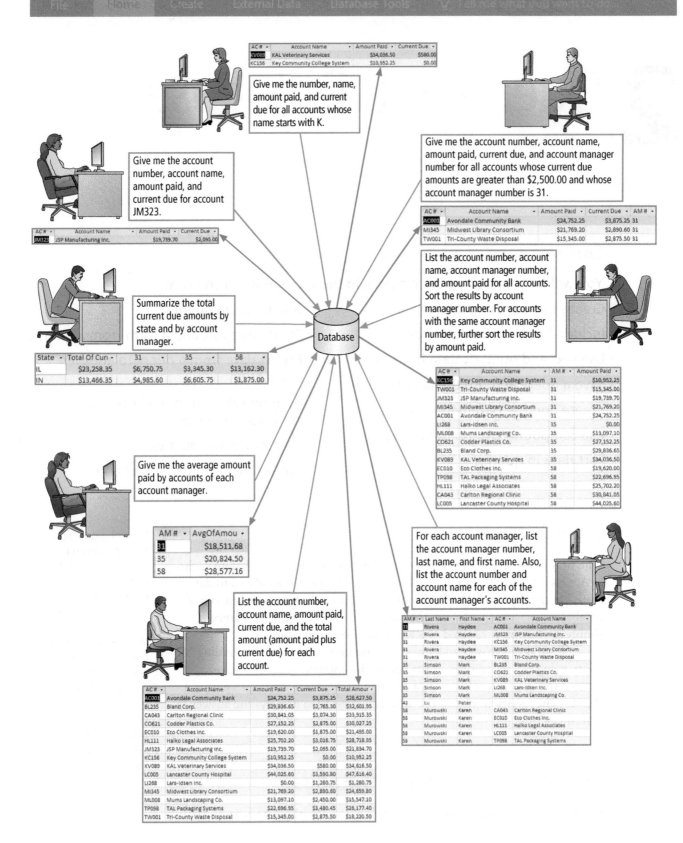

Figure 2–1

In this module, you will learn how to create and use the queries shown in Figure 2–1. The following roadmap identifies general activities you will perform as you progress through this module:

1. CREATE QUERIES in Design view.

2. USE CRITERIA in queries.

3. SORT DATA in queries.

4. JOIN TABLES in queries.

5. EXPORT query RESULTS.

6. PERFORM CALCULATIONS in queries.

7. CREATE a CROSSTAB query.

8. CUSTOMIZE the NAVIGATION PANE.

For an introduction to Office and instructions about how to perform basic tasks in Office apps, read the Office and Windows module at the beginning of this book, where you can learn how to run an application, use the ribbon, save a file, open a file, print a file, exit an application, use Help, and much more.

Creating Queries

As you learned in Module 1, you can use queries in Access to find answers to questions about the data contained in the database. *Note:* In this module, you will save each query example. When you use a query for another task, such as to create a form or report, you will assign a specific name to a query, for example, Manager-Account Query. In situations in which you will not use the query again, you will assign a name using a convention that includes the module number and a query number, for example, m02q01. Queries are numbered consecutively.

BTW
Select Queries
The queries you create in this module are select queries. In a select query, you retrieve data from one or more tables using criteria that you specify and display the data in a datasheet.

1 CREATE QUERIES | 2 USE CRITERIA | 3 SORT DATA | 4 JOIN TABLES | 5 EXPORT RESULTS
6 PERFORM CALCULATIONS | 7 CREATE CROSSTAB | 8 CUSTOMIZE NAVIGATION PANE

To Create a Query in Design View

In Module 1, you used the Simple Query Wizard to create a query. Most of the time, however, you will use Design view, which is the primary option for creating queries. *Why? Once you have created a new query in Design view, you have more options than with the wizard and can specify fields, criteria, sorting, calculations, and so on.* The following steps create a new query in Design view.

1
- Run Access and open the database named PrattLast Associates from your hard disk, OneDrive, or other storage location.

- Click the 'Shutter Bar Open/Close Button' to close the Navigation Pane.

- Click Create on the ribbon to display the Create tab (Figure 2–2).

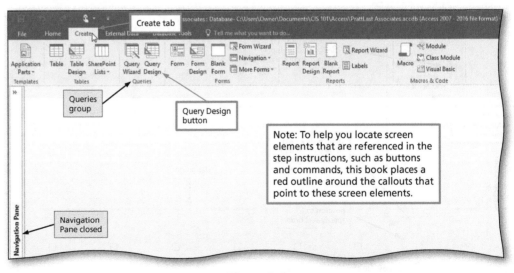

Figure 2–2

2

- Click the Query Design button (Create tab | Queries group) to create a new query (Figure 2–3).

Q&A
Is it necessary to close the Navigation Pane?
No. Closing the pane gives you more room for the query, however, so it is usually a good practice.

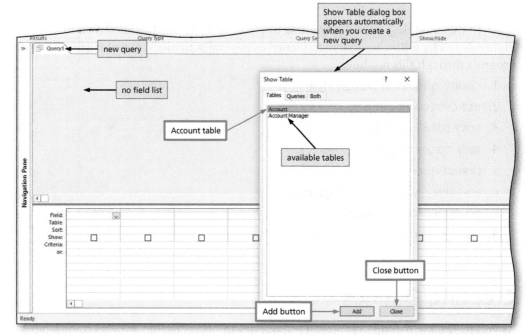

Figure 2–3

3

- Ensure the Account table (Show Table dialog box) is selected. If it is not, click the Account table to select it.
- Click the Add button to add the selected table to the query.
- Click the Close button to remove the dialog box from the screen.

Q&A
What if I inadvertently add the wrong table?
Right-click the table that you added in error and click Remove Table on the shortcut menu. You also can just close the query, indicate that you do not want to save it, and then start over.

- Drag the lower edge of the field list down far enough so all fields in the table appear (Figure 2–4).

Q&A
Is it essential that I resize the field list?
No. You can always scroll through the list of fields using the scroll bar. Resizing the field list so that all fields appear is usually more convenient.

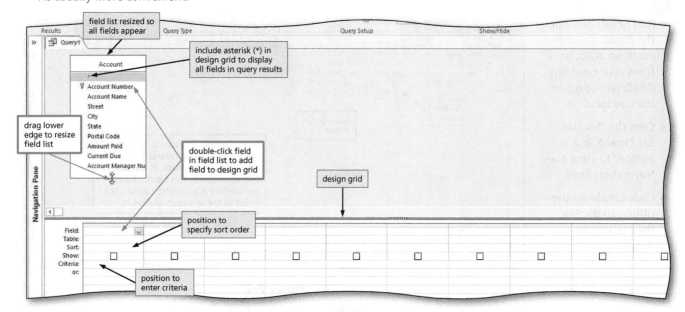

Figure 2–4

To Add Fields to the Design Grid

Once you have a new query displayed in Design view, you are ready to make entries in the **design grid**, the portion of the window where you specify fields and criteria for the query. The design grid is located in the lower pane of the window. You add the fields you want included in the query to the Field row in the grid. *Why add fields to the grid? Only the fields that appear in the design grid are included in the query results.* The following step begins creating a query that PrattLast Associates might use to obtain the account number, account name, amount paid, and current due for a particular account.

1

- Double-click the Account Number field in the field list to add the field to the query.

Q&A What if I add the wrong field? Click just above the field name in the design grid to select the column and then press the DELETE key to remove the field.

- Double-click the Account Name field in the field list to add the field to the query.

- Add the Amount Paid field to the query.

- Add the Current Due field to the query (Figure 2–5).

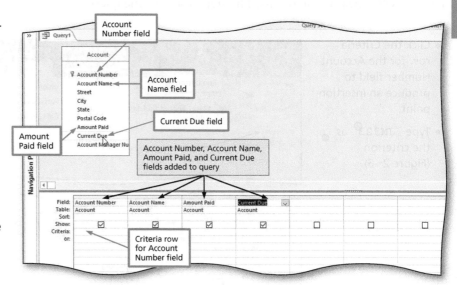

Figure 2–5

Q&A What if I want to include all fields? Do I have to add each field individually?
No. Instead of adding individual fields, you can double-click the asterisk (*) to add the asterisk to the design grid. The asterisk is a shortcut indicating all fields are to be included.

Determining Criteria

When you use queries, usually you are looking for those records that satisfy some criterion. In the simple query you created in the previous module, for example, you entered a criterion to restrict the records to those with the account manager number 35. In another query, you might want the name, amount paid, and current due amounts for the account whose number is JM323, for example, or for those accounts whose names start with the letters, La. You enter criteria in the Criteria row in the design grid below the field name to which the criterion applies. For example, to indicate that the account number must be JM323, you first must add the Account Number field to the design grid. You then would type JM323 in the Criteria row below the Account Number field.

Running the Query

After adding the appropriate fields and defining the query's criteria, you must run the query to get the results. To view the results of the query from Design view, click the Run button to instruct Access to run the query, that is, to perform the necessary actions to produce and display the results in Datasheet view.

1 CREATE QUERIES | 2 USE CRITERIA | 3 SORT DATA | 4 JOIN TABLES | 5 EXPORT RESULTS
6 PERFORM CALCULATIONS | 7 CREATE CROSSTAB | 8 CUSTOMIZE NAVIGATION PANE

To Use Text Data in a Criterion

To use **text data** (data in a field whose data type is Short Text) in criteria, simply type the text in the Criteria row below the corresponding field name, just as you did in Module 1. In Access, you do not need to enclose text data in quotation marks as you do in many other database management systems. *Why? Access will enter the quotation marks automatically, so you can simply type the desired text.* The following steps finish creating a query that PrattLast Associates might use to obtain the account number, account name, amount paid, and current due amount of account JM323. These steps add the appropriate criterion so that only the desired account will appear in the results. The steps also save the query.

1

- Click the Criteria row for the Account Number field to produce an insertion point.

- Type **JM323** as the criterion (Figure 2–6).

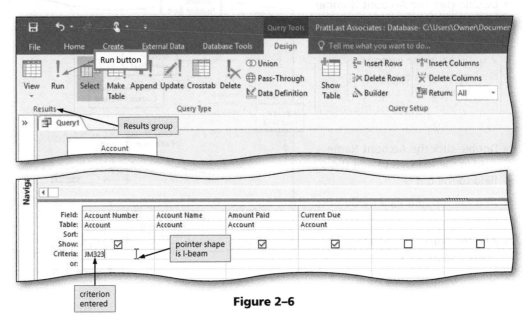

Figure 2–6

2

- Click the Run button (Query Tools Design tab | Results group) to run the query (Figure 2–7).

Q&A Can I also use the View button in the Results group to run the query?
Yes. You can click the View button to view the query results in Datasheet view.

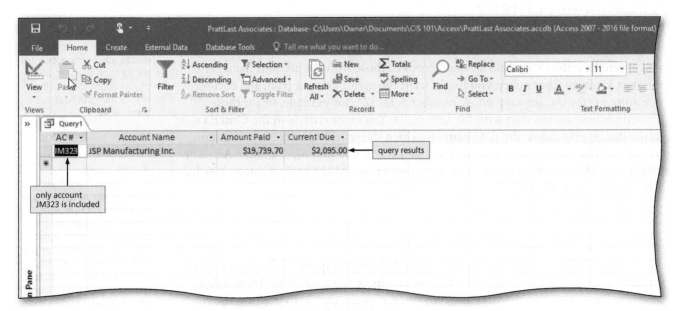

Figure 2–7

3
- Click the Save button on the Quick Access Toolbar to display the Save As dialog box.

- Type **m02q01** as the name of the query (Figure 2–8).

Q&A

Can I also save from Design view?
Yes. You can save the query when you view it in Design view just as you can save it when you view query results in Datasheet view.

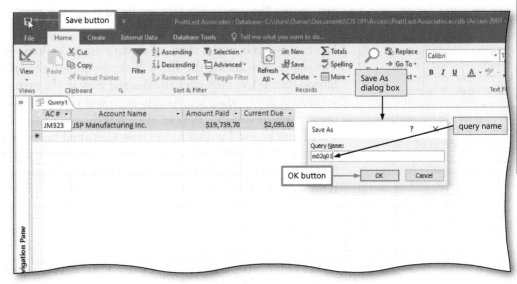

Figure 2–8

4
- Click the OK button (Save As dialog box) to save the query (Figure 2–9).

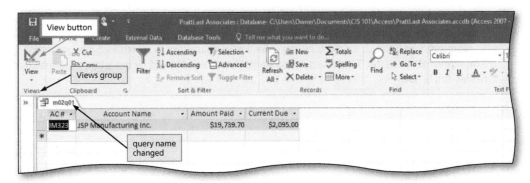

Figure 2–9

Other Ways

1. Right-click query tab, click Save on shortcut menu   2. Press CTRL+S

Using Saved Queries

After you have created and saved a query, you can use it in a variety of ways:

- To view the results of a query that is not currently open, open it by right-clicking the query in the Navigation Pane and clicking Open on the shortcut menu.

- If you want to change the design of a query that is already open, return to Design view and make the changes.

- If you want to change the design of a query that is not currently open, right-click the query in the Navigation Pane and then click Design View on the shortcut menu to open the query in Design view.

- To print the results with a query open, click File on the ribbon, click the Print tab in the Backstage view, and then click Quick Print.

BTW

The Ribbon and Screen Resolution
Access may change how the groups and buttons within the groups appear on the ribbon, depending on the computer or mobile device's screen resolution. Thus, your ribbon may look different from the ones in this book if you are using a screen resolution other than 1366 x 768.

• To print a query without first opening it, be sure the query is selected in the Navigation Pane and click File on the ribbon, click the Print tab in the Backstage view, and then click Quick Print.

• You can switch between views of a query using the View button (Home tab | Views group). Clicking the arrow at the bottom of the button produces the View button menu. You then click the desired view in the menu. The two query views you use in this module are Datasheet view (to see the results) and Design view (to change the design). You can also click the top part of the View button, in which case you will switch to the view identified by the icon on the button. In Figure 2–9, the View button displays the icon for Design view, so clicking the button would change to Design view. For the most part, the icon on the button represents the view you want, so you can usually simply click the button.

Wildcards

Microsoft Access supports wildcards. **Wildcards** are symbols that represent any character or combination of characters. One common wildcard, the **asterisk** (*), represents any collection of characters. Another wildcard symbol is the **question mark (?)**, which represents any individual character.

What does S* represent? What does T?m represent?
S* represents the letter, S, followed by any collection of characters. A search for S* might return System, So, or Superlative. T?m represents the letter, T, followed by any single character, followed by the letter, m. A search for T?m might return the names Tim or Tom.

To Use a Wildcard

1 CREATE QUERIES | 2 USE CRITERIA | 3 SORT DATA | 4 JOIN TABLES | 5 EXPORT RESULTS
6 PERFORM CALCULATIONS | 7 CREATE CROSSTAB | 8 CUSTOMIZE NAVIGATION PANE

The following steps modify the previous query to use the asterisk wildcard so that PrattLast Associates can select only those accounts whose names begin with K. *Why? Because you do not know how many characters will follow the K, the asterisk wildcard symbol is appropriate.* The steps also save the query with a new name using the Save As command.

• Click the View button (Home tab | Views group), shown in Figure 2–9, to return to Design view.

• If necessary, click the Criteria row below the Account Number field to produce an insertion point.

Q&A The text I entered now has quotation marks surrounding it. What happened?
Criteria for text data needs to be enclosed in quotation marks. You do not have to type the quotation marks; Access adds them automatically.

• Use the DELETE or BACKSPACE key as necessary to delete the current entry.

• Click the Criteria row below the Account Name field to produce an insertion point.

• Type **K*** as the criterion (Figure 2–10).

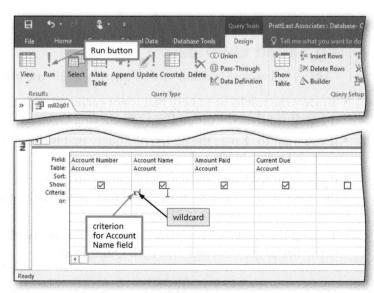

Figure 2–10

2

• Run the query by clicking the Run button (Query Tools Design tab | Results group) (Figure 2–11).

🔍 **Experiment**

• Change the letter K to lowercase in the criterion and run the query to determine whether case makes a difference when entering a wildcard.

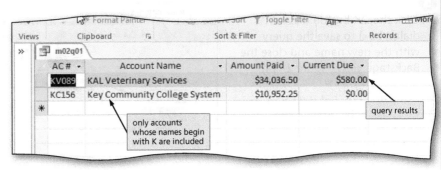

Figure 2–11

3

• Click File on the ribbon to open the Backstage view.

• Click the Save As tab in the Backstage view to display the Save As gallery.

• Click 'Save Object As' in the File Types area (Figure 2–12).

Q&A Can I just click the Save button on the Quick Access Toolbar as I did when saving the previous query?
If you clicked the Save button, you

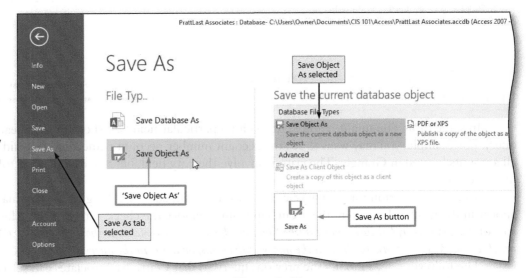

Figure 2–12

would replace the previous query with the version you just created. Because you want to save both the previous query and the new one, you need to save the new version with a different name. To do so, you must use Save Object As, which is available through the Backstage view.

4

• With Save Object As selected in the File Types gallery, click the Save As button to display the Save As dialog box.

• Erase the name of the current query and type m02q02 as the name for the saved query (Figure 2–13).

Q&A The current entry in the As text box is
Query. Could I save the query as some other type of object?
Although you usually would want to save the query as another query, you can also save it as a form or report by changing the entry in the As text box. If you do, Access would create either a simple form or a simple report for the query.

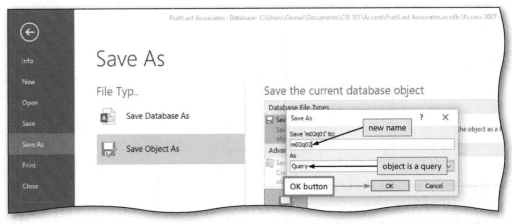

Figure 2–13

5

- Click the OK button (Save As dialog box) to save the query with the new name and close the Backstage view (Figure 2–14).

Q&A
How can I tell that the query was saved with the new name?
The new name will appear on the tab.

Figure 2–14

Other Ways

1. Click Design View button on status bar

To Use Criteria for a Field Not Included in the Results

1 CREATE QUERIES | 2 USE CRITERIA | 3 SORT DATA | 4 JOIN TABLES | 5 EXPORT RESULTS
6 PERFORM CALCULATIONS | 7 CREATE CROSSTAB | 8 CUSTOMIZE NAVIGATION PANE

In some cases, you might require criteria for a particular field that should not appear in the results of the query. For example, you may want to see the account number, account name, amount paid, and current due for all accounts located in Granger. The criteria involve the City field, but you do not want to include the City field in the results.

To enter a criterion for the City field, it must be included in the design grid. Normally, it would then appear in the results. To prevent this from happening, remove the check mark from its check box in the Show row of the grid. *Why? A check mark in the Show check box instructs Access to show the field in the result. If you remove the check mark, you can use the field in the query without displaying it in the query results.*

The following steps modify the previous query so that PrattLast Associates can select only those accounts located in Granger. PrattLast does not want the city to appear in the results, however. The steps also save the query with a new name.

1

- Click the View button (Home tab | Views group), shown in Figure 2–14, to return to Design view.

Q&A
The text I entered is now preceded by the word, Like. What happened?
Criteria that include wildcards need to be preceded by the word, Like. However, you do not have to type it; Access adds the word automatically to any criterion involving a wildcard.

- Erase the criterion in the Criteria row of the Account Name field.

- Add the City field to the query.

- Type **Granger** as the criterion for the City field (Figure 2–15).

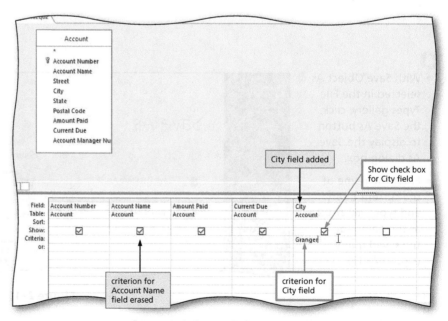

Figure 2–15

2

- Click the Show check box for the City field to remove the check mark (Figure 2–16).

Q&A Could I have removed the check mark before entering the criterion?
Yes. The order in which you perform the two operations does not matter.

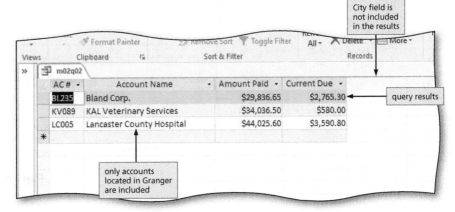

check mark removed from Show check box, indicating that City field will not appear in query results

Access automatically adds quotation marks

Figure 2–16

3

- Run the query (Figure 2–17).

Experiment

- Click the View button to return to Design view, enter a different city name as the criterion, and run the query. Repeat this process with additional city names, including at least one city name that is not in the database. When finished, change the criterion back to Granger.

City field is not included in the results

query results

only accounts located in Granger are included

Figure 2–17

Creating a Parameter Query

If you wanted to find accounts located in Wells instead of Granger, you would either have to create a new query or modify the existing query by replacing Granger with Wells as the criterion. Rather than giving a specific criterion when you first create the query, occasionally you may want to be able to enter part of the criterion when you run the query and then have the appropriate results appear. For example, you might want a query to return the account number, account name, amount paid, and current due for all accounts in a specific city, specifying a different city each time you run the query. A user could run the query, enter Wells as the city, and then see all the accounts in Wells. Later, the user could use the same query but enter Granger as the city, and then see all the accounts in Granger.

To enable this flexibility, you create a **parameter query**, which is a query that prompts for input whenever it is used. You enter a parameter (the prompt for the user) rather than a specific value as the criterion. You create the parameter by enclosing the criterion value in square brackets. It is important that the value in the brackets does not match the name of any field. If you enter a field name in square brackets, Access assumes you want that particular field and does not prompt the user for input. To prompt the user to enter the city name as the input, you could place [Enter City] as the criterion in the City field.

BTW
Designing Queries
Before creating queries, examine the contents of the tables involved. You need to know the data type for each field and how the data for the field is stored. If a query includes a state, for example, you need to know whether state is stored as the two-character abbreviation or as the full state name.

To Create and View a Parameter Query

The following steps create a parameter query. *Why? The parameter query will give users at PrattLast the ability to enter a different city each time they run the query rather than having a specific city as part of the criterion in the query.* The steps also save the query with a new name.

● Return to Design view.

● Erase the current criterion in the City column, and then type **[Enter City]** as the new criterion (Figure 2–18).

Q&A

What is the purpose of the square brackets?
The square brackets indicate that the text entered is not text that the value in the column must match. Without the brackets, Access would search for records in which the city is Enter City.

What if I typed a field name in the square brackets?
Access would simply use the value in that field. To create a parameter query, you must not use a field name in the square brackets.

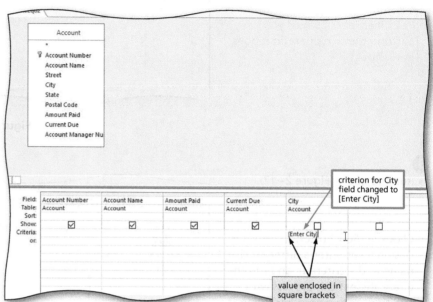

Figure 2–18

● Click the Run button (Query Tools Design tab | Results group) to display the Enter Parameter Value dialog box (Figure 2–19).

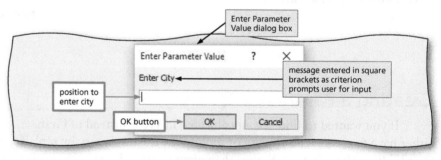

Figure 2–19

● Type **Wells** as the parameter value in the Enter City text box, and then click the OK button (Enter Parameter Value dialog box) to close the dialog box and view the query (Figure 2–20).

Experiment

● Try using other characters between the square brackets. In each case, run the query. When finished, change the characters between the square brackets back to Enter City.

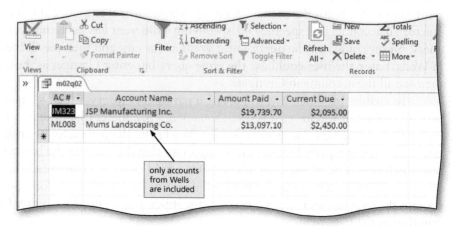

Figure 2–20

4

- Click File on the ribbon to open the Backstage view.

- Click the Save As tab in the Backstage view to display the Save As gallery.

- Click 'Save Object As' in the File Types area.

- With Save Object As selected in the File Types area, click the Save As button to display the Save As dialog box.

- Type **Account-City Query** as the name for the saved query.

- Click the OK button (Save As dialog box) to save the query with the new name and close the Backstage view (Figure 2–21).

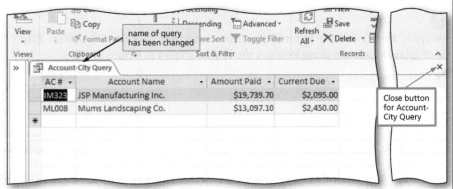

Figure 2–21

5

- Click the Close button for the Account-City Query to close the query.

Break Point: If you wish to take a break, this is a good place to do so. You can exit Access now. To resume later, run Access, open the database called PrattLast Associates, and continue following the steps from this location forward.

To Use a Parameter Query

1 CREATE QUERIES | 2 USE CRITERIA | 3 SORT DATA | 4 JOIN TABLES | 5 EXPORT RESULTS
6 PERFORM CALCULATIONS | 7 CREATE CROSSTAB | 8 CUSTOMIZE NAVIGATION PANE

You use a parameter query like any other saved query. You can open it or you can print the query results. In either case, Access prompts you to supply a value for the parameter each time you use the query. If changes have been made to the data since the last time you ran the query, the results of the query may be different, even if you enter the same value for the parameter. *Why? In addition to the ability to enter different field values each time the parameter query is run, the query always uses the data that is currently in the table.* The following steps use the parameter query named Account-City Query.

1

- Open the Navigation Pane.

- Right-click the Account-City Query to produce a shortcut menu.

- Click Open on the shortcut menu to open the query and display the Enter Parameter Value dialog box (Figure 2–22).

Q&A The title bar for my Navigation Pane contains Tables and Related Views rather than All Access Objects as it did in Module 1. What should I do?
Click the Navigation Pane arrow and then click 'All Access Objects'.

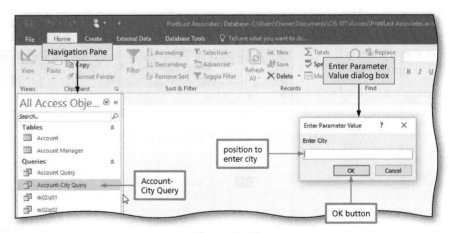

Figure 2–22

I do not have the Search bar at the top of the Navigation Pane that I had in Module 1. What should I do?
Right-click the Navigation Pane title bar arrow to display a shortcut menu, and then click Search Bar.

2

• Type **Wells** in the Enter City text box, and then click the OK button (Enter Parameter Value dialog box) to display the results using Wells as the city, as shown in Figure 2–21.

• Close the query.

To Use a Number in a Criterion

1 CREATE QUERIES | 2 USE CRITERIA | 3 SORT DATA | 4 JOIN TABLES | 5 EXPORT RESULTS
6 PERFORM CALCULATIONS | 7 CREATE CROSSTAB | 8 CUSTOMIZE NAVIGATION PANE

To enter a number in a criterion, type the number without any dollar signs or commas. *Why? If you enter a dollar sign, Access assumes you are entering text. If you enter a comma, Access considers the criterion invalid.* The following steps create a query that PrattLast Associates might use to display all accounts whose current due amount is $0. The steps also save the query with a new name.

1

• Close the Navigation Pane.

• Click Create on the ribbon to display the Create tab.

• Click the Query Design button (Create tab | Queries group) to create a new query.

• If necessary, click the Account table (Show Table dialog box) to select the table.

• Click the Add button to add the selected table to the query.

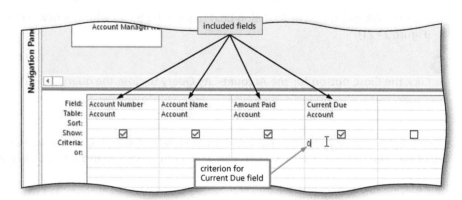

Figure 2–23

• Click the Close button to remove the dialog box from the screen.

• Drag the lower edge of the field list down far enough so all fields in the list are displayed.

• Include the Account Number, Account Name, Amount Paid, and Current Due fields in the query.

• Type **0** as the criterion for the Current Due field (Figure 2–23).

Q&A Do I need to enter a dollar sign and decimal point?
No. Access will interpret 0 as $0 because the data type for the Current Due field is currency.

2

• Run the query (Figure 2–24).

Q&A Why did Access display the results as $0.00 when I only entered 0?
Access uses the format for the field to determine how to display the result. In this case, the format indicated that Access should include the dollar sign, decimal point, and two decimal places.

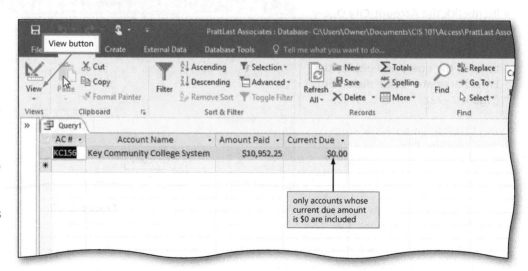

Figure 2–24

3

- Save the query as m02q03.

Q&A How do I know when to use the Save button to save a query or use the Backstage view to perform a Save As?
If you are saving a new query, the simplest way is to use the Save button on the Quick Access Toolbar. If you are saving changes to a previously saved query but do not want to change the name, use the Save button. If you want to save a previously saved query with a new name, you must use the Backstage view and perform a Save Object As.

- Close the query.

Comparison Operators

Unless you specify otherwise, Access assumes that the criteria you enter involve equality (exact matches). In the last query, for example, you were requesting those accounts whose current due amount is equal to 0 (zero). In other situations, you might want to find a range of results; for example, you could request accounts whose current due is greater than $1,000.00. If you want a query to return something other than an exact match, you must enter the appropriate **comparison operator**. The comparison operators are > (greater than), < (less than), >= (greater than or equal to), <= (less than or equal to), and NOT (not equal to).

To Use a Comparison Operator in a Criterion

1 CREATE QUERIES | 2 USE CRITERIA | 3 SORT DATA | 4 JOIN TABLES | 5 EXPORT RESULTS
6 PERFORM CALCULATIONS | 7 CREATE CROSSTAB | 8 CUSTOMIZE NAVIGATION PANE

The following steps use the > operator to create a query that PrattLast Associates might use to find all account managers whose start date is after 1/1/2015. **Why?** *A date greater than 1/1/2015 means the date comes after 1/1/2015.* The steps also save the query with a new name.

1

- Start a new query using the Account Manager table.
- Include the Account Manager Number, Last Name, First Name, and Start Date fields.
- Type **>1/01/2015** as the criterion for the Start Date field (Figure 2–25).

Q&A Why did I not have to type the leading zero in the Month portion of the date?
It is fine as you typed it. You also could have typed 01/1/2015. Some people often type the day using two digits, such as 1/01/2015. You also could have typed a leading zero for both the month and the day: 01/01/2015.

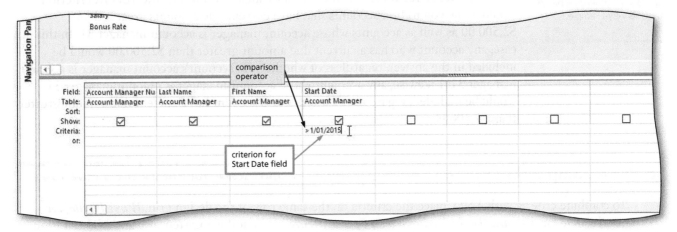

Figure 2–25

2

- Run the query (Figure 2–26).

 Experiment

- Return to Design view. Try a different criterion involving a comparison operator in the Start Date field and run the query. When finished, return to Design view, enter the original criterion (>1/01/2015) in the Start Date field, and run the query.

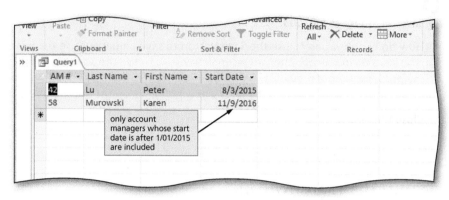

Figure 2–26

Q&A I returned to Design view and noticed that Access changed 1/01/2015 to #1/01/2015#. Why does the date now have number signs around it?

This is the date format in Access. You usually do not have to enter the number signs because in most cases Access will insert them automatically.

My records are in a different order. Is this a problem?

No. The important thing is which records are included in the results. You will see later in this module how you can specify the specific order you want for cases when the order is important.

Can I use the same comparison operators with text data?

Yes. Comparison operators function the same whether you use them with number fields, currency fields, date fields, or text fields. With a text field, comparison operators use alphabetical order in making the determination.

3

- Save the query as m02q04.

- Close the query.

BTW

Queries: Query-by-Example

Query-By-Example, often referred to as QBE, was a query language first proposed in the mid-1970s. In this approach, users asked questions by filling in a table on the screen. The Access approach to queries is based on Query-By-Example.

Using Compound Criteria

Often your search data must satisfy more than one criterion. This type of criterion is called a **compound criterion** and is created using the words AND or OR.

In an **AND criterion**, each individual criterion must be true in order for the compound criterion to be true. For example, an AND criterion would allow you to find accounts that have current due amounts greater than $2,500.00 and whose account manager is manager 31.

An **OR criterion** is true if either individual criterion is true. An OR criterion would allow you to find accounts that have current due amounts greater than $2,500.00 as well as accounts whose account manager is account manager 31. In this case, any account who has a current due amount greater than $2,500.00 would be included in the answer, regardless of whether the account's account manager is account manager 31. Likewise, any account whose account manager is account manager 31 would be included, regardless of whether the account has a current due amount greater than $2,500.00.

To Use a Compound Criterion Involving AND

1 CREATE QUERIES | 2 USE CRITERIA | 3 SORT DATA | 4 JOIN TABLES | 5 EXPORT RESULTS
6 PERFORM CALCULATIONS | 7 CREATE CROSSTAB | 8 CUSTOMIZE NAVIGATION PANE

To combine criteria with AND, place the criteria on the same row of the design grid. *Why? Placing the criteria in the same row indicates that both criteria must be true in Access.* The following steps use an AND criterion to enable PrattLast to find those accounts who have a current due amount greater than $2,500.00 and whose account manager is manager 31. The steps also save the query.

1

- Start a new query using the Account table.
- Include the Account Number, Account Name, Amount Paid, Current Due, and Account Manager Number fields.
- Type >2500 as the criterion for the Current Due field.
- Type 31 as the criterion for the Account Manager Number field (Figure 2–27).

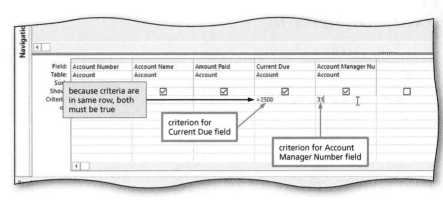

Figure 2–27

2

- Run the query (Figure 2–28).

3

- Save the query as m02q05.

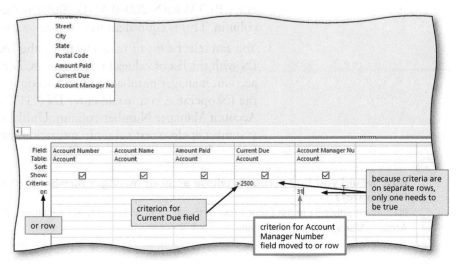

Figure 2–28

To Use a Compound Criterion Involving OR

1 CREATE QUERIES | 2 USE CRITERIA | 3 SORT DATA | 4 JOIN TABLES | 5 EXPORT RESULTS
6 PERFORM CALCULATIONS | 7 CREATE CROSSTAB | 8 CUSTOMIZE NAVIGATION PANE

To combine criteria with OR, each criterion must go on separate rows in the Criteria area of the grid. **Why?** *Placing criteria on separate rows indicates at least one criterion must be true in Access.* The following steps use an OR criterion to enable PrattLast to find those accounts who have a current due amount greater than $2,500.00 or whose account manager is manager 31 (or both). The steps also save the query with a new name.

1

- Return to Design view.
- If necessary, click the Criteria entry for the Account Manager Number field and then use the BACKSPACE key or the DELETE key to erase the entry ("31").
- Click the or row (the row below the Criteria row) for the Account Manager Number field, and then type 31 as the entry (Figure 2–29).

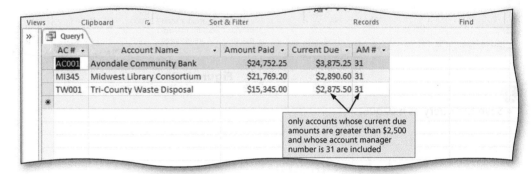

Figure 2–29

● Run the query (Figure 2–30).

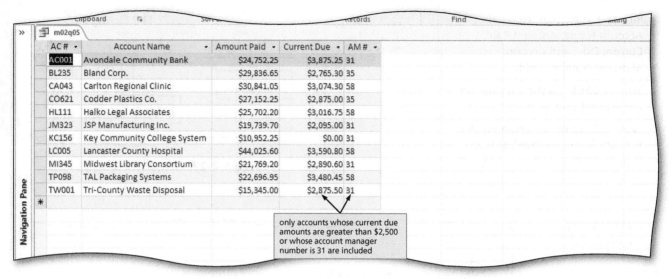

only accounts whose current due amounts are greater than $2,500 or whose account manager number is 31 are included

Figure 2–30

● Save the query as m02q06.

Special Criteria

BTW

Rearranging Fields in a Query

To move a field in the design grid, click the column selector for the field to select the field and drag it to the appropriate location.

You can use three special criteria in queries:

1. If you want to create a criterion involving a range of values in a single field, you can use the **AND operator**. You place the word AND between the individual conditions. For example, if you wanted to find all accounts whose amount paid is greater than or equal to $20,000.00 and less than or equal to $40,000.00, you would enter >= 20000 AND <= 40000 as the criterion in the Amount Paid column.

2. You can select values in a given range by using the **BETWEEN operator**. This is often an alternative to the AND operator. For example, to find all accounts whose amount paid is between $20,000.00 and $40,000.00, inclusive, you would enter BETWEEN 20000 AND 40000 as the criterion in the Amount Paid column. This is equivalent to entering >=20000 and <=40000.

3. You can select a list of values by using the **IN operator**. You follow the word IN with the list of values in parentheses. For example, to find accounts whose account manager number is 31 and accounts whose account manager is 35 using the IN operator, you would enter IN ("31","35") on the Criteria row in the Account Manager Number column. Unlike when you enter a simple criterion, you must enclose text values in quotation marks.

CONSIDER THIS

How would you find accounts whose account manager number is 31 or 35 without using the IN operator?

Place the number 31 in the Criteria row of the Account Manager Number column. Place the number 35 in the or row of the Account Manager Number column.

Sorting

In some queries, the order in which the records appear is irrelevant. All you need to be concerned about are the records that appear in the results. It does not matter which one is first or which one is last.

In other queries, however, the order can be very important. You may want to see the cities in which accounts are located and would like them arranged alphabetically. Perhaps you want to see the accounts listed by account manager number. Further, within all the accounts of any given account manager, you might want them to be listed by amount paid from largest amount to smallest.

To order the records in a query result in a particular way, you **sort** the records. The field or fields on which the records are sorted is called the **sort key**. If you are sorting on more than one field (such as sorting by amount paid within account manager number), the more important field (Account Manager Number) is called the **major key** (also called the **primary sort key**) and the less important field (Amount Paid) is called the **minor key** (also called the **secondary sort key**).

To sort in Microsoft Access, specify the sort order in the Sort row of the design grid below the field that is the sort key. If you specify more than one sort key, the sort key on the left will be the major sort key, and the one on the right will be the minor key.

BTW

Sorting Data in a Query
When sorting data in a query, the records in the underlying tables (the tables on which the query is based) are not actually rearranged. Instead, the DBMS determines the most efficient method of simply displaying the records in the requested order. The records in the underlying tables remain in their original order.

BTW

Clearing the Design Grid
You can also clear the design grid using the ribbon. To do so, click the Home tab, click the Advanced button to display the Advanced menu, and then click Clear Grid on the Advanced menu.

To Clear the Design Grid

1 CREATE QUERIES | 2 USE CRITERIA | 3 SORT DATA | 4 JOIN TABLES | 5 EXPORT RESULTS
6 PERFORM CALCULATIONS | 7 CREATE CROSSTAB | 8 CUSTOMIZE NAVIGATION PANE

Why? *If the fields you want to include in the next query are different from those in the previous query, it is usually simpler to start with a clear grid, that is, one with no fields already in the design grid.* You always can clear the entries in the design grid by closing the query and then starting over. A simpler approach to clearing the entries is to select all the entries and then press the DELETE key. The following steps return to Design view and clear the design grid.

1

- Return to Design view.

- Click just above the Account Number column heading in the grid to select the column.

Q&A I clicked above the column heading, but the column is not selected. What should I do?
You did not point to the correct location. Be sure the pointer changes into a down-pointing arrow and then click again.

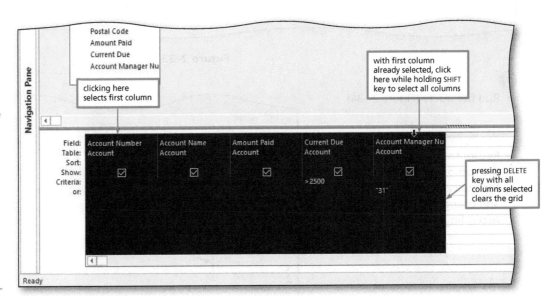

Figure 2–31

- Hold the SHIFT key down and click just above the Account Manager Number column heading to select all the columns (Figure 2–31).

- Press the DELETE key to clear the design grid.

To Sort Data in a Query

If you determine that the query results should be sorted, you will need to specify the sort key. The following steps sort the cities in the Account table by indicating that the City field is to be sorted. The steps specify Ascending sort order. *Why? When sorting text data, Ascending sort order arranges the results in alphabetical order.*

1
- Include the City field in the design grid.
- Click the Sort row in the City field column, and then click the Sort arrow to display a menu of possible sort orders (Figure 2–32).

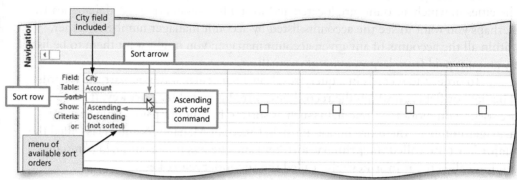

Figure 2–32

2
- Click Ascending to select the sort order (Figure 2–33).

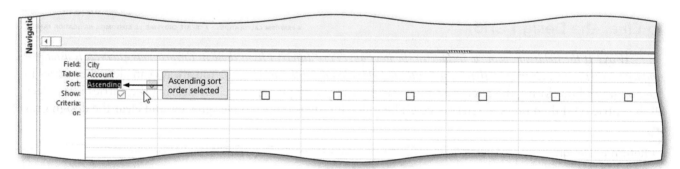

Figure 2–33

3
- Run the query (Figure 2–34).

Experiment
- Return to Design view and change the sort order to Descending. Run the query. Return to Design view and change the sort order back to Ascending. Run the query.

Q&A Why do some cities appear more than once?
More than one account is located in those cities.

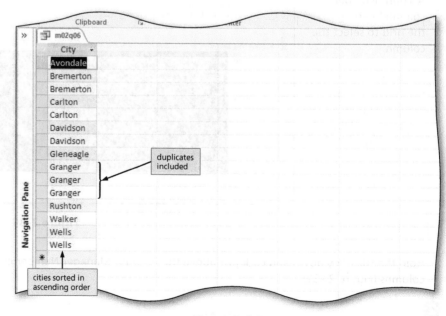

Figure 2–34

To Omit Duplicates

When you sort data, duplicates normally are included. In the query shown in Figure 2–34, for example, Bremerton appears twice. Several other cities appear multiple times as well. You eliminate duplicates using the query's property sheet. A **property sheet** is a window containing the various properties of the object. To omit duplicates, you will use the property sheet to change the Unique Values property from No to Yes.

The following steps create a query that PrattLast Associates might use to obtain a sorted list of the cities in the Account table in which each city is listed only once. *Why? Unless you wanted to know how many accounts were located in each city, the duplicates typically do not add any value.* The steps also save the query with a new name.

1

- Return to Design view.

- Click the second field (the empty field to the right of City) in the design grid to produce an insertion point.

- If necessary, click Design on the ribbon to display the Design tab.

- Click the Property Sheet button (Query Tools Design tab | Show/Hide group) to display the property sheet (Figure 2–35).

Q&A My property sheet looks different. What should I do?
If your sheet looks different, close the property sheet and repeat this step.

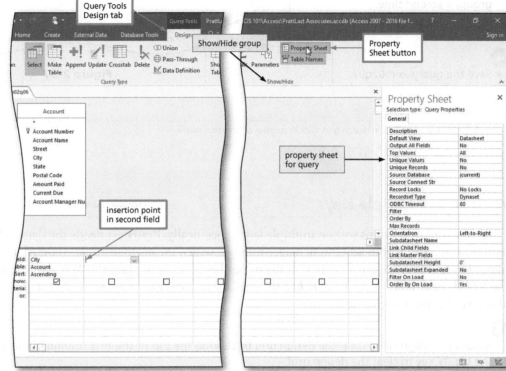

Figure 2–35

2

- Click the Unique Values property box, and then click the arrow that appears to display a list of available choices (Figure 2–36).

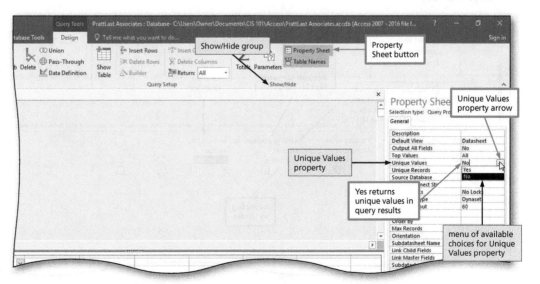

Figure 2–36

• Click Yes to indicate that the query will return unique values, which means that each value will appear only once in the query results.

• Close the Query Properties property sheet by clicking the Property Sheet button (Query Tools Design tab | Show/Hide group) a second time.

• Run the query (Figure 2–37).

• Save the query as m02q07.

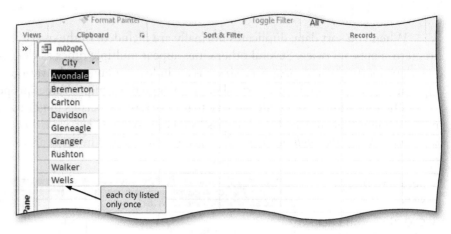

Figure 2–37

Other Ways

1. Right-click second field in design grid, click Properties on shortcut menu

---

To Sort on Multiple Keys

1 CREATE QUERIES | 2 USE CRITERIA | 3 SORT DATA | 4 JOIN TABLES | 5 EXPORT RESULTS
6 PERFORM CALCULATIONS | 7 CREATE CROSSTAB | 8 CUSTOMIZE NAVIGATION PANE

The following steps sort on multiple keys. Specifically, PrattLast needs the data to be sorted by amount paid (low to high) within account manager number, which means that the Account Manager Number field is the major key and the Amount Paid field is the minor key. The steps place the Account Manager Number field to the left of the Amount Paid field. *Why? In Access, the major key must appear to the left of the minor key.* The steps also save the query with a new name.

• Return to Design view. Clear the design grid by clicking the top of the first column in the grid, and then pressing the DELETE key to clear the design grid.

• In the following order, include the Account Number, Account Name, Account Manager Number, and Amount Paid fields in the query.

• Select Ascending as the sort order for both the Account Manager Number field and the Amount Paid field (Figure 2–38).

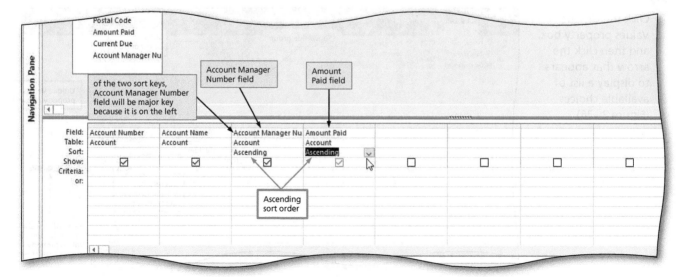

Figure 2–38

2

- Run the query (Figure 2–39).

🔍 **Experiment**

- Return to Design view and try other sort combinations for the Account Manager Number and Amount Paid fields, such as Ascending for Account Manager Number and Descending for Amount Paid. In each case, run the query to see the effect of the changes. When finished, select Ascending as the sort order for both fields.

Q&A What if the Amount Paid field is to the left of the Account Manager Number field?

It is important to remember that the major sort key must appear to the left of the minor sort key in the design grid. If you attempted to sort by amount paid within account manager number, but placed the Amount Paid field to the left of the Account Manager Number field, your results would not accurately represent the intended sort.

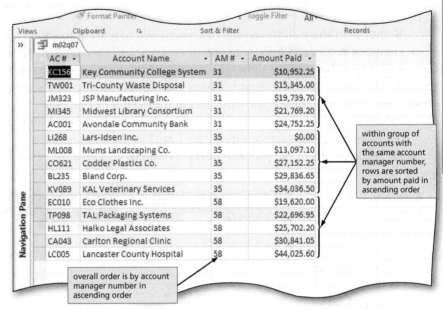

within group of accounts with the same account manager number, rows are sorted by amount paid in ascending order

overall order is by account manager number in ascending order

Figure 2–39

3

- Save the query as m02q08.

Is there any way to sort the records in this same order, but have the Amount Paid field appear to the left of the Account Manager Number field in the query results?

Yes. Remove the check mark from the Account Manager Number field, and then add an additional Account Manager Number field at the end of the query. The first Account Manager Number field will be used for sorting but will not appear in the results. The second will appear in the results, but will not be involved in the sorting process.

How do you approach the creation of a query that might involve sorting?

Examine the query or request to see if it contains words such as *order* or *sort*. Such words imply that the order of the query results is important. If so, you need to sort the query.

- If sorting is required, identify the field or fields on which the results are to be sorted. In the request, look for language such as *ordered by* or *sort the results by*, both of which would indicate that the specified field is a sort key.

- If using multiple sort keys, determine the major and minor keys. If you are using two sort keys, determine which one is the more important, or the major key. Look for language such as *sort by amount paid within account manager number*, which implies that the overall order is by account manager number. In this case, the Account Manager Number field would be the major sort key and the Amount Paid field would be the minor sort key.

- Determine sort order. Words such as *increasing*, *ascending*, or *low-to-high* imply Ascending order. Words such as *decreasing*, *descending*, or *high-to-low* imply Descending order. Sorting in *alphabetical order* implies Ascending order. If there were no words to imply a particular order, you would typically use Ascending.

- Examine the query or request to see if there are any special restrictions. One common restriction is to exclude duplicates. Another common restriction is to list only a certain number of records, such as the first five records.

To Create a Top-Values Query

Rather than show all the results of a query, you may want to show only a specified number of records or a percentage of records. *Why? You might not need to see all the records, just enough to get a general idea of the results.* Creating a **top-values query** allows you to restrict the number of records that appear. When you sort records, you can limit results to those records having the highest (descending sort) or lowest (ascending sort) values. To do so, first create a query that sorts the data in the desired order. Next, use the Return box on the Design tab to change the number of records to be included from All to the desired number or percentage.

The following steps create a query for PrattLast Associates that shows only the first five records that were included in the results of the previous query. The steps also save the resulting query with a new name.

1

- Return to Design view.

- If necessary, click Design on the ribbon to display the Design tab.

- Click the Return arrow (Query Tools Design tab | Query Setup group) to display the Return menu (Figure 2–40).

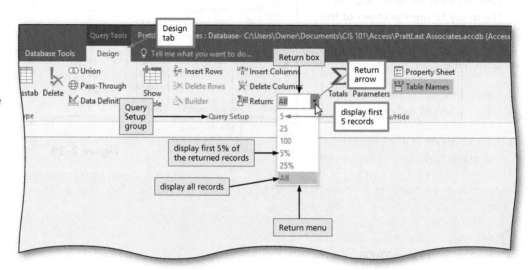

Figure 2–40

2

- Click 5 in the Return menu to specify that the query results should contain the first five rows.

Q&A Could I have typed the 5? What about other numbers that do not appear in the list?
Yes, you could have typed the 5. For numbers not appearing in the list, you must type the number.

- Run the query (Figure 2–41).

3

- Save the query as m02q09.

- Close the query.

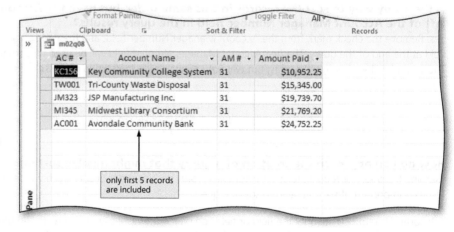

Figure 2–41

Q&A Do I need to close the query before creating my next query?
Not necessarily. When you use a top-values query, however, it is important to change the value in the Return box back to All. If you do not change the Return value back to All, the previous value will remain in effect. Consequently, you might not get all the records you should in the next query. A good practice whenever you use a top-values query is to close the query as soon as you are done. That way, you will begin your next query from scratch, which ensures that the value is reset to All.

Joining Tables

In designing a query, you need to determine whether more than one table is required. For example, if the question being asked involves data from both the Account and Account Manager tables, then both tables are required for the query. For example, you might want a query that gives the number and name of each account (from the Account table) along with the number and name of the account's account manager (from the Account Manager table). Both the Account and Account Manager tables are required for this query. You need to **join** the tables to find records in the two tables that have identical values in matching fields (Figure 2–42). In this example, you need to find records in the Account table and the Account Manager table that have the same value in the Account Manager Number fields.

BTW
Ad Hoc Relationships
When you join tables in a query, you are creating an ad hoc relationship, that is, a relationship between tables created for a specific purpose. In Module 3, you will create general-purpose relationships using the Relationships window.

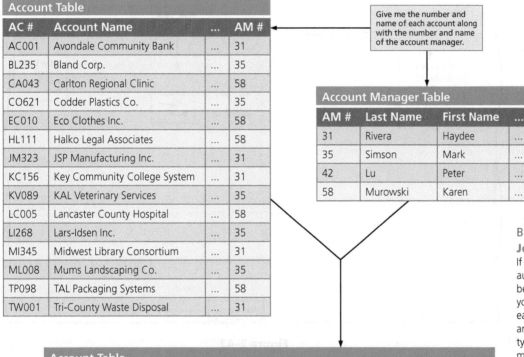

BTW
Join Line
If you do not get a join line automatically, there may be a problem with one of your table designs. Open each table in Design view and make sure that the data types are the same for the matching field in both tables and that one of the matching fields is the primary key in a table. Correct these errors and create the query again.

BTW
Join Types
The type of join that finds records from both tables that have identical values in matching fields is called an inner join. An inner join is the default join in Access. Outer joins are used to show all the records in one table as well as the common records; that is, the records that share the same value in the join field. In a left outer join, all rows from the table on the left are included. In a right outer join, all rows from the table on the right are included.

Figure 2–42

To Join Tables

If you have determined that you need to join tables, you first will bring field lists for both tables to the upper pane of the Query window while working in Design view. Access will draw a line, called a **join line**, between matching fields in the two tables, indicating that the tables are related. You then can select fields from either table. Access joins the tables automatically.

The first step is to create a new query and add the Account Manager table to the query. Then, add the Account table to the query. A join line should appear, connecting the Account Manager Number fields in the two field lists. *Why might the join line not appear? If the names of the matching fields differ from one table to the other, Access will not insert the line. You can insert it manually, however, by clicking one of the two matching fields and dragging the pointer to the other matching field.*

The following steps create a query to display information from both the Account table and the Account Manager table.

- Click Create on the ribbon to display the Create tab.

- Click the Query Design button (Create tab | Queries group) to create a new query.

- If necessary, click the Account Manager table (Show Table dialog box) to select the table.

- Click the Add button (Show Table dialog box) to add a field list for the Account Manager Table to the query (Figure 2–43).

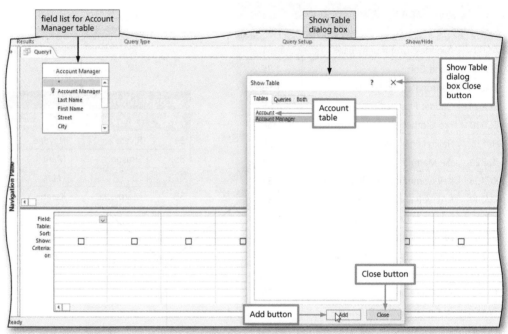

Figure 2–43

- Click the Account table (Show Table dialog box).

- Click the Add button (Show Table dialog box) to add a field list for the Account table.

- Close the Show Table dialog box by clicking the Close button.

- Expand the size of the two field lists so all the fields in the Account Manager and Account tables appear (Figure 2–44).

Q&A | I did not get a join line. What should I do?
Ensure that the names of the matching fields are the same, the data types are the same, and the matching field is the primary key in one of the two tables. If all of these factors are true and you still do not have a join line, you can produce one by pointing to a matching field and dragging to the other matching field.

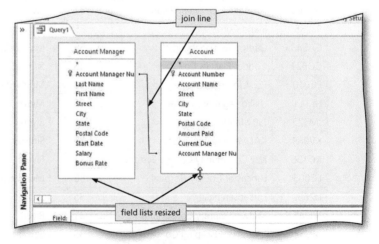

Figure 2–44

3

- In the design grid, include the Account Manager Number, Last Name, and First Name fields from the Account Manager Table as well as the Account Number and Account Name fields from the Account table.

- Select Ascending as the sort order for both the Account Manager Number field and the Account Number field (Figure 2–45).

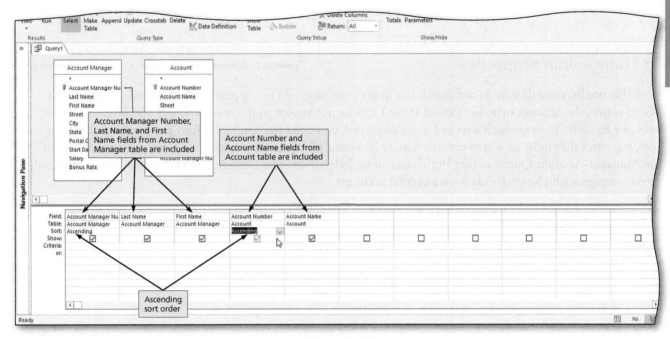

Figure 2–45

4

- Run the query (Figure 2–46).

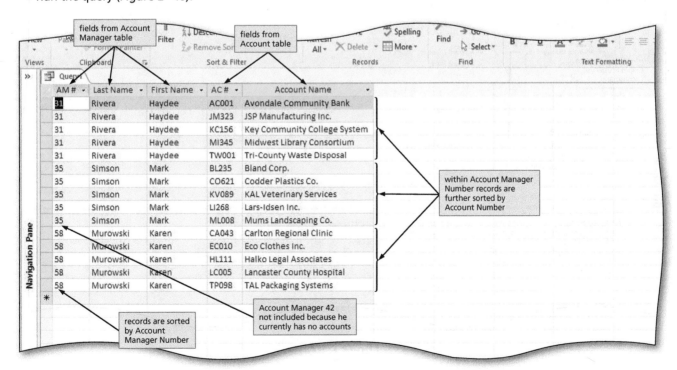

Figure 2–46

● Click the Save button on the Quick Access Toolbar to display the Save As dialog box.

● Type **Manager-Account Query** as the query name.

● Click the OK button (Save As dialog box) to save the query.

To Change Join Properties

Normally, records that do not match the query conditions do not appear in the results of a join query. For example, the account manager named Peter Lu does not appear in the results. *Why? He currently does not have any accounts.* To cause such a record to be displayed, you need to change the **join properties**, which are the properties that indicate which records appear in a join. The following steps change the join properties of the Manager-Account Query so that PrattLast can include all account managers in the results, rather than only those managers who have already been assigned accounts.

● Return to Design view.

● Right-click the join line to produce a shortcut menu (Figure 2–47).

Q&A I do not see Join Properties on my shortcut menu. What should I do?
If Join Properties does not appear on your shortcut menu, you did not point to the appropriate portion of the join line. You will need to point to the correct (middle) portion and right-click again.

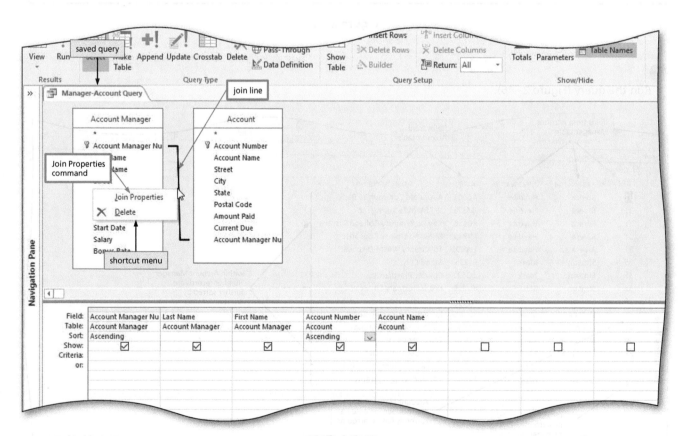

Figure 2–47

2

- Click Join Properties on the shortcut menu to display the Join Properties dialog box (Figure 2–48).

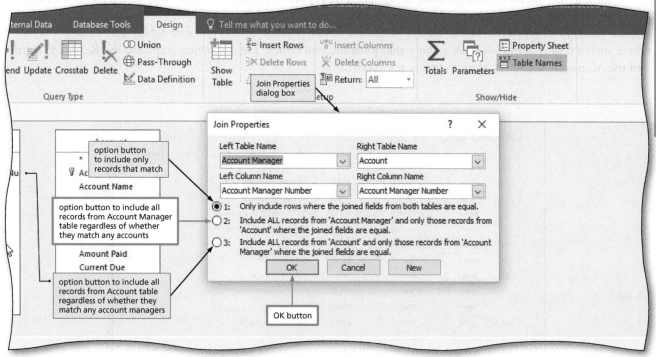

Figure 2–48

3

- Click option button 2 (Join Properties dialog box) to include all records from the Account Manager Table regardless of whether they match any accounts.

- Click the OK button (Join Properties dialog box) to modify the join properties.

- Run the query (Figure 2–49).

🔍 **Experiment**

- Return to Design view, change the Join properties, and select option button 3. Run the query to see the effect of this option. When done, return to Design view, change the join properties, and once again select option button 2.

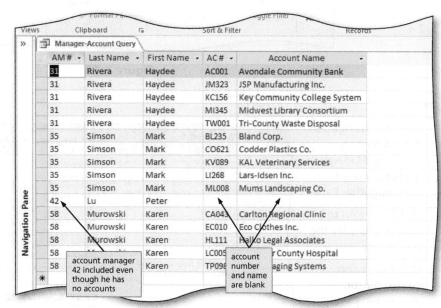

Figure 2–49

4

- Click the Save button on the Quick Access Toolbar to save the changes to the query.

- Close the Manager-Account Query.

Q&A I see a dialog box that asks if I want to save the query. What should I do?
Click the OK button to save the query.

To Create a Report from a Query

You can use queries in the creation of reports. The report in Figure 2–50 involves data from more than one table. *Why? The Last Name and First Name fields are in the Account Manager table. The Account Number and Account Name fields are in the Account table. The Account Manager Number field is in both tables.* The easiest way to create such a report is to base it on a query that joins the two tables. The following steps use the Report Wizard and the Manager-Account Query to create the report.

Manager-Account Report

AM #	Last Name	First Name	AC #	Account Name
31	Rivera	Haydee	AC001	Avondale Community Bank
31	Rivera	Haydee	JM323	JSP Manufacturing Inc.
31	Rivera	Haydee	KC156	Key Community College System
31	Rivera	Haydee	MI345	Midwest Library Consortium
31	Rivera	Haydee	TW001	Tri-County Waste Disposal
35	Simson	Mark	BL235	Bland Corp.
35	Simson	Mark	CO621	Codder Plastics Co.
35	Simson	Mark	KV089	KAL Veterinary Services
35	Simson	Mark	LI268	Lars-Idsen Inc.
35	Simson	Mark	ML008	Mums Landscaping Co.
42	Lu	Peter		
58	Murowski	Karen	CA043	Carlton Regional Clinic
58	Murowski	Karen	EC010	Eco Clothes Inc.
58	Murowski	Karen	HL111	Halko Legal Associates
58	Murowski	Karen	LC005	Lancaster County Hospital
58	Murowski	Karen	TP098	TAL Packaging Systems

Figure 2–50

1

- Open the Navigation Pane, and then select the Manager-Account Query in the Navigation Pane.

- Click Create on the ribbon to display the Create tab.

- Click the Report Wizard button (Create tab | Reports group) to display the Report Wizard dialog box (Figure 2–51).

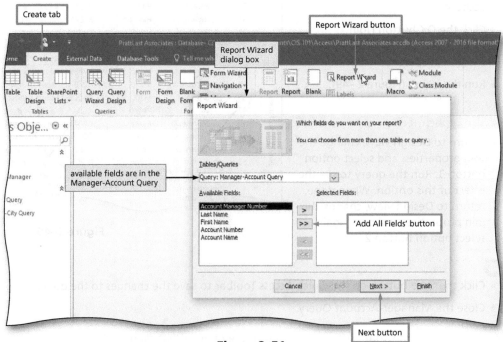

Figure 2–51

2

- Click the 'Add All Fields' button (Report Wizard dialog box) to add all the fields in the Manager-Account Query.

- Click the Next button to display the next Report Wizard screen (Figure 2–52).

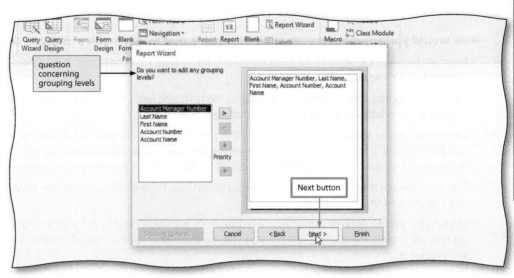

Figure 2–52

3

- Because you will not specify any grouping, click the Next button in the Report Wizard dialog box to display the next Report Wizard screen.

- Because you already specified the sort order in the query, click the Next button again to display the next Report Wizard screen.

- Make sure that Tabular is selected as the Layout and Portrait is selected as the Orientation.

- Click the Next button to display the next Report Wizard screen.

- Erase the current title, and then type **Manager-Account Report** as the new title.

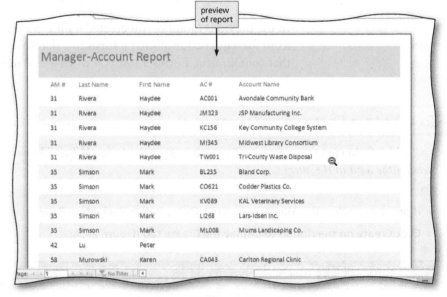

Figure 2–53

- Click the Finish button to produce the report (Figure 2–53).

Q&A My report is very small and does not look like the one in the figure. What should I do?
Click the pointer, which should look like a magnifying glass, anywhere in the report to magnify the report.

- Close the Manager-Account Report.

To Print a Report

The following steps print a hard copy of the report.

1 With the Manager-Account Report selected in the Navigation Pane, click File on the ribbon to open the Backstage view.

2 Click the Print tab in the Backstage view to display the Print gallery.

3 Click the Quick Print button to print the report.

How would you approach the creation of a query that might involve multiple tables?

• Examine the request to see if all the fields involved in the request are in one table. If the fields are in two (or more) tables, you need to join the tables.

• If joining is required, identify within the two tables the matching fields that have identical values. Look for the same column name in the two tables or for column names that are similar.

• Determine whether sorting is required. Queries that join tables often are used as the basis for a report. If this is the case, it may be necessary to sort the results. For example, the Manager-Account Report is based on a query that joins the Account Manager and Account tables. The query is sorted by account manager number and account number.

• Examine the request to see if there are any special restrictions. For example, the user may only want accounts whose current due amount is $0.00.

• Examine the request to see if you only want records from both tables that have identical values in matching fields. If you want to see records in one of the tables that do not have identical values in the other table, then you need to change the join properties.

Creating a Form for a Query

In the previous module, you created a form for the Account table. You can also create a form for a query. Recall that a **form** in a database is a formatted document with fields that contain data. Forms allow you to view and maintain data.

To Create a Form for a Query

1 CREATE QUERIES | 2 USE CRITERIA | 3 SORT DATA | 4 JOIN TABLES | 5 EXPORT RESULTS
6 PERFORM CALCULATIONS | 7 CREATE CROSSTAB | 8 CUSTOMIZE NAVIGATION PANE

The following steps create a form, then save the form. *Why? The form will be available for future use in viewing the data in the query.*

• If necessary, select the Manager-Account Query in the Navigation Pane.

• Click Create on the ribbon to display the Create tab (Figure 2–54).

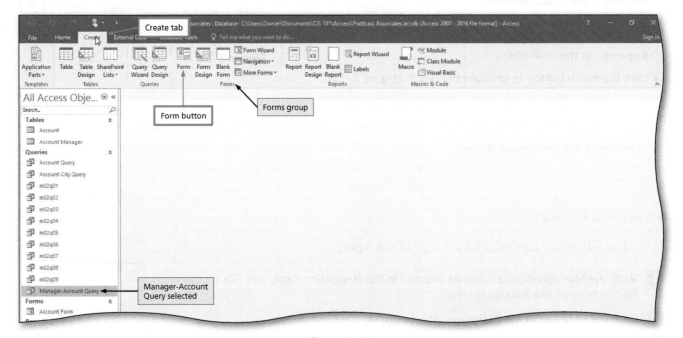

Figure 2–54

2
- Click the Form button (Create tab | Forms group) to create a simple form (Figure 2–55).

Q&A | I see a field list also. What should I do?
Click the Close button for the Field List.

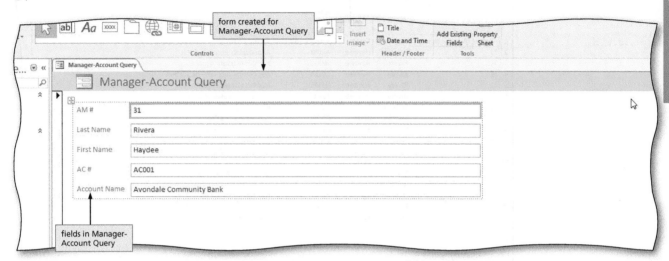

Figure 2–55

3
- Click the Save button on the Quick Access Toolbar to display the Save As dialog box.
- Type **Manager-Account Form** as the form name.
- Click the OK button to save the form.
- Click the Close button for the form to close the form.

Using a Form

After you have saved a form, you can use it at any time by right-clicking the form in the Navigation Pane and then clicking Open on the shortcut menu. If you plan to use the form to enter data, you must ensure you are viewing the form in Form view.

Break Point: If you wish to take a break, this is a good place to do so. You can exit Access now. To resume later, run Access, open the database called PrattLast Associates, and continue following the steps from this location forward.

Exporting Data From Access to Other Applications

You can **export**, or copy, tables or queries from an Access database so that another application (for example, Excel or Word) can use the data. The application that will receive the data determines the export process to be used. You can export to text files in a variety of formats. For applications to which you cannot directly export data, you often can export an appropriately formatted text file that the other application can import. Figure 2–56 shows the workbook produced by exporting the Manager-Account Query to Excel. The columns in the workbook have been resized to best fit the data.

BTW
Exporting Data
You frequently need to export data so that it can be used in other applications and by other users in an organization. For example, the Accounting department might require financial data in an Excel format to perform certain financial functions. Marketing might require a list of account names and addresses in Word or RTF format for marketing campaigns.

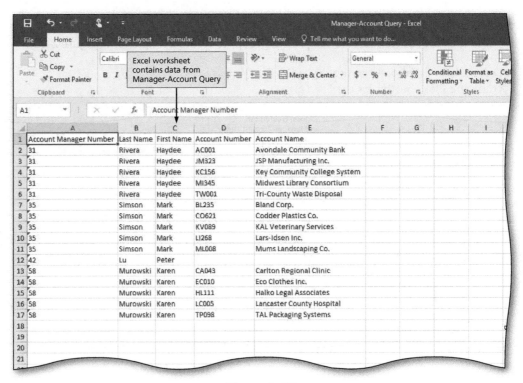

Figure 2–56

1 CREATE QUERIES | 2 USE CRITERIA | 3 SORT DATA | 4 JOIN TABLES | **5 EXPORT RESULTS**
6 PERFORM CALCULATIONS | 7 CREATE CROSSTAB | 8 CUSTOMIZE NAVIGATION PANE

To Export Data to Excel

For PrattLast Associates to make the Manager-Account Query available to Excel users, it needs to export the data. To export data to Excel, select the table or query to be exported and then click the Excel button in the Export group on the External Data tab. The following steps export the Manager-Account Query to Excel and save the export steps. *Why save the export steps?* *By saving the export steps, you could easily repeat the export process whenever you like without going through all the steps.* You would use the saved steps to export data in the future by clicking the Saved Exports button (External Data tab | Export group) and then selecting the steps you saved.

1
- If necessary, click the Manager-Account Query in the Navigation Pane to select it.
- Click External Data on the ribbon to display the External Data tab (Figure 2–57).

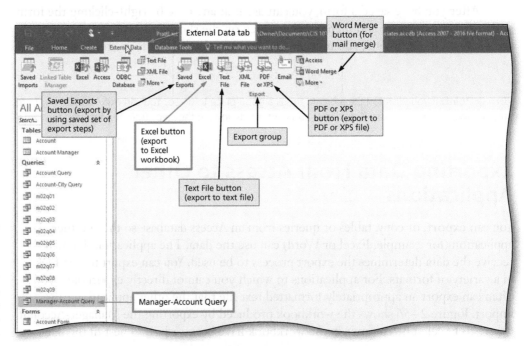

Figure 2–57

2

- Click the Excel button (External Data tab | Export group) to display the Export-Excel Spreadsheet dialog box.

- Click the Browse button (Export-Excel Spreadsheet dialog box), and then navigate to the location where you want to export the query (your hard disk, OneDrive, or other storage location).

- Confirm that the file format is Excel Workbook (*.xlsx), and the file name is Manager-Account Query, and then click the Save button (File Save dialog box) to select the file name and location (Figure 2–58).

Q&A Did I need to browse?
No. You could type the appropriate file location.

Could I change the name of the file?
You could change it. Simply replace the current file name with the one you want.

What if the file I want to export already exists?
Access will indicate that the file already exists and ask if you want to replace it. If you click the Yes button, the file you export will replace the old file. If you click the No button, you must either change the name of the export file or cancel the process.

- Click the OK button (Export-Excel Spreadsheet dialog box) to export the data (Figure 2–59).

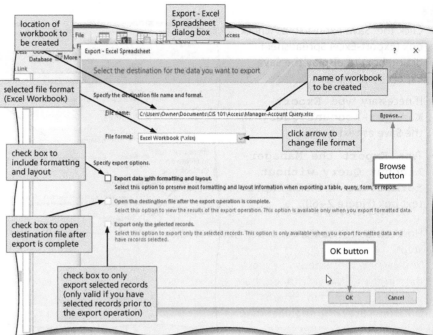

Figure 2–58

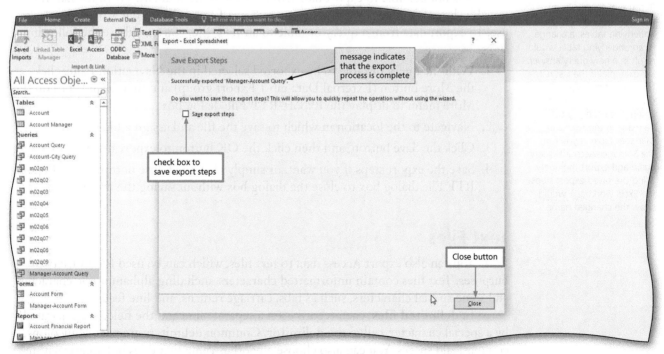

Figure 2–59

3

- Click the 'Save export steps' check box (Export-Excel Spreadsheet dialog box) to display the Save Export Steps options.

- If necessary, type **Export-Manager-Account Query** in the Save as text box.

- Type **Export the Manager-Account Query without formatting** in the Description text box (Figure 2–60).

Q&A

How could I re-use the export steps?

You can use these steps to export data in the future by clicking the Saved Exports button (External Data tab | Export group) and then selecting the steps you saved.

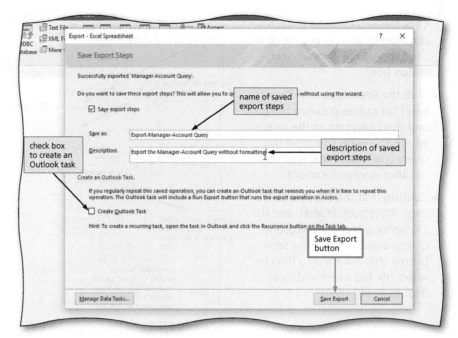

Figure 2–60

4
- Click the Save Export button (Export-Excel Spreadsheet dialog box) to save the export steps.

Other Ways

1. Right-click database object in Navigation Pane, click Export.

TO EXPORT DATA TO WORD

It is not possible to export data from Access to the standard Word format. It is possible, however, to export the data as a rich text format (RTF) file, which Word can use. To export data from a query or table to an RTF file, you would use the following steps.

1. With the query or table to be exported selected in the Navigation Pane, click the More button (External Data tab | Export group) and then click Word on the More menu to display the Export-RTF File dialog box.

2. Navigate to the location in which to save the file and assign a file name.

3. Click the Save button, and then click the OK button to export the data.

4. Save the export steps if you want, or simply click the Close button in the Export-RTF File dialog box to close the dialog box without saving the export steps.

Text Files

You can also export Access data to text files, which can be used for a variety of purposes. Text files contain unformatted characters, including alphanumeric characters, and some special characters, such as tabs, carriage returns, and line feeds.

In **delimited files**, each record is on a separate line and the fields are separated by a special character, called the **delimiter**. Common delimiters are tabs, semicolons, commas, and spaces. You can also choose any other value that does not appear within the field contents as the delimiter. The comma-separated values (CSV) file often used in Excel is an example of a delimited file.

In **fixed-width files**, the width of any field is the same on every record. For example, if the width of the first field on the first record is 12 characters, the width of the first field on every other record must also be 12 characters.

TO EXPORT DATA TO A TEXT FILE

When exporting data to a text file, you can choose to export the data with formatting and layout. This option preserves much of the formatting and layout in tables, queries, forms, and reports. For forms and reports, this is the only option for exporting to a text file.

If you do not need to preserve the formatting, you can choose either delimited or fixed-width as the format for the exported file. The most common option, especially if formatting is not an issue, is delimited. You can choose the delimiter. You can also choose whether to include field names on the first row. In many cases, delimiting with a comma and including the field names is a good choice.

To export data from a table or query to a comma-delimited file in which the first row contains the column headings, you would use the following steps.

1. With the query or table to be exported selected in the Navigation Pane, click the Text File button (External Data tab | Export group) to display the Export-Text File dialog box.
2. Select the name and location for the file to be created.
3. If you need to preserve formatting and layout, be sure the 'Export data with formatting and layout' check box is checked. If you do not need to preserve formatting and layout, make sure the check box is not checked. Once you have made your selection, click the OK button in the Export-Text File dialog box.
4. To create a delimited file, be sure the Delimited option button is selected in the Export Text Wizard dialog box. To create a fixed-width file, be sure the Fixed Width option button is selected. Once you have made your selection, click the Next button.
5. a. If you are exporting to a delimited file, choose the delimiter that you want to separate your fields, such as a comma. Decide whether to include field names on the first row and, if so, click the 'Include Field Names on First Row' check box. If you want to select a text qualifier, select it in the Text Qualifier list. When you have made your selections, click the Next button.

   b. If you are exporting to a fixed-width file, review the position of the vertical lines that separate your fields. If any lines are not positioned correctly, follow the directions on the screen to reposition them. When you have finished, click the Next button.
6. Click the Finish button to export the data.
7. Save the export steps if you want, or simply click the Close button in the Export-Text File dialog box to close the dialog box without saving the export steps.

BTW
Distributing a Document
Instead of printing and distributing a hard copy of a document, you can distribute the document electronically. Options include sending the document via email; posting it on cloud storage (such as OneDrive) and sharing the file with others; posting it on social media, a blog, or other website; and sharing a link associated with an online location of the document. You also can create and share a PDF or XPS image of the document, so that users can view the file in Acrobat Reader or XPS Viewer instead of in Access.

Adding Criteria to a Join Query

Sometimes you will want to join tables, but you will not want to include all possible records. For example, you would like to create a report showing only those accounts whose amount paid is greater than $20,000.00. In this case, you would relate the tables and include fields just as you did before. You will also include criteria. To include only those accounts whose amount paid is more than $20,000.00, you will include >20000 as a criterion for the Amount Paid field.

To Restrict the Records in a Join

The following steps modify the Manager-Account Query so that the results for PrattLast Associates include a criterion. **Why?** *PrattLast wants to include only those accounts whose amount paid is more than $20,000.00.*

1
- Open the Navigation Pane, if necessary, and then right-click the Manager-Account Query to produce a shortcut menu.

- Click Design View on the shortcut menu to open the Manager-Account Query in Design view.

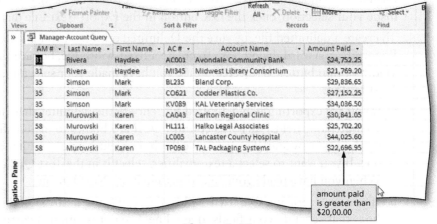

Figure 2–61

- Close the Navigation Pane.

- Add the Amount Paid field to the query.

- Type **>20000** as the criterion for the Amount Paid field (Figure 2–61).

2
- Run the query (Figure 2–62).

3
- Close the query.

- When asked if you want to save your changes, click the No button.

Q&A | What would happen if I saved the changes?
The next time you used this query, you would only see accounts whose amount paid is more than $20,000.00.

Figure 2–62

AM #	Last Name	First Name	AC #	Account Name	Amount Paid
31	Rivera	Haydee	AC001	Avondale Community Bank	$24,752.25
31	Rivera	Haydee	MI345	Midwest Library Consortium	$21,769.20
35	Simson	Mark	BL235	Bland Corp.	$29,836.65
35	Simson	Mark	CO621	Codder Plastics Co.	$27,152.25
35	Simson	Mark	KV089	KAL Veterinary Services	$34,036.50
58	Murowski	Karen	CA043	Carlton Regional Clinic	$30,841.05
58	Murowski	Karen	HL111	Halko Legal Associates	$25,702.20
58	Murowski	Karen	LC005	Lancaster County Hospital	$44,025.60
58	Murowski	Karen	TP098	TAL Packaging Systems	$22,696.95

Calculations

If a special calculation is required for a query, you need to determine whether the calculation is an **individual record calculation** (for example, adding the values in two fields for one record) or a **group calculation** (for example, finding the total of the values in a particular field on all the records).

PrattLast Associates might want to know the total amount (amount paid and current due) for each account. This would seem to pose a problem because the Account table does not include a field for total amount. You can calculate it, however, because the total amount is equal to the amount paid plus the current due. A field that can be computed from other fields is called a **calculated field** or a **computed field** and is not usually included in the table. Including it introduces the possibility for errors in the table. If the value in the field does not happen to match the results of the calculation, the data is inconsistent. A calculated field is an individual record calculation because each calculation only involves fields in a single record.

PrattLast might also want to calculate the average amount paid for the accounts of each account manager. That is, they may want the average for accounts of account manager 31, the average for accounts of account manager 35, and so on. This type of calculation is called a **group calculation** because each calculation involves groups of records. In this example, the accounts of account manager 31 would form one group, the accounts of account manager 35 would be a second group, and the accounts of account manager 58 would form a third group.

To Use a Calculated Field in a Query

1 CREATE QUERIES | 2 USE CRITERIA | 3 SORT DATA | 4 JOIN TABLES | 5 EXPORT RESULTS
6 PERFORM CALCULATIONS | 7 CREATE CROSSTAB | 8 CUSTOMIZE NAVIGATION PANE

If you need a calculated field in a query, you enter a name, or alias, for the calculated field, a colon, and then the calculation in one of the columns in the Field row of the design grid for the query. Any fields included in the expression must be enclosed in square brackets ([ ]). For example, for the total amount, you will type Total Amount:[Amount Paid]+[Current Due] as the expression.

You can type the expression directly into the Field row in Design view. The preferred method, however, is to select the column in the Field row and then use the Zoom command on its shortcut menu. When Access displays the Zoom dialog box, you can enter the expression. *Why use the Zoom command? You will not be able to see the entire entry in the Field row, because the space available is not large enough.*

You can use addition (+), subtraction (-), multiplication (*), or division (/) in calculations. If you have multiple calculations in an expression, you can include parentheses to indicate which calculations should be done first.

The following steps create a query that PrattLast Associates might use to obtain financial information on its accounts, including the total amount (amount paid + current due), which is a calculated field.

1

- Create a query with a field list for the Account table.

- Add the Account Number, Account Name, Amount Paid, and Current Due fields to the query.

- Right-click the Field row in the first open column in the design grid to display a shortcut menu (Figure 2–63).

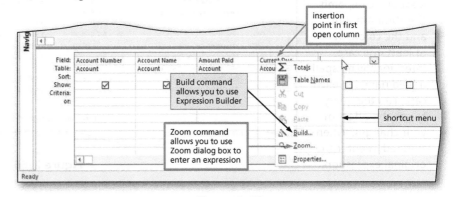

Figure 2–63

2

- Click Zoom on the shortcut menu to display the Zoom dialog box.

- Type `Total Amount:[Amount Paid]+[Current Due]` in the Zoom dialog box (Figure 2–64).

Q&A
Do I always need to put square brackets around field names?
If the field name does not contain spaces, square brackets are technically not required. It is a good practice, however, to get in the habit of using the brackets in field calculations.

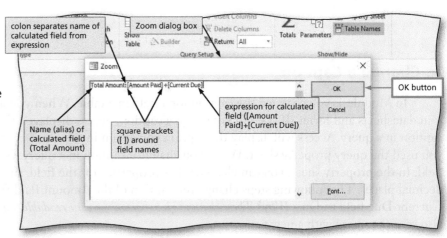

Figure 2–64

3

- Click the OK button (Zoom dialog box) to enter the expression (Figure 2–65).

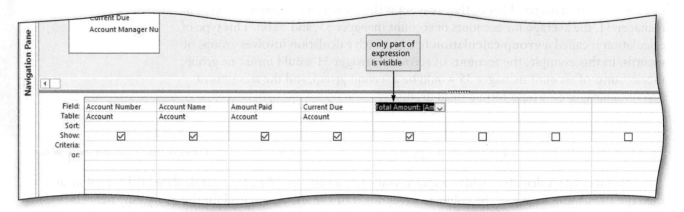

Figure 2–65

4

- Run the query (Figure 2–66).

Experiment

- Return to Design view and try other expressions. In at least one case, omit the Total Amount and the colon. In at least one case, intentionally misspell a field name. In each case, run the query to see the effect of your changes. When finished, reenter the original expression.

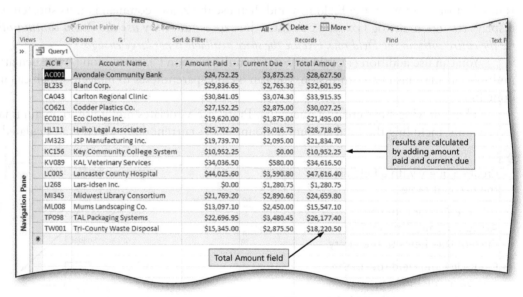

Figure 2–66

Other Ways

1. Press SHIFT+F2

To Change a Caption

1 CREATE QUERIES | 2 USE CRITERIA | 3 SORT DATA | 4 JOIN TABLES | 5 EXPORT RESULTS
6 PERFORM CALCULATIONS | 7 CREATE CROSSTAB | 8 CUSTOMIZE NAVIGATION PANE

In Module 1, you changed the caption for a field in a table. When you assigned a caption, Access displayed it in datasheets and forms. If you did not assign a caption, Access displayed the field name. You can also change a caption in a query. Access will display the caption you assign in the query results. When you omitted duplicates, you used the query property sheet. When you change a caption in a query, you use the property sheet for the field. In the property sheet, you can change other properties for the field, such as the format and number of decimal places. The following steps change the caption of the Amount Paid field to Paid and the caption of the Current Due field to Due. *Why? These changes give shorter, yet very readable, column headings for the fields.* The steps also save the query with a new name.

1

- Return to Design view.

- If necessary, click Design on the ribbon to display the Query Tools Design tab.

- Click the Amount Paid field in the design grid, and then click the Property Sheet button (Query Tools Design tab | Show/Hide group) to display the properties for the Amount Paid field.

- Click the Caption box, and then type **Paid** as the caption (Figure 2–67).

Q&A | My property sheet looks different. What should I do?
Close the property sheet and repeat this step.

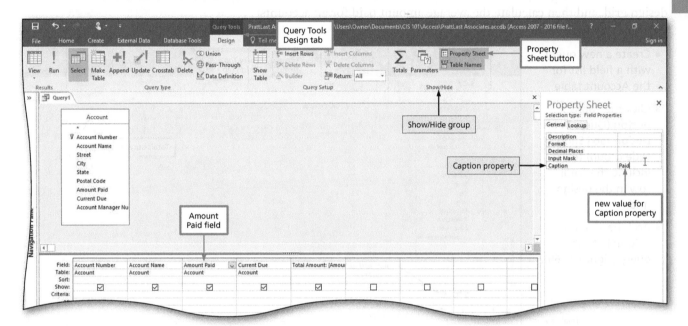

Figure 2–67

2

- Click the Current Due field in the design grid to view its properties in the Property Sheet.

- Click the Caption box, and then type **Due** as the caption.

- Close the Property Sheet by clicking the Property Sheet button a second time.

- Run the query (Figure 2–68).

3

- Save the query as m02q10.

- Close the query.

AC #	Account Name	Paid	Due	Total Amour
AC001	Avondale Community Bank	$24,752.25	$3,875.25	$28,627.50
BL235	Bland Corp.	$29,836.65	$2,765.30	$32,601.95
CA043	Carlton Regional Clinic	$30,841.05	$3,074.30	$33,915.35
CO621	Codder Plastics Co.	$27,152.25	$2,875.00	$30,027.25
EC010	Eco Clothes Inc.	$19,620.00	$1,875.00	$21,495.00
HL111	Halko Legal Associates	$25,702.20	$3,016.75	$28,718.95
JM323	JSP Manufacturing Inc.	$19,739.70	$2,095.00	$21,834.70
KC156	Key Community College System	$10,952.25	$0.00	$10,952.25
KV089	KAL Veterinary Services	$34,036.50	$580.00	$34,616.50
LC005	Lancaster County Hospital	$44,025.60	$3,590.80	$47,616.40
LI268	Lars-Idsen Inc.	$0.00	$1,280.75	$1,280.75
MI345	Midwest Library Consortium	$21,769.20	$2,890.60	$24,659.80
ML008	Mums Landscaping Co.	$13,097.10	$2,450.00	$15,547.10
TP098	TAL Packaging Systems	$22,696.95	$3,480.45	$26,177.40
TW001	Tri-County Waste Disposal	$15,345.00	$2,875.50	$18,220.50

Figure 2–68

Other Ways

1. Right-click field in design grid, click Properties on shortcut menu

To Calculate Statistics

For group calculations, Microsoft Access supports several built-in statistics: COUNT (count of the number of records), SUM (total), AVG (average), MAX (largest value), MIN (smallest value), STDEV (standard deviation), VAR (variance), FIRST (first value), and LAST (last value). These statistics are called aggregate functions. An **aggregate function** is a function that performs some mathematical function against a group of records. To use an aggregate function in a query, you include it in the Total row in the design grid. In order to do so, you must first include the Total row by clicking the Totals button on the Design tab. **Why?** *The Total row usually does not appear in the grid.*

The following steps create a new query for the Account table. The steps include the Total row in the design grid, and then calculate the average amount paid for all accounts.

1

- Create a new query with a field list for the Account table.

- Click the Totals button (Query Tools Design tab | Show/ Hide group) to include the Total row in the design grid.

- Add the Amount Paid field to the query (Figure 2–69).

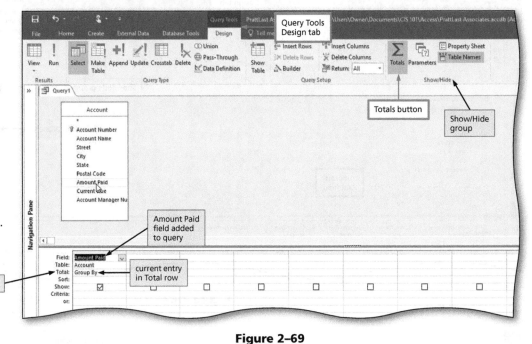

Figure 2–69

2

- Click the Total row in the Amount Paid column to display the Total arrow.

- Click the Total arrow to display the Total list (Figure 2–70).

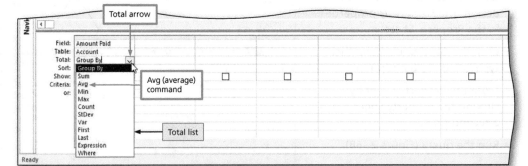

Figure 2–70

3

- Click Avg to select the calculation that Access is to perform (Figure 2–71).

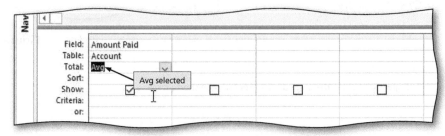

Figure 2–71

4
- Run the query (Figure 2–72).

🔎 **Experiment**
- Return to Design view and try other aggregate functions. In each case, run the query to see the effect of your selection. When finished, select Avg once again.

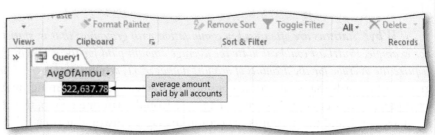

Figure 2–72

To Use Criteria in Calculating Statistics

1 CREATE QUERIES | 2 USE CRITERIA | 3 SORT DATA | 4 JOIN TABLES | 5 EXPORT RESULTS
6 PERFORM CALCULATIONS | 7 CREATE CROSSTAB | 8 CUSTOMIZE NAVIGATION PANE

Why? *Sometimes calculating statistics for all the records in the table is appropriate. In other cases, however, you will need to calculate the statistics for only those records that satisfy certain criteria.* To enter a criterion in a field, first you select Where as the entry in the Total row for the field, and then enter the criterion in the Criteria row. Access uses the word, Where, to indicate that you will enter a criterion. The following steps use this technique to calculate the average amount paid for accounts of account manager 31. The steps also save the query with a new name.

1
- Return to Design view.
- Include the Account Manager Number field in the design grid.
- Click the Total row in the Account Manager Number column.
- Click the Total arrow in the Account Manager Number column to produce a Total list (Figure 2–73).

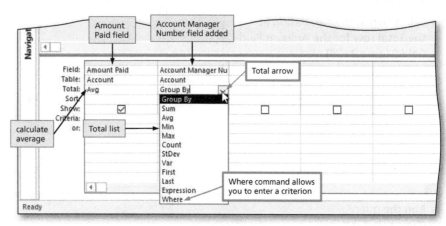

Figure 2–73

2
- Click Where to be able to enter a criterion.
- Type **31** as the criterion for the Account Manager Number field (Figure 2–74).

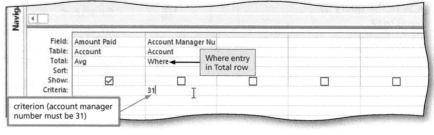

Figure 2–74

3
- Run the query (Figure 2–75).

4
- Save the query as m02q11.

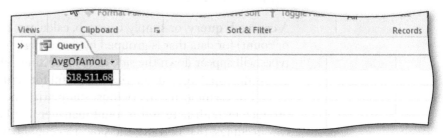

Figure 2–75

To Use Grouping

1 CREATE QUERIES | 2 USE CRITERIA | 3 SORT DATA | 4 JOIN TABLES | 5 EXPORT RESULTS
6 PERFORM CALCULATIONS | 7 CREATE CROSSTAB | 8 CUSTOMIZE NAVIGATION PANE

Why? *Statistics are often used in combination with grouping; that is, statistics are calculated for groups of records. For example, PrattLast could calculate the average amount paid for the accounts of each account manager, which would require the average for the accounts of account manager 31, account manager 35, and so on.* **Grouping** means creating groups of records that share some common characteristic. In grouping by Account Manager Number, for example, the accounts of account manager 31 would form one group, the accounts of account manager 35 would form a second, and the accounts of account manager 58 would form a third group. The calculations are then made for each group. To indicate grouping in Access, select Group By as the entry in the Total row for the field to be used for grouping.

The following steps create a query that calculates the average amount paid for the accounts of each account manager at PrattLast Associates. The steps also save the query with a new name.

1

- Return to Design view and clear the design grid.
- Include the Account Manager Number field in the query.
- Include the Amount Paid field in the query.
- Select Avg as the calculation in the Total row for the Amount Paid field (Figure 2–76).

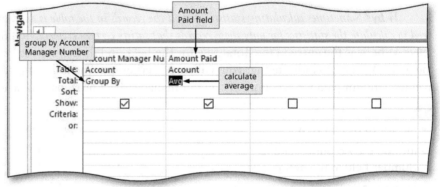

Figure 2–76

Q&A

Why was it not necessary to change the entry in the Total row for the Account Manager Number field?

Group By, which is the initial entry in the Total row when you add a field, is correct. Thus, you did not need to change the entry.

2

- Run the query (Figure 2–77).

3

- Save the query as m02q12.
- Close the query.

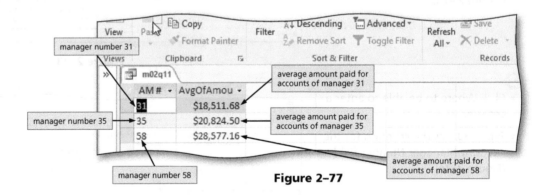

Figure 2–77

Crosstab Queries

A **crosstab query**, or simply, crosstab, calculates a statistic (for example, sum, average, or count) for data that is grouped by two different types of information. One of the types will appear down the side of the resulting datasheet, and the other will appear across the top. Crosstab queries are useful for summarizing data by category or group.

For example, if a query must summarize the sum of the current due amounts grouped by both state and account manager number, you could have states as the row headings, that is, down the side. You could have account manager numbers as the column headings, that is, across the top. The entries within the datasheet represent the total of the current due amounts. Figure 2–78 shows a crosstab in which the total of current due amounts is grouped by both state and account manager number, with states down the left side and account manager numbers across the top. For example, the entry in the row labeled IL and in the column labeled 31 represents the total of the current due amounts by all accounts of account manager 31 who are located in Illinois.

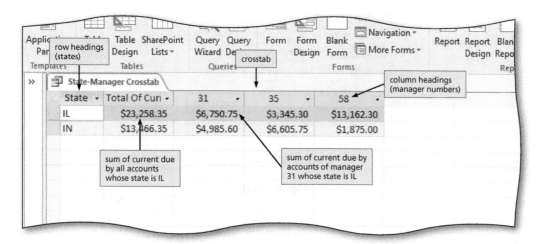

Figure 2–78

How do you know when to use a crosstab query?

If data is to be grouped by two different types of information, you can use a crosstab query. You will need to identify the two types of information. One of the types will form the row headings and the other will form the column headings in the query results.

CONSIDER THIS

To Create a Crosstab Query

1 CREATE QUERIES | 2 USE CRITERIA | 3 SORT DATA | 4 JOIN TABLES | 5 EXPORT RESULTS
6 PERFORM CALCULATIONS | 7 CREATE CROSSTAB | 8 CUSTOMIZE NAVIGATION PANE

The following steps use the Crosstab Query Wizard to create a crosstab query. *Why? PrattLast Associates wants to group data on current due amounts by two types of information: state and account manager.*

1

- Click Create on the ribbon to display the Create tab.
- Click the Query Wizard button (Create tab | Queries group) to display the New Query dialog box (Figure 2–79).

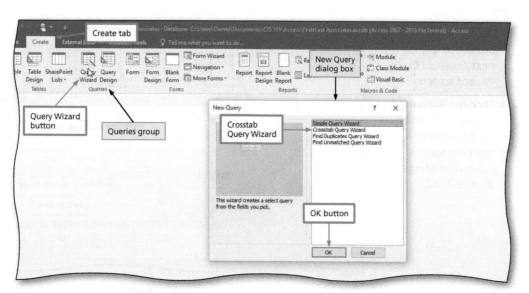

Figure 2–79

- Click Crosstab Query Wizard (New Query dialog box).

- Click the OK button to display the Crosstab Query Wizard dialog box (Figure 2–80).

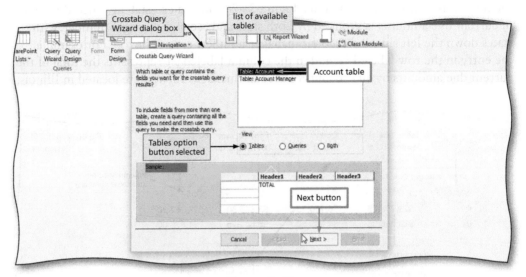

Figure 2–80

- With the Tables option button selected, click Table: Account to select the Account table, and then click the Next button to display the next Crosstab Query Wizard screen.

- Click the State field, and then click the Add Field button to select the State field for row headings (Figure 2–81).

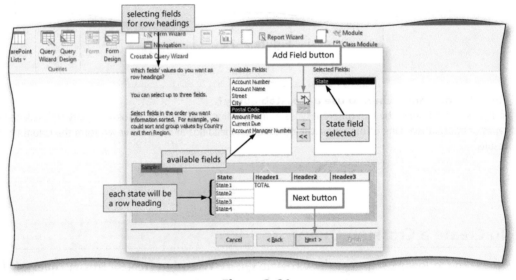

Figure 2–81

④

- Click the Next button to display the next Crosstab Query Wizard screen.

- Click the Account Manager Number field to select the field for column headings (Figure 2–82).

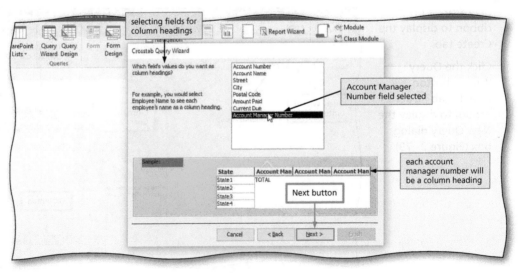

Figure 2–82

5

- Click the Next button to display the next Crosstab Query Wizard screen.

- Click the Current Due field to select the field for calculations.

🔍 **Experiment**

- Click other fields. For each field, examine the list of calculations that are available. When finished, click the Current Due field again.

- Click Sum to select the calculation to be performed (Figure 2–83).

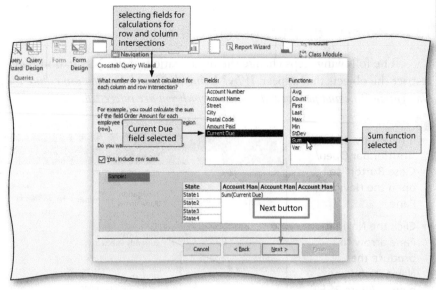

Figure 2–83

 Q&A My list of functions is different. What did I do wrong?
Either you clicked the wrong field, or the Current Due field has the wrong data type. For example, if you mistakenly assigned it the Short Text data type, you would not see Sum in the list of available calculations.

6

- Click the Next button to display the next Crosstab Query Wizard screen.

- Erase the text in the name text box and type **State-Manager Crosstab** as the name of the query (Figure 2–84).

7

- If requested to do so by your instructor, name the crosstab query as FirstName LastName Crosstab where FirstName and LastName are your first and last names.

- Click the Finish button to produce the crosstab shown in Figure 2–78.

- Close the query.

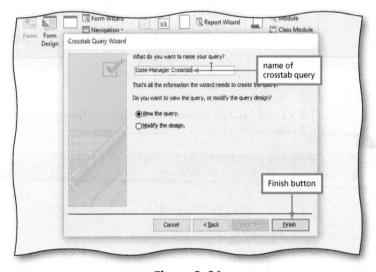

Figure 2–84

Customizing the Navigation Pane

Currently, the entries in the Navigation Pane are organized by object type. That is, all the tables are together, all the queries are together, and so on. You might want to change the way the information is organized. For example, you might want to have the Navigation Pane organized by table, with all the queries, forms, and reports associated with a particular table appearing after the name of the table. You can also use the Search bar to restrict the objects that appear to only those that have a certain collection of characters in their name. For example, if you entered the letters, Ma, only those objects containing Ma somewhere within the name will be included.

BTW

Access Help
At any time while using Access, you can find answers to questions and display information about various topics through Access Help. Used properly, this form of assistance can increase your productivity and reduce your frustrations by minimizing the time you spend learning how to use Access. For instructions about Access Help and exercises that will help you gain confidence in using it, read the Office and Windows module at the beginning of this book.

To Customize the Navigation Pane

The following steps change the organization of the Navigation Pane. They also use the Search bar to restrict the objects that appear. *Why? Using the Search bar, you can reduce the number of objects that appear in the Navigation Pane and just show the ones in which you are interested.*

1

- If necessary, click the 'Shutter Bar Open/ Close Button' to open the Navigation Pane.

- Click the Navigation Pane arrow to produce the Navigation Pane menu (Figure 2–85).

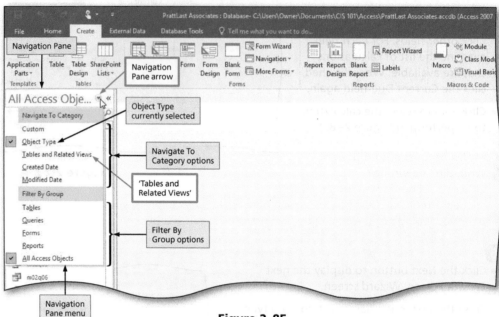

Figure 2–85

2

- Click 'Tables and Related Views' to organize the Navigation Pane by table rather than by the type of object (Figure 2–86).

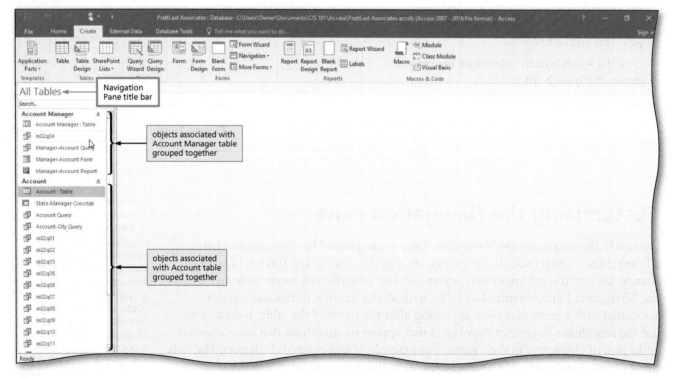

Figure 2–86

3

- Click the Navigation Pane arrow to produce the Navigation Pane menu.
- Click Object Type to once again organize the Navigation Pane by object type.

🔍 **Experiment**

- Select different Navigate To Category options to see the effect of the option. With each option you select, select different Filter By Group options to see the effect of the filtering. When you have finished experimenting, select the 'Object Type Navigate To Category' option and the 'All Access Objects Filter By Group' option.
- If the Search bar does not appear, right-click the Navigation Pane and click Search Bar on the shortcut menu.
- Click in the Search box to produce an insertion point.
- Type **Ma** as the search string to restrict the objects displayed to only those containing the desired string (Figure 2–87).

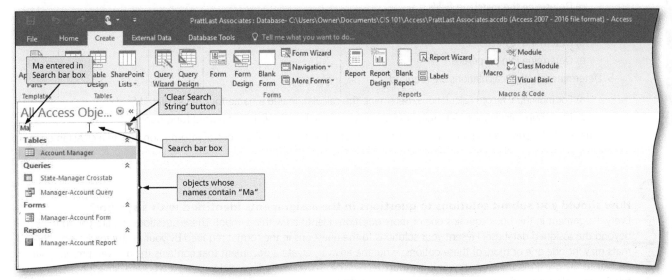

Figure 2–87

4

- Click the 'Clear Search String' button to remove the search string and redisplay all objects.

Q&A Did I have to click the button to redisplay all objects? Could I simply have erased the current string to achieve the same result?

You did not have to click the button. You could have used the DELETE or BACKSPACE keys to erase the current search string.

- If desired, sign out of your Microsoft account.
- Exit Access.

Summary

In this module you have learned to create queries, enter fields, enter criteria, use text and numeric data in queries, use wildcards, use compound criteria, create parameter queries, sort data in queries, join tables in queries, perform calculations in queries, and create crosstab queries. You also learned to create a report and a form that used a query, to export a query, and to customize the Navigation Pane.

CONSIDER THIS

What decisions will you need to make when creating queries?

Use these guidelines as you complete the assignments in this module and create your own queries outside of this class.

1. Identify the fields by examining the question or request to determine which fields from the tables in the database are involved.

2. Identify restrictions or the conditions that records must satisfy to be included in the results.

3. Determine whether special order is required.

    a) Determine the sort key(s).

    b) If using two sort keys, determine the major and minor key.

    c) Determine sort order. If there are no words to imply a particular order, you would typically use Ascending.

    d) Determine restrictions, such as excluding duplicates.

4. Determine whether more than one table is required.

    a) Determine which tables to include.

    b) Determine the matching fields.

    c) Determine whether sorting is required.

    d) Determine restrictions.

    e) Determine join properties.

5. Determine whether calculations are required.

    a) For individual record calculations, determine the calculation and a name for the calculated field.

    b) For group calculations, determine the calculation as well as the field to be used for grouping.

6. If data is to be summarized and the data is to be grouped by two different types of information, create a crosstab query.

CONSIDER THIS

How should you submit solutions to questions in the assignments identified with a symbol?

Every assignment in this book contains one or more questions identified with a symbol. These questions require you to think beyond the assigned database. Present your solutions to the questions in the format required by your instructor. Possible formats may include one or more of these options: write the answer; create a document that contains the answer; present your answer to the class; discuss your answer in a group; record the answer as audio or video using a webcam, smartphone, or portable media player; or post answers on a blog, wiki, or website.

Apply Your Knowledge

Reinforce the skills and apply the concepts you learned in this module.

Using Wildcards in a Query, Creating a Parameter Query, Joining Tables, and Creating a Report

Instructions: Run Access. Open the Apply Friendly Janitorial Services database that you modified in Apply Your Knowledge in Module 1. (If you did not complete the exercise, see your instructor for a copy of the modified database.)

Perform the following tasks:

1. Create a query for the Client table and add the Client Number, Client Name, Amount Paid, and Current Due fields to the design grid. Add a criterion to find all clients whose names start with the letter B. Run the query and then save it as Apply 2 Step 1 Query.

2. Create a query for the Client table and add the Client Number, Client Name, Amount Paid, and Supervisor Number fields to the design grid. Sort the records in descending order by Amount Paid. Add a criterion for the Supervisor Number field that allows the user to enter a different supervisor each time the query is run. Run the query and enter 114 as the supervisor number to test the query. Save the query as Apply 2 Step 2 Query.

3. Create a query for the Client table and add the Client Number, Client Name, and Current Due fields to the design grid. Add a criterion to find all clients whose current due amount is less than $500.00. Run the query and then save it as Apply 2 Step 3 Query.

4. Create a query that joins the Supervisor and Client tables. Add the Supervisor Number, Last Name, and First Name fields from the Supervisor table and the Client Number and Client Name fields from the Client table to the design grid. Sort the records in ascending order by Client Number within Supervisor Number. Run the query and save it as Supervisor-Client Query.

5. Create the report shown in Figure 2–88. The report uses the Supervisor-Client Query.

Supervisor-Client Report

SU #	Last Name	First Name	CL #	Client Name
103	Estevez	Enrique	AT13	Atlas Repair
103	Estevez	Enrique	CP03	Calder Plastics
103	Estevez	Enrique	HC17	Hill Crafts
103	Estevez	Enrique	KD15	Klean n Dri
110	Hillsdale	Rachel	AZ01	AZ Auto
110	Hillsdale	Rachel	BB35	Babbage Bookkeeping
110	Hillsdale	Rachel	CJ45	C Joe Diner
110	Hillsdale	Rachel	HN23	Hurley National Bank
110	Hillsdale	Rachel	PL03	Prime Legal Associates
114	Liu	Chou	CC25	Cramden Co.
114	Liu	Chou	MM01	Moss Manufacturing
114	Liu	Chou	PS67	PRIM Staffing
120	Short	Chris	BL24	Blanton Shoes
120	Short	Chris	KC12	Kady Regional Clinic
120	Short	Chris	TE15	Telton-Edwards

Figure 2–88

6. If requested to do so by your instructor, rename the Supervisor-Client Report in the Navigation Pane as LastName-Client Report where LastName is your last name.

7. Submit the revised database in the format specified by your instructor.

8. ✳ What criteria would you enter in the Street field if you wanted to find all clients whose businesses were on Beard?

Extend Your Knowledge

Extend the skills you learned in this module and experiment with new skills. You may need to use Help to complete the assignment.

Creating Crosstab Queries Using Criteria and Exporting a Query

Note: To complete this assignment, you will be required to use the Data Files. Please contact your instructor for information about accessing the Data Files.

Continued >

STUDENT ASSIGNMENTS

Extend Your Knowledge *continued*

Instructions: Run Access. Open the Extend TAL Maintenance database, which is located in the Data Files. TAL Maintenance is a small business that provides various outdoor maintenance services, such as painting, lawn maintenance, and parking lot re-paving, to commercial customers. The owner has created an Access database in which to store information about the customers the company serves and team leaders working for the company. You will create the crosstab query shown in Figure 2–89. You will also query the database using specified criteria and export a query.

Perform the following tasks:

1. Create the crosstab query shown in Figure 2–89. The crosstab groups the total of customers' balance by city and team leader number.

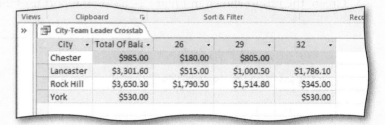

Figure 2–89

2. Create a query to find all customers who are not located in Rock Hill. Include the Customer Number, Customer Name, and Balance fields in the query results. Save the query as Extend 2 Step 2 Query.

3. Create a query to find all team leaders whose first name is either Alex or Alix. Include the Team Leader Number, First Name, and Last Name in the query results. Save the query as Extend 2 Step 3 Query.

4. Create a query to find all customers where the team leader number is either 29 or 32 and the balance is greater than $550.00. Include the Customer Number, Customer Name, Balance, and Team Leader Number fields in the design grid in that order. Use the IN operator in your query design. Sort the results by customer number within team leader number. Save the query as Extend 2 Step 4 Query.

5. Export the City-Team Leader Crosstab as a Word file with the name City-Team Leader Crosstab.rtf and save the export steps.

6. Open the Customer table and change the balance for account C04 to $1,000.50.

7. If requested to do so by your instructor, change the customer name of customer K10 from Kathy's Books to Last Name Books where Last Name is your last name.

8. Use the saved export steps to export the City-Team Leader Crosstab again. When asked if you want to replace the existing file, click Yes.

9. Submit the revised database and the exported RTF file in the format specified by your instructor.

10. ✳ How would you create the query in Step 4 without using the IN operator?

Expand Your World

Create a solution, which uses cloud and web technologies, by learning and investigating on your own from general guidance.

Problem: You are taking a general science course and the instructor would like you to gather some weather statistics and query the statistics as part of the unit on climate change.

Instructions:

1. Examine a website that contains historical weather data, such as accuweather.com or weatherunderground.com. Select weather data for the city in which you were born for the month of January, 2014. If you cannot find your city, then select a large city near your current location.

2. Create a database that contains one table and has the following fields: Day of the month (1 through 31), Day of the week, high temperature for the day, and low temperature for the day. (*Hint:* Use the autonumber data type to record the day of the month.)

3. Create queries that do the following:

   a. Display the five days with the highest high temperature.

   b. Display the five days with lowest low temperature.

   c. Display the average high and low temperature for the entire month.

   d. Calculate the difference between the high and low temperatures for each day.

   e. Display the high and low temperatures for each day in both Fahrenheit and Celsius. (*Hint:* Use the Internet to find the conversion formula.)

4. Submit the revised database in the format specified by your instructor.

5. Use an Internet search engine to find the historical average high and low temperatures in January for your city.

6. ✺ Which websites did you use to gather data and search for the historical averages? How does the query result in Step 3c differ from the historical average?

In the Labs

Design, create, modify, and/or use a database following the guidelines, concepts, and skills presented in this module. Labs are listed in order of increasing difficulty. Labs 1 and 2, which increase in difficulty, require you to create solutions based on what you learned in the module; Lab 3 requires you to apply your creative thinking and problem solving skills to design and implement a solution.

Lab 1: **Querying the Garden Naturally Database**

Problem: The management of Garden Naturally has determined a number of questions it wants the database management system to answer. You must obtain the answers to these questions.

Note: Use the database modified in Lab 1 of Module 1 for this assignment, or see your instructor for information on accessing the required files.

Instructions: Perform the following tasks:

1. Run Access. Open the Lab 1 Garden Naturally database you modified in Module 1 and create a new query for the Customer table. Add the Customer Number, Customer Name, Amount Paid, Balance Due, and Sales Rep Number fields to the design grid, and restrict the query results to only those customers where the sales rep number is 29. Save the query as Lab 2-1 Step 1 Query.

2. Create a query for the Customer table that includes the Customer Number, Customer Name, and Balance Due fields for all customers located in Delaware (DE) with a balance due greater than $1,000.00. Save the query as Lab 2-1 Step 2 Query.

3. Create a query for the Customer table that includes the Customer Number, Customer Name, Address, City, and State fields for all customers located in cities that begin with Ch. Save the query as Lab 2-1 Step 3 Query.

Continued >

In the Labs *continued*

4. Create a query for the Customer table that lists all states in ascending order. Each state should appear only once. Save the query as Lab 2-1 Step 4 Query.

5. Create a query for the Customer table that allows the user to type the name of the desired city when the query is run. The query results should display the Customer Number, Customer Name, Balance Due, and Amount Paid fields in that order. Test the query by searching for those records where the customer is located in Quaker. Save the query as Lab 2-1 Step 5 Query.

6. Create a query for the Sales Rep table that includes the First Name, Last Name, and Start Date for all sales reps who started after June 1, 2015. Save the query as Lab 2-1 Step 6 Query.

7. Create a query that joins the Sales Rep and Customer tables. Include the Sales Rep Number, Last Name, and First Name from the Sales Rep table. Include the Customer Number, Customer Name, and Amount Paid from the Customer table. Sort the records in ascending order by sales rep's last name and then by customer name. All sales reps should appear in the result even if they currently have no customers. Save the query as Lab 2-1 Step 7 Query.

8. Open the Lab 2-1 Step 7 Query in Design view and remove the Sales Rep table from the query. Add the Balance Due field to the design grid. Calculate the total of the balance and amount paid amounts. Assign the alias Total Amount to the calculated field. Change the caption for the Amount Paid field to Paid and the caption for the Balance Due field to Owed. Save the query as Lab 2-1 Step 8 Query.

9. Create a query for the Customer table to display the total amount paid for sales rep 26. Save the query as Lab 2-1 Step 9 Query.

10. Create a query for the Customer table to display the average balance due for each sales rep. Save the query as Lab 2-1 Step 10 Query.

11. Create the crosstab query shown in Figure 2–90. The crosstab groups the average of customers' amount paid by state and sales rep number. Save the crosstab as State-Sales Rep Crosstab.

Views	Clipboard		Sort & Filter		Reco
»	State-Sales Rep Crosstab				
	State ▾	Total Of Am(▾	26 ▾	29 ▾	32 ▾
	DE	$1,431.38		$537.50	$2,325.25
	NJ	$2,503.57	$2,352.61	$2,285.50	$3,325.45
	PA	$1,717.10	$1,190.00	$1,572.50	$2,125.25

Figure 2–90

12. If requested to do so by your instructor, open the Lab 2-1 Step 1 query and change the caption for the Sales Rep Number field to your last name.

13. Submit the revised database in the format specified by your instructor.

14. ✳ How would you modify the query in Step 7 to include only sales reps that currently have customers?

Lab 2: **Querying the Museum Gift Shop Database**

Problem: The manager of the Museum gift shop has determined a number of questions she wants the database management system to answer. You must obtain answers to these questions.

Note: Use the database created in Lab 2 of Module 1 for this assignment or see your instructor for information on accessing the required files.

Instructions: Perform the following tasks:

1. Run Access. Open the Lab 2 Museum Gift Shop database and create a query for the Item table that includes all fields and all records in the Item table. Name the query Lab 2-2 Step 1 Query.

2. Create a query for the Item table that includes the Item Number, Description, Wholesale Cost, and Vendor Code fields for all records where the vendor code is AW. Save the query as Lab 2-2 Step 2 Query.

3. Create a query for the Item table that includes the Item Number and Description fields for all items where the description starts with G. Save the query as Lab 2-2 Step 3 Query.

4. Create a query for the Item table that includes the Item Number and Description for all items with a Wholesale Cost greater than $15.00. Save the query as Lab 2-2 Step 4 Query.

5. Create a query for the Item table that includes the Item Number, Description, and Wholesale Cost fields for all items with a Wholesale Cost between $5.00 and $10.00. Save the query as Lab 2-2 Step 5 Query.

6. Create a query for the Item table that includes the Item Number, Description, On Hand, and Wholesale Cost fields for all items where the number on hand is less than 5 and the wholesale cost is less than $15.00. Save the query as Lab 2-2 Step 6 Query.

7. Create a query for the Item table that includes the Item Number, Description, Wholesale Cost, and Vendor Code for all items that have a Wholesale Cost greater than $20.00 or a Vendor Code of SD. Save the query as Lab 2-2 Step 7 Query.

8. Create a query that joins the Vendor and the Item tables. Include the Vendor Code and Vendor Name from the Vendor table and the Item Number, Description, Wholesale Cost, and Retail Price fields from the Item table. Sort the query in ascending order by Description within Vendor Code. Save the query as Vendor-Item Query.

9. Create a form for the Vendor-Item Query. Save the form as Vendor-Item Form.

10. If requested to do so by your instructor, rename the form in the Navigation Pane as LastName-Item Form where LastName is your last name.

11. Create the report shown in Figure 2–91. The report uses the Vendor-Item Query but does not use all the fields in the query.

Vendor-Item Report

Vendor Name	Description	Wholesale	Retail
Atherton Wholesalers	Amazing Science Fun	$13.50	$24.99
Atherton Wholesalers	Crystal Growing Kit	$6.75	$12.97
Atherton Wholesalers	Discovery Dinosaurs	$12.35	$19.95
Atherton Wholesalers	Gem Nature Guide	$9.50	$14.95
Atherton Wholesalers	Onyx Jar	$7.50	$13.97
Gift Specialties	Agate Bookends	$16.25	$27.97
Gift Specialties	Dinosaur Egg Ornament	$7.50	$14.99
Gift Specialties	Fibonacci Necklace	$16.75	$29.99
Gift Specialties	Gyrobot	$27.99	$49.99
Gift Specialties	Molecule Necklace	$16.25	$29.95
Smith Distributors	Cosmos Uncovered	$8.95	$15.00
Smith Distributors	Fun with Math	$12.95	$24.95
Smith Distributors	Geek Toys Guide	$5.10	$9.99
Smith Distributors	Paper Planes	$7.10	$13.99
Smith Distributors	Slime Time	$15.35	$24.99

Figure 2–91

Continued >

12. Create a query for the Item table that includes the Item Number, Description, Wholesale Cost, and Retail Price. Calculate the difference between Retail Price and Wholesale Cost (Retail Price – Wholesale Cost). Assign the alias Mark Up to the calculated field. Save the query as Lab 2-2 Step 12 Query.

13. Create a query for the Item table that displays the average Wholesale Cost and the average Retail Price of all items. Save the query as Lab 2-2 Step 13 Query.

14. Create a query for the Item table that displays the Item Number, Description, On Hand, and Retail Price for the 5 items with the lowest retail price. Save the query as Lab 2-2 Step 14 Query.

15. Submit the revised database in the format specified by your instructor.

16. ✷ How could you modify the query in step 2 to find all vendors where the vendor code is AW or GS? If there is more than one way to perform this query, list all ways.

Lab 3: **Consider This: Your Turn**

Querying the Camshay Marketing Database

Instructions: Open the Lab 3 Camshay Marketing database you created in Module 1. If you did not create this database, contact your instructor for information about accessing the required files.

Part 1:   Use the concepts and techniques presented in this module to create queries for the following. Save each query.

a.   Find all marketing analysts who started between June 1, 2015 and September 30, 2015. Show the marketing analyst's first name, last name, salary YTD, and incentive YTD.

b.   Find the client name and street address of all clients located in a city that starts with Bu.

c.   Find the client number, client name, amount paid and current due of all clients whose amount paid is $0.00 or whose current due is $0.00.

d.   Find the client number, client name, amount paid, current due, and total amount for all clients located in North Carolina (NC).

e.   Create a parameter query for the Client table that will allow the user to enter a different city each time the query is run. The user should see all fields in the query result.

f.   Create a crosstab query that groups the amount paid total by city and marketing analyst.

g.   Find the marketing analyst for each client. List the marketing analyst number, first name, last name, client number, client name, and current due. Sort the results by client number within marketing analyst number.

h.   Open the query you created in Step g above and restrict retrieval to only those clients whose current due amount is greater than $5,000.00.

i.   Change the organization of the Navigation Pane so that all objects associated with the Client table are grouped together and all objects associated with the Marketing Analyst are grouped together.

Submit your assignment in the format specified by your instructor.

Part 2:   You made several decisions while creating the queries in this assignment, including the parameter query in Step e. What was the rationale behind your decisions? There are two ways to create the query in step e. What are they? Which one did you use?

3 | Maintaining a Database

Objectives

You will have mastered the material in this module when you can:

- Add, change, and delete records
- Search for records
- Filter records
- Update a table design
- Use action queries to update records
- Use delete queries to delete records
- Specify validation rules, default values, and formats

- Create and use single-value lookup fields
- Create and use multivalued lookup fields
- Add new fields to an existing report
- Format a datasheet
- Specify referential integrity
- Use a subdatasheet
- Sort records

Introduction

Once you have created a database and loaded it with data, you must maintain it. **Maintaining the database** means modifying the data to keep it up to date by adding new records, changing the data for existing records, and deleting records. Updating can include mass updates or mass deletions (i.e., updates to, or deletions of, many records at the same time).

Maintenance of a database can also involve the need to **restructure the database** periodically. Restructuring can include adding new fields to a table, changing the characteristics of existing fields, and removing existing fields. Restructuring also includes the creation of validation rules and referential integrity. Validation rules ensure the validity of the data in the database, whereas referential integrity ensures the validity of the relationships between entities. Maintaining a database can also include filtering records, a process that ensures that only the records that satisfy some criterion appear when viewing and updating the data in a table. Changing the appearance of a datasheet is also a maintenance activity.

Project — Maintaining a Database

PrattLast Associates faces the task of keeping its database up to date. As the company takes on new accounts and account managers, it will need to add new records, make changes to existing records, and delete records. PrattLast believes that it can serve its

BTW
Organizing Files and Folders
You should organize and store files in folders so that you easily can find the files later. For example, if you are taking an introductory computer class called CIS 101, a good practice would be to save all Access files in an Access folder in a CIS 101 folder. For a discussion of folders and detailed examples of creating folders, refer to the Office and Windows module at the beginning of this book.

For an introduction to Windows and instructions about how to perform basic Windows tasks, read the Office and Windows module at the beginning of this book, where you can learn how to resize windows, change screen resolution, create folders, move and rename files, use Windows Help, and much more.

accounts better by changing the structure of the database to categorize the accounts by type. The company will do this by adding an Account Type field to the Account table. Account managers also believe they can provide better customer service if the database includes the list of human resource services that are of interest to each account. The company will do so by adding a Services Needed field to the Account table. Because accounts may need more than one service, this field will be a multivalued field, which is a field that can store multiple values or entries. Along with these changes, PrattLast staff wants to change the appearance of a datasheet when displaying data.

PrattLast would like the ability to make mass updates, that is, to update or delete many records in a single operation. It wants rules that make sure users can enter only valid, or appropriate, data into the database. PrattLast also wants to ensure that the database cannot contain the name of an account that is not associated with a specific account manager.

Figure 3–1 summarizes some of the various types of activities involved in maintaining the PrattLast Associates database.

Figure 3–1

For an introduction to Office and instructions about how to perform basic tasks in Office apps, read the Office and Windows module at the beginning of this book, where you can learn how to run an application, use the ribbon, save a file, open a file, print a file, exit an application, use Help, and much more.

In this module, you will learn how to maintain a database by performing the tasks shown in Figure 3–1. The following roadmap identifies general activities you will perform as you progress through this module:

1. UPDATE RECORDS using a form.

2. FILTER RECORDS using various filtering options.

3. CHANGE the STRUCTURE of a table.

4. Make MASS CHANGES to a table.

5. Create VALIDATION RULES.

6. CHANGE the APPEARANCE of a datasheet.

7. Specify REFERENTIAL INTEGRITY.

8. ORDER RECORDS in a datasheet.

Updating Records

Keeping the data in a database current requires updating records in three ways: adding new records, changing the data in existing records, and deleting existing records. In Module 1, you added records to a database using Datasheet view; that is, as you added records, the records appeared on the screen in a datasheet. The data looked like a table. When you need to add additional records, you can use the same techniques.

In Module 1, you used a simple form to view records. You can also use a **split form**, a form that allows you to simultaneously view both simple form and datasheet views of the data. You can use either portion of a split form to add or update records. To add new records, change existing records, or delete records, you use the same techniques you used in Datasheet view.

BTW
The Ribbon and Screen Resolution
Access may change how the groups and buttons within the groups appear on the ribbon, depending on the computer or mobile device's screen resolution. Thus, your ribbon may look different from the ones in this book if you are using a screen resolution other than 1366 x 768.

To Create a Split Form

1 UPDATE RECORDS | 2 FILTER RECORDS | 3 CHANGE STRUCTURE | 4 MASS CHANGES | 5 VALIDATION RULES
6 CHANGE APPEARANCE | 7 REFERENTIAL INTEGRITY | 8 ORDER RECORDS

The following steps create a split form. *Why? With a split form, you have the advantage of seeing a single record in a form, while simultaneously viewing several records in a datasheet.*

- Run Access and open the database named PrattLast Associates from your hard disk, OneDrive, or other storage location.

- Open the Navigation Pane if it is currently closed.

- If necessary, click the Account table in the Navigation Pane to select it.

- Click Create on the ribbon to display the Create tab.

- Click the More Forms button (Create tab | Forms group) to display the More Forms menu (Figure 3–2).

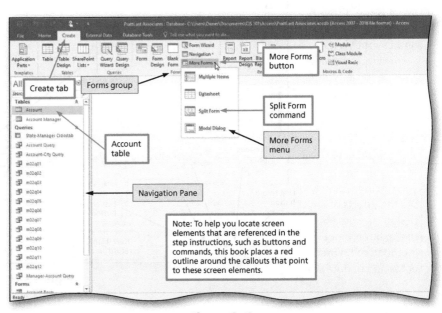

Figure 3–2

2

- Click Split Form to create a split form based on the Account table.
- Close the Navigation Pane (Figure 3–3).

Q&A Is the form automatically saved?
No. You will take specific actions later to save the form.

Q&A A field list appeared when I created the form. What should I do?
Click the 'Add Existing Fields' button (Design tab | Tools group) to remove the field list.

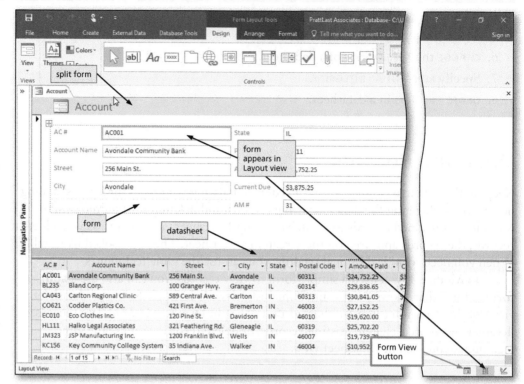

Figure 3–3

3

- Click the Form View button on the Access status bar to display the form in Form view rather than Layout view (Figure 3–4).

Q&A What is the difference between Form view and Layout view?
Form view is the view you use to view, enter, and update data. Layout view is the view you use to make design changes to the form. It shows you the form with data in it so you can immediately see the effects of any design changes you make, but it is not intended to be used to enter and update data.

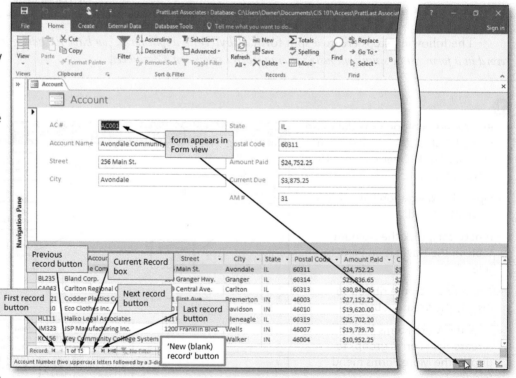

Figure 3–4

Experiment

- Click the various Navigation buttons (First record, Next record, Previous record, Last record, and 'New (blank) record') to see each button's effect. Click the Current Record box, change the record number, and press the ENTER key to see how to move to a specific record.

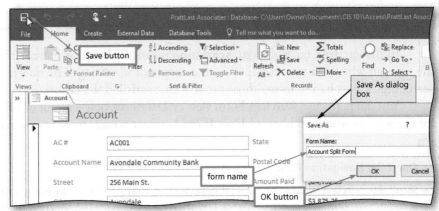

④
- Click the Save button on the Quick Access Toolbar to display the Save As dialog box.
- Type **Account Split Form** as the form name (Figure 3–5).

⑤
- Click the OK button (Save As dialog box) to save the form.

Figure 3–5

Other Ways

1. Right-click tab for form, click Form View on shortcut menu

To Use a Form to Add Records

1 UPDATE RECORDS | 2 FILTER RECORDS | 3 CHANGE STRUCTURE | 4 MASS CHANGES | 5 VALIDATION RULES
6 CHANGE APPEARANCE | 7 REFERENTIAL INTEGRITY | 8 ORDER RECORDS

Once a form or split form is open in Form view, you can add records using the same techniques you used to add records in Datasheet view. In a split form, the changes you make on the form are automatically made on the datasheet. You do not need to take any special action. The following steps use the split form that you just created to add records. *Why? With a split form, as you add a record, you can immediately see the effect of the addition on the datasheet.*

①
- Click the 'New (blank) record' button on the Navigation bar to enter a new record, and then type the data for the new record, as shown in Figure 3–6. Press the TAB key after typing the data in each field, except after typing the data for the final field (Account Manager Number).

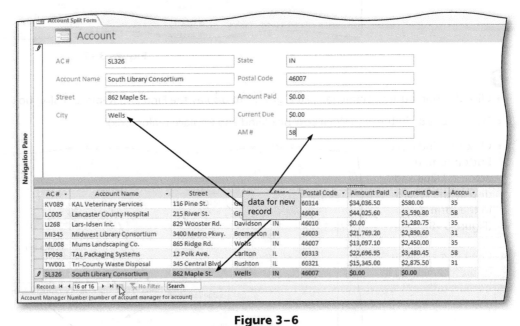

Figure 3–6

②
- Press the TAB key to complete the entry of the record.
- Close the form.

Other Ways

1. Click New button (Home tab | Records group)   2. Press CTRL+PLUS SIGN (+)

To Search for a Record

In the database environment, **searching** means looking for records that satisfy some criteria. Looking for the account whose number is LI268 is an example of searching. The queries in Module 2 were also examples of searching. Access had to locate those records that satisfied the criteria.

You can perform a search in Form view or Datasheet view without creating a query. The following steps search for the account whose number is LI268. *Why? You want to locate the record quickly so you can update this account's record.*

1

- Open the Navigation Pane.
- Scroll down in the Navigation Pane, if necessary, so that Account Split Form appears on your screen, right-click Account Split Form to display a shortcut menu, and then click Open on the shortcut menu to open the form in Form view.

Q&A Which command on the shortcut menu gives me Form view? I see both Layout View and Design View, but no option for Form View.
The Open command opens the form in Form view.

- Close the Navigation Pane (Figure 3–7).

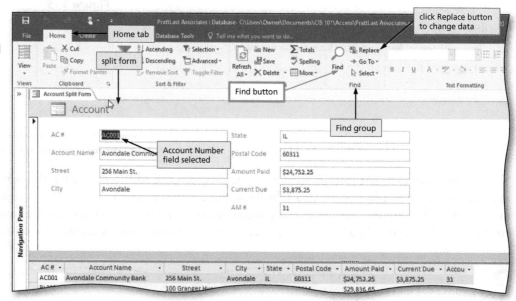

Figure 3–7

2

- Click the Find button (Home tab | Find group) to display the Find and Replace dialog box.
- Type **LI268** in the Find What text box (Find and Replace dialog box).
- Click the Find Next button to find account LI268 and display the record in the form (Figure 3–8).

Q&A Can I find records using this method in both Datasheet view and Form view?
Yes. You use the same process to find records whether you are viewing the data with a split form, in Datasheet view, or in Form view.

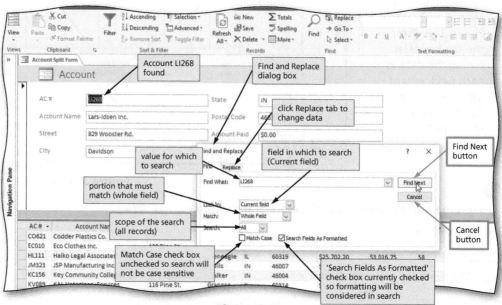

Figure 3–8

3

- Click the Cancel button (Find and Replace dialog box) to remove the dialog box from the screen.

Q&A

Why does the button in the dialog box read, Find Next, rather than simply Find?
In some cases, after locating a record that satisfies a criterion, you might need to find the next record that satisfies the same criterion. For example, if you just found the first account whose account manager number is 31, you might then want to find the second such account, then the third, and so on. To do so, click the Find Next button. You will not need to retype the value each time.

Other Ways
1. Press CTRL+F

Can you replace one value with another using the Find and Replace dialog box?
Yes. Either click the Replace button (Home tab | Find group) or click the Replace tab in the Find and Replace dialog box. You can then enter both the value to find and the new value.

To Update the Contents of a Record

1 UPDATE RECORDS | 2 FILTER RECORDS | 3 CHANGE STRUCTURE | 4 MASS CHANGES | 5 VALIDATION RULES
6 CHANGE APPEARANCE | 7 REFERENTIAL INTEGRITY | 8 ORDER RECORDS

The following step uses Form view to change the name of account LI268 from Lars-Idsen Inc. to Lars-Idsen-Fleming Inc. *Why? PrattLast determined that this account's name was incorrect and must be changed.* After locating the record to be changed, select the field to be changed by clicking the field. You can also press the TAB key repeatedly until the desired field is selected. Then make the appropriate changes. (Clicking the field automatically produces an insertion point. If you use the TAB key, you will need to press the F2 key to produce an insertion point.)

1

- Click in the Account Name field in the form for account LI268 immediately to the right of the n in Idsen.

- Type a hyphen (-) and then type **Fleming** after Idsen.

- Press the TAB key to complete the change and move to the next field (Figure 3–9).

Q&A

Could I have changed the contents of the field in the datasheet portion of the split form?
Yes. You first need to ensure the record to be changed appears in the datasheet. You then can change the value just as in the form.

Do I need to save my change?
No. Once you move to another record or close this form, the change to the name will become permanent.

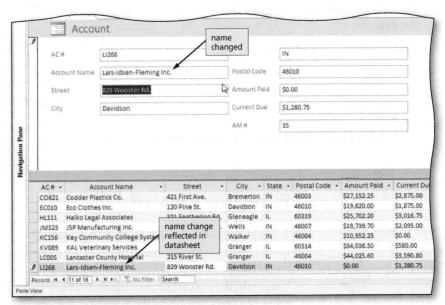

Figure 3–9

To Delete a Record

When records are no longer needed, you should delete the records (remove them) from the table. The following steps delete account JM323. *Why? Account JM323 is no longer served by PrattLast Associates and its final payment has been received, so the record can be deleted.*

1

• With the Account Split Form open, click the record selector in the datasheet for account JM323 to select the record (Figure 3–10).

Q&A That technique works in the datasheet portion. How do I select the record in the form portion?
With the desired record appearing in the form, click the record selector (the triangle in front of the record) to select the entire record.

Q&A What do I do if the record I want to delete does not appear on the screen?
First search for the record you want to delete using the Find and Replace dialog box.

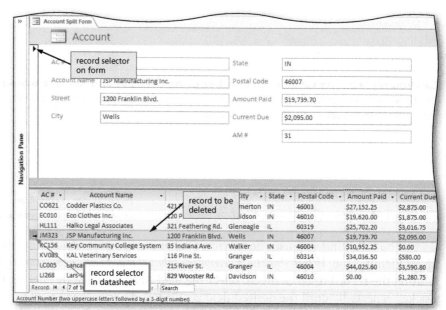

Figure 3–10

2

• Press the DELETE key to delete the record (Figure 3–11).

3

• Click the Yes button to complete the deletion.

• Close the Account Split Form.

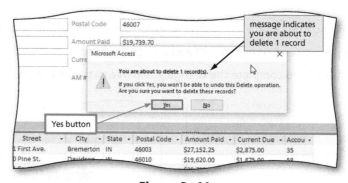

Figure 3–11

Other Ways

1. Click Delete arrow (Home tab | Records group), click Delete Record on Delete menu

---

Filtering Records

You can use the Find button in either Datasheet view or Form view to locate a record quickly that satisfies some criterion (for example, the account number is LI268). All records appear, however, not just the record or records that satisfy the criterion. To have only the record or records that satisfy the criterion appear, use a **filter**. Four types of filters are available: Filter By Selection, Common Filters, Filter By Form, and Advanced Filter/Sort. You can use a filter in either Datasheet view or Form view.

To Use Filter By Selection

To use Filter By Selection, you give Access an example of the data you want by selecting the data within the table. You then choose the option you want on the Selection menu. The following steps use Filter By Selection in Datasheet view to display only the records for accounts in Granger. *Why? Filter by Selection is appropriate for displaying these records and is the simplest type of filter.*

1

- Open the Navigation Pane.
- Open the Account table, and close the Navigation Pane.
- Click the City field on the second record to specify Granger as the city (Figure 3–12).

Q&A Could I have selected the City field on another record where the city is also Granger to select the same city?
Yes. It does not matter which record you select as long as the city is Granger.

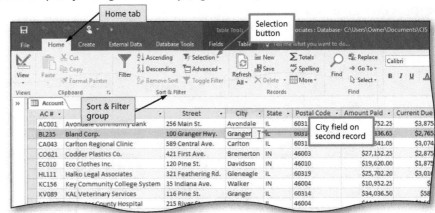

Figure 3–12

2

- Click the Selection button (Home tab | Sort & Filter group) to display the Selection menu (Figure 3–13).

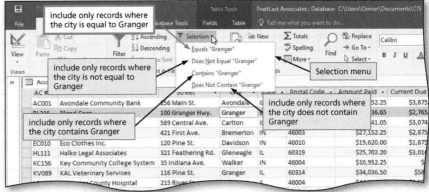

Figure 3–13

3

- Click Equals "Granger" to select only those accounts whose city is Granger (Figure 3–14).

Q&A Can I also filter in Form view?
Yes. Filtering works the same whether you are viewing the data with a split form, in Datasheet view, or in Form view.

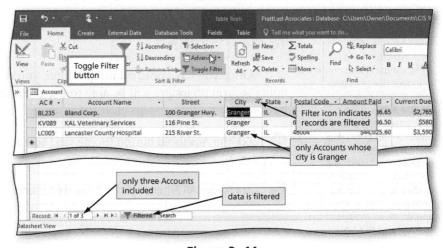

Figure 3–14

1 UPDATE RECORDS | 2 FILTER RECORDS | 3 CHANGE STRUCTURE | 4 MASS CHANGES | 5 VALIDATION RULES
6 CHANGE APPEARANCE | 7 REFERENTIAL INTEGRITY | 8 ORDER RECORDS

To Toggle a Filter

The Toggle Filter button toggles between filtered and unfiltered displays of the records in the table. That is, if only filtered records currently appear, clicking the Toggle Filter button will redisplay all records. If all records are currently displayed and there is a filter that is in effect, clicking the Toggle Filter button will display only the filtered records. If no filter is active, the Toggle Filter button will be dimmed, so clicking it would have no effect.

The following step toggles the filter. *Why? PrattLast wants to once again view all the records.*

1

- Click the Toggle Filter button (Home tab | Sort & Filter group) to toggle the filter and redisplay all records (Figure 3–15).

Q&A Does that action clear the filter?

No. The filter is still in place. If you click the Toggle Filter button a second time, you will again see only the filtered records.

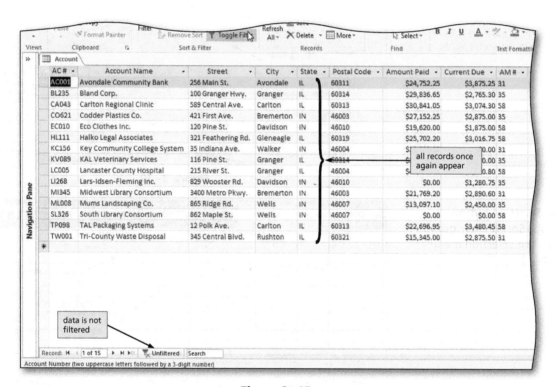

Figure 3–15

BTW

Access Screen Resolution
If you are using a computer or mobile device to step through the project in this module and you want your screens to match the figures in this book, you should change your screen's resolution to 1366 x 768. For information about how to change a computer's resolution, refer to the Office and Windows module at the beginning of this book.

To Clear a Filter

Once you have finished using a filter, you can clear (remove) the filter. After doing so, you no longer will be able to use the filter by clicking the Toggle Filter button. The following steps clear the filter.

1 Click the Advanced button (Home tab | Sort & Filter group) to display the Advanced menu.

2 Click 'Clear All Filters' on the Advanced menu.

To Use a Common Filter

If you have determined you want to include those accounts whose city begins with G, Filter By Selection would not be appropriate. *Why? None of the options within Filter by Selection would support this type of criterion.* You can filter individual fields by clicking the arrow to the right of the field name and using one of the **common filters** that are available for the field. Access includes a collection of filters that perform common filtering tasks; you can modify a common filter by customizing it for the specific field. The following steps customize a common filter to include only those accounts whose city begins with G.

- Click the City arrow to display the common filter menu.
- Point to the Text Filters command to display the custom text filters (Figure 3–16).

Q&A I selected the City field and then clicked the Filter button on the Home tab | Sort & Filter group. My screen looks the same. Is this right?
Yes. That is another way to display the common filter menu.

Q&A If I wanted certain cities included, could I use the check boxes?
Yes. Be sure the cities you want are the only ones checked.

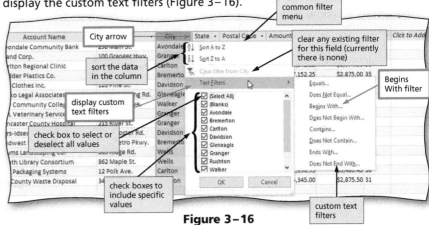

Figure 3–16

❷

- Click Begins With to display the Custom Filter dialog box.
- Type G as the 'City begins with' value (Figure 3–17).

Experiment

- Try other options in the common filter menu to see their effects. When done, once again select those accounts whose city begins with G.

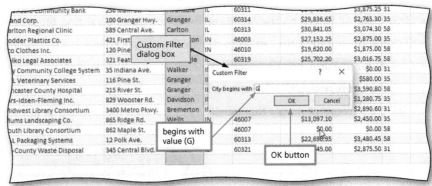

Figure 3–17

❸

- Click the OK button to filter the records (Figure 3–18).

Q&A Can I use the same technique in Form view?
In Form view, you would need to click the field and then click the Filter button to display the Common Filter menu. The rest of the process would be the same.

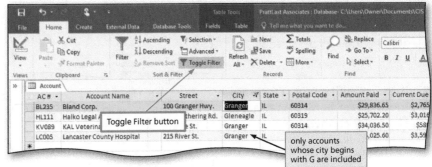

Figure 3–18

❹

- Click the Toggle Filter button (Home tab | Sort & Filter group) to toggle the filter and redisplay all records.

Other Ways

1. Right-click field, click Text Filters on shortcut menu

To Use Filter By Form

Filter By Selection and the common filters method you just used are quick and easy ways to filter by the value in a single field. For filters that involve multiple fields, however, these methods are not appropriate, so you would use Filter By Form. **Why?** *Filter By Form allows you to filter based on multiple fields and criteria.* For example, Filter By Form would allow you to find only those accounts whose current due amounts are less than $2,000.00 and whose account manager number is 35. The following steps use Filter By Form to restrict the records that appear.

1

- Click the Advanced button (Home tab | Sort & Filter group) to display the Advanced menu (Figure 3–19).

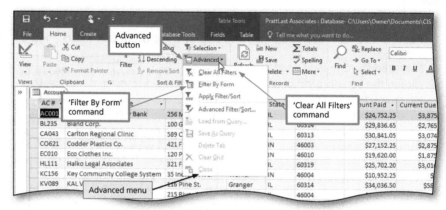

Figure 3–19

2

- Click 'Clear All Filters' on the Advanced menu to clear the existing filter.
- Click the Advanced button again to display the Advanced menu a second time.
- Click 'Filter By Form' on the Advanced menu.
- Click the blank row in the Current Due field, and then type `<2000` to enter a criterion for the Current Due field.
- Click the Account Manager Number (AM #) field, click the arrow that appears, and then click 35 (Figure 3–20).

Q&A Could I have clicked the arrow in the Current Due field and then made a selection rather than typing a criterion?

No. Because your criterion involves something other than equality, you need to type the criterion rather than selecting from a list.

Q&A Is there any difference in the process if I am viewing a table in Form view rather than in Datasheet view?

In Form view, you will make your entries in a form rather than a datasheet. Otherwise, the process is the same.

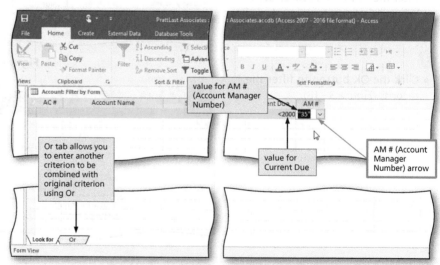

Figure 3–20

● Click the Toggle Filter button (Home tab | Sort & Filter group) to apply the filter (Figure 3–21).

Experiment

● Select 'Filter by Form' again and enter different criteria. In each case, toggle the filter to see the effect of your selection. When done, once again select those accounts whose Current Due amounts are less than (<) 2000 and whose account manager number is 35.

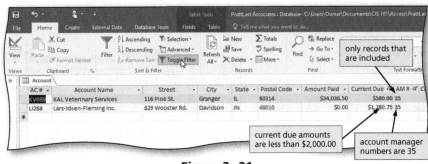

Figure 3–21

Other Ways

1. Click the Advanced button (Home tab | Sort & Filter group), click Apply Filter/Sort on Advanced menu

---

To Use Advanced Filter/Sort

1 UPDATE RECORDS | 2 FILTER RECORDS | 3 CHANGE STRUCTURE | 4 MASS CHANGES | 5 VALIDATION RULES
6 CHANGE APPEARANCE | 7 REFERENTIAL INTEGRITY | 8 ORDER RECORDS

In some cases, your criteria will be too complex even for Filter By Form. You might decide you want to include any account whose current due amounts are greater than $3,000 and whose account manager number is 58. Additionally, you might want to include any account whose current due amount is $0, no matter who the account's manager is. Further, you might want to have the results sorted by account name. The following steps use Advanced Filter/Sort to accomplish this task. *Why? Advanced Filter/Sort supports complex criteria as well as the ability to sort the results.*

● Click the Advanced button (Home tab | Sort & Filter group) to display the Advanced menu, and then click 'Clear All Filters' on the Advanced menu to clear the existing filter.

● Click the Advanced button to display the Advanced menu a second time.

● Click 'Advanced Filter/Sort' on the Advanced menu.

● Expand the size of the field list so all the fields in the Account table appear.

● Add the Account Name field and select Ascending as the sort order to specify the order in which the filtered records will appear.

● Include the Account Manager Number field and enter 58 as the criterion.

● Include the Current Due field and enter >3000 as the criterion in the Criteria row and 0 as the criterion in the or row (Figure 3–22).

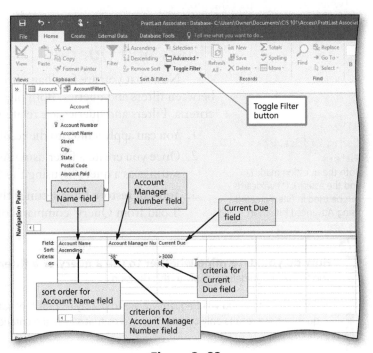

Figure 3–22

2

- Click the Toggle Filter button (Home tab | Sort & Filter group) to toggle the filter so that only records that satisfy the criteria will appear (Figure 3–23).

 Why are those particular records included?

The first, second, fourth, and sixth records are included because the account manager number is 58 and the current due amount is greater than $3,000. The other records are included because the current due amount is $0.00.

 Experiment

- Select 'Advanced Filter/Sort' again and enter different sorting options and criteria. In each case, toggle the filter to see the effect of your selection. When done, change back to the sorting options and criteria you entered in Step 1.

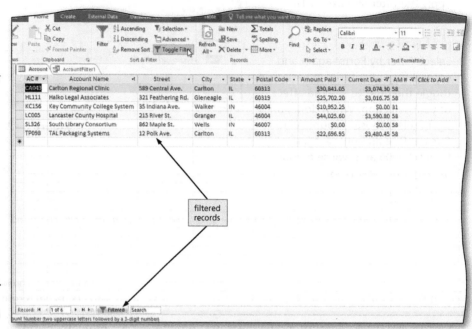

Figure 3–23

3

- Close the Account table. When asked if you want to save your changes, click the No button.

 Should I not have cleared all filters before closing the table?

If you are closing a table and not saving the changes, it is not necessary to clear the filter. No filter will be active when you next open the table.

Filters and Queries

Now that you are familiar with how filters work, you might notice similarities between filters and queries. Both objects are used to locate data that meets specific criteria. Filters and queries are related in three ways.

BTW
Using Wildcards in Filters
Both the question mark(?) and the asterisk (*) wildcards can be used in filters created using Advanced Filter/Sort.

1. You can apply a filter to the results of a query just as you can apply a filter to a table.
2. Once you create a filter using Advanced Filter/Sort, you can save the filter settings as a query by using the 'Save as Query' command on the Advanced menu.
3. You can restore filter settings that you previously saved in a query by using the 'Load from Query' command on the Advanced menu.

 CONSIDER THIS

How do you determine whether to use a query or a filter?
The following guidelines apply to this decision.

- If you think that you will frequently want to display records that satisfy this exact criterion, you should consider creating a query whose results only contain the records that satisfy the criterion. To display those records in the future, simply open the query.

- If you are viewing data in a datasheet or form and decide you want to restrict the records to be included, it is easier to create a filter than a query. You can create and use the filter while you are viewing the data.

- If you have created a filter that you would like to be able to use again, you can save the filter as a query.

Once you have decided to use a filter, how do you determine which type of filter to use?

- If your criterion for filtering is that the value in a particular field matches or does not match a certain specific value, you can use Filter By Selection.
- If your criterion only involves a single field but is more complex (for example, the criterion specifies that the value in the field begins with a certain collection of letters) you can use a common filter.
- If your criterion involves more than one field, use Filter By Form.
- If your criterion involves more than a single And or Or, or if it involves sorting, you will probably find it simpler to use Advanced Filter/Sort.

Break Point: If you wish to take a break, this is a good place to do so. You can quit Access now. To resume at a later time, run Access, open the database called PrattLast Associates, and continue following the steps from this location forward.

Changing the Database Structure

When you initially create a database, you define its **structure**; that is, you assign names and types to all the fields. In many cases, the structure you first define will not continue to be appropriate as you use the database.

Perhaps a field currently in the table is no longer necessary. If no one ever uses a particular field, it is not needed in the table. Because it is occupying space and serving no useful purpose, you should remove it from the table. You would also need to delete the field from any forms, reports, or queries that include it.

More commonly, an organization will find that it needs to add data that was not anticipated at the time the database was first designed. The organization's own requirements may have changed. In addition, outside regulations that the organization must satisfy may change as well. Either case requires the addition of fields to an existing table.

Although you can make some changes to the database structure in Datasheet view, it is usually easier and better to make these changes in Design view.

TO DELETE A FIELD

If a field in one of your tables is no longer needed, you should delete the field; for example, it may serve no useful purpose, or it may have been included by mistake. To delete a field, you would use the following steps.

1. Open the table in Design view.
2. Click the row selector for the field to be deleted.
3. Press the DELETE key.
4. When Access displays the dialog box requesting confirmation that you want to delete the field, click the Yes button.

TO MOVE A FIELD

If you decide you would rather have a field in one of your tables in a different position in the table, you can move it. To move a field, you would use the following steps.

1. Open the table in Design view.
2. Click the row selector for the field to be deleted.
3. Drag the field to the desired position.
4. Release the mouse button to place the field in the new position.

BTW
Using the Find Button
You can use the Find button (Home tab | Find group) to search for records in datasheets, forms, query results, and reports.

BTW
Changing Data Types
It is possible to change the data type for a field that already contains data. Before doing so, you should consider the effect on other database objects, such as forms, queries, and reports. For example, you could convert a Short Text field to a Long Text field if you find that you do not have enough space to store the data that you need. You also could convert a Number field to a Currency field or vice versa.

To Add a New Field

You can add fields to a table in a database. The following steps add the Account Type field to the Account table immediately after the Postal Code field. *Why? PrattLast Associates has decided that it needs to categorize its accounts by adding an additional field, Account Type. The possible values for Account Type are SER (which indicates the account is a service organization), NON (which indicates the account is a nonprofit), or IND (which indicates the account is an industrial/manufacturing company).*

- If necessary, open the Navigation Pane, open the Account table in Design view, and then close the Navigation Pane.
- Right-click the row selector for the Amount Paid field, and then click Insert Rows on the shortcut menu to insert a blank row above the selected field (Figure 3–24).

- Click the Field Name column for the new field to produce an insertion point.
- Type **Account Type** as the field name and then press the TAB key.

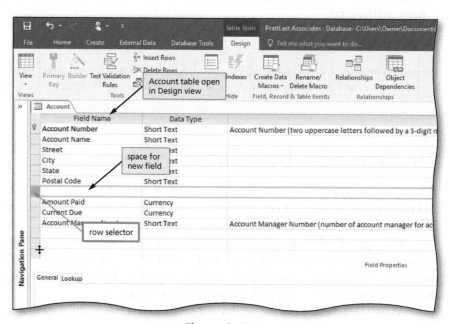

Figure 3–24

Other Ways

1. Click Insert Rows button (Table Tools Design tab | Tools group)

To Create a Lookup Field

A **lookup field** allows the user to select from a list of values when updating the contents of the field. The following steps make the Account Type field a lookup field. *Why? The Account Type field has only three possible values, making it an appropriate lookup field.*

- If necessary, click the Data Type column for the Account Type field, and then click the Data Type arrow to display the menu of available data types (Figure 3–25).

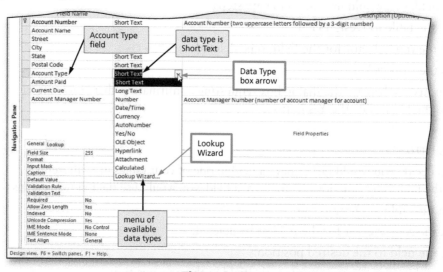

Figure 3–25

2

- Click Lookup Wizard, and then click the 'I will type in the values that I want.' option button (Lookup Wizard dialog box) to indicate that you will type in the values (Figure 3–26).

Q&A
When would I use the other option button?
You would use the other option button if the data to be entered in this field were found in another table or query.

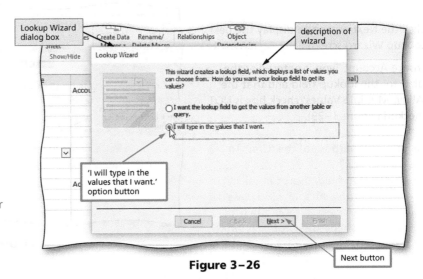

Figure 3–26

3

- Click the Next button to display the next Lookup Wizard screen (Figure 3–27).

Q&A
Why did I not change the field size for the Account Type field?
You could have changed the field size to 3, but it is not necessary. When you create a lookup field and indicate specific values for the field, you automatically restrict the field size.

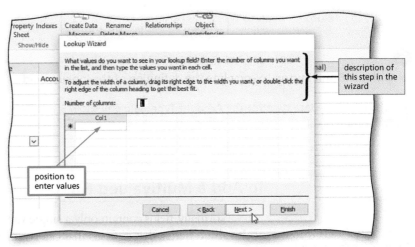

Figure 3–27

4

- Click the first row of the table (below Col1), and then type SER as the value in the first row.

- Press the DOWN ARROW key, and then type NON as the value in the second row.

- Press the DOWN ARROW key, and then type IND as the value in the third row (Figure 3–28).

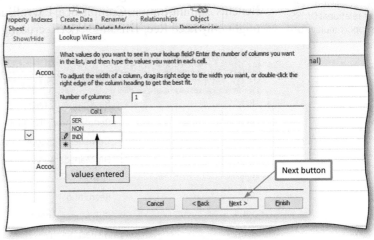

Figure 3–28

5

- Click the Next button to display the next Lookup Wizard screen.

- Ensure Account Type is entered as the label for the lookup field and that the 'Allow Multiple Values' check box is NOT checked (Figure 3–29).

 What is the purpose of the 'Limit To List' check box?

With a lookup field, users can select from the list of values, in which case they can only select items in the list. They can also type their entry, in which case they are not necessarily limited to items in the list. If you check the 'Limit To List' check box, users would be limited to items in the list, even if they type their entry. You will accomplish this same restriction later in this module with a validation rule, so you do not need to check this box.

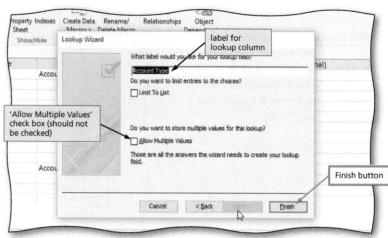

Figure 3–29

6

- Click the Finish button to complete the definition of the lookup field.

 Why does the data type for the Account Type field still show Short Text?

The data type is still Short Text because the values entered in the wizard were entered as text.

To Add a Multivalued Field

Normally, fields contain only a single value. In Access, it is possible to have **multivalued fields**, that is, fields that can contain more than one value. PrattLast Associates wants to use such a field to store the abbreviations of the various services its accounts need (see Table 3–1 for the service abbreviations and descriptions). Unlike the Account Type, where each account had only one type, accounts can require multiple services. One account might need Bck, Ben, Com, Pay, and Rsk (Background Checks, Benefits Administration, Compliance, Payroll, and Risk Management). Another account might only need Rec, Trn, and Wrk (Recruiting, Training, and Workman's Compensation).

Table 3–1 Service Abbreviations and Descriptions	
Service Abbreviation	**Description**
Bck	Background Checks
Ben	Benefits Administration
Com	Compliance (Regulatory)
Mgt	HR Management
Pay	Payroll
Rec	Recruiting
Rsk	Risk Management
Tch	HR Technology
Trn	Training
Wrk	Workman's Compensation

Creating a multivalued field uses the same process as creating a lookup field, with the exception that you check the 'Allow Multiple Values' check box. The following steps create a multivalued field.

1 Right-click the row selector for the Amount Paid field, and then click Insert Rows on the shortcut menu to insert a blank row.

2 Click the Field Name column for the new field, type `Services Needed` as the field name, and then press the TAB key.

3 Click the Data Type arrow to display the menu of available data types for the Services Needed field, and then click Lookup Wizard in the menu of available data types to start the Lookup Wizard.

4 Click the 'I will type in the values that I want.' option button to indicate that you will type in the values.

5 Click the Next button to display the next Lookup Wizard screen.

6 Click the first row of the table (below Col1), and then type `Bck` as the value in the first row.

7 Enter the remaining values from the first column in Table 3–1. Before typing each value, press the DOWN ARROW key to move to a new row.

8 Click the Next button to display the next Lookup Wizard screen.

9 Ensure that Services Needed is entered as the label for the lookup field.

10 Click the 'Allow Multiple Values' check box to allow the user to enter multiple values.

11 Click the Finish button to complete the definition of the Lookup Wizard field.

To Modify Single Valued or Multivalued Lookup Fields

At some point you might want to change the list of choices in a lookup field. If you need to modify a single value or multivalued lookup field, you would use the following steps.

1. Open the table in Design view and select the field to be modified.
2. Click the Lookup tab in the Field Properties pane.
3. Change the list in the Row Source property to the desired list of values.

To Add a Calculated Field

1 UPDATE RECORDS | 2 FILTER RECORDS | 3 CHANGE STRUCTURE | 4 MASS CHANGES | 5 VALIDATION RULES
6 CHANGE APPEARANCE | 7 REFERENTIAL INTEGRITY | 8 ORDER RECORDS

A field that can be computed from other fields is called a **calculated field** or a **computed field**. In Module 2, you created a calculated field in a query that provided total amount data. In Access 2016, it is also possible to include a calculated field in a table. Users will not be able to update this field. *Why? Access will automatically perform the necessary calculation and display the correct value whenever you display or use this field in any way.* The following steps add to the Account table a field that calculates the sum of the Amount Paid and Current Due fields.

1

- Right-click the row selector for the Account Manager Number field, and then click Insert Rows on the shortcut menu to insert a blank row above the selected field.
- Click the Field Name column for the new field.
- Type `Total Amount` as the field name, and then press the TAB key.

BTW

Modifying Table Properties
You can change the properties of a table by opening the table in Design view and then clicking the Property Sheet button. To display the records in a table in an order other than primary key (the default sort order), use the Order By property. For example, to display the Account table automatically in Account Name order, change the Order By property setting to Account.Account Name in the property box, close the property sheet, and save the change to the table design. When you open the Account table in Datasheet view, the records will be sorted in Account Name order.

BTW

Calculated Fields
You can use the Result Type field property to format the calculated field values.

- Click the Data Type arrow to display the menu of available data types (Figure 3–30).

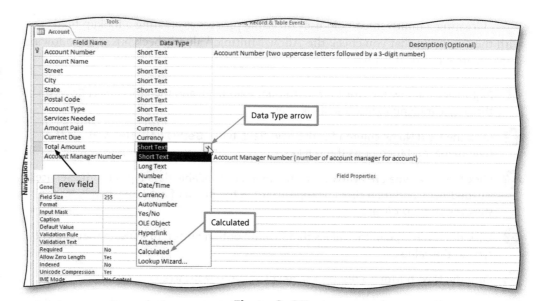

Figure 3–30

2
- Click Calculated to select the Calculated data type and display the Expression Builder dialog box (Figure 3–31).

 I do not have the list of fields in the Expression Categories area. What should I do? Click Account in the Expression Elements area.

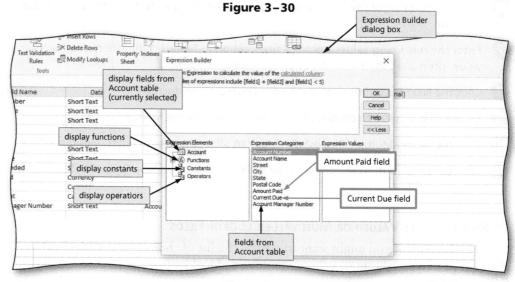

Figure 3–31

3
- Double-click the Amount Paid field in the Expression Categories area (Expression Builder dialog box) to add the field to the expression.

- Type a plus sign (+).

Q&A Could I select the plus sign from a list rather than typing it? Yes. Click Operators in the Expression Elements area to display available operators, and then double-click the plus sign.

- Double-click the Current Due field in the Expression Categories area (Expression Builder dialog box) to add the field to the expression (Figure 3–32).

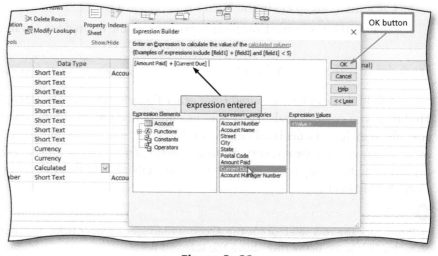

Figure 3–32

4

- Click the OK button (Expression Builder dialog box) to enter the expression in the Expression property of the Total Amount (Figure 3–33).

Q&A Could I have typed the expression in the Expression Builder dialog box rather than selecting the fields from a list?
Yes. You can use whichever technique you find more convenient.

Q&A When I entered a calculated field in a query, I typed the expression in the Zoom dialog box. Could I have used the Expression Builder instead?
Yes. To do so, you would click Build rather than Zoom on the shortcut menu.

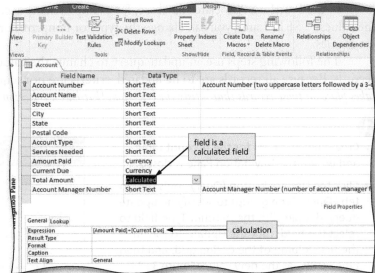

Figure 3–33

To Save the Changes and Close the Table

The following steps save the changes; that is, they save the addition of the new fields and close the table.

1 Click the Save button on the Quick Access Toolbar to save the changes.

2 Close the Account table.

Mass Changes

In some cases, rather than making individual changes to records, you will want to make mass changes. That is, you will want to add, change, or delete many records in a single operation. You can do this with action queries. Unlike the select queries that you created in Module 2, which simply presented data in specific ways, an **action query** adds, deletes, or changes data in a table. An **update query** allows you to make the same change to all records satisfying some criterion. If you omit the criterion, you will make the same changes to all records in the table. A **delete query** allows you to delete all the records satisfying some criterion. You can add the results of a query to an existing table by using an **append query**. You also can add the query results to a new table by using a **make-table query**.

BTW
Database Backup
If you are doing mass changes to a database, be sure to back up the database prior to doing the updates.

To Use an Update Query

1 UPDATE RECORDS | 2 FILTER RECORDS | 3 CHANGE STRUCTURE | 4 MASS CHANGES | 5 VALIDATION RULES
6 CHANGE APPEARANCE | 7 REFERENTIAL INTEGRITY | 8 ORDER RECORDS

The new Account Type field is blank on every record in the Account table. One approach to entering the information for the field would be to step through the entire table, assigning each record its appropriate value. If most of the accounts have the same type, it would be more convenient to use an update query to assign a single value to all accounts and then update the Account Type for those accounts whose type differs. An update query makes the same change to all records satisfying a criterion.

In the PrattLast Associates database, for example, many accounts are type SER. Initially, you can set all the values to SER. Later, you can change the type for nonprofit organizations and industrial/manufacturing companies.

The following steps use an update query to change the value in the Account Type field to SER for all the records. Because all records are to be updated, criteria are not required. ***Why? If there is a criterion, the update only takes place on those records that satisfy the criterion. Without a criterion, the update applies to all records.***

❶

- Create a new query for the Account table, and ensure the Navigation Pane is closed.

- Click the Update button (Query Tools Design tab | Query Type group) to specify an update query, double-click the Account Type field to select the field, click the Update To row in the first column of the design grid, and then type **SER** as the new value (Figure 3–34).

Q&A If I change my mind and do not want an update query, how can I change the query back to a select query?
Click the Select button (Query Tools Design tab | Query Type group).

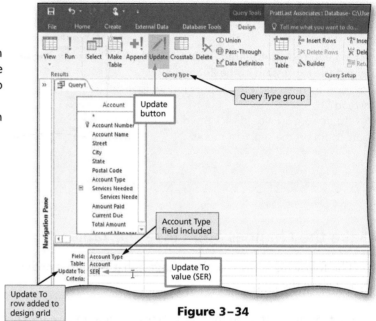

Figure 3–34

❷

- Click the Run button (Query Tools Design tab | Results group) to run the query and update the records (Figure 3–35).

Q&A The dialog box did not appear on my screen when I ran the query. What happened?
If the dialog box did not appear, it means that you did not click the Enable Content button when you first opened the database. Close the database, open it again, and enable the content. Then, create and run the query again.

❸

- Click the Yes button to make the changes.

Experiment

- Create an update query to change the account type to COM. Enter a criterion to restrict the records to be updated, and then run the query. Open the table to view your changes. When finished, create and run an update query to change the account type to SER on all records.

- Close the query. Because you do not need to use this update query again, do not save the query.

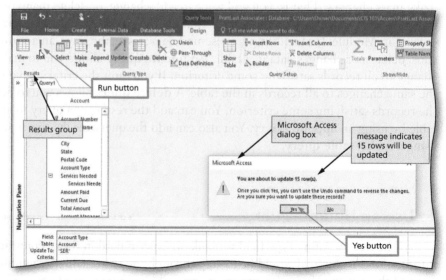

Figure 3–35

Other Ways

1. Right-click any open area in upper pane, point to Query Type on shortcut menu, click Update Query on Query Type submenu

TO USE A DELETE QUERY

In some cases, you might need to delete several records at a time. If, for example, PrattLast no longer services accounts in Indiana (IN), the accounts with this value in the State field can be deleted from the PrattLast Associates database. Instead of deleting these accounts individually, which could be very time-consuming in a large database, you can delete them in one operation by using a delete query, which is a query that deletes all the records satisfying the criteria entered in the query. To create a delete query, you would use the following steps.

1. Create a query for the table containing the records to be deleted.
2. In Design view, indicate the fields and criteria that will specify the records to delete.
3. Click the Delete button (Query Tools Design tab | Query Type group).
4. Run the query by clicking the Run button (Query Tools Design tab | Results group).
5. When Access indicates the number of records to be deleted, click the Yes button.

TO USE AN APPEND QUERY

An append query adds a group of records from one table, called the Source table, to the end of another table, called the Destination table. For example, suppose that PrattLast Associates acquires some new accounts; these new accounts are accompanied by a related database. To avoid entering all this information manually, you can append it to the Account table in the PrattLast Associates database using the append query. To create an append query, you would use the following steps.

1. Create a query for the Source table.
2. In Design view, indicate the fields to include, and then enter any necessary criteria.
3. View the query results to be sure you have specified the correct data, and then return to Design view.
4. Click the Append button (Query Tools Design tab | Query Type group).
5. When Access displays the Append dialog box, specify the name of the Destination table and its location. Run the query by clicking the Run button (Query Tools Design tab | Results group).
6. When Access indicates the number of records to be appended, click the OK button.

TO USE A MAKE-TABLE QUERY

In some cases, you might want to create a new table that contains only records from an existing table. If so, use a make-table query to add the records to a new table. To create a make-table query, you would use the following steps.

1. Create a query for the Source table.
2. In Design view, indicate the fields to include, and then enter any necessary criteria.
3. View the query results to be sure you have specified the correct data, and then return to Design view.
4. Click the Make Table button (Query Tools Design tab | Query Type group).
5. When Access displays the Make Table dialog box, specify the name of the Destination table and its location. Run the query by clicking the Run button (Query Tools Design tab | Results group).
6. When Access indicates the number of records to be inserted, click the OK button.

BTW

Viewing Records Before Updating
You can view records affected by an update query before running the query. To do so, use the Select button to convert the query to a select query, add any additional fields that would help you identify the records, and then view the results. Make any necessary corrections to the query in Design view. When you are satisfied, use the Update button to once again convert the query to an update query.

BTW

Delete Queries
If you do not specify any criteria in a delete query, Access will delete all the records in the table.

BTW

Archive Tables
You can use a make table query to create an archive table. An archive table is a table that contains data that is no longer used in operations but that might still be needed by the organization.

Break Point: If you wish to take a break, this is a good place to do so. You can quit Access now. To resume at a later time, run Access, open the database called PrattLast Associates, and continue following the steps from this location forward.

Validation Rules

You now have created, loaded, queried, and updated a database. Nothing you have done so far, however, restricts users to entering only valid data, that is, data that follows the rules established for data in the database. An example of such a rule would be that account types can only be SER, NON, or IND. To ensure the entry of valid data, you create **validation rules**, or rules that a user must follow when entering the data. When the database contains validation rules, Access prevents users from entering data that does not follow the rules. You can also specify **validation text**, which is the message that appears if a user attempts to violate the validation rule.

Validation rules can indicate a **required field**, a field in which the user *must* enter data; failing to enter data into a required field generates an error. Validation rules can also restrict a user's entry to a certain **range of values**; for example, the values in the Current Due field must be between $0 and $10,000. Alternatively, rules can specify a **default value**, that is, a value that Access will display on the screen in a particular field before the user begins adding a record. To make data entry of account numbers more convenient, you can also have lowercase letters appear automatically as uppercase letters. Finally, validation rules can specify a collection of acceptable values.

To Change a Field Size

The Field Size property for text fields represents the maximum number of characters a user can enter in the field. Because the field size for the Account Number field is five, for example, a user would not be able to enter a sixth character in the field. Occasionally, you will find that the field size that seemed appropriate when you first created a table is no longer appropriate. In the Account table, there is a street name that needs to be longer than 20 characters. To allow this name in the table, you need to change the field size for the Street field to a number that is large enough to accommodate the new name. The following step changes the field size for the Street field from 20 to 25.

1 Open the Account table in Design view and close the Navigation Pane.

2 Select the Street field by clicking its row selector.

3 Click the Field Size property to select it, delete the current entry (20), and then type **25** as the new field size.

To Specify a Required Field

1 UPDATE RECORDS | 2 FILTER RECORDS | 3 CHANGE STRUCTURE | 4 MASS CHANGES | 5 VALIDATION RULES
6 CHANGE APPEARANCE | 7 REFERENTIAL INTEGRITY | 8 ORDER RECORDS

To specify that a field is to be required, change the value for the Required property from No to Yes. The following step specifies that the Account Name field is a required field. *Why? Users will not be able to leave the Account Name field blank when entering or editing records.*

- Select the Account Name field by clicking its row selector.
- Click the Required property box in the Field Properties pane, and then click the down arrow that appears.
- Click Yes in the list to make Account Name a required field (Figure 3–36).

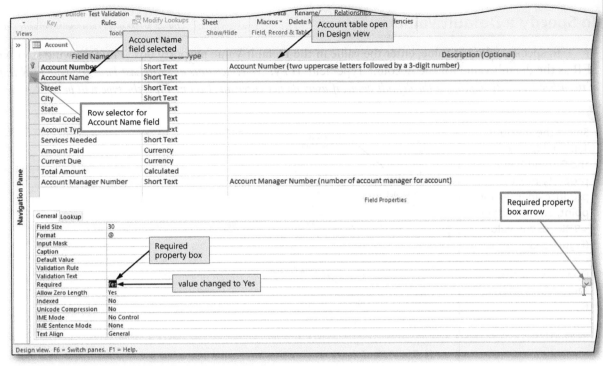

Figure 3–36

To Specify a Range

1 UPDATE RECORDS | 2 FILTER RECORDS | 3 CHANGE STRUCTURE | 4 MASS CHANGES | 5 VALIDATION RULES
6 CHANGE APPEARANCE | 7 REFERENTIAL INTEGRITY | 8 ORDER RECORDS

The following step specifies that entries in the Current Due field must be between $0 and $10,000. To indicate this range, the criterion specifies that the Current Due amount must be both >= 0 (greater than or equal to 0) and <= 10000 (less than or equal to 10,000). **Why?** *Combining these two criteria with the word, and, is logically equivalent to being between $0.00 and $10,000.00.*

1

- Select the Current Due field by clicking its row selector, click the Validation Rule property box to produce an insertion point, and then type **>=0 and <=10000** as the rule.

- Click the Validation Text property box to produce an insertion point, and then type **Must be at least $0.00 and at most $10,000.00** as the text (Figure 3–37).

Q&A What is the effect of this change? Users will now be prohibited from entering a Current Due amount that is either less than $0.00 or greater than $10,000.00 when they add records or change the value in the Current Due field.

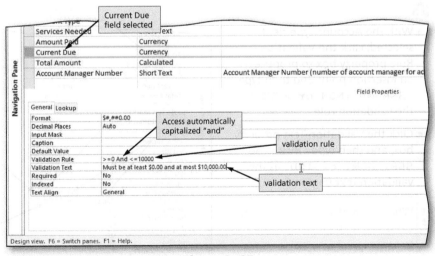

Figure 3–37

To Specify a Default Value

To specify a default value, enter the value in the Default Value property box. The following step specifies SER as the default value for the Account Type field. **Why?** *More accounts at PrattLast have the type SER than either of the other types. By making it the default value, if users do not enter an Account Type, the type will be SER.*

1

- Select the Account Type field, click the Default Value property box to produce an insertion point, and then type **=SER** as the value (Figure 3–38).

Q&A Do I need to type the equal (=) sign? No. You could enter just SER as the default value.

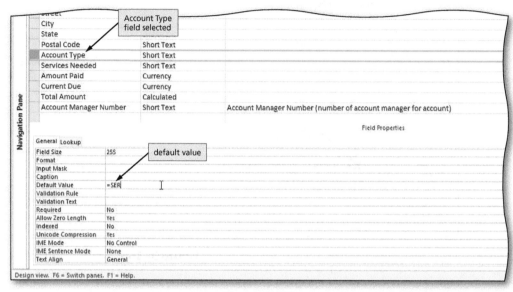

Figure 3–38

To Specify a Collection of Legal Values

The only **legal values**, or **allowable values**, for the Account Type field are SER, NON, and IND. The following step creates a validation rule to specify these as the only legal values for the Account Type field. **Why?** *The validation rule prohibits users from entering any other value in the Account Type field.*

1

- With the Account Type field selected, click the Validation Rule property box to produce an insertion point and then type **=SER or =NON or =IND** as the validation rule.

- Click the Validation Text property box, and then type **Must be SER, NON, or IND** as the validation text (Figure 3–39).

Q&A What is the effect of this change? Users will now only be allowed to enter SER, NON, or IND in the Account Type field when they add records or make changes to this field.

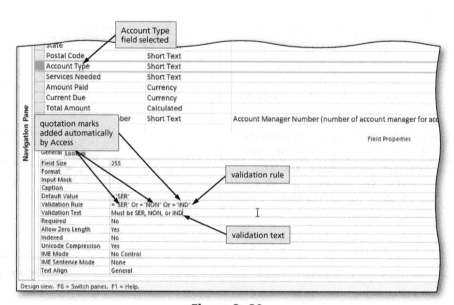

Figure 3–39

Maintaining a Database   **Access Module 3**   **AC** 147

Access Module 3

1 UPDATE RECORDS | 2 FILTER RECORDS | 3 CHANGE STRUCTURE | 4 MASS CHANGES | 5 VALIDATION RULES
6 CHANGE APPEARANCE | 7 REFERENTIAL INTEGRITY | 8 ORDER RECORDS

To Specify a Format

To affect the way data appears in a field, you can use a **format**. To use a format with a Short Text field, you enter a special symbol, called a **format symbol**, in the field's Format property box. The Format property uses different settings for different data types. The following step specifies a format for the Account Number field using the > symbol. *Why? The > format symbol causes Access to display lowercase letters automatically as uppercase letters, which is appropriate for the Account Number field.* There is another symbol, the < symbol, which causes Access to display uppercase letters automatically as lowercase letters.

1

• Select the Account Number field.

• Click the Format property box, erase the current format (@), if it appears on your screen, and then type   >   (Figure 3–40).

Q&A
Where did the current format (@) come from and what does it mean?
Access added this format when you created the table by importing data from an Excel workbook. It simply means any character or a space. It is not needed here.

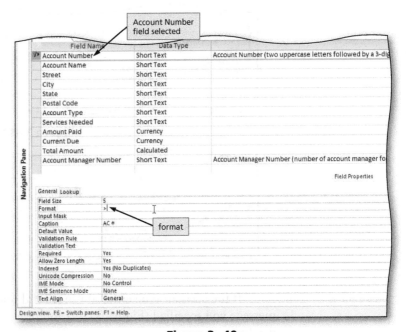

Figure 3–40

To Save the Validation Rules, Default Values, and Formats

The following steps save the validation rules, default values, and formats.

1   Click the Save button on the Quick Access Toolbar to save the changes (Figure 3–41).

2   If a Microsoft Access dialog box appears, click the No button to save the changes without testing current data.

Q&A
When would you want to test current data?
If you have any doubts about the validity of the current data, you should be sure to test the current data.

3   Close the Account table.

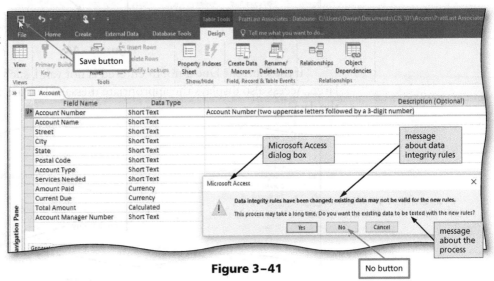

Figure 3–41

Updating a Table that Contains Validation Rules

Now that the PrattLast database contains validation rules, Access restricts the user to entering data that is valid and is formatted correctly. If a user enters a number that is out of the required range, for example, or enters a value that is not one of the possible choices, Access displays an error message in the form of a dialog box. The user cannot update the database until the error is corrected.

If the account number entered contains lowercase letters, such as bc486 (Figure 3–42), Access will display the data automatically as BC486 (Figure 3–43).

Figure 3–42

Figure 3–43

If the account type entered is not valid, such as xxx, Access will display the text message you specified (Figure 3–44) and prevent the data from being entering into the database.

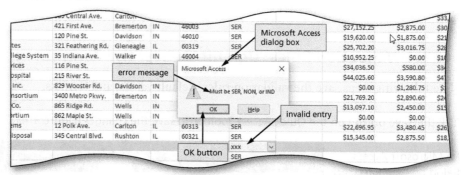

Figure 3–44

If the Current Due amount entered is not valid, such as 50000, which is too large, Access also displays the appropriate message (Figure 3–45) and refuses to accept the data.

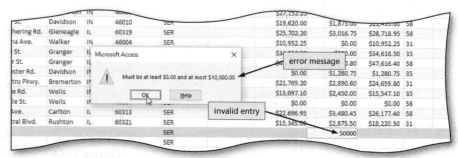

Figure 3–45

If a required field contains no data, Access indicates this by displaying an error message as soon as you attempt to leave the record (Figure 3–46). The field must contain a valid entry before Access will move to a different record.

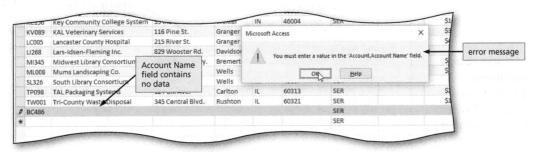

Figure 3–46

When entering invalid data into a field with a validation rule, is it possible that you could not enter the data correctly? What would cause this? If it happens, what should you do?

If you cannot remember the validation rule you created or if you created the rule incorrectly, you might not be able to enter the data. In such a case, you will be unable to leave the field or close the table because you have entered data into a field that violates the validation rule.

If this happens, first try again to type an acceptable entry. If this does not work, repeatedly press the BACKSPACE key to erase the contents of the field and then try to leave the field. If you are unsuccessful using this procedure, press the ESC key until the record is removed from the screen. The record will not be added to the database.

Should the need arise to take this drastic action, you probably have a faulty validation rule. Use the techniques of the previous sections to correct the existing validation rules for the field.

Making Additional Changes to the Database

Now that you have changed the structure and created validation rules, there are additional changes to be made to the database. You will use both the lookup and multivalued lookup fields to change the contents of the fields. You will also update both the form and the report to reflect the changes in the table.

To Change the Contents of a Field

1 UPDATE RECORDS | 2 FILTER RECORDS | 3 CHANGE STRUCTURE | 4 MASS CHANGES | **5 VALIDATION RULES**
6 CHANGE APPEARANCE | 7 REFERENTIAL INTEGRITY | 8 ORDER RECORDS

Now that the size for the Street field has been increased, you can change the Street name for account BL235 from 100 Granger Hwy. to 100 South Granger Hwy. and then resize the column, just as you resized columns in Module 1. *Why? Changing the field size for the field does not automatically increase the width of the corresponding column in the datasheet.* The following steps change the Street name and resize the column in the datasheet to accommodate the new name.

- Open the Account table in Datasheet view and ensure the Navigation Pane is closed.

- Click in the Street field for account BL235 immediately to the left of the letter, G, of Granger to produce an insertion point.

- Change the name of the street from 100 Granger Hwy. to 100 South Granger Hwy. by typing South and a space, and then pressing the TAB key.

I cannot add the extra characters. Whatever I type replaces what is currently in the cell. What happened and what should I do?
You are typing in Overtype mode, not Insert mode. Press the INSERT key and correct the entry.

- Resize the Street column to best fit the new data by double-clicking the right boundary of the field selector for the Street field, that is, the column heading (Figure 3–47).

- Save the changes to the layout by clicking the Save button on the Quick Access Toolbar.

- Close the Account table.

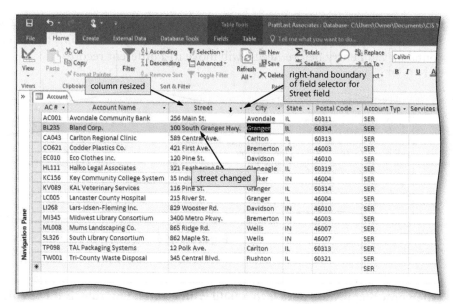

Figure 3–47

To Use a Lookup Field

1 UPDATE RECORDS | 2 FILTER RECORDS | 3 CHANGE STRUCTURE | 4 MASS CHANGES | 5 VALIDATION RULES
6 CHANGE APPEARANCE | 7 REFERENTIAL INTEGRITY | 8 ORDER RECORDS

Earlier, you changed all the entries in the Account Type field to SER. You have created a rule that will ensure that only legitimate values (SER, NON, or IND) can be entered in the field. You also made Account Type a lookup field. ***Why?*** *You can make changes to a lookup field for individual records by simply clicking the field to be changed, clicking the arrow that appears in the field, and then selecting the desired value from the list.* The following steps change the incorrect Account Type values to the correct values.

- Open the Account table in Datasheet view and ensure the Navigation Pane is closed.

- Click in the Account Type field on the second record (BL235) to display an arrow.

- Click the arrow to display the drop-down list of available choices for the Account Type field (Figure 3–48).

I got the drop-down list as soon as I clicked. I did not need to click the arrow. What happened?
If you click in the position where the arrow would appear, you will get the drop-down list. If you click anywhere else, you would need to click the arrow.

Could I type the value instead of selecting it from the list?
Yes. Once you have either deleted the previous value or selected the entire previous value, you can begin typing. You do not have to type the full entry. When you begin with the letter, I, for example, Access will automatically add the ND.

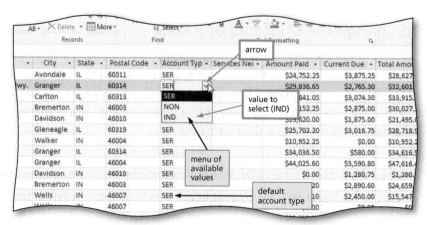

Figure 3–48

2

- Click IND to change the value.

- In a similar fashion, change the values on the other records to match those shown in Figure 3–49.

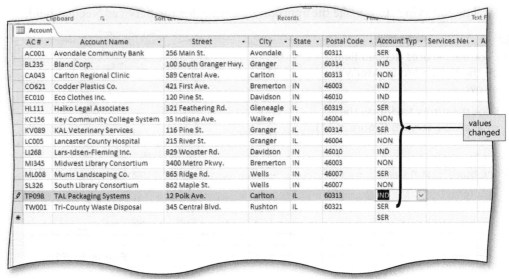

Figure 3–49

To Use a Multivalued Lookup Field

1 UPDATE RECORDS | 2 FILTER RECORDS | 3 CHANGE STRUCTURE | 4 MASS CHANGES | **5 VALIDATION RULES**
6 CHANGE APPEARANCE | 7 REFERENTIAL INTEGRITY | 8 ORDER RECORDS

Using a multivalued lookup field is similar to using a regular lookup field. The difference is that when you display the drop down list, the entries will all be preceded by check boxes. *Why? Having the check boxes allows you to make multiple selections. You check all the entries that you want.* The appropriate entries are shown in Figure 3–50. As indicated in the figure, the services needed for account AC001 are Bck, Ben, Com, Pay, and Rsk.

Account Number	Account Name	Services Needed
AC001	Avondale Community Bank	Bck, Ben, Com, Pay, Rsk
BL235	Bland Corp.	Bck, Mgt, Rsk, Tch, Wrk
CA043	Carlton Regional Clinic	Mgt, Pay, Rsk, Tch
CO621	Codder Plastics Co.	Ben, Pay, Rsk, Trn, Wrk
EC010	Eco Clothes Inc.	Rec, Trn, Wrk
HL111	Halko Legal Associates	Ben, Com, Pay, Rsk, Tch, Trn
KC156	Key Community College System	Ben, Com, Mgt, Rsk, Wrk
KV089	KAL Veterinary Services	Ben, Com, Tch, Trn
LC005	Lancaster County Hospital	Ben, Mgt, Pay, Rsk, Tch, Wrk
LI268	Lars-Idsen-Fleming Inc.	Ben, Pay, Wrk
MI345	Midwest Library Consortium	Bck, Ben, Com, Pay, Tch, Trn
ML008	Mums Landscaping Co.	Bck, Pay, Wrk
SL326	South Library Consortium	Bck, Ben, Com, Pay, Tch, Trn
TP098	TAL Packaging Systems	Ben, Com, Pay, Trn, Wrk
TW001	Tri-County Waste Disposal	Bck, Pay, Rec, Wrk

Figure 3–50

The following steps make the appropriate entries for the Services Needed field.

1

● Click the Services Needed field on the first record to display the arrow.

● Click the arrow to display the list of available services (Figure 3–51).

All the services currently appear in the box. What if there were too many services to fit?
Access would automatically include a scroll bar that you could use to scroll through all the choices.

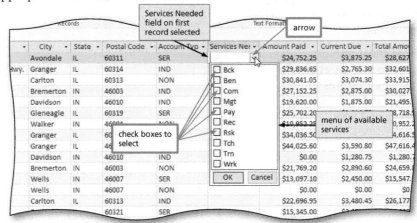

Figure 3–51

2

● Click the Bck, Ben, Com, Pay, and Rsk check boxes to select the services for the first account (Figure 3–52).

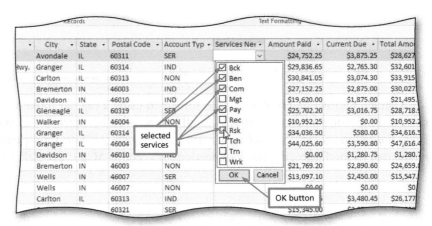

Figure 3–52

3

● Click the OK button to complete the selection.

● Using the same technique, enter the services given in Figure 3–50 for the remaining accounts.

● Double-click the right boundary of the field selector for the Services Needed field to resize the field so that it best fits the data (Figure 3–53).

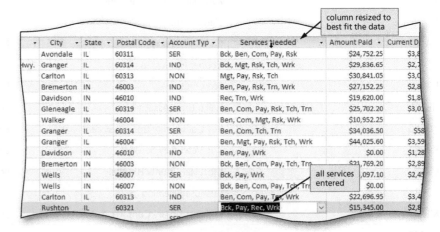

Figure 3–53

4

● Save the changes to the layout by clicking the Save button on the Quick Access Toolbar.

● Close the Account table.

What if I closed the table without saving the layout changes?
You would be asked if you want to save the changes.

To Update a Form to Reflect Changes in the Table

Earlier, you clicked the Form button (Create tab | Forms group) to create a simple form that contained all the fields in the Account table. Now that you have added fields, the form you created, Account Form, no longer contains all the fields in the table. The following steps delete the Account Form and then create it a second time.

1 Open the Navigation Pane, and then right-click the Account Form in the Navigation Pane to display a shortcut menu.

2 Click Delete on the shortcut menu to delete the selected form, and then click the Yes button in the Microsoft Access dialog box to confirm the deletion.

3 Click the Account table in the Navigation Pane to select the table.

4 If necessary, click Create on the ribbon to display the Create tab.

5 Click the Form button (Create tab | Forms group) to create a simple form (Figure 3–54).

6 Click the Save button on the Quick Access Toolbar to save the form.

7 Type **Account Form** as the form name, and then click the OK button to save the form.

8 Close the form.

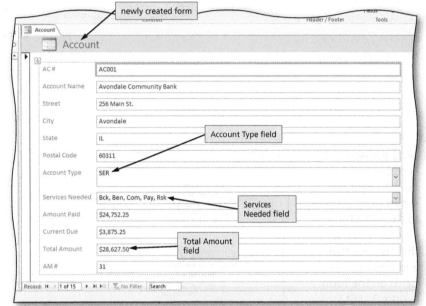

Figure 3–54

To Update a Report to Reflect Changes in the Table

1 UPDATE RECORDS | 2 FILTER RECORDS | 3 CHANGE STRUCTURE | 4 MASS CHANGES | 5 VALIDATION RULES
6 CHANGE APPEARANCE | 7 REFERENTIAL INTEGRITY | 8 ORDER RECORDS

You also might want to include the new fields in the Account Financial Report you created earlier. Just as you did with the form, you could delete the current version of the report and then create it all over again. It would be better, however, to modify the report in Layout view. *Why? There are several steps involved in creating the Account Financial report, so it is more complicated than the process of re-creating the form.* In Layout view, you easily can add new fields. The following steps modify the Account Financial Report by adding the Account Type and Total Amount fields. To accommodate the extra fields, the steps also change the orientation of the report from Portrait to Landscape.

1

- Open the Navigation Pane, if necessary, and then right-click the Account Financial Report in the Navigation Pane to display a shortcut menu.

- Click Layout View on the shortcut menu to open the report in Layout view.

- Close the Navigation Pane.

- Click the 'Add Existing Fields' button (Report Layout Tools Design tab | Tools group) to display a field list (Figure 3–55).

Q&A Why are there two Services Needed fields in the list?

They serve different purposes. If you were to select Services Needed, you would get all the services for a given account on one line. If you were to select Services Needed. Value, each resource would be on a separate line. You are not selecting either one for this report.

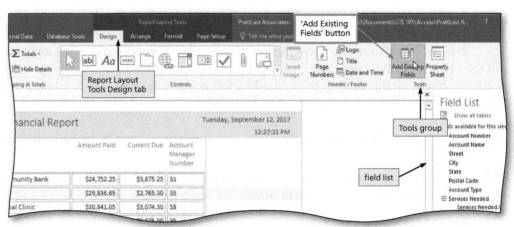

Figure 3-55

❷

- Drag the Account Type field in the field list into the report until the line to the left of the pointer is between the Account Name and Amount Paid fields on the form (Figure 3-56).

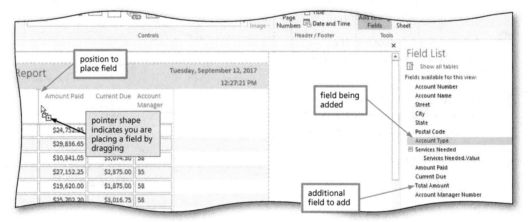

Figure 3-56

❸

- Release the mouse button to place the field.

Q&A What if I make a mistake?

You can delete the field by clicking the column heading for the field, clicking the Select Column command (Report Layout Tools Arrange tab | Rows & Columns group), and then pressing the DELETE key. You can move the field by dragging it to the correct position. As an alternative, you can close the report without saving it and then open it again in Layout view.

- Using the same technique, add the Total Amount field between the Current Due and Account Manager Number fields.

- Click the 'Add Existing Fields' button (Report Layout Tools Design tab | Tools group) to remove the field list from the screen.

Q&A What would I do if the field list covered the portion of the report where I wanted to insert a new field?

You can move the field list to a different position on the screen by dragging its title bar.

- Click Page Setup on the ribbon to display the Report Layout Tools Page Setup tab.

- Click the Landscape button (Report Layout Tools Page Setup tab | Page Layout group) to change the orientation of the report to Landscape (Figure 3–57).

- Click the Save button on the Quick Access Toolbar to save your changes.

- Close the report.

Figure 3–57

To Print a Report

The following steps print the report.

1 With the Account Financial Report selected in the Navigation Pane, click File on the ribbon to open the Backstage view.

2 Click the Print tab in the Backstage view to display the Print gallery.

3 Click the Quick Print button to print the report.

Changing the Appearance of a Datasheet

You can change the appearance of a datasheet in a variety of ways. You can include totals in the datasheet. You can also change the appearance of gridlines or the text colors and font.

To Include Totals in a Datasheet

1 UPDATE RECORDS | 2 FILTER RECORDS | 3 CHANGE STRUCTURE | 4 MASS CHANGES | 5 VALIDATION RULES
6 CHANGE APPEARANCE | 7 REFERENTIAL INTEGRITY | 8 ORDER RECORDS

The following steps first include an extra row, called the Total row, in the datasheet for the Account Manager table. **Why?** *It is possible to include totals and other statistics at the bottom of a datasheet in the Total row.* The steps then display the total of the salaries for all the account managers.

1

- Open the Account Manager table in Datasheet view and close the Navigation Pane.

- Click the Totals button (Home tab | Records group) to include the Total row in the datasheet.

- Click the Total row in the Salary column to display an arrow.

BTW

Distributing a Document

Instead of printing and distributing a hard copy of a document, you can distribute the document electronically. Options include sending the document via email; posting it on cloud storage (such as OneDrive) and sharing the file with others; posting it on social media, a blog, or other website; and sharing a link associated with an online location of the document. You also can create and share a PDF or XPS image of the document, so that users can view the file in Acrobat Reader or XPS Viewer instead of in Access.

- Click the arrow to display a menu of available calculations (Figure 3–58).

Will I always get the same list?

No. You will only get the items that are applicable to the type of data in the column. You cannot calculate the sum of text data, for example.

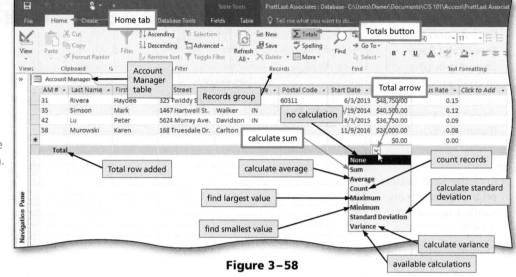

Figure 3–58

- Click Sum to calculate the total of the salary amounts.

- Resize the Salary column to best fit the total amount (Figure 3–59).

 **Experiment**

- Experiment with other statistics. When finished, once again select the sum.

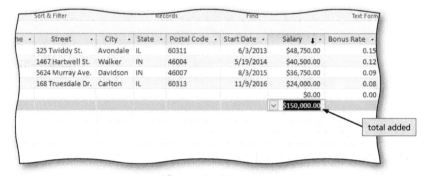

Figure 3–59

To Remove Totals from a Datasheet

If you no longer want the totals to appear as part of the datasheet, you can remove the Total row. The following step removes the Total row.

1. Click the Totals button (Home tab | Records group), which is shown in Figure 3–58, to remove the Total row from the datasheet.

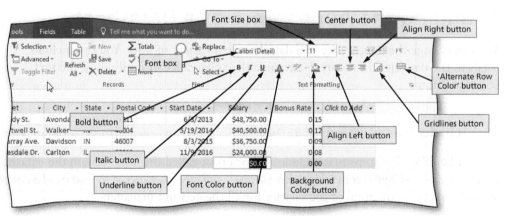

Figure 3–60

Figure 3–60 shows the various buttons, found in the Text Formatting group on the Home tab, that are available to change the datasheet appearance. The changes to the datasheet will be reflected not only on the screen, but also when you print or preview the datasheet.

To Change Gridlines in a Datasheet

1 UPDATE RECORDS | 2 FILTER RECORDS | 3 CHANGE STRUCTURE | 4 MASS CHANGES | 5 VALIDATION RULES
6 CHANGE APPEARANCE | 7 REFERENTIAL INTEGRITY | 8 ORDER RECORDS

The following steps change the datasheet so that only horizontal gridlines are included. *Why? You might prefer the appearance of the datasheet with only horizontal gridlines.*

- Open the Account Manager table in Datasheet view, if it is not already open.

- If necessary, close the Navigation Pane.

- Click the datasheet selector, the box in the upper-left corner of the datasheet, to select the entire datasheet (Figure 3–61).

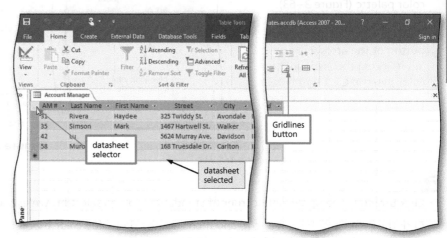

Figure 3–61

- Click the Gridlines button (Home tab | Text Formatting group) to display the Gridlines gallery (Figure 3–62).

Q&A Does it matter whether I click the button or the arrow?
In this case, it does not matter. Either action will display the gallery.

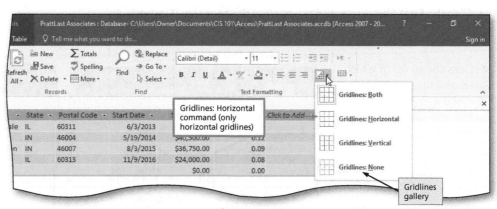

Figure 3–62

- Click Gridlines: Horizontal in the Gridlines gallery to include only horizontal gridlines.

 Experiment

- Experiment with other gridline options. When finished, once again select horizontal gridlines.

To Change the Colors and Font in a Datasheet

1 UPDATE RECORDS | 2 FILTER RECORDS | 3 CHANGE STRUCTURE | 4 MASS CHANGES | 5 VALIDATION RULES
6 CHANGE APPEARANCE | 7 REFERENTIAL INTEGRITY | 8 ORDER RECORDS

You can also modify the appearance of the datasheet by changing the colors and the font. The following steps change the Alternate Fill color, a color that appears on every other row in the datasheet. *Why? Having rows appear in alternate colors is an attractive way to visually separate the rows.* The steps also change the font color, the font, and the font size.

①

- With the datasheet for the Account Manager table selected, click the 'Alternate Row Color' button arrow (Home tab | Text Formatting group) to display the color palette (Figure 3–63).

Q&A Does it matter whether I click the button or the arrow?

Yes. Clicking the arrow produces a color palette. Clicking the button applies the currently selected color. When in doubt, you should click the arrow.

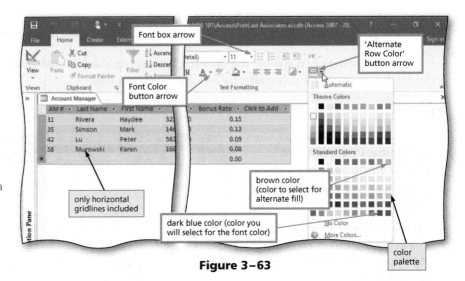

Figure 3–63

②

- Click Brown in the upper-right corner of Standard Colors to select brown as the alternate color.
- Click the Font Color button arrow, and then click the dark blue color that is the second color from the right in the bottom row in the Standard Colors to select the font color.
- Click the Font arrow, scroll down in the list until Bodoni MT appears, and then select Bodoni MT as the font. (If it is not available, select any font of your choice.)
- Click the Font Size arrow and select 10 as the font size (Figure 3–64).

Q&A Does the order in which I make these selections make a difference?

No. You could have made these selections in any order.

⌕ Experiment

- Experiment with other colors, fonts, and font sizes. When finished, return to the options selected in this step.

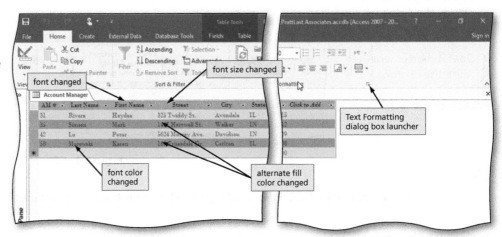

Figure 3–64

Using the Datasheet Formatting Dialog Box

As an alternative to using the individual buttons, you can click the Datasheet Formatting dialog box launcher, which is the arrow at the lower-right of the Text Formatting group, to display the Datasheet Formatting dialog box (Figure 3–65). You can use the various options within the dialog box to make changes to the datasheet format. Once you are finished, click the OK button to apply your changes.

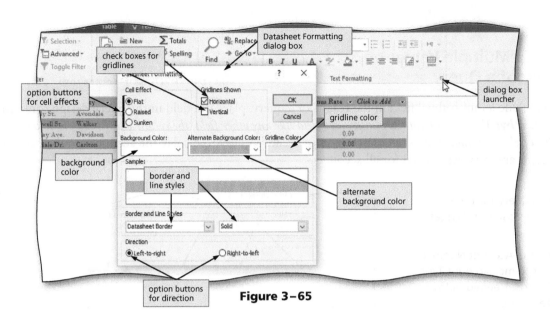

Figure 3–65

To Close the Datasheet without Saving the Format Changes

The following steps close the datasheet without saving the changes to the format. Because the changes are not saved, the next time you open the Account Manager table in Datasheet view it will appear in the original format. If you had saved the changes, the changes would be reflected in its appearance.

1 Close the Account Manager table.

2 Click the No button in the Microsoft Access dialog box when asked if you want to save your changes.

What kind of decisions should I make in determining whether to change the format of a datasheet?

- Would totals or other calculations be useful in the datasheet? If so, include the Total row and select the appropriate computations.

- Would another gridline style make the datasheet more useful? If so, change to the desired gridlines.

- Would alternating colors in the rows make them easier to read? If so, change the alternate fill color.

- Would a different font and/or font color make the text stand out better? If so, change the font color and/or the font.

- Is the font size appropriate? Can you see enough data at one time on the screen and yet have the data be readable? If not, change the font size to an appropriate value.

- Is the column spacing appropriate? Are some columns wider than they need to be? Do some columns not display all the data? Change the column sizes as necessary.

As a general guideline, once you have decided on a particular look for a datasheet, all datasheets in the database should have the same look, unless there is a compelling reason for a datasheet to differ.

CONSIDER THIS

Multivalued Fields in Queries

You can use multivalued fields in queries in the same way you use other fields in queries. You can choose to display the multiple values either on a single row or on multiple rows in the query results.

To Include Multiple Values on One Row of a Query

1 UPDATE RECORDS | 2 FILTER RECORDS | 3 CHANGE STRUCTURE | 4 MASS CHANGES | 5 VALIDATION RULES
6 CHANGE APPEARANCE | 7 REFERENTIAL INTEGRITY | 8 ORDER RECORDS

To include a multivalued field in the results of a query, place the field in the query design grid just like any other field. *Why? When you treat the multivalued field like any other field, the results will list all of the values for the multivalued field on a single row.* The following steps create a query to display the account number, account name, account type, and services needed for all accounts.

1

- Create a query for the Account table and close the Navigation Pane.

- Include the Account Number, Account Name, Account Type, and Services Needed fields (Figure 3–66).

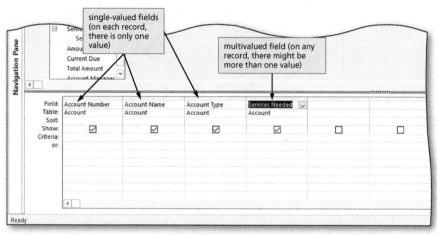

Figure 3–66

2

- Run the query and view the results (Figure 3–67).

Q&A Can I include criteria for the multivalued field?
Yes. You can include criteria for the multivalued field.

3

- Save the query as m03q01.

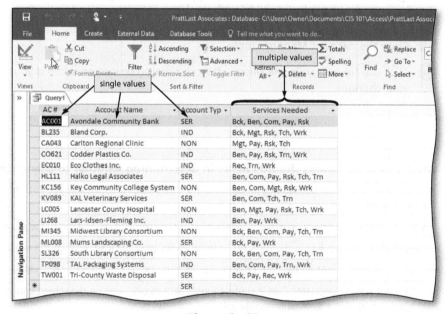

Figure 3–67

To Include Multiple Values on Multiple Rows of a Query

1 UPDATE RECORDS | 2 FILTER RECORDS | 3 CHANGE STRUCTURE | 4 MASS CHANGES | 5 VALIDATION RULES
6 CHANGE APPEARANCE | 7 REFERENTIAL INTEGRITY | 8 ORDER RECORDS

You might want to see the multiple services needed for an account on separate rows rather than a single row. *Why? Each row in the results will focus on one specific service that is needed.* To do so, you need to use the Value property of the Services Needed field by following the name of the field with a period and then the word, Value. The following steps use the Value property to display each service on a separate row.

1

- Return to Design view and ensure that the Account Number, Account Name, Account Type, and Services Needed fields are included in the design grid.

- Click the Services Needed field to produce an insertion point, press the RIGHT ARROW key as necessary to move the insertion point to the end of the field name, and then type a period.

- If the word, Value, did not automatically appear after the period, type the word **Value** after the period following the word, Needed, to use the Value property (Figure 3–68).

Q&A I do not see the word, Services. Did I do something wrong?
No. There is not enough room to display the entire name. If you wanted to see it, you could point to the right boundary of the column selector and then either drag or double-click.

Q&A I see Services Needed.Value as a field in the field list. Could I have deleted the Services Needed field and added the Services Needed.Value field?
Yes. Either approach is fine.

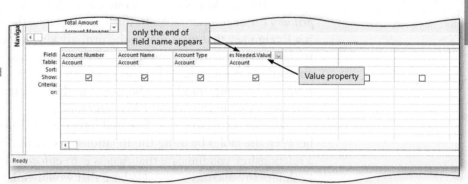

Figure 3–68

2

- Run the query and view the results (Figure 3–69).

Q&A Can I now include criteria for the multivalued field?
Yes. You could enter a criterion just like in any other query.

Q&A Could I sort the rows by account number?
Yes. Select Ascending as the sort order just as you have done in other queries.

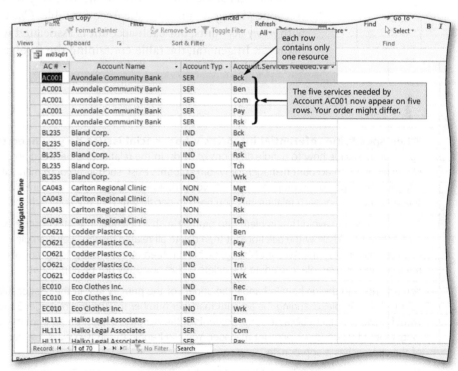

Figure 3–69

3

- Save the query as a new object in the database named m03q02.

- Close the query.

Break Point: If you wish to take a break, this is a good place to do so. You can quit Access now. To resume at a later time, run Access, open the database called PrattLast Associates, and continue following the steps from this location forward.

Referential Integrity

BTW
Using Criteria with Multivalued Fields
To enter criteria in a multivalued field, simply enter the criteria in the Criteria row. For example, to find all accounts who need payroll services, enter Pay in the Criteria row.

When you have two related tables in a database, it is essential that the data in the common fields match. There should not be an account in the Account table whose account manager number is 31, for example, unless there is a record in the Account Manager table whose number is 31. This restriction is enforced through **referential integrity**, which is the property that ensures that the value in a foreign key must match that of another table's primary key.

A **foreign key** is a field in one table whose values are required to match the *primary key* of another table. In the Account table, the Account Manager Number field is a foreign key that must match the primary key of the Account Manager table; that is, the account manager number for any account must exist as an account manager currently in the Account Manager table. An account whose account manager number is 92, for example, should not be stored in the Account table because no such account manager exists in the Account Manager table.

In Access, to specify referential integrity, you must explicitly define a relationship between the tables by using the Relationships button. As part of the process of defining a relationship, you indicate that Access is to enforce referential integrity. Access then prohibits any updates to the database that would violate the referential integrity.

The type of relationship between two tables specified by the Relationships command is referred to as a **one-to-many relationship**. This means that *one* record in the first table is related to, or matches, *many* records in the second table, but each record in the second table is related to only *one* record in the first. In the PrattLast Associates database, for example, a one-to-many relationship exists between the Account Manager table and the Account table. *One* account manager is associated with *many* accounts, but each account is associated with only a single account manager. In general, the table containing the foreign key will be the *many* part of the relationship.

CONSIDER THIS

When specifying referential integrity, what special issues do you need to address?
You need to decide how to handle deletions of fields. In the relationship between accounts and account managers, for example, deletion of an account manager for whom accounts exist, such as account manager number 31, would violate referential integrity. Accounts for account manager 31 would no longer relate to any account manager in the database. You can handle this in two ways. For each relationship, you need to decide which of the approaches is appropriate.

The normal way to avoid this problem is to prohibit such a deletion. The other option is to **cascade the delete.** This means that Access would allow the deletion but then delete all related records. For example, it would allow the deletion of the account manager from the Account Manager table but then automatically delete any accounts related to the deleted account manager. In this example, cascading the delete would obviously not be appropriate.

You also need to decide how to handle the update of the primary key. In the relationship between account managers and accounts, for example, changing the account manager number for account manager 31 to 32 in the Account Manager table would cause a problem because some accounts in the Account table have account manager number 31. These accounts no longer would relate to any account manager. You can handle this in two ways. For each relationship, you need to decide which of the approaches is appropriate.

The normal way to avoid this problem is to prohibit this type of update. The other option is to **cascade the update.** This means to allow the change, but make the corresponding change in the foreign key on all related records. In the relationship between accounts and account managers, for example, Access would allow the update but then automatically make the corresponding change for any account whose account manager number was 31. It will now be 32.

To Specify Referential Integrity

The following steps use the Relationships button on the Database Tools tab to specify referential integrity by explicitly indicating a relationship between the Account Manager and Account tables. The steps also ensure that updates will cascade, but that deletes will not. *Why? By indicating a relationship between tables, and specifying that updates will cascade, it will be possible to change the Account Manager Number for an account manager, and the same change will automatically be made for all accounts of that account manager. By not specifying that deletes will cascade, it will not be possible to delete an account manager who has related accounts.*

- Click Database Tools on the ribbon to display the Database Tools tab. (Figure 3–70).

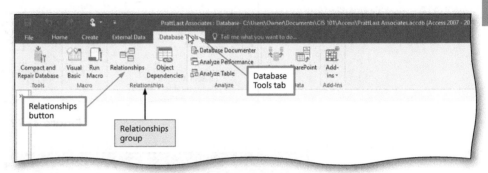

Figure 3–70

- Click the Relationships button (Database Tools tab | Relationships group) to open the Relationships window and display the Show Table dialog box (Figure 3–71).

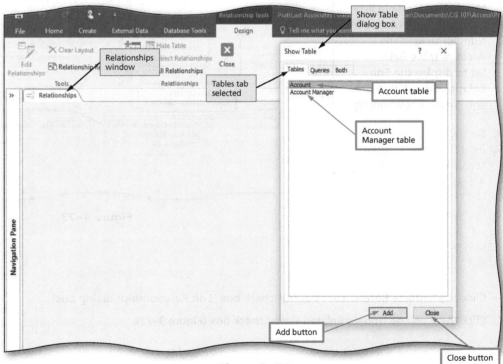

Figure 3–71

- Click the Account Manager table (Show Table dialog box), and then click the Add button to add a field list for the Account Manager table to the Relationships window.

- Click the Account table (Show Table dialog box), and then click the Add button to add a field list for the Account table to the Relationships window.

- Click the Close button (Show Table dialog box) to close the dialog box.

- Resize the field lists that appear so all fields are visible (Figure 3–72).

Q&A Do I need to resize the field lists?
No. You can use the scroll bars to view the fields. Before completing the next step, however, you would need to make sure the Account Manager Number fields in both tables appear on the screen.

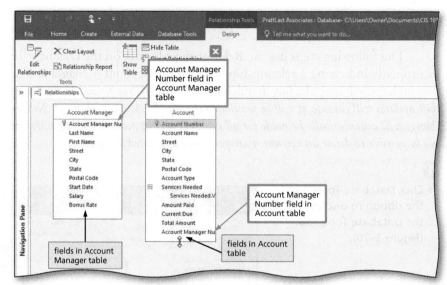

Figure 3–72

4

- Drag the Account Manager Number field in the Account Manager table field list to the Account Manager Number field in the Account table field list to display the Edit Relationships dialog box and create a relationship.

Q&A Do I actually move the field from the Account Manager table to the Account table?
No. The pointer will change shape to indicate you are in the process of dragging, but the field does not move.

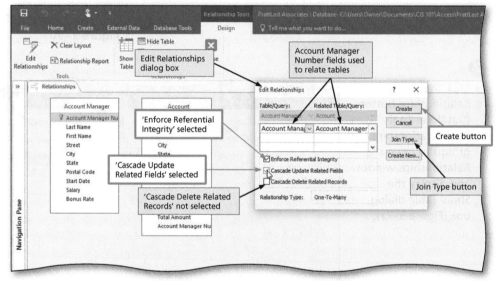

Figure 3–73

- Click the 'Enforce Referential Integrity' check box (Edit Relationships dialog box).

- Click the 'Cascade Update Related Fields' check box (Figure 3–73).

Q&A The Cascade check boxes were dim until I clicked the 'Enforce Referential Integrity' check box. Is that correct?
Yes. Until you have chosen to enforce referential integrity, the cascade options are not applicable.

5

- Click the Create button (Edit Relationships dialog box) to complete the creation of the relationship (Figure 3–74).

Q&A What is the symbol at the lower end of the join line?
It is the mathematical symbol for infinity. It is used here to denote the "many" end of the relationship.

Can I print a copy of the relationship?

Yes. Click the Relationship Report button (Relationship Tools Design tab | Tools group) to produce a report of the relationship. You can print the report. You can also save it as a report in the database for future use. If you do not want to save it, close the report after you have printed it and do not save the changes.

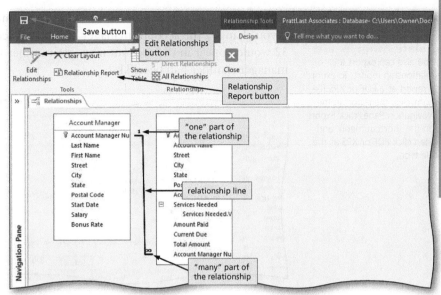

Figure 3–74

6

- Click the Save button on the Quick Access Toolbar to save the relationship you created.
- Close the Relationships window.

◁ **Can I later modify the relationship if I want to change it in some way?**

Yes. Click Database Tools on the ribbon to display the Database Tools tab, and then click the Relationships button (Database Tools tab | Relationships group) to open the Relationships window. To add another table, click the Show Table button on the Design tab. To remove a table, click the Hide Table button. To edit a relationship, select the relationship and click the Edit Relationships button.

Can I change the join type as I can in queries?

Yes. Click the Join Type button in the Edit Relationships dialog box. Click option button 1 to create an INNER join, that is, a join in which only records with matching values in the join fields appear in the result. Click option button 2 to create a LEFT join, that is, a join that includes all records from the left-hand table, but only records from the right-hand table that have matching values in the join fields. Click option button 3 to create a RIGHT join, that is, a join that includes all records from the right-hand table, but only records from the left-hand table that have matching values in the join fields.

CONSIDER THIS

Effect of Referential Integrity

Referential integrity now exists between the Account Manager and Account tables. Access now will reject any number in the Account Manager Number field in the Account table that does not match an account manager number in the Account Manager table. Attempting to change the account manager number for an account to one that does not match any account manager in the Account Manager table would result in the error message shown in Figure 3–75. Similarly, attempting to add an account whose account manager number does not match would produce the same error message.

Access also will reject the deletion of an account manager for whom related accounts exist. Attempting to delete account manager 31 from the Account Manager table, for example, would result in the message shown in Figure 3–76.

Access would, however, allow the change of an account manager number in the Account Manager table. It would then automatically make the corresponding change

BTW
Relationships
You also can use the Relationships window to specify a one-to-one relationship. In a one-to-one relationship, the matching fields are both primary keys. If PrattLast Associates maintained a company car for each account manager, the data concerning the cars might be kept in a Car table, in which the primary key is Account Manager Number — the same primary key as the Account Manager table. Thus, there would be a one-to-one relationship between account managers and cars.

BTW
**Exporting a
Relationship Report**
You also can export a
relationship report. To export
a report as a PDF or XPS file,
right-click the report in the
Navigation Pane, click Export
on the shortcut menu, and
then click PDF or XPS as the
file type.

to the account manager number for all the account manager's accounts. For example, if you changed the account manager number of account manager 31 to 32, the number 32 would appear in the account manager number field for accounts whose account manager number had been 31.

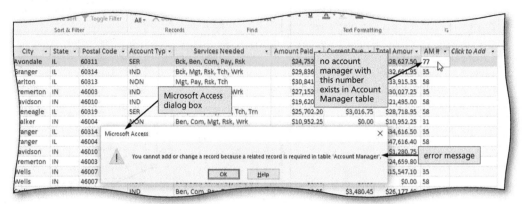

Figure 3–75

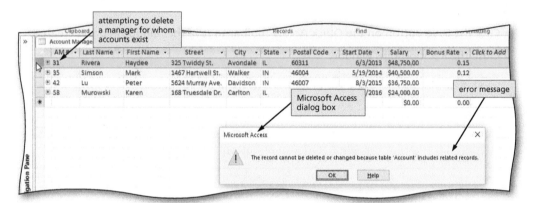

Figure 3–76

To Use a Subdatasheet

1 UPDATE RECORDS | 2 FILTER RECORDS | 3 CHANGE STRUCTURE | 4 MASS CHANGES | 5 VALIDATION RULES
6 CHANGE APPEARANCE | 7 REFERENTIAL INTEGRITY | 8 ORDER RECORDS

One consequence of the tables being explicitly related is that the accounts for an account manager can appear below the account manager in a **subdatasheet**. *Why is a subdatasheet useful? A subdatasheet is useful when you want to review or edit data in joined or related tables.* The availability of such a subdatasheet is indicated by a plus sign that appears in front of the rows in the Account Manager table. The following steps display the subdatasheet for account manager 35.

• Open the Account Manager table in Datasheet view and close the Navigation Pane (Figure 3–77).

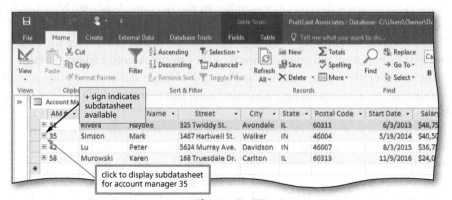

Figure 3–77

- Click the plus sign in front of the row for account manager 35 to display the subdatasheet (Figure 3–78).

How do I hide the subdatasheet when I no longer want it to appear?
When you clicked the plus sign, it changed to a minus sign. Click the minus sign.

Experiment

- Display subdatasheets for other account managers. Display more than one subdatasheet at a time. Remove the subdatasheets from the screen.

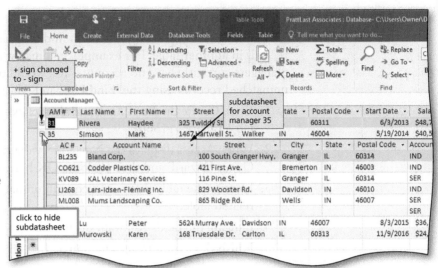

Figure 3–78

❸

- If requested by your instructor, replace the city and state for account manager 35 with your city and state.

- Close the Account Manager table.

Handling Data Inconsistency

In many organizations, databases evolve and change over time. One department might create a database for its own internal use. Employees in another department may decide they need their own database containing much of the same information. For example, the Purchasing department of an organization might create a database of products that it buys and the Receiving department may create a database of products that it receives. Each department is keeping track of the same products. When the organization eventually merges the databases, they might discover inconsistencies and duplication. The Find Duplicates Query Wizard and the Find Unmatched Query Wizard can assist in clearing the resulting database of duplication and errors.

BTW

Database Design: Validation
In most organizations, decisions about what is valid and what is invalid data are made during the requirements gathering process and the database design process.

To Find Duplicate Records

One reason to include a primary key for a table is to eliminate duplicate records. A possibility still exists, however, that duplicate records can get into your database. You would use the following steps to find duplicate records using the 'Find Duplicates Query Wizard'.

1. Click Create on the ribbon, and then click the Query Wizard button (Create tab | Queries group).
2. When Access displays the New Query dialog box, click the 'Find Duplicates Query Wizard' and then click the OK button.
3. Identify the table and field or fields that might contain duplicate information.
4. Indicate any other fields you want displayed.
5. Finish the wizard to see any duplicate records.

TO FIND UNMATCHED RECORDS

Occasionally, you might need to find records in one table that have no matching records in another table. For example, you may want to determine which account managers currently have no accounts. You would use the following steps to find unmatched records using the 'Find Unmatched Query Wizard'.

1. Click Create on the ribbon, and then click the Query Wizard button (Create tab | Queries group).
2. When Access displays the New Query dialog box, click the 'Find Unmatched Query Wizard' and then click the OK button.
3. Identify the table that might contain unmatched records, and then identify the related table.
4. Indicate the fields you want displayed.
5. Finish the wizard to see any unmatched records.

Ordering Records

Normally, Access sequences the records in the Account table by account number whenever listing them because the Account Number field is the primary key. You can change this order, if desired.

To Use the Ascending Button to Order Records

1 UPDATE RECORDS | 2 FILTER RECORDS | 3 CHANGE STRUCTURE | 4 MASS CHANGES | 5 VALIDATION RULES
6 CHANGE APPEARANCE | 7 REFERENTIAL INTEGRITY | 8 ORDER RECORDS

To change the order in which records appear, use the Ascending or Descending buttons. Either button reorders the records based on the field in which the insertion point is located. The following steps order the records by city using the Ascending button. *Why? Using the Ascending button is the quickest and easiest way to order records.*

1

• Open the Account table in Datasheet view.

• Click the City field on the first record to select the field (Figure 3–79).

Q&A
Did I have to click the field on the first record?
No. Any other record would have worked as well.

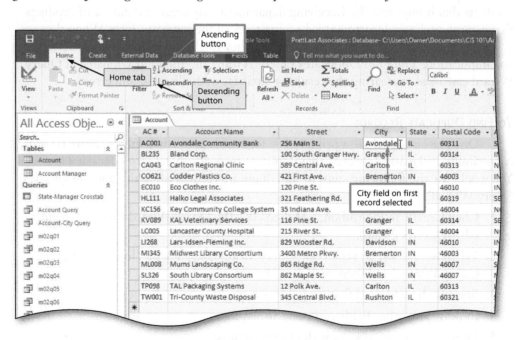

Figure 3–79

2

- Click the Ascending button (Home tab | Sort & Filter group) to sort the records by City (Figure 3–80).

3

- Close the Account table.

- Click the No button (Microsoft Access dialog box) when asked if you want to save your changes.

What if I saved the changes?
The next time you open the table the records will be sorted by city.

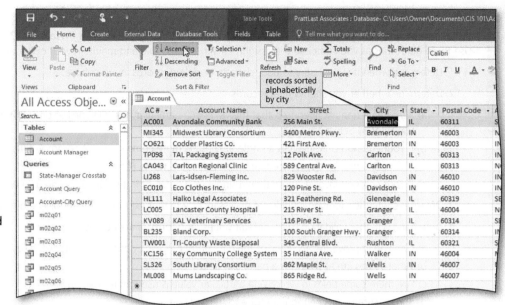

Figure 3–80

- If desired, sign out of your Microsoft account.

- Exit Access.

Other Ways	
1. Right-click field name, click Sort A to Z (for ascending) or Sort Z to A (for descending)	2. Click the field selector arrow and click Sort A to Z or Sort Z to A

TO USE THE ASCENDING BUTTON TO ORDER RECORDS ON MULTIPLE FIELDS

Just as you are able to sort the answer to a query on multiple fields, you can also sort the data that appears in a datasheet on multiple fields. To do so, the major and minor keys must be next to each other in the datasheet with the major key on the left. If this is not the case, you can drag the columns into the correct position. Instead of dragging, however, usually it will be easier to use a query that has the data sorted in the desired order.

To sort on a combination of fields where the major key is just to the left of the minor key, you would use the following steps.

1. Click the field selector at the top of the major key column to select the entire column.

2. Hold down the SHIFT key and then click the field selector for the minor key column to select both columns.

3. Click the Ascending button to sort the records.

Summary

In this module you have learned how to use a form to add records to a table, search for records, delete records, filter records, change the database structure, create and use lookup fields, create calculated fields, create and use multivalued fields, make mass changes, create validation rules, change the appearance of a datasheet, specify referential integrity, and use subdatasheets.

BTW

Access Help
At any time while using Access, you can find answers to questions and display information about various topics through Access Help. Used properly, this form of assistance can increase your productivity and reduce your frustrations by minimizing the time you spend learning how to use Access. For instructions about Access Help and exercises that will help you gain confidence in using it, read the Office and Windows module at the beginning of this book.

CONSIDER THIS

What decisions will you need to make when maintaining your own databases?
Use these guidelines as you complete the assignments in this module and maintain your own databases outside of this class.

1. Determine when it is necessary to add, change, or delete records in a database.

2. Determine whether you should filter records.

   a) If your criterion for filtering is that the value in a particular field matches or does not match a certain specific value, use Filter By Selection.

   b) If your criterion only involves a single field but is more complex, use a common filter.

   c) If your criterion involves more than one field, use Filter By Form.

   d) If your criterion involves more than a single And or Or, or if it involves sorting, use Advanced Filter/Sort.

3. Determine whether additional fields are necessary or whether existing fields should be deleted.

4. Determine whether validation rules, default values, and formats are necessary.

   a) Can you improve the accuracy of the data entry process by enforcing data validation?

   b) What values are allowed for a particular field?

   c) Are there some fields in which one particular value is used more than another?

   d) Should some fields be required for each record?

   e) Are there some fields for which special formats would be appropriate?

5. Determine whether changes to the format of a datasheet are desirable.

   a) Would totals or other calculations be useful in the datasheet?

   b) Would different gridlines make the datasheet easier to read?

   c) Would alternating colors in the rows make them easier to read?

   d) Would a different font and/or font color make the text stand out better?

   e) Is the font size appropriate?

   f) Is the column spacing appropriate?

6. Identify related tables in order to implement relationships between the tables.

   a) Is there a one-to-many relationship between the tables?

   b) If so, which table is the one table?

   c) Which table is the many table?

7. When specifying referential integrity, address deletion and update policies.

   a) Decide how to handle deletions. Should deletion be prohibited or should the delete cascade?

   b) Decide how to handle the update of the primary key. Should the update be prohibited or should the update cascade?

CONSIDER THIS

How should you submit solutions to questions in the assignments identified with a symbol?
Every assignment in this book contains one or more questions identified with a symbol. These questions require you to think beyond the assigned database. Present your solutions to the questions in the format required by your instructor. Possible formats may include one or more of these options: write the answer; create a document that contains the answer; present your answer to the class; discuss your answer in a group; record the answer as audio or video using a webcam, smartphone, or portable media player; or post answers on a blog, wiki, or website.

Apply Your Knowledge
Reinforce the skills and apply the concepts you learned in this module.

Adding Lookup Fields, Specifying Validation Rules, Updating Records, Updating Reports, and Creating Relationships

Instructions: Run Access. Open the Apply Friendly Janitorial Services database that you modified in Apply Your Knowledge in Module 2. (If you did not complete the exercise, see your instructor for a copy of the modified database.)

Perform the following tasks:

1. Open the Client table in Design view.

2. Add a Lookup field called Client Type to the Client table. The field should appear after the Postal Code field. The field will contain data on the type of client. The client types are IND (industrial, manufacturing), RET (retail stores), and SER (service, nonprofit). Save the changes to the Client table.

3. Create the following validation rules for the Client table.

    a. Specify the legal values IND, RET, and SER for the Client Type field. Enter `Must be IND, RET, or SER` as the validation text.

    b. Format the Client Number field to ensure that any letters entered in the field appear as uppercase.

    c. Make the Client Name field a required field.

4. Save the changes and close the table. You do not need to test the current data.

5. Create an update query for the Client table. Change all the entries in the Client Type field to SER. Run the query and save it as Client Type Update Query.

6. Open the Client table in Datasheet view, update the following records, and then close the table:

    a. Change the client type for clients CC25, CP03, MM01, and TE15 to IND.

    b. Change the client type for clients AZ01, BL24, and HC17 to RET.

7. Create a split form for the Client table. Save the form as Client Split Form.

8. Open the Client Split Form in Form view, find client HC17, and change the client name to Hilltop Crafters. Close the form.

9. Open the Client Financial Report in Layout view and add the Client Type field to the report as shown in Figure 3–81. Save the report.

Client Number	Client Name	Client Type	Amount Paid	Current Due	Supervisor Number
AT13	Atlas Repair	SER	$5,400.00	$600.00	103
AZ01	AZ Auto	RET	$9,250.00	$975.00	110
BB35	Babbage Bookkeeping	SER	$8,820.00	$980.00	110

Figure 3–81

10. Establish referential integrity between the Supervisor table (the one table) and the Client table (the many table). Cascade the update but not the delete. Save the relationship.

11. If requested to do so by your instructor, rename the Client Split Form as Split Form for First Name Last Name where First Name Last Name is your name.

12. Submit the revised database in the format specified by your instructor.

13. ✳ The values in the Client Type field are currently in the order IND, RET, SER. How would you reorder the values to SER, IND, RET in the Client Type list?

Extend Your Knowledge

Extend the skills you learned in this module and experiment with new skills. You may need to use Help to complete the assignment.

Creating Action Queries, Changing Table Properties, and Adding Totals to a Datasheet

Note: To complete this assignment, you will be required to use the Data Files. Please contact your instructor for information about accessing the Data Files.

Continued >

Extend Your Knowledge *continued*

Instructions: Babbage Bookkeeping is a small company that provides bookkeeping services to small businesses. PrattLast Associates has been approached about buying Babbage Bookkeeping. PrattLast is interested in knowing how many clients the companies have in common. Babbage also needs to do some database maintenance by finding duplicate records and finding unmatched records.

Perform the following tasks:

1. Run Access and open the Extend Babbage Bookkeeping database. Create a make-table query to create the Potential Accounts table in the Babbage Bookkeeping database shown in Figure 3–82. Run the query and save it as Make Table Query.

Client Numb ▼	Client Name ▼	Street ▼	City ▼	State ▼	Postal Code ▼	Amount Pai(▼	Balance Due ▼	Bookkeeper ▼
A54	Afton Manufac	612 Revere Rd.	Granger	IL	60311	$575.00	$315.00	22
A62	Atlas Distribute	227 Dandelion	Burles	IN	46002	$250.00	$175.00	24
B26	Blake-Scryps	557 Maum St.	Georgetown	IN	46008	$875.00	$250.00	24
D76	Dege Grocery C	446 Linton Ave	Burles	IN	46002	$1,015.00	$325.00	22
G56	Grandston Clea	337 Abelard Rd	Buda	IL	60310	$485.00	$165.00	24
H21	Hill Country Sh	247 Fulton St.	Granger	IL	60311	$0.00	$285.00	34
J77	Jones Plumbin	75 Getty Blvd.	Buda	IL	60310	$685.00	$0.00	22
M26	Mohr Art Suppl	665 Maum St.	Georgetown	IN	46008	$125.00	$185.00	24
S56	SeeSaw Indust	31 Liatris Ave.	Walburg	IN	46006	$1,200.00	$645.00	22
T45	Tate Repair	824 Revere Rd.	Granger	IL	60311	$345.00	$200.00	34
W24	Woody Sportin	578 Central Ave	Walburg	IN	46006	$975.00	$0.00	34
C29	Catering by Jer	123 Second St.	Granger	IL	60311	$0.00	$250.00	34

Figure 3–82

2. Open the Potential Accounts table and change the font to Arial with a font size of 10. Resize the columns to best fit the data. Save the changes to the table and close the table.

3. Open the Bookkeeper table and add the Totals row to the table. Calculate the average hourly rate and the total Earnings YTD. Save the changes to the table layout and close the table.

4. Use the Find Duplicates Query Wizard to find duplicate information in the City field of the Client table. Include the Client Name in the query. Save the query as City Duplicates Query and close the query.

5. Use the Find Unmatched Query Wizard to find all records in the Bookkeeper table that do not match records in the Client table. Bookkeeper Number is the common field in both tables. Include the Bookkeeper Number, Last Name, and First Name in the query. Save the query as Bookkeeper Unmatched Query and close the query.

6. If requested to do so by your instructor, change the client name in the Client table for client number B26 to First Name Last Name where First Name Last Name is your name. If your name is longer than the space allowed, simply enter as much as you can.

7. Submit the revised database in the format specified by your instructor.

8. ✳ What differences, if any, are there between the Client table and the Potential Accounts table you created with the make-table query?

Expand Your World

Create a solution, which uses cloud and web technologies, by learning and investigating on your own from general guidance.

Problem: You own a small business that employs college students to do odd jobs for homeowners in the college town where you live. You created an Access database to keep track of your customers and workers and have been teaching yourself more about database design and how best to use Access to promote and manage your business.

Perform the following tasks:

1. Run Access and open the Expand Odd Jobs database. Edit the relationship between the Worker table and the Customer table to cascade the updates. Save the change to the relationship.

2. Create a relationship report for the relationship and save the report as First Name Last Name Relationship Report where First Name Last Name is your name.

3. Export the relationship as an RTF/Word document to a cloud-based storage location of your choice. Do not save the export steps.

4. Research the web to find a graphic that depicts a one-to-many relationship for a relational database. (*Hint:* Use your favorite search engine and enter keywords such as ERD diagram, entity-relationship diagram, or one to many relationship.)

5. Insert the graphic into the relationship report using an app of your choice, such as Word Online, and save the modified report.

6. Share the modified report with your instructor.

7. Submit the revised database in the format specified by your instructor.

8. ✷ Which cloud-based storage location did you use? How did you locate your graphic? Which app did you use to modify the report?

In the Labs

Design, create, modify, and/or use a database following the guidelines, concepts, and skills presented in this module. Labs are listed in order of increasing difficulty. Labs 1 and 2, which increase in difficulty, require you to create solutions based on what you learned in the module. Lab 3 requires you to apply your creative thinking and problem–solving skills to design and implement a solution.

Lab 1: Maintaining the Garden Naturally Database

Problem: Garden Naturally is expanding rapidly and needs to make some database changes to handle the expansion. The company needs to know more about its customers, such as general types of products needed. It also needs to add validation rules and update records in the database.

Note: Use the database modified in Lab 1 of Module 2 for this assignment, or see your instructor for information on accessing the files required for this book.

Instructions: Perform the following tasks:
1. Open the Lab 1 Garden Naturally database and open the Customer table in Design view.
2. Add a multivalued lookup field, Product Types Needed, to the Customer table. The field should appear after the Postal Code field. Table 3–2 lists the product type abbreviations that management would like in the multivalued field as well as a description. Save the change to the table.

Table 3–2 Product Type Abbreviations and Descriptions	
Product Type Abbreviations	**Product Type Descriptions**
Comp	Composting Needs
Frtl	Fertilizers
Grdn	Garden Supplies
Grnh	Greenhouse Supplies
Lawn	Lawn and Landscaping
Seed	Seeds
Soil	Soils and Nutrients
Watr	Watering Equipment

Continued >

In the Labs *continued*

3. Add a calculated field named Total Amount (Amount Paid + Balance Due) to the Customer table. The field should follow the Balance Due field. Save the change to the table.

4. Create the following rules for the Customer table and save the changes:

   a. Ensure that any letters entered in the Customer Number field appear as uppercase.

   b. Make Customer Name a required field.

   c. Ensure that only the values DE, NJ, and PA can be entered in the State field. Include validation text.

   d. Assign a default value of NJ to the State field.

5. Use Filter By Form to find all records where the city is Gaston and the balance due is $0.00. Delete the record(s). Do not save the filter.

6. Open the Customer table in Datasheet view and add the data shown in Figure 3–83 to the Product Types Needed field. Resize the field to best fit and save the changes to the layout of the table.

Customer Table		
Customer Number	**Customer Name**	**Product Types Needed**
AA30	All About Gardens	Grdn, Seed, Soil, Watr
CT02	Christmas Tree Farm	Comp, Frtl, Seed, Soil, Watr
GG01	Garden Gnome	Frtl, Grdn, Lawn
GT34	Green Thumb Growers	Frtl, Grnh, Seed
LH15	Lawn & Home Store	Comp, Frtl, Grdn, Lawn
ML25	Mum's Landscaping	Frtl, Soil, Watr
OA45	Outside Architects	Grdn, Watr
PL10	Pat's Landscaping	Frtl, Grdn, Watr
PN18	Pyke Nurseries	Comp, Frtl, Grnh, Seed, Soil
SL25	Summit Lawn Service	Grdn, Lawn, Watr
TW34	TAL Wholesalers	Comp, Frtl, Seed, Soil
TY03	TLC Yard Care	Lawn, Watr
YS04	Yard Shoppe	Grdn, Lawn, Watr
YW01	Young's Wholesalers	Comp, Frtl, Grdn, Lawn, Seed, Soil

Figure 3–83

7. Open the Sales Rep table in Design view and change the field size for the Address field to 25. Save the changes and close the table.

8. Open the Sales Rep table in Datasheet view, find the record for sales rep 32, and change the address to 982 Victoria Station Rd. Resize the column to best fit.

9. If requested to do so by your instructor, change the last name for sales rep 35 to your last name. If your last name is longer than 15 characters, simply enter as much as you can.

10. Save the changes to the layout of the table and close the Sales Rep table.

11. Establish referential integrity between the Sales Rep table (the one table) and the Customer table (the many table). Cascade the update but not the delete.

12. Submit the revised database in the format specified by your instructor.

13. ✹ The State field currently has three possible values. How would you add MD to the State field list?

Lab 2: **Maintaining the Museum Gift Shop Database**

Problem: The manager of the Science Museum gift shop needs to change the database structure, add validation rules, and update records. Also, a volunteer at the gift shop was asked to add some items to the database. By mistake, the volunteer created a new database in which to store the items. These items need to be added to the Museum Gift Shop database.

Note: To complete this assignment, you will be required to use the Data Files. Please contact your instructor for information about accessing the Data Files. Use the database modified in Lab 2 of Module 2 for this assignment or see your instructor for information on accessing the files required for this book.

Instructions: Perform the following tasks:

1. Open the Lab 2 Museum Gift Shop database, and then open the Item table in Design view.
2. Add a lookup field, Item Type, to the Item table. The field should appear after the Description field. The field will contain data on the type of item for sale. The item types are ACT (activity, game), BKS (book), and NOV (novelty, gift).
3. Add the following validation rules to the Item table and save the changes:
   a. Make Description a required field.
   b. Specify the legal values ACT, BKS, and NOV for the Item Type field. Include validation text.
   c. Assign ACT as the default value for the Item Type field.
   d. Specify that the number on hand must be between 0 and 50, inclusive. Include validation text.
4. Using a query, assign the value ACT to the Item Type field for all records. Save the query as Update Query.
5. Create a split form for the Item table and save it as Item Split Form.
6. Use the split form to change the item type for items 6234, 6345, and 7123 to BKS. Change the item type for items 3663, 4583, 6185, 8196, and 8344 to NOV.
7. Open the Lab 2 Additional Items database from the Data Files.
8. Create and run a query to append the data in the Additional Items table to the Item table in the Lab 2 Museum Gift Shop database. Save the query as Append Query and close the Lab 2 Additional Items database.
9. Open the Lab 2 Museum Gift Shop database and then open the Item table. The result of the append query will be the table shown in Figure 3–84.

Item Number	Description	Item Type	On Hand	Wholesale	Retail	VC	Click to Add
3663	Agate Bookends	NOV	4	$16.25	$27.97	GS	
3673	Amazing Science Fun	ACT	8	$13.50	$24.99	AW	
3873	Big Book of Why	BKS	12	$7.99	$14.95	AW	
4553	Cosmos Uncovered	ACT	9	$8.95	$15.00	SD	
4573	Crystal Growing Kit	ACT	7	$6.75	$12.97	AW	
4583	Dinosaur Egg Ornament	NOV	12	$7.50	$14.99	GS	
5923	Discovery Dinosaurs	ACT	3	$12.35	$19.95	AW	
6185	Fibonacci Necklace	NOV	5	$16.75	$29.99	GS	
6234	Fun with Math	BKS	16	$12.95	$24.95	SD	
6325	Fun Straws	ACT	20	$4.55	$8.99	SD	
6345	Geek Toys Guide	BKS	20	$5.10	$9.99	SD	
7123	Gem Nature Guide	BKS	12	$9.50	$14.95	AW	
7934	Gyrobot	ACT	24	$27.99	$49.99	GS	
8196	Molecule Necklace	NOV	6	$16.25	$29.95	GS	
8344	Onyx Jar	NOV	2	$7.50	$13.97	AW	
8590	Paper Planes	ACT	22	$7.10	$13.99	SD	
9201	Sidewalk Art and More	ACT	15	$9.35	$16.95	GS	
9458	Slime Time	ACT	15	$15.35	$24.99	SD	
*		ACT					

Figure 3–84

Continued >

10. Create an advanced filter for the Item table. Filter the table to find all items with fewer than 10 items on hand. Sort the filter by Item Type and Description. Save the filter settings as a query and name the filter Reorder Filter. Clear the filter from the Item table.

11. Using a query, delete all records in the Item table where the description starts with the letter M. Run the query and save it as Delete Query.

12. If requested to do so by your instructor, right-click the Item table in the Navigation Pane, click Table Properties, and add a description for the Item table that includes your first and last name and the date you completed this assignment. Save the change to the table property.

13. Specify referential integrity between the Vendor table (the one table) and the Item table (the many table). Cascade the update but not the delete.

14. Add the Item Type field to the Item Status Report. It should follow the Description field.

15. Submit the revised database in the format specified by your instructor.

16. ✳ There are two ways to enter the validation rule in Step 3d. What are they? Which one did you use?

Lab 3: **Consider This: Your Turn**

Maintaining the Camshay Marketing Database

Instructions: Open the Lab 3 Camshay Marketing database you used in Module 2. If you did not use this database, contact your instructor for information about accessing the required files.

Part 1: Use the concepts and techniques presented in this module to modify the database according to the following requirements:

  a. Grant Auction House is no longer a client of Camshay. Use Find or Filter By Selection to delete this record.

  b. A Total Amount field that summed the Amount Paid and Current Due fields would be beneficial for the reports that Camshay needs.

  c. Camshay could better serve its clients by adding a field that would list each client's type of business or organizations. Businesses are nonprofit (NON), service (SER), or retail (RET).

  d. Most businesses are service organizations. Buda Community Clinic, Hendley County Hospital, and Granger Foundation are nonprofit organizations. The Bikeshop and Woody Sporting Goods are retail stores.

  e. The Client Financial Report must show the Total Amount.

  f. An entry should always appear in the Client Name field. Any letters in the Client Number field should appear in uppercase.

  g. A client's current due amount should never exceed $10,000.00.

  h. Camshay has acquired a new client and needs to add the data to the database. Fine Wooden Crafts is a retail store located at 24 Oakley in Buda, NC 27032. Its client number is FW01 with zero amount paid and current due. The client has been assigned to Jeff Scott.

  i. Specify referential integrity. Cascade the update but not the delete.

  j. Camshay would like the records in the Client table to be sorted by client name, not client number.

Submit your assignment in the format specified by your instructor.

Part 2: You made several decisions while including adding a calculated field, Total Amount, to the database. What was the rationale behind your decisions? Does the calculated field actually exist in the database? Are there any issues that you need to consider when you create a calculated field?

4 Creating Reports and Forms

Objectives

You will have mastered the material in this module when you can:

- Create reports and forms using wizards
- Modify reports and forms in Layout view
- Group and sort data in a report
- Add totals and subtotals to a report
- Conditionally format controls
- Resize columns
- Filter records in reports and forms

- Print reports and forms
- Apply themes
- Add a field to a report or form
- Add a date
- Change the format of a control
- Move controls
- Create and print mailing labels

Introduction

One of the advantages to maintaining data in a database is the ability to present the data in attractive reports and forms that highlight certain information. Reports present data in an organized format that is usually printed. The data can come from one or more tables. On the other hand, you usually view forms on the screen, although you can print them. In addition to viewing data, you can also use forms to update data. That is, you can use forms to add records, delete records, or change records. Like reports, the data in the form can come from one or more tables. This module shows how to create reports and forms by creating two reports and a form. There are several ways to create both reports and forms. One approach is to use the Report or Form Wizard. You can also use either Layout view or Design view to create or modify a report or form. In this module, you will use Layout view for this purpose. In later modules, you will learn how to use Design view. You will also use the Label Wizard to produce mailing labels.

Project — Reports and Forms

PrattLast Associates is now able to better keep track of its account information and to target account needs by using the database of accounts and managers. PrattLast hopes to improve their decision-making capability further by using two custom reports that meet their specific needs. Figure 4–1 shows the Account Financial report, which is a modified version of an existing report. The report features

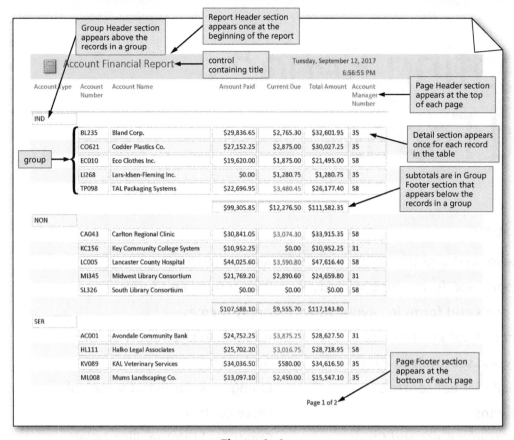

Figure 4–1a

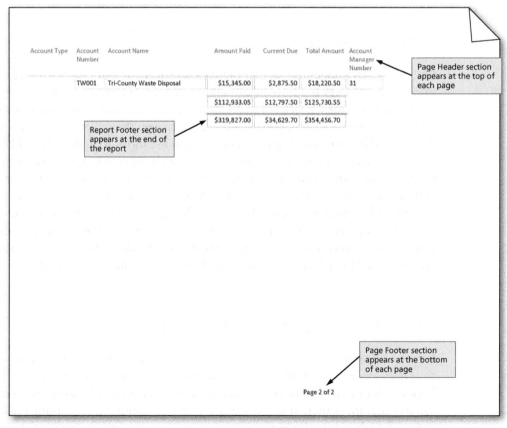

Figure 4–1b

grouping. The report shown in Figure 4–1 groups records by account types. There are three separate groups, one each for the three possible account types: IND, NON, and SER. The appropriate type appears before each group. The totals of the Amount Paid, Current Due, and Total Amount fields for the accounts in the group (called a **subtotal**) appear after the group. At the end of the report are grand totals of the same fields.

Figure 4–2 shows the second report. This report encompasses data from both the Account Manager table and the Account table. Like the report in Figure 4–1, the data is grouped, although this time it is grouped by account manager number. Not only does the manager number appear before each group, but the first name and last name of the manager appear as well. Like the first report, this report contains subtotals.

BTW

Consider Your Audience

Always design reports and forms with your audience in mind. Make your reports and forms accessible to individuals who may have problems with colorblindness or reduced vision.

Accounts by Account Manager

AM #	First Name	Last Name	AC #	Account Name	Amount Paid	Current Due
31	Haydee	Rivera				
			AC001	Avondale Community Bank	$24,752.25	$3,875.25
			KC156	Key Community College System	$10,952.25	$0.00
			MI345	Midwest Library Consortium	$21,769.20	$2,890.60
			TW001	Tri-County Waste Disposal	$15,345.00	$2,875.50
Summary for 'Account Manager Number' = 31 (4 detail records)						
Sum					$72,818.70	$9,641.35
35	Mark	Simson				
			BL235	Bland Corp.	$29,836.65	$2,765.30
			CO621	Codder Plastics Co.	$27,152.25	$2,875.00
			KV089	KAL Veterinary Services	$34,036.50	$580.00
			LI268	Lars-Idsen-Fleming Inc.	$0.00	$1,280.75
			ML008	Mums Landscaping Co.	$13,097.10	$2,450.00
Summary for 'Account Manager Number' = 35 (5 detail records)						
Sum					$104,122.50	$9,951.05
58	Karen	Murowski				
			CA043	Carlton Regional Clinic	$30,841.05	$3,074.30
			EC010	Eco Clothes Inc.	$19,620.00	$1,875.00
			HL111	Halko Legal Associates	$25,702.20	$3,016.75
			LC005	Lancaster County Hospital	$44,025.60	$3,590.80
			SL326	South Library Consortium	$0.00	$0.00
			TP098	TAL Packaging Systems	$22,696.95	$3,480.45
Summary for 'Account Manager Number' = 58 (6 detail records)						
Sum					$142,885.80	$15,037.30
Grand Total					$319,827.00	$34,629.70

Tuesday, September 12, 2017   Page 1 of 1

Figure 4–2

PrattLast also wants to improve the process of updating data by using a custom form, as shown in Figure 4–3. The form has a title and a date. Unlike the form you can create by clicking the Form button, this form does not contain all the fields in the Account table. In addition, the fields are in a different order than in the table. For this form, PrattLast likes the appearance of including the fields in a stacked layout.

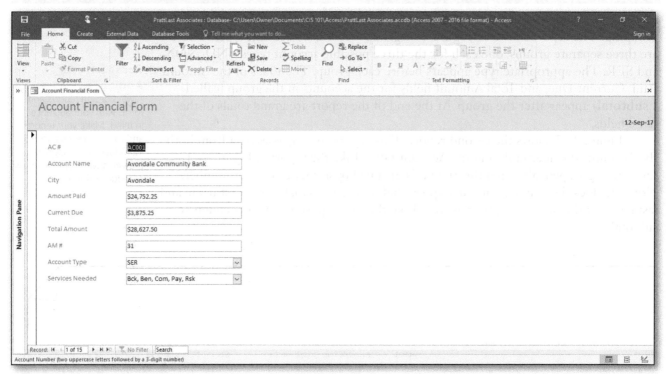

Figure 4–3

PrattLast also wants to be able to produce mailing labels for its accounts. These labels must align correctly with the particular labels PrattLast uses and must be sorted by postal code (Figure 4–4).

Midwest Library Consortium
3400 Metro Pkwy.
Bremerton, IN 46003

Codder Plastics Co.
421 First Ave.
Bremerton, IN 46003

Lancaster County Hospital
215 River St.
Granger, IL 46004

Key Community College System
35 Indiana Ave.
Walker, IN 46004

South Library Consortium
862 Maple St.
Wells, IN 46007

Mums Landscaping Co.
865 Ridge Rd.
Wells, IN 46007

Lars-Idsen-Fleming Inc.
829 Wooster Rd.
Davidson, IN 46010

Eco Clothes Inc.
120 Pine St.
Davidson, IN 46010

Avondale Community Bank
256 Main St.
Avondale, IL 60311

TAL Packaging Systems
12 Polk Ave.
Carlton, IL 60313

Carlton Regional Clinic
589 Central Ave.
Carlton, IL 60313

KAL Veterinary Services
116 Pine St.
Granger, IL 60314

Figure 4–4

In this module, you will learn how to create the reports, forms, and labels shown in Figures 4–1 through 4–4. The following roadmap identifies general activities you will perform as you progress through this module:

1. GROUP, SORT, and TOTAL in a report.

2. CONDITIONALLY FORMAT CONTROLS in a report.

3. FILTER REPORT RECORDS.

4. Create a MULTIPLE-TABLE REPORT.

5. Create a form using the FORM WIZARD.

6. MODIFY CONTROLS in a control layout on a form.

7. FILTER FORM RECORDS.

8. Create MAILING LABELS.

Report Creation

When working with a report in Access, there are four different ways to view the report: Report view, Print Preview, Layout view, and Design view. Report view shows the report on the screen. Print Preview shows the report as it will appear when printed. Layout view is similar to Report view in that it shows the report on the screen, but it also allows you to make changes to the report. Using Layout view is usually the easiest way to make such changes. Design view also allows you to make changes, but it does not show you the actual report. It is most useful when the changes you need to make are complex. In this module, you will use Layout view to modify the report.

Report Sections

A report is divided into various sections to help clarify the presentation of data. A typical report consists of a Report Header section, Page Header section, Detail section, Page Footer section, and Report Footer section (see Figure 4–1). In Design view, which you will use in later modules, you can see the names for each section on the screen. Even though the names of the sections are not visible in Layout view, it is still useful to understand the purpose of the various sections.

The contents of the Report Header section appear once at the beginning of the report. In the Account Financial Report, the report title is in the Report Header section. The contents of the Report Footer section appear once at the end of the report. In the Account Financial Report, the Report Footer section contains the grand totals of Amount Paid, Current Due, and Total Amount. The contents of the Page Header section appear once at the top of each page and typically contain the column headers. The contents of the Page Footer section appear once at the bottom of each page; Page Footer sections often contain a date and a page number. The contents of the Detail section appear once for each record in the table; for example, once for Bland Corp., once for Codder Plastics Co., and so on. In this report, the detail records contain the account number, account name, amount paid, current due, total amount, and account manager number.

When the data in a report is grouped, there are two additional sections. The contents of the Group Header section are printed above the records in a particular group, and the contents of the Group Footer section are printed below the group. In the Account Financial Report, the Group Header section contains the Account Type, and the Group Footer section contains the subtotals of Amount Paid, Current Due, and Total Amount.

BTW

The Ribbon and Screen Resolution
Access may change how the groups and buttons within the groups appear on the ribbon, depending on the computer's screen resolution. Thus, your ribbon may look different from the ones in this book if you are using a screen resolution other than 1366 x 768.

BTW

Touch Screen Differences
The Office and Windows interfaces may vary if you are using a touch screen. For this reason, you might notice that the function or appearance of your touch screen differs slightly from this module's presentation.

BTW

Enabling the Content
For each of the databases you use in this module, you will need to enable the content.

To Group and Sort in a Report

In Layout view of the report, you can specify both grouping and sorting by using the Group & Sort button on the Design tab. The following steps open the Account Financial Report in Layout view and then specify both grouping and sorting in the report. *Why? PrattLast has determined that the records in the report should be grouped by account type. That is, all the accounts of a given type should appear together immediately after the type. Within the accounts in a given type, accounts are to be ordered by account number.*

1

- Run Access and open the database named PrattLast Associates from your hard disk, OneDrive, or other storage location. If you do not have the PrattLast Associates database, see your instructor.

- Right-click the Account Financial Report in the Navigation Pane to produce a shortcut menu.

- Click Layout View on the shortcut menu to open the report in Layout view.

- Close the Navigation Pane.

- If a field list appears, close the field list by clicking the 'Add Existing Fields' button (Report Layout Tools Design tab | Tools group).

- Click the Group & Sort button (Report Layout Tools Design tab | Grouping & Totals group) to display the Group, Sort, and Total pane (Figure 4–5).

Q&A | My report is in a different order. Do I need to change it?
No. You will change the order of the records in the following steps.

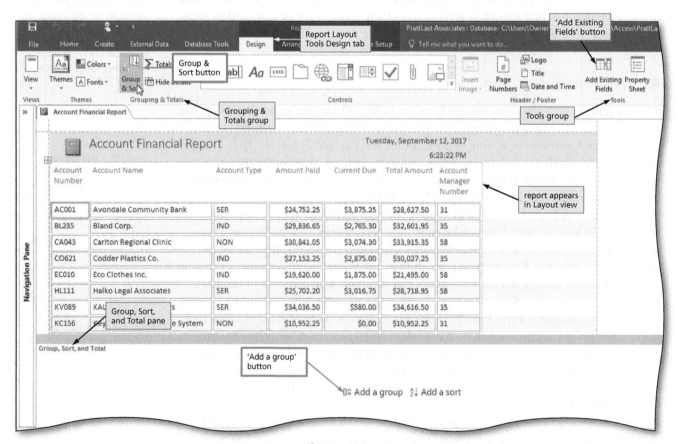

Figure 4–5

2

• Click the 'Add a group' button to add a group (Figure 4–6).

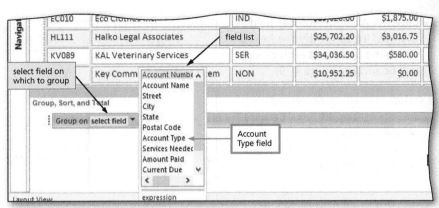

Figure 4–6

3

• Click the Account Type field in the field list to select a field for grouping and group the records on the selected field (Figure 4–7).

Q&A

Does the field on which I group have to be the first field?
No. If you select a field other than the first field, Access will move the field you select into the first position.

Figure 4–7

4

• Click the 'Add a sort' button to add a sort (Figure 4–8).

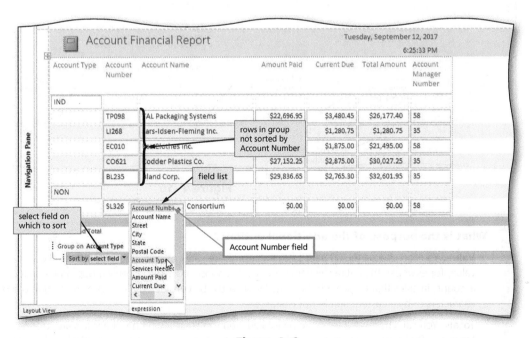

Figure 4–8

5

- Click the Account Number field in the field list to specify the field on which the records in each group will be sorted (Figure 4–9).

I thought the report would be sorted by Account Type, because I chose to group on that field. What is the effect of choosing to sort by Account Number?
This sort takes place within groups. You are specifying that within the list of accounts of the same type, the accounts will be ordered by account number.

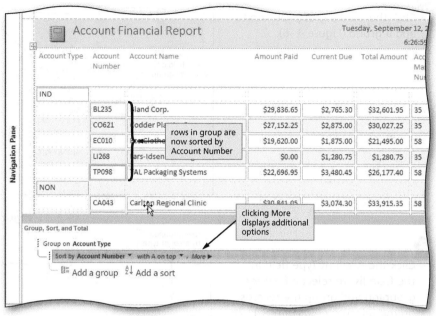

Figure 4–9

Other Ways

1. Right-click column header for field on which to group, click Group On (field name)

Grouping and Sorting Options

For both grouping and sorting, you can click the More button to specify additional options (see Figure 4–10).

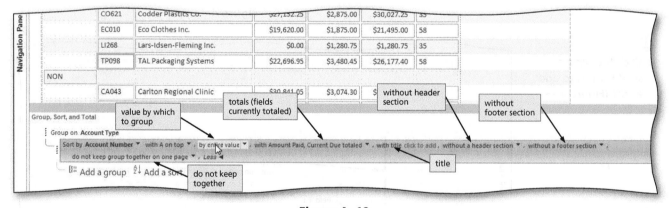

Figure 4–10

What is the purpose of the additional options?

- **Value.** You can choose the number of characters of the value on which to group. Typically, you would group by the entire value, for example, the entire city name. You could choose, however, to only group on the first character, in which case all accounts in cities that begin with the same letter would be considered a group. You could also group by the first two characters or by a custom number of characters.

- **Totals.** You can choose the values to be totaled. You can specify whether the totals are to appear in the group header or in the group footer and whether to include a grand total. You can also choose whether to show group totals as a percentage of the grand total.

- **Title.** You can customize the group title.
- **Header section.** You can include or omit a header section for the group.
- **Footer section.** You can include or omit a footer section for the group.
- **Keep together.** You can indicate whether Access should attempt to keep portions of a group together on the same page. The default setting does not keep portions of a group together, but you can specify that Access should keep a whole group together on one page, when possible. If the group will not fit on the remainder of the page, Access will move the group header and the records in a group to the next page. Finally, you can choose to have Access keep the header and the first record together on one page. If the header would fit at the bottom of a page, but there would not be room for the first record, Access will move the header to the next page.

Report Controls

The various objects on a report are called **controls.** You can manipulate these controls to modify their location and appearance. The report title, column headers, contents of various fields, subtotals, and so on are all contained in controls. When working in Layout view, as you will do in this module, Access handles details concerning placement, sizing, and format of these controls for you automatically. When working in Design view, you will see and manipulate the controls. Even when working in Layout view, however, it is useful to understand the concepts of controls.

The report shown in Figure 4–1 has a control containing the title, Account Financial Report. The report also includes controls containing each column header (Account Type, Account Number, Account Name, Amount Paid, Current Due, Total Amount, and Account Manager Number). A control in the Group Header section displays the account type.

There are three controls in the Group Footer section: One control displays the subtotal of Amount Paid, a second displays the subtotal of Current Due, and a third displays the subtotal of Total Amount. The Detail section has controls containing the account number, account name, amount paid, current due, total amount, and account manager number.

Access has three types of controls: bound controls, unbound controls, and calculated controls. **Bound controls** are used to display data that comes from the database, such as the account number and name. **Unbound controls** are not associated with data from the database and are used to display such things as the report's title. Finally, **calculated controls** are used to display data that is calculated from other data, such as a total.

BTW
Grouping
You should allow sufficient white space between groups. If you feel the amount is insufficient, you can add more space by enlarging the group header or group footer.

BTW
Report Design Considerations
The purpose of any report is to present specific information. Make sure that the meaning of the row and column headings is clear. You can use different fonts and sizes by changing the appropriate properties, but do not overuse them. Finally, be consistent when creating reports. Once you decide on a general report style or theme, stick with it throughout your database.

To Add Totals and Subtotals

1 GROUP, SORT, & TOTAL | 2 CONDITIONALLY FORMAT CONTROLS | 3 FILTER REPORT RECORDS | 4 MULTIPLE-TABLE REPORT
5 FORM WIZARD | 6 MODIFY CONTROLS | 7 FILTER FORM RECORDS | 8 MAILING LABELS

To add totals or other statistics, use the Totals button on the Design tab. You then select from a menu of aggregate functions, which are functions that perform some mathematical function against a group of records. The available aggregate functions, or calculations, are Sum (total), Average, Count Records, Count Values, Max (largest value), Min (smallest value), Standard Deviation, and Variance. Because the report is grouped, each group will have a **subtotal,** that is, a total for just the records in the group. At the end of the report, there will be a **grand total,** that is, a total for all records.

The following steps specify totals for three of the fields. *Why? Along with determining to group data in this report, PrattLast has also determined that subtotals and grand totals of the Amount Paid, Current Due, and Total Amount fields should be included.* Even though totals were previously specified for the Amount Paid and Current Due fields, you need to do so again because of the grouping.

1

- Click the Amount Paid column header to select the field.

Does it have to be the column header?
No, you could click the Amount Paid field on any record.

- Click the Totals button (Report Layout Tools Design tab | Grouping & Totals group) to display the list of available calculations (Figure 4–11).

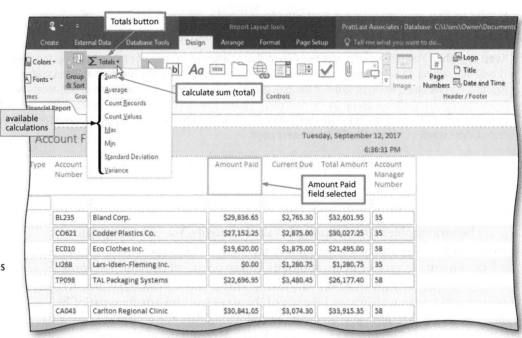

Figure 4–11

2

- Click Sum to calculate the sum of the Amount Paid values.

- If the subtotal does not appear completely, click the subtotal and then drag the lower boundary of the control for the subtotal to the approximate position shown in Figure 4–12.

I moved the control rather than resizing it. What did I do wrong?
You dragged the control rather than dragging its lower boundary. Click the Undo button on the Quick Access Toolbar to undo your change and then drag again, making sure you are pointing to the lower boundary.

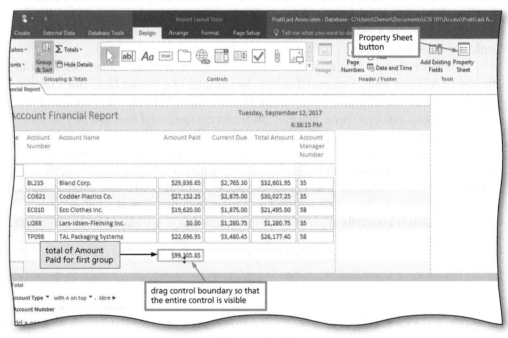

Figure 4–12

3

- Using the same technique as in Steps 1 and 2, add subtotals for the Current Due and Total Amount fields.

- Click the subtotal of the Total Amount field to select it.

- Click the Property Sheet button (Report Layout Tools Design tab | Tools group) to display the property sheet for the subtotal control.

- Click the Format box to produce an arrow, and then click the Format arrow.

- Click Currency to apply the Currency style to the subtotal of the total amount.

- Click the Property Sheet button (Report Layout Tools Design tab | Tools group) to close the property sheet.

- Scroll to the bottom of the report and use the same technique to change the format for the grand total of Total Amount to Currency.

- If necessary, drag the lower boundaries of the controls for the grand totals so that the numbers appear completely (Figure 4–13).

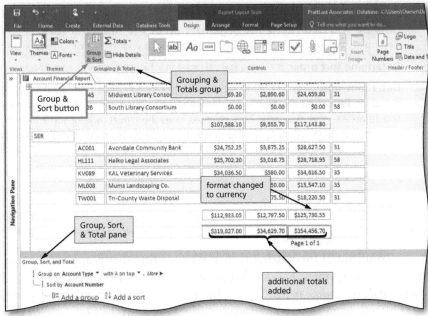

Figure 4–13

Other Ways

1. Right-click column header for field on which to total, click Total (field name)

To Remove the Group, Sort, and Total Pane

1 GROUP, SORT, & TOTAL | 2 CONDITIONALLY FORMAT CONTROLS | 3 FILTER REPORT RECORDS | 4 MULTIPLE-TABLE REPORT
5 FORM WIZARD | 6 MODIFY CONTROLS | 7 FILTER FORM RECORDS | 8 MAILING LABELS

The following step removes the Group, Sort, and Total pane from the screen. *Why? Because you have specified the required grouping and sorting for the report, you no longer need to use the Group, Sort, and Total pane.*

1

- Click the Group & Sort button (Report Layout Tools Design tab | Grouping & Totals group) to remove the Group, Sort, and Total pane (Figure 4–14).

Q&A Do I need to remove the Group, Sort, and Total pane?

No. Doing so provides more room on the screen for the report, however. You can easily display the pane whenever you need it by clicking the Group & Sort button again.

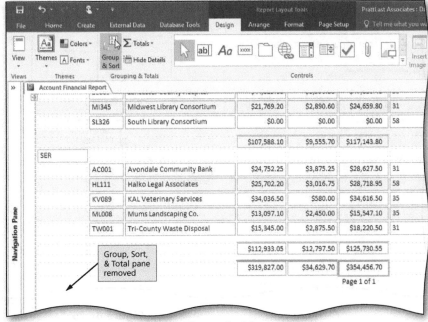

Figure 4–14

Other Ways

1. Click 'Close Grouping Dialog Box' button

CONSIDER THIS

How do you determine the organization of the report or form?

Determine various details concerning how the data in your report or form is to be organized.

Determine sort order. Is there a special order in which the records should appear?

Determine grouping. Should the records be grouped in some fashion? If so, what should appear before the records in a group? If, for example, accounts are grouped by city, the name of the city should probably appear before the group. What should appear after the group? For example, does the report include some fields for which subtotals should be calculated? If so, the subtotals would come after the group. Determine whether you need multiple levels of grouping.

To Conditionally Format Controls

1 GROUP, SORT, & TOTAL | **2 CONDITIONALLY FORMAT CONTROLS** | 3 FILTER REPORT RECORDS | 4 MULTIPLE-TABLE REPORT
5 FORM WIZARD | 6 MODIFY CONTROLS | 7 FILTER FORM RECORDS | 8 MAILING LABELS

Conditional formatting is special formatting that is applied to values that satisfy some criterion. PrattLast management has decided to apply conditional formatting to the Current Due field. *Why? They would like to emphasize values in the Current Due field that are greater than or equal to $3,000 by changing the font color to red.* The following steps conditionally format the Current Due field by specifying a **rule** that states that if the values in the field are greater than or equal to $3,000, such values will be formatted in red.

1

- Scroll to the top of the report.
- Click Format on the ribbon to display the Report Layout Tools Format tab.
- Click the Current Due field on the first record to select the field (Figure 4–15).

Q&A Does it have to be the first record?
No. You could click the field on any record.

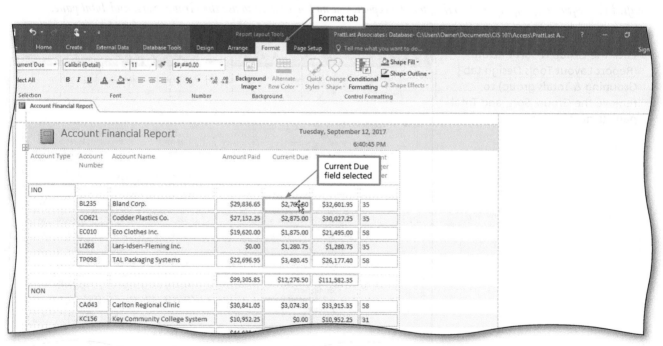

Figure 4–15

2

- Click the Conditional Formatting button (Report Layout Tools Format tab | Control Formatting group) to display the Conditional Formatting Rules Manager dialog box (Figure 4–16).

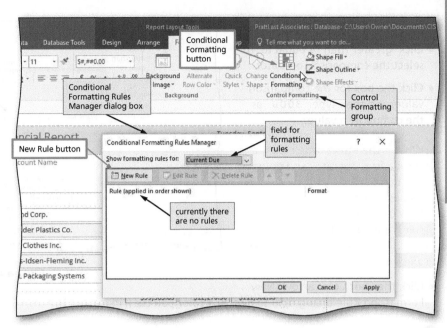

Figure 4–16

3

- Click the New Rule button (Conditional Formatting Rules Manager dialog box) to display the New Formatting Rule dialog box (Figure 4–17).

Q&A

I see that there are two boxes to enter numbers. I only have one number to enter, 3000. Am I on the right screen?

Yes. Next, you will change the comparison operator from 'between' to 'greater than or equal to.' Once you have done so, Access will only display one box for entering a number.

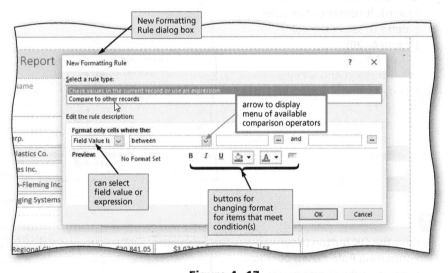

Figure 4–17

4

- Click the arrow to display the list of available comparison operators (New Formatting Rule dialog box) (Figure 4–18).

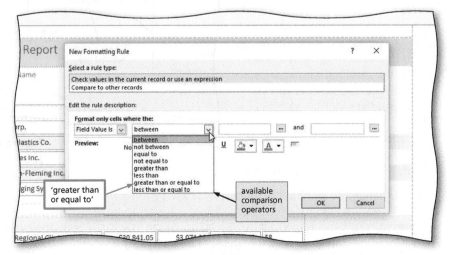

Figure 4–18

• Click 'greater than or equal to' to select the comparison operator.

• Click the box for the comparison value, and then type **3000** as the comparison value.

Q&A
What is the effect of selecting this comparison operator and entering this number?
Values in the field that are greater than or equal to 3000 satisfy this rule. Any formatting that you now specify will apply to those values and no others.

• Click the Font Color arrow (New Formatting Rule dialog box) to display a color palette (Figure 4–19).

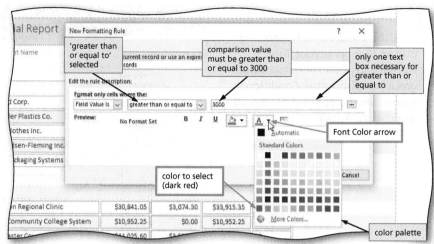

Figure 4–19

• Click the dark red color in the lower-left corner of the color palette to select the color (Figure 4–20).

Q&A
What other changes could I specify for those values that satisfy the rule?
You could specify that the value is bold, italic, and/or underlined. You could also specify a background color.

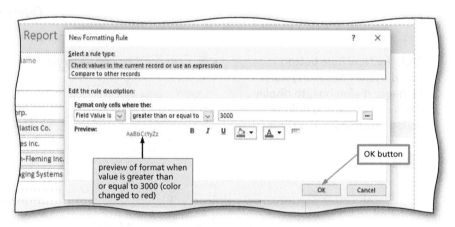

Figure 4–20

7

• Click the OK button (New Formatting Rule dialog box) to enter the rule (Figure 4–21).

Q&A
What if I have more than one rule?
The rules are applied in the order in which they appear in the dialog box. If a value satisfies the first rule, the specified formatting will apply, and no further rules will be tested. If not, the value will be tested against the second rule. If it satisfies the rule, the formatting for the second rule would apply. If not, the value would be tested against the third rule, and so on.

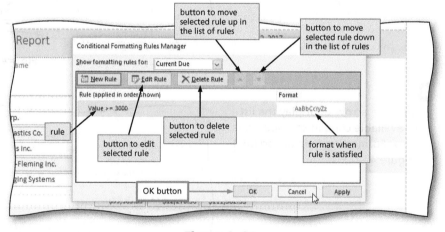

Figure 4–21

Can I change this conditional formatting later?
Yes. Select the field for which you had applied conditional formatting on any record, click the Conditional Formatting button (Report Layout Tools Format tab | Control Formatting group), click the rule you want to change, click the Edit Rule button, and then make the necessary changes. You can also delete the selected rule by clicking the Delete Rule button, or move the selected rule by clicking the Move Up or Move Down buttons.

8

- Click the OK button (Conditional Formatting Rules Manager dialog box) to complete the entry of the conditional formatting rules and apply the rule (Figure 4–22).

9

- Save your changes by clicking the Save button on the Quick Access Toolbar.

Experiment

- After saving your changes, experiment with different rules. Add a second rule that changes the format for any current due amount that is greater than or equal to $500 to a different color to see the effect of multiple rules. Change the order of rules to see the effect of a different order. When you have finished, delete any additional rules you have added so that the report contains only the one rule that you created earlier.

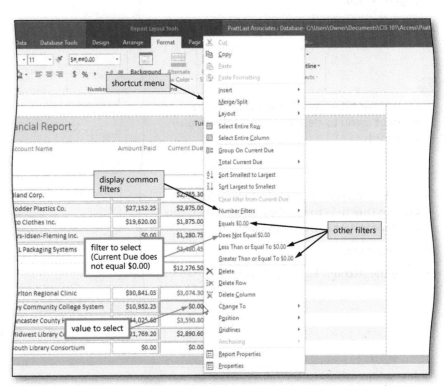

Figure 4–22

To Filter Records in a Report

1 GROUP, SORT, & TOTAL | 2 CONDITIONALLY FORMAT CONTROLS | 3 FILTER REPORT RECORDS | 4 MULTIPLE-TABLE REPORT
5 FORM WIZARD | 6 MODIFY CONTROLS | 7 FILTER FORM RECORDS | 8 MAILING LABELS

You sometimes might want to filter records in a report. *Why? You may want to include in a report only those records that satisfy some criterion and be able to change that criterion easily.* To filter records in a report, you can use the filter buttons in the Sort & Filter group on the Home tab. If the filter involves only one field, however, right-clicking the field provides a simple way to filter. The following steps filter the records in the report to include only those records on which the current due amount is not $0.00.

1

- Right-click the Current Due field on the first record where Current Due is 0 to display the shortcut menu (Figure 4–23).

Q&A

Did I have to pick the first record where the value is $0.00?
No. You could pick any record on which the Current Due value is $0.00.

Figure 4–23

2

- Click 'Does Not Equal $0.00' on the shortcut menu to restrict the records in the report to those on which the Current Due value is not $0.00 (Figure 4–24).

Q&A When would you use Number Filters?
You would use Number Filters if you need filters that are not on the main shortcut menu or if you need the ability to enter specific values other than the ones shown on the shortcut menu. If those filters are insufficient for your needs, you can use Advanced Filter/Sort, which is accessible through the Advanced button (Home tab | Sort & Filter group).

Amount Paid	Current Due	Total Amount	Account Manager Number
$29,836.65	$2,765.30	$32,601.95	35
$27,152.25	$2,875.00	$30,027.25	35
$19,620.00	$1,875.00	$21,495.00	58
$0.00	$1,280.75	$1,280.75	35
$22,696.95	$3,480.45	$26,177.40	58
$99,305.85	$12,276.50	$111,582.35	
$30,841.05	$3,074.30	$33,915.35	58
$44,025.60	$3,590.80	$47,616.40	58
$21,769.20	$2,890.60	$24,659.80	31
$96,635.85	$9,555.70	$106,191.55	

only Current Due values that are not $0.00 are included

Figure 4–24

Other Ways

1. Click Selection button (Home tab | Sort & Filter group)

To Clear a Report Filter

1 GROUP, SORT, & TOTAL | 2 CONDITIONALLY FORMAT CONTROLS | 3 FILTER REPORT RECORDS | 4 MULTIPLE-TABLE REPORT
5 FORM WIZARD | 6 MODIFY CONTROLS | 7 FILTER FORM RECORDS | 8 MAILING LABELS

The following steps clear the filter on the Current Due field. **Why?** *When you no longer want the records to be filtered, you clear the filter so that all records are again included.*

1

- Right-click the Current Due field on the first record to display the shortcut menu (Figure 4–25).

Q&A Did I have to pick the first record?
No. You could pick the Current Due field on any record.

2

- Click 'Clear filter from Current Due' on the shortcut menu to clear the filter and redisplay all records.

🔍 **Experiment**

- Try other filters on the shortcut menu for the Current Due field to see their effect. When you are done with each, clear the filter.

- Save your work.

- Close the Account Financial Report.

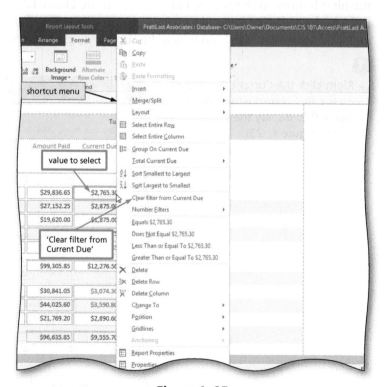

Figure 4–25

Other Ways

1. Click Advanced button (Home tab | Sort & Filter group)

The Arrange and Page Setup Tabs

When working on a report in Layout view, you can make additional layout changes by using the Report Layout Tools Arrange and/or Page Setup tabs. The Arrange tab is shown in Figure 4–26. Table 4–1 shows the buttons on the Arrange tab along with the Enhanced ScreenTips that describe their function.

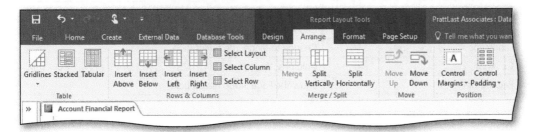

Figure 4–26

Table 4–1 Arrange Tab	
Button	**Enhanced ScreenTip**
Gridlines	Gridlines.
Stacked	Create a layout similar to a paper form, with labels to the left of each field.
Tabular	Create a layout similar to a spreadsheet, with labels across the top and data in columns below the labels.
Insert Above	Insert above.
Insert Below	Insert below.
Insert Left	Insert left.
Insert Right	Insert right.
Select Layout	Select layout.
Select Column	Select column.
Select Row	Select row.
Merge	Merge cells.
Split Vertically	Split the selected control into two rows.
Split Horizontally	Split the selected control into two columns.
Move Up	Move up.
Move Down	Move down.
Control Margins	Specify the location of information displayed within the control.
Control Padding	Set the amount of spacing between controls and the gridlines of a layout.

The Report Layout Tools Page Setup tab is shown in Figure 4–27. Table 4–2 shows the buttons on the Page Setup tab along with the Enhanced ScreenTips that describe their function.

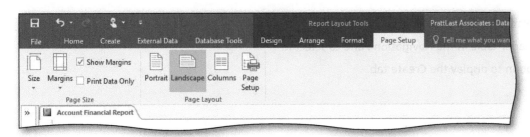

Figure 4–27

Table 4–2 Page Setup Tab	
Button	**Enhanced ScreenTip**
Size	Choose a paper size for the current document.
Margins	Select the margin sizes for the entire document or the current section.
Show Margins	Show margins.
Print Data Only	Print data only.
Portrait	Change to portrait orientation.
Landscape	Change to landscape orientation.
Columns	Columns.
Page Setup	Show the Page Setup dialog box.

TO PRINT A REPORT

If you want to print your report, you would use the following steps.

1. With the report selected in the Navigation Pane, click File on the ribbon to open the Backstage view.

2. Click the Print tab in the Backstage view to display the Print gallery.

3. Click the Quick Print button to print the report.

Q&A How can I print multiple copies of my report?

Click File on the ribbon to open the Backstage view. Click the Print tab, click Print in the Print gallery to display the Print dialog box, increase the number in the Number of Copies box, and then click the OK button (Print dialog box).

Multiple-Table Reports

Sometimes you will create reports that require data from more than one table. You can use the Report Wizard to create a report based on multiple tables just as you can use it to create reports based on single tables or queries.

To Create a Report that Involves Multiple Tables

1 GROUP, SORT, & TOTAL | 2 CONDITIONALLY FORMAT CONTROLS | 3 FILTER REPORT RECORDS | **4 MULTIPLE-TABLE REPORT**
5 FORM WIZARD | 6 MODIFY CONTROLS | 7 FILTER FORM RECORDS | 8 MAILING LABELS

Why? PrattLast needs a report that includes the Account Manager Number, First Name, and Last Name fields from the Account Manager table. In addition, for each account of the manager, they need the Account Number, Account Name, Amount Paid, and Current Due fields from the Account table. The following steps use the Report Wizard to create a report that includes fields from both the Account Manager and Account tables.

● Open the Navigation Pane if it is currently closed.

● Click the Account Manager table in the Navigation Pane to select it.

● Click Create on the ribbon to display the Create tab.

- Click the Report Wizard button (Create tab | Reports group) to start the Report Wizard (Figure 4–28).

Q&A My Navigation Pane does not look like the one in this screen. Is that a problem? How do I change it?
No, this is not a problem, but you should change the Navigation Pane so it matches the screens in this module. To do so, click the Navigation Pane arrow and then click Object Type.

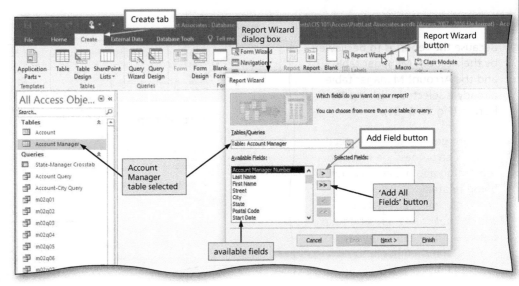

Figure 4–28

❷
- Click the Add Field button to add the Account Manager Number field to the report.
- Add the First Name field by clicking it and then clicking the Add Field button.
- Add the Last Name field in the same manner.
- Click the Tables/Queries arrow, scroll if necessary so that the Account table appears, and then click Table: Account in the Tables/Queries list box (Figure 4–29).

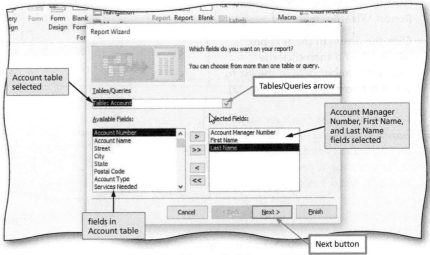

Figure 4–29

❸
- Add the Account Number, Account Name, Amount Paid, and Current Due fields by clicking the field and then clicking the Add Field button.
- Click the Next button (Figure 4–30).

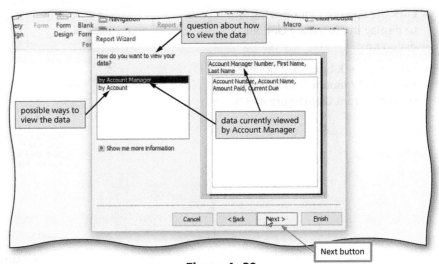

Figure 4–30

4

- Because the report is to be viewed by the Account Manager table, and the Account Manager table already is selected, click the Next button (Figure 4–31).

Q&A I did not get this screen. Instead, I got an error message that said something about the tables not being related.
The tables must be related. If you did not create a relationship between these tables earlier, do so now, and then begin these steps again.

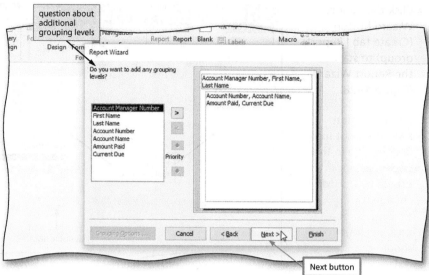

Figure 4–31

5

- Because you do not need to add any grouping levels, click the Next button to move to the next Report Wizard screen.

- Click the arrow in the text box labeled 1, and then click the Account Number field in the list to select the sort order (Figure 4–32).

Q&A When would I use the Summary Options button?
You would use the Summary Options button if you want to specify subtotals or other calculations for the report while using the wizard. You can also use it to produce a summary report by selecting Summary Only, which will omit all detail records from the report.

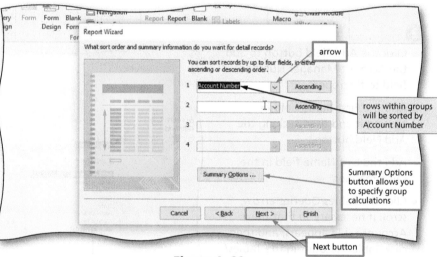

Figure 4–32

6

- Click the Summary Options button to display the Summary Options dialog box.

- Click the check boxes to calculate the sum of Amount Paid and the sum of Current Due (Figure 4–33).

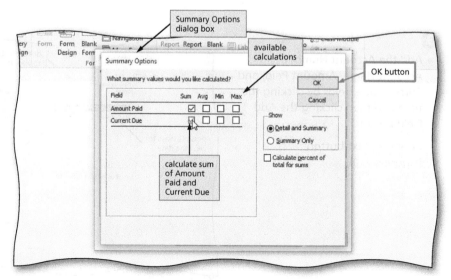

Figure 4–33

7

- Click the OK button (Summary Options dialog box).

- Click the Next button, be sure the Stepped layout is selected, and then click the Landscape option button to select the orientation (Figure 4–34).

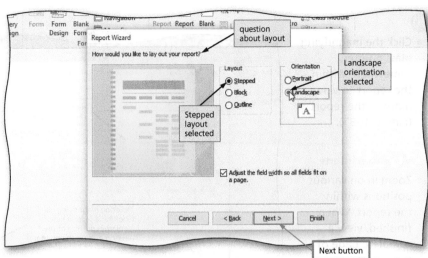

Figure 4–34

8

- Click the Next button to move to the next Report Wizard screen, and then type **Accounts by Account Manager** as the report title (Figure 4–35).

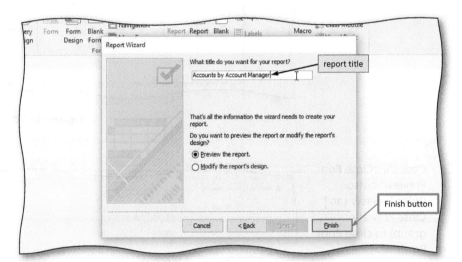

Figure 4–35

9

- Click the Finish button to produce the report (Figure 4–36).

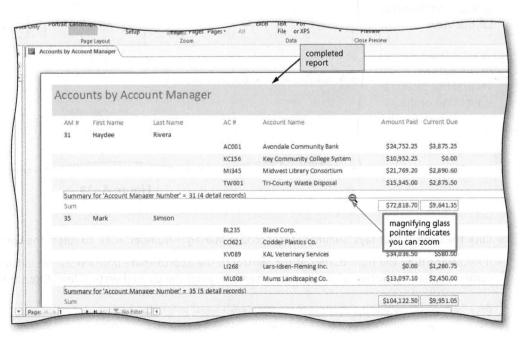

Figure 4–36

10

- Click the magnifying glass pointer somewhere within the report to view more of the report (Figure 4–37).

🔍 **Experiment**

- Zoom in on various positions within the report. When finished, view a complete page of the report.

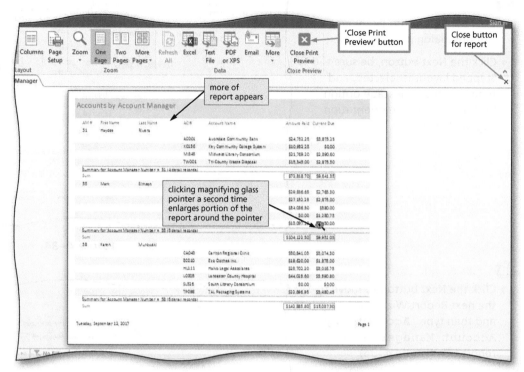

Figure 4–37

11

- Click the 'Close Print Preview' button (Print Preview tab | Close Preview group) to close Print Preview.

- Click the View arrow (Design tab | Views group), and then click Layout View.

Q&A What is the purpose of the dashed vertical line near the right edge of the screen?
The line shows the right border of the amount of the report that will print on one page. If any portion of the report extends beyond the line, the report may not print correctly.

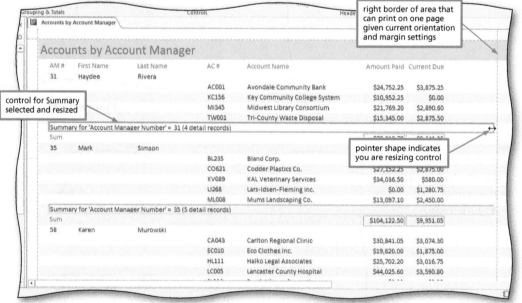

Figure 4–38

- Click the control that says 'Summary for 'Account Manager Number' = 31' to select the control.

- If necessary, drag the right border of the control to the approximate position shown in Figure 4–38 to resize the control so that no portion of the control extends beyond the dashed vertical line. Close the field list, if necessary.

Q&A Do I have to resize all the controls that begin with Summary individually?
No. When you resize one of them, the others will all be resized the same amount automatically.

- Ensure that the control for the Page Number is visible, click the Page number to select it, and then drag it to the left, if necessary, so that no portion of the control extends beyond the dashed line.

- Save your work.

- Click the Close button for the report to close the report and remove it from the screen.

CONSIDER THIS

How do you determine the tables and fields that contain the data needed for the report?

First you need to know the requirements for the report. Precisely what data is the report intended to convey? Once you understand those requirements, follow these guidelines:

Examine the requirements for the report to determine the tables. Do the requirements only relate to data in a single table, or does the data come from multiple tables? What is the relationship between the tables?

Examine the requirements for the report to determine the fields necessary. Look for all the data items specified for the report. Each should correspond to a field in a table or be able to be computed from fields in a table. This information gives you the list of fields to include.

Determine the order of the fields. Examine the requirements to determine the order in which the fields should appear. Be logical and consistent in your ordering. For example, in an address, the city should come before the state and the state should come before the postal code, unless there is some compelling reason for another order.

Creating a Report in Layout View

You can use the Report button initially to create a report containing all the fields in a table. You can then delete the unwanted fields so that the resulting report contains only the desired fields. At that point you can use Layout view to modify the report and produce the report you want.

You can also use Layout view to create single- or multiple-table reports from scratch. To do so, you would first create a blank report and display a field list for the table containing the first fields you want to include on the report (Figure 4–39).

BTW
Multicolumn Reports
There are times when you might want to create a report that has multiple columns. For example, a telephone list with employee name and phone number could print in multiple columns. To do so, create the report using Layout view or Design view and then click the Page Setup tab, click the Columns button, enter the number of columns, select the desired column layout, and then click the OK button.

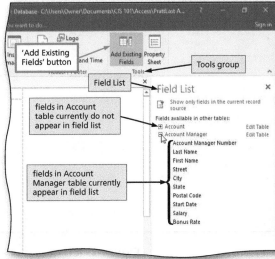

Figure 4–39

You then would drag any fields you want from the table onto the report in the order you want them to appear (Figure 4–40).

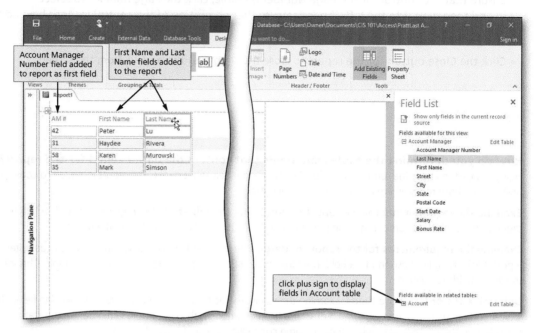

Figure 4–40

If the report involves a second table, you display the fields from the second table in the field list and then drag the fields from the second table onto the report in the desired order (Figure 4–41).

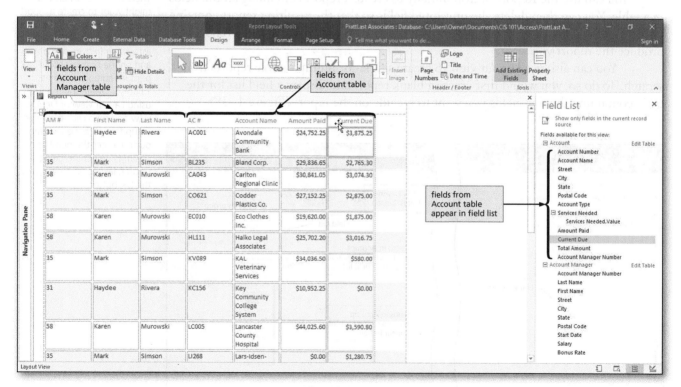

Figure 4–41

When you create a report in Layout view, the report does not automatically contain a title, but you can add one by clicking the Title button (Report Layout Tools Design tab | Header/Footer group) (Figure 4–42).

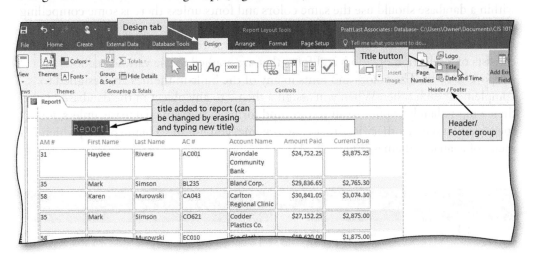

Figure 4–42

Once you have added the title, you can type whatever title you want for the report.

TO CREATE A REPORT IN LAYOUT VIEW BY CREATING A BLANK REPORT

If you wanted to create a report in Layout view, you would use the following steps.

1. Click Create on the ribbon to display the Create tab.
2. Click the Blank Report button (Create tab | Reports group) to create a blank report.
3. If a field list does not appear, display a field list by clicking the 'Add Existing Fields' button (Report Layout Tools Design tab | Tools group).
4. If the tables do not appear in the field list, click 'Show all tables'.
5. If the fields in a table do not appear, click the plus sign in front of the name of the table.
6. Drag the fields from the field list onto the report in the desired order.
7. If the report involves a second table, be sure the fields in the second table appear, and then drag the fields from the second table onto the report in the desired order. (If the field list covers the portion of the report where you want to drag the fields, move the field list to a different position by dragging its title bar.)
8. To add a title to the report, click the Title button (Report Layout Tools Design tab | Header/Footer group) and then type the desired title.

Using Themes

The most important characteristic of a report or form is that it presents the desired data in a useful arrangement. Another important characteristic, however, is the general appearance of the form. The colors and fonts that you use in the various sections of a report or form contribute to this look. You should keep in mind two important goals when assigning colors and fonts. First, the various colors and fonts

BTW

Using Themes
Office themes are designed to enhance an organization's brand identity. Many organizations consistently use themes, styles, and color schemes to visually assist in identifying their products and/or services.

should complement each other. A clash of colors or two fonts that do not go well together can produce a report that looks unprofessional or is difficult to read. Second, the choice of colors and fonts should be consistent. That is, all the reports and forms within a database should use the same colors and fonts unless there is some compelling reason for a report or form to look different from the others.

Fortunately, Access themes provide an easy way to achieve both goals. A **theme** consists of a selection of colors and fonts that are applied to the various sections in a report or form. The colors and fonts in any of the built-in themes are designed to complement each other. When you assign a theme to any object in the database, the theme immediately applies to all reports and forms in the same database, unless you specifically indicate otherwise. To assign a theme, you use the Theme picker, which is a menu of available themes (Figure 4–43).

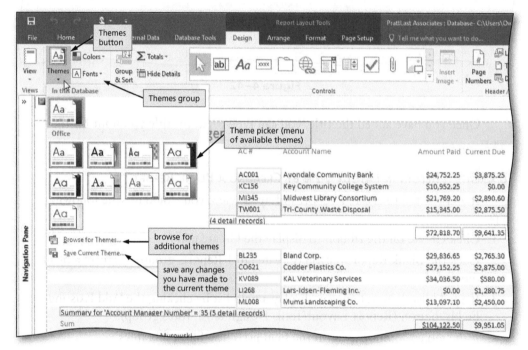

Figure 4–43

If you point to any theme in the Theme picker, you will see a ScreenTip giving the name of the theme. When you select a theme, the colors and fonts represented by that theme will immediately apply to all reports and forms. If you later decide that you would prefer a different theme, you can change the theme for all of the objects in the database by repeating the process with a different theme.

You can also use the Browse for Themes command to browse for themes that are not listed as part of a standard Access installation, but which are available for download. You can also create your own customized theme by specifying a combination of fonts and colors and using the Save Current Theme command to save your combination. If, after selecting a theme using the Themes button, you do not like the colors in the current theme, you can change the theme's colors. Click the Colors button (Report Layout Tools Design tab | Themes group) (Figure 4–44), and then select an alternative color scheme.

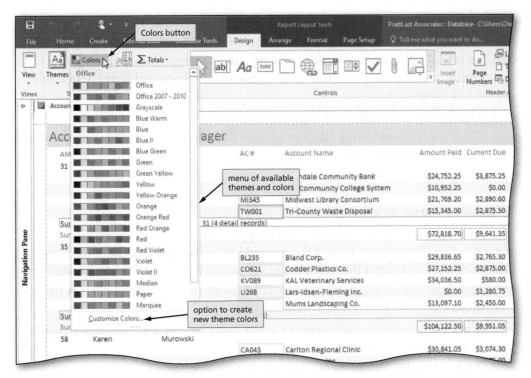

Figure 4–44

Similarly, if you do not like the fonts in the current theme, you can click the Fonts button (Report Layout Tools Design tab | Themes group) (Figure 4–45). You can then select an alternative font for the theme.

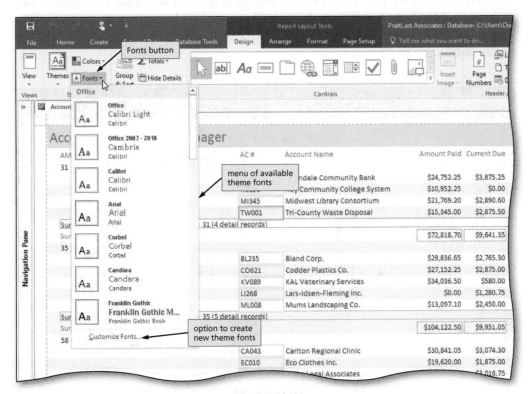

Figure 4–45

To Assign a Theme to All Objects

To assign a theme, it is easiest to use Layout view. You can use Design view as well, but it is easier to see the result of picking a theme when you are viewing the report or form in Layout view. To assign a theme to all reports and forms, you would use the following steps.

1. Open any report or form in Layout view.
2. Click the Themes button (Report Layout Tools Design tab | Themes group) to display the Theme picker.
3. Click the desired theme.

To Assign a Theme to a Single Object

In some cases, you might only want to apply a theme to the current report or form, while all other reports and forms would retain the characteristics from the original theme. To assign a theme to a single object, you would use the following steps.

1. Open the specific report or form to which you want to assign a theme in Layout view.
2. Click the Themes button (Report Layout Tools Design tab | Themes group) to display the Theme picker.
3. Right-click the desired theme to produce a shortcut menu.
4. Click the 'Apply Theme to This Object Only' command on the shortcut menu to apply the theme to the single object on which you are working.

Live Preview for Themes

When selecting themes, Access provides a **live preview** of what the report or form will look like with the theme before you actually select and apply the theme. The report or form will appear as it would in the theme to which you are currently pointing (Figure 4–46). If you like that theme, you then can select the theme by clicking the left mouse button.

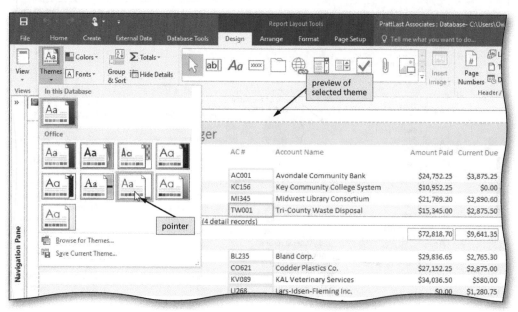

Figure 4–46

To Create a Summary Report

A report that includes group calculations such as subtotals, but does not include the individual detail lines, is called a **summary report**. *Why? You might need a report that only shows the overall group calculations, but not all the records.* The following steps hide the detail lines in the Accounts by Account Manager report, thus creating a summary report.

- Open the Accounts by Account Manager report in Layout view and close the Navigation Pane.

- Click the Hide Details button (Report Layout Tools Design tab | Grouping & Totals group) to hide the details in the report (Figure 4–47).

Q&A How can I see the details once I have hidden them?
Click the Hide Details button a second time.

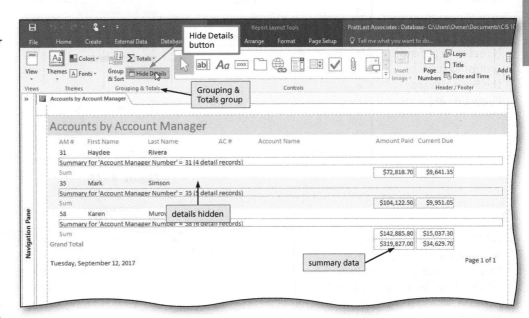

Figure 4–47

- Close the report without saving your changes.

Q&A What would happen if I saved the report?
The next time you view the report, the details would still be hidden. If that happened and you wanted to show all the details, just click the Hide Details button a second time.

Break Point: If you wish to take a break, this is a good place to do so. You can quit Access now. To resume at a later time, run Access, open the database called PrattLast Associates, and continue following the steps from this location forward.

Form Creation

You can create a simple form consisting of all the fields in the Account table using the Form button (Create tab | Forms group). To create more customized forms, you can use the Form Wizard. Once you have used the Form Wizard to create a form, you can modify that form in either Layout view or Design view.

BTW
Summary Reports
You can create a summary report in either Layout view or Design view.

To Use the Form Wizard to Create a Form

The following steps use the Form Wizard to create an initial version of the Account Financial Form. *Why? Using the Form Wizard is the easiest way to create this form.* The initial version will contain the Account Number, Account Name, Account Type, Services Needed, Amount Paid, Current Due, Total Amount, and Account Manager Number fields.

1

- Open the Navigation Pane and select the Account table.
- Click Create on the ribbon to display the Create tab.
- Click the Form Wizard button (Create tab | Forms group) to start the Form Wizard (Figure 4–48).

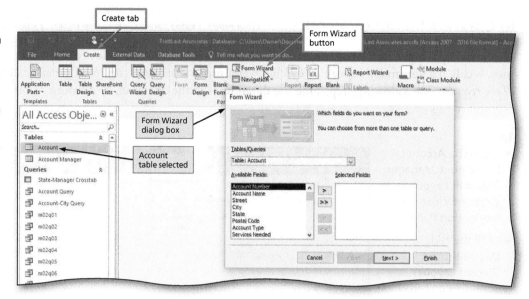

Figure 4–48

2

- Add the Account Number, Account Name, Account Type, Services Needed, Amount Paid, Current Due, Total Amount, and Account Manager Number fields to the form (Figure 4–49).

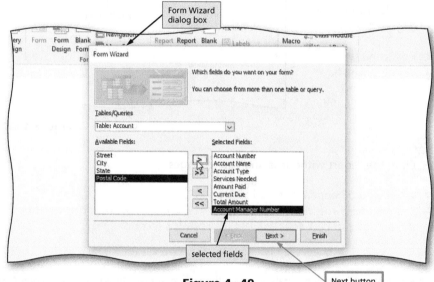

Figure 4–49

- Click the Next button to display the next Form Wizard screen (Figure 4–50).

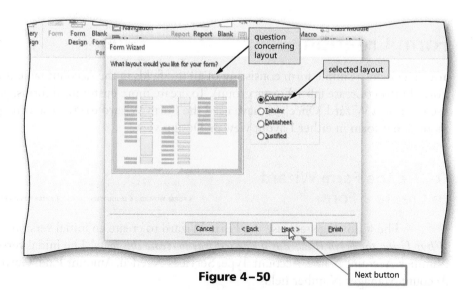

Figure 4–50

- Be sure the Columnar layout is selected, click the Next button to display the next Form Wizard screen, and then type **Account Financial Form** as the title for the form (Figure 4–51).

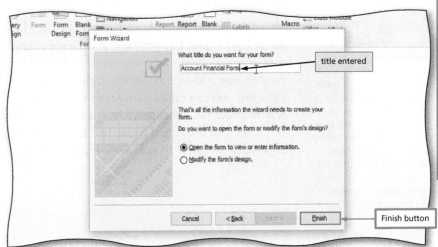

Figure 4–51

- Click the Finish button to complete and display the form (Figure 4–52).

- Click the Close button for the Account Financial Form to close the form.

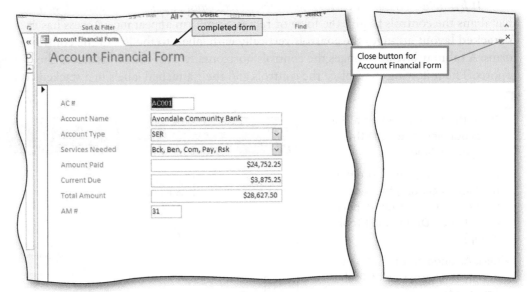

Figure 4–52

Form Sections

A form typically has only three sections. The Form Header section appears at the top of the form and usually contains the form title. It may also contain a logo and/or a date. The body of the form is in the Detail section. The Form Footer section appears at the bottom of the form and is often empty.

Form Controls

Just as with reports, the various items on a form are called controls. Forms include the same three types of controls: bound controls, unbound controls, and calculated controls. Bound controls have attached labels that typically display the name of the field that supplies the data for the control. The **attached label** for the Account Number field, for example, is the portion of the screen immediately to the left of the field. It contains the words, Account Number (AC#).

BTW
Form Design Considerations
Forms should be appealing visually and present data logically and clearly. Properly designed forms improve both the speed and accuracy of data entry. Forms that are too cluttered or contain too many different effects can be hard on the eyes. Some colors are more difficult than others for individuals to see. Be consistent when creating forms. Once you decide on a general style or theme for forms, stick with it throughout your database.

Views Available for Forms

When working with a form in Access, there are three different ways to view the form: Form view, Layout view, and Design view. Form view shows the form on the screen and allows you to use the form to update data. Layout view is similar to Form view in that it shows the form on the screen. In Layout view, you cannot update the data, but you can make changes to the layout of the form, and it is usually the easiest way to make such changes. Design view also allows you to make changes, but it does not show you the actual form. It is most useful when the changes you need to make are especially complex. In this module, you will use Layout view to modify the form.

To Place Controls in a Control Layout

1 GROUP, SORT, & TOTAL | 2 CONDITIONALLY FORMAT CONTROLS | 3 FILTER REPORT RECORDS | 4 MULTIPLE-TABLE REPORT
5 FORM WIZARD | 6 MODIFY CONTROLS | **7 FILTER FORM RECORDS** | **8 MAILING LABELS**

Why? *To use Layout view with a form, the controls must be placed in a control layout.* A **control layout** is a guide that aligns the controls to give the form or report a uniform appearance. Access has two types of control layouts. A **stacked layout** arranges the controls vertically with labels to the left of the control and is commonly used in forms. A **tabular layout** arranges the controls horizontally with the labels across the top and is typically used in reports. The following steps place the controls and their attached labels in a stacked control layout.

1

- Open the Account Financial Form in Layout view and close the Navigation Pane.

- If a field list appears, close the field list by clicking the 'Add Existing Fields' button (Report Layout Tools Design tab | Tools group).

- Click Arrange on the ribbon to display the Form Layout Tools Arrange tab.

- Click the attached label for the Account Number control to select the control.

- While holding the SHIFT key down, click the remaining attached labels and all the controls (Figure 4–53).

Q&A Did I have to select the attached labels and controls in that order?
No. As long as you select all of them, the order in which you selected them does not matter.

When I clicked some of the controls, they moved so they are no longer aligned as well as they are in the figure. What should I do?
You do not have to worry about it. Once you complete the next step, they will once again be aligned properly.

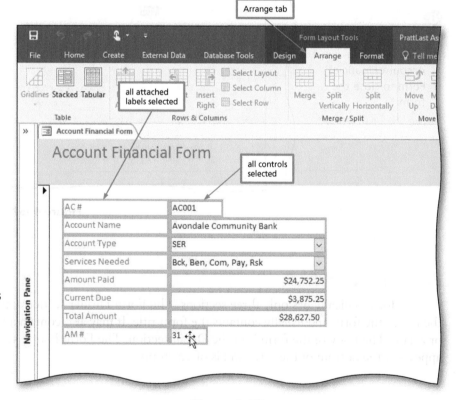

Figure 4–53

②

- Click the Stacked button (Form Layout Tools Arrange tab | Table group) to place the controls in a stacked layout (Figure 4–54).

Q&A How can I tell whether the controls are in a control layout? Look for the Control Layout indicator in the upper-left corner of the control layout.

What is the difference between stacked layout and tabular layout? In a stacked layout, which is more often used in forms, the controls are placed vertically with the labels to the left of the controls. In a tabular layout, which is more often used in reports, the controls are placed horizontally with the labels above the controls.

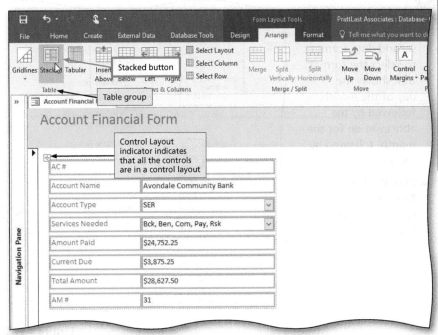

Figure 4–54

To Enhance a Form by Adding a Date

1 GROUP, SORT, & TOTAL | 2 CONDITIONALLY FORMAT CONTROLS | 3 FILTER REPORT RECORDS | 4 MULTIPLE-TABLE REPORT
5 FORM WIZARD | 6 MODIFY CONTROLS | **7 FILTER FORM RECORDS** | 8 MAILING LABELS

Why? To enhance the look or usability of a report or form, you can add special items, such as a logo or title. You can also add the date and/or the time. In the case of reports, you can add a page number as well. To add any of these items, you use the appropriate button in the Header/Footer group of the Design tab. The following steps use the 'Date and Time' button to add a date to the Account Financial Form.

①

- Click Design on the ribbon to display the Form Layout Tools Design tab.
- Click the 'Date and Time' button (Form Layout Tools Design tab | Header/Footer group) to display the Date and Time dialog box (Figure 4–55).

Q&A What is the purpose of the various check boxes and option buttons? If the Include Date check box is checked, you must pick a date format from the three option buttons underneath the check box. If it is not checked, the option buttons will be dimmed. If the Include Time check box is checked, you must pick a time format from the three option buttons underneath the check box. If it is not checked, the option buttons will be dimmed.

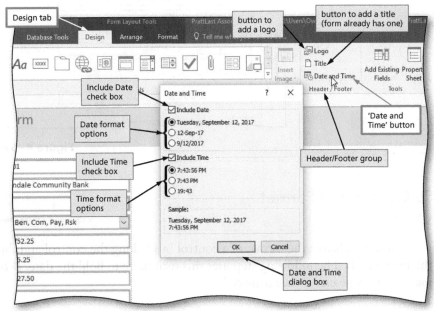

Figure 4–55

2

- Click the option button for the second date format to select the format that shows the day of the month, followed by the abbreviation for the month, followed by the year.

- Click the Include Time check box to remove the check mark (Figure 4–56).

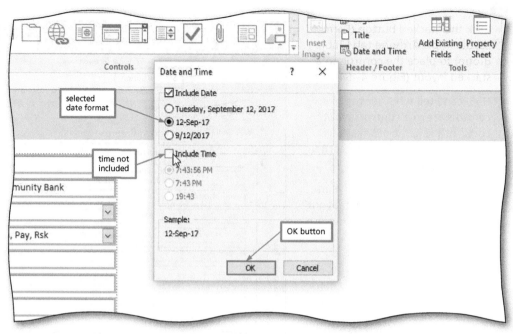

Figure 4–56

3

- Click the OK button (Date and Time dialog box) to add the date to the form (Figure 4–57).

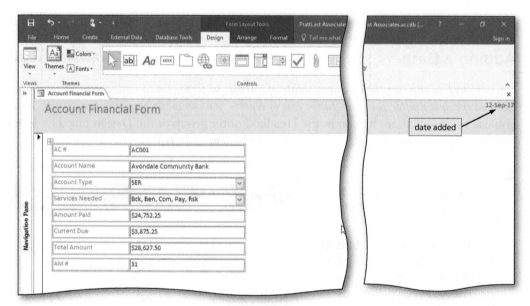

Figure 4–57

To Change the Format of a Control

1 GROUP, SORT, & TOTAL | 2 CONDITIONALLY FORMAT CONTROLS | 3 FILTER REPORT RECORDS | 4 MULTIPLE-TABLE REPORT
5 FORM WIZARD | 6 MODIFY CONTROLS | 7 FILTER FORM RECORDS | 8 MAILING LABELS

You can change the format of a control by clicking the control and then clicking the appropriate button on the Format tab. The following step uses this technique to bold the date. *Why? Formatting controls on a form lets you visually emphasize certain controls.*

1

- Click the Date control to select it.

- Click Format on the ribbon to display the Form Layout Tools Format tab.

- Click the Bold button (Form Layout Tools Format tab | Font group) to bold the date (Figure 4–58).

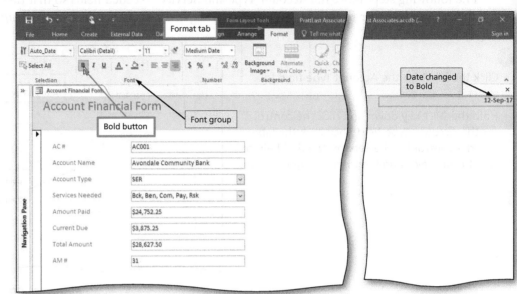

Figure 4–58

To Move a Control

1 GROUP, SORT, & TOTAL | 2 CONDITIONALLY FORMAT CONTROLS | 3 FILTER REPORT RECORDS | 4 MULTIPLE-TABLE REPORT
5 FORM WIZARD | 6 MODIFY CONTROLS | 7 FILTER FORM RECORDS | 8 MAILING LABELS

You can move a control by dragging the control. The following step moves the Date control to the lower edge of the form header. **Why?** *The default location of some controls might not be ideal; moving controls lets you adjust the design to your specifications.*

1

- Point to the Date control so that the pointer changes to a four-headed arrow, and then drag the Date control to the lower boundary of the form header in the approximate position shown in Figure 4–59.

Q&A I moved my pointer a little bit and it became a two-headed arrow. Can I still drag the pointer?
If you drag when the pointer is a two-headed arrow, you will resize the control. To move the control, it must be a four-headed arrow.

Could I drag other objects as well? For example, could I drag the title to the center of the form header?
Yes. Just be sure you are pointing at the object and the pointer is a four-headed arrow. You can then drag the object to the desired location.

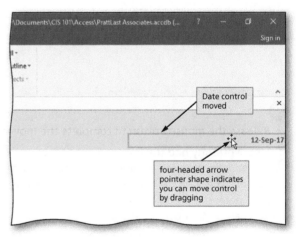

Figure 4–59

To Move Controls in a Control Layout

1 GROUP, SORT, & TOTAL | 2 CONDITIONALLY FORMAT CONTROLS | 3 FILTER REPORT RECORDS | 4 MULTIPLE-TABLE REPORT
5 FORM WIZARD | 6 MODIFY CONTROLS | 7 FILTER FORM RECORDS | 8 MAILING LABELS

Just as you moved the Date control in the previous section, you can move any control within a control layout by dragging the control to the location you want. As you move it, a line will indicate the position where the control will be placed when you release the mouse button or your finger. You can move more than one control in the same operation by selecting multiple controls prior to moving them.

The following steps move the Account Type and Services Needed fields so that they follow the Account Manager Number field. *Why? The requirements for the form place these two fields after the Account Manager Number field.*

● Click the label for the Account Type field to select it.

● Hold the SHIFT key down and click the control for the Account Type field, then click the label and the control for the Services Needed field to select both fields and their labels (Figure 4–60).

Q&A Why did I have to hold the SHIFT key down when I clicked the remaining controls?
If you did not hold the SHIFT key down, you would only select the control for the Services Needed field (the last control selected). The other controls no longer would be selected.

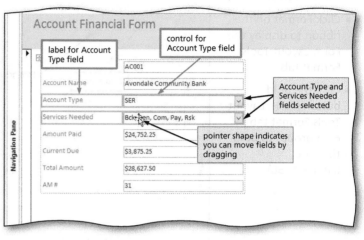

Figure 4–60

② Drag the fields straight down to the position shown in Figure 4–61, making sure that the line by the pointer is under the data. (For illustration purposes, do not release the mouse button yet.)

Q&A What is the purpose of the line by the pointer?
It shows you where the fields will be positioned.

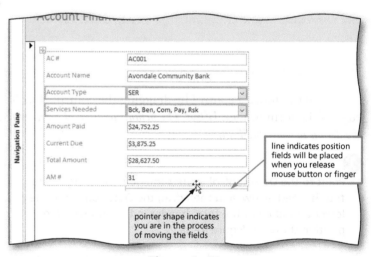

Figure 4–61

③ Release the mouse button to complete the movement of the fields (Figure 4–62).

Q&A I inadvertently had the line under the label rather than the data when I released the mouse button. The data that I moved is now under the field names. How do I fix this?
You can try to move it back where it was, but that can be tricky. The easiest way is to use the Undo button on the Quick Access Toolbar to undo your change.

I inadvertently moved my pointer so that the line became vertical and was located between a label and the corresponding data when I released the mouse button. It seemed to split the form. The data I moved appears right where the line was. It is between a label and the corresponding data. How do I fix this?
Use the Undo button on the Quick Access Toolbar to undo your change.

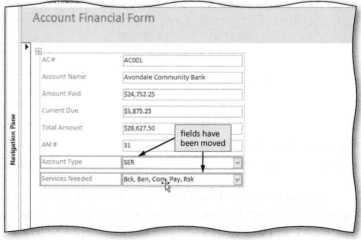

Figure 4–62

To Add a Field

Why? *Just as with a report, once you have created an initial form, you might decide that the form should contain an additional field.* The following steps use a field list to add the City field to the Account Financial Form.

1

- Click Design on the ribbon to display the Form Layout Tools Design tab.
- Click the 'Add Existing Fields' button (Form Layout Tools Design tab | Tools group) to display a field list (Figure 4–63).

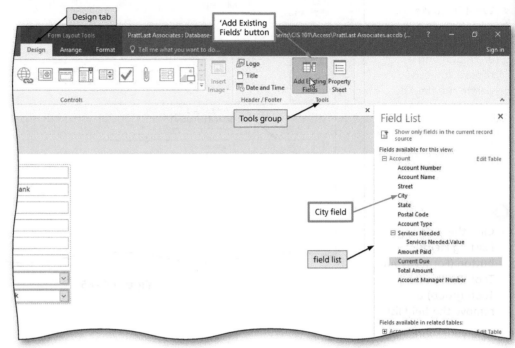

Figure 4–63

2

- Point to the City field in the field list, and then drag the pointer to the position shown in Figure 4–64. For illustration purposes do not release the mouse button yet.

Q&A Does it have to be exact?
The exact pointer position is not critical as long as the line is in the position shown in the figure.

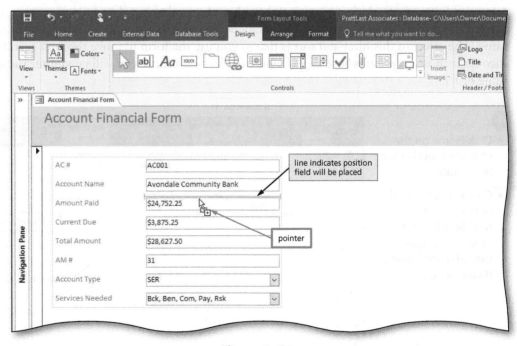

Figure 4–64

3

- Release the mouse button to place the field (Figure 4–65).

Q&A What if I make a mistake?
Just as when you are modifying a report, you can delete the field by clicking the field and then pressing the DELETE key. You can move the field by dragging it to the correct position.

4

- Click the 'Add Existing Fields' button (Form Layout Tools Design tab | Tools group) to remove the field list.

- Save your work.

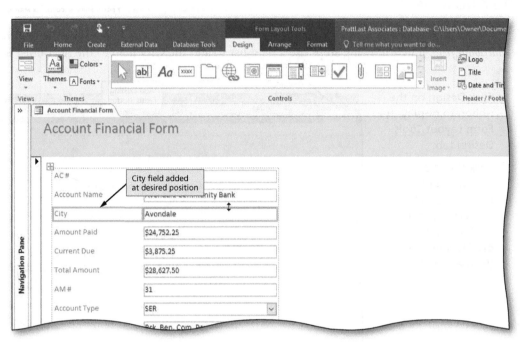

Figure 4–65

To Filter and Sort Using a Form

1 GROUP, SORT, & TOTAL | 2 CONDITIONALLY FORMAT CONTROLS | 3 FILTER REPORT RECORDS | 4 MULTIPLE-TABLE REPORT
5 FORM WIZARD | 6 MODIFY CONTROLS | **7 FILTER FORM RECORDS** | **8 MAILING LABELS**

Why? Just as in a datasheet, you often need to filter and sort data when using a form. You can do so using Advanced Filter/Sort, which is a command on the Advanced menu. The following steps use Advanced Filter/Sort to filter the records to those records whose city begins with the letter, G. They also sort the records by account name. The effect of this filter and sort is that as you use the form to move through accounts, you will only encounter those accounts whose cities begin with G. In addition, you will encounter those accounts in account name order.

1

- Click Home on the ribbon to display the Home tab.

- Click the Advanced button (Home tab | Sort & Filter group) to display the Advanced menu (Figure 4–66).

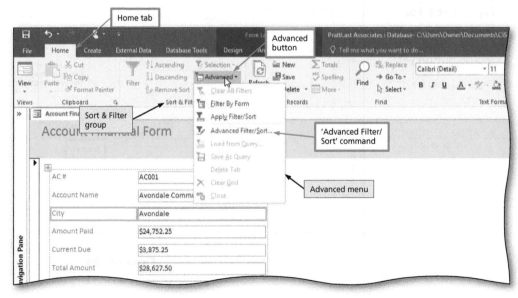

Figure 4–66

2

- Click 'Advanced Filter/Sort' on the Advanced menu.

- If necessary, resize the field list so that the Account Name and City fields appear.

- Add the Account Name field to the design grid and select Ascending sort order.

- Add the City field and type **G*** as the criterion for the City field (Figure 4–67).

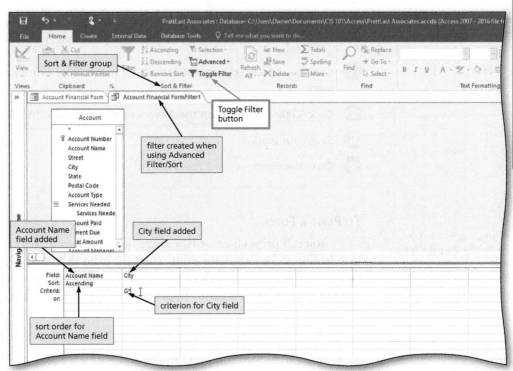

Figure 4–67

3

- Click the Toggle Filter button (Home tab | Sort & Filter group) to filter the records (Figure 4–68).

Q&A I can only see one record at a time in the form. How can I see which records are included?
You need to scroll through the records using the arrows in the Navigation bar.

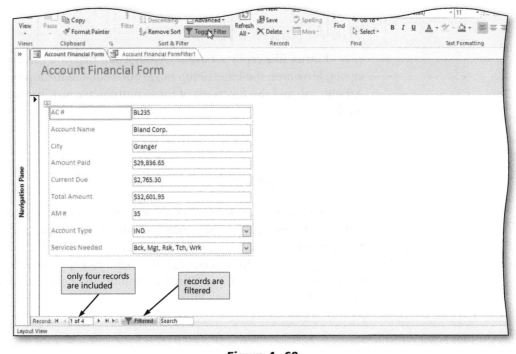

Figure 4–68

To Clear a Form Filter

When you no longer want the records to be filtered, you clear the filter. The following steps clear the current filter for the Account Financial Form.

1 Click the Advanced button (Home tab | Sort & Filter group) to display the Advanced menu.

2 Click 'Clear All Filters' on the Advanced menu to clear the filter.

3 Save your work.

4 Close the Form.

TO PRINT A FORM

You can print all records, a range of records, or a selected record of a form by selecting the appropriate print range. To print the selected record, the form must be open. To print all records or a range of records, you can simply highlight the form in the Navigation Pane. To print a specific record in a form, you would use the following steps.

1. Be sure the desired form is open and the desired record is selected.
2. Click File on the ribbon to open the Backstage view.
3. Click the Print tab in the Backstage view to display the Print gallery.
4. Click the Print button to display the Print dialog box.
5. Click the Selected Record(s) option button in the Print Range section, and then click the OK button.

The Arrange Tab

Forms, like reports, have an Arrange tab that you can use to modify the form's layout. However, the Page Setup tab is not available for forms. The buttons on the Arrange tab and the functions of those buttons are just like the ones described in Table 4–1.

Mailing Labels

Organizations need to send all kinds of correspondence — such as invoices, letters, reports, and surveys — to accounts and other business partners on a regular basis. Using preprinted mailing labels eliminates much of the manual labor involved in preparing mailings. In Access, mailing labels are a special type of report. When this report prints, the data appears on the mailing labels aligned correctly and in the order you specify.

To Create Labels

To create labels, you will typically use the Label wizard. *Why? Using the wizard, you can specify the type and dimensions, the font, and the content of the label.* The following steps create the labels.

- If necessary, open the Navigation Pane and select the Account table.

- Click Create on the ribbon to display the Create tab.

- Click the Labels button (Create tab | Reports group) to display the Label Wizard dialog box.

- Ensure that English is selected as the Unit of Measure and that Avery is selected in the 'Filter by manufacturer' box.

- If necessary, scroll through the product numbers until C2163 appears, and then click C2163 in the Product number list to select the specific type of labels (Figure 4–69).

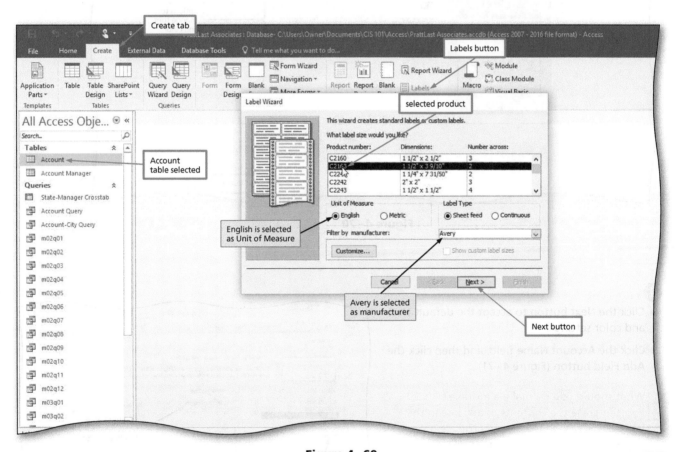

Figure 4–69

● Click the Next button (Figure 4–70).

Q&A | What font characteristics could I change with this screen?
You could change the font, the font size, the font weight, and/or the font color. You could also specify italic or underline.

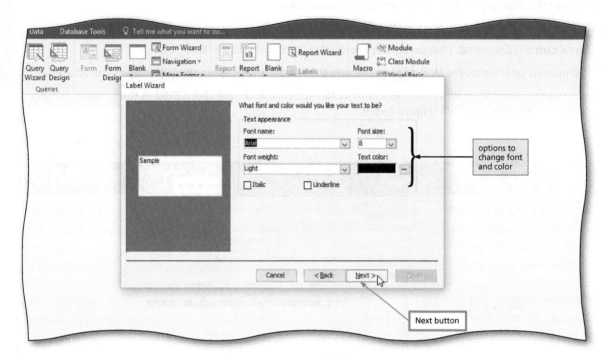

Figure 4–70

● Click the Next button to accept the default font and color settings.

● Click the Account Name field, and then click the Add Field button (Figure 4–71).

Q&A | What should I do if I make a mistake?
You can erase the contents of any line in the label by clicking in the line to produce an insertion point and then using the DELETE or BACKSPACE key to erase the current contents. You then can add the correct field by clicking the field and then clicking the Add Field button.

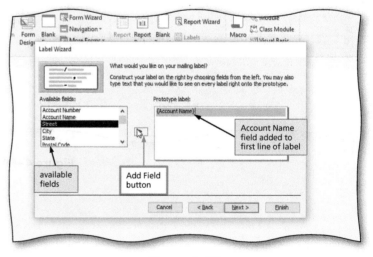

Figure 4–71

4

- Click the second line of the label, and then add the Street field.
- Click the third line of the label.
- Add the City field, type **,** (a comma), press the SPACEBAR, add the State field, press the SPACEBAR, and then add the Postal Code field (Figure 4–72).

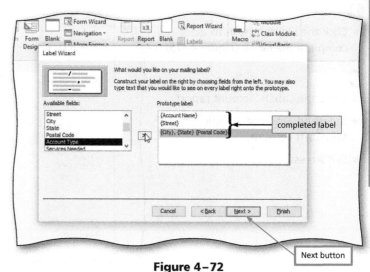

Figure 4–72

5

- Because you have now added all the necessary fields to the label, click the Next button.
- Select the Postal Code field as the field to sort by, and then click the Add Field button (Figure 4–73).

Why am I sorting by postal code?

When you need to do a bulk mailing, that is, send a large number of items using a special postage rate, businesses that provide mailing services often require that the mail be sorted in postal code order.

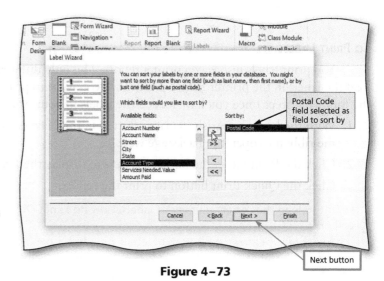

Figure 4–73

6

- Click the Next button.
- Ensure the name for the report (that is, the labels) is Labels Account (Figure 4–74).

If requested to do so by your instructor, name the labels report as Labels FirstName LastName where FirstName and LastName are your first and last names.

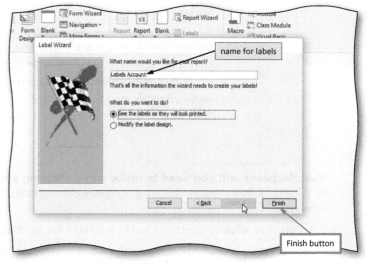

Figure 4–74

7

- Click the Finish button to complete the labels (Figure 4–75).

8

- Close the Labels Account report.

- If desired, sign out of your Microsoft account.

- Exit Access.

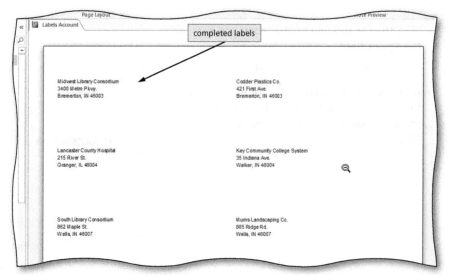

Figure 4–75

TO PRINT LABELS

You print labels just as you print a report. The only difference is that you must load the labels in the printer before printing. If you want to print labels, you would use the following steps once you have loaded the labels in your printer.

1. With the labels you wish to print selected in the Navigation Pane, click File on the ribbon to open the Backstage view.

2. Click the Print tab in the Backstage view to display the Print gallery.

3. Click the Quick Print button to print the report.

Q&A I want to load the correct number of labels. How do I know how many pages of labels will print?

If you are unsure how many pages of labels will print, open the label report in Print Preview first. Use the Navigation buttons in the status bar of the Print Preview window to determine how many pages of labels will print.

BTW

Customizing Mailing Labels
Once you create mailing labels, you can customize them just as you can customize other reports. In Design view, you can add a picture to the label, change the font size, adjust the spacing between controls, or make any other desired changes.

Summary

In this module you have learned to use wizards to create reports and forms, modify the layout of reports and forms using Layout view, group and sort in a report, add totals to a report, conditionally format controls, filter records in reports and forms, resize and move controls, add fields to reports and forms, create a stacked layout for a form, add a date, move controls in a control layout, apply themes, and create mailing labels.

CONSIDER THIS

What decisions will you need to make when creating your own reports and forms?
Use these guidelines as you complete the assignments in this module and create your own reports and forms outside of this class.

1. Determine whether the data should be presented in a report or a form.

   a. Do you intend to print the data? If so, a report would be the appropriate choice.

   b. Do you intend to view the data on the screen, or will the user update data? If so, a form would be the appropriate choice.

2. Determine the intended audience for the report or form.

   a. Who will use the report or form?

   b. Will the report or form be used by individuals external to the organization? For example, many government agencies require reports from organizations. If so, government regulations will dictate the report requirements. If the report is for internal use, the user will have specific requirements based on the intended use.

   c. Adding unnecessary data to a report or form can make the form or report unreadable. Include only data necessary for the intended use.

   d. What level of detail should the report or form contain? Reports used in day-to-day operations need more detail than weekly or monthly reports requested by management.

3. Determine the tables that contain the data needed for the report or form.

   a. Is all the data found in a single table?

   b. Does the data come from multiple related tables?

4. Determine the fields that should appear on the report or form.

5. Determine the organization of the report or form.

   a. In what order should the fields appear?

   b. How should they be arranged?

   c. Should the records in a report be grouped in some way?

   d. Are any calculations required?

   e. Should the report be used to simply summarize data?

   f. Should the data for the report or form be filtered in some way?

6. Determine the format of the report or form.

   a. What information should be in the report or form header?

   b. Do you want a title and date?

   c. Do you want a logo?

   d. What information should be in the body of the report or form?

   e. Is any conditional formatting required?

   f. What style should be applied to the report or form? In other words, determine the visual characteristics that the various portions of the report or form should have.

   g. Is it appropriate to apply a theme to the reports, forms, and other objects in the database?

7. Review the report or form after it has been in operation to determine whether any changes are necessary.

   a. Is the order of the fields still appropriate?

   b. Are any additional fields required?

8. For mailing labels, determine the contents, order, and type of label.

   a. What fields should appear on the label?

   b. How should the fields be arranged?

   c. Is there a certain order (for example, by postal code) in which the labels should be printed?

   d. Who is the manufacturer of the labels and what is the style number for the labels?

   e. What are the dimensions for each label?

   f. How many labels print across a page?

How should you submit solutions to questions in the assignments identified with a symbol?
Every assignment in this book contains one or more questions identified with a symbol. These questions require you to think beyond the assigned database. Present your solutions to the questions in the format required by your instructor. Possible formats may include one or more of these options: write the answer; create a document that contains the answer; present your answer to the class; discuss your answer in a group; record the answer as audio or video using a webcam, smartphone, or portable media player; or post answers on a blog, wiki, or website.

CONSIDER THIS

Apply Your Knowledge

Reinforce the skills and apply the concepts you learned in this module.

Creating Two Reports and a Form

Note: To complete this assignment, you will be required to use the Data Files. Please contact your instructor for information about accessing the Data Files.

Instructions: Run Access. Open the Apply NicelyNeat Services database from the Data Files and enable the content. NicelyNeat Services provides janitorial services to local businesses. The company uses a team-based approach and each team has a team leader or supervisor. You will create two reports and a form for the company's owner.

Perform the following tasks:

1. Open the Client Financial Report in Layout view and modify the report to create the report shown in Figure 4–76. The report is grouped by Client Type and sorted by Client Number. Include subtotals and grand totals for the Amount Paid and Current Due fields. Apply conditional formatting to the Current Due field by changing the font color to dark red for all records where the Current Due is greater than or equal to $2,000.00. Save the changes to the report.

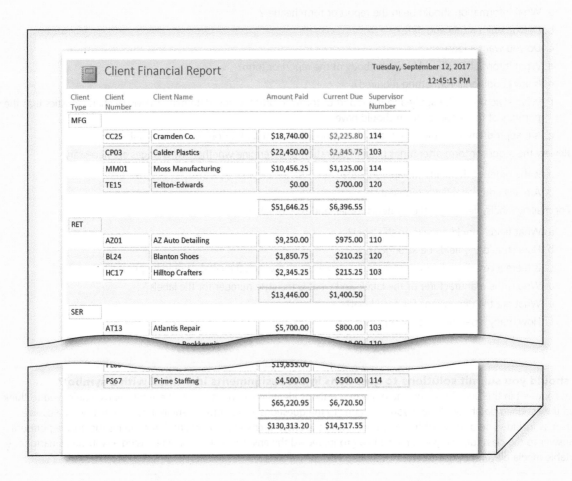

Figure 4–76

2. Create the Clients by Supervisor report shown in Figure 4–77. The report is grouped by supervisor number and sorted by client number. Include a total for the Total Amount field. Be sure to apply the Currency format to the Total Amount subtotals and grand total. Resize the total controls, if necessary. Decrease the size of the total controls so the report prints on one page. Save the report.

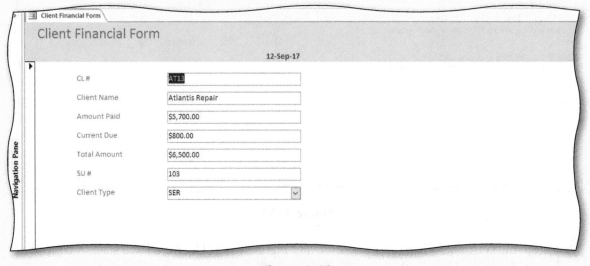

Clients by Supervisor

SU #	Last Name	CL #	Client Name	Total Amount
103	Estevez			
		AT13	Atlantis Repair	$6,500.00
		CP03	Calder Plastics	$24,795.75
		HC17	Hilltop Crafters	$2,560.50
		KD15	Klean n Dri	$2,100.50
Summary for 'Supervisor Number' = 103 (4 detail records)				
Sum				$35,956.75
110	Hillsdale			
		AZ01	AZ Auto Detailing	$10,225.00

			Prime Staffing	~~$9,000.00~~
Summary for 'Supervisor Number' = 114 (3 detail records)				
Sum				$37,547.05
120	Short			
		BL24	Blanton Shoes	$2,061.00
		KC12	Kady Regional Clinic	$9,910.50
		TE15	Telton-Edwards	$700.00
Summary for 'Supervisor Number' = 120 (3 detail records)				
Sum				$12,671.50
Grand Total				$144,830.75

Figure 4–77

3. Create the Client Financial Form shown in Figure 4–78. The form has a stacked layout and includes the current date. Bold the date control. Save the form.

Client Financial Form	
	12-Sep-17
CL #	AT13
Client Name	Atlantis Repair
Amount Paid	$5,700.00
Current Due	$800.00
Total Amount	$6,500.00
SU #	103
Client Type	SER

Navigation Pane

Figure 4–78

Continued >

4. If requested to do so by your instructor, rename the Clients by Supervisor report as Clients by LastName where LastName is your last name.

5. Submit the revised database in the format specified by your instructor.

6. ✸ How would you add the City field to the Client Financial Form so that the field appears below the Client Name field?

Extend Your Knowledge

Extend the skills you learned in this module and experiment with new skills. You may need to use Help to complete the assignment.

Creating a Summary Report and Assigning Themes to Reports and Forms

Note: To complete this assignment, you will be required to use the Data Files. Please contact your instructor for information about accessing the Data Files.

Instructions: Run Access. Open the Extend PowerWashers database from the Data Files. PowerWashers is a company that does power washing of residential properties. You will create a summary report for the PowerWashers database, assign a theme to an existing report, and create a form.

Perform the following tasks:

1. Open the Customer Financial Report in Layout view. Change the theme for the report to Integral and the Theme Colors to Red Violet. Save your changes to the report.

2. Use the Report Wizard to create the summary report shown in Figure 4–79. Name the report Customers by Worker Summary. Group the report by Worker ID and sort by Customer Number within Worker ID. Sum the Amount Owed field. Change the orientation to landscape. Delete the Page control and resize the summary lines so that the report prints on one page. Save your changes to the report. *Note*: The theme you applied in Step 1 will also apply to this report.

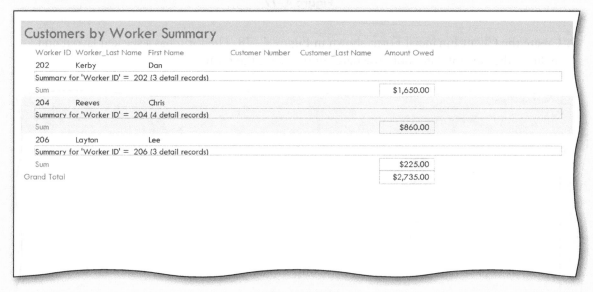

Figure 4–79

3. Create the Customer Financial Form shown in Figure 4–80. The form has a stacked control layout. Apply the Organic theme to this form only. Save the changes to the form.

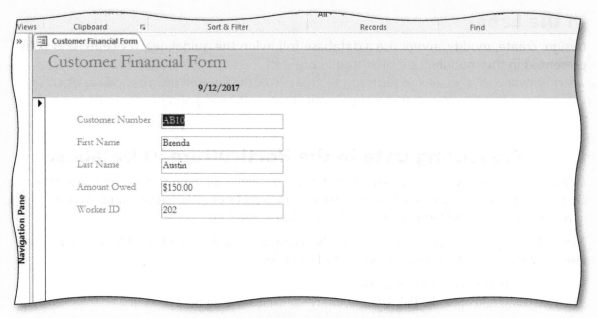

Figure 4–80

4. If requested to do so by your instructor, open the Customer Financial Form in Form view and change the first name and last name for Customer AB10 to your first and last names.

5. Submit the revised database in the format specified by your instructor.

6. ✺ How would you change the theme font for the Customer Financial Form to Arial?

Expand Your World

Create a solution, which uses cloud and web technologies, by learning and investigating on your own from general guidance.

Problem: Reports are often used to present data to individuals outside an organization. Forms are often used to input data and to display data retrieved from a query. When you create reports and forms, it is important to follow certain design guidelines. For example, there are certain fonts that you should use for a title and certain colors that you should avoid because they are harder for individuals to see.

Instructions:

1. Save the PrattLast Associates database as First Name Last Name Associates, where First Name Last Name is your first and last name, to a storage location of your choice.

2. Use a web search engine to research report and form guidelines. Document your research and cite your references in a blog or shared document. For example, the online OneNote or the Word apps.

3. Modify the Account Financial Report to illustrate poor design features for a printed report. In your blog or document explain what design principles were violated.

4. Modify the Account Financial Form to illustrate poor design features for an online form. In your blog or document explain what design principles were violated.

5. Submit the revised database and the blog or document in the format specified by your instructor. Be sure to turn in the document that contains your research references.

6. ✺ Should all reports and forms for a particular company use the same basic design and themes? Why or why not?

In the Labs

Design, create, modify, and/or use a database following the guidelines, concepts, and skills presented in this module. Labs are listed in order of increasing difficulty. Labs 1 and 2, which increase in difficulty, require you to create solutions based on what you learned in the module; Lab 3 requires you to apply your creative thinking and problem solving skills to design and implement a solution.

Lab 1: Presenting Data in the Horticulture4U Database

Problem: Horticulture4U provides products for the gardening community. Sales representatives are responsible for selling to wholesalers, nurseries, and retail stores. Management needs your help in preparing reports and forms to present data for decision making.

Note: To complete this assignment, you will be required to use the Data Files. Please contact your instructor for information about accessing the Data Files.

Instructions: Perform the following tasks:

1. Run Access and open the Lab 1 Horticulture4U database from the Data Files.

2. Open the Customer Financial Report in Layout view and modify the report to create the report shown in Figure 4–81. Add the Total Amount field to the report. Group the report by State and sort by Customer Name within State. Include totals for the Amount Paid, Balance Due, and Total Amount fields. Change the orientation to landscape. Make sure the total controls appear completely and that the Total Amount subtotals and grand total have the currency format.

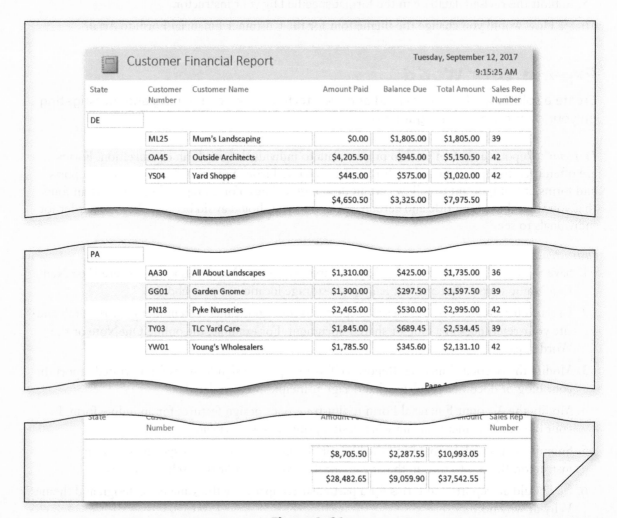

Figure 4–81

3. Create the Customers by Sales Rep report shown in Figure 4–82. Sort by Customer Number and include the average for the Balance Due field. Change the orientation to landscape. If necessary, open the report in Layout view and decrease the size of the summary line so that the report prints on one page. Save the report.

Customers by Sales Rep

SR #	Last Name	First Name	CU #	Customer Name	Balance Due
36	Fitzmyer	Patti			
			AA30	All About Landscapes	$425.00
			LH15	Lawn & Home Stores	$515.25
			PL10	Pat's Landscaping	$180.75
			SL25	Summit Lawn Service	$675.50
			TW34	TAL Wholesalers	$350.00

Summary for 'Sales Rep Number' = 36 (5 detail records)

Avg					$429.30
39	Gupta	Rudy			
			CT02	Christmas Tree Growers	$860.35
			GG01	Garden Gnome	$297.50
			ML25	Mum's Landscaping	$1,805.00
			TY03	TLC Yard Care	$689.45

Summary for 'Sales Rep Number' = 39 (4 detail records)

Avg					$913.08
42	Ortega	Gloria			
			GT34	Green Thumb Growers	$865.50
			OA45	Outside Architects	$945.00
			PN18	Pyke Nurseries	$530.00
			YS04	Yard Shoppe	$575.00
			YW01	Young's Wholesalers	$345.60

Summary for 'Sales Rep Number' = 42 (5 detail records)

Avg					$652.22

Figure 4–82

4. Create the Customer Financial Form shown in Figure 4–83. The form includes the date. Bold the date control. Apply the Slice theme for this form only. Save the form.

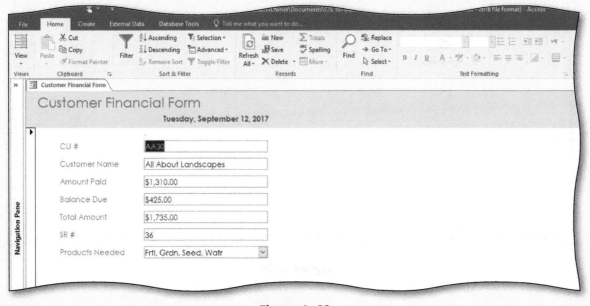

Figure 4–83

Continued >

STUDENT ASSIGNMENTS

In the Labs *continued*

5. Create mailing labels for the Customer table. Use Avery labels C2163 and format the labels with customer name on the first line, street on the second line, and city, state, and postal code on the third line. Include a comma and a space after the city and a space between state and postal code. Sort the labels by postal code.

6. If requested to do so by your instructor, rename the mailing labels as Labels First Name Last Name where First Name and Last Name are your first and last names.

7. Submit the revised database in the format specified by your instructor.

8. ✸ How could you display only the records of sales rep 42 in the Customer Financial Form?

Lab 2: **Presenting Data in the SciTech Sundries Database**

Problem: The local discovery place operates a gift shop that sells science and technology merchandise. The gift shop manager would like to prepare reports and forms for the database.

Note: To complete this assignment, you will be required to use the Data Files. Please contact your instructor for information about accessing the Data Files.

Instructions: Perform the following tasks:

1. Run Access and open the Lab 2 SciTech Sundries database from the Data Files.

2. Open the Item Status Form in Layout view and create the form shown in Figure 4–84. Be sure to place the controls in a stacked control layout. (*Hint:* Place the controls in a control layout before adding the Wholesale Cost field.) If there are fewer than 10 items on hand, the on hand value should appear in a red bold font. Save the changes to the form.

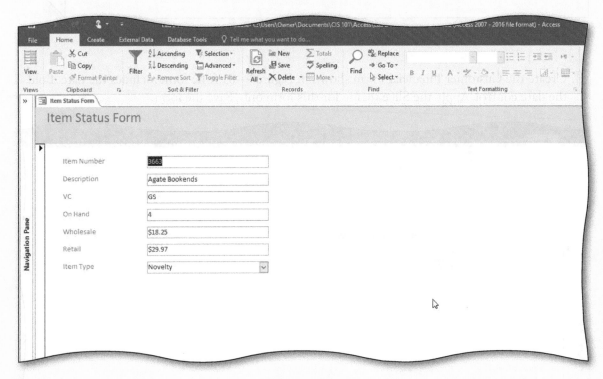

Figure 4–84

3. Open the Item Status Report in Layout view and create the report shown in Figure 4–85. Group the report by Item Type and sort by Description within Item Type. Display the average wholesale cost. If there are 5 or fewer items on hand, the value should appear in a red bold font. Save the changes to the report.

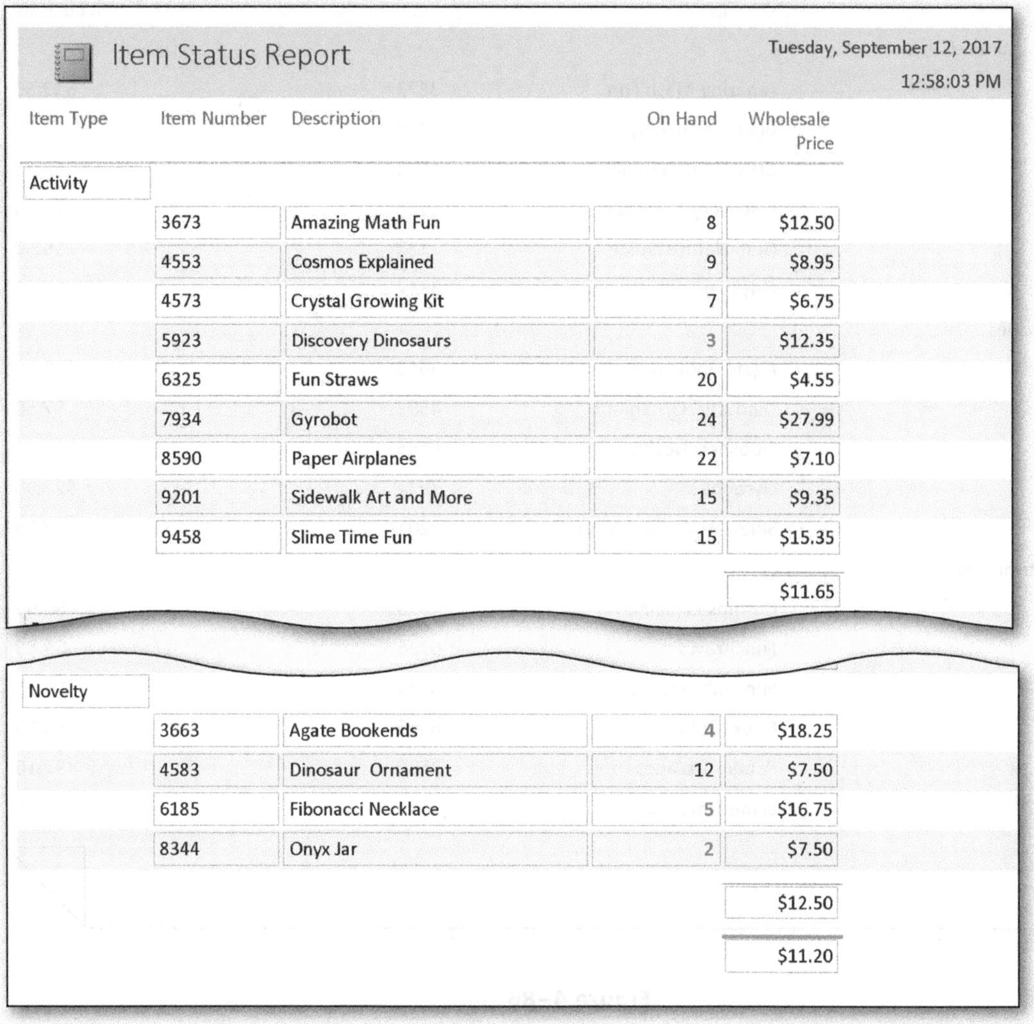

Item Status Report

Tuesday, September 12, 2017
12:58:03 PM

Item Type	Item Number	Description	On Hand	Wholesale Price
Activity				
	3673	Amazing Math Fun	8	$12.50
	4553	Cosmos Explained	9	$8.95
	4573	Crystal Growing Kit	7	$6.75
	5923	Discovery Dinosaurs	3	$12.35
	6325	Fun Straws	20	$4.55
	7934	Gyrobot	24	$27.99
	8590	Paper Airplanes	22	$7.10
	9201	Sidewalk Art and More	15	$9.35
	9458	Slime Time Fun	15	$15.35
				$11.65
Novelty				
	3663	Agate Bookends	4	$18.25
	4583	Dinosaur Ornament	12	$7.50
	6185	Fibonacci Necklace	5	$16.75
	8344	Onyx Jar	2	$7.50
				$12.50
				$11.20

Figure 4–85

4. Filter the report for all items where the number on hand is less than 10. Save the filtered report as Filtered Item Status Report.

5. Use the Report Wizard to create the Items by Vendor report shown in Figure 4–86. The report is grouped by Vendor Name and sorted by Description within Vendor Name. There are no subtotals or totals.

6. If requested to do so by your instructor, rename the Items by Vendor report as Items by First Name Last Name where First Name and Last Name are your first and last names.

7. Submit the revised database in the format specified by your instructor.

8. ✸ How could you modify the Items by Vendor report to display the average wholesale cost?

Continued >

In the Labs *continued*

Items by Vendor

Vendor Name	Description	Item Number	Wholesale
Atherton Wholesalers			
	Amazing Math Fun	3673	$12.50
	Big Book of Why	3873	$7.99
	Crystal Growing Kit	4573	$6.75
	Discovery Dinosaurs	5923	$12.35
	Gem Nature Guide	7123	$9.50
	Onyx Jar	8344	$7.50
Gift Sundries			
	Agate Bookends	3663	$18.25
	Dinosaur Ornament	4583	$7.50
	Fibonacci Necklace	6185	$16.75
	Gyrobot	7934	$27.99
	Sidewalk Art and More	9201	$9.35
Sinz Distributors			
	Cosmos Explained	4553	$8.95
	Fun Straws	6325	$4.55
	Fun with Science	6234	$12.95
	Geek Guide	6345	$5.10
	Paper Airplanes	8590	$7.10
	Slime Time Fun	9458	$15.35

Figure 4–86

Lab 3: **Consider This: Your Turn**

Presenting Data in the JSP Analysis Database

Note: To complete this assignment, you will be required to use the Data Files. Please contact your instructor for information about accessing the Data Files.

Instructions: Open the Lab 3 JSP Analysis database from the Data Files. Then, use the concepts and techniques presented in this module to perform each of the following tasks:

Part 1: JSP Analysis is a small company that provides marketing research services to the nonprofit, service, and retail sectors. You are doing an internship at JSP and the owner has asked you to create two reports and a form.

    a. Modify the Client Financial Report so that the report is grouped by marketing analyst number. Sort the report by client number within marketing analyst number. Use conditional formatting to highlight any values in the Current Due field that are greater than $5,000.00. Include subtotals and totals for the currency fields.

b. Create a report that includes data from both the Marketing Analyst table and the Client table. Include the Marketing Analyst Number, First Name, and Last Name from the Marketing Analyst table. Include the Client Number, Client Name, Amount Paid, and Current Due fields from the Client table. Group the report by marketing analyst number and sort by client number. Include subtotals for the two currency fields. Change the orientation to landscape. Adjust the size of the summary controls and move the page number control so the report prints on one page.

c. Create a form for the Client table. Include the Client Number, Client Name, Amount Paid, Current Due, Total Amount, Marketing Analyst Number, and Client Type fields on the form.

d. Filter the form you created in Step c for all accounts where the Amount Paid is greater than $4,000.00 and sort the results in descending order by amount paid. Save the form as Filtered Form.

e. Create mailing labels for the Client table that are similar to the labels shown in Figure 4–75. Sort the labels by postal code.

f. Submit your assignment in the format specified by your instructor.

Part 2:   You made several decisions while creating these reports and forms, including conditionally formatting values. What was the rationale behind your decisions? Which formatting option did you choose for the conditional formatting? Why? What other options are available?

5 | Multiple-Table Forms

Objectives

You will have mastered the material in this module when you can:

- Add Yes/No, Long Text, OLE Object, and Attachment fields
- Use the Input Mask Wizard
- Update fields and enter data
- Change row and column size
- Create a form with a subform in Design view
- Modify a subform and form design

- Enhance the form title
- Change tab stops and tab order
- Use the form to view data and attachments
- View object dependencies
- Use Date/Time, Long Text, and Yes/No fields in a query
- Create a form with a datasheet

Introduction

This module adds to the PrattLast database several new fields that require special data types. It then creates a form incorporating data from two tables. Recall that the two tables, Account Manager and Account, are related in a one-to-many relationship, with one account manager being related to many accounts, but each account being related to only one account manager. The form that you create will show one account manager at a time, but also will include the many accounts of that account manager. This module also creates queries that use the added fields.

Project — Multiple-Table Forms

PrattLast Associates uses its database to keep records about accounts and account managers. After using the database for several months, however, PrattLast has found that it needs to maintain additional data on its account managers. The company wants to identify those account managers who have reached their Professional in Human Resources (PHR) certification. They also want to include each account manager's special skills as well as the account manager's picture. Additionally, account managers now maintain files about current and potential accounts. These files are separate from the database; some are maintained in Word and others in Excel. PrattLast would like a way to attach these files to the corresponding account manager's record in the database. Finally, PrattLast wants to add the Phone Number field to the Account Manager table. Users should type only the digits in the telephone number and then have Access format the number appropriately. If the user enters 8255553455, for example, Access will format the number as (825) 555–3455.

After the proposed fields have been added to the database, PrattLast wants users to be able to use a form that incorporates the Account and Account Manager tables and includes the newly added fields as well as some of the existing fields in the Account Manager table. The form should also include the account number, name, amount paid, and current due amount for the accounts of each account manager. PrattLast would like to see multiple accounts for each account manager on the screen at the same time (Figure 5–1). The database should allow users to scroll through all the accounts of an account manager and to open any of the attachments concerning the account manager's account notes. Finally, PrattLast requires queries that use the PHR Certification, Start Date, and Special Skills fields.

Figure 5–1

In this module, you will learn how to create and use the form shown in Figure 5–1. The following roadmap identifies general activities you will perform as you progress through this module:

1. ADD FIELDS to the Account Manager table.
2. ENTER DATA into the new fields.
3. CREATE a FORM for the Account Manager table.
4. ADD CONTROLS to the form.
5. ADD a SUBFORM to the form.
6. MODIFY the SUBFORM.
7. ENHANCE the FORM.
8. CREATE QUERIES with the new fields.

Adding Special Fields

Having analyzed its requirements, the management of PrattLast has identified a need for some new fields for the Account Manager table. They need a Phone Number field and they want to assist users in entering the correct format for a phone number, so the field will use an input mask. An **input mask** specifies how data is to be entered and how it will appear. For example, an input mask can indicate that a phone number has parentheses around the first three digits and a hyphen between the sixth and seventh digits.

PrattLast also needs a PHR Certification field, which uses a value of Yes or No to indicate whether an account manager has attained the Professional in Human Resources certification; this field's data type will be Yes/No. They need a Special Skills field that identifies each manager's unique abilities, which will be a Long Text field. The Account Notes field, which must be able to contain multiple attachments for each account manager, will be an Attachment field. The Picture field is the only field whose data type is uncertain — it could be either OLE Object, which can contain objects created by a variety of applications, or Attachment.

Certainly, OLE Object is an appropriate data type for a picture, because when you store an image as an OLE object, the image becomes a part of the database. On the other hand, if an Attachment field contains a picture, the field will display an icon indicating that there is a picture as an attachment. Other types of attachments, such as Word documents and Excel workbooks, would also appear in the Attachment field as an icon representing the type of attachment. You can then open the attachment. In the case of a picture, this action will display the picture. In the case of a Word document, it will open the file in Word. PrattLast Associates has decided to use OLE Object as the Picture field data type for two reasons. First, the form shown in Figure 5–1 contains another field that must be an Attachment field, the Account Notes field. In Datasheet view, an Attachment field appears as a paper clip rather than the field name. Thus, if the Picture field were also an Attachment field, the form would display two paper clips, leading to potential confusion. A second potential problem with using an Attachment field for pictures occurs when you have multiple attachments to a record. Only the first attachment routinely appears in the field on either a datasheet or form. Thus, if the picture were not the first attachment, it would not appear.

BTW

The Ribbon and Screen Resolution
Access may change how the groups and buttons within the groups appear on the ribbon, depending on the computer's screen resolution. Thus, your ribbon may look different from the ones in this book if you are using a screen resolution other than 1366 × 768.

BTW

OLE Object Fields
OLE Object Fields can store video clips, sound, and other objects from Windows-based apps.

BTW

Long Text Fields
Long Text fields can store up to a gigabyte of text. If you need to keep a historical record of changes to a Long Text field, set the value for the Append Only property to Yes. To use formatting such as bold and underline in a Long Text field, set the value for the Text Format property to Rich Text.

BTW

Adding Captions to Attachment Fields
You can add a caption to an Attachment field. To add a caption in Design view, use the Caption property box.

To Add Fields with New Data Types to a Table

1 ADD FIELDS | 2 ENTER DATA | 3 CREATE FORM | 4 ADD CONTROLS | 5 ADD SUBFORM
6 MODIFY SUBFORM | 7 ENHANCE FORM | 8 CREATE QUERIES

You add the new fields to the Account Manager table by modifying the design of the table and inserting the fields at the appropriate position in the table structure. The following steps add the PHR Certification, Special Skills, Picture, and Account Notes fields to the Account Manager table. *Why? PrattLast has determined that they need these fields added to the table.*

1

- Run Access and open the database named PrattLast Associates from your hard disk, OneDrive, or other storage location. If you do not have the PrattLast Associates database, contact your instructor for the required file.

- If necessary, enable the content and open the Navigation Pane.

- Right-click the Account Manager table to display a shortcut menu (Figure 5–2).

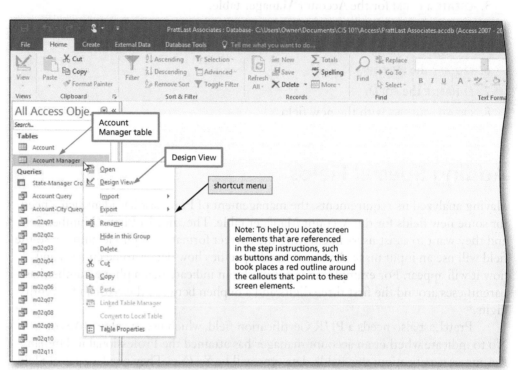

Figure 5–2

2

- Click Design View on the shortcut menu to open the table in Design view (Figure 5–3).

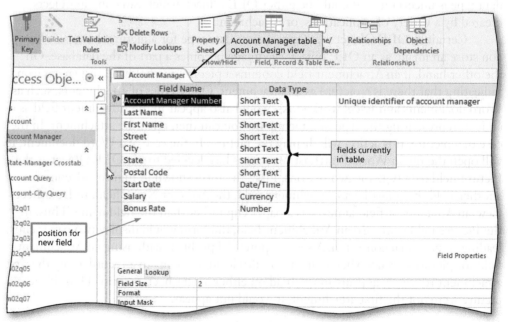

Figure 5–3

3

- Click the first open field to select the position for the first additional field.

- Type **PHR Certification** as the field name, press the TAB key, click the Data Type arrow, select Yes/No as the data type, and then press the TAB key twice to move to the next field.

- Use the same technique to add a field with Special Skills as the field name and Long Text as the data type, a field with Picture as the field name and OLE Object as the data type, and a field with Account Notes as the field name and Attachment as the data type (Figure 5–4).

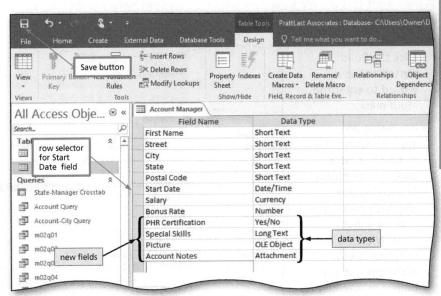

Figure 5–4

4

- Click the Save button on the Quick Access Toolbar to save your changes.

To Use the Input Mask Wizard

1 ADD FIELDS | 2 ENTER DATA | 3 CREATE FORM | 4 ADD CONTROLS | 5 ADD SUBFORM
6 MODIFY SUBFORM | 7 ENHANCE FORM | 8 CREATE QUERIES

As mentioned previously, an input mask specifies how data, such as a phone number, is to be entered and how it will appear. You can enter an input mask directly, but you usually will use the Input Mask Wizard. *Why? The wizard assists you in the creation of the input mask by allowing you to select from a list of the most frequently used input masks.*

To use the Input Mask Wizard, select the Input Mask property in the field's property sheet and then select the Build button. The following steps add the Phone Number field and then specify how the telephone number is to appear by using the Input Mask Wizard.

1

- Right-click the row selector for the Start Date field (shown in Figure 5–4) to produce a shortcut menu, and then click Insert Rows to insert a blank row above Start Date.

- Click the Field Name column for the new field.

- Type **Phone Number** as the field name, and then press the TAB key to enter the field.

- Click the Input Mask property box (Figure 5–5).

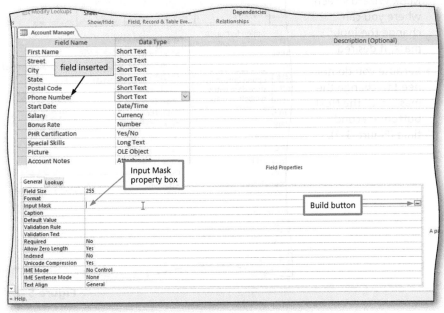

Figure 5–5

Q&A Do I need to change the data type?
No. Short Text is the appropriate data type for the Phone Number field.

2

- Click the Build button to use a wizard to enter the input mask.

- If a dialog box appears asking you to save the table, click the Yes button. (If a dialog box displays a message that the Input Mask Wizard is not installed, check with your instructor before proceeding with the following steps.)

- Ensure that Phone Number is selected (Figure 5–6).

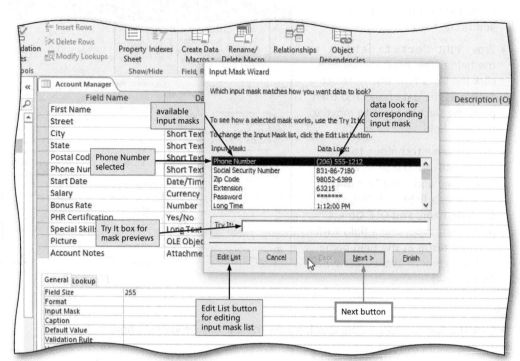

Figure 5–6

 Experiment

- Click different input masks and enter data in the Try It text box to see the effect of the input mask. When you are done, click the Phone Number input mask.

3

- Click the Next button to move to the next Input Mask Wizard screen, where you can change the input mask, if desired.

- Because you do not need to change the mask, click the Next button a second time (Figure 5–7).

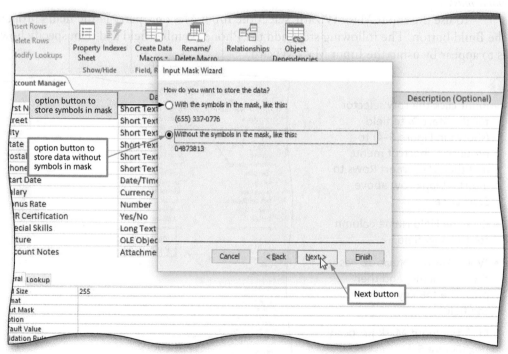

Figure 5–7

4

- Be sure the 'Without the symbols in the mask, like this' option button is selected, click the Next button to move to the next Input Mask Wizard screen, and then click the Finish button (Figure 5–8).

Why does the data type not change to Input Mask?

The data type of the Phone Number field is still Short Text. The only thing that changed is one of the field properties, the Input Mask property.

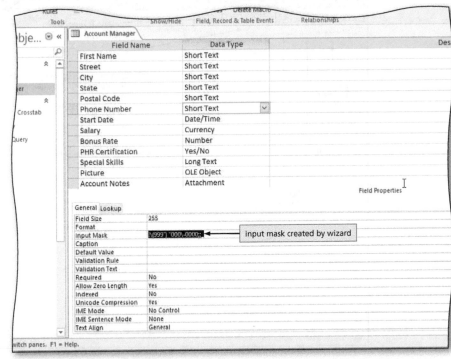

Figure 5–8

Could I have typed the value in the Input Mask property myself, rather than using the wizard?
Yes. Input masks can be complex, however, so it is usually easier and safer to use the wizard.

5

- Click the Save button on the Quick Access Toolbar to save your changes.
- Close the Account Manager table.

Adding Fields in Datasheet View

Previously you added fields to a table using Design view. You can also add fields in Datasheet view. One way to do so is to use the Add & Delete group on the Table Tools Fields tab (Figure 5–9). Select the field that precedes the position where you want to add the new field and then click the appropriate button. You can click the Short Text button to add a Short Text field, the Number button to add a Number field, the Currency button to add a Currency field, and so on. Alternatively, you can click the More Fields button as shown in the figure to display the Data Type gallery. You then can click a data type in the gallery to add a field with that type.

The gallery provides more options for ways to display various types of data. For example, if you click the Check Box version of a Yes/No field, the field will be displayed as a check box, which is the common way to display such a field. If instead you click the Yes/No version of a Yes/No field, the value in the field will be displayed as either the word, Yes, or the word, No.

If you scroll down in the Data Type gallery, you will find a Quick Start section. The commands in this section give you quick ways of adding some common types of fields. For example, clicking Address in the Quick Start section immediately adds several fields: Address, City, State Province, Zip Postal, and Country Region. Clicking Start and End Dates immediately adds both a Start Date field and an End Date field.

BTW

Input Mask Characters
When you create an input mask, Access adds several characters. These characters control the literal values that appear when you enter data. For example, the first backslash in the input mask in Figure 5 -8 displays the opening parenthesis. The double quotes force Access to display the closing parenthesis and a space. The second backslash forces Access to display the hyphen that separates the first and second part of the phone number.

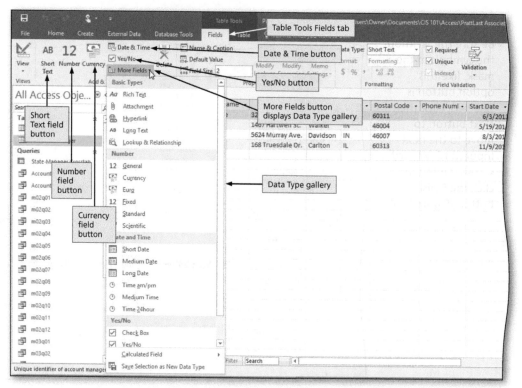

Figure 5–9

In Datasheet view, you can rename fields by right-clicking the field name, clicking Rename Field on the shortcut menu, and then typing the new name. Delete a field by clicking the field and then clicking the Delete button (Table Tools Fields tab | Add & Delete group). Move a field from one location to another by dragging the field.

How do you determine if fields need special data types or an input mask?

Determine whether an input mask is appropriate. Sometimes the data in the field should be displayed in a special way, for example, with parentheses and a hyphen like a phone number, or separated into three groups of digits like a Social Security number. If so, should Access assist the user in entering the data in the right format? For example, by including an input mask in a field, Access can automatically insert the parentheses and a hyphen when a user enters phone number digits.

Determine whether the Yes/No data type is appropriate. A field is a good candidate for the Yes/No data type if the only possible field values are Yes or No, True or False, or On or Off.

Determine whether the Long Text data type is appropriate. A field that contains text that is variable in length and potentially very long is an appropriate use of the Long Text data type. If you want to use special text effects, such as bold and italic, you can assign the field the Long Text data type and change the value of the field's Text Format property from Plain Text to Rich Text. You can also collect history on the changes to a Long Text field by changing the value of the field's Append Only property from No to Yes. If you do so, when you right-click the field and click Show Column History on the shortcut menu, you will see a record of all changes made to the field.

Determine whether the OLE Object data type is appropriate. Does the field contain a picture? Does it contain an object created by other applications that support **OLE (Object Linking and Embedding)?**

Determine whether the Attachment data type is appropriate. Will the field contain one or more attachments that were created in other applications? If so, the Attachment data type is appropriate. It allows you to store multiple attachments on each record. You can view and manipulate these attachments in their original application.

Determine whether the Hyperlink data type is appropriate. A field with the hyperlink data type contains a hyperlink, that is, a link to another location such as a webpage or a file. Will the field contain an email address, links to other Office documents, or links to webpages? If so, Hyperlink is appropriate.

Updating the New Fields

After adding the new fields to the table, the next task is to enter data into the fields. The data type determines the manner in which this is accomplished. The following sections cover the methods for updating fields with an input mask, Yes/No fields, Long Text fields, OLE fields, and Attachment fields. They also show how you would enter data in Hyperlink fields.

1 ADD FIELDS | 2 ENTER DATA | 3 CREATE FORM | 4 ADD CONTROLS | 5 ADD SUBFORM
6 MODIFY SUBFORM | 7 ENHANCE FORM | 8 CREATE QUERIES

To Enter Data Using an Input Mask

Why? *When you are entering data in a field that has an input mask, Access will insert the appropriate special characters in the proper positions. This means Access will automatically insert the parentheses around the area code, the space following the second parenthesis, and the hyphen in the Phone Number field.* The following steps use the input mask to add the telephone numbers.

* Open the Account Manager table and close the Navigation Pane.

* Click at the beginning of the Phone Number field on the first record to display an insertion point in the field (Figure 5–10).

Q&A

I do not see the parentheses and hyphen as shown in the figure. Did I do something wrong?

Depending on exactly where you click, you might not see the symbols. Regardless, as soon as you start typing in the field, the symbols should appear.

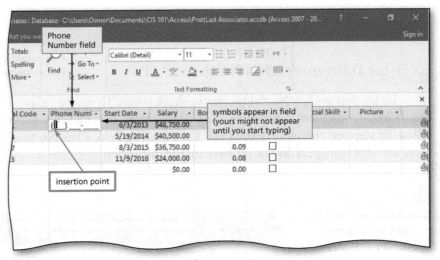

Figure 5–10

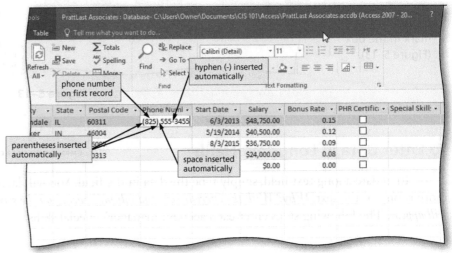

* Type **8255553455** as the telephone number (Figure 5–11).

Figure 5–11

3

- Use the same technique to enter the remaining telephone numbers, as shown in Figure 5–12.
- If requested to do so by your instructor, change the phone number for account manager 42 to your phone number.

Q&A Do I need to click at the beginning of the field?

Yes. If you do not, the data will not be entered correctly.

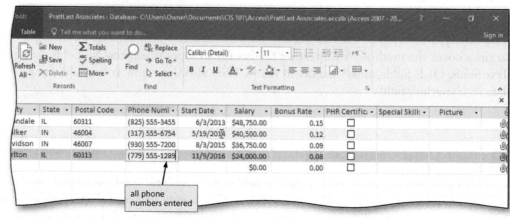

Figure 5–12

To Enter Data in Yes/No Fields

1 ADD FIELDS | 2 ENTER DATA | 3 CREATE FORM | 4 ADD CONTROLS | 5 ADD SUBFORM
6 MODIFY SUBFORM | 7 ENHANCE FORM | 8 CREATE QUERIES

Fields that are Yes/No fields contain check boxes. To set the value to Yes, place a check mark in the check box. **Why?** *A check mark indicates the value is Yes or True.* To set a value to No, leave the check box blank. The following step sets the value of the PHR Certification field, a Yes/No field, to Yes for the first record. The other three account managers do not yet have their certification.

1

- If necessary, click the right scroll arrow (shown in Figure 5–15) until the new fields appear.
- Click the check box in the PHR Certification field on the first record to place a check mark in the box (Figure 5–13).

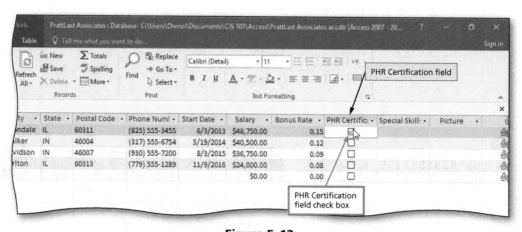

Figure 5–13

To Enter Data in Long Text Fields

1 ADD FIELDS | 2 ENTER DATA | 3 CREATE FORM | 4 ADD CONTROLS | 5 ADD SUBFORM
6 MODIFY SUBFORM | 7 ENHANCE FORM | 8 CREATE QUERIES

To update a long text field, simply type the data in the field. You will later change the spacing to allow more room for the text. **Why?** *With the current row and column spacing on the screen, only a small portion of the text will appear.* The following steps enter each account manager's special skills.

1

- If necessary, click the right scroll arrow so the Special Skills field appears.

- Click the Special Skills field on the first record, and then type `Fluent in Spanish. Excellent organizational and communication skills. Mentors new employees.` as the entry (Figure 5–14).

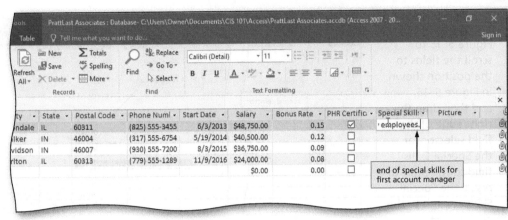

Figure 5–14

2

- Click the Special Skills field on the second record, and then type `Conflict management and negotiation skills. Excels at labor relations.` as the entry.

- Click the Special Skills field on the third record, and then type `Excellent communication skills. Previous IT experience. Familiar with human resources management software.` as the entry.

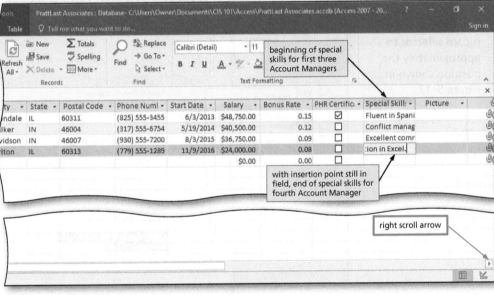

Figure 5–15

- Click the Special Skills field on the fourth record, and then type `Accounting background. Microsoft certification in Excel.` as the entry (Figure 5–15).

To Change the Row and Column Size

1 ADD FIELDS | 2 ENTER DATA | 3 CREATE FORM | 4 ADD CONTROLS | 5 ADD SUBFORM
6 MODIFY SUBFORM | 7 ENHANCE FORM | 8 CREATE QUERIES

Only a small portion of the special skills data appears in the datasheet. To allow more of the information to appear, you can expand the size of the rows and the columns. You can change the size of a column by using the field selector. The **field selector** is the bar containing the field name. To change the size of a row, you use a record's record selector.

The following steps resize the column containing the Special Skills field and the rows of the table. *Why? Resizing the column and the rows allows the entire Special Skills field text to appear.*

1

- Use the right scroll arrow shown in Figure 5–15 to scroll the fields to the position shown in Figure 5–16, and then drag the right edge of the field selector for the Special Skills field to the right to resize the Special Skills column to the approximate size shown in Figure 5–16.

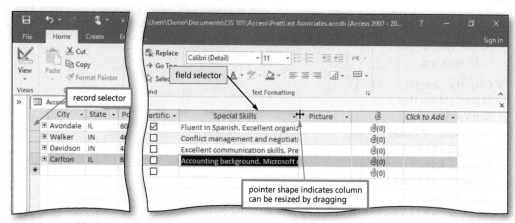

Figure 5–16

2

- Drag the lower edge of the record selector to approximately the position shown in Figure 5–17.

Q&A
Can rows be different sizes?
No. Access formats all rows to be the same size.

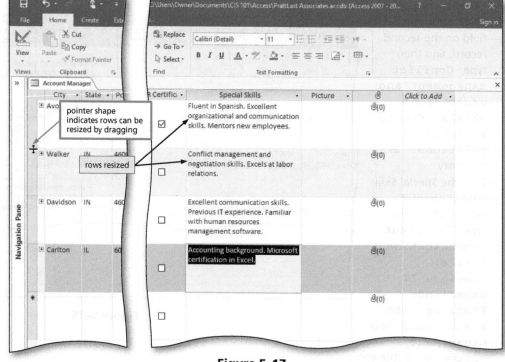

Figure 5–17

Other Ways

1. Right-click record selector, click Row Height to change row spacing
2. Right-click field selector, click Field Width to change column size

BTW
Entering Data in Long Text Fields
You also can enter data in a long text field using the Zoom dialog box. To do so, click the long text field and then press SHIFT+F2 to open the Zoom dialog box.

Undoing Changes to Row Height and Column Width

If you later find that the changes you made to the row height or the column width are no longer appropriate, you can undo them. To undo changes to the row height, right-click the row selector, click Row Height on the shortcut menu, and then click the Standard Height check box in the Row Height dialog box. To undo changes to the column width, right-click the field selector, click Field Width on the shortcut menu, and then click the Standard Width check box in the Column Width dialog box.

To Enter Data in OLE Object Fields

To insert data into an OLE Object field, you use the Insert Object command on the OLE field's shortcut menu. If the object is already created and stored in a file, you could choose to insert it directly from the file. The Insert Object command presents a list of the various types of objects that can be inserted, and it often is better to use one of these types rather than simply inserting from a file. *Why? Depending on your installation of Access, you might be limited to certain types of graphics files.* When you select a type of object to insert, Access will open the corresponding application to create the object. For example, if you select a Bitmap Image object type, Access will open Paint. You then can use that application to create the picture. In the case of Paint, you easily can create the picture by pasting the picture from a file.

The following steps insert pictures into the Picture field. The pictures will be visible as photographs in the form; however, the table will display the text, Bitmap Image, in the Picture field in the datasheet. The steps assume that the pictures are located in the same folder as your database.

1

- Ensure the Picture field appears on your screen, and then right-click the Picture field on the first record to produce a shortcut menu (Figure 5–18).

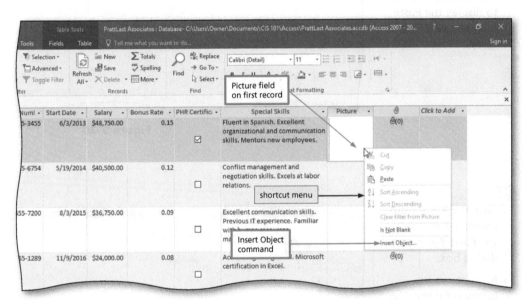

Figure 5–18

2

- Click Insert Object on the shortcut menu to display the Microsoft Access dialog box (Figure 5–19).

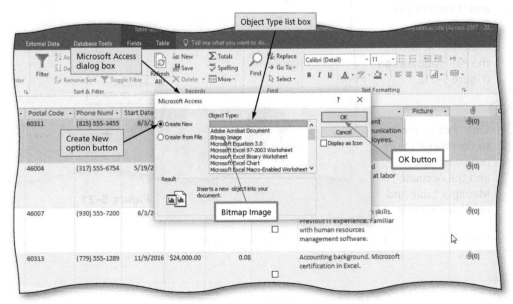

Figure 5–19

• Select the Bitmap Image object type from the Object Type list.

• Click the OK button to open the Paint application.

Unlike the figure, my window is maximized. Does that make a difference?
No. The same steps will work in either case.

• Click the Paste button arrow (Home tab | Clipboard group) in the Paint application to display the Paste menu (Figure 5–20).

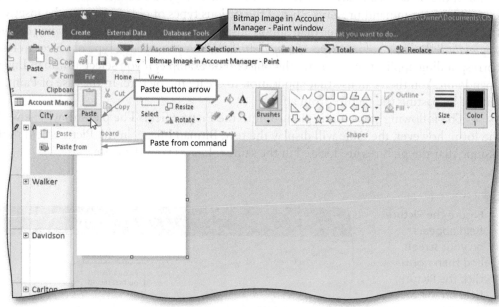

Figure 5–20

• Click the Paste from command to display the Paste From dialog box.

• Navigate to the location for the .jpg file named haydee_rivera, select the file, and then click the Open button.

• Click the File tab in the Paint application (Figure 5–21).

5

• Click 'Exit and return to document' to return to Access and the Account Manager table and insert the picture.

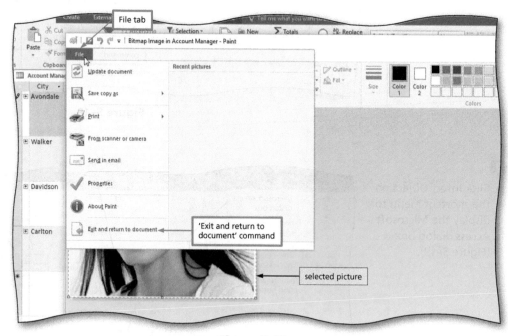

Figure 5–21

I do not see the picture. I just see words. Is that correct?
Yes. You will see the actual picture when you use this field in a form.

How can you insert a picture using the 'Create from File' option button?

If your installation of Access supports adding files of the type you want to insert, you would use the following steps:

1. Click the 'Create from File' option button (Figure 5–19), and then click the Browse button to display the Browse dialog box.

2. Navigate to the folder containing the picture you want to insert.

3. Click the file containing the desired picture, and then click the OK button (Browse dialog box) to select the appropriate picture.

4. Click the OK button to complete the addition of the picture.

If the entries do not change to the words, Bitmap Image, after you move to a different record, your installation does not support the addition of your type of files. In that case, use the steps given under To Enter Data in OLE Object Fields.

To Insert the Remaining Pictures

The following step adds the remaining pictures.

① Insert the pictures into the second, third, and fourth records using the techniques illustrated in the previous set of steps. For the second record, select the picture named mark_simson. For the third record, select the picture named peter_lu. For the fourth record, select karen_murowski.

Q&A I see Paintbrush Picture rather than Bitmap Image. Did I do something wrong?
The entries will initially be Paintbrush Picture, but they should change to the words, Bitmap Image, after you move to another record. They should also change after you close and reopen the table.

To Enter Data in Attachment Fields

1 ADD FIELDS | 2 ENTER DATA | 3 CREATE FORM | 4 ADD CONTROLS | 5 ADD SUBFORM
6 MODIFY SUBFORM | 7 ENHANCE FORM | 8 CREATE QUERIES

To insert data into an Attachment field, you use the Manage Attachments command on the Attachment field's shortcut menu. *Why? The Manage Attachments command displays the Attachments dialog box, which you can use to attach as many files as necessary to the field.* The following steps attach two files to the first account manager and one file to the third account manager. The second and fourth account managers currently have no attachments.

①

• Ensure the Account Notes field, which has a paper clip in the field selector, appears on your screen, and then right-click the Account Notes field on the first record to produce a shortcut menu (Figure 5–22).

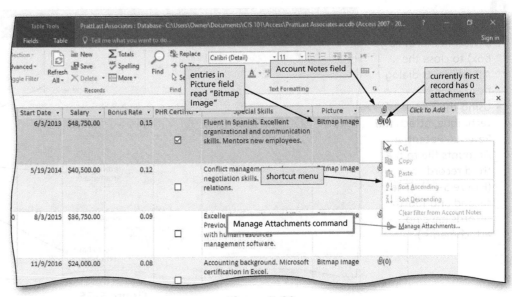

Figure 5–22

2

- Click Manage Attachments on the shortcut menu to display the Attachments dialog box (Figure 5–23).

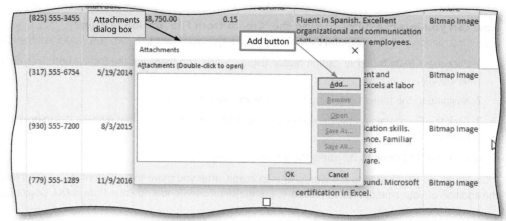

Figure 5–23

3

- Click the Add button (Attachments dialog box) to display the Choose File dialog box, where you can add an attachment.

- Navigate to the location containing your attachment files.

- Click Haydee Rivera Accounts, a Word file, and then click the Open button (Choose File dialog box) to attach the file.

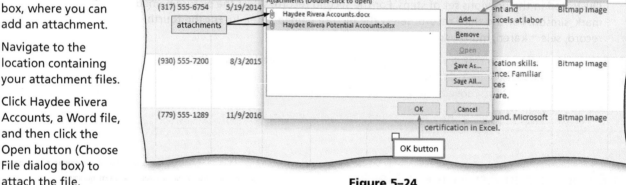

Figure 5–24

- Click the Add button (Attachments dialog box).

- Click Haydee Rivera Potential Accounts, an Excel file, and then click the Open button to attach the second file (Figure 5–24).

4

- Click the OK button (Attachments dialog box) to close the Attachments dialog box.

- Using the same technique, attach the Peter Lu Potential Accounts file to the third record (Figure 5–25). (The second and fourth records have no attachments.)

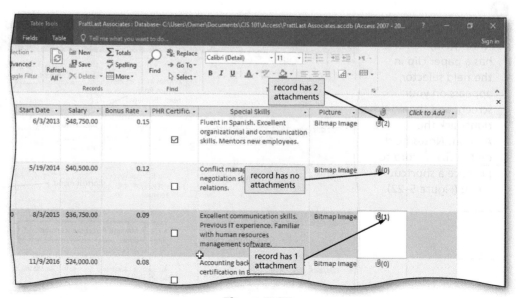

Figure 5–25

TO ENTER DATA IN HYPERLINK FIELDS

If your database contained a Hyperlink field, you would insert data by using the following steps.

1. Right-click the Hyperlink field in which you want to enter data to display a shortcut menu.
2. Point to Hyperlink on the shortcut menu to display the Hyperlink submenu.
3. Click Edit Hyperlink on the Hyperlink submenu to display the Insert Hyperlink dialog box.
4. Type the desired web address in the Address text box.
5. Click the OK button (Insert Hyperlink dialog box).

To Save the Properties

The row and column spacing are table properties. When changing any table properties, the changes apply only as long as the table is active *unless they are saved*. Once you have saved them, they will apply every time you open the table.

The following steps first save the properties and then close the table.

1 Click the Save button on the Quick Access Toolbar to save the changes to the table properties.

2 Close the table.

Viewing Pictures and Attachments in Datasheet View

Although the pictures do not appear on the screen, you can view them within the table. To view the picture of a particular account manager, right-click the Picture field for the account manager. Point to Bitmap Image Object on the shortcut menu, and then click Open. The picture will appear. Once you have finished viewing the picture, close the window containing the picture by clicking its Close button.

You can view the attachments in the Account Notes field by right-clicking the field and then clicking Manage Attachments on the shortcut menu. The attachments then appear in the Attachments dialog box. To view an attachment, click the attachment and then click the Open button (Attachments dialog box). The attachment will appear in its original application. After you have finished viewing the attachment, close the original application and close the dialog box.

Break Point: If you wish to stop working through the module at this point, you can resume the project at a later time by running Access, opening the database called PrattLast Associates, and continuing to follow the steps from this location forward.

Multiple-Table Form Techniques

With the additional fields in place, PrattLast Associates management is ready to incorporate data from both the Account Manager and Account tables in a single form. The form will display data concerning one account manager at a time. It will also display data concerning the many accounts assigned to the account manager. The relationship between account managers and accounts is a one-to-many relationship in which the Account Manager table is the "one" table and the Account table is the "many" table.

To include the data for the many accounts of an account manager on the form, the account data will appear in a **subform**, which is a form that is contained within another form. The form in which the subform is contained is called the **main form**. Thus, the main form will contain account manager data, and the subform will contain account data.

CONSIDER THIS

When a form includes data from multiple tables, how do you relate the tables?
Once you determine that you need data from more than one table, you need to determine the main table and its relationship to any other table.

Determine the main table the form is intended to view and/or update. You need to identify the purpose of the form and the table it is really intended to show, which is the *main* table.

Determine how the additional table should fit into the form. If the additional table is the "many" part of the relationship, the data should probably be in a subform or datasheet. If the additional table is the "one" part of the relationship, the data should probably simply appear as fields on the form.

To Create a Form in Design View

1 ADD FIELDS | 2 ENTER DATA | 3 CREATE FORM | 4 ADD CONTROLS | 5 ADD SUBFORM
6 MODIFY SUBFORM | 7 ENHANCE FORM | 8 CREATE QUERIES

You can create a form in Design view. *Why? Design view gives you increased flexibility in laying out a form by using a blank design on which you place objects in the precise locations you want.* The following steps create a form in Design view.

1

- If necessary, open the Navigation Pane and be sure the Account Manager table is selected.

- Click Create on the ribbon to display the Create tab (Figure 5–26).

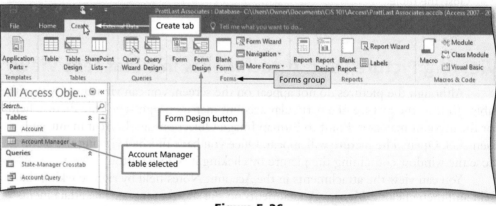

Figure 5–26

2

- Click the Form Design button (Create tab | Forms group) to create a new form in Design view.

- Close the Navigation Pane.

- If a field list does not appear, click the 'Add Existing Fields' button (Form Design Tools Design tab | Tools group) to display a field list (Figure 5–27). If you do not see the tables listed, click, 'Show all tables'. (Your list might show all fields in the Account table.)

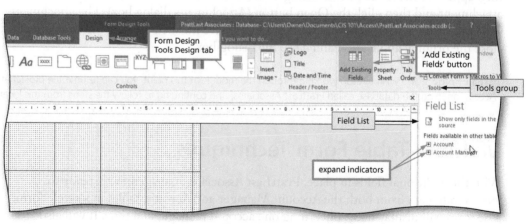

Figure 5–27

1 ADD FIELDS | 2 ENTER DATA | 3 CREATE FORM | 4 ADD CONTROLS | 5 ADD SUBFORM
6 MODIFY SUBFORM | 7 ENHANCE FORM | 8 CREATE QUERIES

To Add a Control for a Field to the Form

To place a control for a field on a form, drag the field from the field list to the desired position. The following steps place the Account Manager Number field on the form. *Why? Dragging is the easiest way to place a field on a form.*

● If necessary, click the expand indicator for the Account Manager table to display the fields in the table. Drag the Account Manager Number field in the field list for the Account Manager table to the approximate position shown in Figure 5–28. (For illustration purposes, do not release the mouse button yet.)

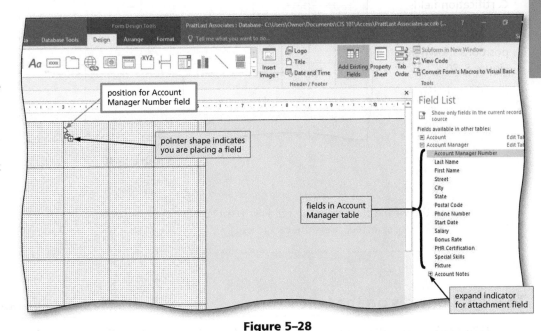

Figure 5–28

Q&A Do I have to be exact?
No. Just be sure you are in the same general location.

● Release the mouse button to place a control for the field (Figure 5–29).

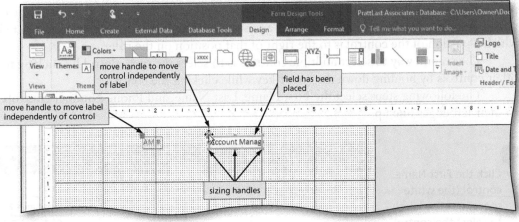

Figure 5–29

1 ADD FIELDS | 2 ENTER DATA | 3 CREATE FORM | 4 ADD CONTROLS | 5 ADD SUBFORM
6 MODIFY SUBFORM | 7 ENHANCE FORM | 8 CREATE QUERIES

To Add Controls for Additional Fields

The following step places controls for the First Name, Last Name, Phone Number, Salary, Bonus Rate, Start Date, and PHR Certification fields on the form by dragging the fields from the field list. *Why? These fields all need to be included in the form.*

1

- Drag the First Name, Last Name, Phone Number, Salary, Bonus Rate, Start Date, and PHR Certification fields and their labels to the approximate positions shown in Figure 5–30.

Q&A
Do I have to align them precisely?
You can, but you do not need to. In the next steps, you will instruct Access to align the fields properly.

What if I drag the wrong field from the field list? Can I delete the control?
Yes. With the control selected, press the DELETE key.

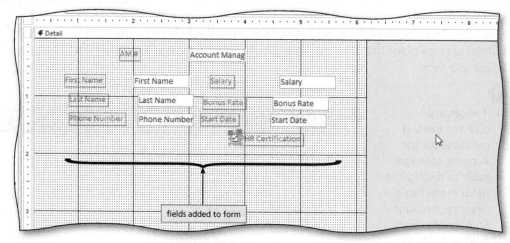

Figure 5–30

To Align Controls on the Left

1 ADD FIELDS | 2 ENTER DATA | 3 CREATE FORM | 4 ADD CONTROLS | 5 ADD SUBFORM
6 MODIFY SUBFORM | 7 ENHANCE FORM | 8 CREATE QUERIES

Why? *Often, you will want form controls to be aligned in some fashion. For example, the controls might be aligned so their right edges are even with each other. In another case, controls might be aligned so their top edges are even.* To ensure that a group of controls is aligned properly with each other, select all of the affected controls, and then use the appropriate alignment button on the Form Design Tools Arrange tab.

You can use one of two methods to select multiple controls. One way is to use a ruler. If you click a position on the horizontal ruler, you will select all the controls for which a portion of the control is under that position on the ruler. Similarly, if you click a position on the vertical ruler, you will select all the controls for which a portion of the control is to the right of that position on the ruler.

The second way to select multiple controls is to select the first control by clicking it. Then, select all the other controls by holding down the SHIFT key while clicking the control.

The following steps select the First Name, Last Name, and Phone Number controls and then align them so their left edges line up.

1

- Click the First Name control (the white space, not the label) to select the control.

- Hold the SHIFT key down and click the Last Name control to select an additional control. Do not release the SHIFT key.

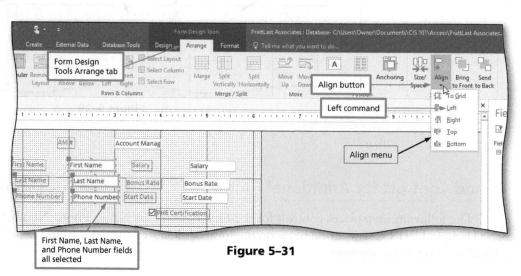

Figure 5–31

- Click the Phone Number control to select a third control, and then release the SHIFT key.

Q&A I selected the wrong collection of fields. How can I start over?
Simply begin the process again, making sure you do not hold the SHIFT key down when you select the first field.

- Click Arrange on the ribbon to display the Form Design Tools Arrange tab.

- Click the Align button (Form Design Tools Arrange tab | Sizing & Ordering group) to display the Align menu (Figure 5–31).

2
- Click the Left command on the Align menu to align the controls on the left (Figure 5–32).

3
- Click outside any of the selected controls to deselect the controls.

- Using the same technique, align the labels for the First Name, Last Name, and Phone Number fields on the left.

- Using the same technique, align the Salary, Bonus Rate, and Start Date fields on the left.

- If necessary, align the labels for the Salary, Bonus Rate, and Start Date fields on the left.

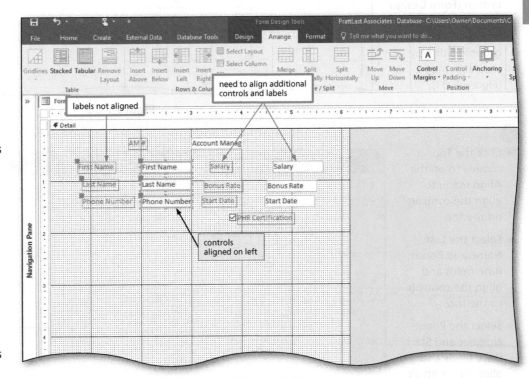

Figure 5–32

Other Ways

1. Right-click selected controls, point to Align

To Align Controls on the Top and Adjust Vertical Spacing

1 ADD FIELDS | 2 ENTER DATA | 3 CREATE FORM | 4 ADD CONTROLS | 5 ADD SUBFORM
6 MODIFY SUBFORM | 7 ENHANCE FORM | 8 CREATE QUERIES

Why? *Aligning the top edges of controls improves the neatness and appearance of a form. In addition, you might want the vertical spacing between controls to be the same.* The following steps align the First Name and Salary controls so that they are aligned on the top. Once these controls are aligned, you adjust the vertical spacing so that the same amount of space separates each row of controls.

- Select the label for the First Name control, the First Name control, the label for the Salary control, and the Salary control.
- Click the Align button (Form Design Tools Arrange tab | Sizing & Ordering group) to display the Align menu (Figure 5–33).

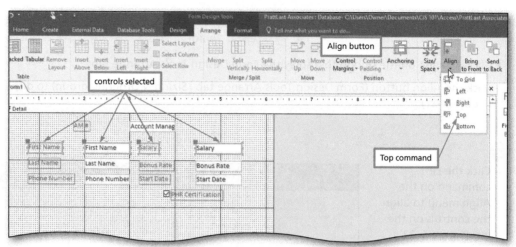

Figure 5–33

- Click the Top command on the Align menu to align the controls on the top.
- Select the Last Name and Bonus Rate fields and align the controls to the top.
- Select the Phone Number and Start Date fields and align the controls to the top.
- Click outside any of the selected controls to deselect the controls.
- Select the First Name, Last Name, Phone Number, Salary, Bonus Rate, and Start Date fields.

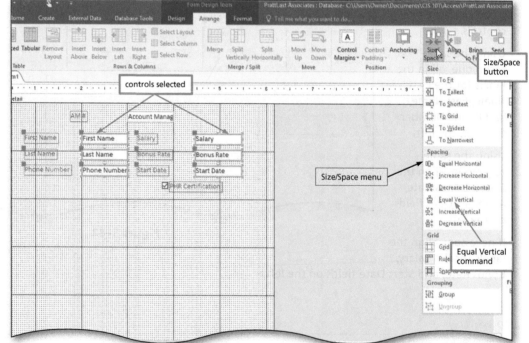

Figure 5–34

- Click the Size/Space button (Form Design Tools Arrange tab | Sizing & Ordering group) to display the Size/Space menu (Figure 5–34).

Q&A Do I need to select the labels too?
No. If you select the control, its label also is selected.

- Click Equal Vertical on the Size/Space menu to specify the spacing.

Q&A What is the purpose of the other commands on the Size/Space menu?
You can adjust the spacing to fit the available space. You can adjust the space to match the tallest, shortest, widest, or narrowest section. You can adjust the space to match the closest grid points. You can specify equal horizontal spacing. Finally, you can increase or decrease either the vertical or the horizontal spacing.

What do you do if the field list obscures part of the form, making it difficult to place fields in the desired locations?
You can move the field list to a different location by dragging its title bar. You can also resize the field list by pointing to the border of the field list so that the mouse pointer changes to a double-headed arrow. You then can drag to adjust the size.

- Because it is a good idea to save the form before continuing, click the Save button on the Quick Access Toolbar.

- Type **Account Manager Master Form** as the name of the form, and then click the OK button to save the form.

To Add Controls for the Remaining Fields

1 ADD FIELDS | 2 ENTER DATA | 3 CREATE FORM | 4 ADD CONTROLS | 5 ADD SUBFORM

6 MODIFY SUBFORM | 7 ENHANCE FORM | 8 CREATE QUERIES

The following steps place controls for the Special Skills, Picture, and Account Notes fields and also move their attached labels to the desired position. *Why? Controls for these fields are to be included in the completed form.*

1

- Drag the control for the Special Skills field from the field list to the approximate position shown in Figure 5–35.

Q&A Is there enough space on the form to add the Special Skills field?
Yes. The size of the form will expand as you drag the field to the form.

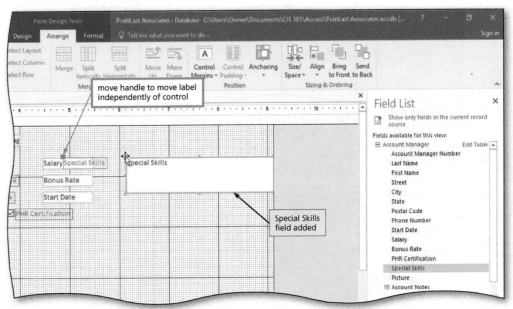

Figure 5–35

2

- Move the label for the Special Skills field to the position shown in Figure 5–36 by dragging its move handle.

Q&A I started to move the label and the control moved along with it. What did I do?
You were not pointing at the handle to move the label independently of the control.
Make sure you are pointing to the little box in the upper-left corner of the label.

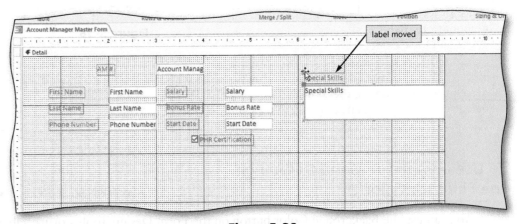

Figure 5–36

- Using the same techniques, move the control for the Picture field to the approximate position shown in Figure 5–37 and move its label to the position shown in the figure.

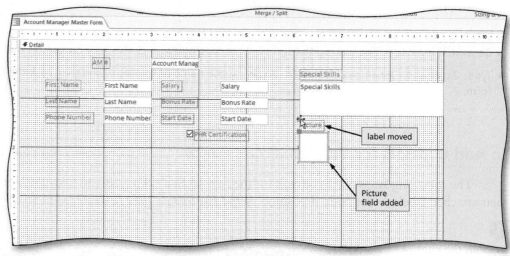

Figure 5–37

- Click the control for the Picture field and drag the lower-right corner to the approximate position shown in Figure 5–38 to resize the control.

- Add the control for the Account Notes field in the position shown in the figure and move its attached label to the position shown in the figure.

Q&A When would I need to click the expand indicator for the Account Notes field?
By clicking the expand indicator, you have access to three special properties of the field: FileData, FileName, and FileType. If you drag one of these onto the form, you will only get the corresponding information in the control. For example, if you drag Account Notes.FileName, the control will display the file name for the attachment. Most of the time, you want the field itself, so you would not use any of these properties.

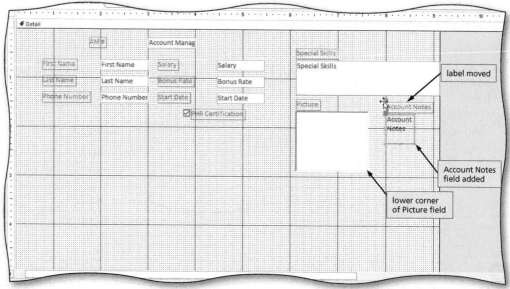

Figure 5–38

To Use a Shortcut Menu to Change the Fill/Back Color

1 ADD FIELDS | 2 ENTER DATA | 3 CREATE FORM | 4 ADD CONTROLS | **5 ADD SUBFORM**
6 MODIFY SUBFORM | 7 ENHANCE FORM | 8 CREATE QUERIES

You can use the Background Color button on the Form Design Tools Format tab to change the background color of a form. You can also use a shortcut menu. The following steps use a shortcut menu to change the background color of the form to gray. **Why?** *Using a shortcut menu is a simple way to change the background color.*

1

- Right-click in the approximate position shown in Figure 5–39 to produce a shortcut menu.

Q&A

Does it matter where I right-click? You can right-click anywhere on the form as long as you are outside of all the controls.

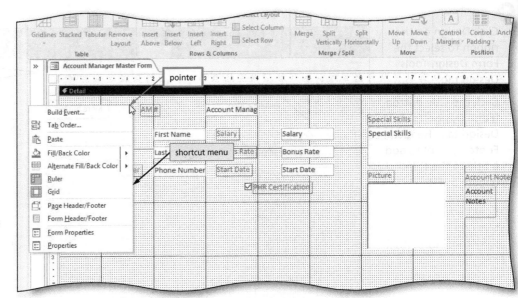

Figure 5–39

2

- Point to the 'Fill/Back Color' arrow on the shortcut menu to display a color palette (Figure 5–40).

3

- Click the gray color (row 3, column 1) shown in Figure 5–40 to change the fill/back color to gray.

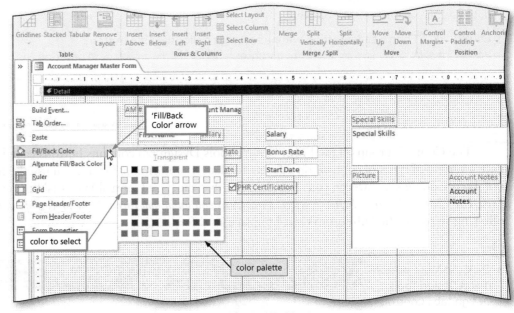

Figure 5–40

1 ADD FIELDS | 2 ENTER DATA | 3 CREATE FORM | 4 ADD CONTROLS | **5 ADD SUBFORM**
6 MODIFY SUBFORM | 7 ENHANCE FORM | 8 CREATE QUERIES

To Add a Title

A form should have a descriptive title. ***Why?*** *The title gives a concise visual description of the purpose of the form.* The following step adds a title to the form.

1

- Click Design on the ribbon to select the Form Design Tools Design tab.

- Click the Title button (Form Design Tools Design tab | Header/Footer group) to add a title to the form (Figure 5–41).

Q&A

Could I change this title if I want something different?
Yes. Change it just like you change any other text.

Why is there a new section?
The form title belongs in the Form Header section. When you clicked the Title button, Access added the Form Header section automatically and placed the title in it.

Could I add a Form Header section without having to click the Title button?
Yes. Right-click anywhere on the form background and click Form Header/Footer on the shortcut menu.

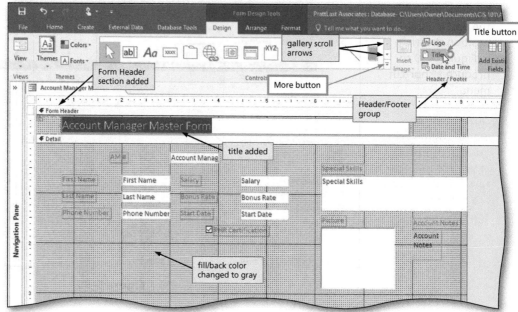

Figure 5–41

To Place a Subform

1 ADD FIELDS | 2 ENTER DATA | 3 CREATE FORM | 4 ADD CONTROLS | **5 ADD SUBFORM**
6 MODIFY SUBFORM | 7 ENHANCE FORM | 8 CREATE QUERIES

The Controls group on the Form Design Tools Design tab contains buttons called tools that you use to place a variety of types of controls on a form. To place a subform on a form, you use the Subform/Subreport tool. Before doing so, however, you should ensure that the 'Use Control Wizards' button is selected. *Why?* *If the 'Use Control Wizards' button is selected, a wizard will guide you through the process of adding the subform.* The following steps use the SubForm Wizard to place a subform.

1

- Click the More button (Form Design Tools Design tab | Controls group) (shown in Figure 5–41) to display a gallery of available tools (Figure 5–42).

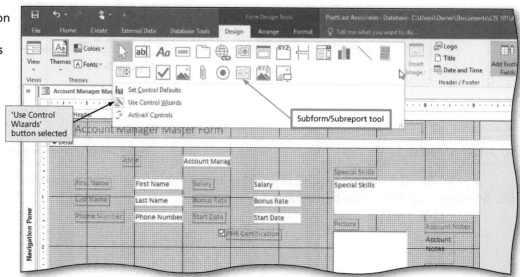

Figure 5–42

2

- Be sure the 'Use Control Wizards' button is selected, click the Subform/ Subreport tool on the Form Design Tools Design tab, and then move the pointer to the approximate position shown in Figure 5–43.

Q&A How can I tell whether the 'Use Control Wizards' button is selected? The icon for the 'Use Control Wizards' button will be highlighted, as shown in Figure 5–42. If it is not, click the 'Use Control Wizards' button to select it, click the More button, and then click the Subform/Subreport tool.

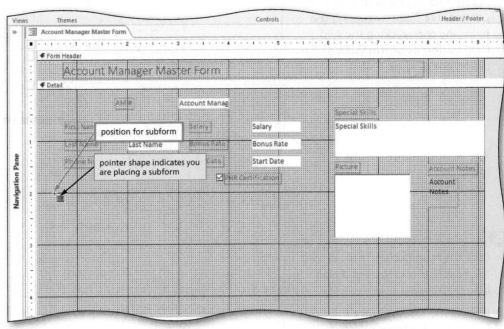

Figure 5–43

3

- Click the position shown in Figure 5–43 and then ensure the 'Use existing Tables and Queries' option button is selected (SubForm Wizard dialog box) (Figure 5–44).

Q&A My control is placed on the screen, but no wizard appeared. What should I do? Press the DELETE key to delete the control you placed. Ensure that the 'Use Control Wizards' button is selected, as described previously.

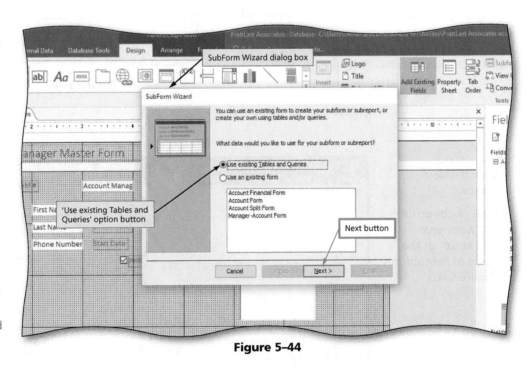

Figure 5–44

4

- Click the Next button.

- If the Account table is not already selected, click the Tables/Queries arrow, and then click the Account table to select it as the table that contains the fields for the subform.

- Add the Account Number, Account Name, Amount Paid, and Current Due fields by clicking the field, and then clicking the Add Field button (SubForm Wizard dialog box) (Figure 5–45).

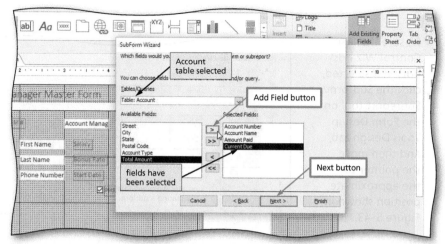

Figure 5–45

- Click the Next button to move to the next SubForm Wizard dialog box.

- Be sure the 'Choose from a list.' option button is selected (Figure 5–46).

Why do I use this option?
Most of the time, Access will have determined the appropriate fields to link the subform and the main form and placed an entry specifying those fields in the list. By choosing from the list, you can take advantage of the information that Access has created for you. The other option is to define your own, in which case you would need to specify the appropriate fields.

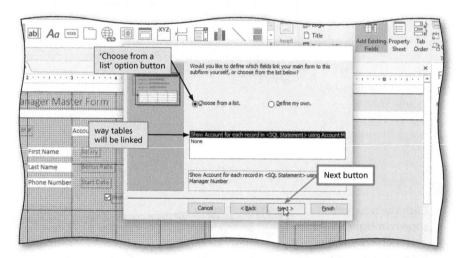

Figure 5–46

6

- Click the Next button.

- Type **Accounts of Account Manager** as the name of the subform (Figure 5–47).

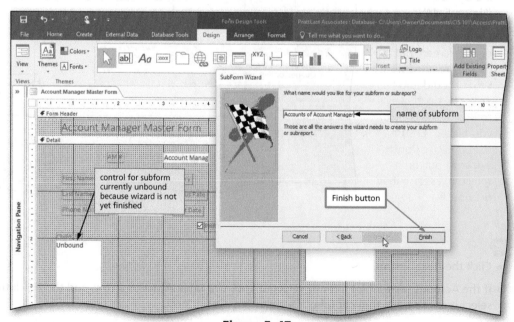

Figure 5–47

7

- Click the Finish button to place the subform.

- If necessary, move the subform control so that it does not overlap any other controls on the form (Figure 5–48).

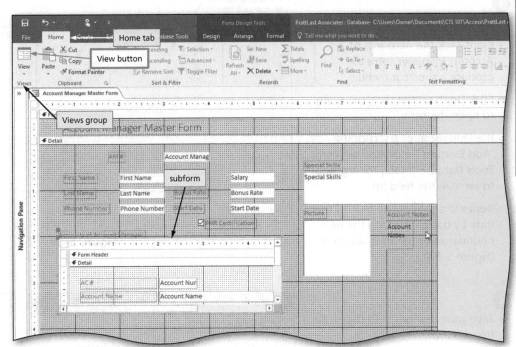

Figure 5–48

8

- Click the View button (Home tab | Views group) to view the form in Form view (Figure 5–49).

Q&A Everything looks good except the subform. I do not see all the fields I should see. What should I do?
You need to modify the subform, which you will do in the upcoming steps.

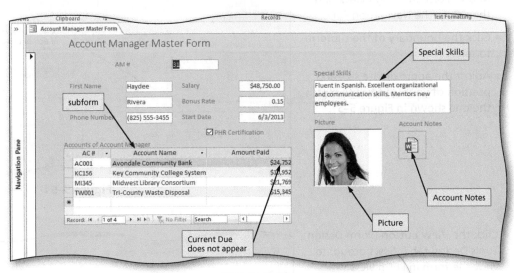

Figure 5–49

9

- Save and then close the form.

Break Point: If you wish to stop working through the module at this point, you can resume the project at a later time by running Access, opening the database called PrattLast Associates, and continuing to follow the steps from this location forward.

To Modify a Subform and Move the Picture

1 ADD FIELDS | 2 ENTER DATA | 3 CREATE FORM | 4 ADD CONTROLS | 5 ADD SUBFORM
6 MODIFY SUBFORM | 7 ENHANCE FORM | 8 CREATE QUERIES

The next task is to resize the columns in the subform, which appears on the form in Datasheet view. The subform exists as a separate object in the database; it is stored independently of the main form. The following steps open the subform and then resize the columns. *Why? The column sizes need to be adjusted so that the data is displayed correctly.* The steps then view the form and finally move and resize the picture.

- Open the Navigation Pane.

- Right-click the Accounts of Account Manager form to produce a shortcut menu.

- Click Open on the shortcut menu to open the form.

- If a field list appears, click the 'Add Existing Fields' button (Form Tools Datasheet tab | Tools group) to remove the field list.

- Resize the columns to best fit the data by double-clicking the right boundaries of the field selectors (Figure 5–50).

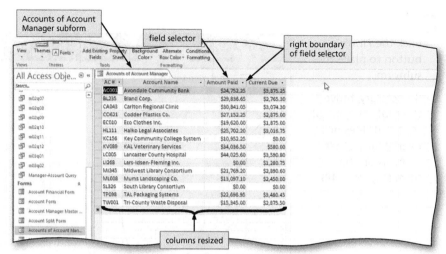

Figure 5–50

- Save your changes, and then close the subform.

- Open the Account Manager Master Form in Design view, and then close the Navigation Pane.

- Click the boundary of the subform to select it.

- Adjust the approximate size and position of your subform to match the one shown in Figure 5–51.

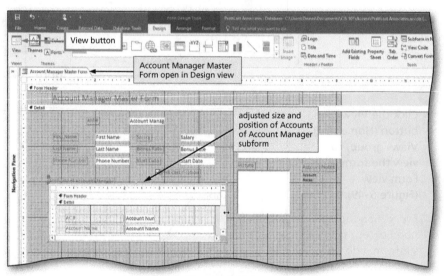

Figure 5–51

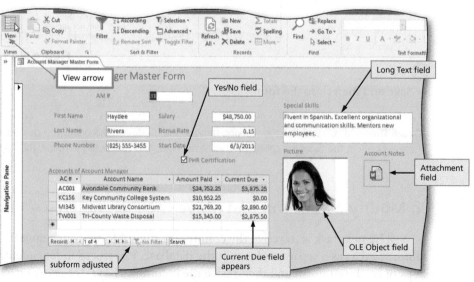

- Click the View button (Form Design Tools Design tab | Views group) to view the form in Form view (Figure 5–52).

Q&A

Could I have clicked the View arrow and then clicked Form View?
Yes. You can always use the arrow. If the icon for the view you want appears on the face of the View button, however, you can just click the button.

The picture seems to be a slightly different size from the one in Figure 5–1. How do I fix this?
You can move and also resize the picture, which you will do in the next step.

Figure 5–52

4

- Return to Design view, and then move and resize your picture to the approximate size and location shown in Figure 5–53.

 How can I tell if the new size and location is correct? View the form. If you are not satisfied with the size or location, return to Design view and make the necessary adjustments. Repeat the process until you are satisfied. You may have to allow a small amount of white on one of the borders of the picture. You will learn about some options you can use to adjust the specific look of the picture later in this module.

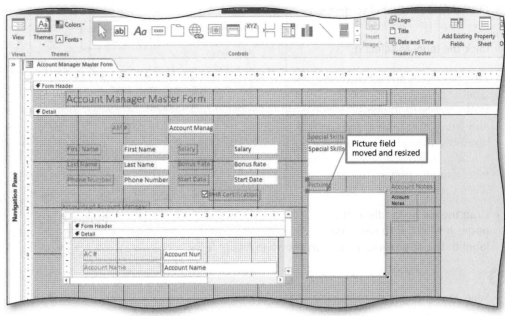

Figure 5–53

To Change a Label

1 ADD FIELDS | 2 ENTER DATA | 3 CREATE FORM | 4 ADD CONTROLS | 5 ADD SUBFORM
6 MODIFY SUBFORM | 7 ENHANCE FORM | 8 CREATE QUERIES

In Datasheet view, shortening the heading for the Account Manager Number column to AM # made sense to save room. Such a change is not necessary in the form. **Why?** *The form has enough room to display the entire field name, so adding the account manager label adds clarity.* In the form, there is plenty of room for the full field name to appear in the label. The following steps change the contents of the label from AM # to Account Manager Number.

1

- If necessary, return to Design view.

- Click the label for the Account Manager Number to select the label.

- Click the label a second time to produce an insertion point.

- Erase the current label (AM #), and then type **Account Manager Number** as the new label (Figure 5–54).

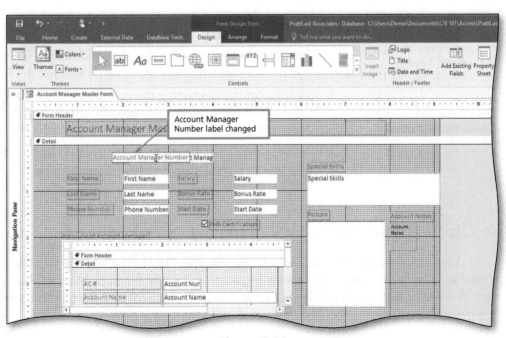

Figure 5–54

2

- Click outside the label to deselect it.

- Click the label to select it.

Why did I need to deselect the label and then select it again? With the insertion point appearing in the label, you could not move the label. By deselecting it and then selecting it again, the label will be selected, but there will be no insertion point.

- Drag the move handle in the upper-left corner to move the label to the approximate position shown in Figure 5–55.

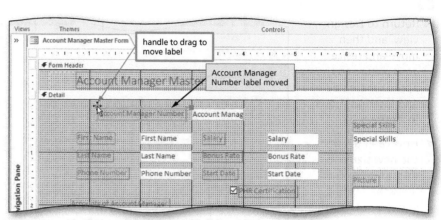

Figure 5–55

3

- Save your changes.

CONSIDER THIS

Is there any way to determine the way pictures fit within the control?

Yes. Access determines the portion of a picture that appears as well as the way it appears using the **size mode** property. The three size modes are as follows:

Clip — This size mode displays only a portion of the picture that will fit in the space allocated to it.

Stretch — This size mode expands or shrinks the picture to fit the precise space allocated on the screen. For photographs, usually this is not a good choice because fitting a photograph to the allocated space can distort the picture, giving it a stretched appearance.

Zoom — This size mode does the best job of fitting the picture to the allocated space without changing the look of the picture. The entire picture will appear and be proportioned correctly. Some white space may be visible either above or to the right of the picture, however.

BTW

Moving Controls

When you are dragging a label or control, you might need to make very small movements. You can use the arrow keys on the keyboard to make fine adjustments to control placement.

TO CHANGE THE SIZE MODE

Currently, the size mode for the picture should be Zoom, which is appropriate. If it were not and you wanted to change it, you would use the following steps.

1. Click the control containing the picture, and then click the Property Sheet button (Form Design Tools Design tab | Tools group) to display the control's property sheet.

2. Click the Size Mode property, and then click the Size Mode property arrow.

3. Click Zoom, and then close the property sheet by clicking its Close button.

To Change Label Effects and Colors

1 ADD FIELDS | 2 ENTER DATA | 3 CREATE FORM | 4 ADD CONTROLS | 5 ADD SUBFORM
6 MODIFY SUBFORM | 7 ENHANCE FORM | **8 CREATE QUERIES**

Access allows you to change many of the characteristics of the labels in the form. You can change the border style and color, the background color, the font, and the font size. You can also apply special label effects, such as raised or sunken. The following steps change the font color of the labels and add special effects. *Why? Modifying the appearance of the labels improves the appearance of the form.*

1

- Click the Account Manager Number label to select it, if necessary.

- Select each of the remaining labels by holding down the SHIFT key while clicking the label. Be sure to include the label for the subform (Figure 5–56).

Q&A Does the order in which I select the labels make a difference?

No. The only thing that is important is that they are all selected when you are done.

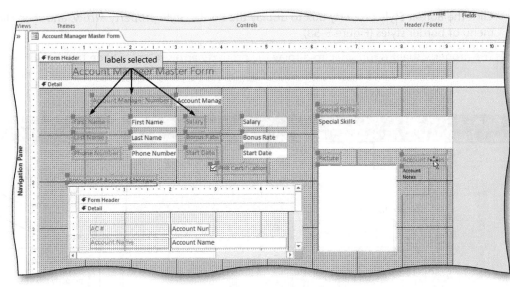

Figure 5–56

2

- Display the Form Design Tools Format tab.

- Click the Font Color arrow (Form Design Tools Format tab | Font group) to display a color palette (Figure 5–57).

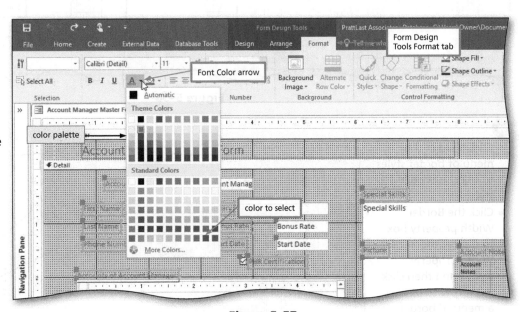

Figure 5–57

3

- Click the blue color in the second position from the right in the bottom row of Standard Colors to change the font color for the labels.

 **Experiment**

- Try other colors by clicking the Font Color arrow and then clicking the other color to see which colors you think would be good choices for the font. View the form to see the effect of your choice, and then return to Design view. When done, select the blue color.

- Display the Form Design Tools Design tab.

- Click the Property Sheet button (Form Design Tools Design tab | Tools group) to produce the property sheet for the selected labels. If your property sheet appears on the left side of the screen, drag it to the right. Make sure the All tab is selected.

- Click the Border Style property box to display the Border Style property arrow, and then click the arrow to display a menu of border styles (Figure 5–58).

Q&A The property sheet is too small to display the property arrow. Can I change the size of the property sheet?
Yes. Point to the border of the property sheet so that the pointer changes to a two-headed arrow. You then can drag to adjust the size.

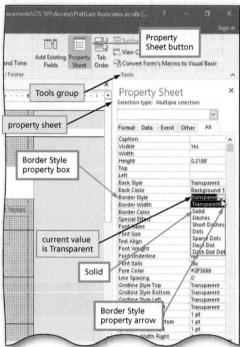
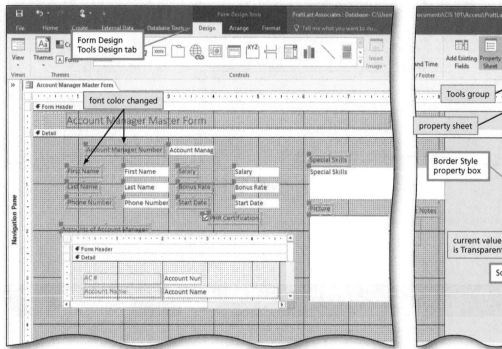

Figure 5–58

- Click Solid in the menu of border styles to select a border style.
- Click the Border Width property box to display the Border Width property arrow, and then click the arrow to display a menu of border widths.
- Click 3 pt to change the border width to 3 pt.
- Click the Special Effect property box to display the Special Effect property arrow, and then click the arrow to display a menu of special effects (Figure 5–59).

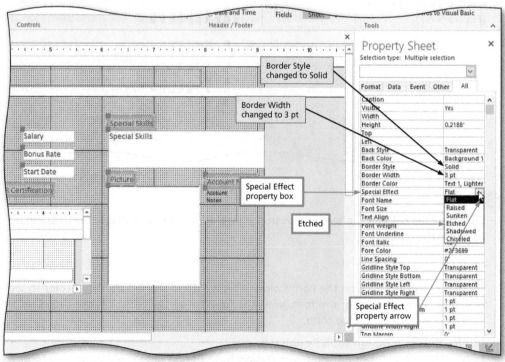

Figure 5–59

5

- Click Etched in the menu of special effects to select a special effect.

Experiment

- Try other special effects. In each case, view the form to see the special effect you selected and then return to Design view. When you are done, select Etched.

- Click the Account Manager Number control (the white space, not the label) to select it.

- Select each of the remaining controls by holding down the SHIFT key while clicking the control. Do not include the subform.

- Select Sunken for the special effect (Figure 5–60).

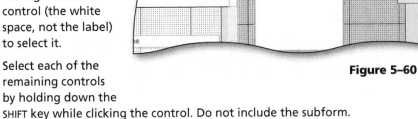

Figure 5–60

6

- Close the property sheet by clicking the Property Sheet button (Form Design Tools Design tab | Tools group).

- Click the View button to view the form in Form view (Figure 5–61).

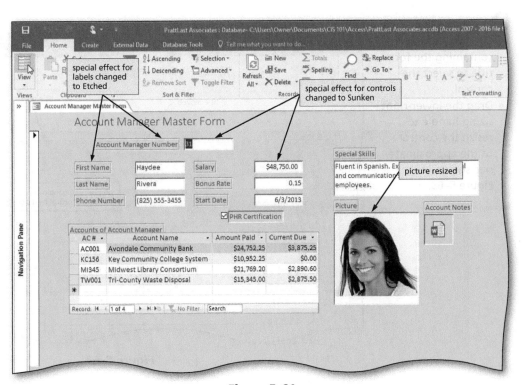

Figure 5–61

To Modify the Appearance of a Form Title

Why? You can enhance the title in a variety of ways by changing its appearance. These options include moving it, *resizing it, changing the font size, changing the font weight, and changing the alignment.* The following steps enhance the form title.

- Return to Design view.
- Resize the Form Header section by dragging down the lower boundary of the section to the approximate position shown in Figure 5–62.

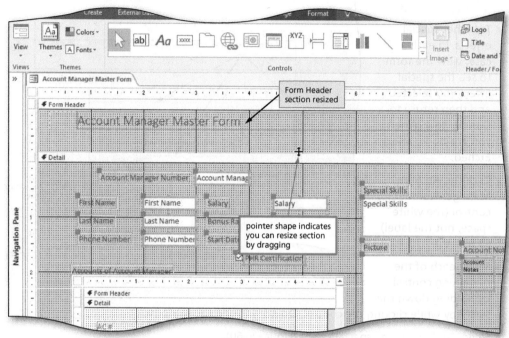

Figure 5–62

- Click the control containing the form title to select the control.
- Drag the lower-right sizing handle to resize the control to the approximate size shown in Figure 5–63.

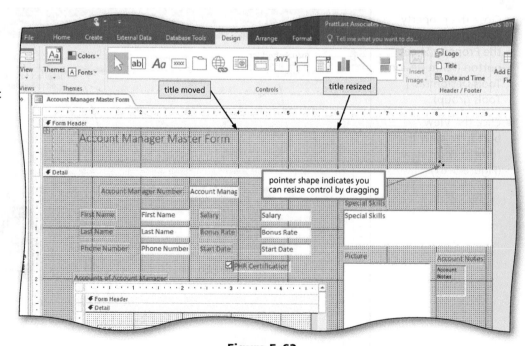

Figure 5–63

- Click the Property Sheet button (Form Design Tools Design tab | Tools group) to display the control's property sheet.

- Click the Font Size property box, click the Font Size property arrow, and then click 28 to change the font size.

- In a similar fashion, change the Text Align property value to Distribute and the Font Weight property value to Semi-bold (Figure 5–64).

- Close the property sheet by clicking the Property Sheet button (Form Design Tools Design tab | Tools group).

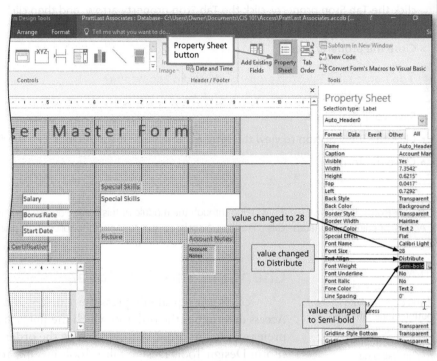

Figure 5–64

Other Ways

1. Enter font size value in Font Size box

1 ADD FIELDS | 2 ENTER DATA | 3 CREATE FORM | 4 ADD CONTROLS | 5 ADD SUBFORM
6 MODIFY SUBFORM | 7 ENHANCE FORM | 8 CREATE QUERIES

To Change a Tab Stop

Users can repeatedly press the TAB key to move through the controls on the form; however, they should bypass the Picture and Account Notes controls because users do not enter data into these fields. To omit these controls from the tab stop sequence, the following steps change the value of the Tab Stop property for the controls from Yes to No. *Why? Changing the Tab Stop property for these fields to No removes them from the Tab Stop sequence.*

1

- Click the Picture control to select it.

- Hold down the SHIFT key while clicking the Account Notes control to select it as well (Figure 5–65).

2

- Click the Property Sheet button (Form Design Tools Design tab | Tools group) to display the property sheet.

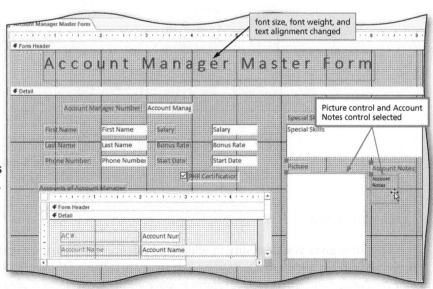

Figure 5–65

- Make sure the All tab (Property Sheet) is selected, click the down scroll arrow until the Tab Stop property appears, click the Tab Stop property, click the Tab Stop property arrow, and then click No to instruct Access to skip the Picture and Account Notes fields in the tab sequence.

- Close the property sheet.

Q&A I do not see the Tab Stop property. What did I do wrong?
You clicked the labels for the controls, not the controls.

- Save your changes.

- Click the View button to view the form in Form view. It should look like the form shown in Figure 5–1.

- Close the form.

Break Point: If you wish to stop working through the module at this point, you can resume the project at a later time by running Access, opening the database called PrattLast Associates, and continuing to follow the steps from this location forward.

BTW
Auto Order Button
If you click the Auto Order button in the Tab Order dialog box, Access will create a top-to-bottom and left-to-right tab order.

Changing the Tab Order

Users can repeatedly press the TAB key to move through the fields on a form. Access determines the order in which the fields are encountered in this process. If you prefer a different order, you can change the order by clicking the Tab Order button (Form Design Tools Design tab | Tools group). You then can use the Tab Order dialog box (Figure 5–66) to change the order by dragging rows (fields) to their desired order as indicated in the dialog box.

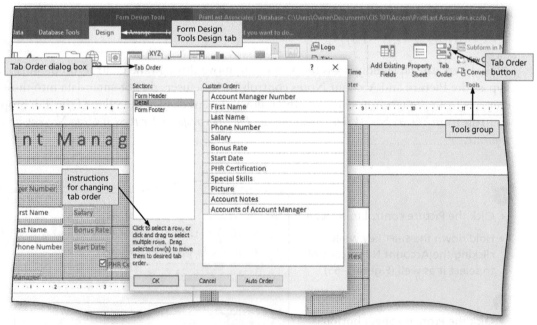

Figure 5–66

To Use the Form

1 ADD FIELDS | 2 ENTER DATA | 3 CREATE FORM | 4 ADD CONTROLS | 5 ADD SUBFORM
6 MODIFY SUBFORM | 7 ENHANCE FORM | **8 CREATE QUERIES**

The form gives you flexibility in selecting both account managers and the accounts of the account manager. *Why? You can use the Navigation buttons at the bottom of the screen to move among account managers. You can use the Navigation buttons in the subform to move among the accounts of the account manager currently shown on the screen.* The following steps use the form to display desired data.

1

- Open the Navigation Pane if it is currently closed.
- Right-click the Account Manager Master Form, and then click Open on the shortcut menu.
- Close the Navigation Pane.
- Right-click the Account Notes field to display a shortcut menu (Figure 5–67).

Figure 5–67

2

- Click the Manage Attachments command on the shortcut menu to display the Attachments dialog box (Figure 5–68).

Q&A How do I use this dialog box?
Select an attachment and click the Open button to view the attachment in its original application. Click the Add button to add a new attachment or the Remove button to remove the selected attachment. By clicking the Save As button, you can save the selected attachment as a file in whatever location you specify. You can save all attachments at once by clicking the Save All button.

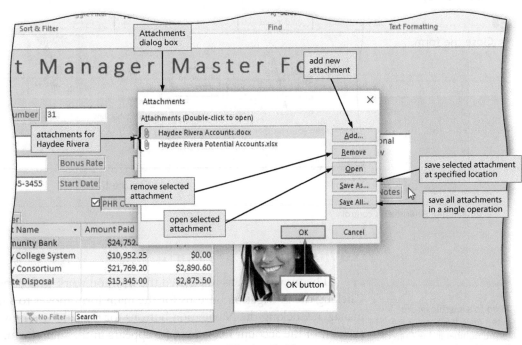

Figure 5–68

Experiment

- Open both attachments to see how they look in the original applications. When finished, close each original application.

3

- Click the OK button to close the Attachments dialog box.

- Click the form's Next record button three times to display the data for account manager 58 (Figure 5–69).

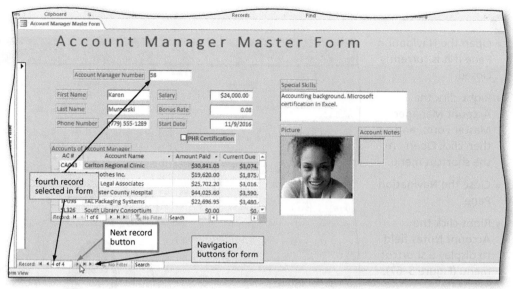

Figure 5–69

4

- Click the subform's Next record button twice to highlight the third account of account manager 58 (Figure 5–70).

5

- Close the form.

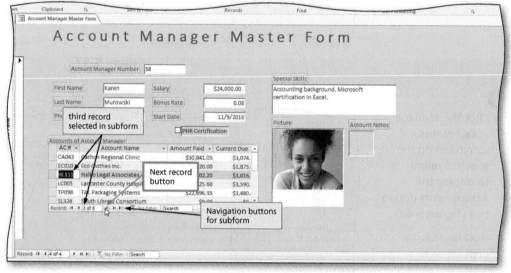

Figure 5–70

Other Ways

1. Double-click Attachments control

Navigation in the Form

BTW

Navigation
To go to a specific record in the main form, enter the record number in the Current Record box for the main form. To go to a specific record in the subform, enter the record number in the Current Record box for the subform.

The previous steps illustrated the way you work with a main form and subform. Clicking the Navigation buttons for the main form moves to a different account manager. Clicking the Navigation buttons for the subform moves to a different account of the account manager who appears in the main form. The following are other actions you can take within the form:

1. To move from the last field in the main form to the first field in the subform, press the TAB key. To move back to the last field in the main form, press SHIFT+TAB.

2. To move from any field in the subform to the first field in the next record's main form, press CTRL+TAB.

3. To switch from the main form to the subform using touch or the mouse, click anywhere in the subform. To switch back to the main form, click any control in the main form. Clicking the background of the main form will not cause the switch to occur.

Object Dependencies

In Access, objects can depend on other objects. For example, a report depends on the table or query on which it is based. A change to the structure of the table or query could affect the report. For example, if you delete a field from a table, any report based on that table that uses the deleted field would no longer be valid.

You can view information on dependencies between database objects. Viewing a list of objects that use a specific object helps in the maintenance of a database and avoids errors when changes are made to the objects involved in the dependency. For example, many items, such as queries and forms, use data from the Account table and thus depend on the Account table. By clicking the Object Dependencies button, you can see what items are based on the object. You also can see the items on which the object depends.

If you are unfamiliar with a database, viewing object dependencies can help you better understand the structure of the database. Viewing object dependencies is especially useful after you have made changes to the structure of tables. If you know which reports, forms, and queries depend on a table, you will be better able to make changes to a table without negatively affecting the related database objects.

To View Object Dependencies

1 ADD FIELDS | 2 ENTER DATA | 3 CREATE FORM | 4 ADD CONTROLS | 5 ADD SUBFORM
6 MODIFY SUBFORM | 7 ENHANCE FORM | **8 CREATE QUERIES**

The following steps view the objects that depend on the Account table. *Why? The objects that depend on the Account might be affected by any change you make to the Account table.*

- Open the Navigation Pane and click the Account table.

- Display the Database Tools tab.

- Click the Object Dependencies button (Database Tools tab | Relationships group) to display the Object Dependencies pane.

- If necessary, click the 'Objects that depend on me' option button to select it (Figure 5–71).

🔎 **Experiment**

- Click the 'Objects that I depend on' option button to see the objects on which the Account table depends. Then try both options for other objects in the database.

- Close the Object Dependencies pane by clicking the Object Dependencies button (Database Tools tab | Relationships group) a second time.

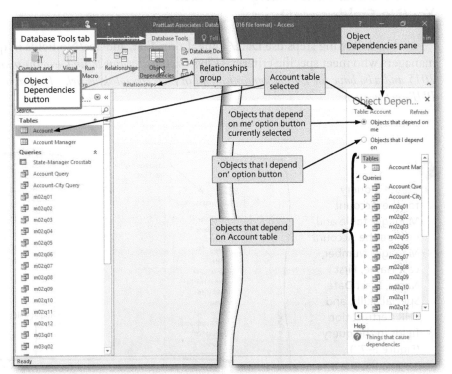

Figure 5–71

BTW

Long Text Fields in Queries

When you query long text fields, consider alternative spellings and phrases. For example, Computer Science also can be referenced as CS.

BTW

Date Fields in Queries

To test for the current date in a query, type Date() in the Criteria row of the appropriate column. Typing <Date() in the Criteria row for the Start Date, for example, finds those account managers who started any time before the date on which you run the query.

Date/Time, Long Text, and Yes/No Fields in Queries

By specifying account manager start dates using Date/Time fields, PrattLast Associates can run queries to find account managers hired before or after a certain date. Another use of the date field might be calculating a rep's length of service by subtracting the start date from the current date. Similarly, management can search for account managers with specific qualifications by adding Long Text and Yes/No fields.

To use Date/Time fields in queries, you simply type the dates, including the slashes. To search for records with a specific date, you must type the date. You can also use comparison operators. To find all the account managers whose start date is after January 5, 2015, for example, you type >1/15/2015 as the criterion.

You can also use Long Text fields in queries by searching for records that contain a specific word or phrase in the Long Text field. To do so, you use wildcards. For example, to find all the account managers who have the word, communication, somewhere in the Special Skills field, you type *communication* as the criterion. The asterisk at the beginning indicates that any characters can appear before the word, communication. The asterisk at the end indicates that any characters can appear after the word, communication.

To use Yes/No fields in queries, type the word, Yes, or the word, No, as the criterion. The following steps create and run queries that use Date/Time, Long Text, and Yes/No fields.

To Use Date/Time, Long Text, and Yes/No Fields in a Query

1 ADD FIELDS | 2 ENTER DATA | 3 CREATE FORM | 4 ADD CONTROLS | 5 ADD SUBFORM
6 MODIFY SUBFORM | 7 ENHANCE FORM | **8 CREATE QUERIES**

The following steps use Date/Time, Long Text, and Yes/No fields in queries to search for account managers who meet specific criteria. *Why? PrattLast wants to find account managers who started after January 1, 2015 and who have the word, communication, in their special skills field. They also want to find reps who have met their PHR certification.*

- Create a query for the Account Manager table and include the Account Manager Number, Last Name, First Name, Start Date, Special Skills, and PHR Certification fields in the query (Figure 5–72).

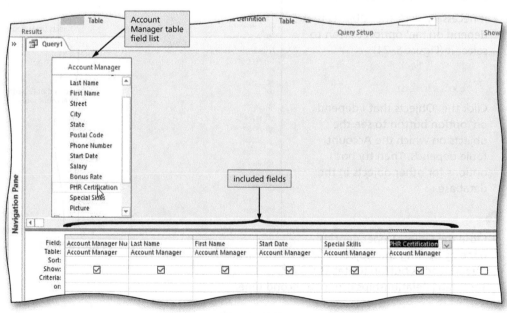

Figure 5–72

2

- Click the Criteria row under the Start Date field, and then type **>1/01/2015** as the criterion.
- Click the Criteria row under the Special Skills field, and then type ***communication*** as the criterion (Figure 5–73).

Why does the date have number signs (#) around it?
This is the date format in Access. Access reformatted the date appropriately as soon as you selected the Criteria row for the Special Skills field.

Are wild card searches in long text fields case-sensitive?
No.

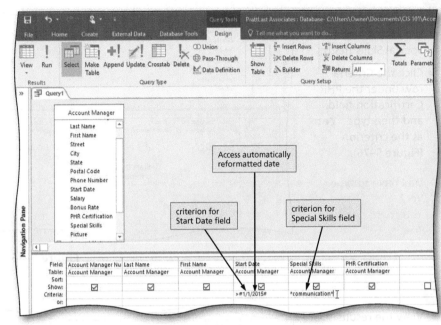

Access automatically reformatted date

criterion for Start Date field

criterion for Special Skills field

Figure 5–73

3

- View the results (Figure 5–74).

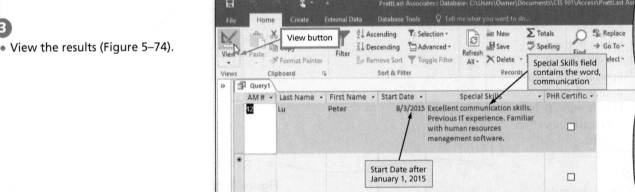

View button

Special Skills field contains the word, communication

Start Date after January 1, 2015

Figure 5–74

4

- Click the View button to return to Design view (Figure 5–75).

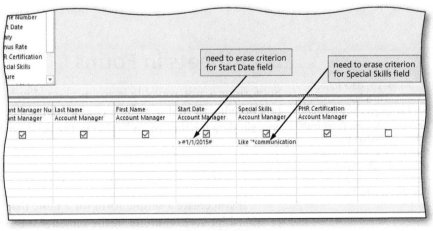

need to erase criterion for Start Date field

need to erase criterion for Special Skills field

Figure 5–75

5

- Erase the criteria in the Start Date and Special Skills fields.

- Click the Criteria row under the PHR Certification field, and then type **Yes** as the criterion (Figure 5–76).

Q&A Do I have to type Yes?
You could also type True.

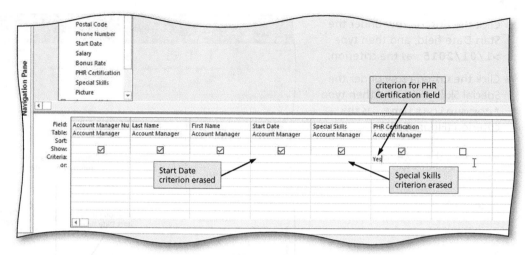

Figure 5–76

6

- View the results (Figure 5–77).

🔍 **Experiment**

- Try other combinations of values in the Start Date field, the Special Skills field, and/or the PHR Certification field. In each case, view the results.

7

- Close the query without saving the results.

- If desired, sign out of your Microsoft account.

- Exit Access.

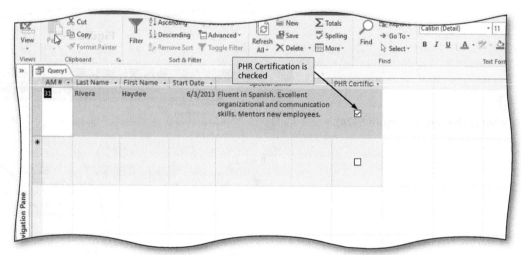

Figure 5–77

BTW
Date Formats
To change the date format for a date in a query, change the format property for the field using the field's property sheet. To change the date format for a field in a table, open the table in Design view and change the format property for the field.

Datasheets in Forms

Subforms are not available in forms created in Layout view, but you can achieve similar functionality to subforms by including datasheets. Like subforms, the datasheets contain data for the "many" table in the relationship.

Creating a Simple Form with a Datasheet

If you create a simple form for a table that is the "one" table in a one-to-many relationship, Access automatically includes the "many" table in a datasheet within the form. If you create a simple form for the Account Manager table, for example, Access will include the Account table in a datasheet within the form, as in Figure 5–78. The accounts in the datasheet will be the accounts of the account manager currently on the screen, in this case, Haydee Rivera.

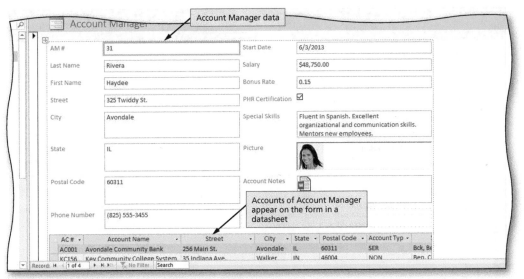

Figure 5–78

TO CREATE A SIMPLE FORM WITH A DATASHEET

To create a simple form with a datasheet, you would use the following steps.

1. Select the table in the Navigation Pane that is the "one" part of a one-to-many relationship.

2. Display the Create tab.

3. Click the Form button (Create tab | Forms group).

Creating a Form with a Datasheet in Layout View

You can create a form with a datasheet in Layout view. To create a form based on the Account Manager table that includes the account number, which is stored in the Account table, you would first use the field list to add the required fields from the "one" table. In Figure 5–79, fields from the Account Manager table have been added to the form.

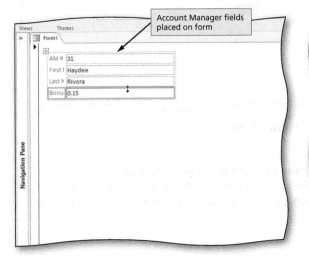

Figure 5–79

Next, you would use the field list to add a single field from the "many" table, as shown in Figure 5–80, in which the Account Number field has been added. Access will automatically create a datasheet containing this field.

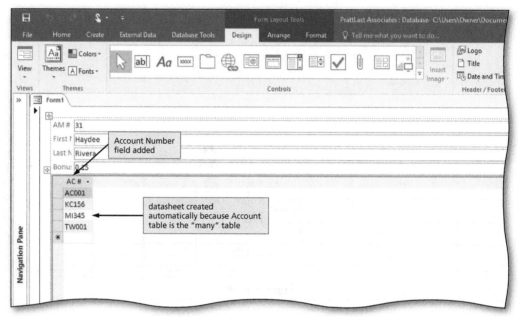

Figure 5–80

Finally, you would click the datasheet to select it and then use the field list to add the other fields from the "many" table that you want to include in the form, as shown in Figure 5–81.

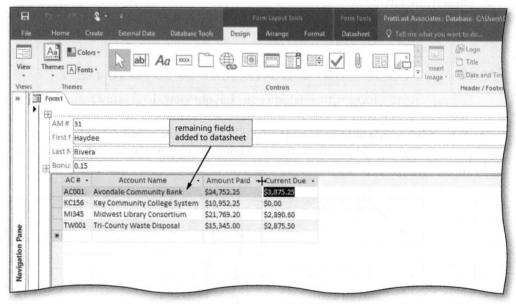

Figure 5–81

Can you modify the form so that the complete labels for the account manager fields appear?
Yes. Click any of the labels for the account manager fields to select the label, and then click the Select Column button (Arrange tab | Rows & Columns group) to select all the labels. You can then drag the right boundary of any of the labels to resize all the labels simultaneously.

CONSIDER THIS

TO CREATE A FORM WITH A DATASHEET IN LAYOUT VIEW

Specifically, to create a form with a datasheet in Layout view, you would use the following steps.

1. Display the Create tab.
2. Click the Blank Form button (Create tab | Forms group) to create a form in Layout view.
3. If a field list does not appear, click the 'Add Existing Fields' button (Form Layout Tools Design tab | Tools group) to display a field list.
4. If necessary, click 'Show all tables' to display the available tables.
5. Click the expand indicator (the plus sign) for the "one" table to display the fields in the table, and then drag the fields to the desired positions.
6. Click the expand indicator for the "many" table and drag the first field for the datasheet onto the form to create the datasheet.
7. Select the datasheet and drag the remaining fields for the datasheet from the field list to the desired locations in the datasheet.

Creating a Multiple-Table Form Based on the Many Table

All the forms discussed so far in this module were based on the "one" table, in this case, the Account Manager table. The records from the "many" table were included in a subform. You can also create a multiple-table form based on the "many" table, in this case, the Account table. Such a form is shown in Figure 5–82.

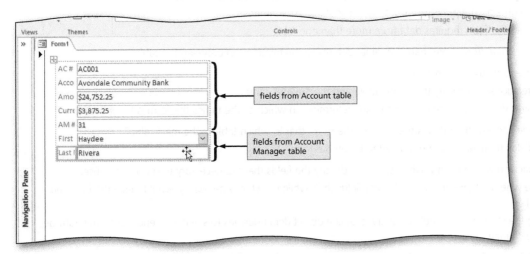

Figure 5–82

In this form, the Account Number, Account Name, Amount Paid, Current Due, and Account Manager Number fields are in the Account table. The First Name and Last Name fields are found in the Account Manager table and are included in the form to help to identify the account manager whose number appears in the Account Manager Number field.

BTW

Distributing a Document

Instead of printing and distributing a hard copy of a document, you can distribute the document electronically. Options include sending the document via email; posting it on cloud storage (such as OneDrive) and sharing the file with others; posting it on a social networking site, blog, or other website; and sharing a link associated with an online location of the document. You also can create and share a PDF or XPS image of the document, so that users can view the file in Acrobat Reader or XPS Viewer instead of in Access.

TO CREATE A MULTIPLE-TABLE FORM BASED ON THE MANY TABLE

To create a multiple-table form based on the "many" table, you would use the following steps.

1. Click the Blank Form button (Create tab | Forms group) to create a form in Layout view.
2. If a field list does not appear, click the 'Add Existing Fields' button on the Design tab to display a field list.
3. Drag the fields for the "many" table to the desired positions.
4. Drag the fields for the "one" table to the desired positions.

Summary

In this module you have learned to use Yes/No, Long Text, OLE Object, and Attachment data types; create and use an input mask; create a form and add a subform; enhance the look of the controls on a form; change tab order and stops; use a form with a subform; create queries involving Yes/No, Date/Time, and Long Text fields; view object dependencies; and create forms containing datasheets in Layout view.

CONSIDER THIS

What decisions will you need to make when creating your own forms?

Use these guidelines as you complete the assignments in this module and create your own forms outside of this class.

1. Determine the purpose of the fields to see if they need special data types.

   a. If the field only contains values such as Yes and No or True and False, it should have Yes/No as the data type.

   b. If the field contains an extended description, it should have Long Text as the data type.

   c. If the field contains a picture or other special object, its data type should be OLE Object.

   d. If the field contains attachments, its data type should be Attachment.

2. Determine whether the form requires data from more than one table.

3. If the form requires data from more than one table, determine the relationship between the tables.

   a. Identify one-to-many relationships.

   b. For each relationship, identify the "one" table and the "many" table.

4. If the form requires data from more than one table, determine on which of the tables the form is to be based.

   a. Which table contains data that is the focus of the form, that is, which table is the main table?

5. Determine the fields from each table that need to be on the form.

   a. Decide exactly how the form will be used, and identify the fields that are necessary to support this use.

   b. Determine whether there are any additional fields that, while not strictly necessary, would make the form more functional.

6. When changing the structure of a table or query, examine object dependencies to see if any report or form might be impacted by the change.

7. Determine the tab order for form controls.

   a. Change the tab order if the form requires a certain progression from one control to the next.

   b. Remove tab stops for those controls for which form navigation is not required.

8. Review the form to determine whether any changes are necessary.

   a. Are there visual changes, such as different colors or a larger font, that would make the form easier to use?

   b. Does the form have a similar look to other forms in the database?

   c. Does the form conform to the organization's standards?

How should you submit solutions to questions in the assignments identified with a symbol?
Every assignment in this book contains one or more questions identified with a symbol. These questions require you to think beyond the assigned database. Present your solutions to the questions in the format required by your instructor. Possible formats may include one or more of these options: write the answer; create a document that contains the answer; present your answer to the class; discuss your answer in a group; record the answer as audio or video using a webcam, smartphone, or portable media player; or post answers on a blog, wiki, or website.

Apply Your Knowledge

Reinforce the skills and apply the concepts you learned in this module.

Adding Phone Number, Yes/No, Long Text, and OLE Object Fields, Using an Input Mask Wizard, and Querying Long Text Fields

Note: To complete this assignment, you will be required to use the Data Files. Please contact your instructor for information about accessing the Data Files.

Instructions: Run Access, and then open the Apply NicelyNeat Services database that you used in Module 4. If you did not use this database, see your instructor about accessing the required files.

Perform the following tasks:

1. Open the Supervisor table in Design view.

2. Add the Phone Number, Safety Training, Other Skills, and Picture fields to the Supervisor table structure, as shown in Figure 5–83. Be sure the Phone Number field appears after the Postal Code field and create an input mask for the new field. Store the phone number data without symbols. Safety Training is a field that indicates whether the supervisor has completed all required safety courses.

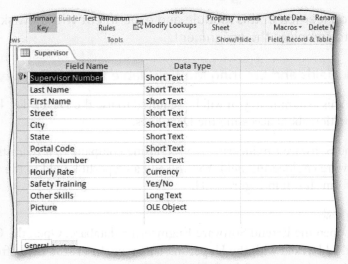

Figure 5–83

Continued >

Apply Your Knowledge *continued*

3. Add the data shown in Table 5–1 to the Supervisor table. Adjust the row and column spacing to best fit the data. Save the changes to the layout of the table.

Table 5–1 Data for Supervisor Table				
Supervisor Number	**Phone Number**	**Safety Training**	**Other Skills**	**Picture**
103	615-555-2222	Yes	Has construction experience. Helps to train new employees.	Pict2.jpg
110	931-555-4433	Yes	Has an Associate's degree. Previous experience as a school custodian.	Pict1.jpg
114	423-555-8877	No	Has construction experience. Excellent mechanical skills.	Pict3.jpg
120	931-555-5498	No	Working on an Associate's degree in supervisory management.	Pict4.jpg

4. If requested to do so by your instructor, change the phone number for supervisor number 103 to your phone number.

5. Query the Supervisor table to find all supervisors who have construction experience. Include the Supervisor Number, Last Name, First Name, and Phone Number fields in the query result. Save the query as Apply 5 Step 5 Query.

6. Query the Supervisor table to find all supervisors with construction experience who have completed all safety courses. Include the Supervisor Number, Last Name, First Name, and Other Skills fields in the query result. Save the query as Apply 5 Step 6 Query.

7. Submit the revised database in the format specified by your instructor.

8. ✳ What value did you enter in the criteria row for the Safety Training field in the query in Step 6 above? Could you have entered the criteria differently? If yes, then how would you enter the criteria?

Extend Your Knowledge

Extend the skills you learned in this module and experiment with new skills. You may need to use Help to complete the assignment.

Adding Hyperlink Fields and Creating Multiple-Table Forms Using Layout View

Note: To complete this assignment, you will be required to use the Data Files. Please contact your instructor for information about accessing the Data Files.

Instructions: Extend Software Engineering is a recruiting company that recruits employees for positions in the software engineering field. You will add a Hyperlink field to the Client table. You will also create the form shown in Figure 5–84.

Perform the following tasks:
1. Run Access and open the Extend Software Engineering database. Open the Client table in Design view and add a field with the Hyperlink data type. Insert the field after the Postal Code field. Use Website as the name of the field.

2. Open the Client table in Datasheet view and add data for the Website field to the first record. Use your school website as the URL. If necessary, resize the column so the complete URL is displayed.

3. If requested to do so by your instructor, enter your name as the client name for the first record of the Client table.

4. Use Layout view to create the multiple-table form shown in Figure 5–84. The Client table appears as a subform in the form. The Recruiter table is the "one" table in the form. Use Clients by Recruiter Form as the form name.

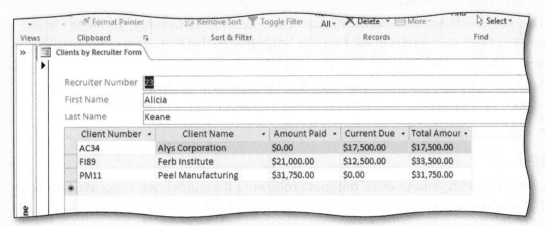

Figure 5–84

5. Submit the revised database in the format specified by your instructor.

6. ✻ How would you add a field for an email address to the Recruiter table?

Expand Your World

Create a solution, which uses cloud and web technologies, by learning and investigating on your own from general guidance.

Problem: Beach Vacations is a database of vacation rentals at a resort beach location. To understand the difference between Attachment and OLE Object data types, you will add those fields to the Rental Unit table. Then, you will insert images that you download from the Internet. Finally, you will create a multiple-table form for the database.

Note: To complete this assignment, you will be required to use the Data Files. Please contact your instructor for information about accessing the Data Files.

Instructions: Perform the following tasks:

1. Access any website containing royalty-free images and search the images to find four different pictures of beach properties for rent.

2. Save these images to a storage location of your choice.

3. Open the Expand Beach Vacations database and open the Rental Unit table in Design view. Add a Property Image field with an OLE Object data type. Add a Picture field with an Attachment data type. Assign the caption, Picture, to the Picture field. The fields should appear before the Owner Code field.

4. Use the techniques shown in the module to add the images to the Property Image field. Add the same images as attachments to the Picture field.

Continued >

Expand Your World *continued*

5. Create a multiple-table form based on the Rental Unit table. Include the Unit Number, Bedrooms, Weekly Rate, and For Sale fields from the Rental Unit table. Include the owner code, and the owner's first and last name on the form.

6. Include a title for the form and the current date. Save the form as Rental Unit Form, and then open the form in Design view.

7. Add the Property Image field and the Picture field to the form. If necessary, use the size mode property to adjust your images in the Property Image field so that they appear appropriately.

8. Submit the revised database in the format specified by your instructor.

9. ✳ In this assignment you stored images as OLE Object and Attachment fields. What differences did you notice on the form? Which storage method do you prefer and why?

In the Labs

Design, create, modify, and/or use a database following the guidelines, concepts, and skills presented in this module. Labs are listed in order of increasing difficulty. Labs 1 and 2, which increase in difficulty, require you to create solutions based on what you learned in the module. Lab 3 requires you to apply your creative thinking and problem solving skills to design and implement a solution.

Lab 1: Adding Fields and Creating Multiple-Table Forms for the Horticulture4U Database

Problem: Horticulture4U needs to maintain additional data on sales reps. Management needs to store notes about each sales rep, indicate whether the sales rep is eligible for a bonus, and display a picture of the sales rep. They also need to store the phone number of each sales rep. Management wants a form that displays sales rep information and the customers for whom they are responsible.

Note: To complete this assignment, you will be required to use the Data Files. Please contact your instructor for information about accessing the Data Files.

Instructions: Perform the following tasks:
1. Run Access and open the Lab 1 Horticulture4U database you used in Module 4. If you did not use this database, see your instructor about accessing the required files.

2. Add the Eligibility, Special Skills, and Picture fields to the end of the Sales Rep table. Eligibility is Yes/No field; Special Skills is a Long Text field; and Picture is an OLE Object Type field. Insert the Phone Number field after the Postal Code field and create the input mask shown in Figure 5–85 for the Phone Number field. Save the changes to the structure of the table.

3. Add the data shown in Table 5–2 to the Sales Rep table. Adjust the row and column spacing to best fit the data. Save the changes to the layout of the table.

Table 5–2 Data for Sales Rep Table				
Sales Rep Number	Phone Number	Eligibility	Special Skills	Picture
36	610-555-2212	Yes	Certified Master Gardener. President of local gardening club.	Pict1.jpg
39	215-555-4343	Yes	Previously owned a plant nursery. Has many contacts in business community.	Pict2.jpg
42	201-555-8787	No	Has a BS in Horticulture. Provides volunteer landscaping services to local library.	Pict4.jpg
45	302-555-9854	No	Lectures on organic gardening to local organizations.	Pict3.jpg

4. If requested to do so by your instructor, change the phone number for sales rep 36 to your phone number.

5. Create the form shown in Figure 5–85. Use Sales Rep Master Form as the name of the form, and Customers of Sales Rep as the name of the subform. The form has a background color of gray. The labels have a solid 3 pt border style with a raised special effect and blue font color. All controls except the subform control are sunken. Users should not be able to tab through the Picture control. The title is centered with a font weight of bold and a font size of 24.

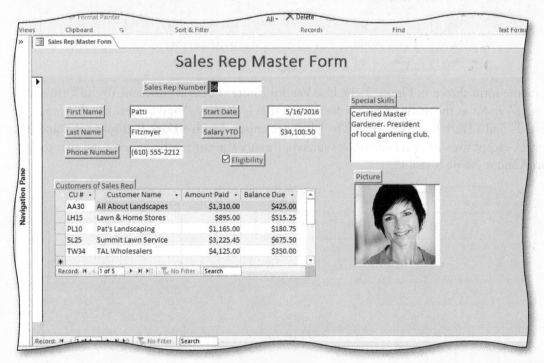

Figure 5–85

6. Query the Sales Rep table to find all sales reps who started before January 1, 2016 and who are eligible for a bonus. Include the Sales Rep Number, Last Name, and First Name in the query results. Save the query as Lab 5–1 Step 6 Query.

7. Submit the revised database in the format specified by your instructor.

8. ⊛ The Sales Rep table includes a Start Date field in the format, mm/dd/yyyy. How could you add an input mask for the Start Date field?

Continued >

In the Labs *continued*

Lab 2: Adding Fields and Creating Multiple-Table Forms for the SciTech Sundries Database

Problem: The management of SciTech Sundries has found that they need to maintain additional data on vendors. Management needs to keep track of whether the vendor accepts returns, and whether the vendor allows online ordering. Management would also like to attach to each vendor's record Excel files that contain historical cost data. SciTech Sundries requires a form that displays information about the vendors as well as the items that are purchased from vendors.

Note: To complete this assignment, you will be required to use the Data Files. Please contact your instructor for information about accessing the Data Files.

Instructions: Perform the following tasks:
1. Run Access and open the Lab 2 SciTech Sundries database you used in Module 4. If you did not use this database, see your instructor about accessing the required files.
2. Add the Returns, Online Ordering, and Cost History fields to the end of the Vendor table structure.
3. Add the data shown in Table 5–3 to the Vendor table.

Table 5–3 Data for Vendor Table

Vendor Code	Returns	Online Ordering	Cost History
AW	Yes	No	AW_History.xlsx
GS	No	Yes	GS_History.xlsx
SD	Yes	Yes	SD_History.xlsx

4. Create the form shown in Figure 5–86. Use Vendor Master Form as the name of the form and Items of Vendor as the name of the subform. The title is shadowed and centered with a font size of 24 and a Dark Red font color. The labels are chiseled with a Dark Red font color and the controls, except the subform control, are sunken. Be sure the entire title appears and that the entire Vendor Name is visible.

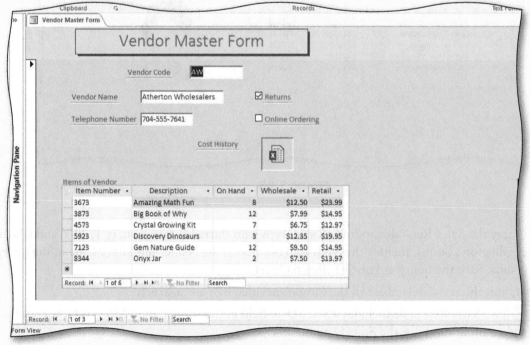

Figure 5–86

5. If requested to do so by your instructor, change the name for Vendor Code AW to your first and last name.

6. Open the Vendor Master Form and then open the cost history for Gift Sundries. Change the previous cost for item 7934 to $24.50. Save the change to the workbook.

7. Query the Vendor table to find all vendors that accept returns and allow online ordering. Include the Vendor Code and Vendor Name in the query results. Save the query as Lab 5–2 Step 7 Query.

8. Submit the revised database in the format specified by your instructor.

9. ✸ What additional field(s) would you add to the Vendor table to assist with online ordering?

Lab 3: **Consider This: Your Turn**

Adding Fields and Creating Multiple-Table Forms for the JSP Analysis Database

Instructions: Open the Lab 3 JSP Analysis database that you used in Module 4. If you did not create this database, see your instructor about accessing the required files.

Part 1: The management of JSP Analysis would like you to add some fields to the Marketing Analyst table. They would also like to create a form for the Marketing Analyst table that shows the clients of each analyst. Use the concepts and techniques presented in this module to perform each of the following tasks:

a. Add a phone number field, a picture field, and a notes field to the Marketing Analyst table. The phone number field should have an input mask.

b. Add the data for these fields to the Marketing Analyst table. Create phone numbers to store in the phone number field. For the pictures, select pictures from the Data Files or use your own photos. For the Notes field, add the notes shown in Table 5–4. Make sure all data appears in the datasheet.

Table 5–4 Data for Marketing Analyst Table	
Marketing Analyst Number	**Notes**
31	Master's degree in Marketing Research; treasurer of a national marketing association.
34	Bachelor's degree in Business Administration; veteran; has database experience.
47	Working on a Master's degree in Management Information Systems.
54	Bachelor's degree in Marketing.

c. Create a Marketing Analyst Master Form for the Marketing Analyst table that is similar in design to the form shown in Figure 5–1. Include the Marketing Analyst Number, First Name, Last Name, Phone Number, Salary YTD, Incentive YTD, Start Date, Picture, and Notes fields from the Marketing Analyst table on the form. The subform should display the Client

Continued >

In the Labs *continued*

Number, Client Name, Amount Paid, and Current Due fields from the Client table. Customize the form by adding special effects to controls and labels and by changing the background color of the form. Add a title and the current date to the form header.

d. Create a query that finds all marketing analysts who started before January 1, 2016 and have a degree in information systems.

Submit your assignment in the format specified by your instructor.

Part 2: You made several decisions while adding the fields and creating the form for this assignment. What was the rationale behind your decisions? Would you add any additional fields to the Marketing Analyst table?

6 Advanced Report Techniques

Objectives

You will have mastered the material in this module when you can:

- Create and relate additional tables
- Create queries for reports
- Create reports in Design view
- Add fields and text boxes to a report
- Format report controls
- Group and ungroup report controls
- Update multiple report controls

- Add and modify a subreport
- Modify section properties
- Add a title, page number, and date to a report
- Preview, print, and publish a report
- Add totals and subtotals to a report
- Include a conditional value in a report

Introduction

In Module 5, you created forms in Design view. In this module, you will create two reports in Design view. Both reports feature grouping and sorting. The first report contains a subreport, which is a report that is contained within another report. The subreport contains data from a query and is related to data in the main report. The second report uses aggregate functions to calculate subtotals and grand totals. It also uses a function to calculate a value where the actual calculation will vary from record to record depending on whether a given criterion is true.

Project — Creating Detailed Reports

PrattLast Associates wants a master list of account managers. This list should be available as an Access report and will have the name, Account Manager Master List. For each account manager, the report will include full details for all the accounts assigned to the account manager. In addition to offering its human resource services, PrattLast offers workshops designed to educate organizations on various aspects of human resource laws as well as ways to better manage employees. Data on workshop participation is stored in the database. For accounts who are participating in workshops, the report should list the specific workshops being offered to the account.

The Account Manager Master List report is shown in Figure 6–1a. The report is organized by account manager, with the data for each manager beginning on a new page. For each account manager, the report lists the account manager number, first name, and last name; the report then lists data for each account served by that account manager. The account data includes the number, name, street, city, state, postal code, account type, services needed, amount paid, current due, and total

Account Manager Master List

Page 1   9/12/2017

Account Manager Number 31   Name   **Haydee Rivera**

Account Number   **AC001**

Account Name	**Avondale Community Bank**	Account Type	**SER**
Street	**256 Main St.**	Services Needed	**Bck, Ben, Com, Pay, Rsk**
City	**Avondale**	Amount Paid	**$24,752.25**
State	**IL**	Current Due	**$3,875.25**
Postal Code	**60311**	Total Amount	**$28,627.50**

Workshop Code	Workshop Description	Total Hours	Hours Spent	Hours Remaining
W01	**Dealing with Unacceptable Employee Behavior**	**6**	**2**	**4**
W02	**Writing Effective Policies and Procedures**	**8**	**4**	**4**
W03	**Payroll Law**	**3**	**0**	**3**

Account Number   **KC156**

Account Name	**Key Community College System**	Account Type	**NON**
Street	**35 Indiana Ave.**	Services Needed	**Ben, Com, Mgt, Rsk, Wrk**
City	**Walker**	Amount Paid	**$10,952.25**
State	**IN**	Current Due	**$0.00**
Postal Code	**46004**	Total Amount	**$10,952.25**

Workshop Code	Workshop Description	Total Hours	Hours Spent	Hours Remaining
W08	**Workers' Compensation**	**16**	**8**	**8**

Figure 6–1a Account Manager Master List

D i s c o u n t   R e p o r t

Manager Number	First Name	Last Name	Account Number	Account Name	Amount Paid	Current Due	Discount
31	Haydee	Rivera					
			AC001	Avondale Community Bank	$24,752.25	$3,875.25	$155.01
			KC156	Key Community College System	$10,952.25	$0.00	$0.00
			MI345	Midwest Library Consortium	$21,769.20	$2,890.60	$115.62
			TW001	Tri-County Waste Disposal	$15,345.00	$2,875.50	$115.02
				Subtotals	$72,818.70	$9,641.35	
35	Mark	Simson					
			BL235	Bland Corp.	$29,836.65	$2,765.30	$110.61
			CO621	Codder Plastics Co.	$27,152.25	$2,875.00	$115.00
			KV089	KAL Veterinary Services	$34,036.50	$580.00	$23.20
			LI268	Lars-Idsen-Fleming Inc.	$0.00	$1,280.75	$25.62
			ML008	Mums Landscaping Co.	$13,097.10	$2,450.00	$98.00
				Subtotals	$104,122.50	$9,951.05	
58	Karen	Murowski					
			CA043	Carlton Regional Clinic	$30,841.05	$3,074.30	$122.97
			EC010	Eco Clothes Inc.	$19,620.00	$1,875.00	$75.00
			HL111	Halko Legal Associates	$25,702.20	$3,016.75	$120.67
			LC005	Lancaster County Hospital	$44,025.60	$3,590.80	$143.63
			SL326	South Library Consortium	$0.00	$0.00	$0.00
			TP098	TAL Packaging Systems	$22,696.95	$3,480.45	$139.22

Page 1   9/12/2017

Figure 6–1b Discount Report

amount. For each workshop the account is taking, the report lists the workshop code, description, total hours the workshop requires, hours already spent, and hours remaining.

To attract new accounts and reward current accounts, many companies offer discounts. PrattLast is considering the effect of offering a discount on the current due amount to its current accounts. The exact amount of the discount depends on how much the account has already paid. If the amount paid is more than $20,000, the discount will be 4 percent of the current due amount. If the amount paid is $20,000 or less, then the discount will be 2 percent of the current due amount. To assist in determining the discount, PrattLast needs a report like the one shown in Figure 6–1b. The report groups accounts by account manager. It includes subtotals of both the Amount Paid and Current Due fields. In addition, although not visible in the figure, it includes grand totals of both fields at the end of the report. Finally, it shows the discount amount, which is calculated by multiplying the current due amount by .04 (4 percent) for those accounts for whom the amount paid is more than $20,000.00 and by .02 (2 percent) for all others.

In this module, you will learn how to create the reports shown in Figure 6–1. The following roadmap identifies general activities you will perform as you progress through this module:

1. CREATE and relate additional TABLES.
2. CREATE QUERIES for a report.
3. CREATE a REPORT.
4. SPECIFY GROUPING AND SORTING.
5. Add fields and TEXT BOXES to the report.
6. ADD a SUBREPORT to the report.
7. ADD a TITLE, PAGE NUMBER, AND DATE to the report.
8. CREATE a SECOND REPORT.

Additional Tables

PrattLast managers are frequently asked to present workshops on various aspects of human resources law as well as ways to better manage employees. PrattLast would like to incorporate the workshop data into the PrattLast Associates database.

Before creating the reports, you need to create two additional tables for the PrattLast Associates database. The first table, Workshop, is shown in Tables 6–1a and 6–1b. As described in Table 6–1a, each workshop has a code and a description. The table also includes the total hours for which the workshop is usually offered and its increments; that is, the standard time blocks in which the workshop is usually offered. Table 6–1b contains the specific workshops that the account managers at PrattLast Associates offer to their accounts. The first row, for example, indicates that workshop W01 is called Dealing with Unacceptable Employee Behavior. It is typically offered in two-hour increments for a total of four hours.

Table 6–1a Structure of Workshop Table			
Field Name	**Data Type**	**Field Size**	**Description**
Workshop Code	Short Text	3	Primary Key
Workshop Description	Short Text	50	
Hours	Number	Integer	
Increments	Number	Integer	

Table 6–1b Workshop Table

Workshop Code	Workshop Description	Hours	Increments
W01	Dealing with Unacceptable Employee Behavior	4	2
W02	Writing Effective Policies and Procedures	8	4
W03	Payroll Law	3	1
W04	Workplace Safety	16	4
W05	The Recruitment Process	24	4
W06	Diversity in the Workplace	12	3
W07	Americans with Disabilities Act (ADA)	4	2
W08	Workers' Compensation	16	4

The second table, Workshop Offerings, is described in Table 6–2a and contains an account number, a workshop code, the total number of hours that the workshop is scheduled for the account, and the number of hours already spent in the workshop. The primary key of the Workshop Offerings table is a combination of the Account Number and Workshop Code fields.

Table 6–2a Structure of Workshop Offerings Table

Field Name	Data Type	Field Size	Description
Account Number	Short Text	5	Part of Primary Key
Workshop Code	Short Text	3	Part of Primary Key
Total Hours	Number	Integer	
Hours Spent	Number	Integer	

Table 6–2b gives the data for the Workshop Offerings table. For example, the first record shows that account number AC001 currently has scheduled workshop W01 (Dealing with Unacceptable Employee Behavior). The workshop is scheduled for six hours, and they have so far spent two hours in class.

Table 6–2b Workshop Offerings Table

Account Number	Workshop Code	Total Hours	Hours Spent
AC001	W01	6	2
AC001	W02	8	4
AC001	W03	3	0
EC010	W05	24	12
KC156	W08	16	8
KV089	W07	4	0
LC005	W02	8	4
LC005	W06	12	6
ML008	W03	3	1
ML008	W04	16	4
SL326	W05	24	16
SL326	W06	12	3
SL326	W07	4	2
TP098	W03	3	0
TP098	W08	16	4
TW001	W01	4	2

BTW

Enabling the Content
For each of the databases you use in this module, you will need to enable the content.

BTW

AutoNumber Field as Primary Key
When you create a table in Datasheet view, Access automatically creates an ID field with the AutoNumber data type as the primary key field. As you add records to the table, Access increments the ID field so that each record will have a unique value in the field. AutoNumber fields are useful when there is no data field in a table that is a suitable primary key.

BTW

Copying the Structure of a Table
If you want to create a table that has a structure similar to an existing table, you can copy the structure of the table only. Select the table in the Navigation Pane and click Copy, then click Paste. In the Paste Table As dialog box, type the new table name and click the Structure Only option button. Then, click the OK button. To modify the new table, open it in Design view.

If you examine the data in Table 6–2b, you see that the Account Number field cannot be the primary key for the Workshop Offerings table. The first and second records, for example, both have an account number of AC001. The Workshop Code field also cannot be the primary key. The second and seventh records, for example, both have workshop code W02. Rather, the primary key is the combination of both Account Number and Workshop Code.

To Create the New Tables

1 CREATE TABLES | 2 CREATE QUERIES | 3 CREATE REPORT | 4 SPECIFY GROUPING & SORTING | 5 ADD FIELDS
6 ADD SUBREPORT | 7 ADD TITLE, PAGE NUMBER, & DATE | 8 CREATE SECOND REPORT

You will use Design view to create the new tables. The steps to create the new tables are similar to the steps you used previously to add fields to an existing table and to define primary keys. The only difference is the way you specify a primary key. *Why? In the Workshop Offerings table, the primary key consists of more than one field, which requires a slightly different process.* To specify a primary key containing more than one field, you must select both fields that make up the primary key by clicking the row selector for the first field, and then hold down the SHIFT key while clicking the row selector for the second field. Once the fields are selected, you can use the Primary Key button to indicate that the primary key consists of both fields.

The following steps create the tables in Design view.

1

- Run Access and open the database named PrattLast Associates from your hard disk, OneDrive, or other storage location.

- If necessary, close the Navigation Pane.

- Display the Create tab (Figure 6–2).

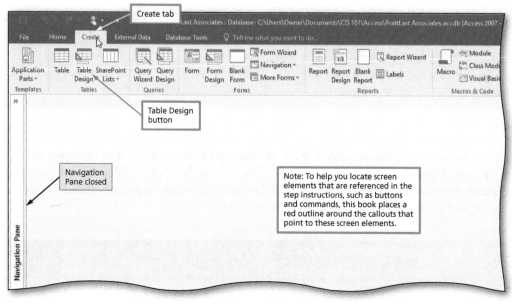

Figure 6–2

2

- Click the Table Design button (Create tab | Tables group) to create a table in Design view.

- Enter the information for the fields in the Workshop table as indicated in Table 6–1a, selecting Workshop Code as the primary key, and selecting the indicated field sizes.

- Save the table using the name **Workshop** and close the table.

- Display the Create tab and then click the Table Design button (Create tab | Tables group) to create a second table in Design view.

- Enter the information for the fields in the Workshop Offerings table as indicated in Table 6–2a.

- Click the row selector for the Account Number field.

- Hold down the SHIFT key and then click the row selector for the Workshop Code field so both fields are selected.

- Click the Primary Key button (Table Tools Design tab | Tools group) to select the combination of the two fields as the primary key (Figure 6–3).

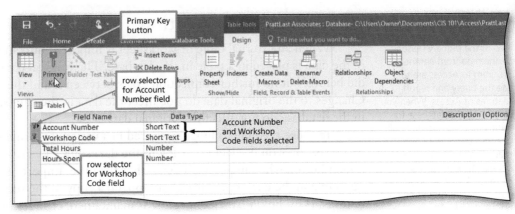

Figure 6–3

- Save the table using the name Workshop Offerings and close the table.

Q&A I realized I designated the wrong fields as the primary key. How can I correct the primary key?
Click any field that currently participates in the primary key, and click the Primary Key button to remove the primary key. You can then specify the correct primary key.

To Import the Data

Now that the tables have been created, you need to add data to them. You could enter the data manually, or if the data is already in electronic form, you could import the data. The data for the Workshop and Workshop Offerings tables is included in the Data Files. The files are text files formatted as delimited files. The Workshop data is in a tab-delimited text (.txt) file, and the Workshop Offerings data is in a comma-separated values (.csv) file, which is also a delimited text file. The following steps import the data.

1. With the PrattLast Associates database open, display the External Data tab and then click the Text File button (External Data tab | Import & Link group) to display the Get External Data - Text File dialog box.

2. Click the Browse button (Get External Data - Text File dialog box) and then navigate to the location containing the text file (for example, the Access folder in the CIS 101 folder).

3. Select the Workshop file and click the Open button.

4. Select the 'Append a copy of the records to the table' option button, select the Workshop table from the drop-down list, and then click the OK button. With the Delimited option button selected, click the Next button.

5. With the Tab option button selected, click the 'First Row Contains Field Names' check box, click the Next button, and then click the Finish button.

6. Click the Close button to close the Get External Data - Text Box dialog box without saving the import steps.

7. Use the technique shown in Steps 1 through 6 to import the Workshop Offerings.csv file into the Workshop Offerings table. Be sure the Comma option button is selected and there is a check mark in the 'First Row Contains Field Names' check box.

Q&A I got an error message after I clicked the Finish button that indicated there were errors. The data was not imported. What should I do?
First, click the Cancel button to terminate the process. Then, review the structure of the table in Design view to ensure that the field names are all spelled correctly and that the data types are correct. Correct any errors you find, save your work, and then redo the steps to import the data.

BTW
Many-to-Many Relationships
There is a many-to-many relationship between the Account table and the Workshop table. To implement a many-to-many relationship in a relational database management system such as Access, you create a third table, often called a junction or intersection table, that has as its primary key the combination of the primary keys of each of the tables involved in the many-to-many relationship. The primary key of the Workshop Offerings table is the combination of the Account Number and the Workshop Code fields.

BTW
Linking
Two of the primary reasons to link data from another program to Access are to use the query and report features of Access. When you link an Access database to data in another program, all changes to the data must be made in the source program. For example, if you link an Excel workbook to an Access database, you cannot edit the linked table in Access. You must make all changes to the data in Excel.

Linking versus Importing

When an external table or worksheet is imported into an Access database, a copy of the data is placed in a table in the database. The original data still exists, just as it did before, but no further connection exists between it and the data in the database. Changes to the original data do not affect the data in the database. Likewise, changes in the database do not affect the original data.

It is also possible to link data stored in a variety of formats to Access databases. To do so, you would select the 'Link to the data source by creating a linked table' option button when importing data, rather than the 'Import the source data into a new table in the current database' or 'Append a copy of the records to the table' option buttons. With linking, the connection is maintained; changes made to the data in the external table or worksheet affect the Access table.

To identify that a table is linked to other data, Access displays an arrow in front of the table in the Navigation Pane. In addition, an icon is displayed in front of the name that indicates the type of file to which the data is linked. For example, an Excel icon in front of the name indicates that the table is linked to an Excel worksheet.

TO MODIFY LINKED TABLES

After you link tables between a worksheet and a database or between two databases, you can modify many of the linked table's features. To rename the linked table, set view properties, and set links between tables in queries, you would use the following steps.

1. Click the 'Linked Table Manager' button (External Data tab | Import & Link group) to update the links.
2. Select the linked table for which you want to update the links.
3. Click the OK button.

To Relate the New Tables

1 CREATE TABLES | 2 CREATE QUERIES | 3 CREATE REPORT | 4 SPECIFY GROUPING & SORTING | 5 ADD FIELDS
6 ADD SUBREPORT | 7 ADD TITLE, PAGE NUMBER, & DATE | 8 CREATE SECOND REPORT

The following steps relate, or create a relationship between, the tables. *Why? The new tables need to be related to the existing tables in the PrattLast Associates database. The Account and Workshop Offerings tables are related through the Account Number field that exists in both tables. The Workshop and Workshop Offerings tables are related through the Workshop Code fields in both tables.*

1

- If necessary, close any open datasheet on the screen by clicking its Close button, and then display the Database Tools tab.

- Click the Relationships button (Database Tools tab | Relationships group) to open the Relationships window (Figure 6–4).

Q&A I only see one table, did I do something wrong?
Click the All Relationships button to display all the tables in relationships.

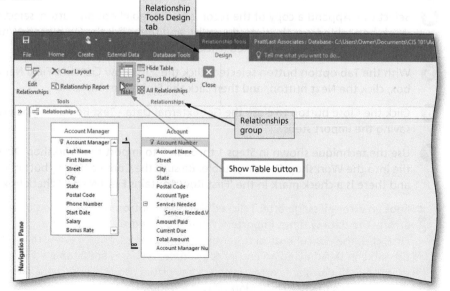

Figure 6–4

2
- Click the Show Table button (Relationship Tools Design tab | Relationships group) to display the Show Table dialog box (Figure 6–5).

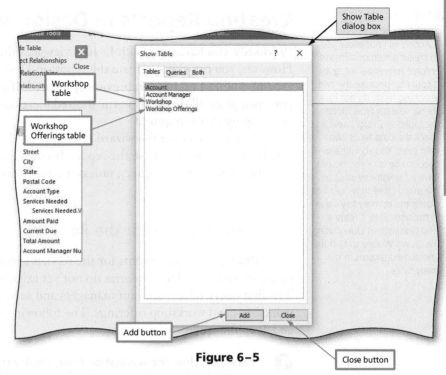

Figure 6–5

3
- Click the Workshop Offerings table, click the Add button (Show Table dialog box), click the Workshop table, click the Add button again, and then click the Close button to add the tables to the Relationships window.

Q&A
I cannot see the Workshop Offerings table. Should I repeat the step?
If you cannot see the table, it is behind the dialog box. You do not need to repeat the step.

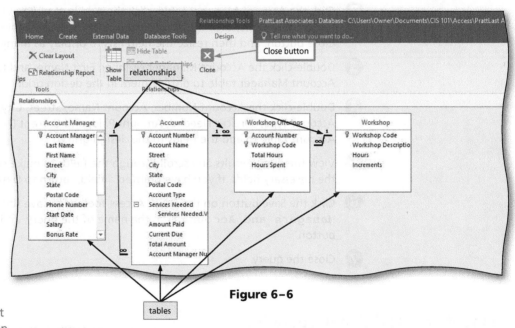

Figure 6–6

- Drag the Account Number field in the Account table to the Account Number field in the Workshop Offerings table to display the Edit Relationships dialog box. Click the 'Enforce Referential Integrity' check box (Edit Relationships dialog box) and then click the Create button to create the relationship.

- Drag the Workshop Code field from the Workshop table to the Workshop Code field in the Workshop Offerings table. Click the 'Enforce Referential Integrity' check box (Edit Relationships dialog box) and then click the Create button to create the relationship (Figure 6–6).

4
- Save the changes and then click the Close button (Relationship Tools Design tab | Relationships group).

BTW
Invalid Relationships
If Access will not allow you to create a relationship and enforce referential integrity, it could be because the two matching fields do not have the same data type. Open the tables in Design view and check the data types and field sizes. You should also check to be sure you do not have a foreign key value in the many table that does not match the primary key value in the one table. Create a Find Unmatched Query using the Query Wizard to find the unmatched records in the many table.

Creating Reports in Design View

Previously, you have used both Layout view and the Report Wizard to create reports. However, you can simply create the report in Design view. You can also use Design view to modify a report you previously created. If you create a report in Design view, you must place all the fields in the desired locations. You must also specify any sorting or grouping that is required.

Whether you use the wizard or simply use Design view, you must determine on which table or query to base the report. If you decide to base the report on a query, you must first create the query, unless it already exists.

To Create a Query for the Report

PrattLast's requirements for the reports specify that it would be convenient to use two queries. These queries do not yet exist, so you will need to create them. The first query relates account managers and accounts, and the second query relates workshops and workshop offerings. The following steps create the Account Managers and Accounts query.

1 If necessary, close the Navigation Pane, display the Create tab, and then click the Query Design button (Create tab | Queries group) to create a new query.

2 Click the Account Manager table, click the Add button (Show Table dialog box), click the Account table, click Add button, close the Show Table dialog box by clicking its Close button, and then resize the field lists to display as many fields as possible.

3 Double-click the Account Manager Number, First Name, and Last Name fields from the Account Manager table to display them in the design grid.

4 Double-click the Account Number, Account Name, Street, City, State, Postal Code, Account Type, Services Needed, Amount Paid, and Current Due fields from the Account table to add the fields to the design grid.

5 View the query results and scroll through the fields to make sure you have included all the necessary fields. If you have omitted a field, return to Design view and add it.

6 Click the Save button on the Quick Access Toolbar to save the query, type **Account Managers and Accounts** as the name of the query, and then click the OK button.

7 Close the query.

To Create an Additional Query for the Report Using Expression Builder

1 CREATE TABLES | 2 CREATE QUERIES | 3 CREATE REPORT | 4 SPECIFY GROUPING & SORTING | 5 ADD FIELDS
6 ADD SUBREPORT | 7 ADD TITLE, PAGE NUMBER, & DATE | 8 CREATE SECOND REPORT

The following steps create the Workshop Offerings and Workshops query, which includes a calculated field for hours remaining, that is, the total number of hours minus the hours spent. *Why? PrattLast Associates needs to include in the Account Manager Master List the number of hours that remain in a workshop offering.*

1
- Display the Create tab and then click the Query Design button (Create tab | Queries group) to create a new query.
- Click the Workshop table, click the Add button (Show Table dialog box), click the Workshop Offerings table, click the Add button, and then click the Close button to close the Show Table dialog box.
- Double-click the Account Number and Workshop Code fields from the Workshop Offerings table to add the fields to the design grid.

- Double-click the Workshop Description field from the Workshop table.

- Double-click the Total Hours and Hours Spent fields from the Workshop Offerings table to add the fields to the design grid.

- Click the Field row in the first open column in the design grid to select it.

- Click the Builder button (Query Tools Design tab | Query Setup group) to display the Expression Builder dialog box (Figure 6–7).

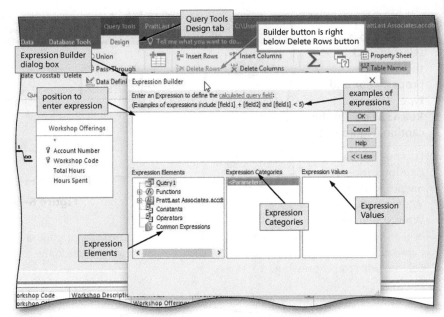

Figure 6–7

- Double-click PrattLast Associates in the Expression Elements section to display the categories of objects within the PrattLast Associates database, and then double-click Tables to display a list of tables.

- Click the Workshop Offerings table to select it.

- Double-click the Total Hours field to add it to the expression.

- Type a minus sign (–) to add it to the expression.

- Double-click the Hours Spent field to add it to the expression (Figure 6–8).

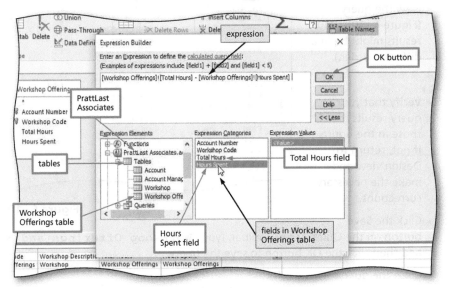

Figure 6–8

Q&A

Why are the fields preceded by a table name and an exclamation point?
This notation qualifies the field; that is, it indicates to which table the field belongs.

Could I type the expression instead of using the Expression Builder?
Yes. You could type it directly into the design grid. You could also right-click the column and click Zoom to allow you to type the expression in the Zoom dialog box. Finally, you could use the Expression Builder, but simply type the expression rather than clicking any buttons. Use whichever method you find most convenient.

- Click the OK button (Expression Builder dialog box) to close the dialog box and add the expression you entered to the design grid.

- With the field in the grid containing the expression selected, click the Property Sheet button (Query Tools Design tab | Show/Hide group) to display the property sheet for the new field.

- Ensure that the General tab is selected, click the Caption property box and type **Hours Remaining** as the caption (Figure 6–9).

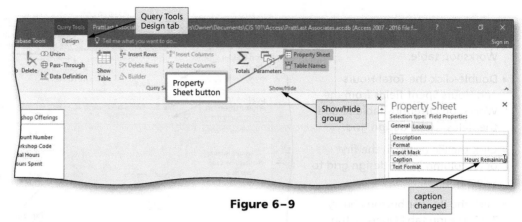

Figure 6–9

Q&A

I do not have a Caption property in my property sheet. What went wrong? What should I do?

You either inadvertently clicked a different location in the grid, or you have not yet completed entering the expression. The easiest way to ensure you have done both is to click any other column in the grid and then click the column with the expression.

4

- Close the property sheet and then view the query (Figure 6–10). (Your results might be in a different order.)

5

- Verify that your query results match those in the figure. If not, return to Design view and make the necessary corrections.

Account Nur ▾	Workshop C ▾	Workshop D ▾	Total Hours ▾	Hours Spent ▾	Hours Rema ▾
AC001	W01	Dealing with U	6	2	4
TW001	W01	Dealing with U	4	2	2
AC001	W02	Writing Effecti	8	4	4
LC005	W02	Writing Effecti	8	4	4
AC001	W03	Payroll Law	3	0	3
ML008	W03	Payroll Law	3	1	2
TP098	W03	Payroll Law	3	0	3
ML008	W04	Workplace Safe	16	4	12
EC010	W05	The Recruitme	24	12	12
SL326	W05	The Recruitme	24	16	8
LC005	W06	Diversity in the	12	6	6
SL326	W06	Diversity in the	12	3	9
KV089	W07	Americans witl	4	0	4
SL326	W07	Americans witl	4	2	2
KC156	W08	Workers' Comp	16	8	8
TP098	W08	Workers' Comp	16	4	12

Figure 6–10

- Click the Save button on the Quick Access Toolbar, type **Workshop Offerings and Workshops** as the name of the query, and then click the OK button to save the query.

- Close the query.

Other Ways

1. Right-click field in grid, click Build

CONSIDER THIS

How do you determine the tables and fields for the report?

If you determine that data should be presented as a report, you need to then determine what tables and fields contain the data for the report.

Examine the requirements for the report in general to determine the tables. Do the requirements only relate to data in a single table, or does the data come from multiple tables? Is the data in a query, or could you create a query that contains some or all of the fields necessary for the report?

Examine the specific requirements for the report to determine the fields necessary. Look for all the data items that are specified for the report. Each item should correspond to a field in a table, or it should be able to be computed from a field or fields in a table. This information gives you the list of fields to include in the query.

Determine the order of the fields. Examine the requirements to determine the order in which the fields should appear. Be logical and consistent in your ordering. For example, in an address, the city should come before the state, and the state should come before the postal code, unless there is some compelling reason for another order.

What decisions do you make in determining the organization of the report?
Determine sort order. Is there a special order in which the records should appear?

Determine grouping. Should the records be grouped in some fashion? If so, what information should appear before the records in a group? If, for example, accounts are grouped by account manager number, the number of the account manager should probably appear before the group. Should the account manager name also appear? What should appear after the group? For example, are there some fields for which subtotals should be calculated? If so, the subtotals would come after the group.

Determine whether to include a subreport. Rather than use grouping, you can include a subreport, as shown in the Account Manager Master List shown in Figure 6–1a. The data concerning workshop offerings for the account could have been presented by grouping the workshop offerings' data by account number. The headings currently in the subreport would have appeared in the group header. Instead, it is presented in a subreport. Subreports, which are reports in their own right, offer more flexibility in formatting than group headers and footers. More importantly, in the Account Manager Master List, some accounts do not have any workshop offerings. If this information were presented using grouping, the group header will still appear for these accounts. With a subreport, accounts that have no workshop offerings do not appear.

To Create an Initial Report in Design View

1 CREATE TABLES | 2 CREATE QUERIES | 3 CREATE REPORT | 4 SPECIFY GROUPING & SORTING | 5 ADD FIELDS
6 ADD SUBREPORT | 7 ADD TITLE, PAGE NUMBER, & DATE | 8 CREATE SECOND REPORT

Creating the report shown in Figure 6–1a from scratch involves creating the initial report in Design view, adding the subreport, modifying the subreport separately from the main report, and then making the final modifications to the main report.

When you want to create a report from scratch, you use Design view rather than the Report Wizard. *Why? The Report Wizard is suitable for simple, customized reports. With Report Design, you can make advanced design changes, such as adding subreports.*

The following steps create the initial version of the Account Manager Master List and select the **record source** for the report; that is, the table or query that will furnish the data for the report. The steps then specify sorting and grouping for the report.

- Display the Create tab.

- Click the Report Design button (Create tab | Reports group) to create a report in Design view.

- Ensure the selector for the entire report, the box in the upper-left corner of the report, contains a small black square, which indicates that the report is selected.

- Click the Property Sheet button (Report Design Tools Design tab | Tools group) to display a property sheet.

Q&A Can I make the property sheet box wider so I can see more of the items in the Record Source list?
Yes, you can make the property sheet wider by dragging its left or right border.

- Drag the left border, if necessary, to increase the width of the property sheet.

- With the All tab (Property Sheet) selected, click the Record Source property box arrow to display the list of available tables and queries (Figure 6–11).

Q&A Can I move the property sheet?
Yes, you can move the property sheet by dragging its title bar.

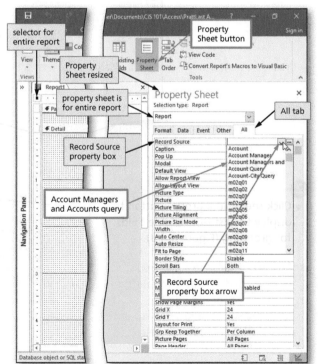

Figure 6–11

2

- Click the Account Managers and Accounts query to select the query as the record source for the report.
- Close the property sheet by clicking the Property Sheet button (Report Design Tools Design tab | Tools group).

Other Ways

1. Right-click report selector, click Properties

1 CREATE TABLES | 2 CREATE QUERIES | 3 CREATE REPORT | 4 SPECIFY GROUPING & SORTING | 5 ADD FIELDS
6 ADD SUBREPORT | 7 ADD TITLE, PAGE NUMBER, & DATE | 8 CREATE SECOND REPORT

To Group and Sort

In Design view of the report, you can specify both grouping and sorting by using the Group & Sort button on the Design tab, just as you did in Layout view. The following steps specify both grouping and sorting in the report. *Why? PrattLast has determined that the records in the report should be grouped by account manager number. That is, all the accounts of a given account manager should appear together. Within the accounts of a given account manager, they have determined that accounts are to be ordered by account number.*

1

- Click the Group & Sort button (Report Design Tools Design tab | Grouping & Totals group) to display the Group, Sort, and Total pane (Figure 6–12).

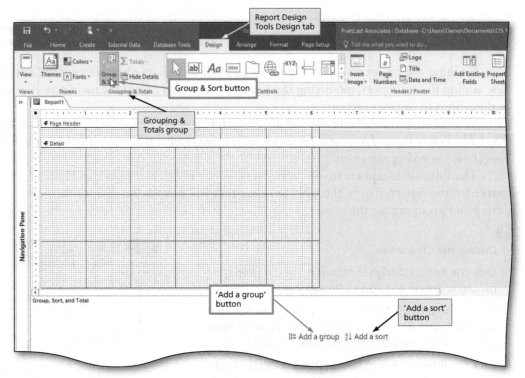

Figure 6–12

2

- Click the 'Add a group' button to display the list of available fields for grouping (Figure 6–13).

Q&A
The list of fields disappeared before I had a chance to select a field. What should I do?
Click the select field arrow to once again display the list of fields.

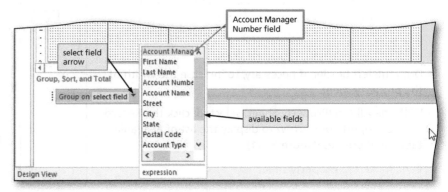

Figure 6–13

3
- Click the 'Account Manager Number' field to group by account manager number (Figure 6–14).

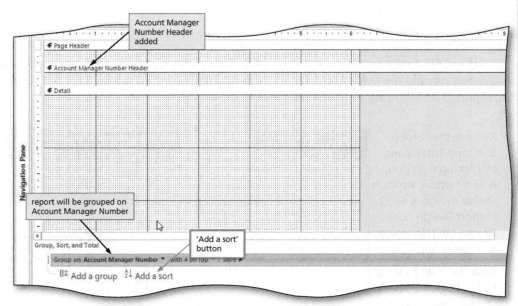

Figure 6–14

4
- Click the 'Add a sort' button to display the list of available fields for sorting (Figure 6–15).

5
- Click the Account Number field to sort by account number.
- Save the report, using **Account Manager Master List** as the report name.

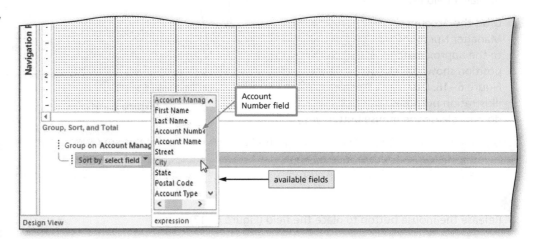

Figure 6–15

Other Ways

1. Right-click any open area of the report, click Sorting & Grouping

Controls and Sections

Recall from Module 4 that a report contains three types of controls: bound controls, unbound controls, and calculated controls. As you learned previously, reports contain standard sections, including the Report Header, Report Footer, Page Header, Page Footer, and Detail sections. When the data in a report is grouped, there are two additional possible sections. The contents of the **Group Header section** are printed before the records in a particular group, and the contents of the **Group Footer section** are printed after the group. In the Discount Report (Figure 6–1b), for example, which is grouped by account manager number, the Group Header section contains the account manager number and name, and the Group Footer section contains subtotals of the Amount Paid and Current Due fields.

BTW
Default Names for Controls
Because each control has properties associated with it, Access assigns a default name to each new control. The default name includes a control identifier and a number. For example, if you create a text box on a report, the default name could be Text32. You should change the default name to something meaningful to make it easier to remember the purpose of the control.

To Add Fields to the Report in Design View

Why? *Once you have determined the fields that are necessary for the report, you need to add them to the report design.* You can add the fields to the report by dragging them from the field list to the appropriate position on the report. The following steps add the fields to the report.

1

- Remove the 'Group, Sort, and Total' pane by clicking the Group & Sort button, which is shown in Figure 6–12 (Report Design Tools Design tab | Grouping & Totals group).

- Click the 'Add Existing Fields' button (Report Design Tools Design tab | Tools group) to display a field list.

- Drag the Account Manager Number field to the approximate position shown in Figure 6–16. (For illustration purposes, do not release the mouse button yet.)

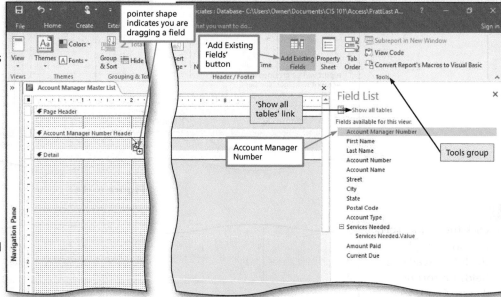

Figure 6–16

Q&A
My field list does not look like the one in the figure. It has several tables listed, and at the top it has 'Show only fields in the current record source.' Yours has 'Show all tables.' What should I do?

Click the 'Show only fields in the current record source' link. Your field list should then match the one in the figure.

2

- Release the mouse button to place the field (Figure 6–17).

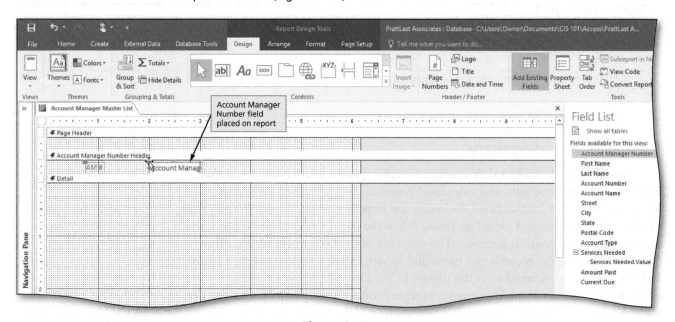

Figure 6–17

③

- Place the remaining fields in the positions shown in Figure 6–18.

- Adjust the positions of the labels to those shown in the figure. If any field is not in the correct position, drag it to its correct location. To move the control or the attached label separately, drag the large handle in the upper-left corner of the control or label. You can align controls using the Align button (Report Design Tools Arrange tab | Sizing & Ordering group) or adjust spacing by using the Size/Space button (Report Design Tools Arrange tab | Sizing & Ordering group).

Q&A

Sometimes I find it hard to move a control a very small amount. Is there a simpler way to do this other than dragging it with a mouse?
Yes. Once you have selected the control, you can use the arrow keys to move the control a very small amount in the desired direction.

Could I drag several fields from the field list at once?
Yes. You can select multiple fields by selecting the first field, holding down the CTRL key and selecting the additional fields. Once you have selected multiple fields, you can drag them all at once. How you choose to select fields and drag them onto the report is a matter of personal preference.

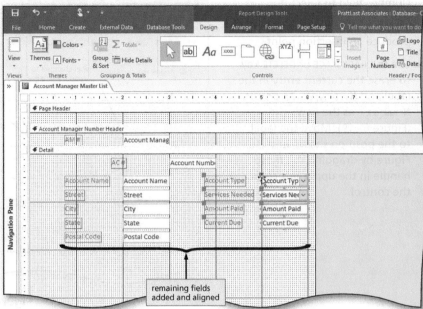

Figure 6–18

 Experiment

- Select more than one control and then experiment with the Size/Space and the Align buttons (Report Design Tools Arrange tab | Sizing & Ordering group) to see their effects. After trying each one, click the Undo button to undo the change. If you used the Arrange tab, redisplay the Design tab.

To Change Labels

1 CREATE TABLES | 2 CREATE QUERIES | 3 CREATE REPORT | 4 SPECIFY GROUPING & SORTING | 5 ADD FIELDS
6 ADD SUBREPORT | 7 ADD TITLE, PAGE NUMBER, & DATE | 8 CREATE SECOND REPORT

The labels for the Account Manager Number and Account Number fields currently contain the captions AM # and AC # for the fields. The following step changes the contents of the label for the Account Manager Number field from AM # to Account Manager Number. It also changes the contents of the label for the Account Number field from AC # to Account Number. *Why? Because there is plenty of room on the report to display longer names for both fields, you can make the report more descriptive by changing the labels.*

①

- Click the label for the Account Manager Number field to select the label.

- Click the label for the Account Manager Number field a second time to produce an insertion point.

- Use the BACKSPACE or DELETE key to erase the current entry in the label, and then type **Account Manager Number** as the new entry.

- Click outside the label to deselect the label and then click the label a second time to select it.

- Move the label to the position indicated in Figure 6–19 by dragging the move handle in the upper-left corner of the label.

- Click the label for the Account Number field to select it.

- Click the label a second time to produce an insertion point.

- Use the BACKSPACE or DELETE key to erase the current entry in the label and then type **Account Number** as the new entry (Figure 6–19). Move the label to the position shown in the Figure by dragging the move handle in the upper-left corner of the control.

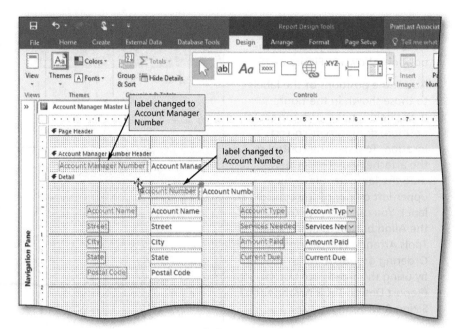

Figure 6–19

Using Other Tools in the Controls Group

Previously, you used the Subform/Subreport tool within the Controls group on the Design tab to place special controls on a form. The Controls group has additional tools available that can be used with forms and reports. A description of the additional tools appears in Table 6–3.

Table 6–3 Additional Tools in the Controls Group	
Tool	**Description**
Select	Select to be able to size, move, or edit existing controls. If you click another tool and want to cancel the effect of the tool before using it, you can click the Select tool.
Text Box	Create a text box for entering, editing, and displaying data. You can also bind the text box to a field in the underlying table or query.
Label	Create a label, a box containing text that cannot be edited and is independent of other controls, such as a title.
Button	Create a command button.
Tab Control	Create a tab control, which contains a series of tabbed pages. Each tabbed page can contain its own controls.
Hyperlink	Inserts a hyperlink to an existing file, Web page, database object, or email address.
Option Group	Create an option group, which is a rectangle containing a collection of option buttons. To select an option, you click the corresponding option button.
Insert or Remove Page Break	Insert or remove a physical page break (typically in a report).
Combo Box	Create a combo box, which is a combination of a text box and a list box.
Chart	Create a chart.
Line	Draw a line on a form or report.
Toggle Button	Add a toggle button. With a toggle button, a user can make a Yes/No selection by clicking the button. The button either appears to be pressed (for Yes) or not pressed (for No).
List Box	Create a list box, a box that allows the user to select from a list of options.
Rectangle	Create a rectangle.
Check Box	Insert a check box. With a check box a user can make multiple Yes/No selections.
Unbound Object Frame	Insert an OLE object (for example, a graph, picture, sound file, or video) that is not contained in a field in a table within the database.

Attachment	Insert an Attachment field.
Option Button	Insert an option button. With an option button, a user can make a single Yes/No selection from among a collection of at least two choices.
Subform/Subreport	Create a subform (a form contained within another form) or a subreport (a report contained within another report).
Bound Object Frame	Insert an OLE object (for example, a graph, picture, sound file, or video) that is contained in a field in a table within the database.
Image	Insert a frame into which you can insert a graphic. The graphic will be the same for all records.

To Add Text Boxes

1 CREATE TABLES | 2 CREATE QUERIES | 3 CREATE REPORT | 4 SPECIFY GROUPING & SORTING | 5 ADD FIELDS
6 ADD SUBREPORT | 7 ADD TITLE, PAGE NUMBER, & DATE | 8 CREATE SECOND REPORT

You can place a text box on a report or form by using the Text Box tool in the Controls group on the Design tab. The text box consists of a control that is initially unbound and an attached label. The next step is to update the **control source**, which is the source of data for the control. You can do so by entering the appropriate expression in the text box or by updating the Control Source property in the property sheet with the expression.

Once you have updated the control source property with the expression, the control becomes a **calculated control**. If the expression is just a single field (for example, =[Amount Paid]), the control would be a **bound control**. **Why?** *The control is bound (tied) to the corresponding field.* The process of converting an unbound control to a bound control is called **binding**. Expressions can also be arithmetic operations: for example, calculating the sum of amount paid and current due. Many times, you need to **concatenate**, or combine, two or more text data items into a single expression; the process is called **concatenation**. To concatenate text data, you use the **ampersand (&)** operator. For example, [First Name]&' '&[Last Name] indicates the concatenation of a first name, a single blank space, and a last name.

The following steps add text boxes and create calculated controls.

1
- Click the Text Box tool (Report Design Tools Design tab | Controls group) and move the pointer to the approximate position shown in Figure 6–20.

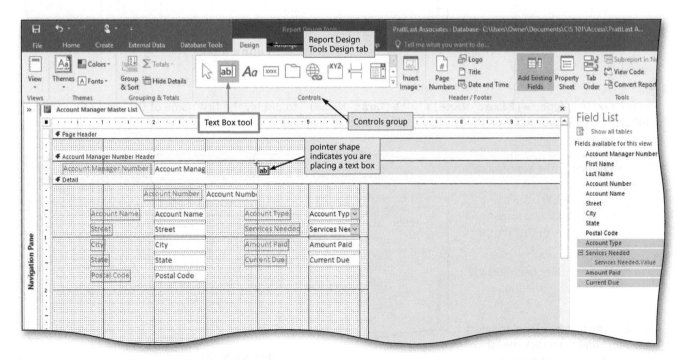

Figure 6–20

2

- Click the position shown in Figure 6–20 to place a text box on the report (Figure 6–21).

Q&A
My text box overlapped an object already on the screen. Is that a problem?
No. You can always move and/or resize your text box to the desired location and size later.

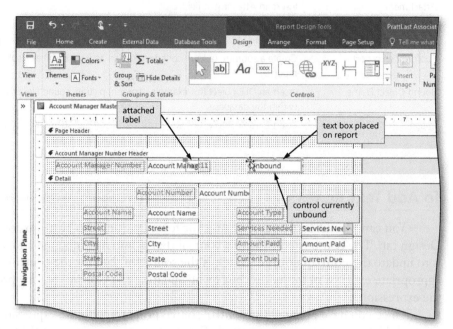

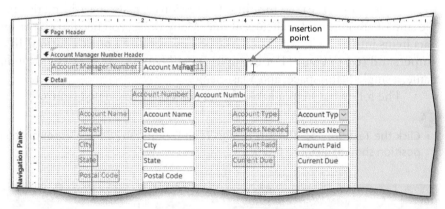

Figure 6–21

3

- Click in the text box to produce an insertion point (Figure 6–22).

Q&A
I inadvertently clicked somewhere else, so the text box was no longer selected. When I clicked the text box a second time, it was selected, but there was no insertion point. What should I do?
Simply click another time.

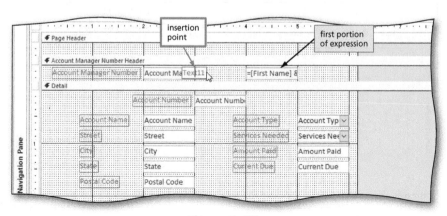

Figure 6–22

4

- In the text box, type   `=[First Name]&' '&[Last Name]`   to display the first name of the account manager, followed by a space, and then the last name of the account manager.

Q&A
Could I use the Expression Builder instead of typing the expression?
Yes. Click the Property Sheet button and then click the Build button, which contains three dots, next to the Control Source property.

Do I need to use single quotes (')?
No. You could also use double quotes (").

- Click in the text box label to select the label and then click the label a second time to produce an insertion point (Figure 6–23).

Figure 6–23

5

- Use the BACKSPACE or DELETE key to erase the current entry in the label and then type **Name** as the new entry.

- Click outside the label to deselect it and then drag the label to the position shown in the Figure by dragging the Move handle in the upper-left corner of the label (Figure 6–24).

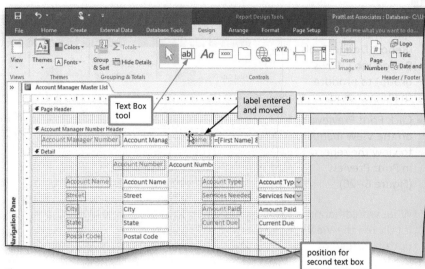

Figure 6–24

6

- Use the techniques in Steps 1 through 5 to place a second text box in the position indicated in Figure 6–24. Type **= [Amount Paid] + [Current Due]** as the expression in the text box, drag the label to the position shown in the figure, erase the contents of the label, and type **Total Amount** in the label (Figure 6–25).

Q&A My label is not in the correct position. What should I do?
Click outside the label to deselect it, click the label, and then drag it to the desired position.

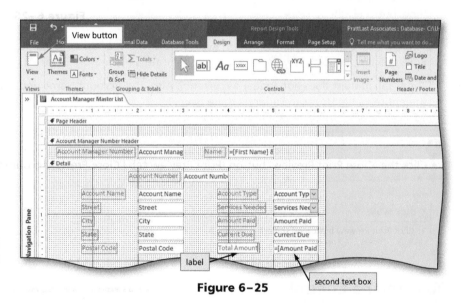

Figure 6–25

CONSIDER THIS

Total Amount is already a calculated field in the Account table. Why would you add the calculation to the report rather than just using the calculated field?

One reason is that if you later decide to move this database to another database management system, such as a SQL Server, the new DBMS may not allow calculated fields.

---

1 CREATE TABLES | 2 CREATE QUERIES | 3 CREATE REPORT | 4 SPECIFY GROUPING & SORTING | 5 ADD FIELDS
6 ADD SUBREPORT | 7 ADD TITLE, PAGE NUMBER, & DATE | 8 CREATE SECOND REPORT

To View the Report in Print Preview

The following steps view the report in Print Preview. *Why? As you are working on a report in Design view, it is useful to periodically view the report to gauge how it will look containing data. One way to do so is to use Print Preview.*

1

- Click the View button arrow (Report Design Tools Design tab | Views group) to produce the View menu.

- Click Print Preview on the View menu to view the report in Print Preview (Figure 6–26).

Q&A

What would happen if I clicked the View button instead of the View button arrow?

The icon on the View button is the icon for Report View, so you would view the results in Report view. This is another useful way to view a report, but compared with Print Preview, Report View does not give as accurate a picture of how the final printed report will look.

The total amount does not appear as currency. Also, the Account Name and Services Needed fields do not display the entire value. How can I address these issues?

You will address these issues in the next sections.

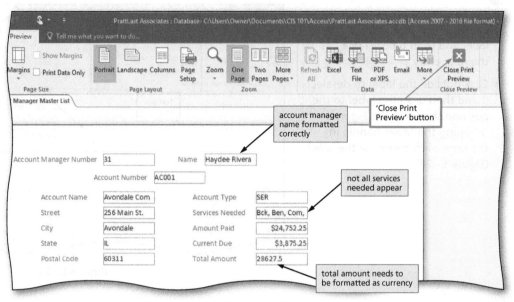

Figure 6–26

2

- Click the 'Close Print Preview' button (Print Preview tab | Close Preview group) to return to Design view.

Other Ways

1. Click Print Preview button on status bar

---

1 CREATE TABLES | 2 CREATE QUERIES | 3 CREATE REPORT | 4 SPECIFY GROUPING & SORTING | 5 ADD FIELDS
6 ADD SUBREPORT | 7 ADD TITLE, PAGE NUMBER, & DATE | 8 CREATE SECOND REPORT

To Format a Control

Why? *When you add a calculated control to a report, you often need to format the control, for example, to display a currency value with a dollar sign, decimal point, and two decimal places.* You can use a control's property sheet to change the value in the appropriate property. If a property does not appear on the screen, you have two choices. You can click the tab on which the property is located. For example, if it were a control related to data, you would click the Data tab to show only data-related properties. Many people, however, prefer to click the All tab, which shows all properties, and then simply scroll through the properties, if necessary, until locating the appropriate property. The following steps change the format of the Total Amount control to Currency by changing the value of the Format property and the Decimal Places property.

1
- Because you will not be using the field list, remove it by clicking the 'Add Existing Fields' button (Report Design Tools Design tab | Tools group).

- Click the control containing the expression for Total Amount to select it, and then click the Property Sheet button (Report Design Tools Design tab | Tools group) to display the property sheet.

- If necessary, click the All tab (Figure 6–27).

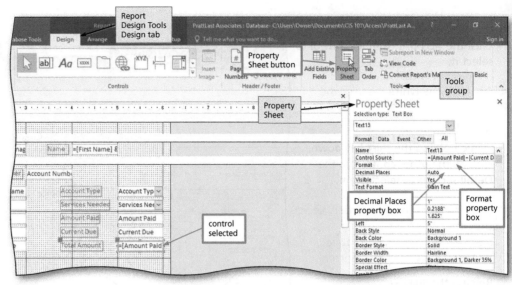

Figure 6–27

 Experiment
- Click the other tabs in the property sheet to see the types of properties on each tab. When finished, once again click the All tab.

2
- Click the Format property box, click the arrow that appears, and then click Currency to select Currency as the format.

- Click the Decimal Places property box, click the arrow that appears, and then click 2 to select two decimal places.

- Remove the property sheet by clicking the Property Sheet button (Report Design Tools Design tab | Tools group) a second time.

- Preview the report using Print Preview to see the effect of the property changes.

- Click the 'Close Print Preview' button (Print Preview tab | Close Preview group) to return to Design view.

Other Ways
1. Right-click control, click Properties

To Group Controls

1 CREATE TABLES | 2 CREATE QUERIES | 3 CREATE REPORT | 4 SPECIFY GROUPING & SORTING | 5 ADD FIELDS
6 ADD SUBREPORT | 7 ADD TITLE, PAGE NUMBER, & DATE | 8 CREATE SECOND REPORT

The following steps group the controls within the Detail section. *Why? If your report contains a collection of controls that you will frequently want to format in the same way, you can simplify the process of selecting all the controls by grouping them. Once they are grouped, selecting any control in the group automatically selects all of the controls in the group. You can then apply the desired change to all the controls.*

1

- Click the Account Number control to select it.

Do I click the white space or the label?
Click the white space.

- While holding the SHIFT key down, click all the other controls in the Detail section to select them.

Does it matter in which order I select the other controls?
No. It is only important that you ultimately select all the controls.

- Release the SHIFT key.

- Display the Report Design Tools Arrange tab.

- Click the Size/Space button (Report Design Tools Arrange tab | Sizing & Ordering group) to display the Size/Space menu (Figure 6–28).

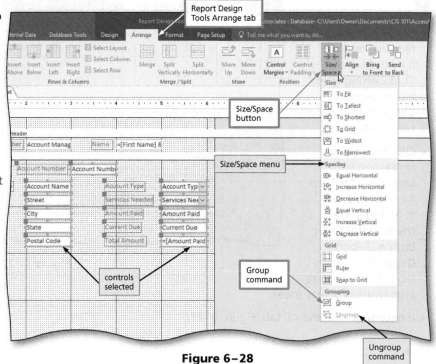

Figure 6–28

2

- Click Group on the Size/Space button menu to group the controls.

What if I make a mistake and group the wrong collection of controls?
Ungroup the controls using the following steps, and then group the correct collection of controls.

TO UNGROUP CONTROLS

If you no longer need to simultaneously modify all the controls you have placed in a group, you can ungroup the controls. To do so, you would use the following steps.

1. Click any of the controls in a group to select the entire group.
2. Display the Report Design Tools Arrange tab.
3. Click the Size/Space button (Report Design Tools Arrange tab | Sizing & Ordering group) to display the Size/Space button menu.
4. Click the Ungroup button on the Size/Space button menu to ungroup the controls.

Can you group controls in forms?
Yes. The process is identical to the process of grouping controls in reports.

To Modify Grouped Controls

1 CREATE TABLES | 2 CREATE QUERIES | 3 CREATE REPORT | 4 SPECIFY GROUPING & SORTING | 5 ADD FIELDS
6 ADD SUBREPORT | 7 ADD TITLE, PAGE NUMBER, & DATE | 8 CREATE SECOND REPORT

To modify grouped controls, click any control in the group to select the entire group. *Why? Any change you make then affects all controls in the group.* The following steps bold the controls in the group, resize them, and then change the border style.

- If necessary, click any one of the grouped controls to select the group.
- Display the Report Design Tools Format tab.
- Click the Bold button (Report Design Tools Format tab | Font group) to bold all the controls in the group (Figure 6–29).

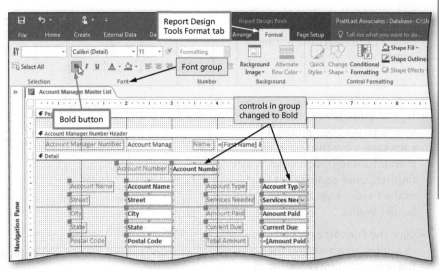

Figure 6–29

- Display the Report Design Tools Design tab.
- Drag the right sizing handle of the Services Needed control to the approximate position shown in Figure 6–30 to resize all the controls in the group.

Q&A Do I need to use the Services Needed field or could I use another field?
Any field in the group will work.

How do I change only one control in the group?
Double-click the control to select just the one control and not the entire group. You then can make any change you want to that control.

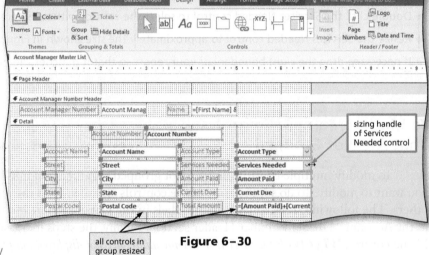

Figure 6–30

3

- Click the Property Sheet button (Report Design Tools Design tab | Tools group) to display the property sheet for the grouped controls.
- With the All tab (Property Sheet) selected, ensure the Border Style property is set to Solid. If it is not, click the Border Style property box to display an arrow, click the arrow to display the list of available border styles, and click Solid.
- Click the Border Width property box to display an arrow and then click the arrow to display the list of available border widths (Figure 6–31).

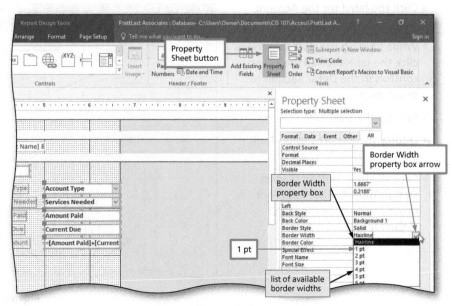

Figure 6–31

● Click 1 pt to select the border width.

Experiment

● Try the other border styles and widths to see their effects. In each case, view the report and then return to Design view. When finished, once again select Solid as the border style and 1 pt as the border width.

● Click the Font Size property box to display an arrow and then click the arrow to display the list of available font sizes.

● Click 10 to change the font size to 10.

● Close the property sheet.

● Double-click the Services Needed control to select the control without selecting the entire group.

● Resize the Services Needed control to approximately the size shown in Figure 6–32.

● If necessary, drag the right boundary of your report so that it matches the one shown in Figure 6–32.

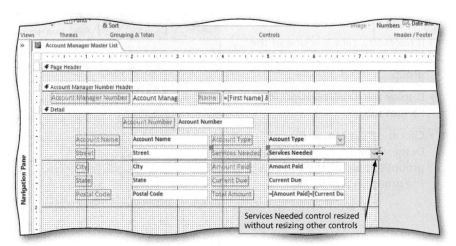

Figure 6–32

To Modify Multiple Controls That Are Not Grouped

1 CREATE TABLES | 2 CREATE QUERIES | 3 CREATE REPORT | 4 SPECIFY GROUPING & SORTING | 5 ADD FIELDS
6 ADD SUBREPORT | 7 ADD TITLE, PAGE NUMBER, & DATE | 8 CREATE SECOND REPORT

To modify multiple controls that are not grouped together, you must simultaneously select all the controls you want to modify. To do so, click one of the controls and then hold the SHIFT key down while selecting the others. The following steps italicize all the labels in the Detail section and then bold all the controls and labels in the Account Manager Number Header section. Finally, the steps increase the size of the Account Manager Name control. *Why? With the current size, some names are not displayed completely.*

1

● Click the label for the Account Number control to select it.

● While holding the SHIFT key down, click the labels for all the other controls in the Detail section to select them.

● Release the SHIFT key.

● Display the Report Design Tools Format tab.

● Click the Italic button (Report Design Tools Format tab | Font group) to italicize the labels (Figure 6–33).

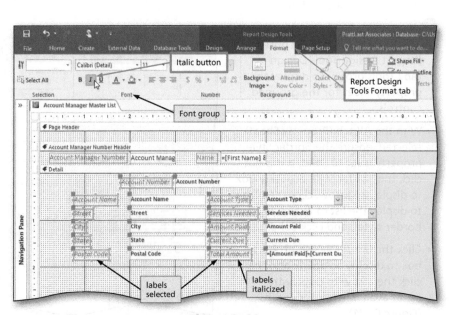

Figure 6–33

2

- Click in the vertical ruler to the left of the Account Manager Number control to select all the controls in the section.

Q&A What exactly is selected when I click in the vertical ruler?
If you picture a horizontal line through the point you clicked, any control that intersects that horizontal line would be selected.

- Use the buttons on the Report Design Tools Arrange tab to align the controls on the top, if necessary.

- Display the Report Design Tools Format tab, if necessary, and then click the Bold button (Report Design Tools Format tab | Font group) to bold all the selected controls (Figure 6–34).

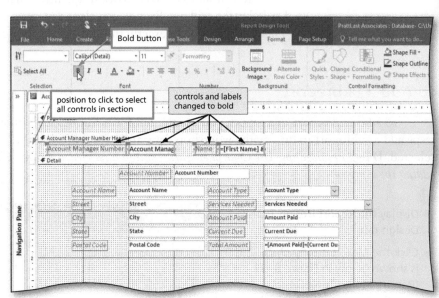

Figure 6–34

3

- Click outside the selected controls to deselect them. Click the control containing the expression for the account manager's name to select it.

Q&A Why do I have to deselect the controls and then select one of them a second time?
If you do not do so, any action you take would apply to all the selected controls rather than just the one you want.

- Drag the right sizing handle of the selected control to the approximate position shown in Figure 6–35.

- View the report in Print Preview and then make any necessary adjustments.

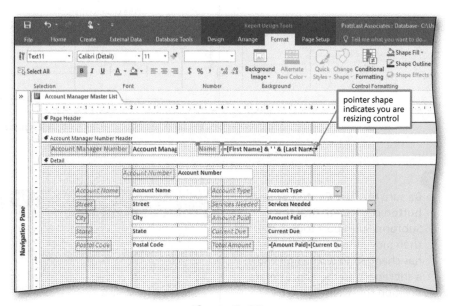

Figure 6–35

Undoing and Saving

Remember that if you make a mistake, you can often correct it by clicking the Undo button on the Quick Access Toolbar. Clicking the Undo button will reverse your most recent change. You can also click the Undo button more than once to reverse multiple changes.

You should save your work frequently. That way, if you have problems that the Undo button will not fix, you can close the report without saving it and open it again. The report will be in exactly the state it was in the last time you saved it.

To Add a Subreport

To add a subreport to a report, you use the Subform/Subreport tool on the Design tab. The following steps add a subreport to display the workshop data, after first ensuring the 'Use Control Wizards' button is selected. *Why? Provided the 'Use Control Wizards' button is selected, a wizard will guide you through the process of adding the subreport.*

1
- Display the Report Design Tools Design tab.
- Click the More button, which is shown below in Figure 6–37 (Report Design Tools Design tab | Controls group), to display a gallery of available tools (Figure 6–36).

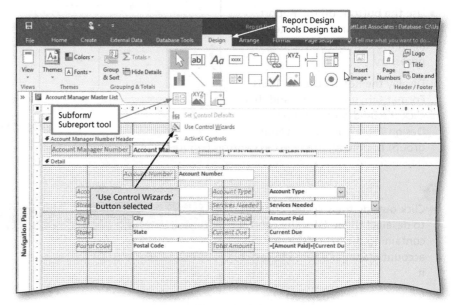

Figure 6–36

2
- Be sure the 'Use Control Wizards' button is selected, click the Subform/Subreport tool, and then move the pointer, which has changed to a plus sign with a subreport, to the approximate position shown in Figure 6–37.

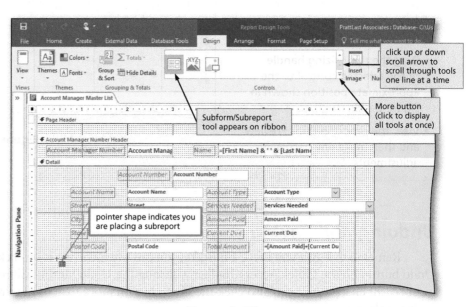

Figure 6–37

3

- Click the position shown in Figure 6–37 to place the subreport and display the SubReport Wizard dialog box. Be sure the 'Use existing Tables and Queries' option button is selected (Figure 6–38).

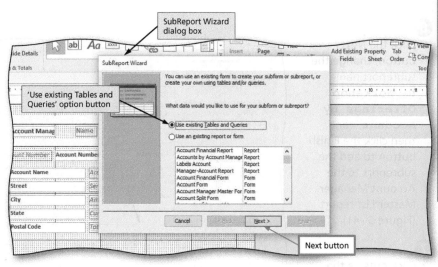

Figure 6–38

4

- Click the Next button.
- Click the Tables/Queries box arrow.
- Scroll down until Query: Workshop Offerings and Workshops is visible, click 'Query: Workshop Offerings and Workshops,' and then click the 'Add All Fields' button to select all the fields in the query (Figure 6–39).

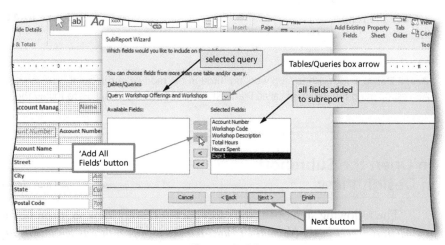

Figure 6–39

5

- Click the Next button and then ensure the 'Choose from a list.' option button is selected (Figure 6–40).

Q&A What is the purpose of this dialog box?

You use this dialog box to indicate the fields that link the main report (referred to as a "form") to the subreport (referred to as a "subform"). If the fields have the same name, as they often will, you can simply select 'Choose from a list' and then accept the selection Access already has made.

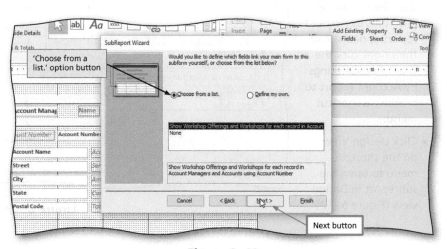

Figure 6–40

- Click the Next button, change the subreport name to **Workshop Offerings by Account,** and then click the Finish button to add the subreport to the Account Manager Master List report (Figure 6–41).

- Click outside the subreport to deselect the subreport.

- Save your changes.

- Close the report.

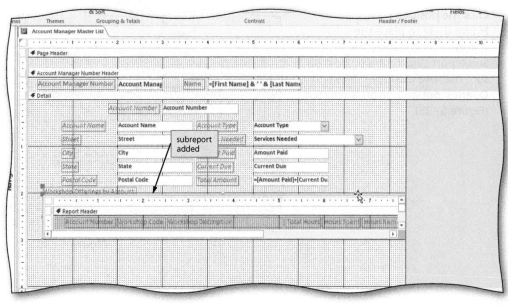

Figure 6–41

Break Point: If you wish to stop working through the module at this point, you can resume the project at a later time by running Access, opening the database called PrattLast Associates, and continuing to follow the steps from this location forward.

To Open the Subreport in Design View

1 CREATE TABLES | 2 CREATE QUERIES | 3 CREATE REPORT | 4 SPECIFY GROUPING & SORTING | 5 ADD FIELDS

6 ADD SUBREPORT | **7 ADD TITLE, PAGE NUMBER, & DATE | 8 CREATE SECOND REPORT**

The following step opens the subreport in Design view so it can be modified. *Why? The subreport appears as a separate report in the Navigation Pane. You can modify it just as you modify any other report.*

1

- Open the Navigation Pane, scroll down so that the Workshop Offerings by Account report appears, and then right-click the Workshop Offerings by Account report to produce a shortcut menu.

- Click Design View on the shortcut menu to open the subreport in Design view (Figure 6–42).

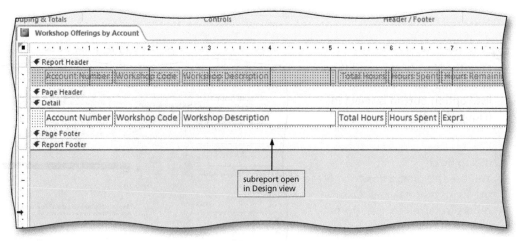

Figure 6–42

Print Layout Issues

If there is a problem with your report, for example, a report that is too wide for the printed page, the report will display a green triangular symbol in the upper-left corner. The green triangle is called an **error indicator**. Clicking it displays an 'Error Checking Options' button. Clicking the 'Error Checking Options' button produces the 'Error Checking Options menu,' as shown in Figure 6–43.

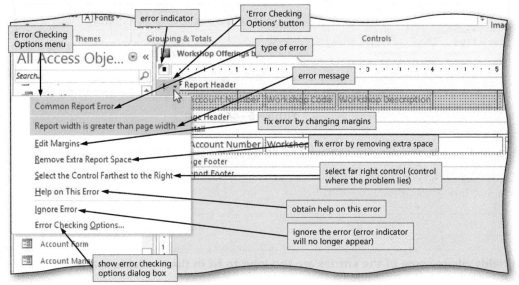

Figure 6–43

The first line in the menu is simply a statement of the type of error that occurred. The second is a description of the specific error, in this case, the fact that the report width is greater than the page width. This situation could lead to data not appearing where you expect it to, as well as the printing of some blank pages.

The next three lines provide potential solutions to the error. You could change the margins to allow more space for the report. You could remove some extra space. You could select the control farthest to the right and move it. The fourth line gives more detailed help on the error. The Ignore Error command instructs Access to not consider this situation an error. Selecting Ignore Error would cause the error indicator to disappear without making any changes. The final line displays the Error Checking Options dialog box, where you can make other changes.

Later in this module, you will fix the problem by changing the width of the report, so you do not need to take any action at this time.

BTW

Subreports
Subreports provide more control in presenting data effectively than multiple levels of grouping can. Because grouping places headers in columns, it often can be difficult to determine the relationship between the group header and the detail. Also, you might want to present subreports side by side. You cannot do that with grouping.

To Modify the Controls in the Subreport

1 CREATE TABLES | 2 CREATE QUERIES | 3 CREATE REPORT | 4 SPECIFY GROUPING & SORTING | 5 ADD FIELDS
6 ADD SUBREPORT | 7 ADD TITLE, PAGE NUMBER, & DATE | 8 CREATE SECOND REPORT

The following step modifies the subreport by deleting the Account Number control and revising the appearance of the column headings. *Why? Because the account number appears in the main report, it does not need to be duplicated in the subreport. In addition, the column headers in the subreport should extend over two lines, as shown in Figure 6–1a.*

- Close the Navigation Pane.

- Click the Account Number control in the Detail section to select the control. Hold the SHIFT key down and click the Account Number control in the Report Header section to select both controls.

- With both controls selected, press the DELETE key to delete the controls.

- Adjust the labels in the Report Header section to match those shown in Figure 6–44. To extend a heading over two lines, click in front of the second word to produce an insertion point and then press SHIFT+ENTER to move the second word to a second line.

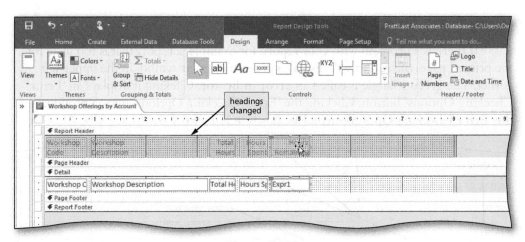

Figure 6–44

- Change the sizes and positions of the controls to match those in the figure by selecting the controls and dragging the sizing handles.

Why does Expr1 appear in the Detail section under the Hours Remaining label?

Expr1 indicates that Hours Remaining is a calculated control.

How can you adjust fields where some of the entries are too long to fit in the available space?

This problem can be addressed in several ways.

1. Move the controls to allow more space between controls. Then, drag the appropriate handles on the controls that need to be expanded to enlarge them.

2. Use the Font Size property to select a smaller font size. This will allow more data to fit in the same space.

3. Use the Can Grow property. By changing the value of this property from No to Yes, the data can be spread over two lines, thus allowing all the data to print. Access will split data at natural break points, such as commas, spaces, and hyphens.

To Change the Can Grow Property

1 CREATE TABLES | 2 CREATE QUERIES | 3 CREATE REPORT | 4 SPECIFY GROUPING & SORTING | 5 ADD FIELDS
6 ADD SUBREPORT | 7 ADD TITLE, PAGE NUMBER, & DATE | 8 CREATE SECOND REPORT

The third approach to handling entries that are too long is the easiest to use and also produces a very readable report. The following steps change the Can Grow property for the Workshop Description field. *Why? Changing the Can Grow property allows Access to optimize the size of fields in reports.*

1

- Click the View button arrow and then click Print Preview to preview the report (Figure 6–45). If an error message appears, indicating the report is too wide, click the OK button.

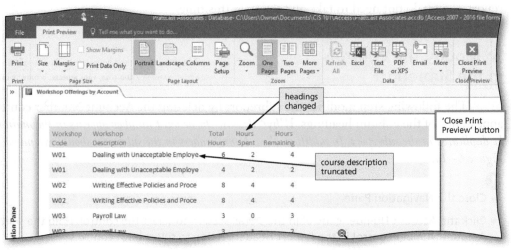

Figure 6–45

2

- Click the 'Close Print Preview' button (Print Preview tab | Close Preview group) to return to Design view.
- Click outside all of the selected controls to deselect the controls.
- Click the Workshop Description control in the Detail section to select it.
- Click the Property Sheet button (Report Design Tools Design tab | Tools group) to display the property sheet.
- With the All tab selected, scroll down until the Can Grow property appears, and then click the Can Grow property box arrow to display the list of possible values for the Can Grow property (Figure 6–46).

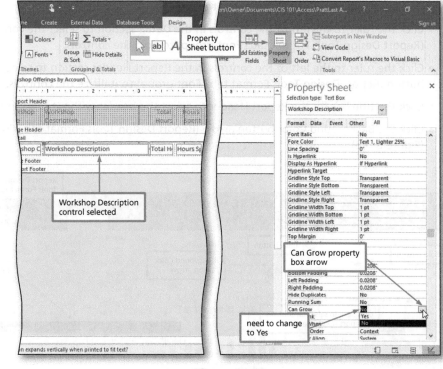

Figure 6–46

Q&A What is the effect of the Can Shrink property?

If the value of the Can Shrink property is set to Yes, Access will remove blank lines that occur when the field is empty.

3

- Click Yes in the list to allow the Workshop Description control to grow as needed.
- Close the property sheet.

To Change the Appearance of the Controls in the Subreport

1 CREATE TABLES | 2 CREATE QUERIES | 3 CREATE REPORT | 4 SPECIFY GROUPING & SORTING | 5 ADD FIELDS
6 ADD SUBREPORT | 7 ADD TITLE, PAGE NUMBER, & DATE | 8 CREATE SECOND REPORT

Why? *PrattLast Associates prefers certain formatting for the subreport controls.* The following steps change the controls in the Detail section to bold and the controls in the Report Header section to italic. They also change the background color in the Report Header section to white.

1

- Drag the right boundary of the subreport to the approximate position shown in Figure 6–47.

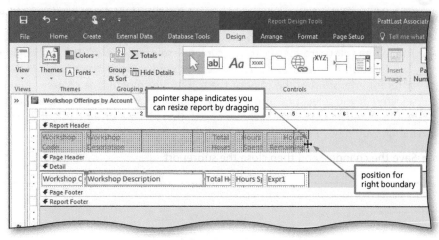

Figure 6–47

2

- Display the Report Design Tools Format tab.

- Click the ruler to the left of the controls in the Detail section to select the controls, and then click the Bold button (Report Design Tools Format tab | Font group) to bold the controls.

- Click the ruler to the left of the controls in the Report Header section to select the controls, and then click the Italic button (Report Design Tools Format tab | Font group) to italicize the controls.

- Click the title bar for the Report Header to select the header without selecting any of the controls in the header.

- Click the Background Color button arrow (Report Design Tools Format tab | Font group) to display a color palette (Figure 6–48).

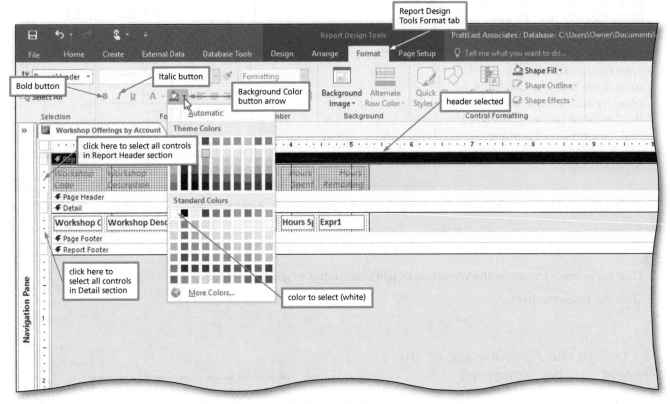

Figure 6–48

3

- Click White in the first row, first column of the Standard Colors to change the background color to white.

Q&A What is the difference between clicking a color in the Theme colors and clicking a color in the Standard Colors?
The theme colors are specific to the currently selected theme. The first column, for example, represents "background 1," one of the selected background colors in the theme. The various entries in the column represent different intensities of the color at the top of the column. The colors would be different if a different theme were selected. If you select one of the theme colors and a different theme is selected in the future, the color you selected would change to the color in the same location. On the other hand, if you select a standard color, a change of theme would have no effect on the color.

- Save the changes, and then close the subreport.

To Resize the Subreport and the Report in Design View

The following steps resize the subreport control in the main report. They then reduce the height of the detail section. *Why? Any additional white space at the bottom of the detail section appears as extra space at the end of each detail line in the final report.* Finally, the steps reduce the width of the main report.

- Open the Navigation Pane.

- Open the Account Manager Master List in Design view.

- Close the Navigation Pane.

- Click the subreport and drag the right sizing handle to change the size to the approximate size shown in Figure 6–49, and then drag the subreport to the approximate position shown in the figure.

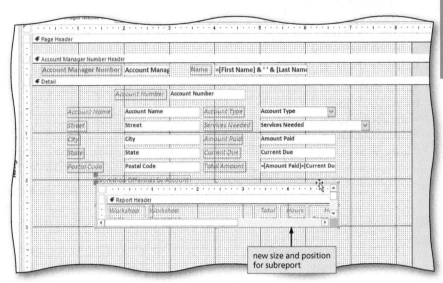

Figure 6–49

- Scroll down in the main report so that the lower boundary of the Detail section appears, and then drag the lower boundary of the section so that the amount of space below the subreport resembles that shown in Figure 6–50.

Q&A   I scrolled down to see the lower boundary of the Detail section, and the controls are no longer on the screen. What is the easiest way to drag the boundary when the position to which I want to drag it is not visible?
You do not need to see the location to drag to it. As you get close to the top of the visible portion of the screen, Access will automatically scroll. You might find it easier, however, to drag the boundary near the top of the visible portion of the report, use the scroll bar to scroll up, and then drag some more. You might have to scroll a couple of times.

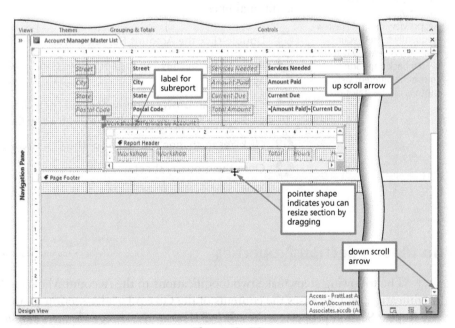

Figure 6–50

3

- If necessary, scroll back up to the top of the report, click the label for the subreport (the label that reads Workshop Offerings by Account), and then press the DELETE key to delete the label.

- Resize the report by dragging its right border to the location shown in Figure 6–51.

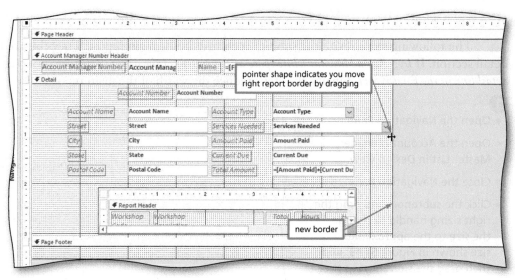

Figure 6–51

BTW
Viewing Report Modifications
As you work through this module, switch between Design view and either Report view or Print Preview frequently to view your changes. An easy way to switch back and forth is to use the different view buttons on the status bar.

To Change the Can Grow Property

The following steps change the Can Grow property for the Account Name control so that names that are too long to fit in the available space will extend to additional lines.

1 Double-click the Account Name control.

2 If necessary, display the property sheet and scroll down until the Can Grow property appears.

3 Click the Can Grow property box and then click the Can Grow property box arrow to display the menu of available values for the Can Grow property.

4 Click Yes to change the value for the Can Grow property.

5 Close the property sheet.

To Modify Section Properties

1 CREATE TABLES | 2 CREATE QUERIES | 3 CREATE REPORT | 4 SPECIFY GROUPING & SORTING | 5 ADD FIELDS
6 ADD SUBREPORT | 7 ADD TITLE, PAGE NUMBER, & DATE | 8 CREATE SECOND REPORT

The following steps make two modifications to the Account Manager Number Header section. The first modification, which causes the contents of the Group Header section to appear at the top of each page, changes the Repeat Section property to Yes. *Why? Without this change, the account manager number and name would only appear at the beginning of the group of accounts of that account manager. If the list of accounts occupies more than one page, it would not be apparent on subsequent pages which account manager is associated with those accounts.* The second modification changes the Force New Page property to Before Section, causing each section to begin at the top of a page.

1

- Click the Account Manager Number Header bar to select the header, and then click the Property Sheet button (Report Design Tools Design tab | Tools group) to display the property sheet.

- With the All tab selected, click the Repeat Section property box, click the arrow that appears, and then click Yes to cause the contents of the group header to appear at the top of each page of the report.

- Click the Force New Page property box, and then click the arrow that appears to display the menu of possible values (Figure 6–52).

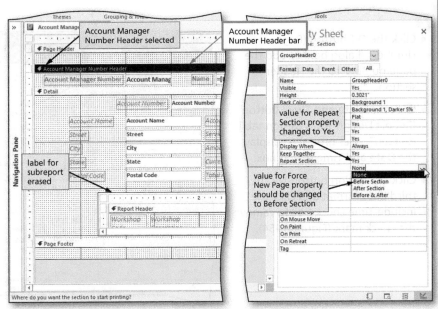

Figure 6–52

2

- Click Before Section to cause a new group to begin at the top of the next page.

- Close the property sheet.

To Add a Title, Page Number, and Date

1 CREATE TABLES | 2 CREATE QUERIES | 3 CREATE REPORT | 4 SPECIFY GROUPING & SORTING | 5 ADD FIELDS
6 ADD SUBREPORT | **7 ADD TITLE, PAGE NUMBER, & DATE** | **8 CREATE SECOND REPORT**

You can add a title, page number, and date to a report using buttons on the Design tab. The following steps add a title, page number, and date to the Account Manager Master List report. The steps move the date to the page header by first cutting the date from its original position and then pasting it into the page header. *Why? The date is automatically added to the report header, which means it only would appear once at the beginning of the report. If it is in the page header, the date will appear at the top of each page.*

1

- Display the Report Design Tools Design tab, if necessary, and then click the Title button (Report Design Tools Design tab | Header/Footer group) to add a title.

Q&A
The title is the same as the name of the report object. Can I change the report title without changing the name of the report object in the database?
Yes. The report title is a label, and you can change it using any of the techniques that you used for changing column headings and other labels.

- Click the Page Numbers button (Report Design Tools Design tab | Header/Footer group) to display the Page Numbers dialog box.

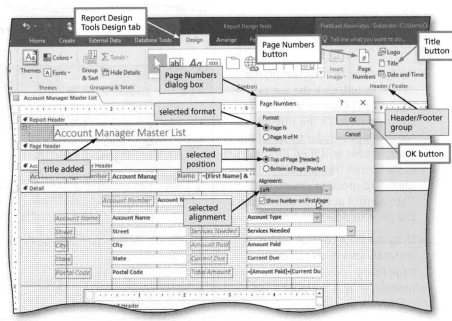

Figure 6–53

- Be sure the Page N and 'Top of Page [Header]' option buttons are selected.

- If necessary, click the Alignment arrow and select Left (Figure 6–53).

2

- Click the OK button (Page Numbers dialog box) to add the page number to the Header section.

- Click the 'Date and Time' button (Report Design Tools Design tab | Header/Footer group) to display the Date and Time dialog box.

- Click the option button for the third date format and click the Include Time check box to remove the check mark (Figure 6–54).

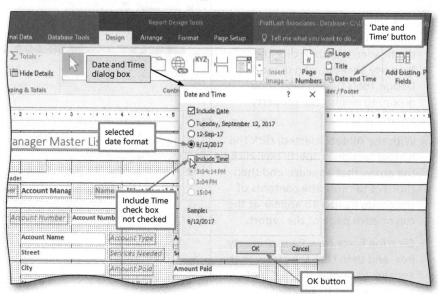

Figure 6–54

3

- Click the OK button (Date and Time dialog box) to add the date to the Report Header.

- Display the Home tab.

- If the Date control is no longer selected, click the Date control to select it (Figure 6–55).

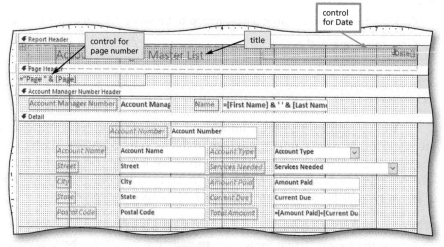

Figure 6–55

4

- With the control containing the date selected, click the Cut button (Home tab | Clipboard group) to cut the date, click the title bar for the Page Header to select the page header, and then click the Paste button (Home tab | Clipboard group) to paste the Date control at the beginning of the page header.

- Drag the Date control, which is currently sitting on top of the Page Number control, to the position shown in Figure 6–56.

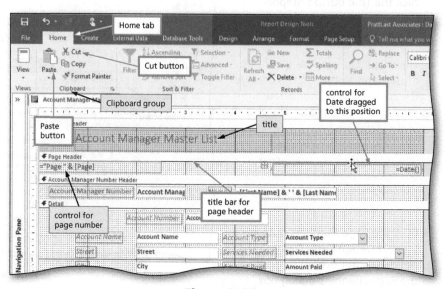

Figure 6–56

To Remove the Header Background Color and the Alternate Color

The report header currently has a blue background, whereas the desired report does not have such a background. In addition, the report has alternate colors. An **alternate color** is a color different from the main color that appears on every other line in a datasheet or report. Using alternate colors can sometimes make a datasheet or report more readable.

The following steps first remove the color from the report header. They then remove the alternate colors from the various sections in the report, starting with the Detail section. *Why? Access automatically assigns alternate colors within the report. In reports with multiple sections, the alternate colors can be confusing. If you do not want these alternate colors, you must remove them.*

①

- Right-click the title bar for the Report Header to select the header without selecting any of the controls in the header.

- Point to the 'Fill/Back Color' arrow to display a color palette (Figure 6–57).

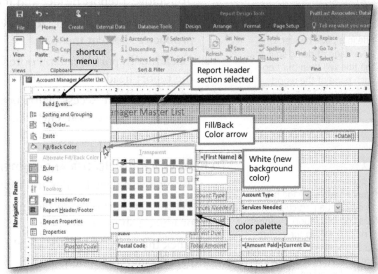

Figure 6–57

②

- Click White in the first row, first column of the color palette.

- Right-click a blank area of the Detail section to produce a shortcut menu.

- Point to the 'Alternate Fill/Back Color' arrow to produce a color palette (Figure 6–58).

③

- Click None on the color palette to remove the alternate color for the selected section.

- Using the same techniques, remove the alternate color from all other sections. (For some sections, the command may be dimmed, in which case you need take no further action.)

- Save and then close the report.

- Open the subreport in Design view.

- Remove the header background color and the alternate color from the subreport, just as you removed them from the main report.

- Save and then close the subreport.

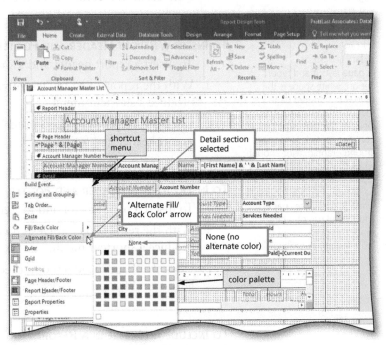

Figure 6–58

Q&A | How can I be sure I removed all the background colors?
Open the report in Print Preview to check that all color has been removed from the report.

Headers and Footers

Access gives you some options for including or omitting headers and footers in your reports. They go together, so if you have a report header, you will also have a report footer. If you do not want one of the sections to appear, you can shrink its size so there is no room for any content, or you can remove the header or footer from your report altogether. If you later decide you want to include them, you once again can add them. You have similar options with page headers and page footers.

TO REMOVE A REPORT HEADER AND FOOTER

To remove a report header and footer, you would use the following steps.

1. With the report open in Design view, right-click any open area of the report to produce a shortcut menu.
2. Click the 'Report Header/Footer' command on the shortcut menu to remove the report header and footer.
3. If the Microsoft Access dialog box appears, asking if it is acceptable to delete any controls in the section, click the Yes button.

TO REMOVE A PAGE HEADER AND FOOTER

To remove a page header and footer, you would use the following steps.

1. With the report open in Design view, right-click any open area of the report to produce a shortcut menu.
2. Click the 'Page Header/Footer' command on the shortcut menu to remove the page header and footer.
3. If the Microsoft Access dialog box appears, asking if it is acceptable to delete any controls in the section, click the Yes button.

TO INSERT A REPORT HEADER AND FOOTER

To insert a report header and footer, you would use the following steps.

1. With the report open in Design view, right-click any open area of the report to produce a shortcut menu.
2. Click the 'Report Header/Footer' command on the shortcut menu to insert a report header and footer.

TO INSERT A PAGE HEADER AND FOOTER

To insert a page header and footer, you would use the following steps.

1. With the report open in Design view, right-click any open area of the report to produce a shortcut menu.
2. Click the 'Page Header/Footer' command on the shortcut menu to insert a page header and footer.

TO INCLUDE AN IMAGE IN A REPORT

You can include a picture (image) in a report. You can also use a picture (image) as the background on a report. To include an image in a report, you would use the following steps.

1. Open the report in Design view or Layout view.
2. Click the Insert Image button (Report Design Tools Design tab | Controls group), and then click the Browse command.
3. Select the desired image.
4. Click the desired location to add the image to the report.

TO USE AN IMAGE AS BACKGROUND FOR A REPORT

To include an image as a background for a report, you would use the following steps.

1. Open the report in Design view or Layout view.
2. Click anywhere in the report, click the Background Image button (Report Design Tools Format tab | Background group), and then click the Browse command.
3. Select the desired image for the background.

TO PUBLISH A REPORT

You can make a report available as an external document by publishing the report as either a PDF or XPS file. If you wanted to do so, you would use the following steps.

1. Select the report to be published in the Navigation Pane.
2. Display the External Data tab.
3. Click the PDF or XPS button (External Data tab | Export group) to display the Publish as PDF or XPS dialog box.
4. Select the appropriate Save as type (either PDF or XPS).
5. Select either 'Standard (publishing online and printing)' or 'Minimum size (publishing online).'
6. If you want to publish only a range of pages, click the Options button and select the desired range.
7. Click the Publish button to publish the report in the desired format.
8. If you want to save the export steps, click the 'Save export steps' check box, then click the Save Export button. If not, click the Close button.

BTW

Distributing a Document
Instead of printing and distributing a hard copy of a document, you can distribute the document electronically. Options include sending the document via email; posting it on cloud storage (such as OneDrive) and sharing the file with others; posting it on a social networking site, blog, or other website; and sharing a link associated with an online location of the document. You also can create and share a PDF or XPS image of the document, so that users can view the file in Acrobat Reader or XPS Viewer instead of in Access.

Break Point: If you wish to stop working through the module at this point, you can resume the project at a later time by running Access, opening the database called PrattLast Associates, and continuing to follow the steps from this location forward.

Creating a Second Report

PrattLast Associates would also like a report that groups accounts by account manager. The report should include subtotals and grand totals. Finally, it should show the discount amount for each account. The discount amount is based on the current due amount. Accounts that owe more than $20,000 will receive a 4 percent discount, and accounts that owe $20,000 or less will receive a 2 percent discount.

To Create a Second Report

The following steps create the Discount Report, select the record source, and specify grouping and sorting options.

1 If necessary, close the Navigation Pane.

2 Display the Create tab and then click the Report Design button (Create tab | Reports group) to create a report in Design view.

3 Ensure the selector for the entire report, which is the box in the upper-left corner of the report, contains a small black square indicating it is selected, and then click the Property Sheet button (Report Design Tools Design tab | Tools group) to display a property sheet.

4 With the All tab selected, click the Record Source property box arrow, and then click the Account Managers and Accounts query to select the query as the record source for the report.

5 Close the property sheet.

6 Click the Group & Sort button (Report Design Tools Design tab | Grouping & Totals group) to display the 'Group, Sort, and Total' pane.

7 Click the 'Add a group' button to display the list of available fields for grouping, and then click the Account Manager Number field to group by account manager number.

8 Click the 'Add a sort' button to display the list of available fields for sorting, and then click the Account Number field to sort by account number.

9 Remove the 'Group, Sort, and Total' pane by clicking the Group & Sort button (Report Design Tools Design tab | Grouping & Totals group).

10 Click the Save button on the Quick Access Toolbar, type **Discount Report** as the report name, and click the OK button to save the report.

Q&A   Why save it at this point?
You do not have to save it at this point. It is a good idea to save it often, however. Doing so will give you a convenient point from which to restart if you have problems. If you have problems, you could close the report without saving it. When you reopen the report, it will be in the state it was in when you last saved it.

To Add and Move Fields in a Report

1 CREATE TABLES | 2 CREATE QUERIES | 3 CREATE REPORT | 4 SPECIFY GROUPING & SORTING | 5 ADD FIELDS
6 ADD SUBREPORT | 7 ADD TITLE, PAGE NUMBER, & DATE | **8 CREATE SECOND REPORT**

As with the previous report, you can add a field to the report by dragging the field from the field list. After adding a field to a report, you can adjust the placement of the field's label, separating it from the control to which it is attached by dragging the move handle in its upper-left corner. This technique does not work, however, if you want to drag the attached label to a section different from the control's section. If you want the label to be in a different section, you must select the label, cut the label, select the section to which you want to move the label, and then paste the label. You then can move the label to the desired location.

The following steps add the Account Manager Number field to the Account Manager Number Header section and then move the label to the Page Header section. *Why? The label should appear at the top of each page, rather than in the group header.*

1

- Click the 'Add Existing Fields' button (Report Design Tools Design tab | Tools group) to display a field list. (Figure 6–59).

Q&A My field list displays 'Show only fields in the current record source,' not 'Show all tables,' as in the figure. What should I do? Click the 'Show only fields in the current record source' link at the top of the field list to display only those fields in the Account Managers and Accounts query.

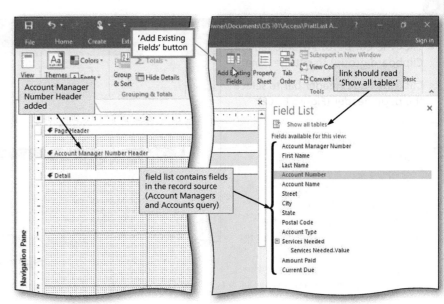

Figure 6–59

2

- Drag the Account Manager Number field to the approximate position shown in Figure 6–60.

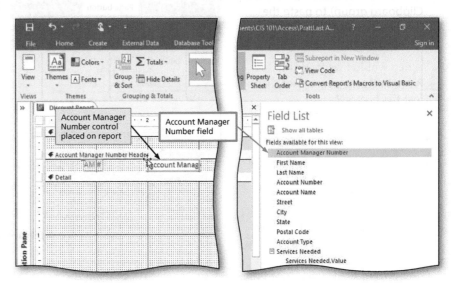

Figure 6–60

3

- Click the label for the Account Manager Number control to select it (Figure 6–61).

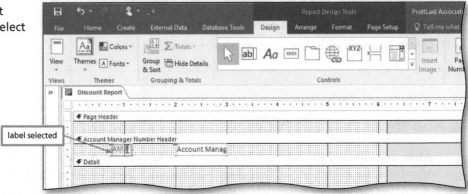

Figure 6–61

4

- Display the Home tab.

- Click the Cut button (Home tab | Clipboard group) to cut the label.

- Click the Page Header bar to select the page header (Figure 6–62).

Q&A
Do I have to click the bar, or could I click somewhere else within the section?
You could also click within the section. Clicking the bar is usually safer, however. If you click in a section intending to select the section, but click within one of the controls in the section, you will select the control rather than the section. Clicking the bar always selects the section.

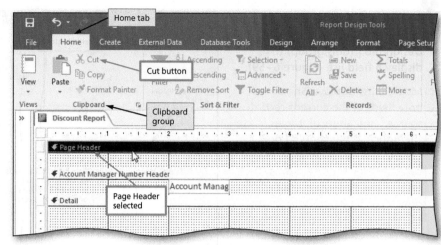

Figure 6–62

5

- Click the Paste button (Home tab | Clipboard group) to paste the label in the Page Header section (Figure 6–63).

Q&A
When would I want to click the Paste button arrow rather than just the button?
Clicking the arrow displays the Paste button menu, which includes the Paste command and two additional commands. Paste Special allows you to paste data into different formats. Paste Append, which is available if you have cut or copied a record, allows you to paste the record to a table with a similar structure.
If you want the simple Paste command, you can just click the button.

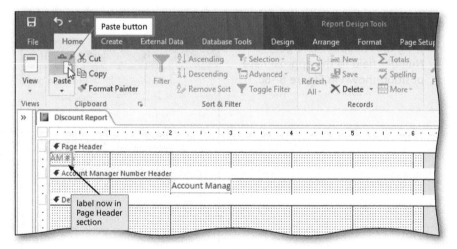

Figure 6–63

6

- Click in the label to produce an insertion point, use the BACKSPACE or DELETE key to erase the current entry in the label, and then type **Manager Number** as the new entry.

- Click in the label in front of the word, Number, to produce an insertion point.

- Press SHIFT+ENTER to move the word, Number, to a second line.

To Add the Remaining Fields

1 CREATE TABLES | 2 CREATE QUERIES | 3 CREATE REPORT | 4 SPECIFY GROUPING & SORTING | 5 ADD FIELDS
6 ADD SUBREPORT | 7 ADD TITLE, PAGE NUMBER, & DATE | **8 CREATE SECOND REPORT**

After first resizing the Account Manager Number control and label, the following steps add all the remaining fields for the report by dragging them into the Detail section. *Why? Dragging them gets them onto the report, where you can now move the controls and labels individually to the desired locations.* The next steps move the labels into the Page Header section, and move the controls containing the fields to the appropriate locations.

1

- Resize and move the Account Manager Number control to the approximate size and position shown in Figure 6–64.

- If necessary, resize the Account Manager Number label to the size shown in the figure.

- Drag the First Name, Last Name, Account Number, Account Name, Amount Paid, and Current Due fields into the Detail section, as shown in the figure.

Q&A Could I drag them all at once?
Yes. You can select multiple fields by selecting the first field, holding down the SHIFT key, and then selecting other adjacent fields. To select fields that are not adjacent to each other, hold down the CTRL key and select the additional fields. Once you have selected multiple fields, you can drag them all at once. How you choose to select fields and drag them onto the report is a matter of personal preference.

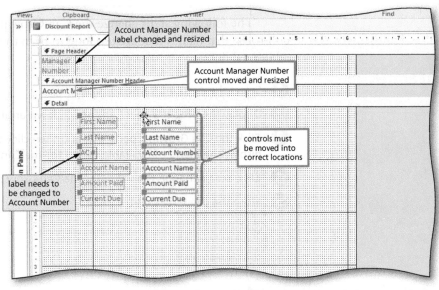

Figure 6–64

2

- Close the field list.

- One at a time, cut each of the labels, paste the label into the Page Header section, and then resize, reformat, and move the labels to the approximate positions shown in Figure 6–65.

Q&A When I paste the label, it is always placed at the left edge, superimposing the Account Manager Number control. Can I change where Access places it? Unfortunately, when you paste to a different section, Access places the control at the left edge. You will need to drag each control to its proper location after pasting it into the Page Header section.

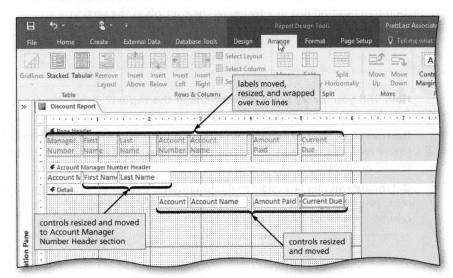

Figure 6–65

- One at a time, resize and move the First Name and Last Name controls to the approximate positions in the Account Manager Number Header section shown in the figure.

- One at a time, resize and move the Account Number, Account Name, Amount Paid, and Current Due controls to the approximate positions in the Detail section shown in the figure.

- Display the Report Design Tools Arrange tab.

- Use the Align button (Report Design Tools Arrange tab | Sizing & Ordering group) as necessary to align all the controls as shown in Figure 6–65.

To Change the Can Grow Property

The following steps change the Can Grow property for the Account Name control so that names that are too long to fit in the available space will extend to additional lines.

1 Select the Account Name control.

2 Display the property sheet and scroll down until the Can Grow property appears.

3 Click the Can Grow property box and then click the Can Grow property box arrow to display the menu of available values for the Can Grow property.

4 Click Yes to change the value for the Can Grow property.

5 Close the property sheet.

To Resize the Detail Section

1 CREATE TABLES | 2 CREATE QUERIES | 3 CREATE REPORT | 4 SPECIFY GROUPING & SORTING | 5 ADD FIELDS
6 ADD SUBREPORT | 7 ADD TITLE, PAGE NUMBER, & DATE | **8 CREATE SECOND REPORT**

The following step resizes the Detail section of the Discount Report to remove most of the extra space below the controls in the section. **Why?** *The extra space would appear after each detail line in the report, which adds unnecessary length to the report. The desired report (Figure 6–1b) does not include such space.*

1

- Scroll down so that the lower boundary of the Detail section appears, and then drag the lower boundary of the section to a position just slightly below the controls in the section.

How will you incorporate calculations in the report?
Determine details concerning any calculations required for the report.

Determine whether to include calculations in the group and report footers. The group footers or report footers might require calculated data such as subtotals or grand totals. Determine whether the report needs other statistics that must be calculated (for example, average).

Determine whether any additional calculations are required. If so, determine the fields that are involved and how they are to be combined. Determine whether any of the calculations depend on a true or false state for a criterion, in which case the calculations are conditional.

CONSIDER THIS

BTW
Arguments
An argument is a piece of data on which a function operates. For example, in the expression = SUM ([Amount Paid]), Amount Paid is the argument because the SUM function will calculate the total of Amount Paid.

Totals and Subtotals

To add totals or other statistics to a footer, add a text box control. You can use any of the aggregate functions in a text box: COUNT, SUM, AVG (average), MAX (largest value), MIN (smallest value), STDEV (standard deviation), VAR (variance), FIRST, and LAST. To use a function, type an equal (=) sign, followed by the function name. You then include a set of parentheses containing the item for which you want to perform the calculation. If the item name contains spaces, such as Amount Paid, you must enclose it in square brackets. For example, to calculate the sum of the amount paid values, the expression would be =SUM([Amount Paid]).

Access will perform the calculation for the appropriate collection of records. If you enter this expression in the Account Manager Number Footer section, Access will only calculate the total for accounts with the given account manager; that is, it will calculate the appropriate subtotal. If you enter the expression in the Report Footer section, Access will calculate the total for all accounts.

Grouping and Sorting Options

As you learned in Module 4, clicking the More button in the Group, Sort, and Total pane allows you to specify additional options for grouping and sorting. The additional options are: Value, which lets you choose the amount of the value on which to group; Totals, which lets you choose the values to be totaled; Title, which lets you customize the group title; Header section, which lets you include or omit a header section for the group; Footer section, which lets you include or omit a footer section for the group; and Keep together, which lets you specify whether Access is to attempt to keep portions of a group together on a page.

To Add Totals and Subtotals

1 CREATE TABLES | 2 CREATE QUERIES | 3 CREATE REPORT | 4 SPECIFY GROUPING & SORTING | 5 ADD FIELDS
6 ADD SUBREPORT | 7 ADD TITLE, PAGE NUMBER, & DATE | **8 CREATE SECOND REPORT**

The following steps first display the Account Manager Number Footer section and then add the total of amount paid and current due to both the Account Manager Number Footer section and the Report Footer section. The steps label the totals in the Account Manager Number Footer section as subtotals and the totals in the Report Footer section as grand totals. The steps change the format of the new controls to currency and the number of decimal places to 2. *Why? The requirements at PrattLast indicate that the Discount Report should contain subtotals and grand totals of amounts paid and current due.*

1
- If necessary, display the Report Design Tools Design tab.
- Click the Group & Sort button (Report Design Tools Design tab | Grouping & Totals group) to display the Group, Sort, and Total pane.
- If necessary, click 'Group on Account Manager Number' to select Group on Account Manager Number (Figure 6–66).

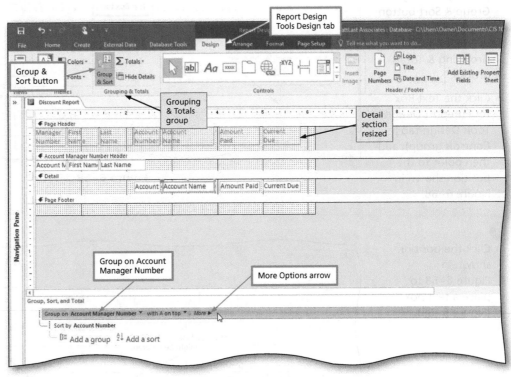

Figure 6–66

2

- Click the More arrow to display additional options for grouping.
- Click the 'without a footer section' arrow to display the available options (Figure 6–67).

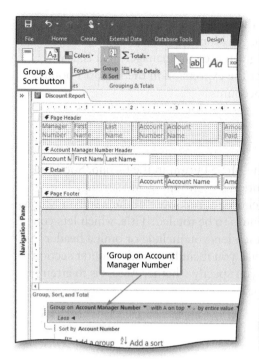

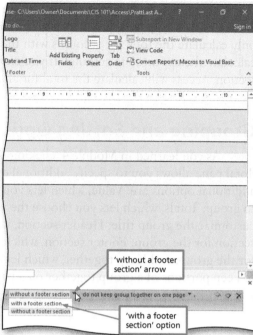

Figure 6–67

3

- Click 'with a footer section' to add a footer.
- Close the Group, Sort, and Total pane by clicking the Group & Sort button (Report Design Tools Design tab | Grouping & Totals group).
- Click the Text Box tool (Report Design Tools Design tab | Controls group), and then point to the position shown in Figure 6–68.

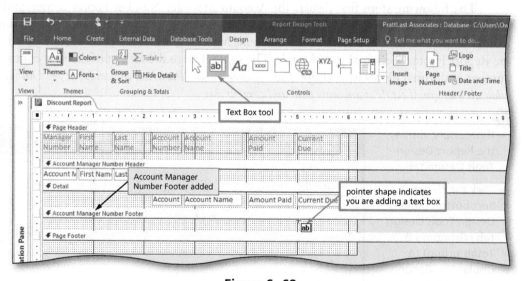

Figure 6–68

4

- Click the position shown in Figure 6–68 to place a text box (Figure 6–69).

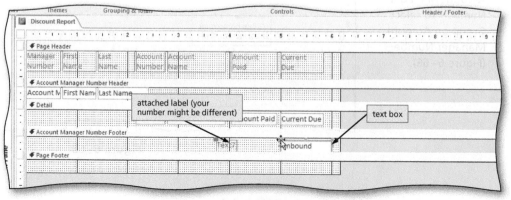

Figure 6–69

5

- Click the text box to produce an insertion point.
- Type **=Sum([Current Due])** in the control to enter the expression calculation, and then press the ENTER key.
- Click the text box label to select it.
- Click the label a second time to produce an insertion point.
- Use the DELETE or BACKSPACE key to delete the Text7 label (your number might be different).

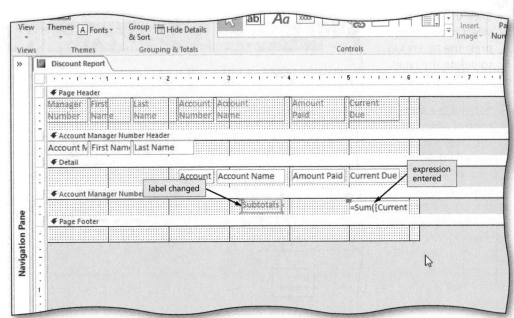

Figure 6–70

- Type **Subtotals** as the label. Click outside the label to deselect it and then drag the label to the position shown in the Figure 6–70.

 6

- Click the Text Box tool (Report Design Tools Design tab | Controls group), and then click in the Account Manager Number Footer section just to the left of the control for the sum of Current Due to place another text box.
- Click the text box to produce an insertion point, type **=Sum([Amount Paid])** in the control, and then press the ENTER key to enter the expression (Figure 6–71).

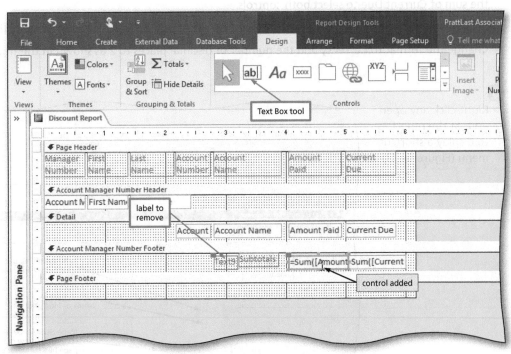

Figure 6–71

Q&A Could I add the controls in the other order?

Yes. The only problem is that the label of the second control overlaps the first control. Adding the controls in the order shown in the steps reduces the overlap. It is not a major difference, however.

7

- Click the label to select it, and then press the DELETE key to delete the label.

I inadvertently deleted the other control rather than the label. What should I do? First, click the Undo button on the Quick Access Toolbar to reverse your deletion. You can then delete the correct control. If that does not work, you can simply delete the remaining control or controls in the section and start these steps over.

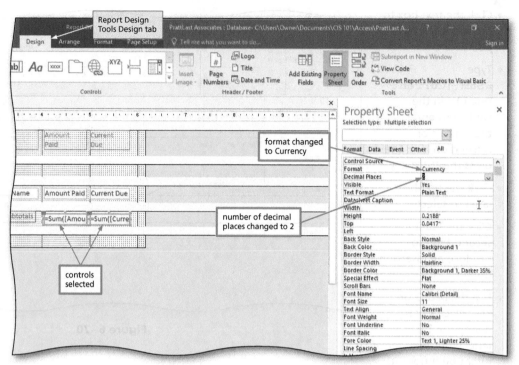

Figure 6–72

- Resize and align the Amount Paid and Current Due controls in the Detail section and the Account Manager Number Footer section to the positions shown in Figure 6–72.

- Click the control for the sum of Amount Paid to select it, and then hold down the SHIFT key and click the control for the sum of Current Due to select both controls.

- Click the Property Sheet button (Report Design Tools Design tab | Tools group) to display the property sheet.

- Change the format to Currency and the number of decimal places to 2 as shown in the figure.

8

- Right-click any open area of the report to display a shortcut menu (Figure 6–73).

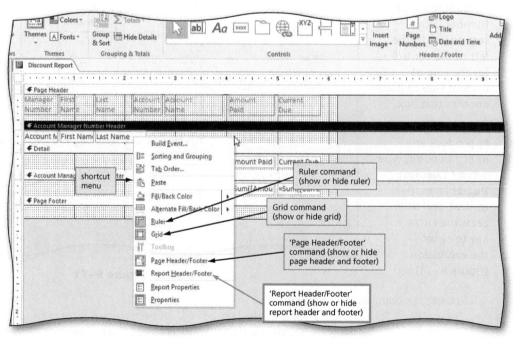

Figure 6–73

9
- Click 'Report Header/ Footer' to display the Report Header and Footer sections.
- Click the ruler in the Account Manager Number Footer to the left of the controls in the section to select the controls.
- Display the Home tab.
- Click the Copy button (Home tab | Clipboard group) to copy the selected controls to the Clipboard (Figure 6–74).

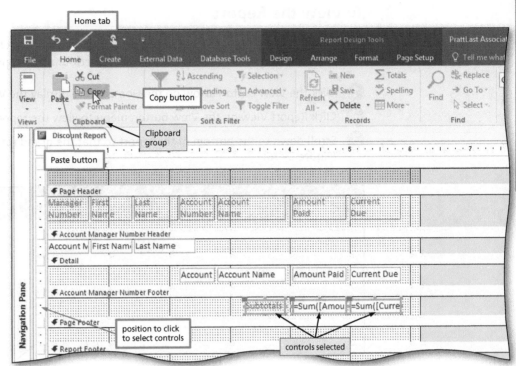

Figure 6–74

10
- Click the Report Footer bar to select the footer, and then click the Paste button (Home tab | Clipboard group) to paste a copy of the controls into the report footer.
- Move the controls to the positions shown in Figure 6–75.
- Click the label in the Report Footer section to select the label, and then click a second time to produce an insertion point.

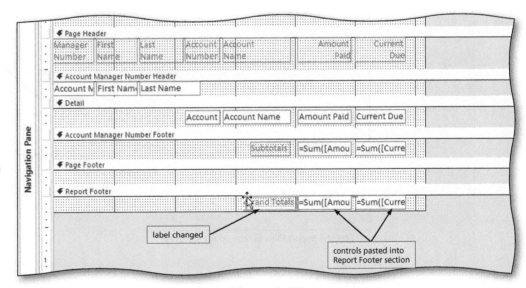

Figure 6–75

- Use the BACKSPACE or DELETE key to erase the current contents, type **Grand Totals** to change the label, and then move the label to the position shown in Figure 6–75.

Q&A Could I enter the controls just as I did earlier, rather than copying and pasting?
Yes. Copying and pasting is simpler, but it is a matter of personal preference.

To View the Report

The following steps view the report in Report view, which is sometimes more convenient when you want to view the lower portion of the report.

1 Click the View button arrow on the Home tab to display the View button menu.

2 Click Report View on the View button menu to view the report in Report view.

3 Scroll down to the bottom of the report so that the grand totals appear on the screen (Figure 6–76).

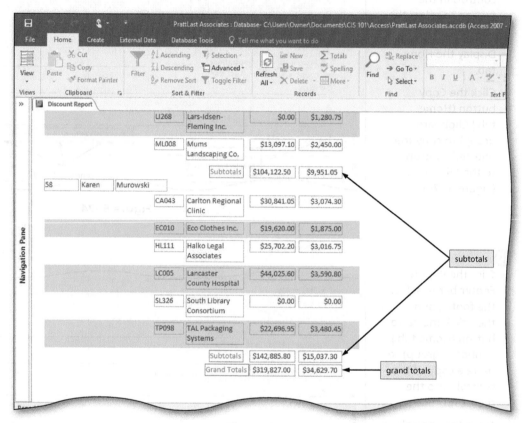

Figure 6–76

Other Ways

1. Click the Report View button on the status bar

To Remove the Color from the Report Header

The following steps remove the color from the Report Header section by changing the background color for the header to white.

1 Click the View button arrow and then click Design View to return to Design view.

2 Right-click the report header to produce a shortcut menu.

3 Point to the 'Fill/Back Color' arrow on the shortcut menu to display a color palette.

4 Click White in the first row, first column to change the background color to white.

To Assign a Conditional Value

The PrattLast requirements for this report also involved a conditional value related to the amount of an account's discount. *Why? PrattLast has determined that the amount of the discount depends on the amount paid. If the amount paid is greater than $20,000, the discount on the current due amount is 4 percent. If not, the discount is 2 percent.*

To assign a conditional value, you will use the IIf function. The IIf function consists of the letters IIf followed by three items, called **arguments**, in parentheses. The first argument is a criterion; the second and third arguments are expressions. If the criterion is true, the function assigns the value of the expression in the second argument. If the criterion is false, the function assigns the value of the expression in the third argument. The IIf function you will use is IIf([Amount Paid]>20000, .04*[Current Due], .02*[Current Due]). This function applies the following rules: If the amount paid is greater than $20,000, the value assigned is .04*[Current Due], that is, 4 percent of the current due amount. If the amount paid is not greater than $20,000, the value assigned is .02*[Current Due], that is, 2 percent of the current due amount.

The following steps add a text box and then use the Expression Builder to enter the appropriate IIf function in the text box. The steps then change the format of the text box and modify and move the label for the text box. They also add a title, page number, and date, and then change the alignment of the title. The steps then change the size of the report.

1

- If necessary, display the Report Design Tools Design tab.

- Click the Text Box tool (Report Design Tools Design tab | Controls group) and point to the approximate position shown in Figure 6–77.

Q&A

How can I place the control accurately when there are no gridlines?
When you click the position for the control, Access will automatically expand the grid. You can then adjust the control using the grid.

Can I automatically cause controls to be aligned to the grid?
Yes. Click the Size/Space button (Report Design Tools Arrange tab | Sizing & Ordering group) and then click Snap to Grid on the Size/Space menu. From that point on, any controls you add will be automatically aligned to the grid.

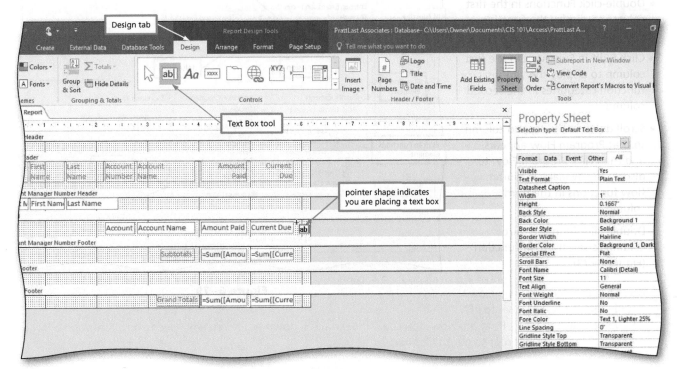

Figure 6–77

● Click the position shown in Figure 6–77 to place a text box.

● Click the attached label to select it, and then press the DELETE key to delete the attached label.

● Click the text box to select it, and then click the Property Sheet button (Report Design Tools Design tab | Tools group), if necessary, to display a property sheet.

● If necessary, display the All tab, and then click the Control Source property to select it (Figure 6–78).

Q&A Why did I choose Control Source instead of Record Source?
You use Record Source to select the source of the records in a report, usually a table or a query. You use the Control Source property to specify the source of data for the control. This allows you to bind an expression or field to a control.

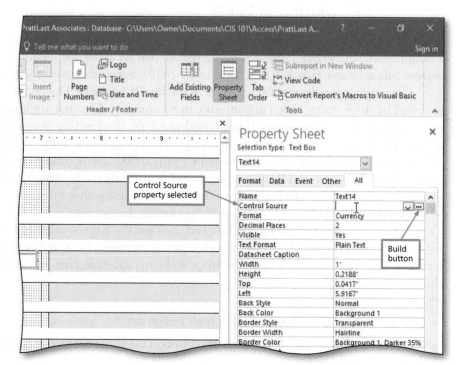

Figure 6–78

3

● Click the Build button to display the Expression Builder dialog box.

● Double-click Functions in the first column to display the function subfolders.

● Click Built-In Functions in the first column to display the various function categories in the second column.

● Scroll down in the second column so that Program Flow appears, and then click Program Flow to display the available program flow functions in the third column.

● Double-click IIf in the third column to select the IIf function (Figure 6–79).

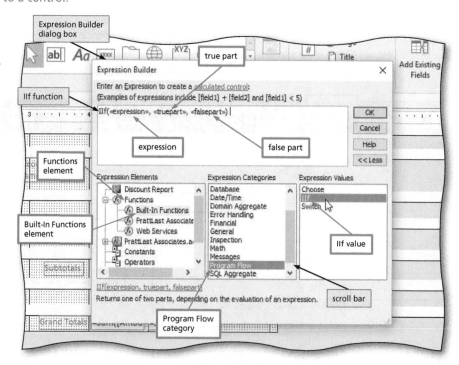

Figure 6–79

Q&A Do I have to select Program Flow? Could I not just scroll down to IIf?
You do not have to select Program Flow. You could indeed scroll down to IIf. You will have to scroll through a large number of functions in order to get to IIf, however.

4
- Click the <<expression>> argument to select it and type **[Amount Paid]>20000** as the expression.

- Click the <<truepart>> argument to select it and type **0.04*[Current Due]** as the true part.

- Click the <<falsepart>> argument to select it and type **0.02*[Current Due]** as the false part (Figure 6–80).

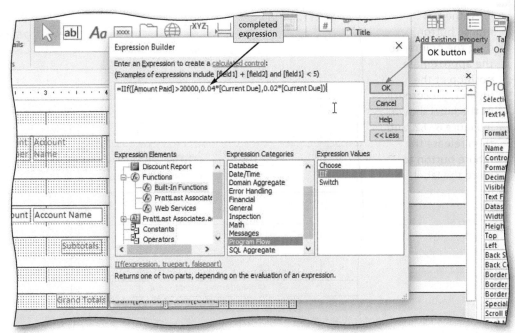

Figure 6–80

Q&A Are there other ways I could enter the expression?

Yes. You could just type the whole expression. On the other hand, you could select the function just as in these steps, and, when entering each argument, you could select the fields from the list of fields and click the desired operators.

5
- Click the OK button (Expression Builder dialog box) to specify the expression as the control source for the text box.

Q&A My property sheet is covering my OK button. What should I do?

Click in the Expression Builder dialog box to bring the entire dialog box in front of the property sheet.

- Change the Format to Currency.

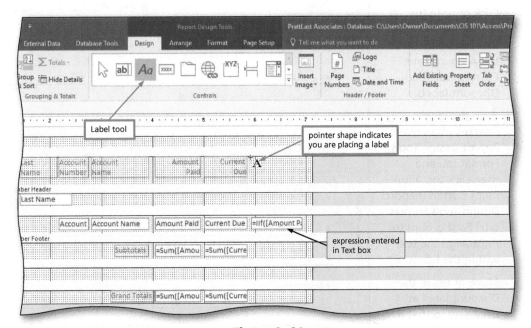

Figure 6–81

- Change the number of decimal places to 2.

- Close the property sheet by clicking the Property Sheet button.

- Click the Label tool on the Report Design Tools Design tab and point to the approximate position shown in Figure 6–81.

6

- Press the left mouse button, drag the pointer to the approximate position at the lower-right corner of the label shown in Figure 6–82, and then release the mouse button to place the label.

Q&A
I made the label the wrong size. What should I do?
With the label selected, drag the sizing handles to resize the label as needed. Drag the control in a position away from the sizing handles if you need to move the label.

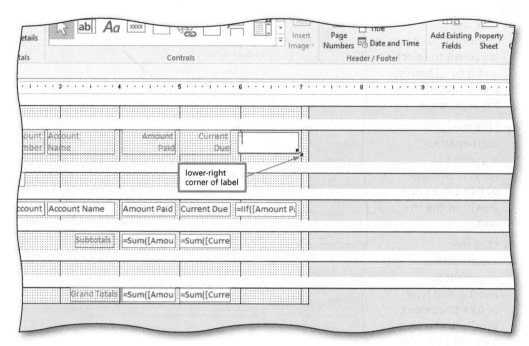

Figure 6–82

7

- Type **Discount** to enter the name of the label.

- Click outside the label to deselect the label and then select the Amount Paid, Current Due, and Discount labels.

- With the labels selected, display the Report Design Tools Format tab and then click the Align Right button (Report Design Tools Format tab | Font group) to right-align the text within the labels.

- Move or resize the Discount label as necessary so that it aligns with the text box containing the IIf statement and with the other controls in the Page Header section.

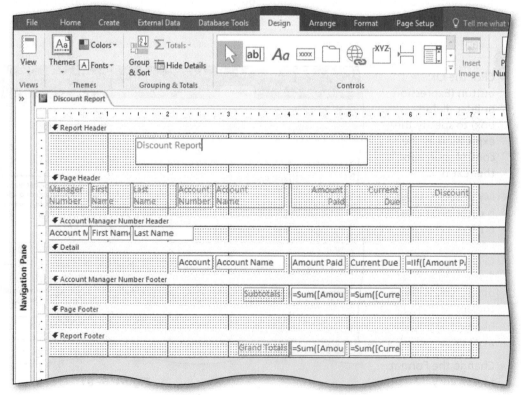

Figure 6–83

- Expand the Report Header section to the approximate size shown in Figure 6–83, place a label in the approximate position shown in the figure, and then type **Discount Report** in the label.

8

- Click outside the label to deselect it and then click the label in the report header to select the entire label.

- Display the property sheet, change the font size to 20 and the text align property to Distribute, which spreads the letters evenly throughout the label. Change the font weight to Semibold, and then close the property sheet.

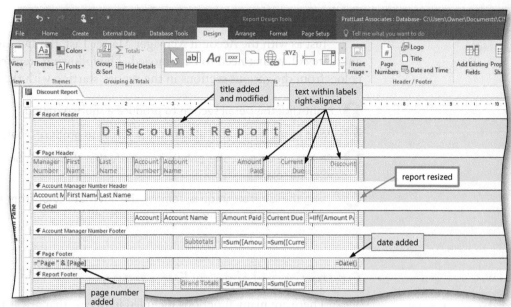

Figure 6–84

- If necessary, increase the size of the Discount Report label so that the entire title is displayed.

- Using the Report Design Tools Design tab, add a page number on the left side of the page footer, then add a date (use the same format you have used previously in this module).

- Cut the date, and then paste it into the page footer. Drag the date so that the date is positioned in the approximate position shown in Figure 6–84.

- Drag the right boundary of the report to the position shown in the Figure to reduce the width of the report, if necessary.

Q&A The report size was correct before. Why would I need to resize it?

When you move a control and a portion of the control extends into the area to the right of the right boundary of the report, the report will be resized. The new larger size will remain even if you move the control back to the left. Thus, it is possible that your report has a larger size than it did before. If this is the case, you need to drag the right boundary to resize the report.

To Change the Border Style

If you print or preview the report, you will notice that all the controls have boxes around them. The box is the border, which you can select and modify if desired. The following steps remove the boxes around the controls by changing the border style to transparent.

1 Select all controls in the report. You can click the first one, and then hold the SHIFT key down while clicking all the others. Alternatively, you can click in the ruler to the left of the Report Header section and then hold the SHIFT key down while clicking to the left of all the other sections.

2 Display the Report Design Tools Design tab.

3 Click the Property Sheet button (Report Design Tools Design tab | Tools group) to display the property sheet.

4 Click the Border Style property box and then click the Border Style property box arrow to display the menu of available border styles.

5 Click Transparent to change the border style. Close the property sheet.

To Remove the Alternate Color

Just as with the Account Manager Master List, the Discount Report also has alternate colors that need to be removed. The following steps remove the alternate colors from the various sections in the report, starting with the Detail section.

1 Right-click the Detail section to produce a shortcut menu.

2 Point to the Alternate Fill/Back Color arrow to produce a color palette.

3 Click None on the color palette to specify that there is to be no alternate color for the selected section.

4 Using the same techniques, remove the alternate color from all other sections. (For some sections, the command may be dimmed.)

Obtaining Help on Functions

There are many functions included in Access that are available for a variety of purposes. To see the list of functions, display the Expression Builder. (See Figure 6–78 for one way to display the Expression Builder.) Double-click Functions in the first column and then click Built-In Functions. You can then scroll through the entire list of functions in the third column. Alternatively, you can click a function category in the second column, in which case the third column will only contain the functions in that category. To obtain detailed help on a function, highlight the function in the third column and click the Help button. The Help presented will show the syntax of the function, that is, the specific rule for how you must type the function and any arguments. It will give you general comments on the function as well as examples illustrating the use of the function.

Report Design Tools Page Setup Tab

You can use the buttons on the Report Design Tools Page Setup tab to change margins, orientation, and other page setup characteristics of the report (Figure 6–85a). If you click the Margins button, you can choose from among some predefined margins or set your own custom margins (Figure 6–85b). If you click the Columns button, you will see the Page Setup dialog box with the Columns tab selected (Figure 6–85c). You can use this tab to specify multiple columns in a report as well as the column spacing. If you click the Page Setup button, you will see the Page Setup dialog box with the Print Options tab selected (Figure 6–85d). You can use this tab to specify custom margins. You can specify orientation by clicking the Page tab (Figure 6–85e). You can also select paper size, paper source, and printer using this tab.

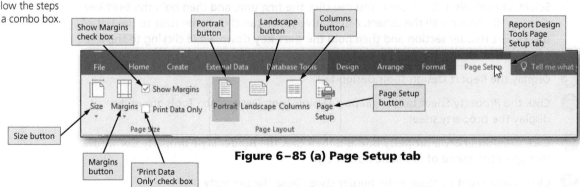

Figure 6–85 (a) Page Setup tab

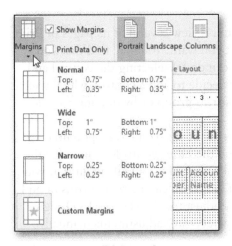

Figure 6–85 (b) Margins menu

Figure 6–85 (c) Columns tab

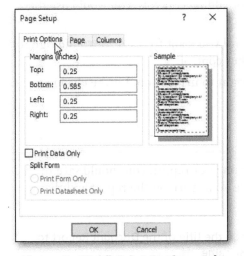

Figure 6–85 (d) Print Options tab

Figure 6–85 (e) Page tab

To Change the Report Margins

If you look at the horizontal ruler in Figure 6–84, you will notice that the report width is slightly over 7 inches. Because the report will probably print on standard 8½" x 11" paper, a 7-inch report with 1-inch margins on the left and right, which would result in a 9-inch width, will not fit. To allow the report to fit on the page, you could change the orientation from Portrait to Landscape or you could reduce the margins. There are two ways to change the margins. You can click the Margins button on the Report Design Tools Page Setup tab and then select from some predefined options. If you want more control, you can click the Page Setup button to display the Page Setup dialog box. You can then specify your own margins, change the orientation, and also specify multiple columns if you want a multicolumn report.

The following steps use the Margins button to select Narrow margins.

1 Display the Report Design Tools Page Setup tab.

2 Click the Margins button (Report Design Tools Page Setup tab | Page Size group).

3 If necessary, click Narrow to specify the Narrow margin option.

Fine-Tuning a Report

When you have finished a report, you should review several of its pages in Print Preview to make sure the layout is precisely what you want. You may find that you need to increase the size of a control, which you can do by selecting the control and dragging the appropriate sizing handle. You may decide to add a control, which you could do by using the appropriate tool in the Controls group or by dragging a field from the field list.

In both cases, if the control is between other controls, you have a potential problem. You may not have enough space between the other controls to increase the size or to add an additional control. If the control is part of a control layout that you had when you modified earlier reports in Layout view, you can resize controls or add new fields, and the remaining fields automatically adjust for the change. In Design view with individual controls, you must make any necessary adjustments manually.

TO MAKE ROOM FOR RESIZING OR ADDING CONTROLS

To make room for resizing a control or for adding controls, you would use the following steps.

1. Select all controls to the right of the control you want to resize, or to the right of the position where you want to add another control.
2. Drag any of the selected controls to the right to make room for the change.

To Save and Close a Report

Now that you have completed your work on your report, you should save the report and close it. The following steps first save your work on the report and then close the report.

1. If instructed to do so by your instructor, change the title of the Discount Report to LastName Report where LastName is your last name.

2. Click the Save button on the Quick Access Toolbar to save your work.

3. Close the Discount Report.

4. Preview and then print the report.

5. If desired, sign out of your Microsoft account.

6. Exit Access.

Summary

In this module you have learned to create and relate additional tables; create queries for a report; create reports in Design view; add fields and text boxes to a report; format controls; group and ungroup controls; modify multiple controls; add and modify a subreport; modify section properties; add a title, page number, and date; add totals and subtotals; use a function in a text box; and publish a report.

What decisions will you need to make when creating your own reports?

Use these guidelines as you complete the assignments in this module and create your own reports outside of this class.

1. Determine the intended audience and purpose of the report.

    a. Identify the user or users of the report and determine how they will use it.

    b. Specify the necessary data and level of detail to include in the report.

2. Determine the source of data for the report.

    a. Determine whether all the data is in a single table or whether it comes from multiple related tables.

3. Determine whether the data is stored in a query.

    a. You might need to create multiple versions of a report for a query where the criterion for a field changes, in which case, you would use a parameter query and enter the criterion when you run the report.

    b. If the data comes from multiple related tables, you might want to create a query and use the query as a source of data.

4. Determine the fields that belong on the report.

    a. Identify the data items that are needed by the user of the report.

5. Determine the organization of the report.

    a. The report might be enhanced by displaying the fields in a particular order and arranged in a certain way.

    b. Should the records in the report be grouped in some way?

    c. Should the report contain any subreports?

6. Determine any calculations required for the report.

    a. Should the report contain totals or subtotals?

    b. Are there any special calculations?

    c. Are there any calculations that involve criteria?

7. Determine the format and style of the report.

    a. What information should be in the report heading?

    b. Do you want a title and date?

    c. Do you want special background colors or alternate colors?

    d. Should the report contain an image?

    e. What should be in the body of the report?

How should you submit solutions to questions in the assignments identified with a symbol?

Every assignment in this book contains one or more questions identified with a symbol. These questions require you to think beyond the assigned database. Present your solutions to the questions in the format required by your instructor. Possible formats may include one or more of these options: write the answer; create a document that contains the answer; present your answer to the class; discuss your answer in a group; record the answer as audio or video using a webcam, smartphone, or portable media player; or post answers on a blog, wiki, or website.

Apply Your Knowledge

Reinforce the skills and apply the concepts you learned in this module.

Adding a Table and Creating a Report with a Subreport

Note: To complete this assignment, you will be required to use the Data Files. Please contact your instructor for information about accessing the Data Files

Instructions: Run Access. Open the Apply NicelyNeat Services database that you modified in Module 5. (If you did not complete the exercise, see your instructor for a copy of the modified database.)

Perform the following tasks:
1. Create a table in which to store data about cleaning services performed for clients. Use Services as the name of the table. The Services table has the structure shown in Table 6–4.

Table 6–4 Structure of Services Table			
Field Name	**Data Type**	**Field Size**	**Description**
Client Number	Short Text	4	Part of Primary Key
Service Date	Date/Time (Change Format property to Short Date)		Part of Primary Key
Hours Worked	Number (Change Format property to Fixed and Decimal Places to 2)	Single	

2. Import the Cleaning Services.txt file into the Services table. The file is delimited by tabs and the first row contains the field names. Do not save the import steps.

3. Create a one-to-many relationship (enforce referential integrity) between the Client table and the Services table. Save the relationship and close the Relationships window.

4. Create a query that joins the Supervisor and Client tables. Include the Supervisor Number, First Name, and Last Name fields from the Supervisor table. Include all fields except Total Amount and Supervisor Number from the Client table. Save the query as Supervisors and Clients.

5. Create the report shown in Figure 6–86. The report uses the Supervisors and Clients query as the basis for the main report and the Services table as the basis for the subreport. Use the name Supervisor Master List for the report. The report title has a Text Align property value of Center. The Border Width property for the detail controls is 1 pt and the subreport name is Services by Client. The report is similar in style to the Account Manager Master List shown in Figure 6–1a.

6. If requested to do so by your instructor, change the title for the report to First Name Last Name Master List where First Name and Last Name are your first and last names.

7. Submit the revised database in the format specified by your instructor.

8. ✷ How would you change the font weight of the report title to bold?

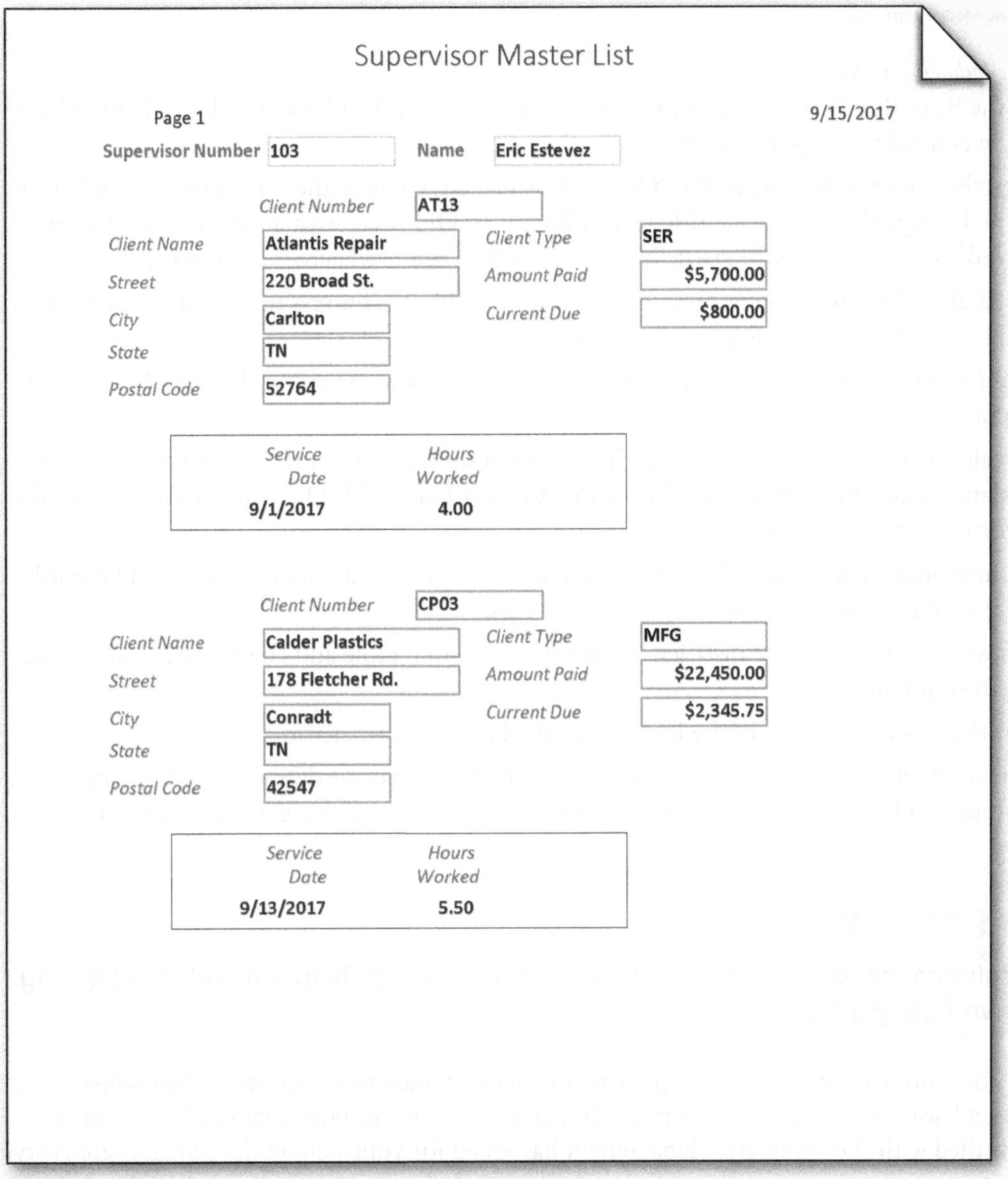

Supervisor Master List

Page 1   9/15/2017

Supervisor Number 103   Name   **Eric Estevez**

Client Number   **AT13**

Client Name   **Atlantis Repair**   *Client Type*   **SER**

Street   **220 Broad St.**   *Amount Paid*   **$5,700.00**

City   **Carlton**   *Current Due*   **$800.00**

State   **TN**

Postal Code   **52764**

Service Date	*Hours Worked*
9/1/2017	**4.00**

Client Number   **CP03**

Client Name   **Calder Plastics**   *Client Type*   **MFG**

Street   **178 Fletcher Rd.**   *Amount Paid*   **$22,450.00**

City   **Conradt**   *Current Due*   **$2,345.75**

State   **TN**

Postal Code   **42547**

Service Date	*Hours Worked*
9/13/2017	**5.50**

Figure 6–86

Extend Your Knowledge

Extend the skills you learned in this module and experiment with new skills.
You may need to use Help to complete the assignment.

Modifying Reports

Note: To complete this assignment, you will be required to use the Data Files. Please
contact your instructor for information about accessing the Data Files.

Instructions: Run Access. Open the Extend Earth Clothes database. Earth Clothes is a
company that manufactures and sells casual clothes made from earth-friendly fabrics.

Continued >

Extend Your Knowledge *continued*

Perform the following tasks:

1. Open the Sales Rep Master List in Design view. Change the date format to Long Date. Move the Date control to the page footer section.

2. Change the report title to Sales Rep/Orders Master List. Change the report header background to white. Change the font of the title text to Bookman Old Style with a font weight of semi-bold. Make sure the entire title is visible and the title is centered across the report.

3. Add a label to the report footer section. The label should contain text to indicate the end of the report, for example, End of Report or similar text.

4. Delete the Postal Code label and field. Remove any extra white space in the Detail section of the report.

5. Add a calculated control, Total Amount. The control should contain the sum of Amount Paid and Balance. Place this new control under the Amount Paid field. The control should have the same format as the Balance field.

6. Use conditional formatting to format the total amount value in a bold red font for all records where the value is equal to or greater than $1,500.00.

7. If requested to do so by your instructor, open the Sales Rep table and change the name of sales rep 44 to your name.

8. Submit the revised database in the format specified by your instructor.

9. ✹ Do you think the borders surrounding the controls enhance or detract from the appearance of the report? How would you remove the borders on all controls except the subreport?

Expand Your World

Create a solution, which uses cloud and web technologies, by learning and investigating on your own from general guidance.

Problem: You work part-time for a company that provides landscaping services. The company has two reports, a Customer Financial Report and Supervisor Master Report, that need to be more clearly identified with the company. Management has asked for your help in designing a report style that they can use.

Perform the following tasks:

1. Run Access and open the Expand Local Landscaping database from the Data Files.

2. Link the Landscape Rates Excel workbook to the database.

3. Search the web to find a suitable royalty-free background image the company can use for its reports, or create your own background image.

4. Open the Customer Financial Report in Design view and delete any alternate background color in the report. Add the background image to the report.

5. Search the web to find a suitable royalty-free logo or image the company can use for its reports, or create your own logo or image.

6. Add the logo or image to the Supervisor Master Report.

7. Add a hyperlink to the Supervisor Master Report that takes the user to a landscaping company website in your local area.

8. Submit the revised database in the format specified by your instructor.

9. ✹ What did you select as a background image and as a logo? What website did you use or did you create your own? Justify your selection.

In the Labs

Design, create, modify, and/or use a database following the guidelines, concepts, and skills presented in this module. Labs are listed in order of increasing difficulty. Labs 1 and 2, which increase in difficulty, require you to create solutions based on what you learned in the module; Lab 3 requires you to apply your creative thinking and problem solving skills to design and implement a solution.

Lab 1: Adding Tables and Creating Reports for the Horticulture4U Database

Problem: The management of Horticulture4U needs to maintain data on a weekly basis on the open orders for its customers. These are orders that have not yet been delivered. To track this information, the company requires a new table – an Open Orders table. The company also needs a report that displays sales rep information as well as information about customers and any open orders that the customer has. The company would like to show its appreciation to current customers by discounting the amount customers currently owe.

Note: To complete this assignment, you will be required to use the Data Files. Please contact your instructor for information about accessing the Data Files.

Instructions: Perform the following tasks:
1. Run Access and open the Lab 1 Horticulture4U database you used in Module 5. If you did not use this database, see your instructor about accessing the required files.
2. Create the Open Orders table using the structure shown in Table 6-5.

Table 6–5 Structure of Open Orders Table			
Field Name	**Data Type**	**Field Size**	**Description**
Order Number	Short Text	6	Primary Key
Amount	Currency		
Customer Number	Short Text	4	Foreign Key; matches primary key of Customer table

3. Import the Open Orders.txt file into the Open Orders table. The file is delimited by tabs and the first row contains the field names. Do not save the import steps.
4. Create a one-to-many relationship between the Customer table and the Open Orders table. Save the relationship.
5. Create a query that joins the Sales Rep table and the Customer table. Include the Sales Rep Number, First Name, and Last Name from the Sales Rep table. Include all fields except Total Amount and Sales Rep Number from the Customer table. Save the query as Sales Reps and Customers.

Continued >

In the Labs *continued*

6. Create the report shown in Figure 6–87. The report uses the Sales Reps and Customers query as the basis for the main report and the Open Orders table as the basis for the subreport. Use Open Orders as the name for the subreport. Change the Can Grow property for the Products Needed field to Yes. The Date control uses the Medium Date format, the title uses Distribute as the Text Align property, and there are no borders around the controls in the Detail section. The report is similar to the Account Manager Master List shown in Figure 6–1a.

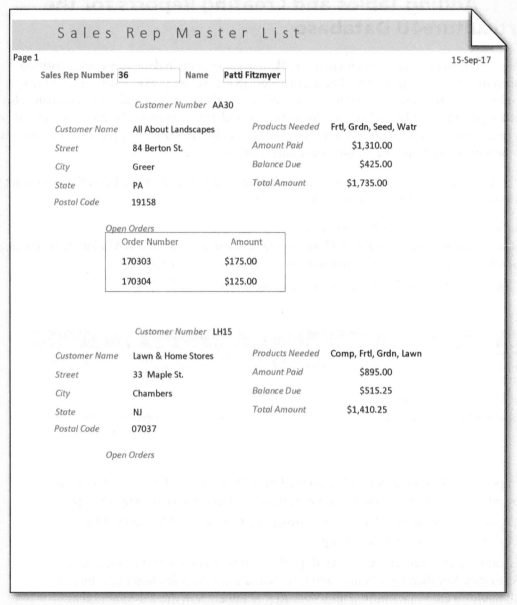

Figure 6–87

7. Create the Customer Discount Report shown in Figure 6–88. The report uses the Sales Reps and Customers query. Customers who have paid $2,000.00 or more will receive a 2 percent discount on the remaining balance, and clients who have paid less than $2,000.00 will receive a 1 percent discount on the remaining balance. The report includes subtotals and grand totals for the Amount Paid and Balance Due fields and is similar in style to the Discount Report shown in Figure 6–1b.

Customer Discount Report

Sales Rep Number	First Name	Last Name	Customer Number	Customer Name	Amount Paid	Balance Due	Discount
36	Patti	Fitzmyer					
			AA30	All About Landscapes	$1,310.00	$425.00	$4.25
			LH15	Lawn & Home Stores	$895.00	$515.25	$5.15
			PL10	Pat's Landscaping	$1,165.00	$180.75	$1.81
			SL25	Summit Lawn Service	$3,225.45	$675.50	$13.51
			TW34	TAL Wholesalers	$4,125.00	$350.00	$7.00
				Subtotals	$10,720.45	$2,146.50	
39	Rudy	Gupta					
			CT02	Christmas Tree Growers	$2,390.75	$860.35	$17.21
			GG01	Garden Gnome	$1,300.00	$297.50	$2.98
			ML25	Mum's Landscaping	$0.00	$1,805.00	$18.05
			TY03	TLC Yard Care	$1,845.00	$689.45	$6.89
				Subtotals	$5,535.75	$3,652.30	
42	Gloria	Ortega					
			GT34	Green Thumb Growers	$3,325.45	$865.50	$17.31
			OA45	Outside Architects	$4,205.50	$945.00	$18.90
			PN18	Pyke Nurseries	$2,465.00	$530.00	$10.60
			YS04	Yard Shoppe	$445.00	$575.00	$5.75
			YW01	Young's Wholesalers	$1,785.50	$345.60	$3.46
				Subtotals	$12,226.45	$3,261.10	
				Grand Totals	$28,482.65	$9,059.90	

Page 1   9/15/2017

Figure 6–88

8. If instructed to do so by your instructor, change the title for the Customer Discount Report to First Name Last Name Report where First Name and Last Name are your first and last name.

9. Submit the revised database in the format specified by your instructor.

10. ✳ How could you concatenate the Street, City, State, and Postal Code fields to display the complete address on one line?

Continued >

In the Labs *continued*

Lab 2: Adding Tables and Creating Reports for the SciTech Sundries Database

Problem: The gift shop manager of SciTech Sundries needs to track items that are being reordered from vendors. The report should indicate the date an item was ordered and the quantity ordered. She also needs a report that displays vendor information as well as information about items and the order status of items. SciTech Sundries is considering running a sale of items within the store; the sale price will be determined by the item's original retail price. The manager would like a report that shows the retail price as well as the sale price of all items.

Note: To complete this assignment, you will be required to use the Data Files. Please contact your instructor for information about accessing the Data Files.

Instructions: Perform the following tasks:

1. Run Access and open the Lab 2 SciTech Sundries database you used in Module 5. If you did not use this database, see your instructor about accessing the required files.

2. Create a table in which to store the item reorder information using the structure shown in Table 6–6. Use Reorder as the name of the table.

Table 6–6 Structure of Reorder Table

Field Name	Data Type	Field Size	Description
Item Number	Short Text	4	Part of Primary Key
Date Ordered	Date/Time (Use Short Date format)		Part of Primary Key
Number Ordered	Number	Integer	

3. Import the data from the Reorder.xlsx workbook to the Reorder table.

4. Add the Reorder table to the Relationships window and establish a one-to-many relationship between the Item table and the Reorder table. Save the relationship.

5. Create a query that joins the Vendor table and the Item table. Include the Vendor Code and Vendor Name from the Vendor table. Include all fields except the Vendor Code from the Item table. Save the query as Vendors and Items.

6. Create the report shown in Figure 6–89. The report uses the Vendors and Items query as the basis for the main report and the Reorder table as the basis for the subreport. Use the name Vendor Master List as the name for the report and the name Items on Order as the name for the subreport. The report uses the same style as that demonstrated in the module project. Use conditional formatting to display the on-hand value in bold red font color for all items with fewer than 10 items on hand. Change the Border Style property to Transparent. Change the Text Align property for the title to Center.

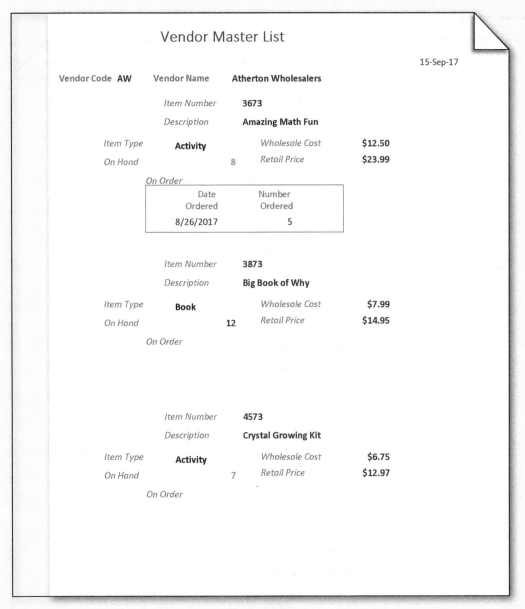

Figure 6–89

7. Create the Item Discount Report shown in Figure 6–90. The report uses the Vendors and Items Query and calculates the sale price for each item. Items with a retail price of more than $20 have a 4 percent discount; otherwise, the discount is 2 percent. Note that the report shows the sale price, not the discount. The report is similar to the Discount Report shown in Figure 6–1b. However, there are no group subtotals or report grand totals. The page number and current date appear in the page footer section. Change the Can Grow property for the Description field to Yes.

Continued >

In the Labs *continued*

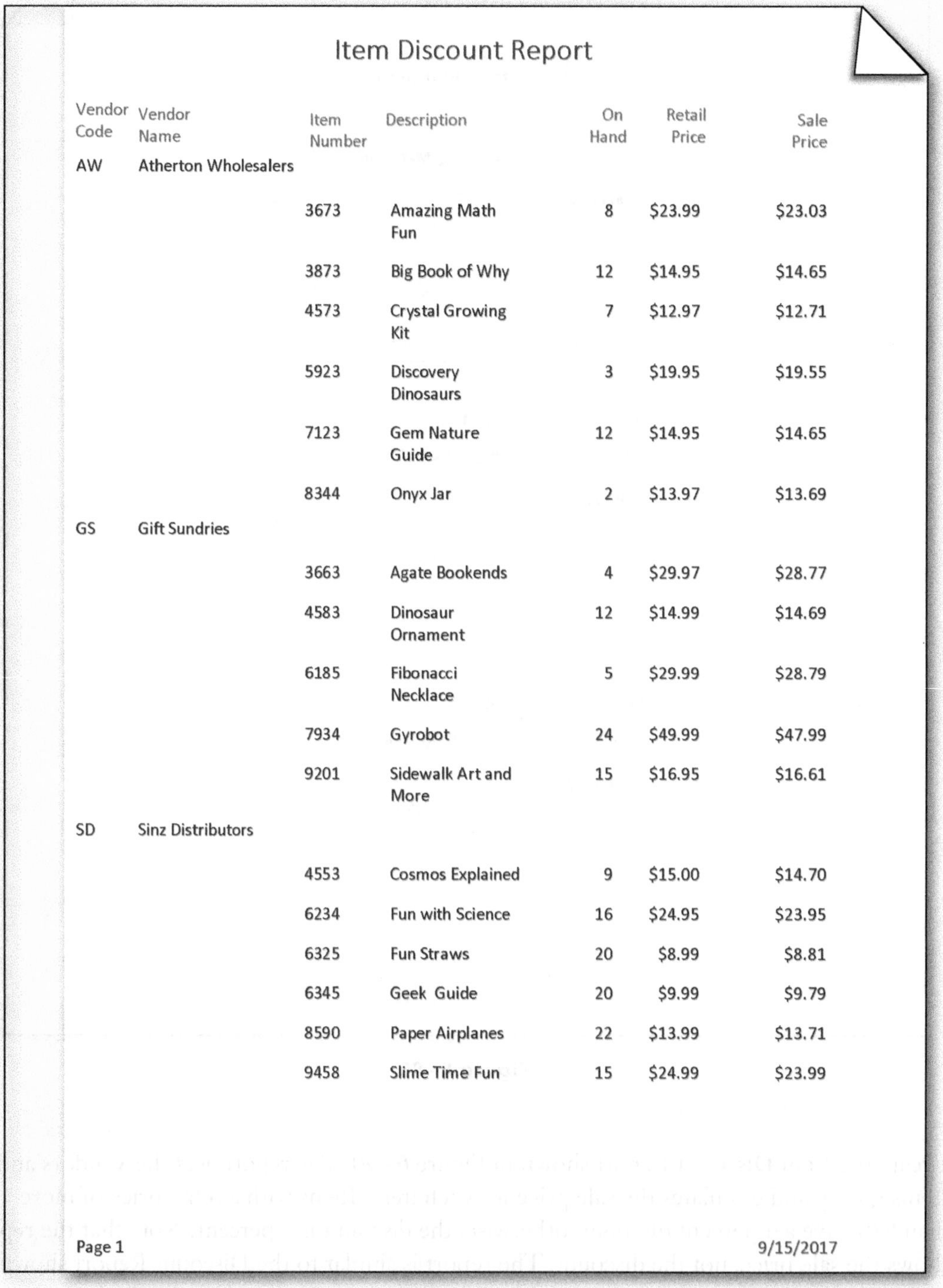

Item Discount Report

Vendor Code	Vendor Name	Item Number	Description	On Hand	Retail Price	Sale Price
AW	Atherton Wholesalers					
		3673	Amazing Math Fun	8	$23.99	$23.03
		3873	Big Book of Why	12	$14.95	$14.65
		4573	Crystal Growing Kit	7	$12.97	$12.71
		5923	Discovery Dinosaurs	3	$19.95	$19.55
		7123	Gem Nature Guide	12	$14.95	$14.65
		8344	Onyx Jar	2	$13.97	$13.69
GS	Gift Sundries					
		3663	Agate Bookends	4	$29.97	$28.77
		4583	Dinosaur Ornament	12	$14.99	$14.69
		6185	Fibonacci Necklace	5	$29.99	$28.79
		7934	Gyrobot	24	$49.99	$47.99
		9201	Sidewalk Art and More	15	$16.95	$16.61
SD	Sinz Distributors					
		4553	Cosmos Explained	9	$15.00	$14.70
		6234	Fun with Science	16	$24.95	$23.95
		6325	Fun Straws	20	$8.99	$8.81
		6345	Geek Guide	20	$9.99	$9.79
		8590	Paper Airplanes	22	$13.99	$13.71
		9458	Slime Time Fun	15	$24.99	$23.99

Page 1   9/15/2017

Figure 6–90

8. If instructed to do so by your instructor, add a label to the report footer with your first and last name.

9. Submit the revised database in the format specified by your instructor.

10. ✳ What expression did you use to create the Sale Price calculated field?

Lab 3: **Consider This: Your Turn**

Adding Tables and Creating Reports for the JSP Analysis Database

Note: To complete this assignment, you will be required to use the Data Files. Please contact your instructor for information about accessing the Data Files.

Instructions: Open the Lab 3 JSP Analysis database you used in Module 5. If you did not use this database, contact your instructor for information about accessing the required files.

Part 1: JSP Analysis offers seminars to its clients to explain applications of data mining. Management needs to maintain data on these seminars. They need a report that lists market analysts as well as the clients they serve and any seminar offerings the client is currently taking. Use the concepts and techniques presented in this module to perform each of the following tasks:

a. Create two tables in which to store data about the seminars requested by clients. The Seminar table contains data about the seminars that JSP Analysis offers. The structure of the table is similar to the Workshop table shown in in Table 6–1a. Replace Workshop with Seminar, name the table Seminar, and import the Seminar.txt file. The Seminar Offerings table has the same structure as the Workshop Offerings table shown in Table 6–2a except that the Account Number field is Client Number with a field size of 4 and Workshop Code is Seminar Code. Create the Seminar Offerings table and import the Seminar Offerings. csv file. Determine the relationships between the Seminar table, the Seminar Offerings table, and the Client table. Enforce referential integrity between the appropriate tables.

b. Create a query that joins the Marketing Analyst and the Client tables. Include the Marketing Analyst Number, First Name, and Last Name fields from the Marketing Analyst table. Include all fields from the Client table except Total Amount and Marketing Analyst Number. Save the query.

c. Create a query that joins the Seminar and Seminar Offerings tables. Include the Client Number and Seminar Code fields from the Seminar Offerings table, the Seminar Description from the Seminar table, and the Total Hours and Hours Spent fields from the Seminar Offerings table. Add a calculated field that contains the difference between Total Hours and Hours Spent. Save the query.

d. Create a Marketing Analyst Master Report that uses the query from Step b above as the basis for the main report and the query from Step c above as the basis for the subreport. The report should be similar in style to that shown in Figure 6–1a. Add a total amount field to the main report that sums the Amount Paid and Current Due fields for each record.

Submit your assignment in the format specified by your instructor.

Part 2: You made several decisions, such as adding new relationships, creating and modifying a subreport, and adding a calculated control, while adding these tables and creating the report. What was the rationale behind your decisions? How could you add a logo to the report?`

7 | Advanced Form Techniques

Objectives

You will have mastered the material in this module when you can:

- Add combo boxes that include selection lists
- Add combo boxes for searching
- Format and resize controls
- Apply formatting characteristics with the Format Painter
- Add command buttons
- Modify buttons and combo boxes

- Add a calculated field
- Use tab controls to create a multipage form
- Add and modify a subform
- Insert charts
- Modify a chart type
- Format a chart

Introduction

In previous modules, you created basic forms using the Form Wizard and you created more complex forms using Design view. In this module, you will create two new forms that feature more advanced form elements. The first form contains two combo boxes, one for selecting data from a related table and one for finding a record on the form. It also contains command buttons to accomplish various tasks.

The second form you will create is a **multipage form**, a form that contains more than one page of information. The form contains a tab control that allows you to access two different pages. Clicking the first tab displays a page containing a subform. Clicking the second tab displays a page containing two charts.

Project — Advanced Form Techniques

PrattLast Associates wants two additional forms to use with its Account and Account Manager tables. The first form, Account View and Update Form (Figure 7–1a), contains the fields in the Account table. The form has five command buttons: Next Record, Previous Record, Add Record, Delete Record, and Close Form. Clicking any of these buttons causes the action indicated on the button to occur.

The form also contains a combo box for the Account Manager Number field that assists users in selecting the correct manager (Figure 7–1b).

To assist users in finding an account when they know the account's name, the form also includes a combo box they can use for this purpose (Figure 7–1c).

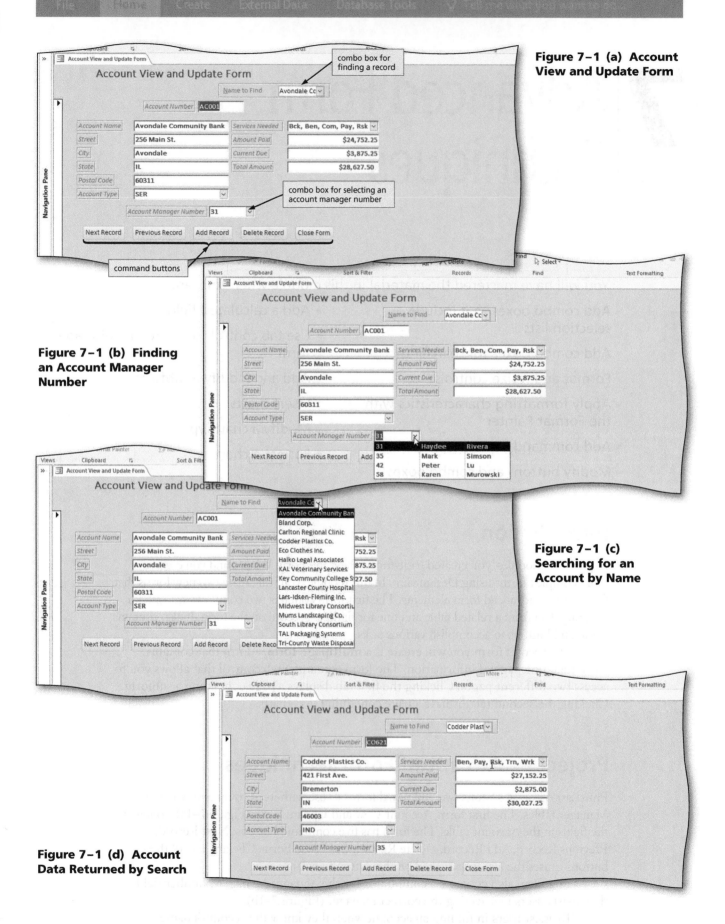

Figure 7–1 (a) Account View and Update Form

Figure 7–1 (b) Finding an Account Manager Number

Figure 7–1 (c) Searching for an Account by Name

Figure 7–1 (d) Account Data Returned by Search

After displaying the list of accounts by clicking the arrow, the user can simply select the account they want to find; Access will then locate the account and display that account's data in the form (Figure 7–1d).

For the second new form, PrattLast Associates needs a multipage form that lists the numbers and names of managers. Each of the two pages that make up the form is displayed in its own tab page. Selecting the first tab, the one labeled Datasheet, displays a subform listing information about the workshop offerings for accounts of the selected manager (Figure 7–2a).

Selecting the other tab, the one labeled Charts, displays two charts that illustrate the total hours spent and hours remaining by the manager for the various workshops (Figure 7–2b). In both charts, the slices of the pie represent the various workshops. They are color-coded and the legend at the bottom indicates the meaning of the various colors. The size of the pie slice gives a visual representation of the portion of the hours spent or hours remaining by the manager for that particular workshop. The chart also includes specific percentages. If you look at the purple slice in the Hours Spent by Workshop Offering chart, for example, you see that the color represents workshop W02. It signifies 25 percent of the total. Thus, for all the hours already spent on the various workshop offerings by manager 31, 25 percent have been spent on workshop W02.

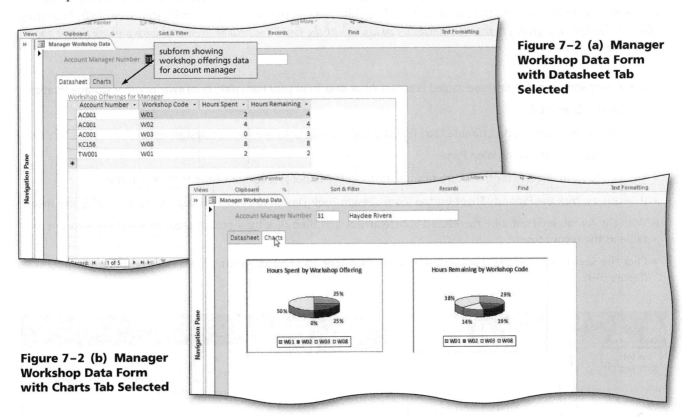

Figure 7–2 (a) Manager Workshop Data Form with Datasheet Tab Selected

Figure 7–2 (b) Manager Workshop Data Form with Charts Tab Selected

In this module, you will learn how to create the forms shown in Figures 7–1 and 7–2. The following roadmap identifies general activities you will perform as you progress through this module:

1. CREATE FORM containing a calculated field.
2. ADD COMBO BOXES, one for selecting data from a related table and one for finding a record on the form.

3. Add COMMAND BUTTONS to the form.

4. MODIFY a MACRO for one of the buttons so that the button works correctly.

5. MODIFY the COMBO BOX for finding a record so that the combo box works correctly.

6. CREATE a SECOND FORM, one that contains a tab control.

7. ADD a SUBFORM to one of the tabbed pages.

8. ADD a CHART to the other tabbed page.

Creating a Form with Combo Boxes and Command Buttons

After planning a form, you might decide that including features such as combo boxes and command buttons will make the form easier to use. You can include such items while modifying the form in Design view.

To Create a Form in Design View

1 CREATE FORM | 2 ADD COMBO BOXES | 3 COMMAND BUTTONS | 4 MODIFY MACRO
5 MODIFY COMBO BOX | 6 CREATE SECOND FORM | 7 ADD SUBFORM | 8 ADD CHART

As you have previously learned, Access provides several differing ways to create a form, including tools such as the Form Wizard and the Form button. The following steps create a form in Design view. *Why? Creating a form in Design view gives you the most flexibility in laying out the form. You will be presented with a blank design on which to place objects.*

- Run Access and open the database named PrattLast Associates from your hard disk, OneDrive, or other storage location.

- Display the Create tab.

- Click the Form Design button (Create tab | Forms group) to create a new form in Design view.

- If necessary, close the Navigation Pane.

- Ensure the form selector for the entire form, the box in the upper-left corner of the form, is selected.

- If necessary, click the Property Sheet button (Form Design Tools Design tab | Tools group) to display a property sheet.

- With the All tab selected, click the Record Source arrow, and then click the Account table to select the Account table as the record source.

- Click the Save button on the Quick Access Toolbar, then type **Account Master Form** as the form name (Figure 7–3).

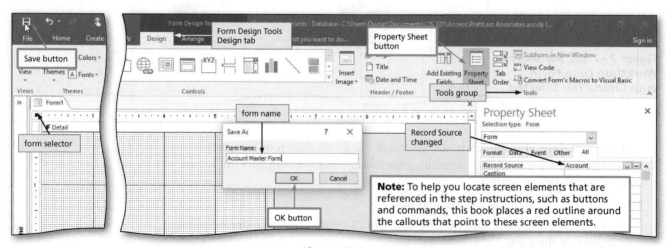

Figure 7–3

2

- Click the OK button (Save As dialog box) to save the form.

- Click the Caption property in the property sheet, and then type **Account View and Update Form** as the new caption.

- Close the property sheet by clicking the Property Sheet button on the Form Design Tools Design tab.

- Click the 'Add Existing Fields' button (Form Design Tools Design tab | Tools group) to display the field list (Figure 7–4).

Q&A Why does the name on the tab not change to the new caption, Account View and Update Form?
The name on the tab will change to the new caption in Form view. In Design view, you still see the name of the form object.

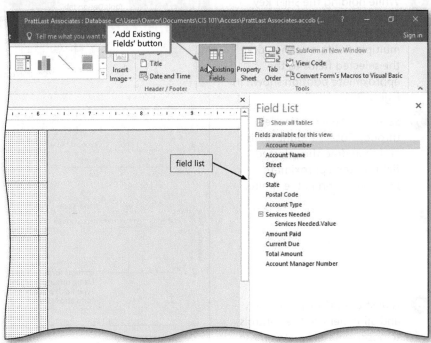

Figure 7–4

To Add Fields to the Form Design

After deciding which fields to add to the Account View and Update Form, you can place them on the form by dragging the fields from the field list to the desired position. The following steps first display only the fields in the Account table in the field list, and then place the appropriate fields on the form.

1 If necessary, click the 'Show only fields in the current record source' link at the top of the field list to change the link to 'Show all tables' and display only the fields in the Account table.

2 Drag the Account Number field from the field list to the top-center area of the form.

3 Click the label once to select it and then click it a second time to produce an insertion point, use the BACKSPACE or DELETE key as necessary to erase the current entry (AC #), and then type **Account Number** as the new label.

4 Click outside the label to deselect it, click the label to select it a second time, and then drag the sizing handle in the upper-left corner of the label to move it to the approximate position shown Figure 7–5.

Q&A I thought the caption for Account Number was changed to AC # so that this short caption would appear in datasheets, on forms, and on reports. Why am I now changing it back?
In these forms, there is plenty of room for the entire field name. Thus, there is no need for the short captions.

5 Click the Account Name field in the field list.

6 While holding the SHIFT key down, click the Account Type field in the field list to select multiple fields, and then drag the selected fields to the approximate position shown in Figure 7–5.

7 Select the Services Needed through Total Amount fields and then drag the selected fields to the approximate position shown in the figure.

Q&A I added the Account Manager Number field by mistake. Can I delete the control?

Yes, select the control and press the DELETE key.

8 Adjust the sizing, placement, and alignment of the controls to approximately match those in the figure. If controls for any of the fields are not aligned properly, align them by dragging them to the desired location or by using the alignment buttons on the Form Design Tools Arrange tab.

9 Close the field list.

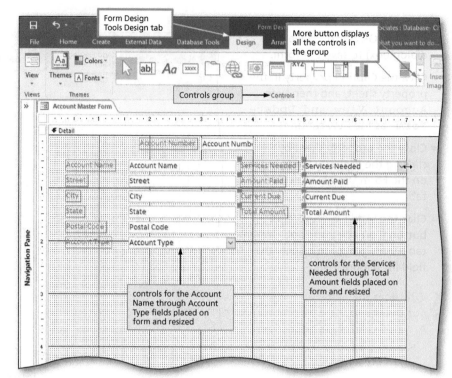

Figure 7–5

How do you decide on the contents of a form?

To design and create forms, follow these general guidelines:

Determine the fields that belong on the form. If you determine that data should be presented as a form, you then need to determine what tables and fields contain the data for the form.

Examine the requirements for the form in general to determine the tables. Do the requirements only relate to data in a single table, or does the data come from multiple tables? How are the tables related?

Examine the specific requirements for the form to determine the fields necessary. Look for all the data items that are specified for the form. Each item should correspond to a field in a table or be able to be computed from a field in a table. This information gives you the list of fields.

Determine whether there are any special calculations required, such as adding the values in two fields or combining the contents of two text fields. If special calculations are needed, what are they? What fields are involved and how are they to be combined?

Combo Boxes

When entering a manager number, the value must match the number of a manager currently in the Account Manager table. To assist users in entering this data, the form will contain a combo box. A **combo box** combines the properties of a **text box,** which is a box into which you can type an entry, and a **list box,** which is a box you can use to display a list from which to select a value. With a combo box, the user can either type the data or click the combo box arrow to display a list of possible values and then select an item from the list.

BTW

Combo Boxes
You also can create combo boxes for reports.

1 CREATE FORM | 2 ADD COMBO BOXES | 3 COMMAND BUTTONS | 4 MODIFY MACRO
5 MODIFY COMBO BOX | 6 CREATE SECOND FORM | 7 ADD SUBFORM | 8 ADD CHART

To Add a Combo Box That Selects Values

If you have determined that a combo box displaying values from a related table would be useful on your form, you can add the combo box to a form using the Combo Box tool in the Controls group on the Form Design Tools Design tab. Before doing so, you should make sure the 'Use Control Wizards' button is selected. *Why? A combo box that allows the user to select a value from a list is a convenient way to enter data.* The following steps place on the form a combo box that displays values from a related table for the Account Manager Number field.

1

• Click the Form Design Tools Design tab and then click the More button (Form Design Tools Design tab | Controls group) (see Figure 7–5) to display all the available tools in the Controls group (Figure 7–6).

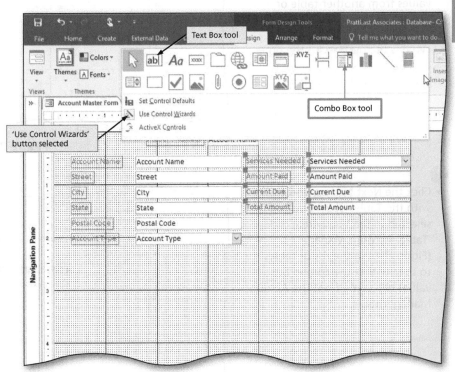

Figure 7–6

2

• With the 'Use Control Wizards' button in the Controls group on the Form Design Tools Design tab selected, click the Combo Box tool (Form Design Tools Design tab | Controls group), and then move the pointer, whose shape has changed to a small plus symbol accompanied by a combo box, to the position shown in Figure 7–7.

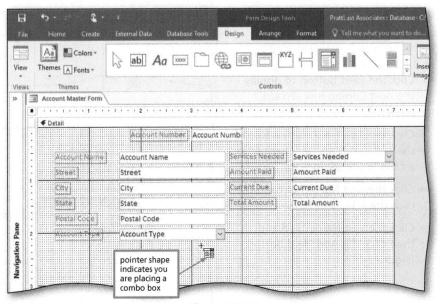

Figure 7–7

Click the position shown in Figure 7–7 to place a combo box and display the Combo Box Wizard dialog box.

- If necessary, in the Combo Box Wizard dialog box, click the 'I want the combo box to get the values from another table or query.' option button (Figure 7–8).

Q&A What is the purpose of the other options?
Use the second option if you want to type a list from which the user will choose. Use the third option if you want to use the combo box to search for a record.

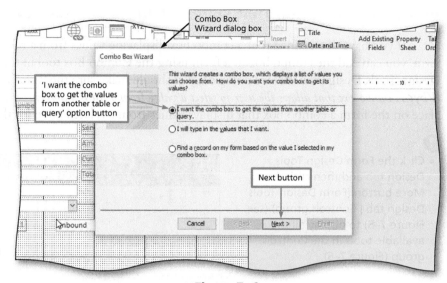

Figure 7–8

- Click the Next button, and then, with the Tables option button selected in the View area, click 'Table: Account Manager' (Figure 7–9) in the list of tables to specify that the combo box values will come from the Account Manager table.

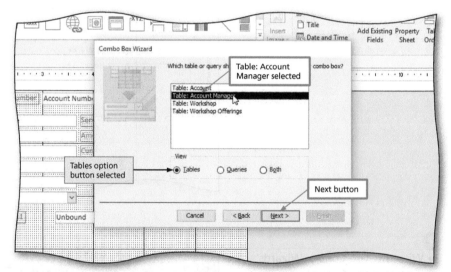

Figure 7–9

- Click the Next button to display the next Combo Box Wizard screen.

- Click the Add Field button to add the Account Manager Number as a field in the combo box.

- Click the First Name field and then click the Add Field button.

- Click the Last Name field and then click the Add Field button (Figure 7–10).

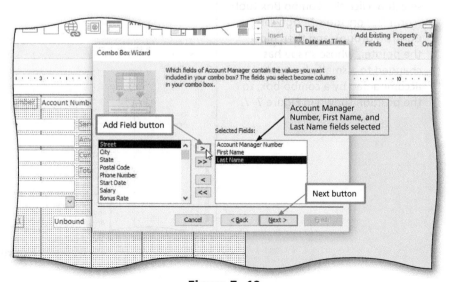

Figure 7–10

6
- Click the Next button to display the next Combo Box Wizard screen.
- Click the arrow in the first text box, and then select the Account Manager Number field to sort the data by account manager number (Figure 7–11).

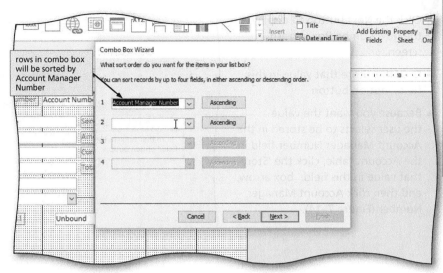

rows in combo box will be sorted by Account Manager Number

Figure 7–11

7
- Click the Next button to display the next Combo Box Wizard screen (Figure 7–12).

Q&A What is the key column? Do I want to hide it?

The key column would be the Account Manager Number, which is the column that identifies both a first name and a last name. Because the purpose of this combo box is to update manager numbers, you want the account manager numbers to be visible.

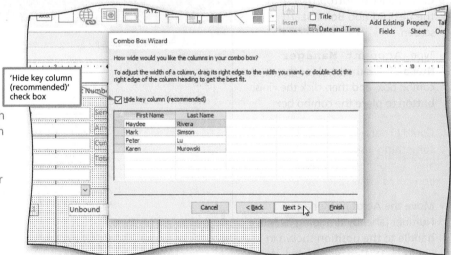

'Hide key column (recommended)' check box

Figure 7–12

8
- Click the 'Hide key column (recommended)' check box to remove the check mark so that the Account Manager Number field will appear along with the First Name and Last Name fields.
- Click the Next button to display the next Combo Box Wizard screen (Figure 7–13).

Q&A Do I need to make any changes here?

No. The Account Manager Number field, which is the field you want to store, is already selected.

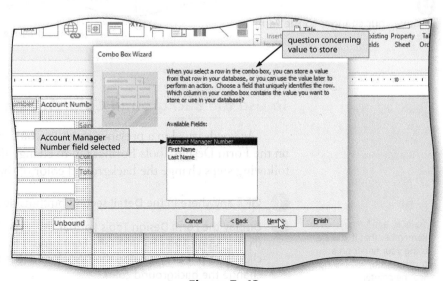

question concerning value to store

Account Manager Number field selected

Figure 7–13

● Click the Next button to display the next Combo Box Wizard screen.

● Click the 'Store that value in this field:' option button.

● Because you want the value the user selects to be stored in the Account Manager Number field in the Account table, click the 'Store that value in this field:' box arrow, and then click Account Manager Number (Figure 7–14).

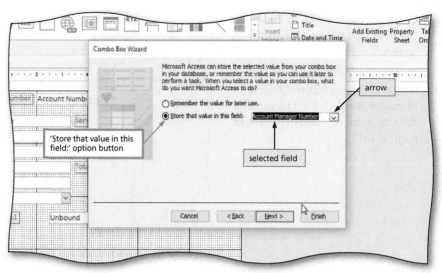

Figure 7–14

● Click the Next button to display the next Combo Box Wizard screen.

● Type **Account Manager Number** as the label for the combo box, and then click the Finish button to place the combo box.

Q&A Could I change the label to something else?
Yes. If you prefer a different label, you could change it.

● Move the Account Manager Number label by dragging its Move handle to the position shown in Figure 7–15. Resize the label, if necessary, to match the figure.

● Save your changes to the form.

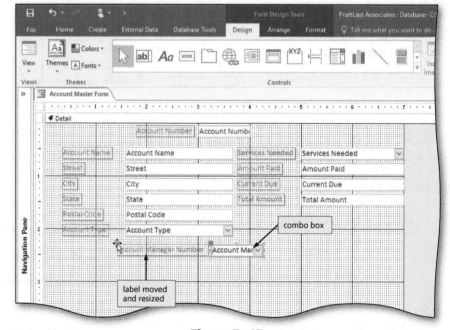

Figure 7–15

To Use the Background Color Button

As you learned in a previous module, you can use the Background Color button on the Form Design Tools Format tab to change the background color of a form. The following steps change the background color of the form to a light gray.

1 Click anywhere in the Detail section but outside all the controls to select the section.

2 Display the Form Design Tools Format tab, click the Background Color button arrow (Form Design Tools Format tab | Font group) to display a color palette, and then click the Light Gray 2 color, the first color in the third row under Standard Colors, to change the background color.

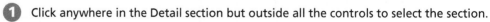

Advanced Form Techniques   Access Module 7   **AC** 371

1 CREATE FORM | 2 ADD COMBO BOXES | 3 COMMAND BUTTONS | 4 MODIFY MACRO
5 MODIFY COMBO BOX | 6 CREATE SECOND FORM | 7 ADD SUBFORM | 8 ADD CHART

Access Module 7

To Format a Control

You can use buttons on the Form Design Tools Design tab to format a control in a variety of ways. The following steps use the property sheet, however, to make a variety of changes to the format of the Account Number control. *Why? Using the property sheet gives you more choices over the types of changes you can make to the form controls than you have with simply using the buttons.*

1

- Display the Form Design Tools Design tab.

- Click the Account Number control (the white space, not the label) to select it.

- Click the Property Sheet button (Form Design Tools Design tab | Tools group) to display the property sheet.

- Change the value of the Font Weight property to Semi-bold.

- Change the value of the Special Effect property to Sunken.

- Click the Fore Color property box to select it, and then click the Build button (the three dots) to display a color palette (Figure 7–16).

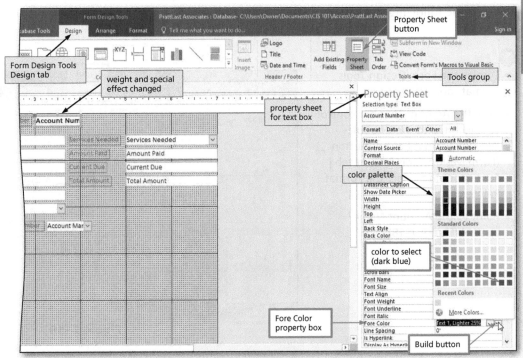

Figure 7–16

2

- Click the Dark Blue color (the second color from the right in the bottom row under Standard Colors) to select it as the foreground color, which is the font color.

- Click the label for the Account Number field to select it.

- Change the value of the Font Italic property to Yes.

- Change the Special Effect property to Etched (Figure 7–17).

3

- Close the property sheet.

Q&A Should I not have closed the property sheet before selecting different control?
You could have, but it is not necessary. The property sheet displayed on the screen always applies to the currently selected control or group of controls.

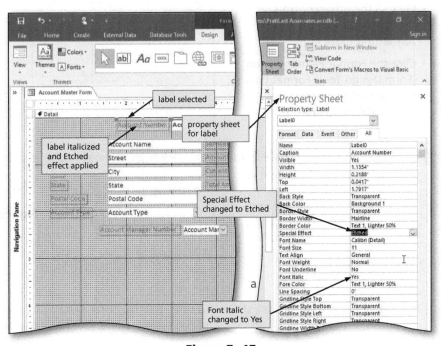

Figure 7–17

To Use the Format Painter

Once you have formatted a control and its label the way you want, you can format other controls in exactly the same way by using the format painter. ***Why?*** *If you click the control whose format you want to copy, click the Format Painter button on the Format tab, and then click another control, Access will automatically apply the characteristics of the first control to the second one.* If you want to copy the format to more than one other control, double-click the Format Painter button instead of simply clicking the button, and then click each of the controls that you want to change. The following steps copy the formatting of the Account Number control and label to the other controls.

- Display the Form Design Tools Format tab.

- Click the Account Number control to select it, and then double-click the Format Painter button (Form Design Tools Format tab | Font group) to select the Format Painter.

- Point to the Account Name control (Figure 7–18).

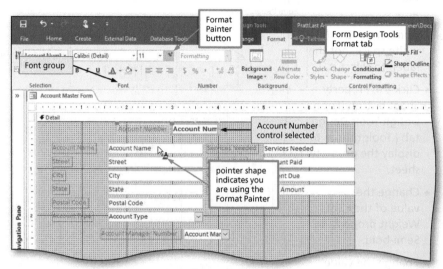

Figure 7–18

- Click the Account Name control to assign to it the same formatting as the Account Number control.

- Click all the other controls on the form to assign the same formatting to them.

- Click the Format Painter button (Form Design Tools Format tab | Font group) to deselect the Format Painter (Figure 7–19).

Q&A Do I always have to click the Format Painter button when I have finished copying the formatting?
If you double-clicked the Format Painter button to enable you to copy the formatting to multiple controls, you need to click the Format Painter button again to turn off the copying. If you single-clicked the Format Painter button to enable you to copy the formatting to a single control, you do not need to click the button again. As soon as you copy the formatting to the single control, the copying will be turned off.

Does the order in which I click the other controls matter?
No. The only thing that is important is that you ultimately click all the controls whose formatting you want to change.

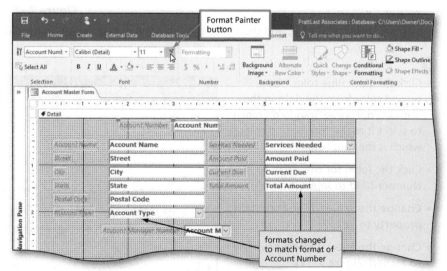

Figure 7–19

❸

- Save your changes to the form.

Advanced Form Techniques   **Access Module 7**   **AC** 373

1 CREATE FORM | 2 ADD COMBO BOXES | 3 COMMAND BUTTONS | 4 MODIFY MACRO
5 MODIFY COMBO BOX | 6 CREATE SECOND FORM | 7 ADD SUBFORM | 8 ADD CHART

Access Module 7

To View the Form

The following steps view the form in Form view and then return to Design view. *Why? As you are working on the design of a form, it is a good idea to periodically view the form in Form view to see the effects of your changes.*

1
- Display the Form Design Tools Design tab.
- Click the View button (Form Design Tools Design tab | Views group) to view the form in Form view (Figure 7–20).

Q&A Why did I have to change from the Format tab to the Design tab?
The Format tab does not have a View button.

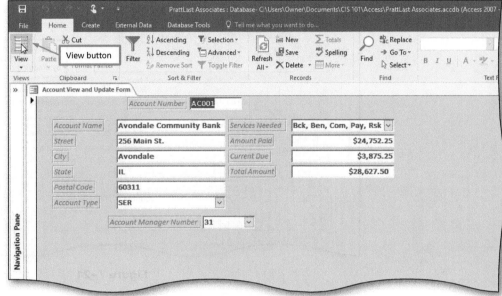

Figure 7–20

2
- Click the View button arrow (Home tab | Views group) to produce the View button menu.
- Click Design View on the View menu to return to Design view.

Q&A Could I simply click the View button?
No. The icon on the View button is the one for Layout view. Clicking the button would show you the form in Layout view, but you are working on the form in Design view.

Other Ways
1. Click Form View button on status bar	2. Click Design View button on status bar

To Add a Title and Expand the Form Header Section

The following steps insert the Form Header and Form Footer sections, and then add a title to the Form Header section. They also expand the Form Header section.

1 Click the Title button (Form Design Tools Design tab | Header/Footer group) to add a Form Header section and to add a control for the title to the Form Header section.

2 Drag the lower boundary of the Form Header section down to the approximate position shown in Figure 7–21.

3 Select the title control, display the Form Design Tools Format tab, and then click the Bold button (Form Design Tools Format tab | Font group) to make the title bold.

4 Drag the right sizing handle to the approximate position shown in the figure to resize the control to the appropriate size for the title.

BTW
Font versus Foreground Color
The font color also is called the foreground color. When you change the font color using the ribbon, you click the Font Color button. If you use the property sheet to change the color, you click the Fore Color property, click the Build button, and then click the desired color.

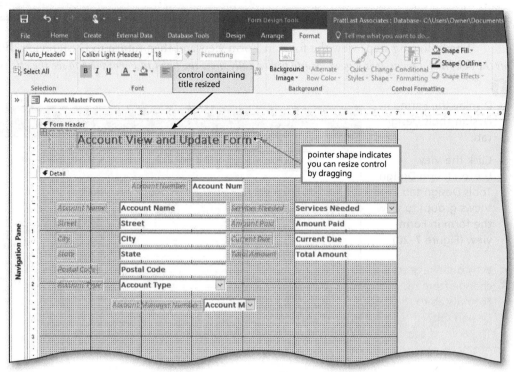

Figure 7–21

To Change the Background Color of the Form Header

BTW
Drop-Down Boxes
Combo boxes also are called drop-down boxes because a list drops down when you click the combo box arrow.

The background color of the form header in the form in Figure 7–1 is the same as the rest of the form. The following steps change the background color of the form header appropriately.

1. Click anywhere in the Form Header section but outside all the controls to select the section.

2. If necessary, display the Form Design Tools Format tab.

3. Click the Background Color button arrow (Form Design Tools Format tab | Font group) to display a color palette.

4. Click the Light Gray 2 color, the first color in the third row under Standard Colors, to change the background color.

5. Save your changes to the form.

Headers and Footers

Just like with reports, you have control over whether your forms contain a form header and footer. They go together, so if you have a form header, you will also have a form footer. If you do not want the sections to appear, you can shrink the size so there is no room for any content. You can also remove the sections from your form altogether. If you later decide you want to include them, you can once again add them. You have similar options with page headers and page footers, although typically page headers and page footers are only used with reports. If you had a very long form that spanned several pages on the screen, you might choose to use page headers and footers, but it is not common to do so.

TO REMOVE A FORM HEADER AND FOOTER

To remove a form header and footer, you would use the following steps.

1. With the form open in Design view, right-click any open area of the form to produce a shortcut menu.
2. Click the Form Header/Footer command on the shortcut menu to remove the form header and footer.
3. If the Microsoft Access dialog box appears, asking if it is acceptable to delete any controls in the section, click the Yes button.

TO REMOVE A PAGE HEADER AND FOOTER

To remove a page header and footer, you would use the following steps.

1. With the form open in Design view, right-click any open area of the form to produce a shortcut menu.
2. Click the Page Header/Footer command on the shortcut menu to remove the page header and footer.
3. If the Microsoft Access dialog box appears, asking if it is acceptable to delete any controls in the section, click the Yes button.

BTW
Hyperlink Controls
You can add a hyperlink to forms. To add a hyperlink, click the Hyperlink tool, enter the hyperlink in the Address text box (Insert Hyperlink dialog box) and click the OK button. If necessary, move the hyperlink control to the desired location on the form.

TO INSERT A FORM HEADER AND FOOTER

To insert a form header and footer, you would use the following steps.

1. With the form open in Design view, right-click any open area of the form to produce a shortcut menu.
2. Click the Form Header/Footer command on the shortcut menu to insert a form header and footer.

TO INSERT A PAGE HEADER AND FOOTER

To insert a page header and footer, you would use the following steps.

1. With the form open in Design view, right-click any open area of the form to produce a shortcut menu.
2. Click the Page Header/Footer command on the shortcut menu to insert a page header and footer.

Images

You can include a picture (image) in a form. You can also use a picture (image) as the background for a form.

TO INCLUDE AN IMAGE IN A FORM

To include an image in a form, you would use the following steps.

1. Open the form in Design view or Layout view.
2. Click the Insert Image button (Form Design Tools Design tab | Controls group) and then click the Browse command.
3. Select the desired image.
4. Click the desired location to add the image to the form.

To Use an Image as Background for a Form

To include an image as background for a form, you would use the following steps.

1. Open the form in Design view or Layout view.
2. Click anywhere in the form, click the Background Image button (Form Design Tools Format tab | Background group), and then click the Browse command.
3. Select the desired image for the background.

Break Point: If you wish to stop working through the module at this point, you can quit Access now. You can resume the project later by running Access, opening the database called PrattLast Associates, opening the Account Master Form in Design view, and continuing to follow the steps from this location forward.

BTW
Record Order
When you use the Next Record button to move through the records, recall that the records are in order by Account Number, which is the primary key, and not alphabetical order.

Command Buttons

Command buttons are buttons placed on a form that users can click to carry out specific actions. To add command buttons, you use the Button tool in the Controls group on the Form Design Tools Design tab. When using the series of Command Button Wizard dialog boxes, you indicate the action that should be taken when the command button is clicked, for example, go to the next record. Within the Command Button Wizard, Access includes several categories of commonly used actions.

CONSIDER THIS

When would you include command buttons in your form?
You can make certain actions more convenient for users by including command buttons. Buttons can carry out record navigation actions (for example, go to the next record), record operation actions (for example, add a record), form operation actions (for example, close a form), report operation actions (for example, print a report), application actions (for example, quit application), and some miscellaneous actions (for example, run a macro).

To Add Command Buttons to a Form

1 CREATE FORM | 2 ADD COMBO BOXES | **3 COMMAND BUTTONS** | **4 MODIFY MACRO**
5 MODIFY COMBO BOX | 6 CREATE SECOND FORM | 7 ADD SUBFORM | 8 ADD CHART

You may find that you can improve the functionality of your form by adding command buttons. *Why? Command buttons enable users to accomplish tasks with a single click.* Before adding the buttons, you should make sure the 'Use Control Wizards' button is selected.

In the Record Navigation action category, you will select the 'Go To Next Record' action for one of the command buttons. From the same category, you will select the 'Go To Previous Record' action for another. Other buttons will use the 'Add New Record' and the Delete Record actions from the Record Operations category. The Close Form button will use the Close Form action from the Form Operations category.

The following steps add command buttons to move to the next record, move to the previous record, add a record, delete a record, and close the form.

1

- Display the Form Design Tools Design tab, click the More button in the control gallery, and then ensure the 'Use Control Wizards' button is selected.

- Click the Button tool (Form Design Tools Design tab | Controls group) and then move the pointer to the approximate position shown in Figure 7–22.

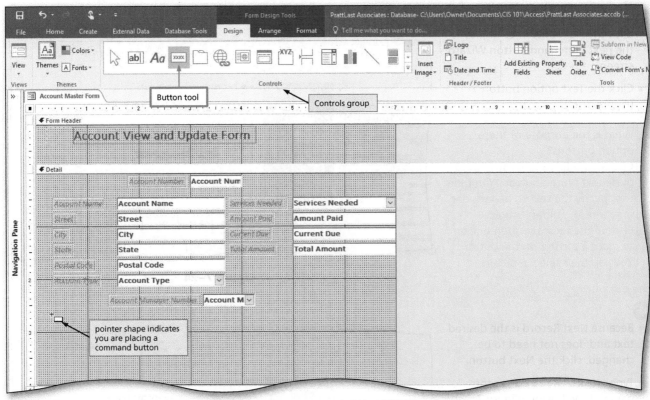

Figure 7–22

2
- Click the position shown in Figure 7–22 to display the Command Button Wizard dialog box.
- With Record Navigation selected in the Categories box, click 'Go To Next Record' in the Actions box (Figure 7–23).

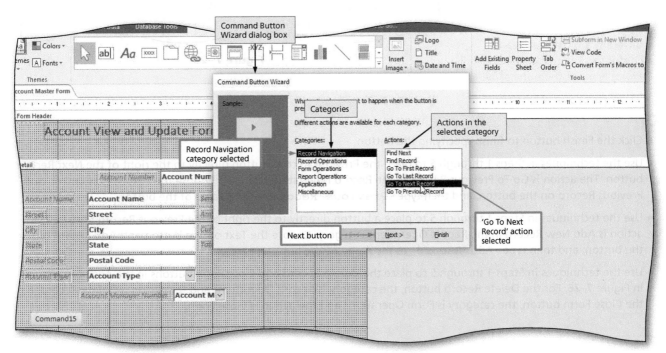

Figure 7–23

3

- Click the Next button to display the next Command Button Wizard screen.

- Click the Text option button (Figure 7–24).

What is the purpose of these option buttons?
Choose the first option button to place text on the button. You then can specify the text to be included or accept the default choice. Choose the second option button to place a picture on the button. You can then select a picture.

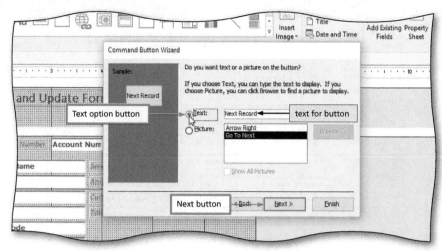

Figure 7–24

4

- Because Next Record is the desired text and does not need to be changed, click the Next button.

- Type **Next Record** as the name of the button (Figure 7–25).

Does the name of the button have to be the same as the text that appears on the face of the button?
No. The text is what will appear on the screen. You use the name when you need to refer to the specific button. They can be different, but this can lead to confusion. Thus, many people will typically make them the same.

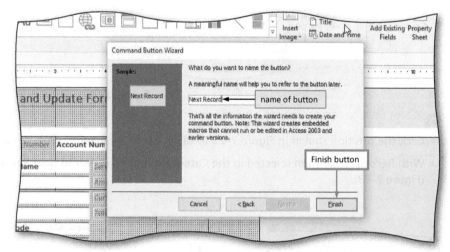

Figure 7–25

5

- Click the Finish button to finish specifying the button.

- Use the techniques in Steps 1 through 5 to place the Previous Record button directly to the right of the Next Record button. The action is Go To Previous Record in the Record Navigation category. Choose the Text option button and Previous Record on the button, and then type **Previous Record** as the name of the button.

- Use the techniques in Steps 1 through 5 to place a button directly to the right of the Previous Record button. The action is Add New Record in the Record Operations category. Choose the Text option button and Add Record on the button, and then type **Add Record** as the name of the button.

- Use the techniques in Steps 1 through 5 to place the Delete Record and Close Form buttons in the positions shown in Figure 7–26. For the Delete Record button, the category is Record Operations and the action is Delete Record. For the Close Form button, the category is Form Operations and the action is Close Form.

Q&A My buttons are not aligned like yours are. What should I do?
If your buttons are not aligned properly, you can drag them to the correct positions. You can also use the buttons in the Sizing & Ordering group on the Form Design Tools Arrange tab.

• Save the changes to the form.

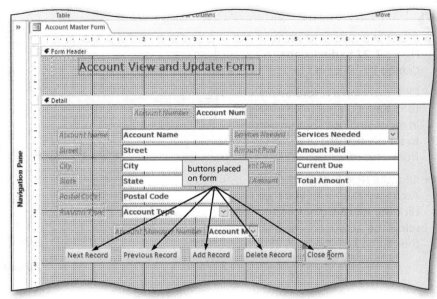

Figure 7–26

To Add a Combo Box for Finding a Record

1 CREATE FORM | 2 ADD COMBO BOXES | 3 COMMAND BUTTONS | 4 MODIFY MACRO
5 MODIFY COMBO BOX | 6 CREATE SECOND FORM | 7 ADD SUBFORM | 8 ADD CHART

Although you can use the Find button (Home tab | Find group) to locate records on a form or a report, it is often more convenient to use a combo box. **Why?** *You can type the account's name directly into the box. Alternatively, you can click the combo box arrow to display a list and then select the desired entry from the list.*

To create a combo box, use the Combo Box tool in the Controls group on the Design tab. The Combo Box Wizard then will guide you through the steps of adding the combo box. The following steps place a combo box for names on the form.

1
• Click the More button (Form Design Tools Design tab | Controls group) to display all the controls.

• With the 'Use Control Wizards' button selected, click the Combo Box tool (Form Design Tools Design tab | Controls group) and then move the pointer, whose shape has changed to a small plus sign with a combo box, to the position shown in Figure 7–27.

Q&A Why is the combo box located in the Form Header section?
Including the combo box in the Form Header section rather than in the Detail section indicates that the contents of the combo box are not changed or updated by the user.

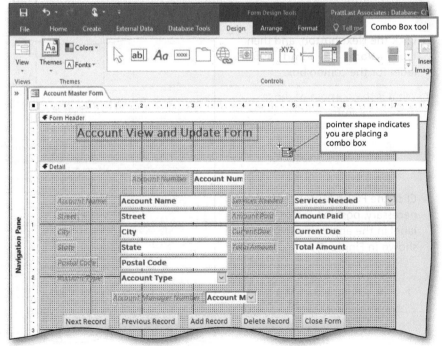

Figure 7–27

- Click the position shown in Figure 7–27 to display the Combo Box Wizard.

- Click the 'Find a record on my form based on the value I selected in my combo box.' option button to specify that the user will select from a list of values.

- Click the Next button, click the Account Name field, and then click the Add Field button to select the Account Name field for the combo box (Figure 7–28).

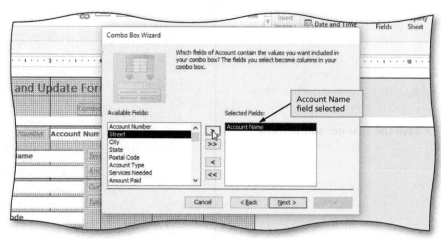

Figure 7–28

- Click the Next button.

- Drag the right boundary of the column heading to the approximate size shown in Figure 7–29.

Q&A Can I also resize the column to best fit the data by double-clicking the right boundary of the column heading?
Yes.

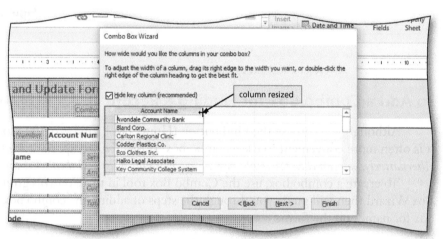

Figure 7–29

- Click the Next button, and then type **&Name to Find** as the label for the combo box.

Q&A What is the purpose of the ampersand in front of the letter, N?
The ampersand (&) in front of the letter, N, indicates that users can select the combo box by pressing ALT+N.

- Click the Finish button, and, if necessary, position the control and label in the approximate position shown in Figure 7–30.

Q&A Why is the letter, N, underlined?
The underlined letter, N, in the word, Name, indicates that you can press ALT+N to select the combo box. It is underlined because you preceded the letter, N, with the ampersand.

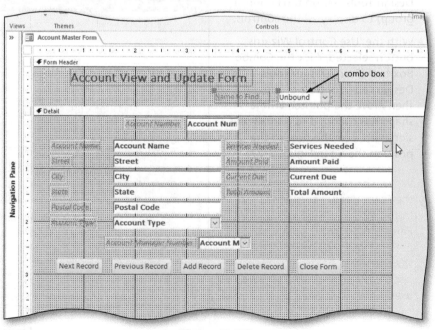

Figure 7–30

When would you include a combo box in your form?

A combo box is a combination of a text box, where users can type data, and a list box, where users can click an arrow to display a list. Would a combo box improve the functionality of the form? Is there a place where it would be convenient for users to enter data by selecting the data from a list, either a list of predefined items or a list of values from a related table? If users need to search for records, including a combo box can assist in the process.

1 CREATE FORM | 2 ADD COMBO BOXES | 3 COMMAND BUTTONS | 4 MODIFY MACRO
5 MODIFY COMBO BOX | 6 CREATE SECOND FORM | 7 ADD SUBFORM | 8 ADD CHART

To Place a Rectangle

The following steps use the Rectangle tool to place a rectangle. *Why? To emphasize an area of a form, you can place a rectangle around it as a visual cue.*

1
- Click the More button (Form Design Tools Design tab | Controls group) to display all the controls (Figure 7–31).

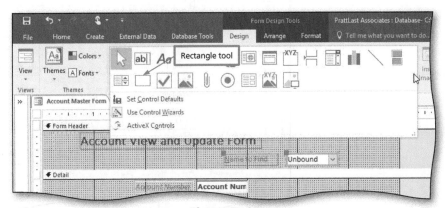

Figure 7–31

2
- Click the Rectangle tool, which is the second tool in the second row, point to the position for the upper-left corner of the rectangle shown in Figure 7–32, and drag to the lower-right corner of the rectangle to place the rectangle.

3
- Click the Property Sheet button (Form Design Tools Design tab | Tools group) to display the property sheet for the rectangle.

- If necessary, change the value of the Special Effect property to Etched.

- Make sure the value of the Back Style property is Transparent, so the combo box will appear within the rectangle.

Q&A What if the value is not Transparent?
If the value is not Transparent, the rectangle would cover the combo box completely and the combo box would not be visible.

- Close the property sheet.

- Save and then close the form.

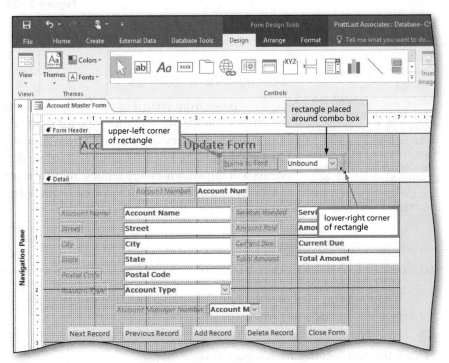

Figure 7–32

BTW
VBA
Visual Basic for Applications (VBA) is a programming language that can be used with Access. As with other programming languages, programs in VBA consist of code; that is, a collection of statements, also called commands, which are instructions that will cause actions to take place when the program executes. VBA is included with all Microsoft Office apps.

To Open the Account View and Update Form

Once you have created the form, you can use it at any time by opening it. The following steps open the Account View and Update Form.

1 Open the Navigation Pane, and then right-click the Account Master Form to display the shortcut menu.

2 Click Open on the shortcut menu to open the form.

3 Close the Navigation Pane (Figure 7–33).

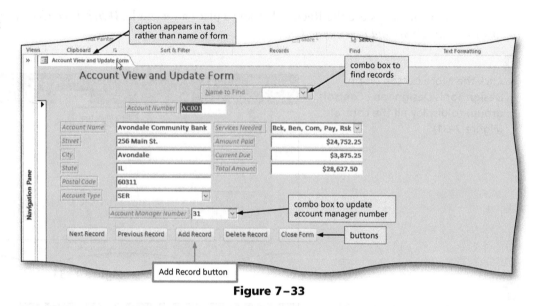

Figure 7–33

BTW
Converting Macros to VBA Code
You can convert macros that are attached to forms to VBA (Visual Basic for Applications) code. To do so, open the form in Design view and click the 'Convert Form's Macros to Visual Basic' button. You also can convert macros that are attached to reports.

Using the Buttons

To move from record to record on the form, you can use the buttons to perform the actions you specify. To move forward to the next record, click the Next Record button. Click the Previous Record button to move back to the previous record. Clicking the Delete Record button will delete the record currently on the screen. Access will display a message requesting that you verify the deletion before the record is actually deleted. Clicking the Close Form button will remove the form from the screen.

To Test the Add Record Button

1 CREATE FORM | 2 ADD COMBO BOXES | 3 COMMAND BUTTONS | 4 MODIFY MACRO
5 MODIFY COMBO BOX | 6 CREATE SECOND FORM | 7 ADD SUBFORM | 8 ADD CHART

The following step uses the Add Record button. **Why?** *Clicking the Add Record button will clear the contents of the form so you can add a new record.*

1

• Click the Add Record button (Figure 7–34).

 There is no insertion point in the Account Number field. How would I begin entering a new record?
To begin entering a record, you would have to click the Account Number field before you can start typing.

Why does SER appear in the Account Type field?
The value SER is the default value assigned to the Account Type field.

Experiment

- Try each of the other buttons to see their effects. Do not delete any records. After clicking the Close Form button, open the form once again and close the Navigation Pane.

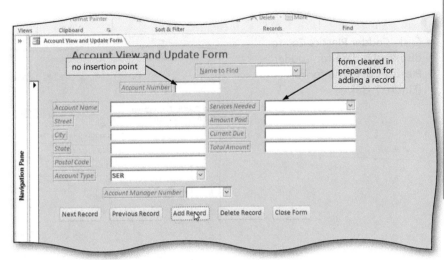

Figure 7–34

To Use the Combo Box

Using the combo box, you can search for an account in two ways. First, you can click the combo box arrow to display a list of account names, and then select the name from the list by clicking it. It is also easy to search by typing the name. **Why?** *As you type, Access will automatically display the name that begins with the letters you have typed. Once the correct name is displayed, you can select the name by pressing the TAB key.* Regardless of the method you use, the data for the selected account appears on the form once the selection is made.

The following steps first locate the account whose name is Codder Plastics Co., and then use the Next Record button to move to the next account.

1

- Click the 'Name to Find' arrow to display a list of account names (Figure 7–35).

Q&A Why does the list not appear in alphabetical order? It would be more useful and easier to use if it were alphabetized.
You will change the combo box later so that the names appear in alphabetical order.

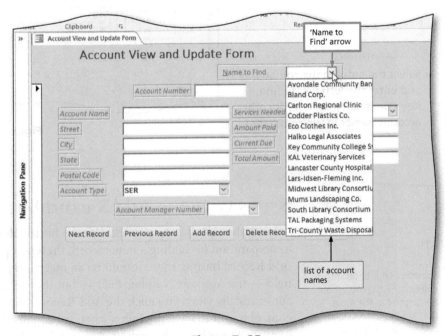

Figure 7–35

2

- Click 'Codder Plastics Co.' to display the data for Codder Plastics Co. in the form (Figure 7–36).

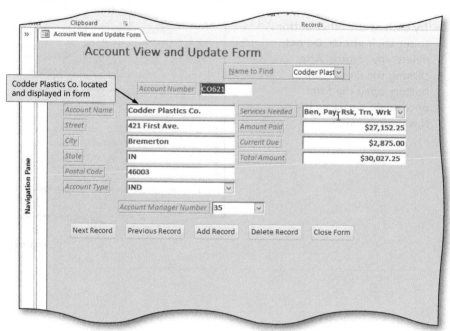

Figure 7–36

3

- Click the Next Record button to display the next record (Figure 7–37).

Q&A Why does the combo box still contain Codder Plastics Co., rather than Eco Clothes Inc.?
This is a problem with the combo box. You will address this issue later.

Experiment

- Select the entry in the combo box and enter the letter, k, to find Key Community College. Try other account names in the combo box.

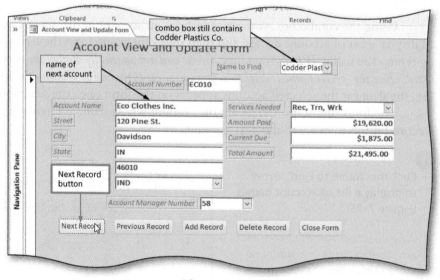

Figure 7–37

Issues with the Add Record Button

BTW
Focus
Sometimes it is difficult to determine which object on the screen has the focus. If a field has the focus, an insertion point appears in the field. If a button has the focus, a small rectangle appears inside the button.

Although clicking the Add Record button does erase the contents of the form in preparation for adding a new record, there is a problem with it. After clicking the Add Record button, there should be an insertion point in the control for the first field — the Account Number field — but there is not. To display an insertion point automatically when you click the Add Record button, you need to change the focus. A control is said to have the **focus** when it becomes active; that is, when it becomes able to receive user input through mouse, touch, or keyboard actions. At any point in time, only one item on the form has the focus. In addition to adding a new record, clicking the Add Record button needs to update the focus to the Account Number field.

Issues with the Combo Box

The combo box has the following issues. First, if you examine the list of names in Figure 7–35, you will see that they are not in alphabetical order (for example, Key Community College comes before KAL Veterinary Services). Second, when you move to a record without using the combo box, such as when navigating using the buttons, the name in the combo box does not change to reflect the name of the account currently on the screen. Third, you should not be able to use the TAB key to change the focus to the combo box, because that does not represent a field to be updated.

Macros

To correct the problem with the Add Record button not displaying an insertion point, you will update a **macro**, which is a series of actions that Access performs when a particular event occurs, in this case when the Add Record button is clicked. (In the next module, you will create macros on your own. In this case, Access has already created the macro; you just need to add a single action to it.)

Specifically, you need to add an action to the macro that will move the focus to the control for the Account Number field. The appropriate action is GoToControl. Like many actions, the GoToControl action requires additional information, called arguments. The argument for the GoToControl action is the name of the control, in this case, the Account Number control.

BTW
Events
Events are actions that have happened or are happening at the present time. An event can result from a user action. For example, one of the events associated with a button on a form is clicking the button. The corresponding event property is On Click. If you associate VBA code or a macro with the On Click event property, the code or macro will execute any time you click the button. Using properties associated with events, you can tell Access to run a macro, call a Visual Basic function, or run an event procedure in response to an event.

To Modify the Macro for the Add Record Button

1 CREATE FORM | 2 ADD COMBO BOXES | 3 COMMAND BUTTONS | 4 MODIFY MACRO
5 MODIFY COMBO BOX | 6 CREATE SECOND FORM | 7 ADD SUBFORM | 8 ADD CHART

The following steps first change the name of the control to remove spaces (a requirement in VBA, which you will use later), and then modify the macro that is associated with the Add Record button. *Why? Modifying the macro lets you add an action that changes the focus to the Account Number field.* You can use different methods of changing control names so that they do not contain spaces. One approach is to simply remove the space. This approach would change Account Number to AccountNumber, for example. The approach you will use is to insert an underscore (_) in place of the space. For example, you will change Account Number to Account_Number.

After changing the name of the control, you will complete an action that changes the focus to the control for the Account Number field.

1
- Click the View button arrow and then click Design View to return to Design view.
- Click the control for the Account Number field (the white space, not the label), and then click the Property Sheet button (Form Design Tools Design tab | Tools group) to display the property sheet.
- If necessary, click the All tab. Ensure the Name property is selected, click immediately following the word, Account, press the DELETE key to delete the space, and then type an underscore (_) to change the name to Account _Number (Figure 7–38).

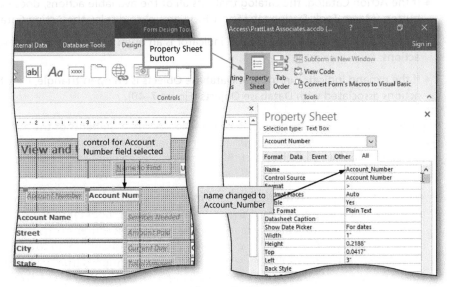

Figure 7–38

Q&A Could I just erase the old name and type Account_Number?
Yes. Use whichever method you find most convenient.

- Close the property sheet and then right-click the Add Record button to display a shortcut menu (Figure 7–39).

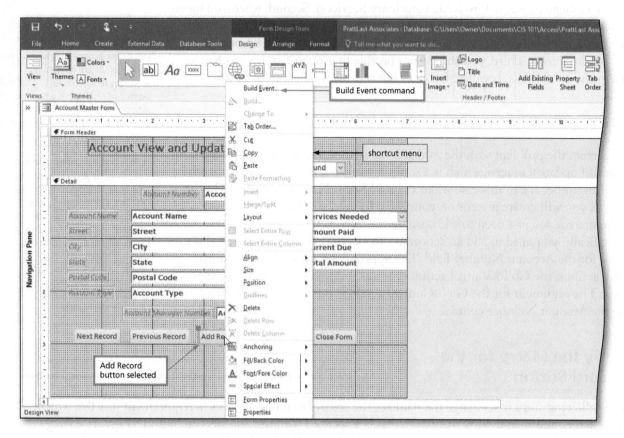

Figure 7–39

❷
- Click Build Event on the shortcut menu to display the macro associated with the On Click event that Access created automatically.

- If the Action Catalog, the catalog that lists all of the available actions, does not appear, click the Action Catalog button (Macro Tools Design tab | Show/Hide group) to display the Action Catalog.

- In the Action Catalog, if the expand indicator is an open triangle in front of Actions, click the triangle to display all actions.

- If the expand indicator in front of Database Objects is an open triangle, click the expand indicator to display all actions associated with Database Objects (Figure 7–40).

Q&A How can I recognize actions? How can I recognize the arguments of the actions?
The actions are in bold. The arguments for the action follow the action and are not bold. The value for an argument appears to the right of the argument. The value for the 'Go to' argument of the OnError action is Next, for example.

What is the purpose of the actions currently in the macro?
The first action indicates that, if there is an error, Access should proceed to the next action in the macro rather than immediately stopping the macro. The second action causes Access to go to the record indicated by the values in the arguments. The value, New, indicates that Access should to go to a new record. Because the final action has a condition, the action will be executed only if the condition is true, that is, the error code contains a value other than 0. In that case, the MsgBox action will display a description of the error.

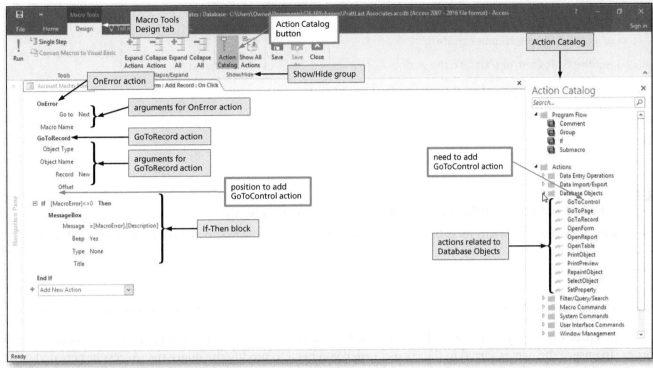

Figure 7–40

3

- Drag the GoToControl action from the Action Catalog to the position shown in Figure 7–40.

- Type **Account_Number** as the Control Name argument (Figure 7–41).

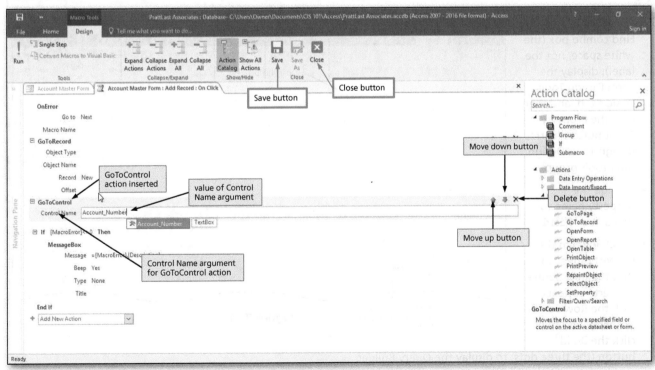

Figure 7–41

Q&A

What is the effect of the GoToControl action?

When Access executes this action, the focus will move to the control indicated in the Control Name argument, in this case, the Account_Number control.

I added the GoToControl action to the wrong place in the macro. How do I move it?

To move it up in the list, click the Move up button. To move it down, click the Move down button.

I added the wrong action. What should I do?

Click the Delete button to delete the action you added, and then add the GoToControl action. If you decide you would rather start over instead, click the Close button (Macro Tools Design tab | Close group) and then click the No button when asked if you want to save your changes. You can then begin again from Step 2.

4

- Click the Save button (Macro Tools Design tab | Close group) to save your changes.

- Click the Close button (Macro Tools Design tab | Close group) to close the macro and return to the form design.

To Modify the Combo Box

1 CREATE FORM | 2 ADD COMBO BOXES | 3 COMMAND BUTTONS | 4 MODIFY MACRO
5 MODIFY COMBO BOX | 6 CREATE SECOND FORM | 7 ADD SUBFORM | 8 ADD CHART

In a previous step, you discovered that the combo box does not display account names in alphabetical order. To ensure the data is sorted in the correct order, you need to modify the query that Access has created for the combo box so the data is sorted by account name. Also, the combo box does not update the name in the combo box to reflect the name of accounts currently on the screen, which will require you to modify the VBA (Visual Basic for Applications) code associated with what is termed the On Current event property of the entire form. ***Why?*** *The modification to the On Current event property will ensure that the combo box remains current with the rest of the form; that is, it contains the name of the account whose number currently appears in the Account Number field.* The following steps modify the query and then the code associated with the On Current event property appropriately. The final step changes the Tab Stop property for the combo box from Yes to No.

1

- Click the Name to Find combo box (the white space, not the label), display the Form Design Tools Design tab, and then click the Property Sheet button (Form Design Tools Design tab | Tools group).

- Change the property name to **Name_to_Find**.

- Scroll down in the property sheet so that the Row Source property appears, click the Row Source property, and then click the Build button (the three dots) to display the Query Builder.

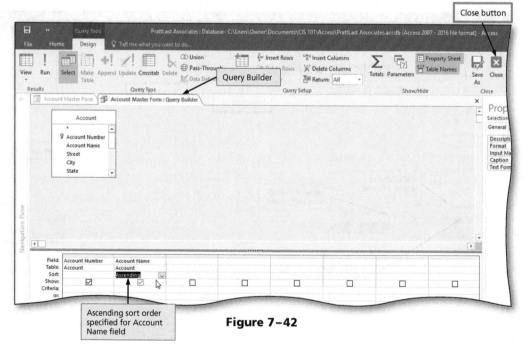

Figure 7–42

- Click the Sort row in the Account Name field, click the arrow that appears, and then click Ascending to change the order and display account names in alphabetical order in the combo box (Figure 7–42).

2

- Click the Save button on the Quick Access Toolbar to save your changes.
- Close the Query Builder window by clicking the Close button on the Design tab.
- Click the form selector (the box in the upper-left corner of the form) to select the form.
- Click the Property Sheet button (Form Design Tools Design tab | Tools group), scroll down until the On Current property appears, and then click the On Current property.

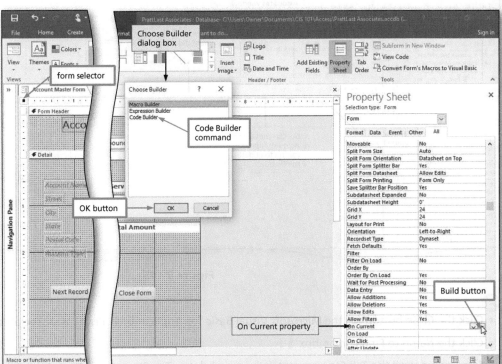

- Click the Build button (the three dots) to display the Choose Builder dialog box (Figure 7–43).

Figure 7–43

3

- Click Code Builder in the Choose Builder dialog box, and then click the OK button to display the VBA code generated for the form's On Current event property (Figure 7–44).

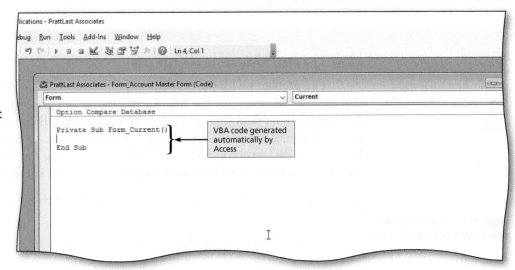

Figure 7–44

4

- Press the TAB key and then type **Name_to_Find = Account_Number ' Update the combo box** as shown in Figure 7–45, to create the command and a comment that describes the effect of the command.

Q&A How would I construct a command like this in my own form?

Begin with the name you assigned to the combo box, followed by an equal sign, and then the name of the control containing the primary key of the table. The portion of the statement following the single quotation mark is a comment describing the purpose of the command. You could simply type the same thing that you see in this command.

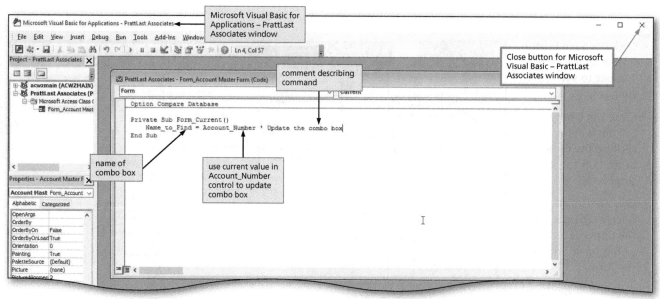

Figure 7–45

- Click the Close button for the Microsoft Visual Basic for Applications - PrattLast Associates window.

- Click the Name to Find combo box.

- Scroll down until the Tab Stop property appears, click the Tab Stop property, and then click the Tab Stop property box arrow.

- Click No to change the value of the Tab Stop property, which skips over the combo box in the tab sequence, and then close the property sheet.

- Save your changes and then close the form.

BTW
Comments in Macros
You can use the Comment action in the Action Catalog to place comments in macros.

Using the Modified Form

The problems with the Add Record button and the combo box are now corrected. When you click the Add Record button, an insertion point appears in the Account Number field (Figure 7–46a). When you click the 'Name to Find' box arrow, the list of names is in alphabetical order (Figure 7–46b). After using the 'Name to Find' box to find an account (Figure 7–46c) and clicking the Next Record button, the 'Name to Find' box is updated with the correct account name (Figure 7–46d).

Figure 7–46 (a) Using the Add Record button

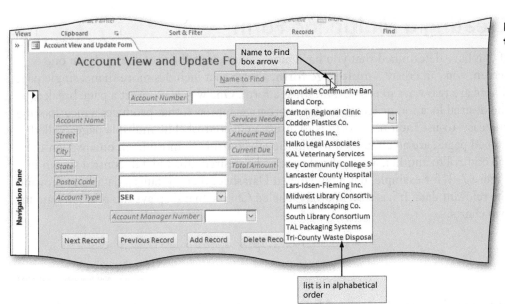

Figure 7–46 (b) Using the Name to Find box

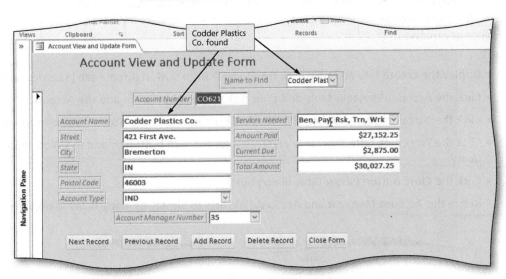

Figure 7–46 (c) Results of using the Name to Find box

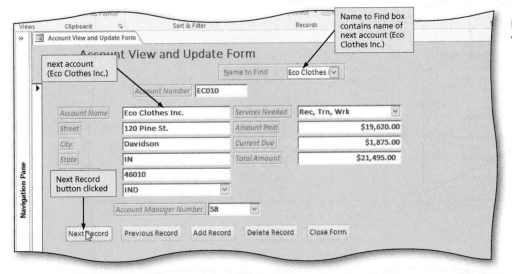

Figure 7–46 (d) Using the Next Record button

Break Point: If you wish to stop working through the module at this point, you can quit Access now. You can resume the project later by running Access, opening the database called PrattLast Associates, and continuing to follow the steps from this location forward.

BTW
Tab Controls
By default, Access places two tabbed pages in a tab control. To add additional tabbed pages, right-click any tab control and click Insert Pages on the shortcut menu.

Creating a Multipage Form

If you have determined that you have more data than will fit conveniently on one screen, you can create a **multipage form**, a form that includes more than a single page. There are two ways to create a multipage form. One way is to insert a page break at the desired location or locations. An alternative approach that produces a nice-looking and easy-to-use multipage form is to insert a tab control. The multiple pages, called tabbed pages, are all contained within the tab control. To move from one page in the tab control to another, a user simply clicks the desired tab. The tab control shown in Figure 7–2, for example, has a tab labeled Datasheet that contains a datasheet showing the relevant data. It has a second tab, labeled Charts, that displays the relevant data in two charts.

To Create a Query

1 CREATE FORM | 2 ADD COMBO BOXES | 3 COMMAND BUTTONS | 4 MODIFY MACRO
5 MODIFY COMBO BOX | 6 CREATE SECOND FORM | 7 ADD SUBFORM | 8 ADD CHART

Why? *The second form contains data from the Account Manager, Account, and Workshop Offerings tables. The simplest way to incorporate this data is to create a query that joins all three tables.* The following steps create the necessary query.

1
- Display the Create tab, and then click the Query Design button (Create tab | Queries group) to create a query.
- Click the Account Manager table and then click the Add button to add the Account Manager table to the query.
- Click the Account table and then click the Add button to add the Account table to the query.
- Click the Workshop Offerings table and then click the Add button to add the Workshop Offerings table to the query.
- Click the Close button (Show Table dialog box).
- Resize the Account Manager and Account field lists to display as many fields as possible (Figure 7–47).

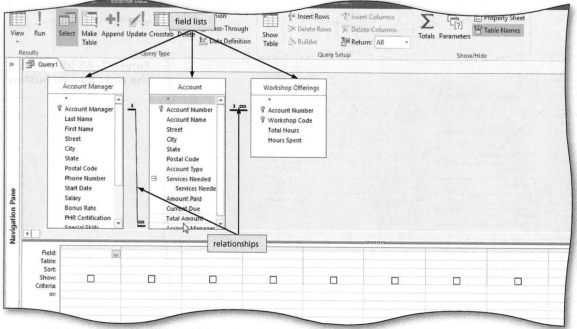

Figure 7–47

2

- Double-click the Account Manager Number field from the Account Manager table and the Account Number field from the Account table.

- Double-click the Workshop Code and Hours Spent fields from the Workshop Offerings table.

- Right-click the Field row in the first open column of the design grid to produce a shortcut menu.

- Click Zoom on the shortcut menu to display the Zoom dialog box and then type **Hours Remaining:[Total Hours]- [Hours Spent]** in the Zoom dialog box to enter the expression for the field (Figure 7–48).

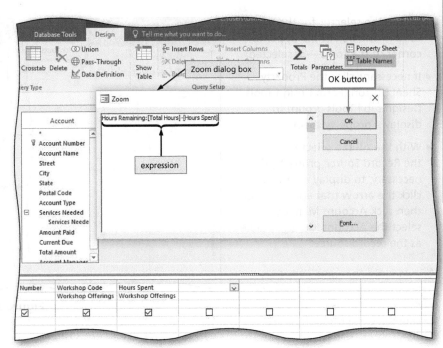

Figure 7–48

3

- Click the OK button and then view the results to ensure they are correct. The order of your records may differ.

- Click the Save button on the Quick Access Toolbar and type **Managers and Workshop Offerings** as <u>the</u> name of the query (Figure 7–49).

4

- Click the OK button to save the query.

- Close the query.

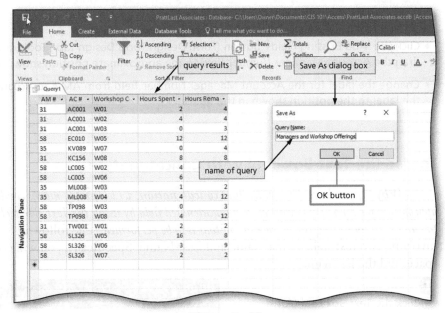

Figure 7–49

To Create a Second Form in Design View

1 CREATE FORM | 2 ADD COMBO BOXES | 3 COMMAND BUTTONS | 4 MODIFY MACRO
5 MODIFY COMBO BOX | 6 CREATE SECOND FORM | 7 ADD SUBFORM | 8 ADD CHART

Why? *The second form will contain the tab control including two tabs: one that displays a datasheet and another that displays two charts.* The following step begins the process by creating a form for the Account Manager table in Design view.

1

- If necessary, close the Navigation Pane.

- Display the Create tab.

- Click the Form Design button (Create tab | Forms group) to create a new form in Design view.

- Ensure the selector for the entire form — the box in the upper-left corner of the form — is selected.

- If necessary, click the Property Sheet button (Form Design Tools Design tab | Tools group) to display a property sheet.

- With the All tab selected, click the Record Source property, if necessary, to display an arrow, click the arrow that appears, and then click Account Manager to select the Account Manager table as the record source.

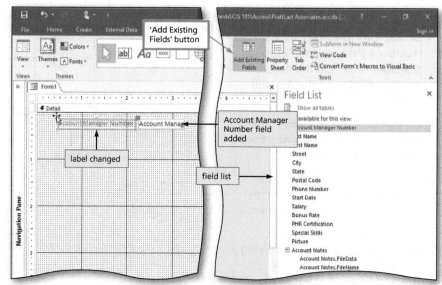

Figure 7–50

Q&A I see more than one choice that begins with the same letters as Account Manager. How do I know I am selecting the right one?

There are two ways to find out if you are selecting the right choice. You could click one of them to produce an insertion point and then repeatedly press or hold down the RIGHT ARROW key to see the remainder of the name. If it is not the correct one, select another. The other way is to expand the width of the property sheet so that more of the property name is visible. You do so by dragging the left border further to the left.

- Close the property sheet.

- Click the 'Add Existing Fields' button (Form Design Tools Design tab | Tools group) to display a field list and then drag the Account Manager Number field to the approximate position shown in Figure 7–50.

- Change the label for the Account Manager Number field from AM # to Account Manager Number. Resize and move the label to the position shown in the figure.

To Use the Text Box Tool with Concatenation

1 CREATE FORM | 2 ADD COMBO BOXES | 3 COMMAND BUTTONS | 4 MODIFY MACRO
5 MODIFY COMBO BOX | 6 CREATE SECOND FORM | **7 ADD SUBFORM** | 8 ADD CHART

Why? *If you have determined that* **concatenation,** *which simply means combining objects together in a series, is appropriate for a form, you can create a concatenated field by using the Text Box tool in the Controls group on the Design tab and then indicating the concatenation that is to be performed.* The following steps add a concatenated field, involving two text fields, First Name and Last Name. Specifically, you will concatenate the first name, a single space, and the last name.

1

- Click the Text Box tool (Form Design Tools Design tab | Controls group) and then move the pointer, whose shape has changed to a small plus symbol accompanied by a text box, to the position shown in Figure 7–51.

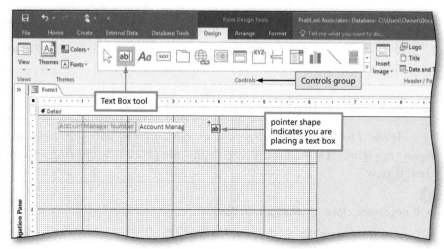

Figure 7–51

- Click the position shown in Figure 7–51 to place a text box on the report.
- Click in the text box to produce an insertion point.
- Type `=[First Name]&' '&[Last Name]` as the entry in the text box.
- Click the attached label to select it (Figure 7–52).

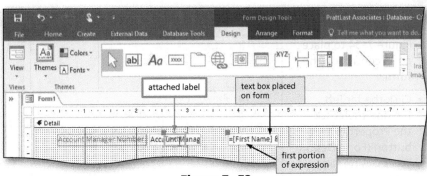

Figure 7–52

- Press the DELETE key to delete the attached label.
- Resize the Account Manager Number control to the approximate size shown in Figure 7–53.
- Click the text box to select it, drag it to the position shown in Figure 7–53, and then drag the right sizing handle to the approximate position shown in the figure.

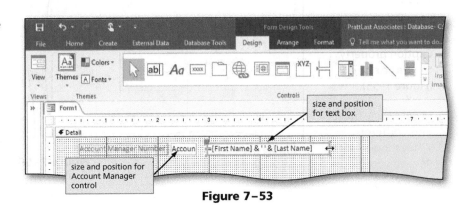

Figure 7–53

- Close the field list by clicking the 'Add Existing Fields' button (Form Design Tools Design tab | Tools group).
- Save the form using the name, Manager Workshop Data.

To Use Tab Controls to Create a Multipage Form

1 CREATE FORM | 2 ADD COMBO BOXES | 3 COMMAND BUTTONS | 4 MODIFY MACRO

5 MODIFY COMBO BOX | 6 CREATE SECOND FORM | 7 ADD SUBFORM | 8 ADD CHART

Why? *To use tabs on a form, you need to insert a tab control.* The following steps insert a tab control with two tabs: Datasheet and Charts. Users will be able to click the Datasheet tab in the completed form to view workshop offerings in Datasheet view. Clicking the Charts tab will display two charts representing the same workshop data as in the Datasheet tab.

- Click the Tab Control tool (Form Design Tools Design Tab | Controls group) and move the pointer to the approximate location shown in Figure 7–54.

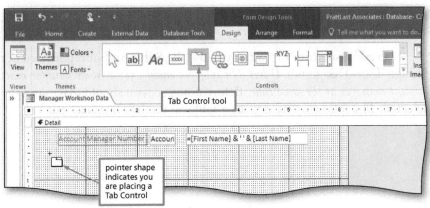

Figure 7–54

2

- Click the position shown in Figure 7–54 to place a tab control on the form.

- Click the far left tab and then click the Property Sheet button (Form Design Tools Design tab | Tools group) to display a property sheet.

- Change the value for the Caption property to **Datasheet** (Figure 7–55).

My property sheet looks different. What should I do?
Be sure you clicked the far left tab before displaying the property sheet. The highlight should be within the border of the tab, as shown in the figure.

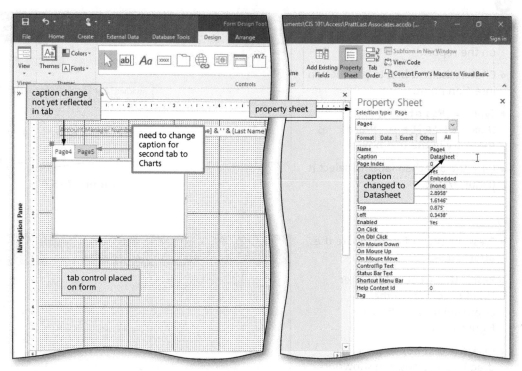

Figure 7–55

3

- Click the second tab without closing the property sheet.

- Change the value for the Caption property to **Charts**.

- Close the property sheet.

When would you include a tab control in your form?
If the form contains more information than will conveniently fit on the screen at a time, consider adding a tab control. With a tab control, you can organize the information within a collection of tabbed pages. To access any of the tabbed pages, users need only click the corresponding tab.

CONSIDER THIS

---

1 CREATE FORM | 2 ADD COMBO BOXES | 3 COMMAND BUTTONS | 4 MODIFY MACRO
5 MODIFY COMBO BOX | 6 CREATE SECOND FORM | 7 ADD SUBFORM | 8 ADD CHART

To Add a Subform

To add a subform to a form, you use the Subform/Subreport tool in the Controls group on the Form Design Tools Design tab. *Why? The subform enables you to show data for multiple workshop offerings for a given account manager at the same time.* Before doing so, you should make sure the 'Use Control Wizards' button is selected. The following steps place a subform on the Datasheet tab.

1

- Click the Datasheet tab.

- Resize the tab control to the approximate size shown in Figure 7–56 by dragging the appropriate sizing handles.

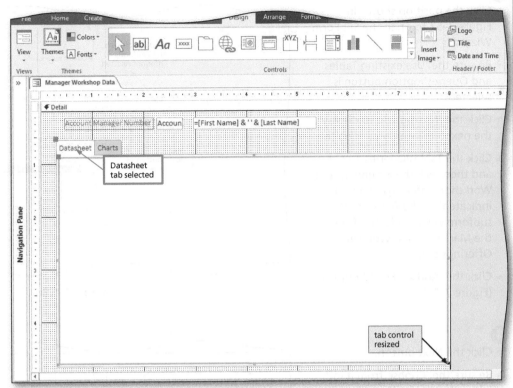

Figure 7–56

2

- Click the More button (Form Design Tools Design tab | Controls group).

- With the 'Use Control Wizards' button selected, click the Subform /Subreport tool (Form Design Tools Design tab | Controls group) and then move the pointer to the approximate position shown in Figure 7–57.

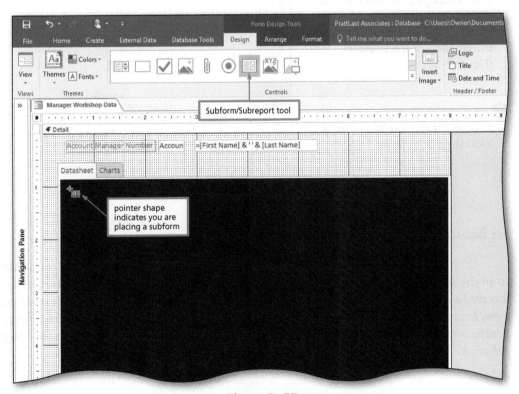

Figure 7–57

3

- Click the position shown in Figure 7–57 to open the SubForm Wizard.

- Be sure the 'Use existing Tables and Queries' option button is selected.

- Click the Next button to display the next SubForm Wizard screen.

- Click the Tables/Queries arrow and then click the Managers and Workshop Offerings query to indicate that the fields for the subform will be selected from the Managers and Workshop Offerings query.

- Click the 'Add All Fields' button (Figure 7–58).

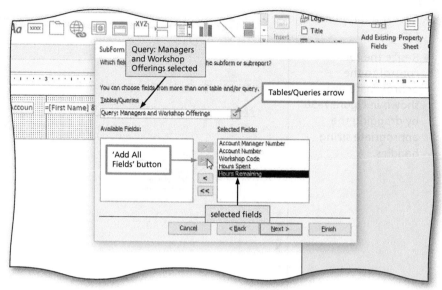

Figure 7–58

4

- Click the Next button.

- Be sure the 'Choose from a list' option button is selected.

- Click the Next button.

- Type **Workshop Offerings for Manager** as the name of the subform and then click the Finish button to complete the creation of the subform (Figure 7–59).

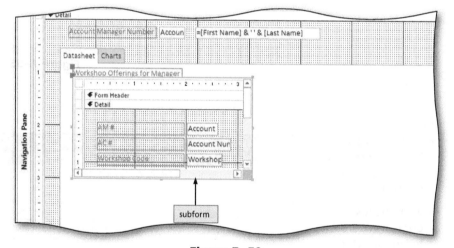

Figure 7–59

5

- Save and then close the Manager Workshop Data form.

To Modify a Subform

1 CREATE FORM | 2 ADD COMBO BOXES | 3 COMMAND BUTTONS | 4 MODIFY MACRO
5 MODIFY COMBO BOX | 6 CREATE SECOND FORM | 7 ADD SUBFORM | 8 ADD CHART

The next task is to modify the subform. The first step is to remove the Account Manager Number field from the subform. *Why? The Account Manager Number field needed to be included initially in the subform because it is the field that is used to link the data in the subform to the data in the main form. It is not supposed to appear in the form, however.* In addition, the remaining columns need to be resized to appropriate sizes. The following step first removes the Account Manager Number field. You then switch to Datasheet view to resize the remaining columns.

- Open the Navigation Pane, right-click the Workshop Offerings for Manager form, and then click Design View on the shortcut menu.

- Click the Account Manager Number control, and then press the DELETE key to delete the control.

- Change the label for the Account Number control from AC # to Account Number.

- Save the subform and close it.

- Right-click the subform in the Navigation Pane and click Open on the shortcut menu.

- Resize each column to best fit the data by double-clicking the right boundary of the column's field selector (Figure 7–60).

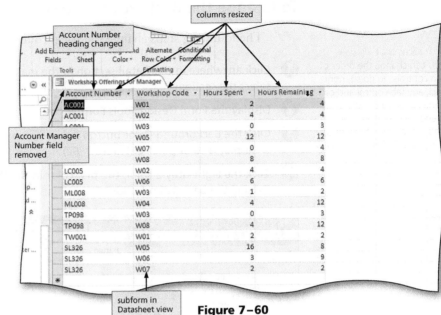

Figure 7–60

②
- Save the subform and then close it.

To Resize the Subform

1 CREATE FORM | 2 ADD COMBO BOXES | 3 COMMAND BUTTONS | 4 MODIFY MACRO
5 MODIFY COMBO BOX | 6 CREATE SECOND FORM | 7 ADD SUBFORM | 8 ADD CHART

The following step resizes the subform. **Why?** *The size should match the size shown in Figure 7–2a.*

①
- If necessary, open the Navigation Pane, right-click the Manager Workshop Data form and then click Design View on the shortcut menu.

- Close the Navigation Pane.

- Resize the subform to the size shown in Figure 7–61 by dragging the right sizing handle.

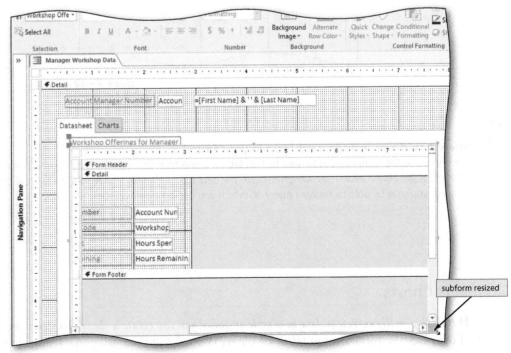

Figure 7–61

To Change the Background Color

The following steps change the background color of the form to a light gray.

1. Click anywhere in the Detail section in the main form but outside all the controls to select the section.

2. Display the Form Design Tools Format tab.

3. Click the Background Color button arrow (Form Design Tools Format tab | Font group) to display a color palette (Figure 7–62).

4. Click the Light Gray 2 color, the first color in the third row under Standard Colors, to change the background color.

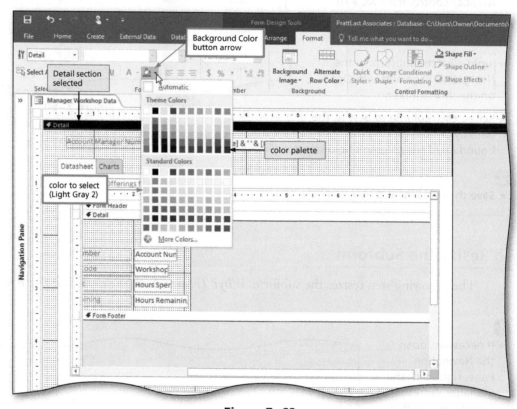

Figure 7–62

CONSIDER THIS

When would you include a subform in your form?
If the fields for the form come from exactly two tables, a one-to-many relationship exists between the two tables, and the form is based on the "one" table, you will often place the data for the "many" table in a subform. If there are more than two tables involved, you may be able to create a query on which you can base the subform.

To Insert Charts

1 CREATE FORM | 2 ADD COMBO BOXES | 3 COMMAND BUTTONS | 4 MODIFY MACRO
5 MODIFY COMBO BOX | 6 CREATE SECOND FORM | 7 ADD SUBFORM | **8 ADD CHART**

Why? *To visually represent data in a table or query, you can create a chart.* To insert a chart, use the Chart tool on the Form Design Tools Design tab. The Chart Wizard will then ask you to indicate the fields to be included on the chart and the type of chart you want to insert. The following steps insert a chart that visually represents the amount of time managers have spent in their various workshops.

1

- Display the Form Design Tools Design tab.
- Click the Charts tab on the tab control.
- Click the More button (Form Design Tools Design tab | Controls group).
- Click the Chart tool.
- Move the pointer to the approximate position shown in Figure 7–63.

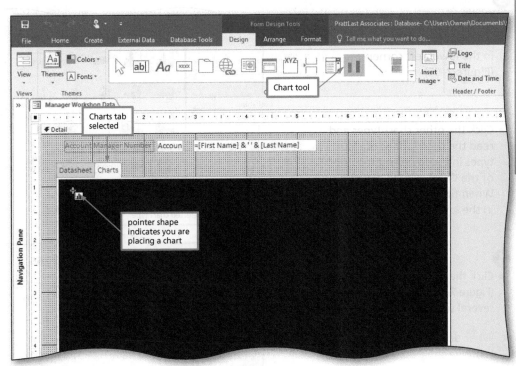

Figure 7–63

2

- Click the position shown in Figure 7–63 to display the Chart Wizard dialog box.
- Click the Queries option button in the Chart Wizard dialog box to indicate that the data will come from a query, scroll down so that the Managers and Workshop Offerings query appears, and then click the Managers and Workshop Offerings query to indicate the specific query containing the desired fields.
- Click the Next button.
- Select the Workshop Code and Hours Spent fields by clicking them and then clicking the Add Field button (Figure 7–64).

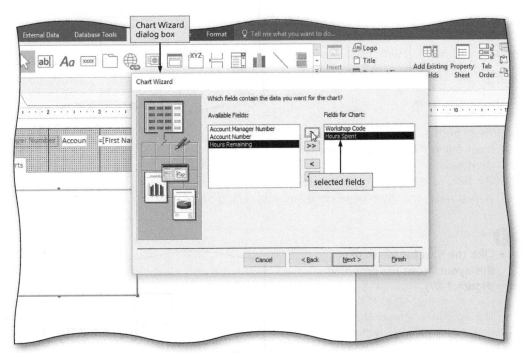

Figure 7–64

- Click the Next button.
- Click the Pie Chart, the chart in the lower-left corner (Figure 7–65).

 Experiment

- Click the other chart types and read the descriptions of chart types in the lower-right corner of the Chart Wizard dialog box. When finished, click the Pie Chart in the lower-left corner.

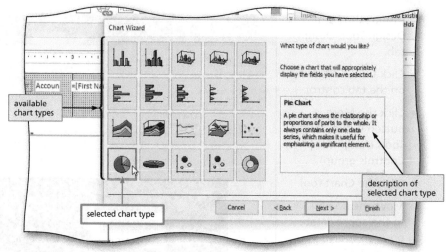

Figure 7–65

- Click the Next button to create the chart (Figure 7–66). Your screen might take several seconds to refresh.

Q&A What do these positions represent? Can I change them?

The field under the chart represents the data that will be summarized by slices of the pie. The other field is used to indicate the series. In this example, the field for the series is the workshop code, and the sizes of the slices of the pie will represent the sum of the number of hours spent. You can change these by dragging the fields to the desired locations.

These positions make sense for a pie chart. What if I selected a different chart type?

The items on this screen will be relevant to the particular chart type you select. Just as with the pie chart, the correct fields will often be selected automatically. If not, you can drag the fields to the correct locations.

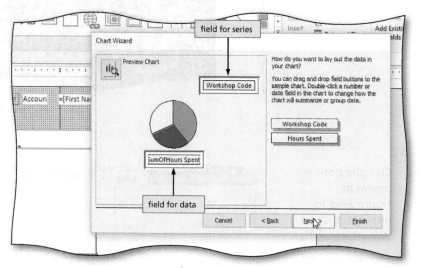

Figure 7–66

5

- Click the Next button to select the layout Access has proposed (Figure 7–67).

Q&A The Account Manager Number field does not appear in my chart. Can I still use it to link the form and the chart?

Yes. Even though the Account Manager Number does not appear, it is still included in the query on which the chart is based. In fact, it is essential that it is included so that you can link the document (that is, the form) and the chart. Linking the document and the chart ensures that the chart will

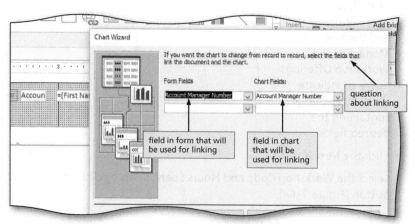

Figure 7–67

accurately reflect the data for the correct manager, that is, the manager who currently appears in the form.

6

- Click the Next button, type **Hours Spent by Workshop Offering** as the title, and then click the Finish button (Figure 7–68).

 The data does not look right. What is wrong and what do I need to do to fix it?

The data in your chart might be fictitious, as in Figure 7–68. In that case, the data simply represents the general way the chart will look. When you view the actual form, the data represented in the chart should be correct.

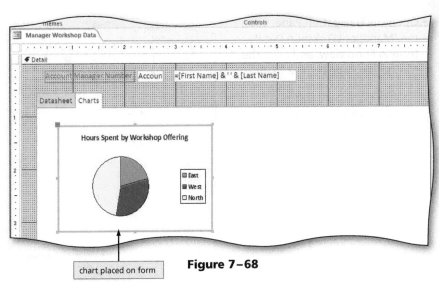

Figure 7–68

7

- Use the techniques shown in Steps 1 through 6 to add a second chart at the position shown in Figure 7–69. In this chart, which is also based on the Managers and Workshop Offerings query, select Hours Remaining instead of Hours Spent and type **Hours Remaining by Workshop Code** as the title of the chart instead of Hours Spent by Workshop Offering.

- Resize the two charts to the size shown in the figure, if necessary, by clicking the chart and then dragging an appropriate sizing handle.

- If requested to do so by your instructor, add a title with your first and last name to the form.

- Save your changes and close the form.

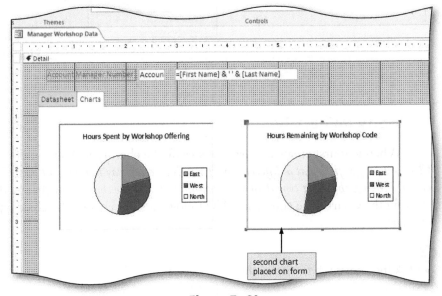

Figure 7–69

1 CREATE FORM | 2 ADD COMBO BOXES | 3 COMMAND BUTTONS | 4 MODIFY MACRO
5 MODIFY COMBO BOX | 6 CREATE SECOND FORM | 7 ADD SUBFORM | **8 ADD CHART**

To Use the Form

You use this form just like the other forms you have created and used. When using the form, it is easy to move from one tabbed page to another. *Why? All you have to do is to click the tab for the desired tabbed page.* The following step uses the form to view the workshop data.

1

- Open the Navigation Pane, open the 'Manager Workshop Data' form in Form view, and close the Navigation Pane (Figure 7–70).

Q&A What is the purpose of the navigation buttons in the subform?

These navigation buttons allow you to move within the records in the subform, that is, within the workshop offerings for the manager whose number and name appear at the top of the form.

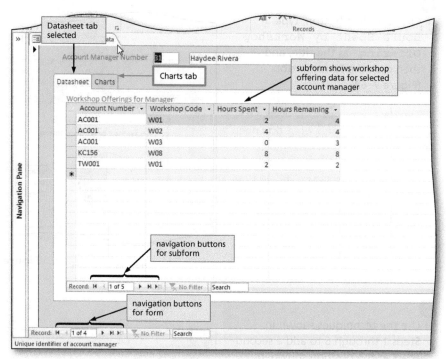

Figure 7–70

To Modify a Chart Type

1 CREATE FORM | 2 ADD COMBO BOXES | 3 COMMAND BUTTONS | 4 MODIFY MACRO
5 MODIFY COMBO BOX | 6 CREATE SECOND FORM | 7 ADD SUBFORM | **8 ADD CHART**

When you first create a chart, you specify the chart type. You sometimes will later want to change the type. *Why? You might find that a different chart type is a better way to represent data. In addition, you have more options when you later change the chart type than when you first created the chart.* You change the type by editing the chart and selecting the Chart Type command. The following steps change the chart type by selecting a different style of pie chart.

1

- Click the Charts tab to display the charts.

- Return to Design view.

- Click the Charts tab, if necessary, to display the charts in Design view (Figure 7–71).

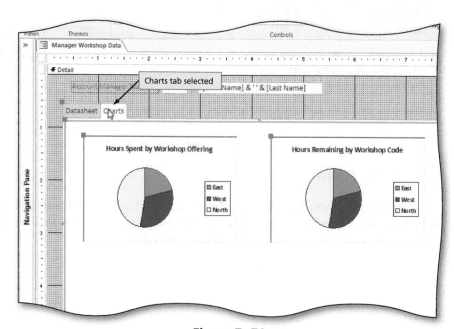

Figure 7–71

2

- Click the 'Hours Spent by Workshop Offering' chart to select it, and then right-click the chart to display a shortcut menu (Figure 7–72).

Q&A Does it matter where I right-click? You should right-click within the rectangle but outside any of the items within the rectangle, in other words, in the white space.

My shortcut menu is very different. What should I do? Click the View button arrow, then click Design View to ensure that you are viewing the form in Design view, and then try again.

- Point to Chart Object on the shortcut menu to display the Chart Object submenu (Figure 7–72).

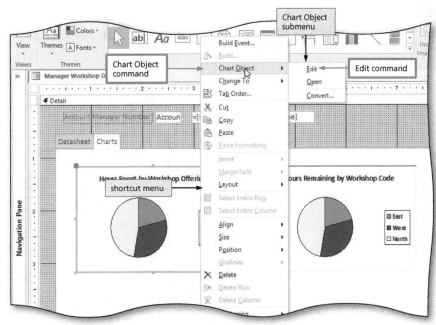

Figure 7–72

3

- Click Edit on the Chart Object submenu to edit the chart. Access will automatically display the underlying chart data in Datasheet view (Figure 7–73).

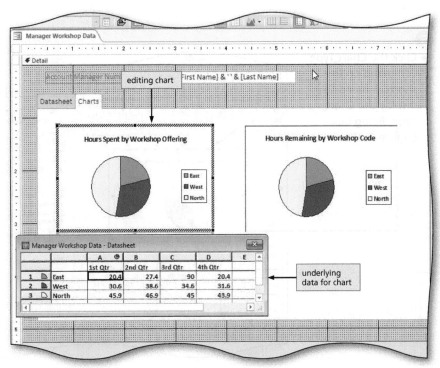

Figure 7–73

4

- Right-click the chart to display the shortcut menu for editing the chart (Figure 7–74).

Q&A Does it matter where I right-click?
You should right-click within the rectangle but outside any of the items within the rectangle, in other words, in the white space.

What types of changes can I make if I select Format Chart Area?
You can change things such as border style, color, fill effects, and fonts.

How do I make other changes?
By clicking Chart Options on the shortcut menu, you can change titles, legends, and labels. For 3-D charts, by clicking 3-D View on the shortcut menu, you can change the elevation and rotation of the chart. You can also format specific items on the chart, as you will see in the next section.

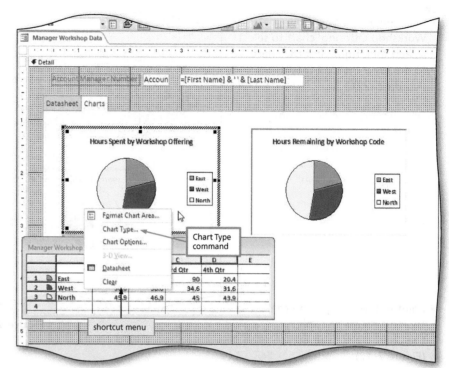

Figure 7–74

5

- Click the Chart Type command on the shortcut menu to display the Chart Type dialog box (Figure 7–75).

Q&A What is the relationship between the Chart type and the Chart sub-type?
You can think of Chart types as categories of charts. There are column charts, bar charts, line charts, and so on. Once you have selected a category, the chart sub-types are those charts in that category. If you have selected the Pie chart category, for example, the charts within the category are the ones shown in the list of chart sub-types in Figure 7–75.

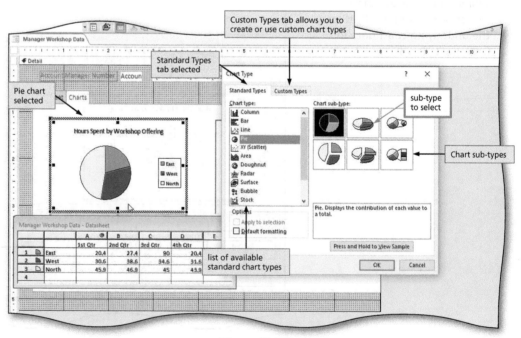

Figure 7–75

6

- Click the chart sub-type in the middle of the first row of chart sub-types to select it as the chart sub-type.

Experiment

- Click each of the chart types and examine the chart sub-types associated with that chart type. When finished, select Pie as the chart type and the sub-type in the middle of the first row as the chart sub-type.

- Click the OK button to change the chart sub-type.

- Click outside the chart and the datasheet to deselect the chart.

- Make the same change to the other chart (Figure 7–76).

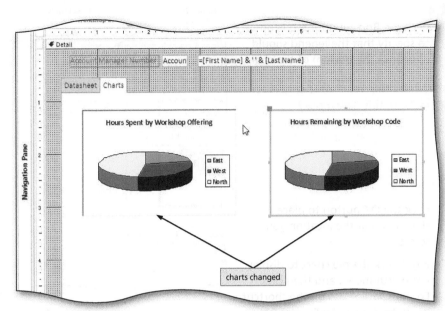

Figure 7–76

To Format a Chart

1 CREATE FORM | 2 ADD COMBO BOXES | 3 COMMAND BUTTONS | 4 MODIFY MACRO
5 MODIFY COMBO BOX | 6 CREATE SECOND FORM | 7 ADD SUBFORM | **8 ADD CHART**

By right-clicking a chart, pointing to Chart Object, and then clicking Edit, you have many formatting options available. You can change the border style, color, fill effects, and fonts by using the Format Chart Area command. You can change titles, legends, and labels by using the Chart Options command. You can also format specific portions of a chart by right-clicking the portion you want to format and then clicking the appropriate command on the shortcut menu. The following steps use this technique to move the legend so that it is at the bottom of the chart. They also include percentages in the chart. **Why?** *Percentages provide valuable information in a pie chart.*

1

- Right-click the 'Hours Spent by Workshop Offering' chart to display a shortcut menu, point to Chart Object on the shortcut menu to display the Chart Object submenu, and then click Edit on the Chart Object submenu.

- Right-click the legend to display a shortcut menu, and then click Format Legend on the shortcut menu to display the Format Legend dialog box.

- Click the Placement tab (Figure 7–77).

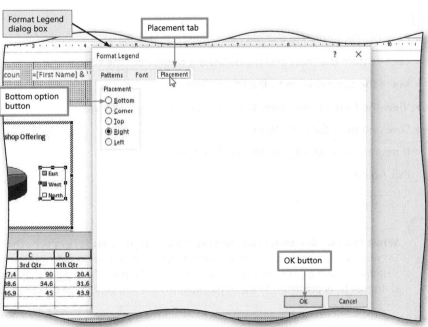

Figure 7–77

2

- Click the Bottom option button to specify that the legend should appear at the bottom of the chart.

Q&A What other types of changes can I make in this dialog box?
Click the Patterns tab to change such things as border style, color, and fill effects. Click the Font tab to change the font and/or font characteristics.

- Click the OK button to place the legend at the location you selected.

- Right-click the pie chart to display a shortcut menu, and then click Format Data Series on the shortcut menu to display the Format Data Series dialog box.

- Click the Data Labels tab.

- Click the Percentage check box to specify that percentages are to be included (Figure 7–78).

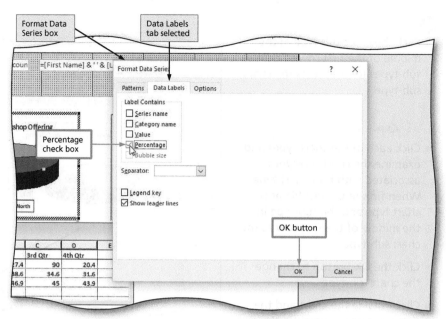

Figure 7–78

Q&A I see a Patterns tab just as with the legend, but how would I use the Options tab? Also, does the fact that these are check boxes rather than option buttons mean that I can select more than one?
Use the Options tab to indicate whether the color is to vary by slice and to specify the angle of the first slice in the pie. Because these are check boxes, you can select as many as you want. Selecting too many can clutter the chart, however.

These options make sense for a pie chart, but what about other chart types?
The options that you see will vary from one chart type to another. They will be relevant for the selected chart type.

3

- Click the OK button to include percentages on the chart.

- Click outside the chart and the datasheet to deselect the chart.

- Make the same change to the other chart.

- View the form in Form view to see the effect of your changes.

- Save and then close the form.

- If desired, sign out of your Microsoft account.

- Exit Access.

BTW
Distributing a Document
Instead of printing and distributing a hard copy of a document, you can distribute the document electronically. Options include sending the document via email; posting it on cloud storage (such as OneDrive) and sharing the file with others; posting it on a social networking site, blog, or other website; and sharing a link associated with an online location of the document. You also can create and share a PDF or XPS image of the document, so that users can view the file in Acrobat Reader or XPS Viewer instead of in Access.

CONSIDER THIS

What type of decisions should you make when considering whether to use a chart?
Do you want to represent data in a visual manner? If so, you can include a chart. If you decide to use a chart, you must determine which type of chart would best represent the data. If you want to represent total amounts, for example, a bar chart may be appropriate. If instead you want to represent portions of the whole, a pie chart may be better.

Summary

In this module you have learned how to create a form in Design view, add a combo box that displays information from a related table as well as a combo box that is used to find records on a form, format controls and use the Format Painter, add command buttons to a form, modify a button and a combo box, add a calculated field to a form, use a tab control to create a multipage form, add and modify a subform, insert charts, change chart types, and format charts.

What decisions will you need to make when creating your own forms?
Use these guidelines as you complete the assignments in this module and create your own forms outside of this class.

1. Determine the intended audience and the purpose of the form.

    a. Who will use the form?

    b. How will they use it?

    c. What data do they need?

    d. What level of detail do they need?

2. Determine the source of data for the form.

    a. Determine whether data comes from a single table or from multiple related tables.

    b. Which table or tables contain the data?

3. Determine the fields that belong on the form.

    a. What data items are needed by the user of the form?

4. Determine any calculations required for the form.

    a. Decide whether the form should contain any special calculations, such as adding two fields.

    b. Determine whether the form should contain any calculations involving text fields, such as concatenating (combining) the fields.

5. Determine the organization of the form.

    a. In what order should the fields appear?

    b. How should they be arranged?

    c. Does the form need multiple pages?

6. Determine any additional controls that should be on the form.

    a. Should the form contain a subform?

    b. Should the form contain a chart?

    c. Should the form contain command buttons to assist the user in performing various functions?

    d. Should the form contain a combo box to assist the user in searching for a record?

7. Determine the format and style of the form.

    a. What should be in the form heading?

    b. Do you want a title?

    c. Do you want an image?

    d. What should be in the body of the form?

    e. What visual characteristics, such as background color and special effects, should the various portions of the form have?

How should you submit solutions to questions in the assignments identified with a symbol?
Every assignment in this book contains one or more questions identified with a symbol. These questions require you to think beyond the assigned database. Present your solutions to the questions in the format required by your instructor. Possible formats may include one or more of these options: write the answer; create a document that contains the answer; present your answer to the class; discuss your answer in a group; record the answer as audio or video using a webcam, smartphone, or portable media player; or post answers on a blog, wiki, or website.

Apply Your Knowledge

Reinforce the skills and apply the concepts you learned in this module.

Creating a Multipage Form for the Apply NicelyNeat Services Database

Instructions: Run Access. Open the Apply NicelyNeat Services database that you modified in Module 6. If you did not use this database, contact your instructor for information on accessing the database required for this exercise.

Perform the following tasks:

1. Create a query that joins the Supervisor, Client, and Services tables. Include the Supervisor Number field from the Supervisor table, the Client Number from the Client table, and the Service Date and Hours Worked fields from the Services table. Sort the query in ascending order by Supervisor Number, Client Number, and Service Date. Save the query as Clients and Services.

2. Create the Supervisor Services Data form shown in Figure 7–79. Concatenate the first and last name of the supervisor and change the background color to Light Gray 1 (the first color in row 2 of the Standard Colors.) The Datasheet tab displays a subform listing information about services for clients of the supervisor (Figure 7–79a). Data for the subform is based on the Clients and Services query. Data for the Chart tab is also based on the Clients and Services query and displays the total hours of service for each client (Figure 7–79b).

3. If requested to do so by your instructor, rename the Supervisor Services Data form as LastName Services Data where LastName is your last name.

4. Submit the revised database in the format specified by your instructor.

5. ✷ How can you add a title to the Supervisor Services Data form?

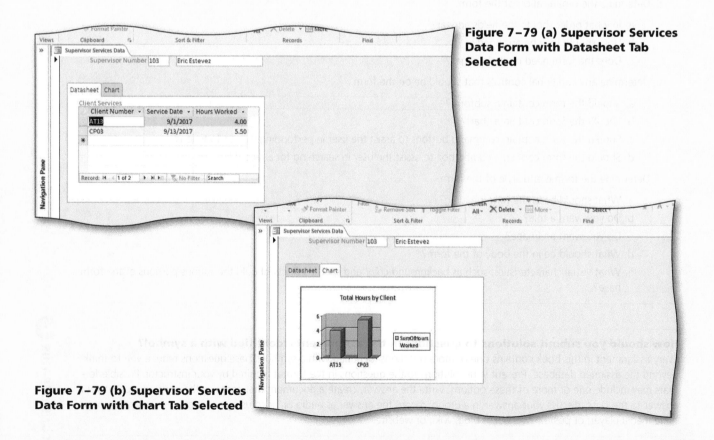

Figure 7–79 (a) Supervisor Services Data Form with Datasheet Tab Selected

Figure 7–79 (b) Supervisor Services Data Form with Chart Tab Selected

Extend Your Knowledge

Extend the skills you learned in this module and experiment with new skills. You may need to use Help to complete the assignment.

Modifying Forms

Note: To complete this assignment, you will be required to use the Data Files. Please contact your instructor for information about accessing the Data Files.

Instructions: Run Access. Open the Extend Landscaping database. The Extend Landscaping database contains information about a company that provides landscaping services to commercial customers.

Perform the following tasks:

1. Open the Supervisor Request Data form in Design view. Add a title to the form and insert the current date in the form header. Bold the label for Supervisor Number.
2. Add a third tab control to the form. Name the tab control, Customers.
3. Add a subform to the Customers tab control. The Customer table is the basis of the subform. Display the Customer Number, Customer Name, and Balance fields in a datasheet on the subform. Accept the default name for the subform and delete the label that appears above the datasheet. Change the label for the Customer Number control from CU # to Customer Number. Resize the datasheet so that all columns appear in the control.
4. Move the Customers tab control so that it appears after the Datasheet tab control. Rename the Datasheet tab control as Service Requests.
5. Add a command button to close the form and use the picture option to place a picture on the button. Save the changes and close the form.
6. Open the Customer Master Form in Design view and change the font color of the title to Dark Red (Standard colors) and format the title as bold. Add a Shadowed special effect. Save the changes to the form.
7. If requested to do so by your instructor, open the Supervisor table in Datasheet view and change the first and last name of supervisor 52 to your first and last name.
8. Submit the revised database in the format specified by your instructor.
9. ☀ How could you change the pie charts in the Charts tab to exploded pie charts with a 3-D visual effect?

Expand Your World

Create a solution, which uses cloud and web technologies, by learning and investigating on your own from general guidance.

Problem: Crafts is a database maintained by a college that is renowned for its school of arts and crafts. Students can sell their designs online through the college bookstore. You will modify the Item Master Form to include a background image and a hyperlink. You will also add images to command buttons.

Note: To complete this assignment, you will be required to use the Data Files. Please contact your instructor for information about accessing the Data Files.

Continued >

Expand Your World *continued*

Perform the following tasks:

1. Open the Expand Crafts database from the Data Files.

2. Open the Item Master Form in Design view. Add a combo box for the Student Code field.

3. Access any website containing royalty-free images to find a suitable background image the college can use for its forms that emphasizes arts and crafts or create your own background image.

4. Add the background image to the form.

5. Add a hyperlink for your school's website to the Form Header.

6. Access any website containing royalty-free images and search for an image suitable to use on a Close Form command button; for example, a Stop sign or a door. Save the image to a storage location of your choice.

7. Add a Close Form command button to the form using the image you downloaded.

8. Save your changes to the Item Master Form.

9. Submit the revised database in the format specified by your instructor.

10. ✸ What image did you choose as the background for your form? What image did you choose for the command button? Why did you make those choices?

In the Labs

Design, create, modify, and/or use a database following the guidelines, concepts, and skills presented in this module. Labs are listed in order of increasing difficulty. Labs 1 and 2, which increase in difficulty, require you to create solutions based on what you learned in the module; Lab 3 requires you to apply your creative thinking and problem solving skills to design and implement a solution.

Lab 1: Applying Advanced Form Techniques to the Horticulture4U Database

Problem: The management of Horticulture4U needs a form for the Customer table that allows users to update data in the table. Horticulture4U also needs a form to display open orders data for sales reps.

Note: Use the database modified in the Lab 1 of Module 6 for this assignment. If you did not use the database, contact your instructor for information on accessing the database required for this exercise.

Instructions: Perform the following tasks:

1. Create the Customer View and Update Form shown in Figure 7–80. Save the form with the name, Customer Master Form. The form includes a title, command buttons, a combo box for the Sales Rep Number field, and a combo box to search for customers by name. Be sure to sort the customer names in alphabetical order, place a rectangle around the combo box, and update the combo box. The user should not be able to tab to the combo box. When the Add Record

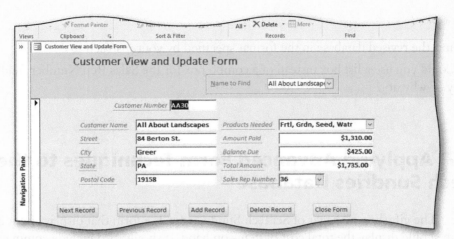

Figure 7–80

button is clicked, the insertion point should be in the Customer Number field. The title is bold. The background of the Detail section of the form is Light Gray 1 (Standard colors). The controls have a semi-bold font weight and a sunken special effect. The labels are italicized with a chiseled special effect. The form is similar in style to that shown in Figure 7–1.

2. Create a query that includes the Sales Rep Number from the Sales Rep table, the Customer Number from the Customer table, and the Order Number and Amount fields from the Open Orders table. Sort the query in ascending order by Sales Rep Number, Customer Number, and Order Number. Save the query as Sales Reps and Open Orders.

3. Create the Sales Rep Order Data form shown in Figure 7–81. The subform that appears in the Datasheet tab uses the Sales Reps and Open Orders query (Figure 7–81a). The chart in the Charts tab uses the same query (Figure 7–81b). Be sure to concatenate the first and last names of the sales rep. Change the background color to Light Gray 2. The form is similar in style to that shown in Figure 7–2.

4. If instructed to do so by your instructor, open the Sales Rep table and change the first and last name of sales rep 39 to your first and last name.

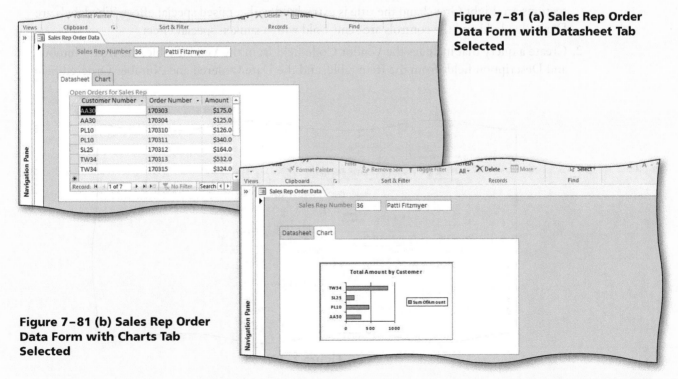

Figure 7–81 (a) Sales Rep Order Data Form with Datasheet Tab Selected

Figure 7–81 (b) Sales Rep Order Data Form with Charts Tab Selected

Continued >

In the Labs *continued*

5. Submit the revised database in the format specified by your instructor.

6. ✳ Could you use a list box instead of a combo box for the Sales Rep Number field in the form? Why or why not?

Lab 2: Applying Advanced Form Techniques to the SciTech Sundries Database

Problem: The gift shop manager of SciTech Sundries needs a form that displays item information. The form should display the total cost of items on hand. It should also include command buttons to perform common operations, a combo box to search for items by description, and a combo box for vendor code. Management also needs a form that displays vendor information as well as items on order and all items associated with a vendor.

Note: Use the database you used in Lab 2 of Module 6 for this assignment. If you did not use this database, contact your instructor for information on accessing the database required for this exercise.

Instructions: Perform the following tasks:

1. Create the Item Master Form shown in Figure 7–82. Use the caption Item View and Update Form for the form. The form includes command buttons, a drop-down box (combo box) for the Vendor Code field, and combo box to search for items by name. Inventory Value is the result of multiplying On Hand by Wholesale Cost. Format Inventory Value as currency with two decimal places. Change the tab order for the controls in the Detail section so that Vendor Code follows Item Type. Be sure to sort the item names alphabetically, place a rectangle around the combo box, and update the combo box. The user should not be able to tab to the combo box. When the Add Record button is clicked, the insertion point should be in the Item Number field. The form is similar in style to that shown in Figure 7–1. The form header and detail sections are Light Gray 2 and the title is extra-bold with a raised special effect. The labels are Dark Blue bold and the controls are semi-bold with a sunken special effect.

2. Create a query that includes the Vendor Code field from the Vendor table, the Item Number and Description fields from the Item table, and the Date Ordered and Number Ordered fields

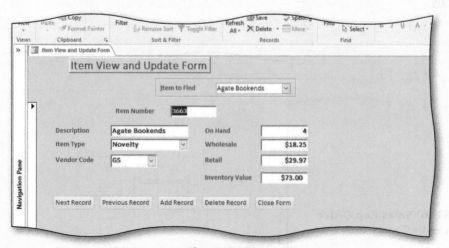

Figure 7–82

from the Reorder table. Sort the query in ascending order by Vendor Code, Item Number, and Date Ordered. Save the query as Vendors and Orders.

3. Create the Vendor Orders Data form shown in Figure 7–83. The In Stock tab uses the Item table for the subform (Figure 7–83a). The On Order tab (Figure 7–83b) uses the Vendors and Orders query for the subform. Note that the labels for Vendor Code and Vendor Name have been removed and that there is a title on the form. The form title and the labels in the Detail section are bold and have the raised special effect. The controls have the sunken special effect. You can use the Format Painter to copy formatting for controls and labels.

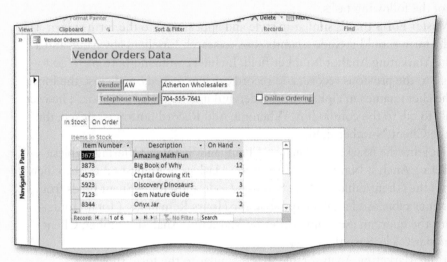

Figure 7–83 (a) Vendor Orders Data Form with In Stock Tab Selected

Figure 7–83 (b) Vendor Orders Data Form with On Order Tab Selected

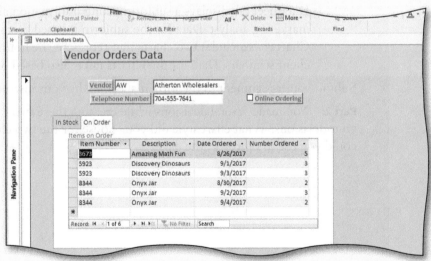

4. If instructed to do so by your instructor, change the phone number for vendor GS to your phone number.

5. Submit the revised database in the format specified by your instructor.

6. ✹ How could you rearrange the tab controls for the Vendor Orders Data form so that the On Order tab appears before the In Stock tab?

Continued >

In the Labs *continued*

Lab 3: **Consider This: Your Turn**

Applying Advanced Form Techniques to the JSP Analysis Database

Part 1: The management of JSP Analysis needs a form to use to update client data. They also need a form to track seminar offerings by marketing analyst. Open the Lab 3 JSP Analysis database that you modified in Module 6. If you did not modify this database, contact your instructor for information about accessing the required database. Then, use the concepts and techniques presented in this module to perform each of the following tasks:

a. Create a Client Master Form that is similar in style and appearance to the form shown in Figure 7–1. The form should include a combo box to search for clients by name and a combo box for the Marketing Analyst Number field. Include command buttons to go to the next record, go to the previous record, add records, delete records, and close the form. Be sure to sort the client names in alphabetical order and update the combo box. The user should not be able to tab to the combo box. When the Add Record button is clicked, the focus should be the Client Number field.

b. Create a query that joins the Marketing Analyst, Client, and Seminar Offerings tables. Include the Marketing Analyst Number field from the Marketing Analyst table, the Client Number field from the Client table, and the Seminar Code and Hours Spent fields from the Seminar Offerings table. Add a calculated field for Hours Remaining (Total Hours – Hours Spent). Sort the query in ascending order by Marketing Analyst Number, Client Number, and Seminar Code. Save the query.

c. Create a form for the Marketing Analyst table that is similar to the form shown in Figure 7–2a. The form should have two tabs, a Datasheet tab and a Charts tab. The Datasheet tab displays a subform listing information about seminars for clients of the marketing analyst. Data for the subform is based on the query you created in Step b. The Charts tab includes two charts that represent the hours spent and hours remaining for client seminars. Data for the Charts tab is also based on the query created in Step b.

Submit your assignment in the format specified by your instructor.

Part 2: You made several decisions while creating these two forms. What was the rationale behind your decisions? What chart style did you choose for the two charts? Why? What other chart styles could you use to represent the data?

8 | Macros, Navigation Forms, and Control Layouts

Objectives

You will have mastered the material in this module when you can:

- Create and modify macros and submacros
- Create a menu form with command buttons
- Create a menu form with an option group
- Create a macro for the option group
- Use an IF statement in a macro
- Create datasheet forms

- Create user interface (UI) macros
- Create navigation forms
- Add tabs to a navigation form
- Create data macros
- Create and remove control layouts
- Use the Arrange tab to modify control layouts on forms and reports

Introduction

In this module, you will learn how to create and test macros that open forms and that preview reports and export reports. You will create a menu form with command buttons as well as a menu form with an **option group**, which is an object that enables you to make a selection by choosing the option button corresponding to your choice. You will also create and use user interface (UI) macros in forms. PrattLast Associates requires a navigation form that will allow users to open forms and reports simply by clicking appropriate tabs and buttons. You will learn about the use of data macros for ensuring that updates to the database are valid. Finally, you will learn how to use control layouts on forms and reports.

Project—Macros, Navigation Forms, and Control Layouts

PrattLast Associates would like its users to be able to access forms and reports by simply clicking tabs and buttons, rather than by using the Navigation Pane. A **navigation form** like the one shown in Figure 8–1a is a form that includes tabs to display forms and reports. This navigation form contains several useful features. With the Account tab selected, you can click the account number on any row to see the data for the selected account displayed in the Account View and Update Form (Figure 8–1b). The form does not appear in a tabbed sheet, the way tables, queries, forms, and reports normally do. Rather, it appears as a **pop-up form**, a form that stays on top of other open objects, even when another object is active.

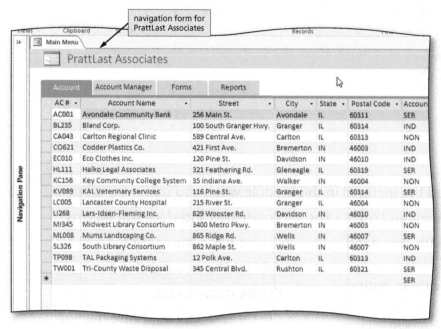

navigation form for PrattLast Associates

Figure 8–1(a) Navigation Form

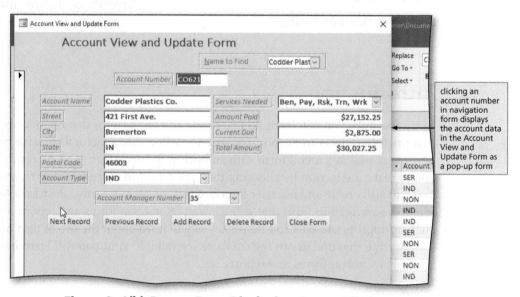

clicking an account number in navigation form displays the account data in the Account View and Update Form as a pop-up form

Figure 8–1(b) Pop-up Form Displaying Account Data

Clicking the Account Manager tab of the navigation form displays account manager data. As with accounts, clicking the account manager number on any record displays data for that account manager in a pop-up form.

Clicking the Forms tab in the PrattLast Associates navigation form displays buttons for each of the available forms (Figure 8–1c). You can open the desired form by clicking the appropriate button.

Clicking the Reports tab displays an option group for displaying reports (Figure 8–1d). You can preview or export any of the reports one at a time by clicking the corresponding option button. PrattLast plans to use the navigation form because they believe it will improve the user-friendliness of the database, thereby improving employee satisfaction and efficiency.

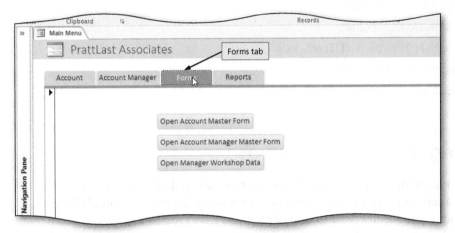

Figure 8–1(c) Forms Tab

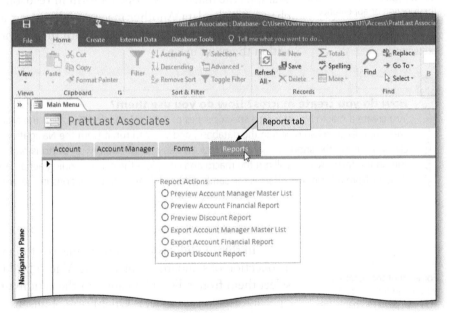

Figure 8–1(d) Reports Tab

Before creating the navigation form, PrattLast will create **macros**, which are collections of actions designed to carry out specific tasks. To perform the actions in a macro, you run the macro. When you run a macro, Access will execute the various steps, called **actions**, in the order indicated by the macro. You run the navigation form macros by clicking certain buttons in the form.

BTW
The Ribbon and Screen Resolution
Access may change how the groups and buttons within the groups appear on the ribbon, depending on the computer's screen resolution. Thus, your ribbon may look different from the ones in this book if you are using a screen resolution other than 1366 x 768.

PrattLast will also create another type of macro, a data macro. A **data macro** is a special type of macro that enables you to add logic to table events such as adding, changing, or deleting data. You typically use data macros to ensure data validity.

In this module, you will learn how to create and use the navigation form shown in Figure 8–1. The following roadmap identifies general activities you will perform as you progress through this module:

1. Create and modify a MACRO WITH SUBMACROS
2. Create a menu FORM with COMMAND BUTTONS
3. Create a menu FORM with an OPTION GROUP
4. Create a MACRO for the OPTION GROUP
5. Create DATASHEET FORMS
6. Create USER INTERFACE (UI) MACROS
7. Create a NAVIGATION FORM
8. Create a DATA MACRO

Creating and Using Macros

BTW
Touch Screen Differences
The Office and Windows interfaces may vary if you are using a touch screen. For this reason, you might notice that the function or appearance of your touch screen differs slightly from this module's presentation.

Similar to other Office apps, Access allows you to create and use macros. A macro consists of a series of actions that Access performs when the macro is run. When you create a macro, you specify these actions. Once you have created a macro, you can simply run the macro, and Access will perform the various actions you specified. For example, the macro might open a form in read-only mode, a mode that prohibits changes to the data. Another macro might export a report as a PDF file. You can group related macros into a single macro, with the individual macros existing as submacros within the main macro.

CONSIDER THIS

How do you create macros? How do you use them?
You create a macro by entering a specific series of actions in a window called the Macro Builder window. Once a macro is created, it exists as an object in the database, and you can run it from the Navigation Pane by right-clicking the macro and then clicking Run on the shortcut menu. Macros can also be associated with buttons on forms. When you click the corresponding button on the form, Access will run the macro and complete the corresponding action. Whether a macro is run from the Navigation Pane or from a form, the effect is the same: Access will execute the actions in the order in which they occur in the macro.

BTW
Enabling the Content
For each of the databases you use in this module, you will need to enable the content.

In this module, you will create macros for a variety of purposes. Access provides a collection of standard actions in the Macro Builder; as you enter actions, you will select them from a list. The names of the actions are self-explanatory. The action to open a form, for example, is OpenForm. Thus, it is not necessary to memorize the specific actions that are available.

To Begin Creating a Macro

1 MACRO WITH SUBMACROS | 2 FORM COMMAND BUTTONS | 3 FORM OPTION GROUP | 4 MACRO FOR OPTION GROUP
5 DATASHEET FORMS | 6 USER INTERFACE MACROS | 7 NAVIGATION FORM | 8 DATA MACRO

The following steps begin creating a macro. *Why? Once you have created the macro, you will be able to add the appropriate actions.*

- Run Access and open the database named PrattLast Associates from your hard disk, OneDrive, or other storage location.
- If necessary, close the Navigation Pane.
- Display the Create tab (Figure 8–2).

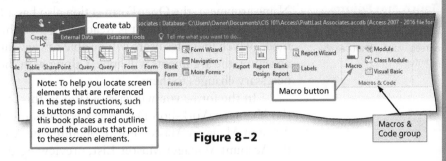

Figure 8–2

②

- Click the Macro button (Create tab | Macros & Code group) to create a new macro.
- Click the Action Catalog button (Macro Tools Design tab | Show/Hide group) if necessary to display the action catalog (Figure 8–3).

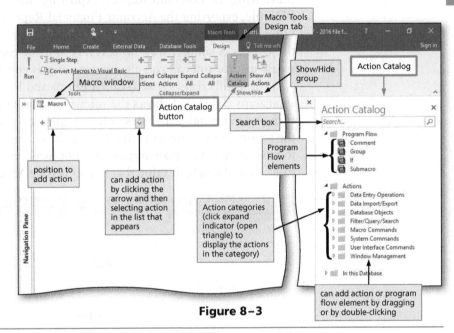

Figure 8–3

The Macro Builder Window

You create a macro by adding actions in the macro window, shown in Figure 8–3. You can add actions by clicking the 'Add New Action' arrow and selecting the desired action from the list of possible actions. You can also use the Action Catalog, which is a list of macro actions organized by type. If the Action Catalog does not appear, click the Action Catalog button (Macro Tools Design tab | Show/Hide group) to display it. You can add an action by double-clicking the action in the Action Catalog or by dragging it.

Access arranges the available actions in categories. To see the actions in a category, click the **expand indicator** (the open triangle) in front of the category. The actions will appear and the expand indicator will change to a solid triangle. To hide the actions in a category, click the solid triangle.

BTW
Macros
A macro is a series of commands used to automate repeated tasks. You can create macros in other Office apps, such as Word and Excel.

How can you find an action if you are not sure which category contains the action?
You can search the list by typing in the Search box. Access will then reduce the list of actions displayed to only those actions whose names or descriptions contain the text you have typed.

Many actions require additional information, called the **arguments** of the action. For example, if the action is OpenForm, Access needs to know which form is to be opened. You indicate the form to be opened by setting the value of the Form Name argument to the desired form. If the value for the Form Name argument for the OpenForm action is Manager Workshop Data, then Access will open the Manager Workshop Data form when it executes this action.

CONSIDER THIS

BTW
Touch and Pointers
Remember that if you are
using your finger on a touch
screen, you will not see the
pointer.

Actions can have more than one argument. For example, in addition to the Form Name argument, the OpenForm action also has a Data Mode argument. If the value of the Data Mode argument is Read Only, then the form will be opened in read-only mode, which indicates users will be able to view but not change data. When you select an action, the arguments will appear along with the action, and you can make any necessary changes to them.

In the forms you will create later in this module, you need macros for opening the Manager Workshop Data form as read-only (to prevent updates), opening the Account Manager Master Form, opening the Account Master Form, previewing the Account Manager Master List, previewing the Account Financial Report, previewing the Discount Report, exporting the Account Manager Master List as a PDF file, exporting the Account Financial Report as a PDF file, and exporting the Discount Report as a PDF file. You could create nine separate macros to accomplish these tasks. A simpler way, however, is to make each of these a submacro within a single macro. You can run a submacro just as you can run a macro.

You will create a macro called Forms and Reports that contains these nine submacros. Table 8–1 shows the submacros. Submacros can contain many actions, but each one in this table includes only a single action. For each submacro, the table gives the action, those arguments that need to be changed, and the values you need to assign to those arguments. If an argument is not listed, then you do not need to change the value from the default value that is assigned by Access.

Table 8–1 Forms and Reports Macro		
Submacro	**Action**	**Arguments to be Changed**
Open Manager Workshop Data		
	OpenForm	Form Name: Manager Workshop Data Data Mode: Read Only
Open Account Manager Master Form		
	OpenForm	Form Name: Account Manager Master Form
Open Account Master Form		
	OpenForm	Form Name: Account Master Form
Preview Account Manager Master List		
	OpenReport	Report Name: Account Manager Master List View: Print Preview
Preview Account Financial Report		
	OpenReport	Report Name: Account Financial Report View: Print Preview
Preview Discount Report		
	OpenReport	Report Name: Discount Report View: Print Preview
Export Account Manager Master List		
	ExportWithFormatting	Object Type: Report Object Name: Account Manager Master List Output Format: PDF Format (*.pdf)
Export Account Financial Report		
	ExportWithFormatting	Object Type: Report Object Name: Account Financial Report Output Format: PDF Format (*.pdf)
Export Discount Report		
	ExportWithFormatting	Object Type: Report Object Name: Discount Report Output Format: PDF Format (*.pdf)

To Add an Action to a Macro

To continue creating the Forms and Reports macro, enter the actions in the Macro Builder. In these steps, you will enter actions by double-clicking the action in the Action Catalog. *Why? The actions in the Action Catalog are organized by function, making it easier to locate the action you want.* Access will add the action to the Add New Action box. If there is more than one Add New Action box, you need to ensure that the one where you want to add the action is selected before you double-click.

The following steps add the first action. They also make the necessary changes to any arguments. Finally, the steps save the macro.

1

- Double-click the Submacro element from the Program Flow section of the Action Catalog to add a submacro and then type **Open Manager Workshop Data** as the name of the submacro (Figure 8–4).

Q&A How can I tell the purpose of the various actions?
If necessary, expand the category containing the action so that the action appears. Point to the action. An expanded ScreenTip will appear, giving you a description of the action.

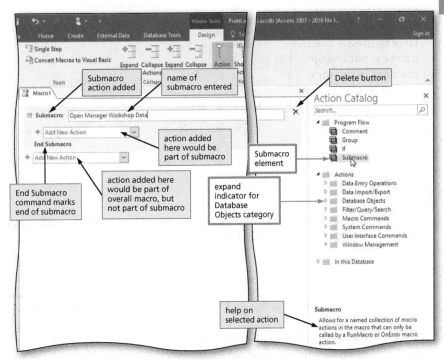

Figure 8–4

2

- Click the expand indicator for the Database Objects category of actions to display the actions within the category.

- Double-click the OpenForm action to add it to the submacro (Figure 8–5).

Q&A What should I do if I add an action in the wrong position? What should I do if I add the wrong action?
If you add an action in the wrong position, use the Move up or Move down buttons to move it to the correct position. If you added the wrong action, click the DELETE button to delete the action, and then fix the error by adding the correct action.

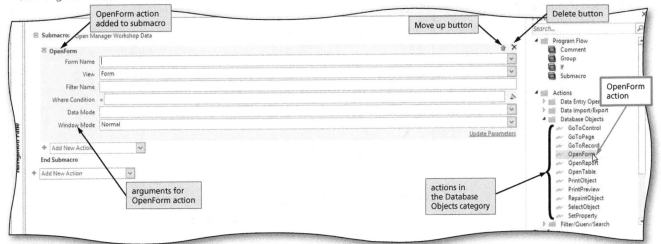

Figure 8–5

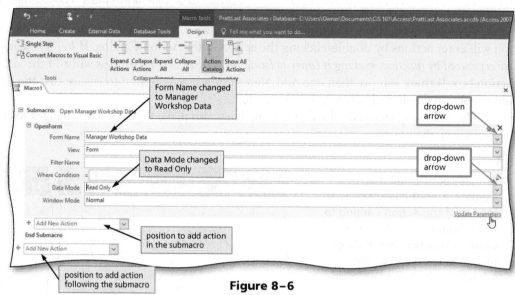

3

- Click the drop-down arrow for the Form Name argument and then select Manager Workshop Data as the name of the form to be opened.

- Click the drop-down arrow for the Data Mode argument and then select Read Only to specify that users cannot change the data in the form (Figure 8–6).

Q&A

What is the effect of the other Data Mode options?

Add allows viewing records and adding new records, but not updating records. Edit allows viewing records, adding new records, and updating existing records.

Figure 8–6

4

- Click the Save button on the Quick Access Toolbar, type **Forms and Reports** as the name of the macro, and then click the OK button to save the macro.

To Add More Actions to a Macro

1 MACRO WITH SUBMACROS | 2 FORM COMMAND BUTTONS | 3 FORM OPTION GROUP | 4 MACRO FOR OPTION GROUP
5 DATASHEET FORMS | 6 USER INTERFACE MACROS | 7 NAVIGATION FORM | 8 DATA MACRO

To complete the macro, you need to add the additional actions shown in Table 8–1. You add the additional actions just as you added the first action. Initially, Access displays all the actions you have added with their arguments clearly visible. After you have added several actions, you might want to collapse some or all of the actions. **Why?** *Collapsing actions makes it easier to get an overall view of your macro.* You can always expand any action later to see details concerning the arguments. The following steps add additional actions to a macro, collapsing existing actions when necessary to provide a better view of the overall macro structure.

1

- Click the minus sign (–) in front of the OpenForm action to collapse the action (Figure 8–7).

Q&A

Could I also use the buttons on the ribbon?

Yes, you can use the buttons in the Collapse/Expand group on the Macro Tools Design tab. Click the Expand Actions button to expand the selected action, or click the Collapse Actions button to collapse the selected action. You can expand all actions at once by clicking the Expand All button, or you can collapse all actions at once by clicking the Collapse All button.

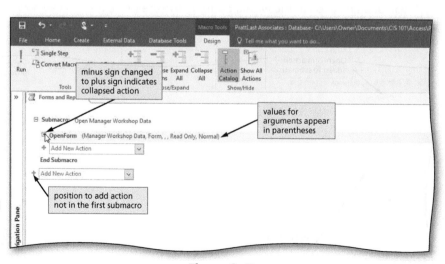

Figure 8–7

2

- Double-click the Submacro element from the Program Flow section of the Action Catalog to add a submacro and then type **Open Account Manager Master Form** as the name of the submacro.

- Double-click the OpenForm action to add it to the submacro.

- Click the drop-down arrow for the Form Name argument and then select 'Account Manager Master Form.'

- In a similar fashion, add the 'Open Account Master Form' submacro.

- Add the OpenForm action to the submacro.

- Select Account Master Form as the value for the Form Name argument (Figure 8–8).

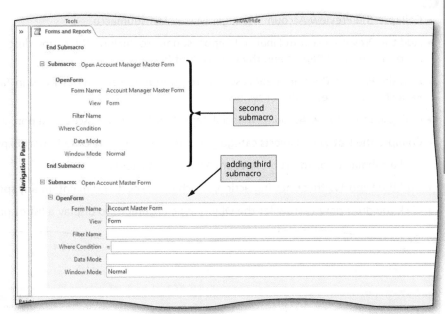

Figure 8–8

Q&A Do I have to change the values of any of the other arguments?
No. The default values that Access sets are appropriate.

3

- For each of the submacros, click the minus sign in front of the submacro to collapse the submacro.

- Add a submacro named Preview Account Manager Master List.

- Add the OpenReport action to the macro.

- Select Account Manager Master List as the report name.

- Select Print Preview as the view (Figure 8–9).

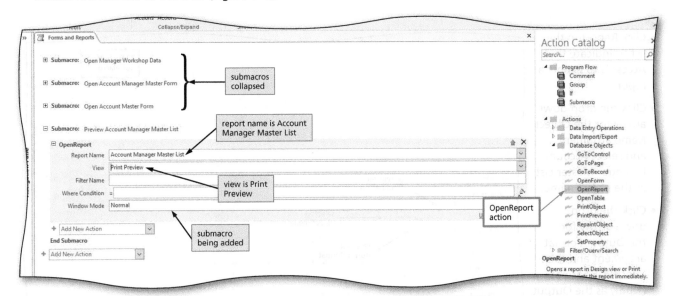

Figure 8–9

- Collapse the Preview Account Manager Master List submacro.
- Add the Preview Account Financial Report submacro. Include the action described in Table 8–1. The report name is Account Financial Report and the view is Print Preview.
- Add the Preview Discount Report submacro. Include the action described in Table 8–1. The report name is Discount Report and the view is Print Preview.
- Collapse the Preview Account Financial Report and Preview Discount Report submacros.
- Collapse the Database Objects category and then expand the Data Import/Export category.
- Add a submacro called Export Account Manager Master List.
- Add the ExportWithFormatting action, which will export and maintain any special formatting in the process.
- Click the drop-down arrow for the Object Type argument to display a list of possible object types (Figure 8–10).

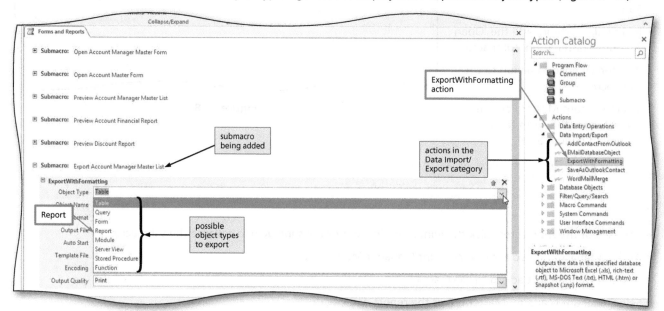

Figure 8–10

- Click Report in the list to indicate that Access is to export a report.

- Click the drop-down arrow for the Object Name argument and select Account Manager Master List as the object name.

- Click the drop-down arrow for the Output Format argument and then select PDF Format (*.pdf) as the Output Format to export the report in PDF format (Figure 8–11).

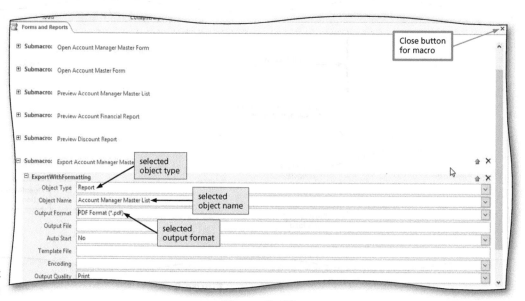

Figure 8–11

- Add the Export Account Financial Report submacro and the action from Table 8–1.

- Select Report as the Object Type and select Account Financial Report as the report name.

- Select PDF Format (*.pdf) as the Output Format to export the report in PDF format.

- Add the Export Discount Report submacro and the action from Table 8–1.

- Select Report as the Object Type and Discount Report as the report name.

- Select PDF Format (*.pdf) as the Output Format to export the report in PDF format.

- Save the macro.

- Close the macro by clicking its Close button, shown in Figure 8–11.

Opening Databases Containing Macros

It is possible that a macro stored in a database can contain a computer virus. By default, Access disables macros when it opens a database and displays a Security Warning. If the database comes from a trusted source and you are sure that it does not contain any macro viruses, click the Enable Content button. You can make adjustments to Access security settings by clicking File on the ribbon to open the Backstage view, and then clicking Options to display the Access Options dialog box, clicking Trust Center, clicking Trust Center Settings, and then clicking Macro Settings.

Errors in Macros

Macros can contain errors. The macro may abort. It might open the wrong table or produce a wrong message. If you have problems with a macro, you can **single-step the macro**, that is, proceed through a macro a step at a time in Design view.

Figure 8–12 shows a macro open in Design view. This macro first has an action to open the Account table in Datasheet view in Read Only mode. It then changes the view to Print Preview. Next, it opens the Account table in Datasheet view, this time in Edit mode. Finally, it opens the Manager-Account Query in Datasheet view in Edit mode. The macro in the figure is a common type of macro that opens several objects at once. To open all these objects, the user only has to run the macro. Unfortunately, this macro contains an error. The name of the Account table is written as "Accounts" in the second OpenTable action.

BTW
Converting a Macro to VBA Code
If you want to use many of the resources provided by Windows or communicate with another Windows app, you will need to convert any macros to VBA (Visual Basic for Applications) code. To convert a macro to VBA code, open the macro in Design view and click the 'Convert Macros to Visual Basic' button (Macro Tools Design tab | Tools group). When the Convert Macro dialog box appears, select the appropriate options, and then click Convert.

Figure 8–12

BTW
Saving a Macro as a VBA Module
You can save a macro as a VBA module using the 'Save Object As' command in Backstage view. Open the macro in Design view, click File on the ribbon to open Backstage view, and then click Save As. When the Save As gallery appears, click 'Save Object As' in the File Types area, and then click the Save As button. When the Save As dialog box appears, click Module in the As text box and then click the OK button.

To run this macro in single-step mode, you would first click the Single Step button (Macro Tools Design tab | Tools group). You would next click the Run button (Macro Tools Design tab | Tools group) to run the macro. Because you clicked the Single Step button, Access would display the Macro Single Step dialog box (Figure 8–13). The dialog box shows the action to be executed and the values of the various arguments. You can click the Step button to proceed to the next step.

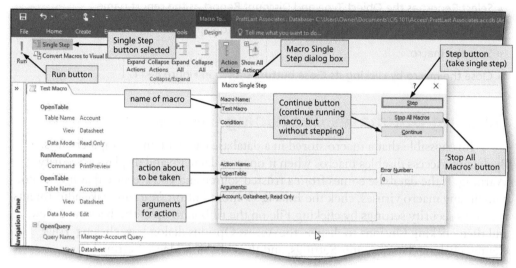

Figure 8–13

BTW
Program Flow Actions
Actions in the Program Flow category can change the order macro actions are executed or help structure a macro.

With this macro, after you clicked the Step button twice, you would arrive at the screen shown in Figure 8–14. Access is about to execute the OpenTable command. The arguments are Accounts, Datasheet, and Edit. At this point, you might spot the fact that "Accounts" is misspelled. It should be "Account." If so, you could click the 'Stop All Macros' button and then correct the object name.

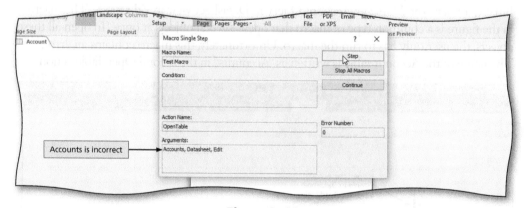

Figure 8–14

If you instead click the Step button, the misspelled name will cause the macro to abort. Access would display the appropriate error message in the Microsoft Access dialog box (Figure 8–15). This error indicates that Access could not find the object named Accounts. Armed with this knowledge, you can click the OK button, stop the macro, and then make the necessary change.

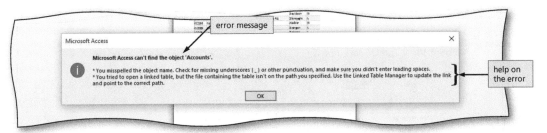

Figure 8–15

You do not need to step through a macro to discover the error. You can simply run the macro, either by clicking the Run button (Macro Tools Design tab | Tools group) with the macro open or by right-clicking the macro in the Navigation Pane and clicking Run. In either case, Access will run the macro until it encounters the error. When it does, it will display the same message shown in Figure 8–15. Just as with stepping through the macro, you would click the OK button, stop the macro, and then make the necessary change.

> **Break Point:** If you wish to stop working through the module at this point, you can resume the project later by running Access, opening the database called PrattLast Associates, and continuing to follow the steps from this location forward.

Creating and Using a Navigation Form

Figure 8–1a showed a navigation form for PrattLast Associates. A navigation form is a form that contains a **navigation control**, a control that can display a variety of forms and reports. Like the form in Figure 8–1, navigation controls contain tabs. Clicking the tab displays the corresponding form or report. The tabs can be arranged across the top and/or down the sides.

You can only include forms and reports on the tabs; you cannot include either tables or queries. The navigation form in Figure 8–1, however, appears to have a tab corresponding to the Account table. If you would find it desirable to display tables or queries on a navigation control tab, you can make it appear as though the navigation form contains these objects by creating a datasheet form based on the table or query. Figure 8–1 actually shows a datasheet form based on the Account table and does not show the Account table itself.

Before creating the navigation form, you have some other forms to create. For example, you might want the users to be able to click a tab in the navigation form and then choose from a list of forms or reports. Figure 8–16 shows a list of forms presented as buttons; the user would click the button for the desired form. Clicking the 'Open Account Master Form' button, for example, would display the Account View and Update Form as shown in Figure 8–17.

BTW
Navigation Forms
A navigation form often is used as a switchboard or main page for a database to reduce clutter and target the most commonly used database objects. A navigation form contains a navigation control and a subform control. After you create a navigation form, you can use the Navigation Where Clause property associated with a navigation control to automatically apply a filter.

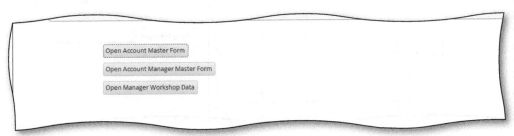

Figure 8–16

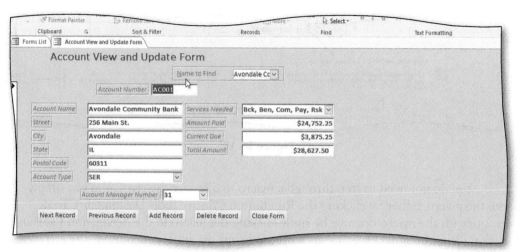

Figure 8–17

To implement options like these, you create blank forms and add either the command buttons or the option group. You then include the form you have created in the navigation form. When users click the corresponding tab, Access displays the form and users can then click the appropriate button.

To Create a Menu Form Containing Command Buttons

1 MACRO WITH SUBMACROS | 2 FORM COMMAND BUTTONS | 3 FORM OPTION GROUP | 4 MACRO FOR OPTION GROUP
5 DATASHEET FORMS | 6 USER INTERFACE MACROS | 7 NAVIGATION FORM | 8 DATA MACRO

Why? A menu form in which you make a selection by clicking the appropriate command button provides a convenient way to select a desired option. You can create a menu form by adding command buttons to the form. The following steps use this technique to create a menu form with three buttons: 'Open Account Master Form,' 'Open Account Manager Master Form,' and 'Open Manager Workshop Data.' The actions assigned to each button will run a macro that causes the desired action to occur. For example, the action for the Open Account Master Form button will run the Open Account Master Form submacro, which in turn will open the Account Master Form.

The following steps create a form in Design view and then add the necessary buttons.

- Display the Create tab.

- Click the Form Design button (Create tab | Forms group) to create a blank form in Design view.

- If a field list appears, click the 'Add Existing Fields' button (Form Design Tools Design tab | Tools group) to remove the field list.

- If a property sheet appears, click the Property Sheet button (Form Design Tools Design tab | Tools group) to remove the property sheet (Figure 8–18).

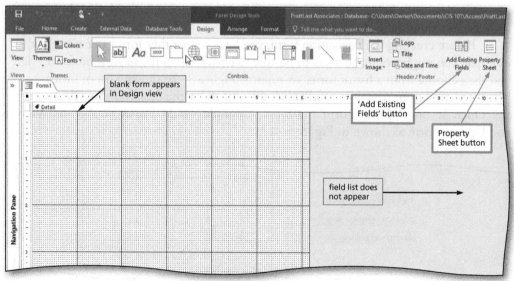

Figure 8–18

• Make sure the 'Use Control Wizards' button is selected.

• Click the Button tool (Form Design Tools Design tab | Controls group) and move the pointer to the approximate position shown in Figure 8–19.

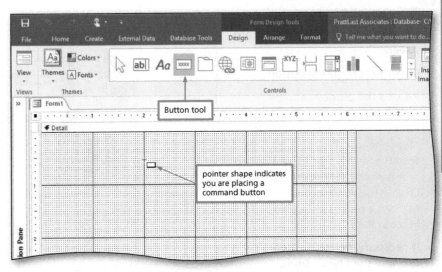

Figure 8–19

• Click the position shown in Figure 8–19 to display the Command Button Wizard dialog box.

• Click Miscellaneous in the Categories box, and then click Run Macro in the Actions box (Figure 8–20).

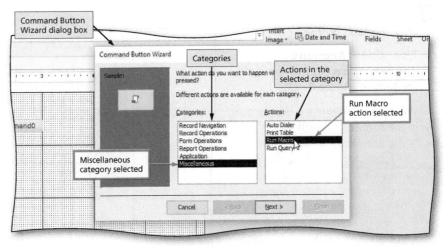

Figure 8–20

• Click the Next button to display the next screen in the wizard.

• Click Forms and Reports.Open Account Master Form to select the macro to be run (Figure 8–21).

Q&A | What does this notation mean?
The portion before the period is the macro and the portion after the period is the submacro. Thus, this notation means the Open Account Master Form submacro within the Forms and Reports macro.

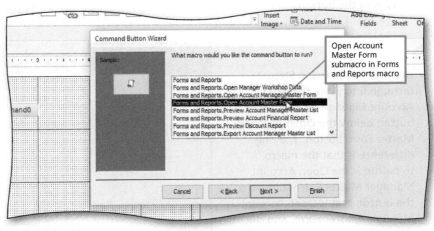

Figure 8–21

- Click the Next button to display the next Command Button Wizard screen.

- Click the Text option button.

Q&A What is the purpose of these option buttons?
Choose the first option button to place text on the button. You can then specify the text to be included or accept the default choice. Choose the second option button to place a picture on the button. You can then select a picture.

- If necessary, delete the default text and then type **Open Account Master Form** as the text (Figure 8–22).

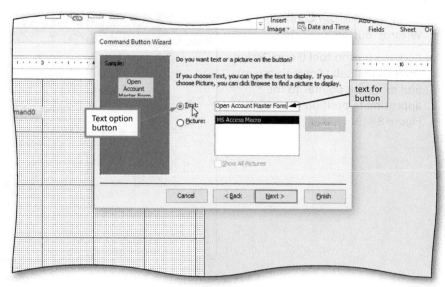

Figure 8–22

- Click the Next button.

- Type **Open_Account_Master_Form** as the name of the button (Figure 8–23).

Q&A Why do you include the underscores in the name of the button?
If you are working with macros or VBA, you cannot have spaces in names. One way to avoid spaces and still make readable names is to include underscores where you would normally use spaces. Thus, Open Account Master Form becomes Open_Account_Master_Form.

- Click the Finish button to finish specifying the button.

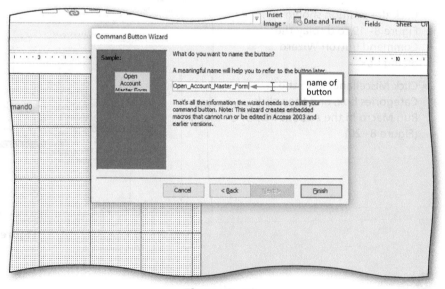

Figure 8–23

7

- Use the techniques in Steps 2 through 6 to place the Open Account Manager Master Form button below the Open Account Master Form button. The only difference is that the macro to be run is the Open Account Manager Master Form submacro, the button text is Open Account Manager Master Form, and the name of the button is Open_Account_Manager_Master_Form.

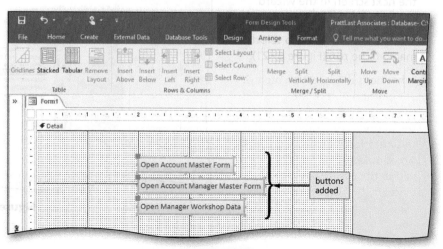

Figure 8–24

- Use the techniques in Steps 2 through 6 to place the Open Manager Workshop Data button below the Open Account Manager Master Form button. The only difference is that the macro to be run is the Open Manager Workshop Data submacro, the text is Open Manager Workshop Data, and the name of the button is Open_Manager_Workshop_Data.

- Adjust the size and spacing of the buttons to approximately match those in Figure 8–24, using the Arrange tab, if necessary.

- Save the form using the name, Forms List.

Q&A How can I test the buttons to make sure the macros work?
Right-click the Forms List form in the Navigation Pane and click Open. Click each of the buttons on the form. If there are errors in any of the macros, open the macro in the Macro Builder window and correct the errors.

 Experiment

- Test each of the buttons on the form. Ensure that the correct form opens. If there are errors, correct the corresponding macro.

8

- Close the form.

Option Groups

You might find it useful to allow users to make a selection from some predefined options by including an option group. An **option group** is a rectangle containing a collection of option buttons. To perform an action, you simply click the corresponding option button. Figure 8–25 shows a list of reports presented in an option group where the user would click the desired option button. Notice that the user could click an option button to preview a report. The user could click a different option button to export the report as a PDF file. Clicking the 'Preview Account Manager Master List' option button, for example, would display a preview of the Account Manager Master List (Figure 8–26). Clicking the Close Print Preview button would return you to the option group.

BTW
Viewing VBA Code
You can view VBA code that is attached to a form or report. To do so, open the form or report in Design view and click the View Code button (Report Design Tools Design tab | Tools group) for reports or (Form Design Tools Design tab | Tools group) for forms.

Figure 8–25

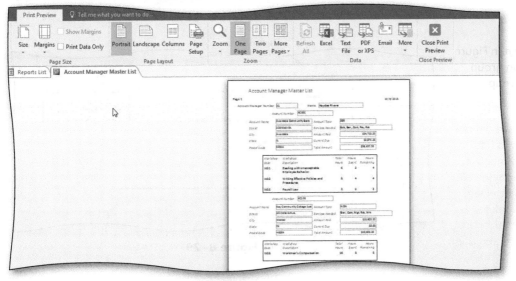

Figure 8–26

To Create a Menu Form Containing an Option Group

The form you are creating will contain an option group. *Why? The option group allows users to select an option button to indicate either a report to preview or a report to export.*

The following steps use the Option Group tool to create the option group named Form Options.

1

- Display the Create tab.

- Click the Form Design button (Create tab | Forms group) to create a blank form in Design view.

- If a field list appears, click the 'Add Existing Fields' button (Form Design Tools Design tab | Tools group) to remove the field list (Figure 8–27).

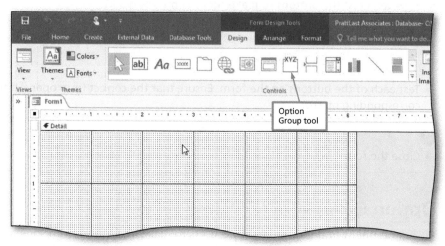

Figure 8–27

2

- With the 'Use Control Wizards' button selected, click the Option Group tool (Form Design Tools Design tab | Controls group) and then move the pointer to the approximate position shown in Figure 8–28.

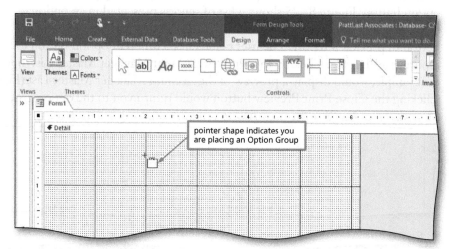

Figure 8–28

3

- Click the position shown in Figure 8–28 to place an option group and start the Option Group Wizard (Figure 8–29).

 The Option Group Wizard did not start for me. What should I do?
You must not have had the 'Use Control Wizards' button selected. With the option group selected, press the DELETE key to delete the option group. Select the 'Use Control Wizards' button, and then add the option group a second time.

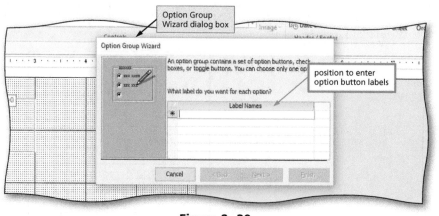

Figure 8–29

- Type **Preview Account Manager Master List** in the first row of label names and press the DOWN ARROW key to specify the label for the first button in the group.

- Type **Preview Account Financial Report** in the second row of label names and press the DOWN ARROW key.

- Type **Preview Discount Report** in the third row of label names and press the DOWN ARROW key.

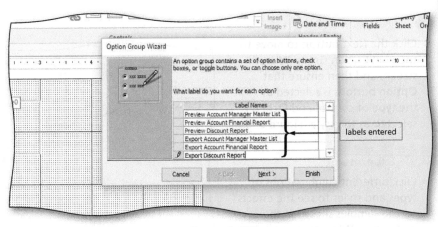

Figure 8–30

- Type **Export Account Manager Master List** in the fourth row of label names and press the DOWN ARROW key.

- Type **Export Account Financial Report** in the fifth row of label names and press the DOWN ARROW key.

- Type **Export Discount Report** in the sixth row of label names (Figure 8–30).

- Click the Next button to move to the next Option Group Wizard screen.

- Click the 'No, I don't want a default.' option button to select it (Figure 8–31).

Q&A
What is the effect of specifying one of the options as the default choice?
The default choice will initially be selected when you open the form. If there is no default choice, no option will be selected.

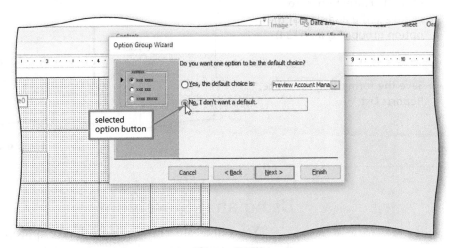

Figure 8–31

- Click the Next button to move to the next Option Group Wizard screen and then verify that the values assigned to the labels match those shown in Figure 8–32.

Q&A
What is the purpose of the values that appear for each option?
You can use the values in macros or VBA. You will use them in a macro later in this module.

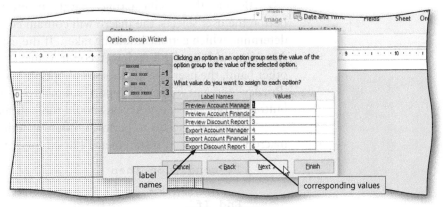

Figure 8–32

6

- Click the Next button to move to the next Option Group Wizard screen, and then ensure that Option buttons is selected as the type of control and Etched is selected as the style (Figure 8–33).

 Experiment

- Click different combinations of types and styles to see the effects on the samples shown in the dialog box. When finished, select Option buttons as the type and Etched as the style.

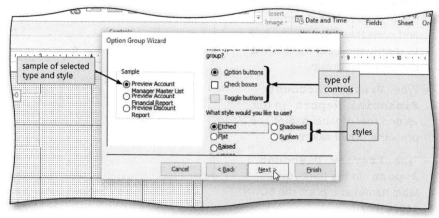

Figure 8–33

7

- Click the Next button to move to the next Option Group Wizard screen and then type **Report Actions** as the caption.

- Click the Finish button to complete the addition of the option group (Figure 8–34).

8

- Save the form using the name, Reports List.

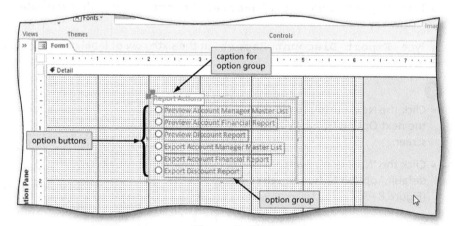

Figure 8–34

Using an If Statement

You will create a macro that will take appropriate action when the user updates the option group, that is, when the user clicks an option button in the group. The macro will run the appropriate submacro, depending on which option the user has selected.

Because the specific actions that the macro will perform depend on the option button the user selects, the macro will contain conditions. The conditions will determine which action should be taken. If the user selects the first option button, Access should run the 'Preview Account Manager Master List' submacro. If, on the other hand, the user selects the second option button, Access should instead run the 'Preview Account Financial Report' submacro. For each of the six possible option buttons a user can select, Access should run a different submacro.

To instruct Access to perform different actions based on certain conditions, the macro will contain an If statement. The simplest form of an If statement is:

```
If condition Then
        action
End If
```

If the condition is true, Access will take the indicated action. If the condition is false, no action will be taken. For example, the condition could be that the user selects the first option button, and the action could be to run the Account Manager Master List submacro. No action would be taken if the user selects any other button.

Another form of the If statement contains an Else clause. This form is:

```
If condition Then
        first action
Else
        second action
End If
```

If the condition is true, the first action is taken; if the condition is false, the second action is taken. For example, the condition could be that the user selects option button 1; the first action could be to run the 'Preview Account Manager Master List' submacro, and the second action could be to run the 'Preview Account Financial Report' submacro. If the user selects option button 1, Access would run the 'Preview Account Manager Master' list submacro. If the user selects any other option button, Access would run the 'Preview Account Financial Report' submacro. Because there are six option buttons, the macro needs to use an If statement with multiple Else Ifs to account for all of the options. This type of If statement has the form:

```
If first condition Then
        first action
Else If second condition Then
        second action
Else If third condition Then
        third action
...

End If
```

The first condition could be that the user selects the first option button; the second condition could be that the user selects the second option button; the third condition could be that the user selects the third option button, and so on. The first action could be that Access runs the first submacro; the second action could be that it runs the second submacro; and the third could be that it runs the third submacro. In this case, there are six option buttons and six submacros. For six conditions, as required in this macro, the If statement will contain five Else Ifs. The If statement along with the five Else Ifs will collectively contain six conditions: one to test if the user selected option 1, one for option 2, one for option 3, one for option 4, one for option 5, and one for option 6.

To Create a Macro with a Variable for the Option Group

1 MACRO WITH SUBMACROS | 2 FORM COMMAND BUTTONS | 3 FORM OPTION GROUP | 4 MACRO FOR OPTION GROUP

5 DATASHEET FORMS | 6 USER INTERFACE MACROS | 7 NAVIGATION FORM | 8 DATA MACRO

The following steps begin creating the macro and add an action to set a variable to the desired value. *Why? The expression that contains the option number is [Forms]![Account Master Form]![Form_Options]. Because this expression is fairly lengthy, the macro will begin by setting a temporary variable to this expression.* A **variable** is a named location in computer memory. You can use a variable to store a value that you can use later in the macro. You will assign the name Optno (short for option number) as the variable name for the expression. This location can contain a value, in this case, the option number on the form. In each of the conditions, you can then use Optno rather than the full expression.

①

- With the option group selected, display a property sheet.
- If necessary, click the All tab.
- Change the name of the option group to Form_Options (Figure 8–35).

Q&A Why this name?

The name Form_Options reflects the fact that these are options that control the action that will be taken on this form. The underscore keeps the name from containing a space.

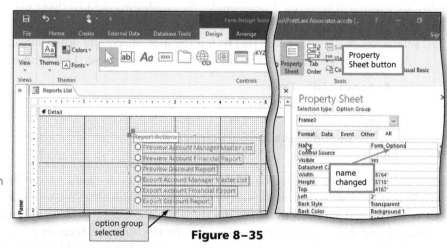

Figure 8–35

②

- Click the After Update property.
- Click the Build button to display the Choose Builder dialog box (Figure 8–36).

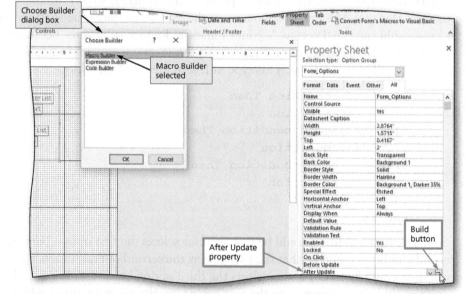

Figure 8–36

③

- With Macro Builder selected in the Choose Builder dialog box, click the OK button to create a macro.
- If necessary, click the Action Catalog button (Macro Tools Design tab | Show/Hide group) to display the Action Catalog.
- If necessary, collapse any category that is expanded.
- Expand the Macro Commands action category.
- Double-click the SetTempVar action in the Action Catalog to add the SetTempVar action to the macro.
- Type **Optno** as the value for the Name argument.
- Type **[Form_Options]** as the value for the Expression argument (Figure 8–37).

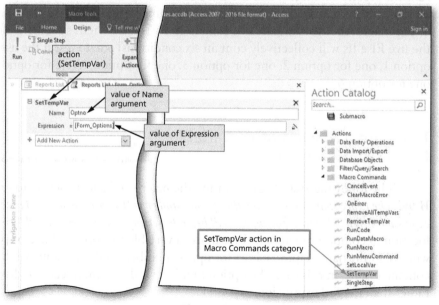

Figure 8–37

How does Access make it easier to enter values for arguments?
Access helps you in three ways. First, if you point to the argument, Access displays a description of the argument. Second, many arguments feature a drop-down list, where you can display the list and then select the desired value. Finally, if you begin typing an expression, a feature called IntelliSense will suggest possible values that start with the letters you have already typed and that are appropriate in the context of what you are typing. If you see the value you want in the list, you can simply click it to select the value.

Macro for Option Group

As mentioned previously, the macro contains six conditions. The first is [TempVars]! [Optno]=1, which simply means the value in the temporary variable Optno is equal to 1. In other words, the user selected the first option button. The action associated with this condition is RunMacro. The argument is the name of the macro. Because the macro to be run is a submacro, the name of the macro includes both the name of the macro containing the submacro, a period, and then the name of the submacro. Because the submacro to be run is Preview Account Manager Master List and is contained in the Forms and Reports macro, the value of the Macro Name argument is Forms and Reports.Preview Account Manager Master List.

The conditions and actions for options 2 through 6 are similar to the first submacro. The only difference is which submacro is associated with each option button. The conditions, actions, and arguments that you will change for the Form_ Options macro are shown in Table 8–2. If the option number is 1, for example, the action is RunMacro. For the RunMacro action, you will change the Macro Name argument. You will set the Macro Name argument to the Preview Account Manager Master List submacro in the Forms and Reports macro. On the other hand, if the option number is 2, for example, the action is again RunMacro. If the option number is 2, however, you will set the Macro Name argument to the Preview Account Financial Report submacro in the Forms and Reports macro. Similar actions take place for the other possible values for the Optno variable, that is, for option buttons 3-6. Because the temporary variable, Optno, is no longer needed at the end of the macro, the macro concludes with the RemoveTempVar command to remove this variable.

Table 8–2 Macro for After Update Property of the Option Group		
Condition	**Action**	**Arguments to be Changed**
	SetTempVar	Name: Optno Expression: [Form_Options]
If [TempVars]![Optno]=1		
	RunMacro	Macro Name: Forms and Reports.Preview Account Manager Master List
Else If [TempVars]![Optno]=2		
	RunMacro	Macro Name: Forms and Reports.Preview Account Financial Report
Else If [TempVars]![Optno]=3		
	RunMacro	Macro Name: Forms and Reports.Preview Discount Report
Else If [TempVars]![Optno]=4		
	RunMacro	Macro Name: Forms and Reports.Export Account Manager Master List
Else If [TempVars]![Optno]=5		
	RunMacro	Macro Name: Forms and Reports.Export Account Financial Report
Else If [TempVars]![Optno]=6		
	RunMacro	Macro Name: Forms and Reports.Export Discount Report
End If		
	RemoveTempVar	Name: Optno

To Add Actions to the Form Options Macro

The following steps add the conditions and actions to the Form_Options macro. *Why? The macro is not yet complete. Adding the conditions and actions will complete the macro.*

1

- Double-click the If element from the Program Flow section of the Action Catalog to add an If statement to the submacro and then type `[TempVars]![Optno]=1` as the condition in the If statement.

- With the Macro Commands category expanded, double-click RunMacro to add the RunMacro action.

- Click the drop-down arrow for the Macro Name argument and select the 'Preview Account Manager Master List' submacro within the Forms and Reports macro as the value for the argument (Figure 8–38).

Q&A What should I do if I add an action in the wrong position? What should I do if I add the wrong action?

If you add an action in the wrong position, use the Move up or Move down buttons to move it to the correct position. If you added the wrong action, click the DELETE button to delete the action, and then fix the error by adding the correct action.

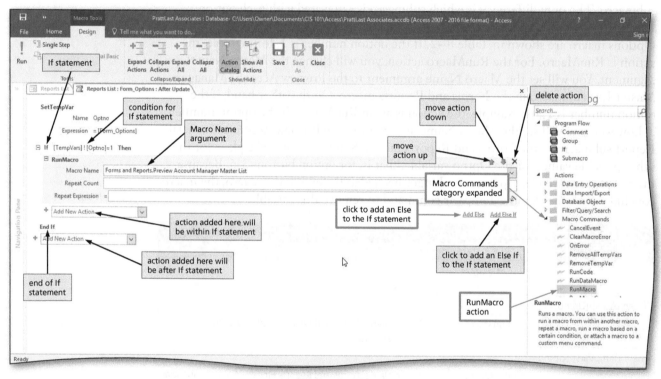

Figure 8–38

2

- Click 'Add Else If' to add an Else If clause to the If statement.

- Add the conditions and actions associated with options 2, 3, 4, 5, and 6 as described in Table 8–2, and specify the arguments for the actions. Click 'Add Else If' after adding each action except for the last one.

Q&A

Do I have to enter all these actions? They seem to be very similar to the ones associated with option 1.

You can copy and paste the action for option 1. Right-click the action to select it and display a shortcut menu. Click Copy on the shortcut menu. Right-click the action just above where you want to insert the selected action and then click Paste. If the new action is not inserted in the correct position, select the new action and then click either the Move up or Move down buttons to move it to the correct location. Once the action is in the correct location, you can make any necessary changes to the arguments.

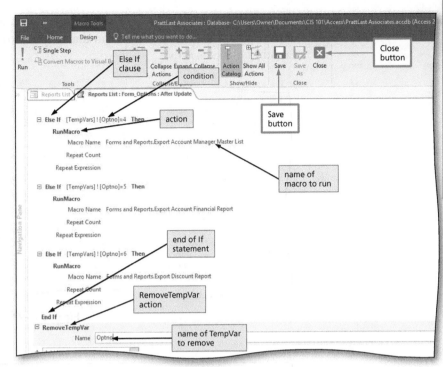

Figure 8–39

- Add the RemoveTempVar action and argument after the end of the If statement, as shown in Figure 8–39.
- Type **Optno** as the name of the TempVar to remove.

Q&A

Do I need to remove the temporary variable?

Technically, no. In fact, if you plan to use this temporary variable in another macro and want it to retain the value you assigned in this macro, you would definitely not remove it. If you do not plan to use it elsewhere, it is a good idea to remove it, however.

- Click the Save button (Macro Tools Design tab | Close group) to save the macro.
- Click the Close button (Macro Tools Design tab | Close group) to close the macro and return to the form.
- Close the property sheet, save the form, and close the form.

Experiment

- Test each of the buttons in the option group. If you do not preview or export the correct report, correct the error in the corresponding macro. If you get an error indicating that the section width is greater than the page width, you have an error in the corresponding report. Correct the error using the instructions in the Errors in Macros section of this module.

Break Point: If you wish to stop working through the module at this point, you can resume the project at a later time by running Access, opening the database called PrattLast Associates, and continuing to follow the steps from this location forward.

User Interface (UI) Macros

A **user interface (UI) macro** is a macro that is attached to a user interface object, such as a command button, an option group, or a control on a form. The macro you just created for the option group is thus a UI macro, as were the macros you attached to command buttons. A common use for UI macros is to associate actions with the clicking of a control on a form. In the Account form shown in Figure 8–40, for example, if you click the account number on the row in the datasheet where the account number is CO621, Access displays the data for that account in a pop-up form (Figure 8–41), that is, a form that stays on top of other open objects, even when another object is active.

AC #	Account Name	Street	City	State	Postal Code	Account Typ	Services Need
AC001	Avondale Community Bank	256 Main St.	Avondale	IL	60311	SER	Bck, Ben, Com, Pay,
BL235	Bland Corp.	100 South Granger Hwy.	Granger	IL	60314	IND	Bck, Mgt, Rsk, Tch,
CA043	Carlton Regional Clinic	589 Central Ave.	Carlton	IL	60313	NON	Mgt, Pay, Rsk, Tch
CO621	Codder Plastics Co.	421 First Ave.	Bremerton	IN	46003	IND	Ben, Pay, Rsk, Trn,
EC010	Eco Clothes Inc.	120 Pine St.	Davidson	IN	46010	IND	Rec, Trn, Wrk
HL111	Halko Legal Associates	321 Feathering Rd.	Gleneagle	IL	60319	SER	Ben, Com, Pay, Rsk,
KC156	Key Community College System	35 Indiana Ave.	Walker	IN	46004	NON	Ben, Com, Mgt, Rsk,
KV089	KAL Veterinary Services	116 Pine St.	Granger	IL	60314	SER	Ben, Com, Tch, Trn
LC005	Lancaster County Hospital	215 River St.	Granger	IL	46004	NON	Ben, Mgt, Pay, Rsk, Tc
LI268	Lars-Idsen-Fleming Inc.	829 Wooster Rd.	Davidson	IN	46010	IND	Ben, Pay, Wrk
MI345	Midwest Library Consortium	3400 Metro Pkwy.	Bremerton	IN	46003	NON	Bck, Ben, Com, Pay, T
ML008	Mums Landscaping Co.	865 Ridge Rd.	Wells	IN	46007	SER	Bck, Pay, Wrk
SL326	South Library Consortium	862 Maple St.	Wells	IN	46007	NON	Bck, Ben, Com, Pay,
TP098	TAL Packaging Systems	12 Polk Ave.	Carlton	IL	60313	IND	Ben, Com, Pay, Trn,
TW001	Tri-County Waste Disposal	345 Central Blvd.	Rushton	IL	60321	SER	Bck, Pay, Rec, Wrk

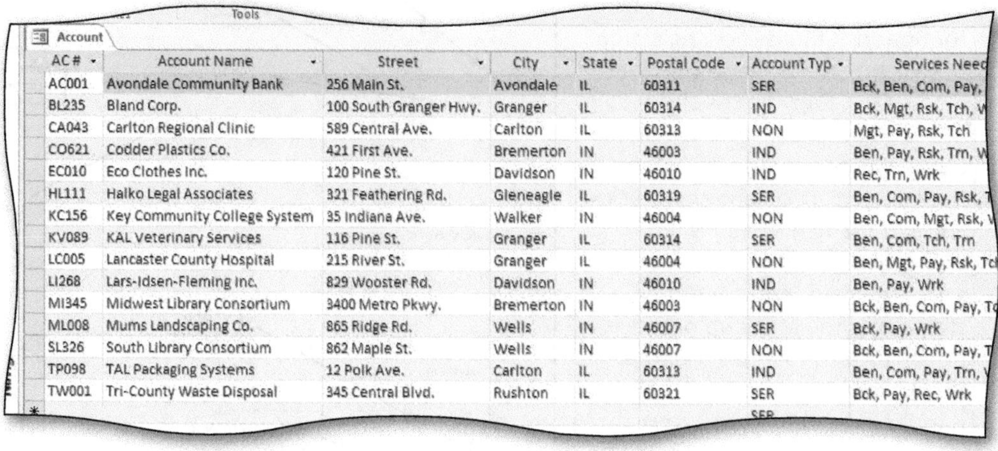

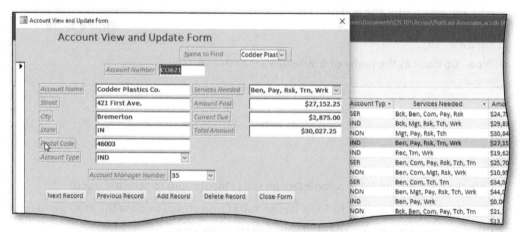

Figure 8–40

Figure 8–41

Similarly, in the Account Manager form shown in Figure 8–42, for example, if you click the account manager number on the row in the datasheet where the account manager number is 58, Access displays the data for that account manager in a pop-up form (Figure 8–43).

AM #	Last Name	First Name	Street	City	State	Postal Code	Phone Numl	Start Date	Salary	Bonus Rate
31	Rivera	Haydee	325 Twiddy St.	Avondale	IL	60311	(825) 555-3455	6/3/2013	$48,750.00	0.15
35	Simson	Mark	1467 Hartwell St.	Walker	IN	46004	(317) 555-6754	5/19/2014	$40,500.00	0.12
42	Lu	Peter	5624 Murray Ave.	Davidson	IN	46007	(930) 555-7200	8/3/2015	$36,750.00	0.09
58	Murowski	Karen	168 Truesdale Dr.	Carlton	IL	60313	(779) 555-1289	11/9/2016	$24,000.00	0.08
									$0.00	0.00

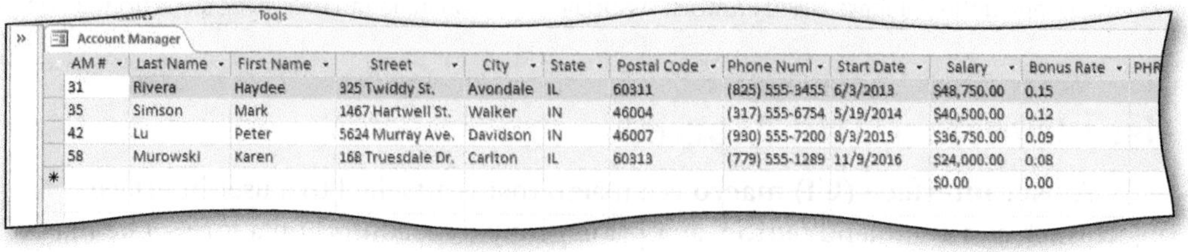

Figure 8–42

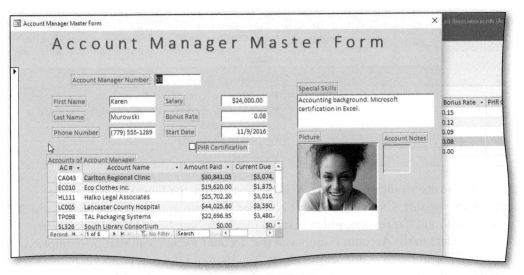

Figure 8–43

Recall that you can only use forms and reports for the tabs in a navigation form, yet the Account tab appears to display the Account table in Datasheet view. You can make it appear as though you are displaying the Account table in Datasheet view by creating a datasheet form that you will call Account. You will create a UI macro in this Account datasheet form. The UI macro that will be associated with the clicking of the account number on some record in the Account form will display the selected account in the Account Master Form.

To display the Account Master Form, the UI macro will use the OpenForm action. You must set the Form Name argument of the OpenForm action to the actual name of the form to be opened, Account Master Form. (Account View and Update Form is just the form caption.) PrattLast wants to prevent the user from updating data using this form, so the Data Mode argument is set to Read Only. The form should appear as a pop-up, which you accomplish by setting the value of the Window Mode argument to Dialog.

The form should display only the record that the user selected. If the user clicks account number CO621 in the Account form, for example, the form should display only the data for account CO621. To restrict the record that appears in the form, you include the Where Condition argument in the UI macro. The condition needs to indicate that the Account Number in the form to be opened, Account Master Form, needs to be equal to the Account Number the user selected in the Account form.

In the Where Condition, you can simply refer to a control in the form to be opened by using its name. If the name has spaces, you must enclose it in square brackets. Thus, the name for the Account Number in the Account Master Form is simply [Account Number]. To reference a control that is part of any other form, the expression must include both the name of the form and the name of the control, separated by an exclamation point. Thus, the Account Number in the Account form would be [Account]![Account Number]. This declaration works correctly when you are programming a macro that simply opens the Account form. However, when you associate the Account form with a tab in the navigation form, the Account form becomes a subform, which requires modification to the expression. This means that a form that works correctly when you open the form may not work correctly when the form is assigned to a tab in a navigation form. A safer approach avoids these issues by using a temporary variable.

Table 8–3 shows the UI macro for the Account form. It is associated with the On Click event for the Account Number control. When a user clicks an account number, the UI macro will display the data for the selected account in the Account Master Form. The main function of the macro is to open the appropriate form using the OpenForm action.

BTW
Distributing a Document
Instead of printing and distributing a hard copy of a document, you can distribute the document electronically. Options include sending the document via email; posting it on cloud storage (such as OneDrive) and sharing the file with others; posting it on a social networking site, blog, or other website; and sharing a link associated with an online location of the document. You also can create and share a PDF or XPS image of the document, so that users can view the file in Acrobat Reader or XPS Viewer instead of in Access.

Table 8–3 UI Macro Associated with On Click Event in the Account Form		
Condition	**Action**	**Arguments to Be Changed**
	SetTempVar	Name: AN Expression: [Account Number]
	OpenForm	Form Name: Account Master Form Where Condition: [Account Number]=[TempVars]![AN] Data Mode: Read Only Window Mode: Dialog
	RemoveTempVar	Name: AN

In the macro shown in Table 8–3, the first action, SetTempVar, assigns the temporary variable AN to the Account Number. The two arguments are Name, which is set to AN, and Expression, which is set to [Account Number]. The AN temporary variable refers to the Account Number in the Account form; recall that the completed macro will open the Account Master Form. You then can use that temporary variable in the Where Condition argument. The expression is thus [Account Number]=[TempVars]![AN]. The [Account Number] portion refers to the Account Number in the Account Master Form. The [TempVars]![AN] portion is the temporary variable that has been set equal to the Account Number in the Account form. The macro ends by removing the temporary variable.

Table 8–4 shows the macro for the Account Manager form, which is very similar to the macro for the Account form.

Table 8–4 UI Macro Associated with On Click Event in the Account Manager Form		
Condition	**Action**	**Arguments to Be Changed**
	SetTempVar	Name: MN Expression: [Account Manager Number]
	OpenForm	Form Name: Account Manager Master Form Where Condition: [Account Manager Number]=[TempVars]![MN] Data Mode: Read Only Window Mode: Dialog
	RemoveTempVar	Name: MN

To Create Datasheet Forms

1 MACRO WITH SUBMACROS | 2 FORM COMMAND BUTTONS | 3 FORM OPTION GROUP | 4 MACRO FOR OPTION GROUP
5 DATASHEET FORMS | 6 USER INTERFACE MACROS | 7 NAVIGATION FORM | 8 DATA MACRO

The following steps create two datasheet forms, one for the Account table and one for the Account Manager table. **Why?** *The datasheet forms enable the Account and Account Manager tables to appear as if displayed in Datasheet view, despite the Access restriction that prevents tables from being used on tabs in a navigation form.*

- Open the Navigation Pane and select the Account table.

- Display the Create tab and then click the More Forms button (Create tab | Forms group) to display the More Forms gallery (Figure 8–44).

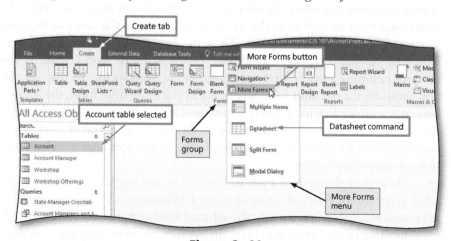

Figure 8–44

● Click Datasheet to create a datasheet form.

● Save the form using the name, Account.

 Is it acceptable to use the same name for the form as for the table?

Yes. In this case, you want it to appear to the user that the Account table is open in Datasheet view. One way to emphasize this fact is to use the same name as the table.

What is the difference between this form, Account, and the form named Account Form?
The Account Form is a simple form that displays only one record at a time. The form you just created displays all of the account data in a datasheet.

● Use the same technique to create a datasheet form named Account Manager for the Account Manager table.

● Close both forms.

To Create UI Macros for the Datasheet Forms

1 MACRO WITH SUBMACROS | 2 FORM COMMAND BUTTONS | 3 FORM OPTION GROUP | 4 MACRO FOR OPTION GROUP

5 DATASHEET FORMS | 6 USER INTERFACE MACROS | **7 NAVIGATION FORM** | 8 DATA MACRO

The following steps create the UI macro for the Account datasheet form shown in Table 8–3 and the UI macro for the Account Manager datasheet form shown in Table 8–4. *Why? The UI macros will cause the appropriate pop-up forms to appear as a result of clicking the appropriate position on the forms.*

● Open the Account datasheet form and then close the Navigation Pane.

● Click the Account Number (AC #) heading to select the Account Number column in the datasheet.

● If necessary, click the Property Sheet button (Form Tools Datasheet tab | Tools group) to display a property sheet.

● Click the Event tab to display only event properties.

 Why click the Event tab? Why not just use the All tab as we have before?

You can always use the All tab; however, if you know the category that contains the property in which you are interested, you can greatly reduce the number of properties that Access will display by clicking the tab for that category. That gives you fewer properties to search through to find the property you want. Whether you use the All tab or one of the other tabs is strictly a matter of personal preference.

● Click the On Click event and then click the Build button (the three dots) to display the Choose Builder dialog box (Figure 8–45).

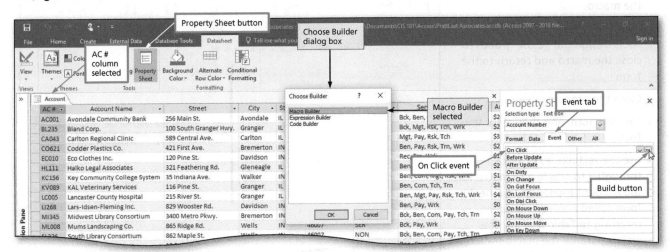

Figure 8–45

2

- Click the OK button (Choose Builder dialog box) to display the Macro Builder window.

- Add the SetTempVar action to the macro, enter **AN** as the value for the Name argument, and enter **[Account Number]** as the value for the Expression argument.

- Add the OpenForm action to the macro, select Account Master Form as the value for the Form Name argument, leave the value of the View argument set to Form, enter **[Account Number] = [TempVars] ! [AN]** as the value for the Where Condition argument, select Read Only as the value for the Data Mode argument, and select Dialog as the value for the Window Mode argument.

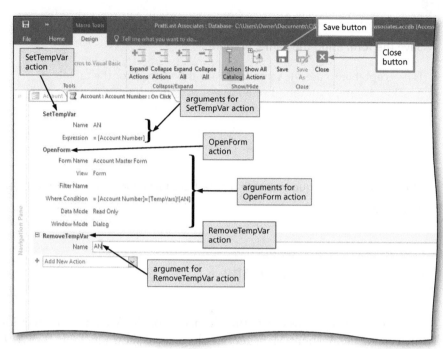

Figure 8–46

Q&A | What does this expression mean?

The portion before the equal sign, [Account Number], refers to the Account Number in the form just opened, that is, in the Account Master Form. The portion to the right of the equal sign, [TempVars]![AN], is the temporary variable that was set equal to the Account Number on the selected record in the Account form. This Where Condition guarantees that the record displayed in the Account Master Form will be the record with the same Account Number as the one selected in the Account form.

- Add the RemoveTempVar action to the macro and enter **AN** as the value for the Name argument (Figure 8–46).

Q&A | Why do you need to remove the temporary variable?

Technically, you do not. It has fulfilled its function, however, so it makes sense to remove it at this point.

3

- Click the Save button (Macro Tools Design tab | Close group) to save the macro.

- Click the Close button (Macro Tools Design tab | Close group) to close the macro and return to the form.

- Close the property sheet.

- Save the form and then close the form.

- Use the techniques in Steps 1 through 3 to create a UI macro for the Account Manager datasheet form called Account Manager, referring to Table 8–4 for the actions. Create the macro shown in Figure 8–47 associated with clicking the Account Manager Number (AM #) column.

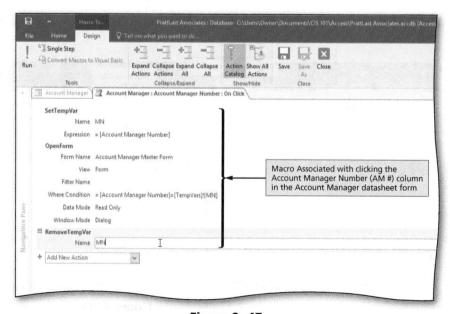

Figure 8–47

4

- Click the Save button (Macro Tools Design tab | Close group) to save the macro.
- Click the Close button (Macro Tools Design tab | Close group) to close the macro and return to the datasheet form.
- Close the property sheet.
- Save the form and then close the form.

To Create a Navigation Form

1 MACRO WITH SUBMACROS | 2 FORM COMMAND BUTTONS | 3 FORM OPTION GROUP | 4 MACRO FOR OPTION GROUP
5 DATASHEET FORMS | 6 USER INTERFACE MACROS | **7 NAVIGATION FORM** | **8 DATA MACRO**

You now have all the forms you need to include in the navigation form. The following steps create the navigation form using horizontal tabs. *Why? Horizontal tabs are common on navigation forms and are easy to use.* The steps then save the form and change the title.

1

- If necessary, open the Navigation Pane.
- Click the Create tab and then click the Navigation button (Create tab | Forms group) to display the gallery of available navigation forms (Figure 8–48).

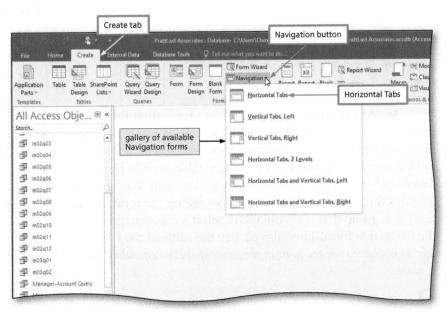

Figure 8–48

2

- Click Horizontal Tabs in the gallery to create a form with a navigation control in which the tabs are arranged horizontally in a single row.
- If a field list appears, click the 'Add Existing Fields' button (Form Layout Tools Design tab | Tools group) to remove the field list (Figure 8–49).

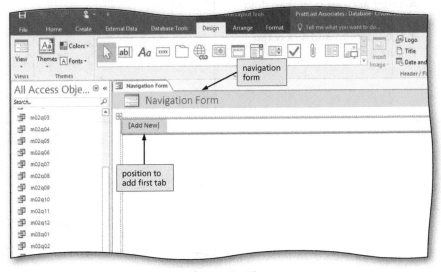

Figure 8–49

- Save the form using the name, Main Menu.

- Click the form title twice: once to select it and the second time to produce an insertion point.

- Erase the current title and then type **PrattLast Associates** as the new title (Figure 8–50).

- Save the form.

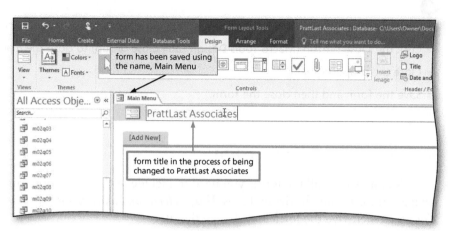

Figure 8–50

To Add Tabs to a Navigation Form

1 MACRO WITH SUBMACROS | 2 FORM COMMAND BUTTONS | 3 FORM OPTION GROUP | 4 MACRO FOR OPTION GROUP
5 DATASHEET FORMS | 6 USER INTERFACE MACROS | **7 NAVIGATION FORM** | **8 DATA MACRO**

To add a form or report to a tab in a navigation form, be sure the Navigation Pane is open and then drag the form or report to the desired tab. As a result, users can display that form or report by clicking the tab. For the PrattLast Associates navigation form, you will drag four forms to the tabs. The Account form is a datasheet form that appears to display the Account table open in Datasheet view. Similarly, the Account Manager form is a datasheet form that appears to display the Account Manager table open in Datasheet view. The Forms List form contains three buttons users can click to display the form of their choice. Finally, the Reports List form contains an option group that users can use to select a report to preview or export. The following steps add the tabs to the navigation form. They also change the name of the Forms List and Reports List tabs. *Why? The names of the tabs do not have to be the same as the name of the corresponding forms. By changing them, you can often make tabs more readable.*

- Scroll down in the Navigation Pane so that the form named Account appears, and then drag the form to the position shown in the figure to add a new tab (Figure 8–51).

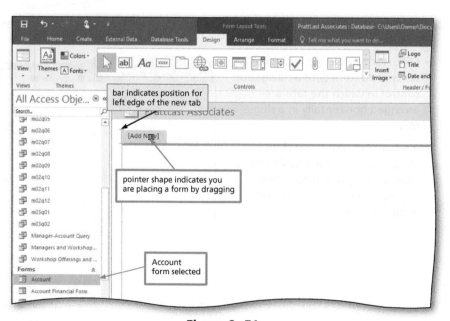

Figure 8–51

2

- Release the left mouse button to add the Account form as the first tab.
- Drag the Account Manager form to the position shown in the figure to add a new tab (Figure 8–52).

 Q&A What should I do if I made a mistake and added a form or report to the wrong location? You can rearrange the tabs by dragging them. Often, the simplest way to correct a mistake is to click the Undo button to reverse your most recent action, however. You can also choose to simply close the form without saving it and then start over.

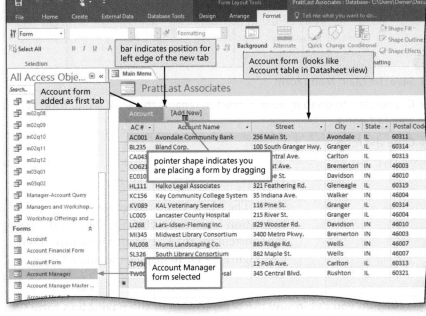

Figure 8–52

3

- Release the left mouse button to add the Account Manager form as the second tab.
- Using the techniques illustrated in Steps 1 and 2, add the Forms List form as the third tab and the Reports List form as the fourth tab (Figure 8–53).

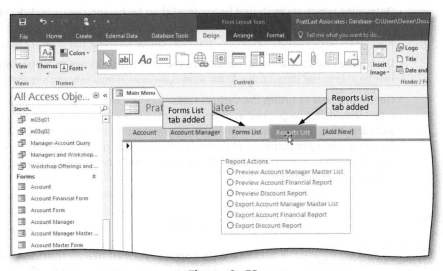

Figure 8–53

4

- Click the Forms List tab twice: once to select it and the second time to produce an insertion point.
- Change the name from Forms List to Forms.
- In a similar fashion, change the name of the Reports List tab from Reports List to Reports (Figure 8–54).

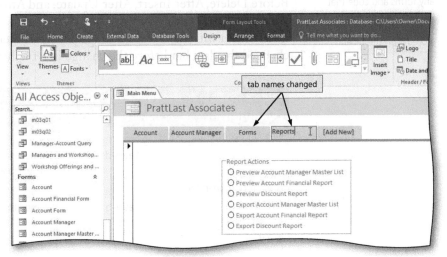

Figure 8–54

I created these two forms using the names Forms List and Reports List. Now I have changed the names to Forms and Reports. Why not call them Forms and Reports in the first place, so I would not have to rename the tabs?
Because the words, forms and reports, have specific meaning in Access, you cannot use these names when creating the forms. Thus, you needed to use some other names, like Forms List and Reports List. Because tabs within forms are not database objects, you can rename them to be any name you want.

5

- Save the Main Menu form.

- If requested to do so by your instructor, rename the Main Menu form as LastName Main Menu where LastName is your last name.

- Close the form.

Using a Navigation Form

The Main Menu navigation form is complete and ready for use. To use the navigation form, right-click the form in the Navigation Pane, and then click Open on the shortcut menu. The Main Menu form then will appear with the first tabbed object (see Figure 8–1). To display the other forms, simply click the appropriate tab.

CONSIDER THIS

How do you determine the organization of the navigation form?
Once you decide you want a navigation form, you need to decide how to organize the form.

- **Determine which tasks should be accomplished by having the user click tabs or buttons in the navigation form.** Which forms should be opened? Which reports should be opened? Are there any tables or queries that you need to be able to open in the navigation form? If so, you must create forms for the tables or queries.

- **Determine any special requirements for the way the tasks are to be performed.** When a form is opened, should a user be able to edit data, or should the form open as read-only? Should a report be exported or simply viewed on the screen?

- **Determine how to group the various tasks.** Should forms or reports simply be assigned to the tabs in the navigation form? Should they be grouped as buttons on a menu form? Should they be placed as options within an option group? (For consistency, you would usually decide on one of these approaches and use it throughout. In this module, one menu form uses command buttons, and the other uses an option group simply to illustrate both approaches.) As far as the navigation form is concerned, is a single set of horizontal tabs sufficient, or would you also like vertical tabs? Would you like two rows of horizontal tabs?

BTW
Data Macros
Data macros are similar to SQL triggers. You attach logic to record or table events and any forms and code that update those events inherit the logic. Data macros are stored with the table.

Data Macros

A data macro is a special type of macro that is associated with specific table-related events, such as updating a record in a table. The possible events are Before Change, Before Delete, After Insert, After Update, and After Delete. Data macros allow you to add logic to these events. For example, the data macro shown in Table 8–5 is associated with the Before Change event, an event that occurs after the user has changed the data but before the change is actually made in the database.

Table 8–5 Data Macro for Before Change Event		
Condition	**Action**	**Arguments to Be Changed**
If [Hours Spent]>[Total Hours]		
	SetField	Name: [Hours Spent] Value: [Total Hours]
Else If [Hours Spent]<0		
	SetField	Name: [Hours Spent] Value: 0
End If		

This macro will examine the value in the Hours Spent field in the Workshop Offerings table. If the user's update would cause the value in the Hours Spent field to be greater than the value in the Total Hours field, the macro will change the value in the Hours Spent field so that it is equal to the value in the Total Hours field. Likewise, if the update would cause the value in the Hours Spent field to be less than zero, the macro will set the value in the Hours Spent field to 0. These changes take place after the user has made the change on the screen but before Access commits the change to the database, that is, before the data in the database is actually changed.

There are other events to which you can assign data macros. The actions in a data macro associated with the Before Delete event will take place after a user has indicated that he or she wants to delete a record, but before the record is actually removed from the database. The actions in a macro associated with the After Insert event will take place immediately after a record physically is added to the database. The actions in a macro associated with the After Update event will take place immediately after a record is physically changed in the database. The actions in a macro associated with the After Delete event will take place immediately after a record is physically removed from the database.

To Create a Data Macro

1 MACRO WITH SUBMACROS | 2 FORM COMMAND BUTTONS | 3 FORM OPTION GROUP | 4 MACRO FOR OPTION GROUP
5 DATASHEET FORMS | 6 USER INTERFACE MACROS | 7 NAVIGATION FORM | **8 DATA MACRO**

The following steps create the data macro in Table 8–5, a macro that will be run after a user makes a change to a record in the Workshop Offerings table, but before the record is updated in the database. *Why? PrattLast Associates management wants a way to prevent users from entering invalid data into the database.*

1

- Open the Workshop Offerings table in Datasheet view and close the Navigation Pane.
- Display the Table Tools Table tab (Figure 8–55).

Q&A What is the meaning of the events in the Before Events and After Events groups?
Actions in macros associated with the Before Events group will occur after the user has taken action to change or delete a record, but before the change or deletion is made permanent in the database. Actions in macros associated with the After Events group will occur after the corresponding update has been made permanent in the database.

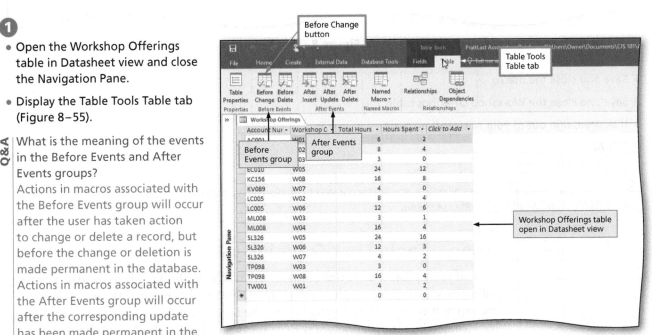

Figure 8–55

● Click the Before Change button (Table Tools Table tab | Before Events group).

● Create the macro shown in Figure 8–56.

Q&A

What happened to all the actions that were in the list? In the previous macros we created, there seemed to be many more actions available.

There are only certain actions that make sense in data macros. Only those actions appear. Therefore, the list of actions that appears is much smaller in a data macro than in other macros.

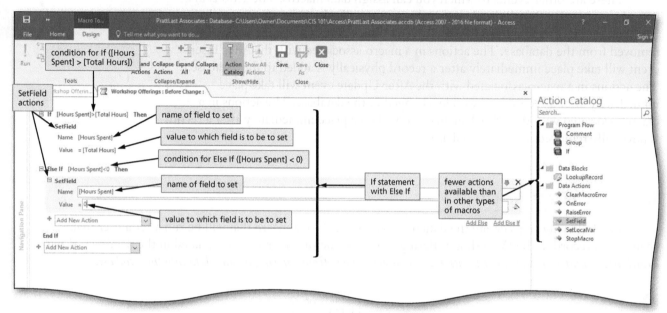

Figure 8–56

● Save and close the macro.

● Save and close the Workshop Offerings table.

● If desired, sign out of your Microsoft account.

● Exit Access.

Note: Unless your instructor indicates otherwise, you are encouraged to simply read the material in this module from this point on for understanding without carrying out any operations.

Using a Table That Contains a Data Macro

If you update a table that contains a data macro, the actions in the data macro will be executed whenever the corresponding event takes place. If the data macro corresponds to the Before Change event, the actions will be executed after the user has changed the data, but before the change is saved in the database. With the data macro you just created, for example, if a user attempts to change the data in such a way that the Hours Spent is greater than the Total Hours (Figure 8–57a), as soon as the user takes an action that would require saving the record, Access makes Hours Spent equal to Total Hours (Figure 8–57b). Likewise, if a user attempts to set Hours Spent to a negative number (Figure 8–58a), as soon as the user takes an action that would require saving the record, Access will set Hours Spent to 0 (Figure 8–58b). This change will take place automatically, regardless of whether the user changes the values in Datasheet view, with a form, in an update query, or in any other fashion.

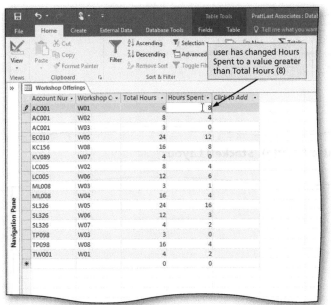

Figure 8–57(a)

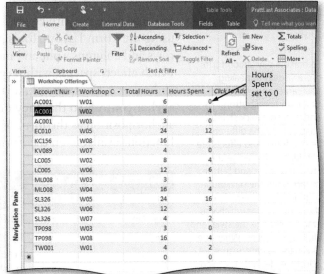

Figure 8–57(b)

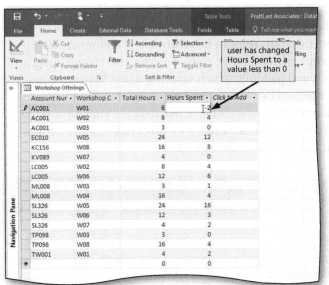

Figure 8–58(a)

Figure 8–58(b)

Using Control Layouts on Forms and Reports

In earlier modules, you worked with control layouts in forms and reports. In a control layout, the data is aligned either horizontally or vertically. The two types of layouts are stacked layouts, which are most commonly used in forms, and tabular layouts, which are most commonly used in reports (Figure 8–59). Using a control layout gives you more options for moving rows or columns than you would have without the layout.

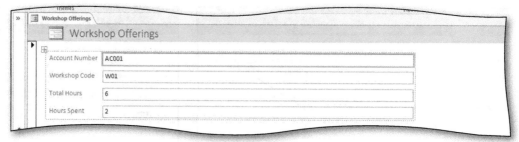

Figure 8–59(a) Stacked Layout

Figure 8–59(b) Tabular Layout

BTW
Quick Styles for Controls
To make a navigation form more visually appealing, you can change the style of a command button and/or tabs. Quick styles change how the different colors, fonts, and effects are combined. To change the style of a command button or tab, open the navigation form in Layout view. Select the control(s) for which you want to change the style, and click Quick Styles. When the Quick Styles gallery appears, select the desired style. You also can change the style of a control in Design view.

In working with control layouts, there are many functions you can perform using the Form Layout Tools Arrange tab. You can insert rows and columns, delete rows and columns, split and merge cells, and move rows. You can also change margins, which affects spacing within cells, and padding, which affects spacing between rows and columns. You can split a layout into two layouts and move layouts. Finally, you can anchor controls so that they maintain the same distance between the control and the anchor position as the form or report is resized. Table 8–6 gives descriptions of the functions available on the Form Layout Tools Arrange tab.

Table 8–6 Arrange Tab	
Button	**Enhanced ScreenTip**
Gridlines	Gridlines
Stacked	Create a layout similar to a paper form, with labels to the left of each field.
Tabular	Create a layout similar to a spreadsheet, with labels across the top and data in columns below the labels.
Insert Above	Insert Above
Insert Below	Insert Below
Insert Left	Insert Left
Insert Right	Insert Right
Select Layout	Select Layout
Select Column	Select Column
Select Row	Select Row
Merge	Merge Cells
Split Vertically	Split the selected layout into two rows.
Split Horizontally	Split the selected layout into two columns.
Move Up	Move Up
Move Down	Move Down
Control Margins	Control Margins
Control Padding	Control Padding
Anchoring	Tie a control to a section or another control so that it moves or resizes in conjunction with movement or resizing of the parent.

TO CREATE A LAYOUT FOR A FORM OR REPORT

If you create a form using the Form button (Create tab | Forms group), Access automatically creates a stacked layout. If you create a report using the Report button (Create tab | Reports group), Access automatically creates a tabular layout. In other cases, you can create a layout using the Form Layout Tools Arrange tab for forms or the Report Layout Tools Arrange tab for reports. If you no longer want controls to be in a control layout, you can remove the layout.

To create a layout in either a form or report, you would use the following steps.

1. Select all the controls that you want to place in a layout.
2. Click the Stacked button (Form Layout Tools Arrange tab | Table group) to create a stacked layout or the Tabular button (Form Layout Tools Arrange tab | Table group) to create a tabular layout.

TO REMOVE A LAYOUT FOR A FORM OR REPORT

To remove a layout from either a form or report, you would use the following steps.

1. Right-click any control in the layout you want to remove to produce a shortcut menu.
2. Point to Layout on the shortcut menu and then click Remove Layout on the submenu to remove the layout.

Using Undo

When making changes with the Form Layout Tools Arrange tab buttons, it is not uncommon to make a change that you did not intend. Sometimes taking appropriate action to reverse the change can prove difficult. If so, remember that you can undo the change by clicking the Undo button on the Quick Access Toolbar. It is also a good idea to save your work frequently. That way, you can always close the form or report without saving. When you reopen the form or report, it will not have any of your most recent changes.

TO INSERT A ROW

You can insert a blank row either above or below a selected row (Figure 8–60). You can then fill in the row by either typing a value or dragging a field from a field

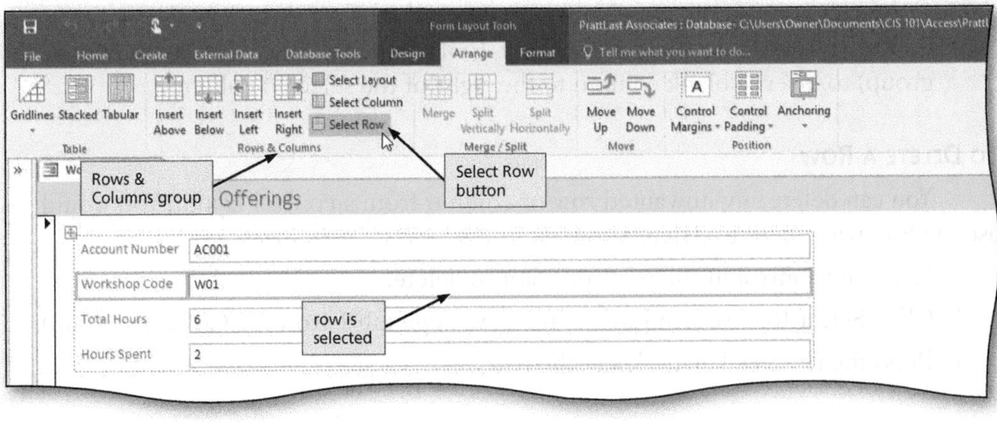

BTW

Change the Shape of a Control
Command buttons and tabs have a default shape. For example, both command buttons and tabs have a rounded rectangle shape as the default shape. You can change the shape of a button or tab control on a navigation form. To do so, open the navigation form in Layout view. Select the control(s) for which you want to change the shape and click Change Shape. When the Change Shape gallery appears, select the desired shape. You also can change the shape of a command button or tab in Design view.

Figure 8–60(a) Selecting a Row

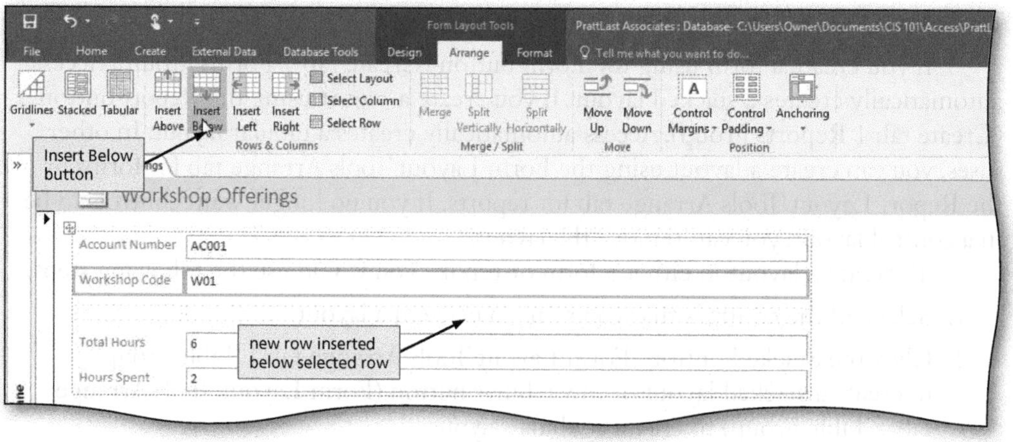

Figure 8–60(b) Inserting a Row

BTW

PivotTables and PivotCharts

PivotTable view and PivotChart view are no longer available in Access. To create a PivotChart or PivotTable, create a new workbook in the Microsoft Excel app, click the From Access button (Data tab | Get External Data group) and follow the directions in the Select Data Source dialog box to import an Access table. You then can use the PivotTable and PivotChart features of Excel.

list. In a similar fashion, you can insert a blank column either to the left or right of a selected column.

You would use the following steps to insert a blank row.

1. Select any control in the row above or below where you want to insert a new row.

2. Click the Select Row button (Form Layout Tools Arrange tab | Rows & Columns group) to select the row.

3. Click the Insert Above button (Form Layout Tools Arrange tab | Rows & Columns group) to insert a blank row above the selected row or the Insert Below button (Form Layout Tools Arrange tab | Rows & Columns group) to insert a blank row below the selected row.

As you have seen earlier in the text, you also can insert a row containing a field by simply dragging the field from the field list to the desired location.

TO INSERT A COLUMN

You would use the following steps to insert a new column.

1. Select any control in the column to the right or left of where you want to insert a new column.

2. Click the Select Column button (Form Layout Tools Arrange tab | Rows & Columns group) to select the column.

3. Click the Insert Left button (Form Layout Tools Arrange tab | Rows & Columns group) to insert a blank column to the left of the selected column or the Insert Right button (Form Layout Tools Arrange tab | Rows & Columns group) to insert a blank column to the right of the selected column.

TO DELETE A ROW

You can delete any unwanted row or column from a control layout. You would use the following steps to delete a row.

1. Click any control in the row you want to delete.

2. Click Select Row (Form Layout Tools Arrange tab | Rows & Columns group).

3. Press the DELETE key to delete the row.

To Delete a Column

You would use the following steps to delete a column.

1. Click any control in the column you want to delete.
2. Click Select Column (Form Layout Tools Arrange tab | Rows & Columns group).
3. Press the DELETE key to delete the column.

Splitting and Merging Cells

You can split a cell into two cells either horizontally, as shown in Figure 8–61, or vertically. You can then enter contents into the new cell. For example, in Figure 8–61, you could type text into the new cell that gives information about account numbers. You can also merge two cells into one.

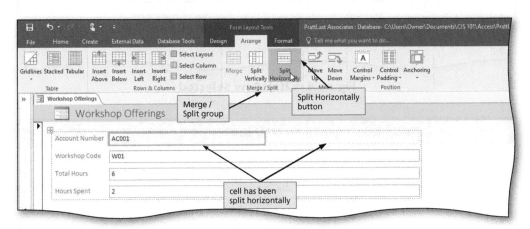

Figure 8–61

To Split a Cell

To split a cell, you would use the following steps.

1. Click the cell to be split.
2. Click the Split Vertically button (Form Layout Tools Arrange tab | Merge / Split group) to split the selected cell vertically or the Split Horizontally button (Form Layout Tools Arrange tab | Merge / Split group) to split the selected cell horizontally.

To Merge Cells

You would use the following steps to merge cells.

1. Select the first cell to be merged.
2. While holding down the CTRL key, click all the other cells to be merged.
3. Click the Merge button (Form Layout Tools Arrange tab | Merge / Split group) to merge the cells.

Moving Cells

You can move a cell in a layout by dragging it to its new position. Most often, however, you will not want to move individual cells, but rather whole rows (Figure 8–62). You can move a row by selecting the row and then dragging it to the new position or you can use the Move buttons on the Form Layout Tools Arrange tab.

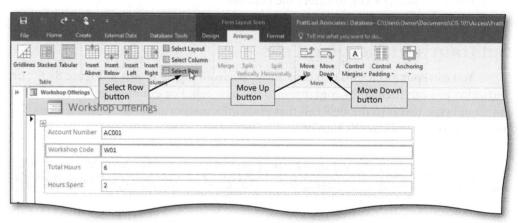

Figure 8–62(a) Row Selected

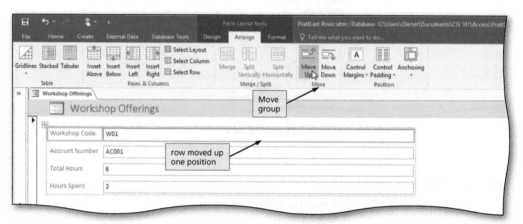

Figure 8–62(b) Row Moved

BTW

Control Padding
The term, padding, refers to the amount of space between a control's border and its contents. Effectively, you can increase or decrease the amount of white space in a control.

TO MOVE ROWS USING THE MOVE BUTTONS

You would use the following steps to move a row.

1. Select any cell in the row to be moved.

2. Click the Select Row button (Form Layout Tools Arrange tab | Rows & Columns group) to select the entire row.

3. Click the Move Up button (Form Layout Tools Arrange tab | Move group) to move the selected row up one row or the Move Down button (Form Layout Tools Arrange tab | Move group) to move the selected row down one row.

Margins and Padding

You can change the spacing within a layout by changing the control margins and the control padding. The control margins, which you change with the Control Margins button, affect the spacing around the text inside a control. Figure 8–63 shows the various options as well as samples of two of the options.

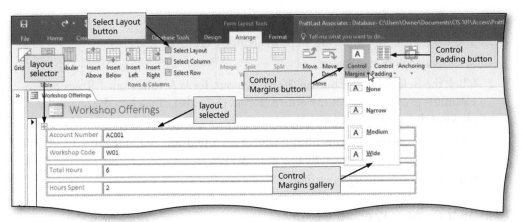

Figure 8–63(a)   Changing Control Margins

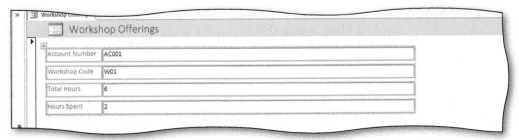

Figure 8–63(b)   Control Margins Set to None

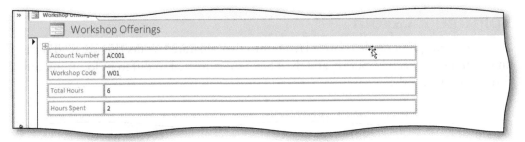

Figure 8–63(c)   Control Margins Set to Medium

The control padding, which you change with the Control Padding button, affects the spacing around the outside of a control. The options are the same as those for control margins. Figure 8–64 shows samples of two of the options.

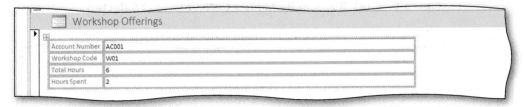

Figure 8–64(a)   Control Padding Set to None

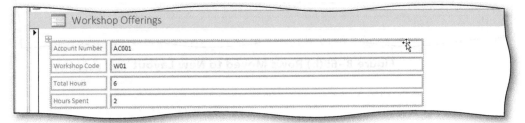

Figure 8–64(b) Control Padding Set to Medium

TO CHANGE CONTROL MARGINS

You would use the following steps to change a control's margins.

1. Select any cell in the layout.
2. Click the Select Layout button (Form Layout Tools Arrange tab | Rows & Columns group) to select the entire layout. (You also can select the layout by clicking the layout selector.)
3. Click the Control Margins button (Form Layout Tools Arrange tab | Position group) to display the available margin settings.
4. Click the desired margin setting.

TO CHANGE CONTROL PADDING

You would use the following steps to change control padding.

1. Select the layout.
2. Click the Control Padding button (Form Layout Tools Arrange tab | Position group) to display the available padding settings.
3. Click the desired padding setting.

Although you can make the margin and padding changes for individual controls, it is much more common to do so for the entire layout. Doing so gives a uniform appearance to the layout.

Splitting a Layout

You can split a single control layout into two separate layouts (Figure 8–65) and then modify each layout separately. They can be moved to different locations and formatted differently.

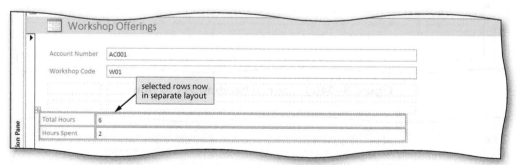

Figure 8–65(a) Rows to Be Moved to New Layout Selected

Figure 8–65(b) Rows Moved to New Layout

TO SPLIT A LAYOUT

To split a layout, you would use the following steps.

1. Select all the cells that you want to move to a new layout.
2. Click the Stacked button (Form Layout Tools Arrange tab | Table group) to place the cells in a stacked layout or the Tabular button (Form Layout Tools Arrange tab | Table group) to place the cells in a tabular layout.

Moving a Layout

You can move a control layout to a different location on the form (Figure 8–66).

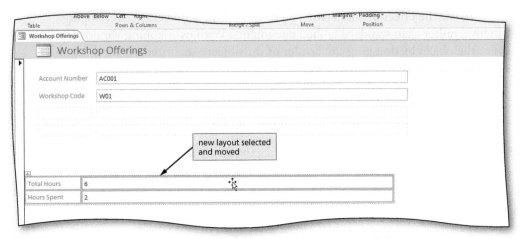

Figure 8–66

TO MOVE A LAYOUT

You would use the following steps to move a layout.

1. Click any cell in the layout to be moved and then click the Select Layout button (Form Layout Tools Arrange tab | Rows & Columns group) to select the layout.
2. Drag the layout to the new location.

Anchoring Controls

The Anchoring button allows you to tie (anchor) controls to a section or to other controls so that they maintain the same distance between the control and the anchor position as the form is resized. To anchor the controls you have selected, you use the Anchoring gallery (Figure 8–67).

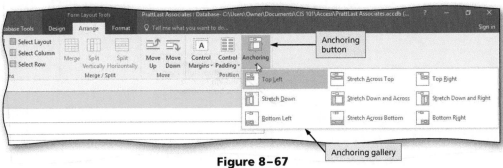

Figure 8–67

The Top Left, Top Right, Bottom Left, and Bottom Right options anchor the control in the indicated position on the form. The other five operations also stretch the controls in the indicated direction.

TO ANCHOR CONTROLS

You would use the following steps to anchor controls.

1. Select the control or controls to be anchored.
2. Click the Anchoring button (Form Layout Tools Arrange tab | Position group) to produce the Anchoring gallery.
3. Select the desired Anchoring option from the Anchoring gallery.

To see the effect of anchoring you need to display objects in overlapping windows rather than standard tabbed documents. With overlapping windows, you can resize the object by dragging the border of the object. Anchored objects keep their same relative position (Figure 8–68).

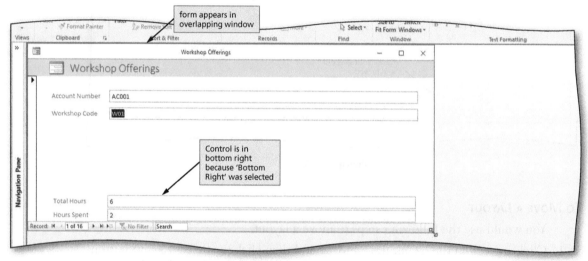

Figure 8–68(a) Form with Anchored Controls Appears in Overlapping Window

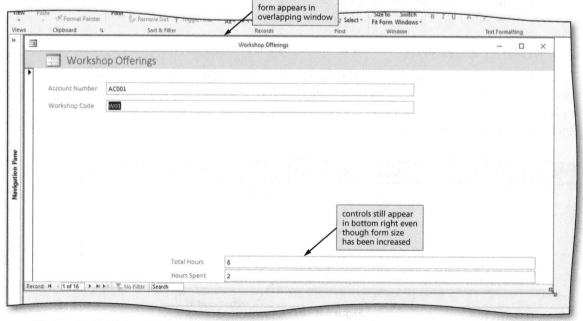

Figure 8–68(b) Resized Form with Anchored Controls Appears in Overlapping Window

If you want to display objects in overlapping windows, you have to modify the appropriate Access option.

TO DISPLAY OBJECTS IN OVERLAPPING WINDOWS

You would use the following steps to overlap windows.

1. Click File on the ribbon to open the Backstage view.
2. Click Options to display the Access Options dialog box.
3. Click Current Database to display the Current Database options.
4. In the Application Options area, click the Overlapping Windows option button.
5. Click the OK button to close the Access Options dialog box.
6. For the changes to take effect, you will need to close and then reopen the database.

You use a similar process to return to displaying objects in tabbed documents.

TO DISPLAY OBJECTS IN TABBED DOCUMENTS

You would use the following steps to display tabbed documents.

1. Click File on the ribbon to open the Backstage view.
2. Click Options to display the Access Options dialog box.
3. Click Current Database to display the Current Database options.
4. In the Application Options area, click the Tabbed Documents option button.
5. Click the OK button to close the Access Options dialog box.
6. For the changes to take effect, you will need to close and then reopen the database.

> **BTW**
> **Overlapping Windows**
> When you display objects in overlapping windows, each database object appears in its own window. When multiple objects are open, these windows overlap each other. By default, Access 2016 displays database objects in a single pane separated by tabs.

Summary

In this module you have learned to create and use macros; create a menu form that uses command buttons for the choices; create a menu form that uses an option group for the choices; create a macro that implements the choices in the option group; create datasheet forms that utilize user interface macros; create a navigation form; add tabs to a navigation form; and create data macros. You also learned to modify control layouts.

What decisions will you need to make when creating your own macros and navigation forms?
Use these guidelines as you complete the assignments in this module and create your own macros and navigation forms outside of this class.

1. Determine when it would be beneficial to automate tasks in a macro.

    a. Are there tasks involving multiple steps that would be more conveniently accomplished by running a macro than by carrying out all the individual steps? For example, opening a form in read-only mode could be accomplished conveniently through a macro.

    b. Are there tasks that are to be performed when the user clicks buttons on a menu form?

    c. Are there tasks to be performed when a user clicks a control on a form?

    d. Are there tasks to be performed when a user updates a table? These tasks can be placed in a macro that can be run when the button is clicked.

2. Determine whether it is appropriate to create a navigation form.

    a. If you want to make it easy and convenient for users to perform a variety of tasks just by clicking tabs and buttons, consider creating a navigation form.

    b. You can associate the performance of the various tasks with the tabs and buttons in the navigation form.

3. Determine the organization of the navigation form.

    a. Determine the various tasks that need to be performed by clicking tabs and buttons.

    b. Decide the logical grouping of the tabs and buttons.

How should you submit solutions to questions in the assignments identified with a symbol?
Every assignment in this book contains one or more questions identified with a symbol. These questions require you to think beyond the assigned database. Present your solutions to the questions in the format required by your instructor. Possible formats may include one or more of these options: write the answer; create a document that contains the answer; present your answer to the class; discuss your answer in a group; record the answer as audio or video using a webcam, smartphone, or portable media player; or post answers on a blog, wiki, or website.

Apply Your Knowledge

Reinforce the skills and apply the concepts you learned in this module.

Creating UI Macros and a Navigation Form

Note: To complete this assignment, you will be required to use the Data Files. Please contact your instructor for information about accessing the Data Files.

Instructions: Run Access. Open the Apply AllAround Services database and enable the content. AllAround Services is a company that provides all types of cleaning and maintenance services for businesses and organizations.

Perform the following tasks:

1. Create a datasheet form for the Client table and name the form Client. Create a UI macro for the Client form. Use CN as the temporary variable name. When a user clicks a client number on a row in the datasheet form, the Client Financial Form should appear in a pop-up form in read-only mode.

2. Create a datasheet form for the Supervisor table and name the form Supervisor. Create a UI macro for the Supervisor form. Use SN as the temporary variable name. When a user clicks a supervisor number on a row in the datasheet form, the Supervisor Master Form should appear in a pop-up form in read-only mode.

3. Create the navigation form shown in Figure 8–69. The purpose of the form is to display the two datasheet forms in the database as horizontal tabs. Name the form Datasheet Forms Menu and change the title to AllAround Services Navigation Form.

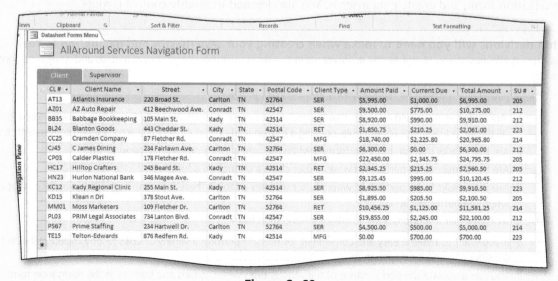

Figure 8–69

4. If requested to do so by your instructor, open the Supervisor datasheet form and change the first and last names of supervisor 212 to your first and last name.

5. Submit the revised database in the format specified by your instructor.

6. ✹ How could you add the Supervisor Services Data form to the navigation form?

Extend Your Knowledge

Extend the skills you learned in this module and experiment with new skills. You may need to use Help to complete the assignment.

Modifying Navigation Forms

Note: To complete this assignment, you will be required to use the Data Files. Please contact your instructor for information about accessing the Data Files.

Instructions: Run Access. Open the Extend Craft Cooperative database and enable the content. Craft Cooperative is run by the local school district to showcase the various crafts made by students.

Perform the following tasks:

1. Open the Main Menu form in Design view and change the theme for this object only to Facet. Expand the size of the form header and add the current date to the form header. Add a command button to the form header that closes the form. Save the changes and switch to Form view. Resize the Price field in the Item datasheet form to best fit, save the changes, and close the form.

2. Open the Reports List form in Design view. Select the Report Options label, and change the font weight to semi-bold and the special effect to Raised. Enlarge the label so that the complete label displays. Select all the option buttons and use the Size/Space menu to adjust the labels to be the same width as the widest label. Select the option group and change the special effect to Shadowed. Change the theme colors to Green for this object only. Use the Background Color button to change the background color of the form to White, Background 1, Darker 5%. Save the changes to the form.

3. Open the Forms List form in Design view and make the same changes that you made to the Reports List form. Save the changes to the form.

4. Convert the Forms and Reports macro to Visual Basic code.

5. Open the Main Menu navigation form in Layout view. Change the shape of the Forms tab to Rounded Rectangle and the shape of the Reports tab to Snip Single Corner Rectangle.

6. If requested to do so by your instructor, add a label to the form header for the Main Menu form with your first and last name.

7. Submit the revised database in the format specified by your instructor.

8. ✹ Why would you convert a macro to Visual Basic code?

Expand Your World

Create a solution which uses cloud and web technologies, by learning and investigating on your own from general guidance.

Problem: The local electric company is actively engaged in educating the community on ways to conserve energy. They regularly provide energy-saving tips and sell devices designed to conserve energy resources. The company has created macros and a navigation form but would like to link a workbook containing fuel usage statistics and add two hyperlinks to a form.

Continued >

Expand Your World *continued*

Note: To complete this assignment, you will be required to use the Data Files. Please contact your instructor for information about accessing the Data Files.

Perform the following tasks:

1. Open your browser and navigate to the U. S. Energy Information Administration website, www. eia.gov/consumption/residential/data/2009/. Select the Housing characteristics tab, and then select Fuels used & end uses. Download the workbook of your choice from the list provided, for example, by type of housing or by region.

2. Open the Expand Electric Company database from the Data Files and link the workbook you downloaded to the database.

3. Access any website containing royalty-free images and search for an energy-related image suitable for a navigation form.

4. Open the Main Menu navigation form in Design view and add the image to the form header. Add a hyperlink to the home page for the U.S. Energy Information Administration website to the form header. Add another link to your local electric utility company.

5. Save your changes.

6. Submit the revised database in the format specified by your instructor.

7. ✸ Which workbook did you download and link? What image did you choose for the navigation form? Why did you make those choices?

In the Labs

Design, create, modify, and/or use a database following the guidelines, concepts, and skills presented in this module. Labs are listed in order of increasing difficulty. Labs 1 and 2, which increase in difficulty, require you to create solutions based on what you learned in the module; Lab 3 requires you to apply your creative thinking and problem solving skills to design and implement a solution.

Lab 1: Creating Macros and a Navigation Form for the Gardening Supply Database

Note: To complete this assignment, you will be required to use the Data Files. Please contact your instructor for information about accessing the Data Files.

Problem: Gardening Supply is a wholesale distributor that supplies businesses such as florists, green houses, and nurseries with plants, pottery, mulch, and other gardening essentials. The company would like an easy way to access the various tables, forms, and reports included in the database. This would make the database easier to maintain and update.

Instructions: Perform the following tasks:

1. Open the Lab 1 Gardening Supply database, enable the content, and create a macro named Forms and Reports that will include submacros to perform the following tasks:
   a. Open the Sales Rep Order Data form in read-only mode.
   b. Open the Sales Rep Master Form. Do not specify a Data Mode.
   c. Open the Customer Master Form. Do not specify a Data Mode.

d. Preview the Sales Rep Master List.
e. Preview the Customer Financial Report.
f. Preview the Customer Discount Report.
g. Export the Sales Rep Master List in PDF format.
h. Export the Customer Financial Report in PDF format.
i. Export the Customer Discount Report in PDF format.

2. Create the menu form shown in Figure 8–70. The command buttons should use the macros you created in Step 1 to open the three forms.

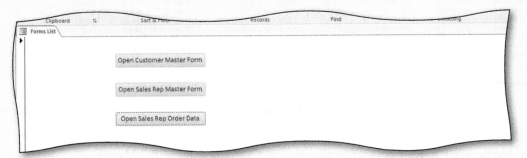

Figure 8–70

3. Create the menu form shown in Figure 8–71. The option group should use the macros you created in Step 1 to preview and export the three reports.

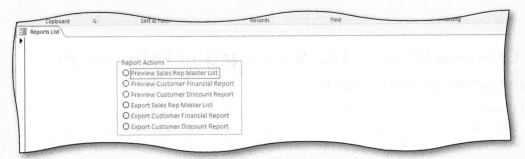

Figure 8–71

4. Create a datasheet form for the Customer table and name the form Customer. Create a UI macro for the Customer form. When a user clicks a customer number on a row in the datasheet, the Customer Master Form should appear in a pop-up, read-only form.

5. Create a datasheet form for the Sales Rep table and name the form Sales Rep. Create a UI macro for the Sales Rep form. When a user clicks a sales rep number on a row in the datasheet, the Sales Rep Master Form should appear in a pop-up, read-only form.

6. Create the navigation form shown in Figure 8–72 for the Gardening Supply database. Use the same design for your navigation form as the one illustrated in this module. For example, the Customer tab should display the Customer form you created in Step 4, and the Sales Rep tab should display the Sales Rep form you created in Step 5. The Forms tab should display the Forms List form you created in Step 2, and the Reports tab should display the Reports List form you created in Step 3.

Continued >

In the Labs *continued*

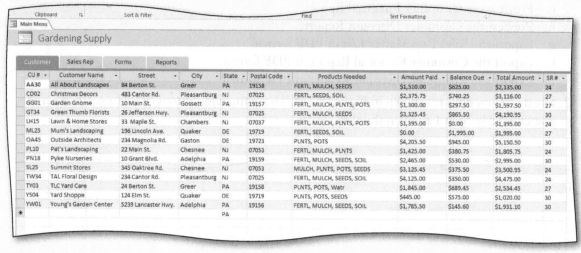

Figure 8–72

7. If requested to do so by your instructor, add your name to the title for the Main Menu navigation form.

8. Submit the revised database in the format specified by your instructor.

9. ✹ In this exercise, you have created both command buttons and option groups to run macros. Which do you prefer? Why?

Lab 2: Creating Macros and a Navigation Form for the Discover Science Database

Problem: Discover Science is an outreach of the local university. Science faculty at the university promote science education through programs at schools, libraries, and special events. As a way to promote science education among young people and raise funds for activities, the university has an online store of science-related items. The store manager would like an easy way to access the various tables, forms, and reports included in the database. This would make the database easier to maintain and update.

Note: To complete this assignment, you will be required to use the Data Files. Please contact your instructor for information about accessing the Data Files.

Instructions: Perform the following tasks:

1. Open the Lab 2 Discover Science database, enable the content, and create a macro named Forms and Reports that will include submacros to perform the following tasks:

   a. Open the Vendor Orders Data form in read-only mode.
   b. Open the Vendor Master Form. Do not specify a Data Mode.
   c. Open the Item Master Form. Do not specify a Data Mode.
   d. Preview the Vendor Master List.
   e. Preview the Item Status Report.
   f. Preview the Item Discount Report.
   g. Export the Vendor Master List in XPS format.

h. Export the Item Status Report in XPS format.

i. Export the Item Discount Report in XPS format.

2. Create the menu form shown in Figure 8–73. The command buttons should use the macros you created in Step 1 to open the three forms. Be sure to include the title on the form.

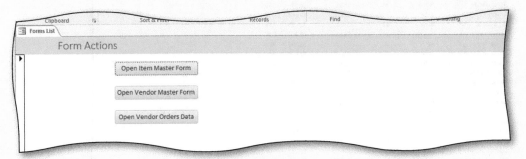

Figure 8–73

3. Create the menu form shown in Figure 8–74. The command buttons should use the macros you created in Step 1 to preview and export the three reports. Be sure to include the title on the form.

Figure 8–74

4. Create a datasheet form for the Item table and name the form Item. Create a UI macro for the Item form. When a user clicks an item number on a row in the datasheet, the Item Master Form should appear in a pop-up form.

5. Create a datasheet form for the Vendor table and name the form Vendor. Create a UI macro for the Vendor form. When a user clicks a vendor code on a row in the datasheet, the Vendor Master Form should appear in a pop-up form.

6. Create the navigation form shown in Figure 8–75 for the Discover Science database. Use the same design for your navigation form as the one illustrated in this module. For example, the Item tab should display the Item form you created in Step 4, and the Vendor tab should display the Vendor form you created in Step 5. The Forms tab should display the Forms List form you created in Step 2, and the Reports tab should display the Reports List form you created in Step 3.

Continued >

In the Labs *continued*

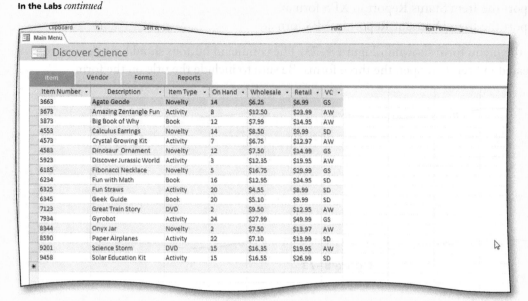

Figure 8–75

7. If requested to do so by your instructor, add your name to the title for the Forms List form.

8. Submit the revised database in the format specified by your instructor.

9. ✹ In this exercise, you exported reports in XPS format. How would you create a macro to export the Item table in Excel format?

Lab 3: **Consider This: Your Turn**

Creating Macros and a Navigation Form for the Marketing Analytics Database

Note: To complete this assignment, you will be required to use the Data Files. Please contact your instructor for information about accessing the Data Files.

Part 1: Marketing Analytics is a marketing research firm that focuses on the needs of small business owners. You are doing an internship with Marketing Analytics and the owners have asked you to create macros and a navigation form to make the database easier to use.

Open the Lab 3 Marketing Analytics database from the Data Files. Then, use the concepts and techniques presented in this module to perform the following tasks:

a. Create a macro that includes submacros to open the Client Master Form, the Marketing Analyst Master Form, and the Analyst Seminar Data form. The Analyst Seminar Data form should open as read-only. The macro should also include submacros to preview and export in PDF format the Client Financial Report, the Marketing Analyst Master Report, and the Clients by Marketing Analyst report.

b. Create a menu form for the forms and a menu form for the reports. Use an option group for each form and include a descriptive title on each form.

c. Create a datasheet form for the Client table and name the form Client. Create a UI macro for the Client form. When a user clicks a client number on a row in the datasheet form, the Client Master Form should appear in a pop-up form.

d. Create a datasheet form for the Marketing Analyst table and name the form Marketing Analyst. Create a UI macro for the Marketing Analyst form. When a user clicks a marketing analyst number on a row in the datasheet form, the Marketing Analyst Master Form should appear in a pop-up form.

e. Create a data macro for the Seminar Offerings table. The macro will examine the value in the Hours Spent field. If the user's update would cause the value to be greater than the Total Hours, the macro will change the value to Total Hours. If the user's update would cause the value to be less than 0, the macro will change the value to 0.

f. Create a navigation form for the Marketing Analytics database. Use the same design for your navigation form as that shown in Figure 8–1a. Include the Client form, the Marketing Analyst form, and the menu forms you created in Step b.

Submit your assignment in the format specified by your instructor.

Part 2:   You made several decisions while completing this assignment, including creating a macro to open a pop-up form. What was the rationale behind your decisions? The window mode to open a form as a pop-up form is Dialog. What would be the effect if the form opened in Normal mode?

9 | Administering a Database System

Objectives

You will have mastered the material in this module when you can:

- Convert a database to and from earlier versions of Access
- Use the Table Analyzer, Performance Analyzer, and Documenter
- Create custom categories and groups in the Navigation Pane
- Use table, database, and field properties
- Create indexes
- Enable and use automatic error checking

- Create custom data type parts
- Create a database for a template
- Create a custom template
- Encrypt a database and set a password
- Lock a database and split a database
- Create a custom web app
- Create custom views for a web app

Introduction

Administering a database system is an important activity that has many facets. Administration activities are an important aspect of database management because they improve the usability, accessibility, security, and efficiency of the database.

Project — Administering a Database System

PrattLast Associates realizes the importance of database administration, that is, the importance of administering its database system properly. Making a database available on the web using a web app (Figure 9–1) is part of this activity. The Customers and Reps database shown in Figure 9–1 is a database that contains information about a software company, a PrattLast subsidiary, that specializes in applications for the health sciences. Figure 9–1a shows the Rep table selected in List view. Not only does the data about the rep appear on the screen, but data concerning the customers of the selected rep does as well. Figure 9–1b shows the Customer table selected in By City view, which has grouped the customers by City. Customers in the selected city, Berridge in this case, appear on the screen. Clicking an individual customer causes all the data for the customer to appear, as shown in Figure 9–1c.

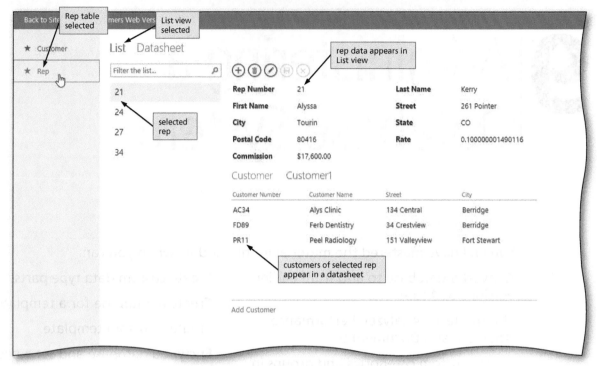

Figure 9–1(a) Rep Table Shown in Web App

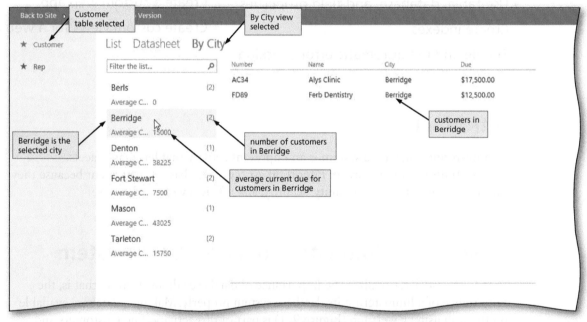

Figure 9–1(b) Customer Table Shown in Web App

Another important activity in administering databases is the creation of custom templates, application parts, and data type parts. **Application parts** and **data type parts** are templates included in Access that you can add to your database to extend its functionality. Clicking an application part adds to your database a predetermined collection of objects such as tables, queries, forms, reports, and/or macros. Clicking a data type part adds a predetermined collection of fields to a table.

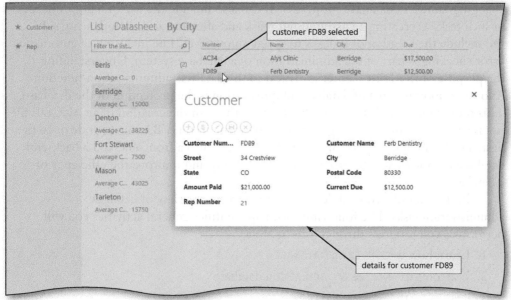

Figure 9–1(c) Customer Details Shown in Web App

Figure 9–2 illustrates the range of activities involved in database administration, including the conversion of an Access database to an earlier version of Access. Database administration usually includes such activities as analyzing tables for potential problems, analyzing performance to see if changes could make the system perform more efficiently, and documenting the various objects in the database. It

BTW
Enabling the Content
For each of the databases you use in this module, you will need to enable the content.

Figure 9–2

BTW
The Ribbon and Screen Resolution
Access may change how the groups and buttons within the groups appear on the ribbon, depending on the computer's screen resolution. Thus, your ribbon may look different from the ones in this book if you are using a screen resolution other than 1366 x 768.

can include creating custom categories and groups in the Navigation Pane as well as changing table and database properties. It can also include the use of field properties in such tasks as creating a custom input mask and allowing zero-length strings. It can include the creation of indexes to speed up retrieval. The inclusion of automatic error checking is part of the administration of a database system. Understanding the purpose of the Trust Center is critical to the database administration function. Another important area of database administration is the protection of the database. This protection includes locking the database through the creation of an ACCDE file to prevent unauthorized changes from being made to the VBA source code or to the design of forms and reports. Splitting the database into a front-end and a back-end database is another way to protect the functionality and improve the efficiency of a database.

In this module, you will learn how to perform a variety of database administration tasks. The following roadmap identifies general activities you will perform as you progress through this module:

1. Learn how to CONVERT a DATABASE
2. Use tools to ANALYZE & DOCUMENT a database
3. CUSTOMIZE the NAVIGATION PANE
4. Use custom PROPERTIES & create INDEXES
5. CREATE a custom DATA PART
6. Create a custom TEMPLATE
7. ENCRYPT, LOCK, & SPLIT a database
8. Learn how to create a custom WEB APP
9. Learn how to create CUSTOM VIEW in a web app

BTW
Converting Databases
If you try to convert a database that contains features specific to a later version of Access, Access displays an error message alerting you that you cannot save the database as an earlier version because it contains features that require the current file format.

Converting Databases

BTW
Maintaining Backward Compatibility
If you plan to share your database with users who may have an earlier version of Access, be sure to maintain backward compatibility. Do not include multivalued fields, attachment fields, or calculated fields in your database design. For example, if there is a calculation that is used frequently, create a query with the calculated field and use the query as the basis for forms and reports rather than adding the field to the table design.

Access 2007, Access 2010, Access 2013, and Access 2016 all use the same file format, the .accdb format. The format is usually referred to as the Access 2007 file format. Thus, in Access 2016, you can use any database created in Access 2007. You should be aware of the following changes in Access 2013 and Access 2016 from the earlier versions.

1. Unlike previous versions, these versions do not support PivotTables or PivotCharts.
2. The Text data type is now Short Text and the Memo data type is now Long Text.
3. Smart Tags are no longer supported.
4. Replication is no longer available.

To convert an Access 2007 database to an earlier version, the database cannot contain any features that are specific to Access 2007, 2010, 2013, or 2016. These include attachments, multivalued fields, offline data, or links to external files not supported in earlier versions of Access. They also include objects published to the web, data macros, and calculated columns. Provided the database does not contain such features, you can convert the database by clicking the Save As tab in the Backstage view (Figure 9–3). You can then choose the appropriate format.

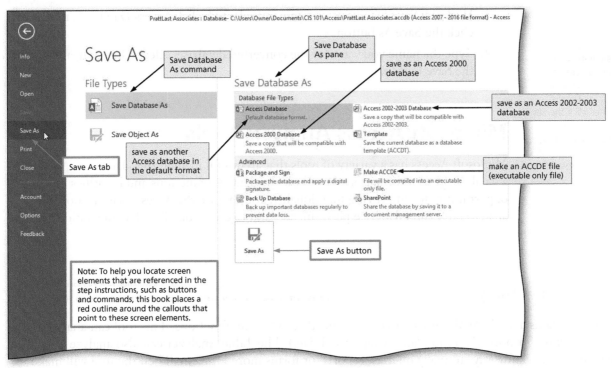

Figure 9–3

To Convert an Access 2007–2016 Database to an Earlier Version

Specifically, to convert an Access 2007–2016 database to an earlier version, you would use the following steps.

1. With the database to be converted open, click File on the ribbon to open the Backstage view.
2. Click the Save As tab.
3. With the 'Save Database As' command selected, click the desired format, and then click the Save As button.
4. Type the name you want for the converted database, select a location in which to save the converted database, and click the Save button.

To Convert an Access 2000 or 2002–2003 Database to an Access 2016 Database

To convert an Access 2000 or Access 2002–2003 database to the default database format for Access 2016, you open the database in Access 2016. Initially, the database is open in compatibility mode, where features that are new to Access 2016 and that cannot easily be displayed or converted are disabled. In this mode, the database remains in its original format. If you want to convert it so that you can use it in Access 2016, you use the Access Database command on the Backstage view. Once the database is converted, the disabled features will be enabled. You will no longer be able to share the database with users of Access 2000 or Access 2002–2003, however.

Specifically, to convert an Access 2000 or 2002–2003 database to the default database format for Access 2016, you would use the following steps.

1. With the database to be converted open, click File on the ribbon to open the Backstage view.
2. Click the Save As tab.

BTW

Saving Databases to External Locations
You also can save a database to an external location such as OneDrive, and to any portable storage device, such as a USB flash drive. To do so, select the desired external location or portable storage device when you browse to specify a location for your database.

BTW

Exporting XML Data
Database administration also may include responsibility for exchanging data between dissimilar systems or apps. Extensible Markup Language (XML) is a data interchange standard for describing and delivering data on the web. With XML, you can describe both the data and the structure (schema) of the data. You can export tables queries, forms, or reports. To export a database object, select the object and click the XML File button (External Data tab | Export group). Select the appropriate options in the Export XML dialog box.

BTW
Creating Databases in Older Formats
To create a database in an older format, create a database and browse to select a location for the database, then click the Save As Type arrow in the File New Database dialog box, and select either 2002-2003 format or 2000 format.

3. With the Save Database As command selected, click Access Database and then click the Save As button.

4. Type the name you want for the converted database, select a location, and click the Save button.

Microsoft Access Analysis Tools

Microsoft Access has a variety of tools that are useful in analyzing databases. Analyzing a database gives information about how the database functions and identifies opportunities for improving functionality. You can use the Access analysis tools to analyze tables and database performance, and to create detailed documentation.

To Use the Table Analyzer

1 CONVERT DATABASE | 2 ANALYZE & DOCUMENT | 3 NAVIGATION PANE | 4 PROPERTIES & INDEXES
5 DATA PART | 6 TEMPLATE | 7 ENCRYPT LOCK & SPLIT | 8 WEB APP | 9 CUSTOM VIEW

Access contains a Table Analyzer tool that performs three separate functions. This tool can analyze tables while looking for potential redundancy (duplicated data). The Table Analyzer can also analyze performance and check for ways to make queries, reports, or forms more efficient. Then the tool will make suggestions for possible changes. The final function of the analyzer is to produce detailed documentation describing the structure and content of the various tables, queries, forms, reports, and other objects in the database.

The following steps use the Table Analyzer to examine the Account table for **redundancy**, or duplicated data. *Why? Redundancy is one of the biggest potential sources of problems in a database.* If redundancy is found, the Table Analyzer will suggest ways to split the table in order to eliminate the redundancy.

1

• Run Access and open the database named PrattLast Associates from your hard disk, OneDrive, or other storage location.

• If necessary, close the Navigation Pane.

• Display the Database Tools tab (Figure 9–4).

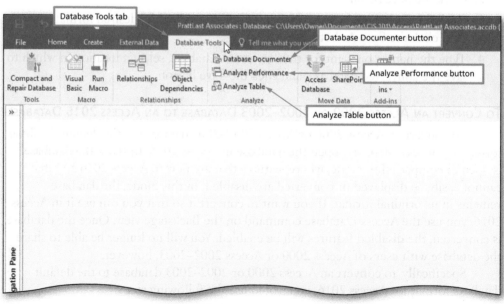

Figure 9–4

2

- Click the Analyze Table button (Database Tools tab | Analyze group) to display the Table Analyzer Wizard dialog box (Figure 9–5).

Q&A Where did the data in the figure come from? It does not look like my data. The data is fictitious. It is just intended to give you an idea of what the data might look like.

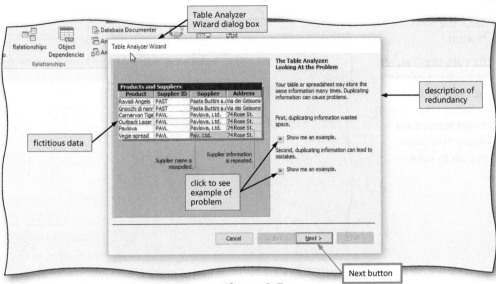

Figure 9–5

3

- Click the Next button to display the next Table Analyzer Wizard screen (Figure 9–6).

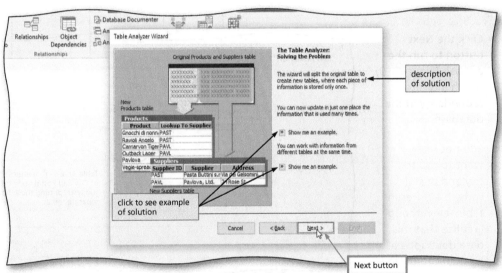

Figure 9–6

4

- Click the Next button to display the next Table Analyzer Wizard screen.

- If necessary, select the Account table (Figure 9–7).

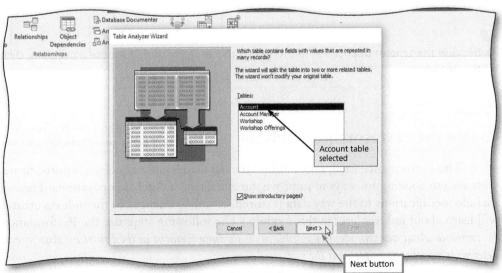

Figure 9–7

5

- Click the Next button.

- Be sure the 'Yes, let the wizard decide.' option button is selected (Figure 9–8) to let the wizard determine what action to take.

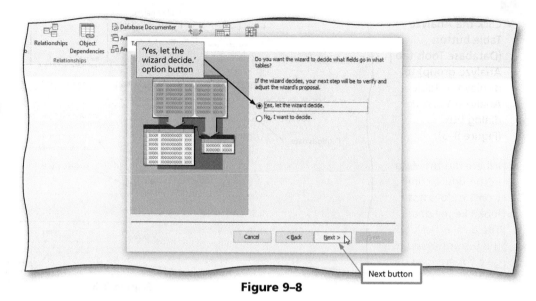

Figure 9–8

6

- Click the Next button to run the analysis (Figure 9–9), which indicates redundancy in the database.

Q&A I do not really want to put the city and postal code in a different table, even though I realize that this data does appear to be duplicated. Do I have to follow this advice?

Certainly not. This is only a suggestion.

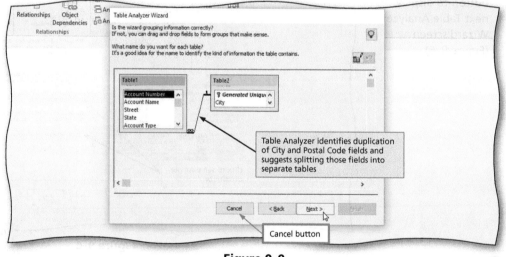

Figure 9–9

7

- Because the type of duplication identified by the analyzer does not pose a problem, click the Cancel button to close the analyzer.

To Use the Performance Analyzer

1 CONVERT DATABASE | 2 ANALYZE & DOCUMENT | 3 NAVIGATION PANE | 4 PROPERTIES & INDEXES
5 DATA PART | 6 TEMPLATE | 7 ENCRYPT LOCK & SPLIT | 8 WEB APP | 9 CUSTOM VIEW

The Performance Analyzer examines the database's tables, queries, reports, forms, and other objects in your system, looking for ways to improve the efficiency of database operations. These improvements could include modifications to the way data is stored, as well as changes to the indexes created for the system. (You will learn about indexes later in this module.) The following steps use the Performance Analyzer. *Why? The Performance Analyzer will identify possible areas for improvement in the PrattLast Associates database. Users then can determine whether to implement the suggested changes.*

1

- Click the Analyze Performance button, shown in Figure 9–4 (Database Tools tab | Analyze group), to display the Performance Analyzer dialog box.

- If necessary, click the Tables tab (Figure 9–10).

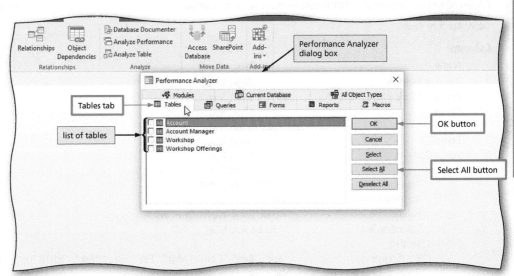

Figure 9–10

2

- Click the Select All button to select all tables.

- Click the OK button to display the results (Figure 9–11).

Q&A What do the results mean?
Because both fields contain only numbers, Access is suggesting that you might improve the efficiency of the table by changing the data types of the fields to Long Integer. As the icon

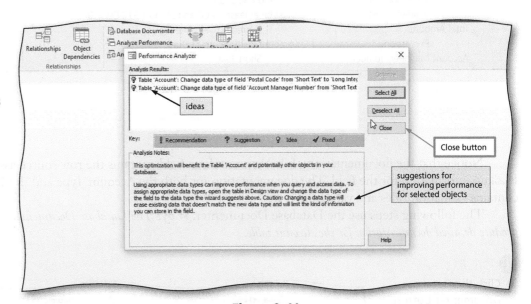

Figure 9–11

in front of the suggestions indicates, this is simply an idea — something to consider. Short Text is a better type for these particular fields, however, so you should ignore this suggestion.

3

- Click the Close button to finish working with the Performance Analyzer.

To Use the Database Documenter

1 CONVERT DATABASE | 2 ANALYZE & DOCUMENT | 3 NAVIGATION PANE | 4 PROPERTIES & INDEXES
5 DATA PART | 6 TEMPLATE | 7 ENCRYPT LOCK & SPLIT | 8 WEB APP | 9 CUSTOM VIEW

The Database Documenter allows you to produce detailed documentation of the various tables, queries, forms, reports, and other objects in your database. Documentation is required by many organizations. It is used for backup, disaster recovery, and planning for database enhancements. Figure 9–12 shows a portion of the documentation for the Account table. The complete documentation is much lengthier than the one shown in the figure.

C:\Users\Owner\Documents\CIS 101\Access\PrattLast Associates.accdb   Tuesday, September 12, 2017

Table: Account Page: 1

Columns

Name	Type	Size
Account Number	Short Text	5
Account Name	Short Text	30
Street	Short Text	25
City	Short Text	20
State	Short Text	2
Postal Code	Short Text	5
Account Type	Short Text	255

    RowSource: "SER";"NON";"IND"
    RowSourceType: Value List
    ValidationRule: ="SER" Or ="NON" Or ="IND"
    ValidationText: Must be SER, NON, or IND

Services Needed		4

    RowSource: "Bck";"Ben";"Com";"Mgt";"Pay";"Rec";"Rsk";"Tch";"Trn";"Wrk"
    RowSourceType: Value List

Amount Paid	Currency	8
Current Due	Currency	8

    ValidationRule: >=0 And <=10000
    ValidationText: Must be at least $0.00 and at most $10,000.00

Total Amount	Currency (Calculated)	8

    Expression: [Amount Paid]+[Current Due]

Account Manager Number	Short Text	2

Figure 9–12

Notice that the documentation of the Account Type field contains the row source associated with the Lookup information for the field. The documentation for both the Account Type and the Current Due fields contains validation rules and validation text.

The following steps use the Database Documenter. **Why?** *The Database Documenter is the easiest way to produce detailed documentation for the Account table.*

1

- Click the Database Documenter button, shown in Figure 9–4 (Database Tools tab | Analyze group), to display the Documenter dialog box.

- If necessary, click the Tables tab and then click the Account check box to specify documentation for the Account table (Figure 9–13).

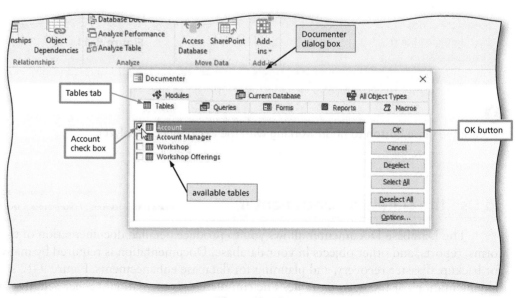

Figure 9–13

2

- Click the OK button to produce a preview of the documentation (Figure 9–14).

Q&A What can I do with this documentation? You could print it by clicking the Print button (Print Preview tab | Print group). You could create a PDF or XPS file containing the documentation by clicking the PDF or XPS button (Print Preview tab | Data group) and following the directions. You could create a Word (RTF) file by clicking the More button (Print Preview tab | Data group), and then clicking Word and following the directions. Whatever option you choose, you may need to use this documentation later if you make changes to the database design.

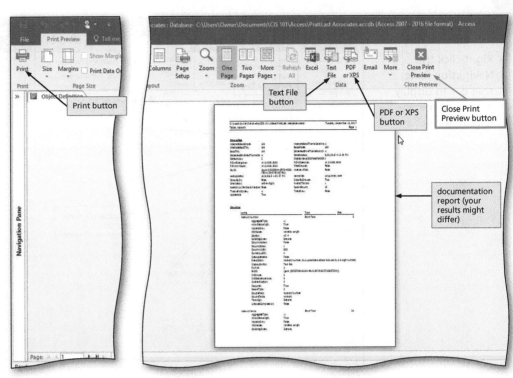

Figure 9–14

- Click the 'Close Print Preview' button (Print Preview tab | Close Preview group) to close the preview of the documentation.

Experiment

- Try other options within the Database Documenter to see the effect of your choice on the documentation produced. Each time, close the preview of the documentation.

BTW
Touch Screen Differences
The Office and Windows interfaces may vary if you are using a touch screen. For this reason, you might notice that the function or appearance of your touch screen differs slightly from this module's presentation.

Navigation Pane Customization

You have already learned how to customize the Navigation Pane by selecting the category and the filter as well as how to use the Search Bar to restrict the items that appear in the Navigation Pane. You can also create custom categories and groups that you can use to categorize the items in the database in ways that are most useful to you.

1 CONVERT DATABASE | 2 ANALYZE & DOCUMENT | **3 NAVIGATION PANE** | 4 PROPERTIES & INDEXES

To Create Custom Categories and Groups

5 DATA PART | 6 TEMPLATE | 7 ENCRYPT LOCK & SPLIT | 8 WEB APP | 9 CUSTOM VIEW

You can create custom categories in the Navigation Pane. You can further refine the objects you place in a category by adding custom groups to the categories. *Why? Custom categories and groups allow you to tailor the Navigation Pane for your own specific needs.* The following steps create a custom category called Financial Items. They then add two custom groups, Detailed and Summary, to the Financial Items category.

1

- Display the Navigation Pane.
- Right-click the Navigation Pane title bar to display a shortcut menu (Figure 9–15).

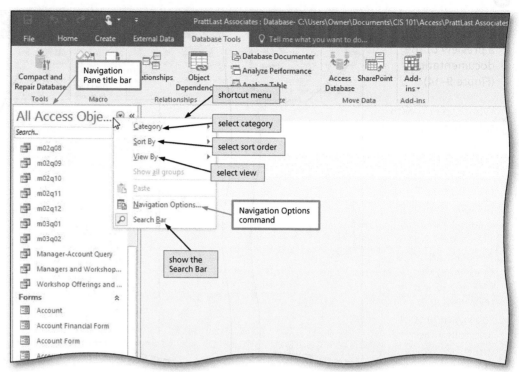

Figure 9–15

2

- Click the Navigation Options command on the shortcut menu to display the Navigation Options dialog box (Figure 9–16).

Q&A What else could I do with the shortcut menu?
You could select a category, select a sort order, or select how to view the items within the Navigation Pane.

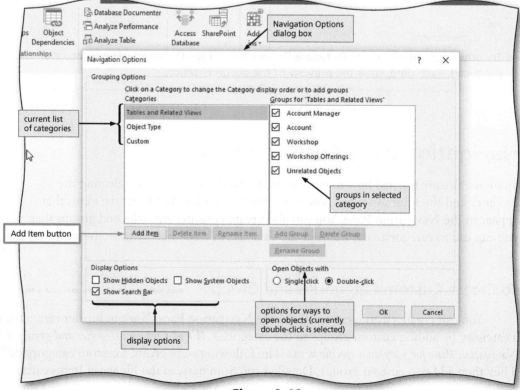

Figure 9–16

- Click the Add Item button to add a new category (Figure 9–17).

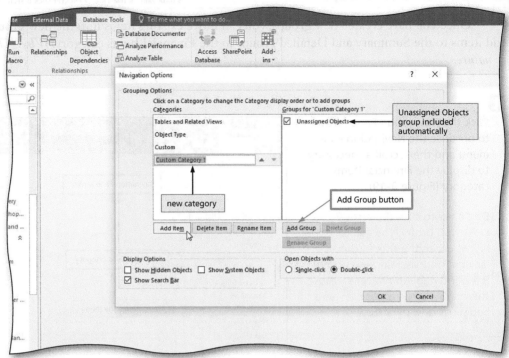

Figure 9–17

- Type **Financial Items** as the name of the category.

- Click the Add Group button to add a group and then type **Detailed** as the name of the group.

- Click the Add Group button to add a group and then type **Summary** as the name of the group (Figure 9–18).

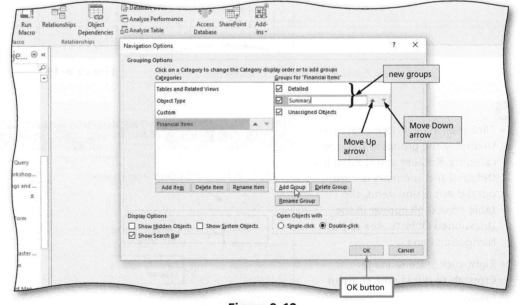

Figure 9–18

Q&A I added the groups in the wrong order. How can I change the order?
Select the group that is in the wrong position. Click the Move Up or Move Down arrow to move the group to the correct location.

If I made a mistake in creating a new category, how can I fix it?
Select the category that is incorrect. If the name is wrong, click the Rename Item button and change the name appropriately. If you do not want the category, click the Delete Item button to delete the category and then click the OK button.

5

- Click the OK button to create the new category and groups.

To Add Items to Groups

Once you have created new groups, you can move existing items into the new groups. The following steps add items to the Summary and Detailed groups in the Financial Items category. *Why? These items are all financial in nature.*

1

● Click the Navigation Pane arrow to produce the Navigation Pane menu and then scroll as necessary to display the Financial Items category (Figure 9–19).

Q&A
Do I have to click the arrow?
No. If you prefer, you can click anywhere in the title bar for the Navigation Pane. Clicking arrows is a good habit, however, because there are many situations where you must click the arrow.

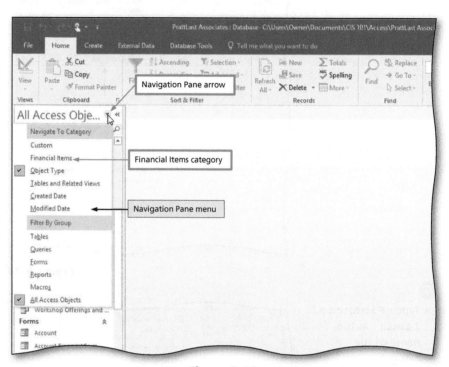

Figure 9–19

2

● Click the Financial Items category to display the groups within the category. Because you created the Detailed and Summary groups but did not assign items, the table objects all appear in the Unassigned Objects area of the Navigation Pane.

● Right-click State-Manager Crosstab to display the shortcut menu.

● Point to the 'Add to group' command on the shortcut menu to display the list of available groups (Figure 9–20).

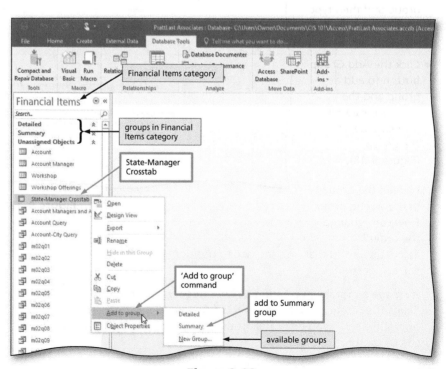

Figure 9–20

Q&A I did not create an Unassigned Objects group. Where did it come from?
Access creates the Unassigned Objects group automatically. Until you add an object to one of the groups you created, it will be in the Unassigned Objects group.

What is the purpose of the New Group on the submenu?
You can create a new group using this submenu. This is an alternative to using the Navigation Options dialog box. Use whichever approach you find most convenient.

③

- Click Summary to add the State-Manager Crosstab to the Summary group.

- Using the same technique, add the items shown in Figure 9–21 to the Detailed and Summary groups.

Q&A What is the symbol that appears in front of the items in the Detailed and Summary groups?
It is the link symbol. You do not actually add an object to your group. Rather, you create a link to the object. In practice, you do not have to worry about this. The process for opening an object in one of your custom groups remains the same.

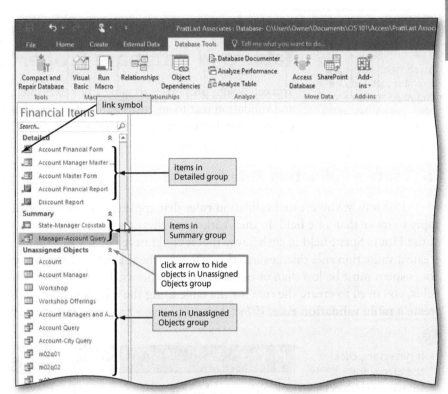

Figure 9–21

④

- Click the arrow in the Unassigned Objects bar to hide the unassigned objects (Figure 9–22).

Q&A Do I have to click the arrow?
No. Just as with the Navigation Pane, you can click anywhere in the Unassigned Objects bar.

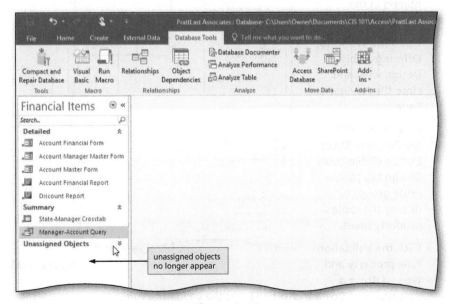

Figure 9–22

Break Point: If you wish to stop working through the module at this point, you can close Access now. You can resume the project at a later time by running Access, opening the PrattLast Associates database, and continuing to follow the steps from this location forward.

What issues do you consider in determining the customization of the Navigation Pane?

The types of issues to consider are the following:

- Would a new category be useful?

- If so, are there new groups that would be useful to include in the new category?

- If you have created a new category and new groups, which items should be included in the new groups, and which should be left uncategorized?

BTW
Touch and Pointers
Remember that if you are using your finger on a touch screen, you will not see the pointer.

Table and Database Properties

You can assign properties to tables. For example, you could assign a validation rule and validation text to an entire table. You can also assign properties to the database, typically for documentation purposes.

To Create a Validation Rule for a Table

1 CONVERT DATABASE | 2 ANALYZE & DOCUMENT | 3 NAVIGATION PANE | 4 PROPERTIES & INDEXES
5 DATA PART | 6 TEMPLATE | 7 ENCRYPT LOCK & SPLIT | 8 WEB APP | 9 CUSTOM VIEW

Previously, you created validation rules that applied to individual fields within a table. Some, however, apply to more than one field. In the Workshop Offerings table, you created a macro that would change the value of the Hours Spent field in such a way that it could never be greater than the Total Hours field. You can also create a validation rule that ensures this will never be the case; that is, the validation rule would require that the hours spent must be less than or equal to the total hours. To create a validation rule that involves two or more fields, you need to create the rule for the table using the table's Validation Rule property. The following steps create a **table validation rule**. *Why? This rule involves two fields, Hours Spent and Total Hours.*

1

- If necessary, click the arrow for Unassigned Objects to display those objects in the Navigation Pane.

- Open the Workshop Offerings table in Design view and close the Navigation Pane.

- If necessary, click the Property Sheet button (Table Tools Design tab | Show /Hide group) to display the table's property sheet.

- Click the Validation Rule property and type `[Hours Spent]<=[Total Hours]` as the validation rule.

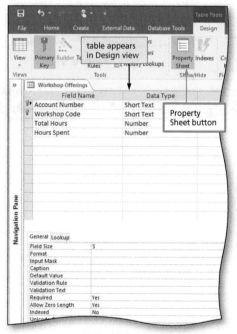

Figure 9–23

- Click the Validation Text property and type `Hours spent cannot exceed total hours` as the validation text (Figure 9–23).

Q&A Could I use the Expression Builder to create the validation rule?

Yes. Use whichever method you find the most convenient.

- Close the property sheet.
- Click the Save button on the Quick Access Toolbar to save the validation rule and the validation text.
- When asked if you want to test existing data, click the No button.
- Close the Workshop Offerings table.

To Create Custom Properties

1 CONVERT DATABASE | 2 ANALYZE & DOCUMENT | 3 NAVIGATION PANE | 4 PROPERTIES & INDEXES
5 DATA PART | 6 TEMPLATE | 7 ENCRYPT LOCK & SPLIT | 8 WEB APP | 9 CUSTOM VIEW

In addition to the general database property categories, you can also use custom properties. *Why? You can use custom properties to further document your database in a variety of ways. If you have needs that go beyond the custom properties, you can create your own original or unique properties.* The following steps **populate** the Status custom property; that is, they set a value for the property. In this case, they set the Status property to Live Version, indicating this is the live version of the database. If the database were still in a test environment, the property would be set to Test Version. The steps also create and populate a new property, Production, which represents the date the database was placed into production.

- Click File on the ribbon to open the Backstage view.
- Ensure the Info tab is selected (Figure 9–24).

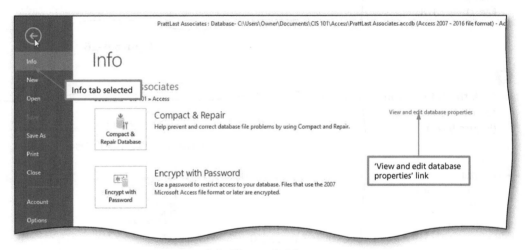

Figure 9–24

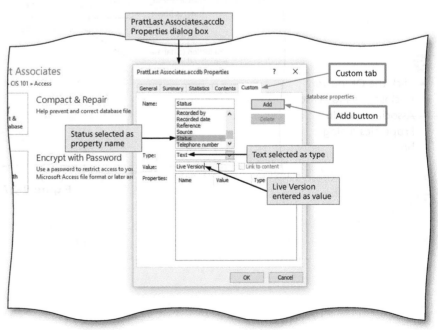

- Click the 'View and edit database properties' link to display the PrattLast Associates.accdb Properties dialog box.
- Click the Custom tab.
- Scroll down in the Name list so that Status appears, and then click Status.
- If necessary, click the Type arrow to set the data type to Text.
- Click the Value box and type **Live Version** as the value to create the custom property (Figure 9–25).

Figure 9–25

- Click the Add button to add the property.

- Type **Production** in the Name box.

- If requested to do so by your instructor, type your first and last name in the Name box.

- Select Date as the Type.

- Type **03/03/2018** as the value (Figure 9–26) to indicate that the database went into production on March 3, 2018.

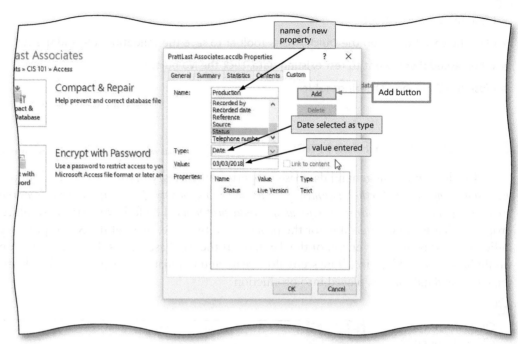

Figure 9–26

- Click the Add button to add the property (Figure 9–27).

Q&A What if I add a property that I decide I do not want?
You can delete it. To do so, click the property you no longer want and then click the Delete button.

- Click the OK button to close the PrattLast Associates.accdb Properties dialog box.

Q&A How do I view these properties in the future?

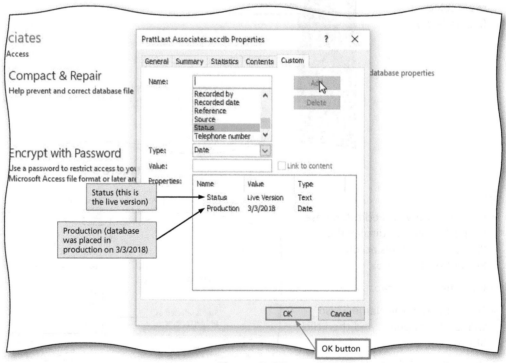

Figure 9–27

The same way you created them. Click File on the ribbon, click the Info tab, and then click the 'View and edit database properties' link. Click the desired tab to see the properties you want.

Special Field Properties

Each field in a table has a variety of field properties available. Recall that field properties are characteristics of a field. Two special field properties, the Custom Input Mask property and the Allow Zero Length property, are described in this section.

Custom Input Masks

One way to help users enter data using a certain format is to use an input mask. You have already used the Input Mask Wizard to create an input mask. Using the wizard, you can select the input mask that meets your needs. This is often the best way to create the input mask.

If the input mask you need to create is not similar to any in the list provided by the wizard, you can create a custom input mask by entering the appropriate characters as the value for the Input Mask property. In doing so, you use the symbols from Table 9–1.

Table 9–1	Input Mask Symbols	
Symbol	**Type of Data Accepted**	**Data Entry**
0	Digits 0 through 9 without plus (+) or minus (–) sign are accepted. Positions left blank appear as zeros.	Required
9	Digits 0 through 9 without plus (+) or minus (–) sign are accepted. Positions left blank appear as spaces.	Optional
#	Digits 0 through 9 with plus (+) or minus (–) sign are accepted. Positions left blank appear as spaces.	Optional
L	Letters A through Z are accepted.	Required
?	Letters A through Z are accepted.	Optional
A	Letters A through Z or digits 0 through 9 are accepted.	Required
a	Letters A through Z or digits 0 through 9 are accepted.	Optional
&	Any character or a space is accepted.	Required
C	Any character or a space is accepted.	Optional
<	Symbol converts any letter entered to lowercase.	Does not apply
>	Symbol converts any letter entered to uppercase.	Does not apply
!	Characters typed in the input mask fill it from left to right.	Does not apply
\	Character following the slash is treated as a literal in the input mask.	Does not apply

For example, to indicate that account numbers must consist of two letters followed by three numbers, you would enter LL999. The Ls in the first two positions indicate that the first two positions must be letters. Using L instead of a question mark indicates that the users are required to enter these letters. If you had used the question mark instead of the L, they could leave these positions blank. The 9s in the last three positions indicate that the users can enter only digits 0 through 9. Using 9 instead of 0 indicates that they could leave these positions blank; that is, they are optional. Finally, to ensure that any letters entered are displayed as uppercase, you would use the > symbol at the beginning of the input mask. The complete mask would be >LL999.

BTW

Changing Data Formats

To create custom data formats, enter various characters in the Format property of a table field. The characters can be placeholders (such as 0 and #), separators (such as periods and commas), literal characters, and colors. You can create custom formats for short text, date, number, and currency fields. Date, number, and currency fields also include a number of standard data formats.

BTW

Table Descriptions

To add a description for a table, right-click the table in the Navigation Pane and then click Table Properties on the shortcut menu. When the Properties dialog box for the table appears, enter the description in the Description property and then click the OK button. To enter a description for a table in Design view, click the Property Sheet button, and then enter a description in the Description property on the property sheet (see Figure 9–23).

To Create a Custom Input Mask

The following step creates a custom input mask for the Account Number field. **Why?** *None of the input masks in the list meet the specific needs for the Account Number field.*

- Open the Navigation Pane, open the Account table in Design view, and then close the Navigation Pane.

- With the Account Number field selected, click the Input Mask property, and then type **>LL999** as the value (Figure 9–28).

Q&A

What is the difference between the Format property and the Input Mask property?
The Format property ensures that data is displayed consistently, for example, always in uppercase. The Input Mask property controls how data is entered by the user.

What is the effect of this input mask?
From this point on, anyone entering an account number will be restricted to letters in the first two positions and numeric digits in the last three. Further, any letters entered in the first two positions will be displayed as uppercase.

In Figure 9–28, the Account Number field has both a custom input mask and a format. Is this a problem?
Technically, you do not need both. When the same field has both an input mask and a format, the format takes precedence. However, because the format specified for the Account Number field is the same as the input mask (uppercase), it will not affect the data.

Figure 9–28

To Not Allow Zero Length

You can use zero-length strings to distinguish data that does not exist from data that is unknown. **Why?** *A zero-length string is different from a field that is blank.* For example, in the Account Manager table, you may want to set the Required property for the Special Skills field to Yes, so that users do not forget to enter an account manager's special skills. If the user forgets to enter a special skill, Access will display an error message and not add the record until the user enters a special skill. If, on the other hand, there are certain account managers for whom no special skill is appropriate, users can enter a **zero-length string** — a string that contains no characters — and Access will accept the record without generating an error message. To enter a zero-length string, you type two quotation marks with no space in between (""). If you enter a zero-length string into a Short Text or Long Text field whose Required property is set to Yes, Access will not report an error.

If you want to ensure that data is entered in the field and a zero-length string is not appropriate, you can set the Required property to Yes and the Allow Zero Length property to No. The following steps set the Allow Zero Length property for the Account Name field to No. (The Required property has already been set to Yes.)

1

- Click the row selector for the Account Name field to select the field.
- Click the 'Allow Zero Length' property and then click the arrow that appears to display a menu.
- Click No in the menu to change the value of the 'Allow Zero Length' property from Yes to No (Figure 9–29).

Q&A Could I just type the word, No? Yes. In fact, you could type the letter, N, and Access would complete the word, No. Use whichever technique you prefer.

2

- Save your changes and click the No button when asked if you want to test existing data.
- Close the table.

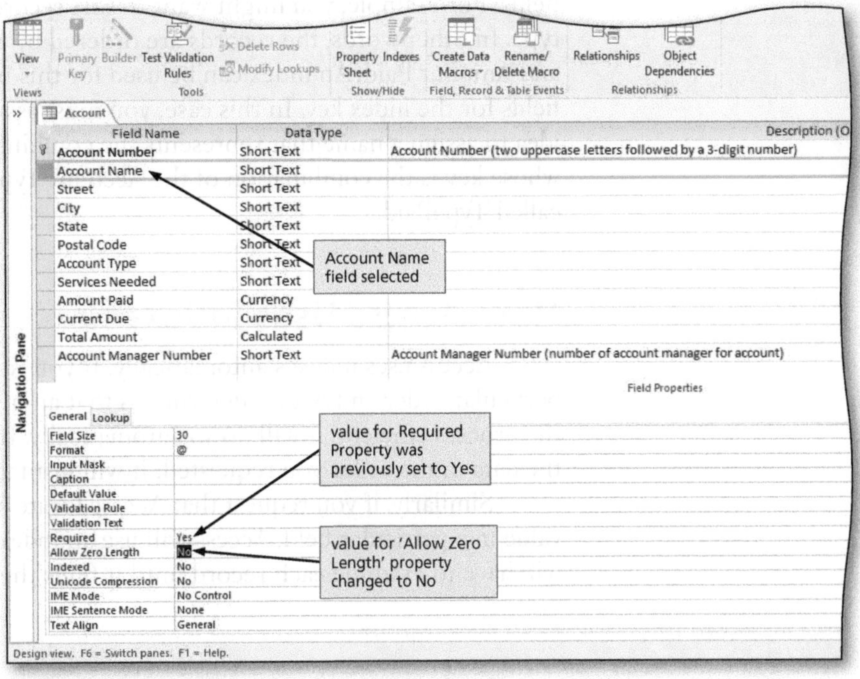

Q&A What is the effect of this change? If the value for the Allow Zero Length property is set to No, an attempt to enter a zero-length string ("") will result in an error message.

Figure 9–29

Creating and Using Indexes

You are already familiar with the concept of an index. The index in the back of a book contains important words or phrases along with a list of pages on which the given words or phrases can be found. An **index** for a table is similar. An index is a database object that is created based on a field or combination of fields. An index on the Account Name field, for example, would enable Access to rapidly locate a record that contains a particular account name. In this case, the items of interest are account names instead of keywords or phrases, as is the case for the index in the back of this book. The field or fields on which the index is built is called the **index key**. Thus, in the index on account names, the Account Name field is the index key.

Each name occurs in the index along with the number of the record on which the corresponding account is located. Further, the names appear in the index in alphabetical order, so Access can use this index to rapidly produce a list of accounts alphabetized by account name.

Another benefit of indexes is that they provide an efficient way to order records. That is, if the records are to appear in a certain order in a database object, Access can use an index instead of physically having to rearrange the records in the database. Physically rearranging the records in a different order can be a very time-consuming process.

To gain the benefits of an index, you must first create one. Access automatically creates an index on some special fields. If, for example, a table contains a field called Postal Code, Access would create an index for this field automatically. You must create any other indexes you determine would improve database performance, indicating the field or fields on which the index is to be built.

BTW

Changing Default Sort Order
To display the records in a table in an order other than the primary key (the default sort order), use the Order By property on the table's property sheet (see Figure 9–23).

BTW

Indexes
The most common structure for high-performance indexes is called a B-tree. It is a highly efficient structure that supports very rapid access to records in the database as well as a rapid alternative to sorting records. Virtually all systems use some version of the B-tree structure.

Although the index key will usually be a single field, it can be a combination of fields. For example, you might want to sort records by amount paid within account type. In other words, the records are ordered by a combination of fields: Account Type and Amount Paid. An index can be used for this purpose by using a combination of fields for the index key. In this case, you must assign a name to the index. It is a good idea to assign a name that represents the combination of fields. For example, an index whose key is the combination of the Account Type and Amount Paid fields might be called TypePaid.

How Access Uses Indexes

Access uses indexes automatically. If you request that data be sorted in a particular order and Access determines that an index is available that it can use to make the process efficient, it will do so automatically. If no index is available, it will still sort the data in the order you requested; it will just take longer than with the index.

Similarly, if you request that Access locate a particular record that has a certain value in a particular field, Access will use an index if an appropriate one exists. If not, it will have to examine each record until it finds the one you want.

To Create a Single-Field Index

1 CONVERT DATABASE | 2 ANALYZE & DOCUMENT | 3 NAVIGATION PANE | 4 PROPERTIES & INDEXES
5 DATA PART | 6 TEMPLATE | 7 ENCRYPT LOCK & SPLIT | 8 WEB APP | 9 CUSTOM VIEW

The following steps create a single-field index on the Account Name field. *Why? This index will make finding accounts based on their name more efficient than it would be without the index. It will also improve the efficiency of sorting by account name.*

- Open the Navigation Pane, open the Account table in Design view, and then close the Navigation Pane.

- Select the Account Name field.

- Click the Indexed property box in the Field Properties pane to select the property.

- Click the arrow that appears to display the Indexed list (Figure 9–30).

- Click Yes (Duplicates OK) in the list to specify that duplicates are to be allowed.

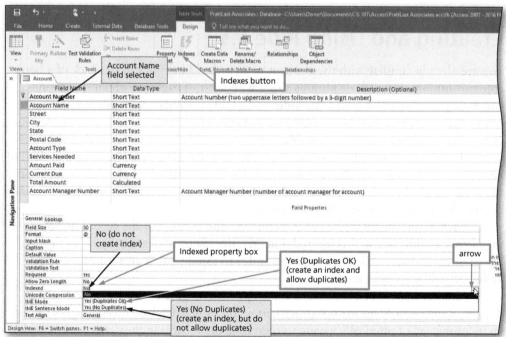

Figure 9–30

To Create a Multiple-Field Index

Creating **multiple-field indexes** — that is, indexes whose key is a combination of fields — involves a different process than creating single-field indexes. To create multiple-field indexes, you will use the Indexes button, enter a name for the index, and then enter the combination of fields that make up the index key. The following steps create a multiple-field index on the combination of Account Type and Amount Paid. *Why? PrattLast needs to sort records on the combination of Account Type and Amount Paid and wants to improve the efficiency of this sort.* The steps assign this index the name TypePaid.

- Click the Indexes button, shown in Figure 9–30 (Table Tools Design tab | Show/Hide group), to display the Indexes: Account window (Figure 9–31).

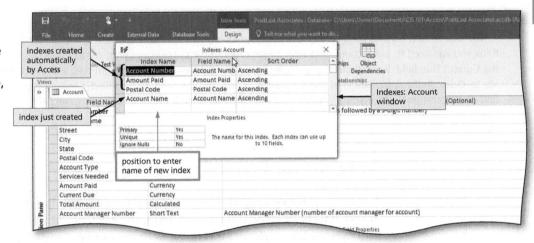

Figure 9–31

- Click the blank row (the row below Account Name) in the Index Name column in the Indexes: Account window to select the position to enter the name of the new index.

- Type **TypePaid** as the index name, and then press the TAB key.

- Click the arrow in the Field Name column to produce a list of fields in the Account table, and then select Account Type to enter the first of the two fields for the index.

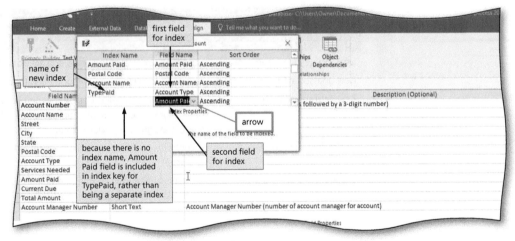

Figure 9–32

- Press the TAB key three times to move to the Field Name column on the following row.

- Select the Amount Paid field in the same manner as the Account Type field (Figure 9–32).

- Close the Indexes: Account window by clicking its Close button.

- Save your changes and close the table.

How do you determine when to use an index?

An index improves efficiency for sorting and finding records. On the other hand, indexes occupy space on your storage device. They also require Access to do extra work. Access must keep current all the indexes that have been created. The following guidelines help determine how and when to use indexes to their fullest advantage.

Create an index on a field (or combination of fields) if one or more of the following conditions are present:

1. The field is the primary key of the table. (Access creates this index automatically.)

2. The field is the foreign key in a relationship you have created.

3. You will frequently need your data to be sorted on the field.

4. You will frequently need to locate a record based on a value in this field.

Because Access handles condition 1 automatically, you only need to concern yourself about conditions 2, 3, and 4. If you think you will need to see account data arranged in order of current due amounts, for example, you should create an index on the Current Due field. If you think you will need to see the data arranged by amount paid within account type, you should create an index on the combination of the Account Type field and the Amount Paid field. Similarly, if you think you will need to find an account given the account's name, you should create an index on the Account Name field.

Automatic Error Checking

Access can automatically check for several types of errors in forms and reports. When Access detects an error, it warns you about the existence of the error and provides you with options for correcting it. The types of errors that Access can detect and correct are shown in Table 9–2.

Table 9–2 Types of Errors	
Error Type	**Description**
Unassociated label and control	A label and control are selected and are not associated with each other.
New unassociated labels	A newly added label is not associated with any other control.
Keyboard shortcut errors	A shortcut key is invalid. This can happen because an unassociated label has a shortcut key, there are duplicate shortcut keys assigned, or a blank space is assigned as a shortcut key.
Invalid control properties	A control property is invalid. For example, the property contains invalid characters.
Common report errors	The report has invalid sorting or grouping specifications, or the report is wider than the page size.

To Enable Error Checking

1 CONVERT DATABASE | 2 ANALYZE & DOCUMENT | 3 NAVIGATION PANE | 4 PROPERTIES & INDEXES
5 DATA PART | 6 TEMPLATE | 7 ENCRYPT LOCK & SPLIT | 8 WEB APP | 9 CUSTOM VIEW

Why? For automatic error checking to take place, it must be enabled. The following steps ensure that error checking is enabled and that errors are found and reported.

1

- Click File on the ribbon and then click the Options tab to display the Access Options dialog box.

- Click Object Designers to display the options for creating and modifying objects.

- Scroll down so that the Error checking area appears.

- Ensure the 'Enable error checking' check box is checked (Figure 9–33).

Q&A

What is the purpose of the other check boxes in the section?
All the other check boxes are checked, indicating that Access will perform all the various types of automatic error checking that are possible. If there were a particular type of error checking that you would prefer to skip, you would remove its check mark before clicking the OK button.

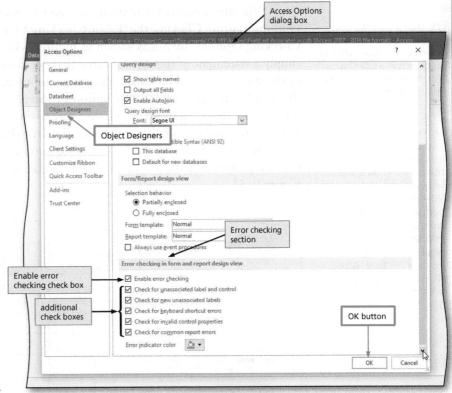

Figure 9–33

2

- Click the OK button to close the Access Options dialog box.

Error Indication

With error checking enabled, if an error occurs, a small triangle called an **error indicator** appears in the appropriate field or control. For example, you could change the label for Account Manager Number in the Account Master Form to include an ampersand (&) before the letter, N, making it a keyboard shortcut for this control. This would be a problem because N is already a shortcut for Name to Find. If this happens, an error indicator appears in both controls in which N is the keyboard shortcut, as shown in Figure 9–34.

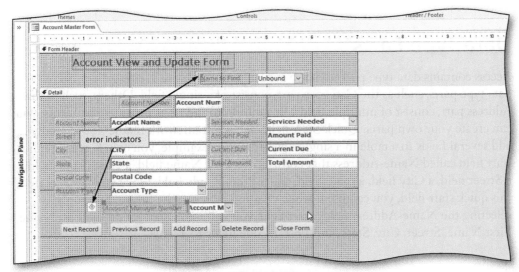

Figure 9–34

BTW

Freezing Fields
The Freeze Fields command allows you to place a column or columns in a table on the left side of the table. As you scroll to the right, the column or columns remain visible. To freeze a column or columns, select the column(s) in Datasheet view, right-click and click Freeze Fields on the shortcut menu. To unfreeze fields, click the 'Unfreeze All Fields' command on the shortcut menu. When you freeze a column, Access considers it a change to the layout of the table. When you close the table, Access will ask you if you want to save the changes.

Selecting a control containing an error indicator displays an 'Error Checking Options' button. Clicking the 'Error Checking Options' button produces the 'Error Checking Options' menu, as shown in Figure 9–35. The first line in the menu is simply a statement of the type of error that occurred, and the second is a description of the specific error. The Change Caption command gives a submenu of the captions that can be changed. The 'Edit Caption Property' command allows you to change the caption directly and is the simplest way to correct this error. The 'Help on This Error' command gives help on the specific error that occurred. You can choose to ignore the error by using the Ignore Error command. The final command, 'Error Checking Options', allows you to change the same error checking options shown in Figure 9–33.

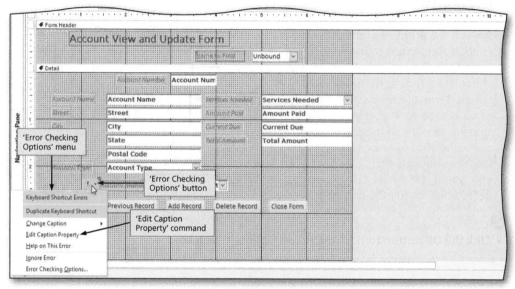

Figure 9–35

The simplest way to fix the duplicate keyboard shortcut error is to edit the caption property. Clicking the 'Edit Caption Property' command produces a property sheet with the Caption property highlighted. You could then change the Caption property of one of the controls, making another letter the shortcut key. For example, you could make the letter, A, the shortcut key by typing `&Account Manager Number` as the entry.

Data Type Parts

Access contains data type parts that are available on the More Fields gallery. Some data type parts, such as the Category part, consist of a single field. Others, such as the Address part, consist of multiple fields. In addition to the parts provided by Access, you can create your own parts. Quick Start fields act as a framework that lets you rapidly add several fields to a table in a single operation. For example, you could create a quick start field called Name-Address that consists of a Last Name field, a First Name field, a Street field, a City field, a State field, and a Postal Code field. Once you have created this quick start field, you can use it when creating tables in the future. By simply selecting the Name-Address quick start field, you will immediately add the Last Name, First Name, Street, City, State, and Postal Code fields to a table.

To Create Custom Data Parts

PrattLast has decided that combining several address-related fields into a single data part would make future database updates easier. To create data parts in the Quick Start category from existing fields, you select the desired field or fields and then select the Save Selection as New Data Type command in the More Fields gallery. If you select multiple fields, the fields must be adjacent.

The following steps create a Quick Start field consisting of the Last Name, First Name, Street, City, State, and Postal Code fields in the Account Manager table. *Why? Once you have created this Quick Start field, users can add this collection of fields to a table by simply clicking the Quick Start field.*

1

- Open the Navigation Pane, open the Account Manager table in Datasheet view, and then close the Navigation Pane.

- Click the column heading for the Last Name field to select the field.

- Hold the SHIFT key down and click the column heading for the Postal Code field to select all the fields from the Last Name field to the Postal Code field.

- Display the Table Tools Fields tab.

- Click the More Fields button (Table Tools Fields tab | Add & Delete group) to display the More Fields gallery (Figure 9–36).

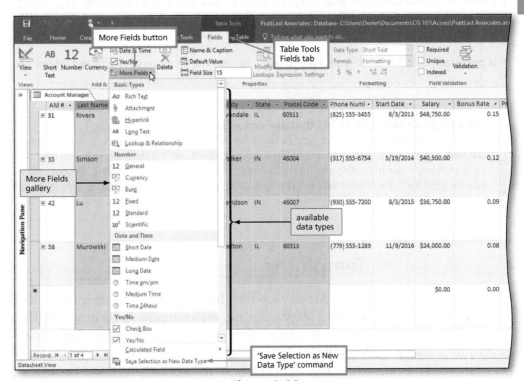

Figure 9–36

2

- Click 'Save Selection as New Data Type' to display the Create New Data Type from Fields dialog box.

- Enter **Name-Address** as the name.

- Enter **Last Name, First Name, Street, City, State, and Postal Code** as the description.

Q&A What is the purpose of the description?
When a user points to the Quick Start field you created, a ScreenTip will appear containing the description you entered.

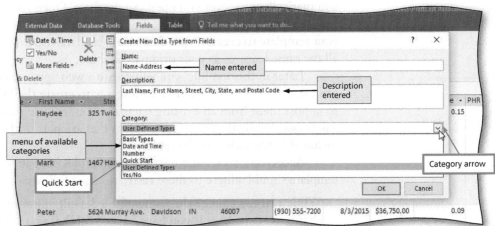

Figure 9–37

- Click the Category arrow to display a list of available categories (Figure 9–37).

- Click Quick Start to indicate the new data type will be added to the Quick Start category.

Q&A What is the difference between the Quick Start and User Defined Types category?

If you select the Quick Start category, the data type you create will be listed among the Quick Start data types that are part of Access. If you select the User Defined Types category, the data type you create will be in a separate category containing only those data types you create. In either case, however, clicking the data type will produce the same result.

- Click the OK button (Create New Data Type from Fields dialog box) to save the data type.

- When Access indicates that your template (that is, your Quick Start field) has been saved, click the OK button (Microsoft Access dialog box).

- Close the table.

- If necessary, click No when asked if you want to save the changes to the layout of the table.

CONSIDER THIS

How do you rearrange fields that are not adjacent?

When adding new data type fields, you can hide the fields that keep your fields from being adjacent. To hide a field, right-click the field to display a shortcut menu, and then click Hide Fields on the shortcut menu. To later unhide a field you have hidden, right-click any column heading and then click Unhide Fields on the shortcut menu. You will see a list of fields with a check box for each field. The hidden field will not have a check mark in the check box. To unhide the field, click the check box for the field.

Templates

BTW

Templates and Application Parts
By default, user-created templates and application parts are stored in the C:\Users*user name*\AppData\Roaming\Microsoft\Templates\Access folder.

Often, Access users find that they create and use multiple databases containing the same objects. You can use a template to create a complete database application containing tables, forms, queries, and other objects. There are many templates available for Access.

You can create your own template from an existing database. To do so, you must first ensure that you have created a database with all the characteristics you want in your template. In this module, the database you create will have two tables, a query, two single-item forms, two datasheet forms that use macros, and a navigation form that will serve as the main menu. In addition, the navigation form will be set to appear automatically whenever you open the database. Once you have incorporated all these features, you will save the database as a template. From that point on, anyone can use your template to create a new database. The database that is created will incorporate all the same features as your original database.

Later in this module, you will create a web app, which is a database that anyone can use through a browser. The easiest way to create the tables for the web app is to import them from an existing database. You will use your template to create such a database. While the queries and forms that are part of the template will not be included in the web app, the tables will.

Access enforces some restrictions to tables used in web apps, so the tables in your template should adhere to these restrictions, as follows:

- While you can change the name of the default autonumber primary key, you cannot change its data type. If you have a text field that you want to be the primary key, the best you can do is to specify that the field must be both required and unique.

- You cannot create relationships as you can do with a typical desktop database. Rather, any relationships must be specified through lookup fields.

To Create a Desktop Database

The following steps create the Customers and Reps **desktop database**, that is, a database designed to run on a personal computer. **Why?** *This database will become the basis for a template.*

- Click File on the ribbon to open the Backstage view.

- Click the New tab.

- Click the 'Blank desktop database' button.

- Type **Customers and Reps** as the name of the database file.

- Click the 'Browse for a location to put your database' button to display the File New Database dialog box, navigate to the desired save location (for example, the Access folder in the CIS 101 folder), and then click the OK button to return to the Backstage view (Figure 9–38).

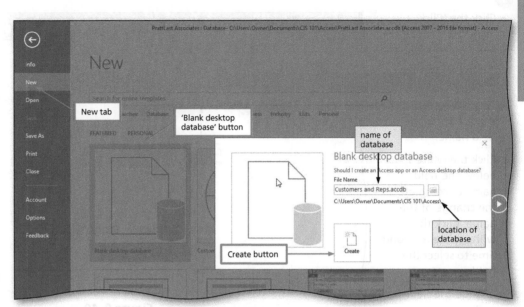

Figure 9–38

- Click the Create button to create the database (Figure 9–39).

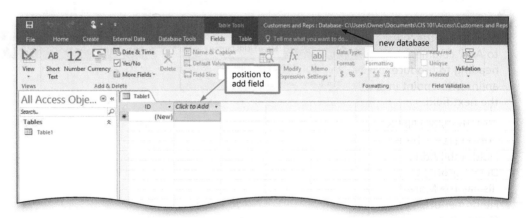

Figure 9–39

To Add Fields to the Table

The tables will have an autonumber ID field as the primary key. **Why?** *You will later import the tables in this database to a web app, and tables in a web app must have an autonumber field as a primary key.* In addition, the field that would normally be the primary key will be designated both required and unique, two characteristics of the primary key.

The following steps add the Rep Number, Last Name, First Name, Street, City, State, Postal Code, Rate, and Commission to a table. The Rate field is a Number field and the Commission field is a Currency field.

The steps designate the Rep Number field as both required and unique. They add the Last Name, First Name, Street, City, State, and Postal Code as a single operation by using the Quick Start field created earlier. After adding the fields, they save the table using the name, Rep. They also change the field size for the Rate field (a Number data type field) to Single so that the field can contain decimal places.

1

- Click the 'Click to Add' column heading and select Short Text as the data type.

- Type **Rep Number** as the field name.

- Click the white space below the field name to complete the change of the name. Click the white space a second time to select the field.

- Change the field size to 2.

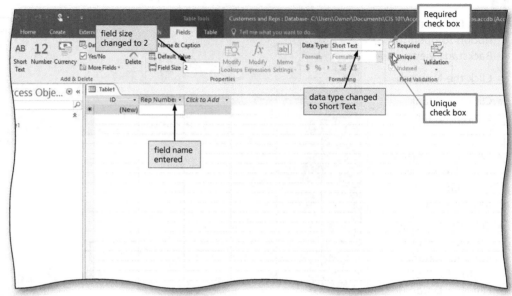

Figure 9–40

- Click the Required check box (Table Tools Fields tab | Field Validation group) to make the field a required field.

- Click the Unique check box (Table Tools Fields tab | Field Validation group) so that Access will ensure that values in the field are unique (Figure 9–40).

2

- Click under the 'Click to Add' column heading to produce an insertion point in the next field.

- Click the More Fields button (Table Tools Fields tab | Add & Delete group) to display the More Fields menu (Figure 9–41).

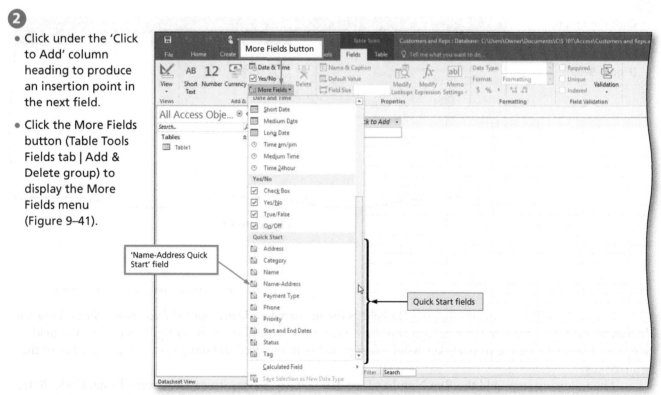

Figure 9–41

● Scroll as necessary to display the Name-Address Quick Start field you created earlier and then click the Name-Address Quick Start field to add the Last Name, First Name, Street, City, State, and Postal Code fields (Figure 9–42).

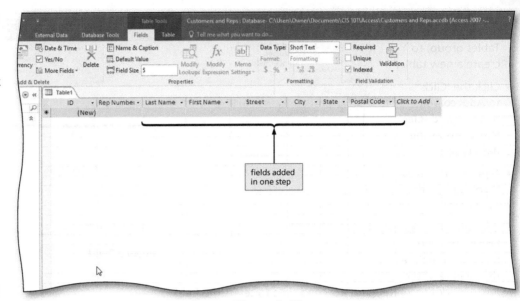

Figure 9–42

● Add the Rate and Commission fields as the last two fields. The Rate field has the Number data type and the Commission field has the Currency data type.

● Save the table, assigning `Rep` as the table name.

● Switch to Design view, select the Rate field, and change the field size to Single so that the Rate field can include decimal places.

● Save and close the table.

To Create a Second Table

1 CONVERT DATABASE | 2 ANALYZE & DOCUMENT | 3 NAVIGATION PANE | 4 PROPERTIES & INDEXES
5 DATA PART | 6 TEMPLATE | 7 ENCRYPT LOCK & SPLIT | 8 WEB APP | 9 CUSTOM VIEW

The following steps create the Customer table. The steps add a lookup field for Rep Number to relate the two tables. *Why? Because the tables will be used in a web app, the relationship between the tables needs to be implemented using a lookup field.*

1

● Display the Create tab (Figure 9–43).

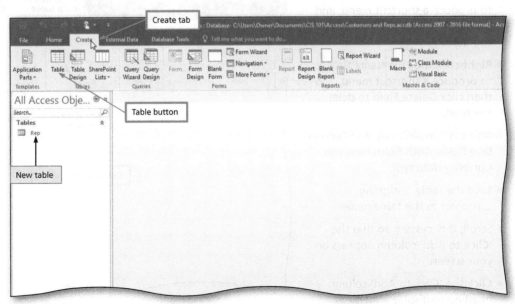

Figure 9–43

2

- Click the Table button (Create tab | Tables group) to create a new table.

- Click the 'Click to Add' column heading and select Short Text as the data type.

- Type **Customer Number** as the field name.

- Click the white space below the field name to complete the change of the name. Click the white space a second time to select the field.

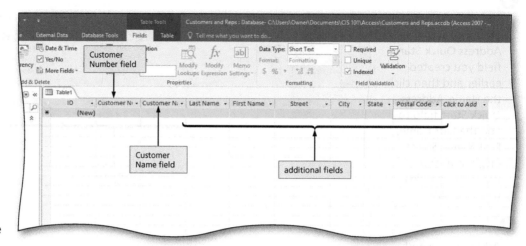

Figure 9–44

- Change the field size to 5.

- Click the Required check box (Table Tools Fields tab | Field Validation group) to make the field a required field.

- Click the Unique check box (Table Tools Fields tab | Field Validation group) so that Access will ensure that values in the field are unique.

- In a similar fashion, add the Customer Name field and change the field size to 30. Do not check the Required or Unique check boxes.

- Click under the 'Click to Add' column heading to produce an insertion point in the next field.

- Click the More Fields button (Table Tools Fields tab | Add & Delete group) to display the More Fields menu (see Figure 9–41).

- Click the Name-Address Quick Start field that you added earlier to add the Last Name, First Name, Street, City, State, and Postal Code fields (Figure 9–44).

3

- Right-click the Last Name field to produce a shortcut menu, and then click Delete Field to delete the field.

- Right-click the First Name field to produce a shortcut menu, and then click Delete Field to delete the field.

- Add the Amount Paid and Current Due fields. Both fields have the Currency data type.

- Save the table, assigning Customer as the table name.

- Scroll, if necessary, so that the 'Click to Add' column appears on your screen.

- Click the 'Click to Add' column heading to display a menu of available data types (Figure 9–45).

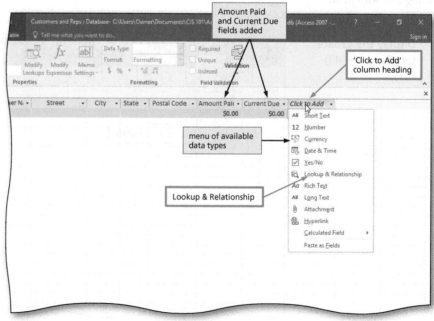

Figure 9–45

- Click Lookup &
  Relationship to
  display the Lookup
  Wizard dialog box
  (Figure 9–46).

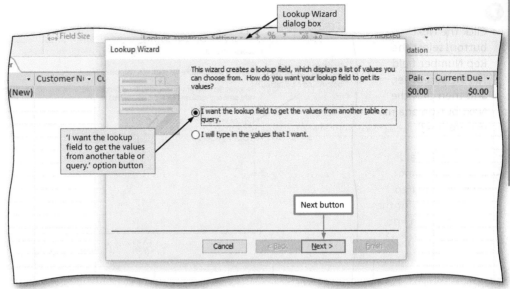

Figure 9–46

- Click the Next
  button to display
  the next Lookup
  Wizard screen, and
  then click the Rep
  table to select it so
  that you can add
  a lookup field for
  the Rep Number to
  the Customer table
  (Figure 9–47).

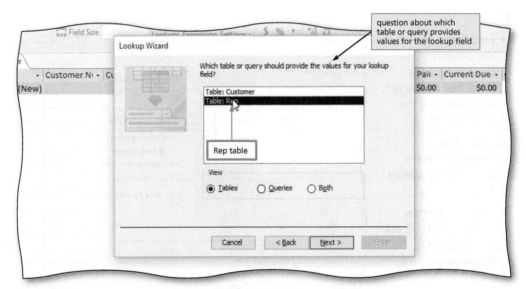

Figure 9–47

- Click the Next
  button, and then
  select the Rep
  Number, First Name,
  and Last Name fields
  for the columns in
  the lookup field
  (Figure 9–48).

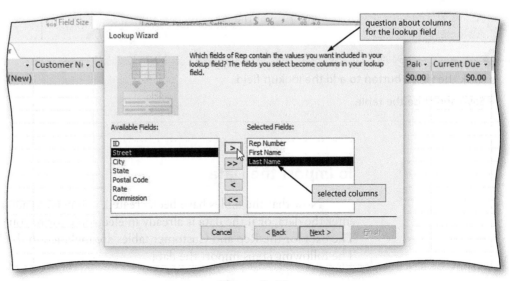

Figure 9–48

● Click the Next
button, select the
Rep Number field
for the sort order,
and then click the
Next button again.
(Figure 9–49).

I see the ID field
listed when I am
selecting the Rep
Number field for the
sort order. Did I do
something wrong?
No. Access
automatically
included the ID field.

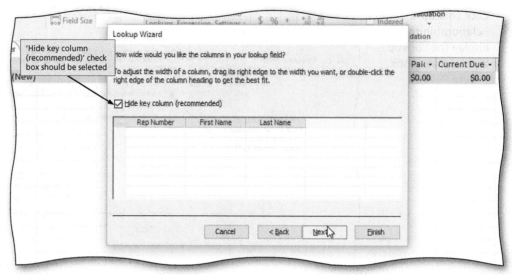

Figure 9–49

● Ensure the 'Hide
key column
(recommended)'
check box is selected,
and then click the
Next button.

● Type **Rep
Number** as the
label for the lookup
field.

● Click the 'Enable
Data Integrity' check
box to select it
(Figure 9–50).

What is the effect
of selecting Enable
Data Integrity?
Access will enforce referential integrity for the Rep Number. That is, Access will not allow a rep number in a
customer record that does not match the number of a rep in the Rep table.

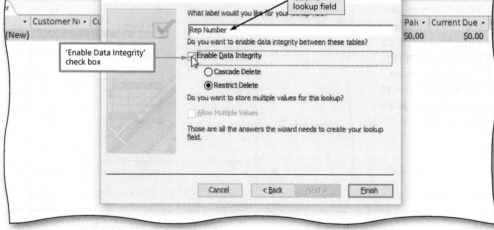

Figure 9–50

● Click the Finish button to add the lookup field.

● Save and close the table.

To Import the Data

Now that the tables have been created, you need to add data to them. You could
enter the data, or if the data is already in electronic form, you could import the data.
The data for the Rep and Customer tables are included in the Data Files as text files.
The following steps import the data.

1 With the Customers and Reps database open, display the External Data tab, and then click the Text File button (External Data tab | Import & Link group) to display the Get External Data - Text File dialog box.

2 Click the Browse button (Get External Data - Text File dialog box) and select the location of the files to be imported (for example, the Access folder in the CIS 101 folder).

3 Select the Rep text file and then click the Open button.

4 Select the 'Append a copy of records to the table' option button, select the Rep table, and then click the OK button.

5 Be sure the Delimited option button is selected, and then click the Next button.

6 Be sure the Comma option button is selected, click the Next button, and then click the Finish button.

7 Click the Close button to close the Get External Data - Text File dialog box without saving the import steps.

8 Use the technique shown in Steps 1 through 7 to import the Customer text file into the Customer table.

BTW
Importing Tables from Other Databases
You can import tables from other Access databases. To do so, click the Access button (External Data tab | Import & Link group) then navigate to the location containing the database and select the database. Click the Open button. Ensure that the 'Import tables, queries, forms, reports, macros, and modules into the current database' option button is selected and click OK. When the Import Object dialog box appears, select the table or tables you want to import and then click OK. You also can import other objects by clicking the appropriate object tabs.

To Create a Query Relating the Tables

The following steps create a query that relates the Customer and Rep tables.

1 Display the Create tab and then click the Query Design button (Create tab | Queries group) to create a new query.

2 Click the Customer table, click the Add button, click the Rep table, click the Add button, and then click the Close button to close the Show Table dialog box.

3 Double-click the Customer Number, Customer Name, and Rep Number fields from the Customer table. Double-click the First Name and Last Name fields from the Rep table to add the fields to the design grid.

4 Click the Save button on the Quick Access Toolbar to save the query, type `Customer-Rep Query` as the name of the query, and then click the OK button.

5 Close the query.

Creating Forms

There are several types of forms that need to be created for this database. The Customer and Rep detail forms show a single record at a time. The Customer, Rep, and Customer-Rep Query forms are intended to look like the corresponding table or query in Datasheet view. Finally, the main menu is a navigation form.

BTW
Rearranging Fields in a Query
If you add fields to a query in the wrong order, you can select the field in the design grid, and drag it to the appropriate location.

To Create Single-Item Forms

The following steps create two single-item forms, that is, forms that display a single record at a time. The first form, called Customer Details, is for the Customer table. The second form is for the Rep table and is called Rep Details.

1 Select the Customer table in the Navigation Pane and then display the Create tab.

2 Click the Form button (Create tab | Forms group) to create a single-item form for the Customer table.

3 Click the Save button on the Quick Access Toolbar and then type `Customer Details` as the name of the form, click the OK button (Save As dialog box) to save the form, and then close the form.

4 Select the Rep table, display the Create tab, and then click the Form button (Create tab | Forms group) to create a single-item form for the Rep table.

5 Save the form, using `Rep Details` as the form name.

6 Close the form.

To Create Datasheet Forms

1 CONVERT DATABASE | 2 ANALYZE & DOCUMENT | 3 NAVIGATION PANE | 4 PROPERTIES & INDEXES
5 DATA PART | 6 TEMPLATE | **7 ENCRYPT LOCK & SPLIT** | 8 WEB APP | 9 CUSTOM VIEW

The following steps create two datasheet forms, that is, forms that display the data in the form of a datasheet. *Why? These forms enable you to make it appear that you are displaying datasheets in a navigation form; recall that navigation forms can display only forms.* The first form is for the Customer table and is also called Customer. The second is for the Rep table and is also called Rep. The steps also create macros that will display the data for a selected record in a single-item form, as you did in Module 8.

1

- Select the Customer table and then display the Create tab.

- Click the More Forms button (Create tab | Forms group) to display the More Forms menu (Figure 9–51).

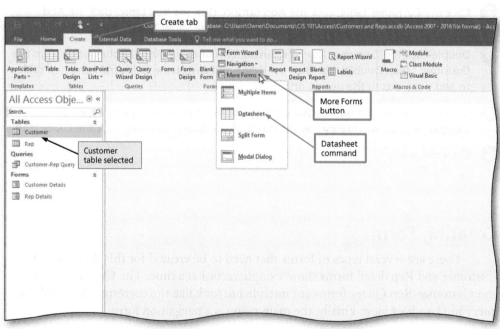

Figure 9–51

2

- Click Datasheet to create a datasheet form for the Customer table.

- Click the Save button on the Quick Access Toolbar and then accept Customer as the default name of the form.

- Click the column heading for the ID field to select the field.

- Display the property sheet and click the Event tab to display only the event properties (Figure 9–52).

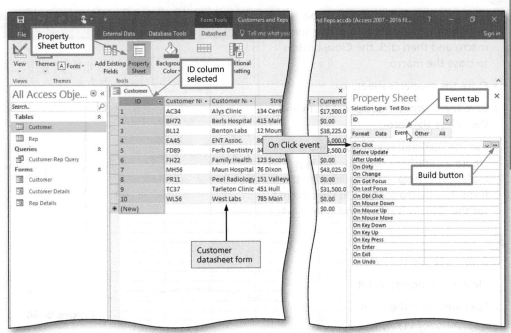

Figure 9–52

3

- Click the Build button (the three dots) for the On Click event, click the OK button (Choose Builder dialog box), and then use the techniques in the User Interface (UI) Macros section of Module 8 to enter the macro shown in Figure 9–53.

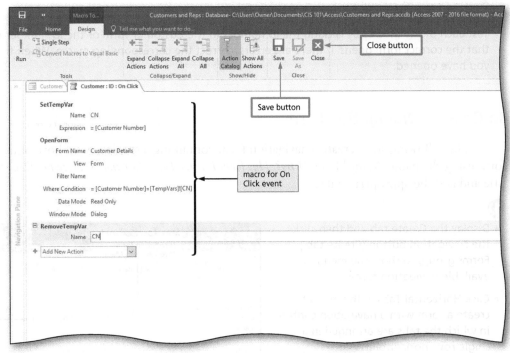

Figure 9–53

• Click the Save button (Macro Tools Design tab | Close group) to save the macro and then click the Close button to close the macro.

• Close the property sheet.

• Save the Customer datasheet form and then close the form.

• Use the techniques in Steps 1 and 2 to create a datasheet form for the Rep table. Use **Rep** as the name for the form. The macro for the On Click event for the ID field is shown in Figure 9–54.

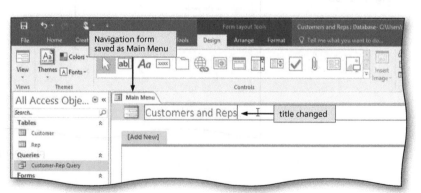

Figure 9–54

• Save and close the macro.

• Close the property sheet.

• Save and close the form.

• Select the Customer-Rep Query.

• Create a datasheet form for the Customer-Rep Query. Save the form, using **Customer-Rep Query** as the form name.

• Close the Customer-Rep Query form.

• Test each of the macros by clicking the ID number in the Customer form or the ID number in the Rep form. Ensure that the correct form opens. If there are errors, correct the corresponding macro. When finished, close any form you have opened.

To Create a Navigation Form

1 CONVERT DATABASE | 2 ANALYZE & DOCUMENT | 3 NAVIGATION PANE | 4 PROPERTIES & INDEXES
5 DATA PART | 6 TEMPLATE | 7 ENCRYPT LOCK & SPLIT | 8 WEB APP | 9 CUSTOM VIEW

The following steps create a navigation form containing a single row of horizontal tabs. The steps save the form using the name, Main Menu. **Why?** *This form is intended to function as a menu.* The steps change the form title and add the appropriate tabs.

• Display the Create tab and then click the Navigation button (Create tab | Forms group) to show the menu of available navigation forms.

• Click Horizontal Tabs in the menu to create a form with a navigation control in which the tabs are arranged in a single row, horizontally.

• If a field list appears, click the 'Add Existing Fields' button (Form Layout Tools Design tab | Tools group) to remove the field list.

Figure 9–55

• Save the navigation form, using Main Menu as the form name.

• Click the form title twice, once to select it and the second time to produce an insertion point.

• Erase the current title and then type **Customers and Reps** as the new title (Figure 9–55).

2

- One at a time, drag the Customer form, the Rep form, the Customer-Rep Query form, the Customer Details form, and the Rep Details form to the positions shown in Figure 9–56.

- Save and close the form.

Q&A What should I do if I made a mistake and added a form to the wrong location?
You can rearrange the tabs by dragging. However, the simplest way to correct a mistake is to click the Undo button to reverse your most recent action. You can also choose to simply close the form without saving it and then start over.

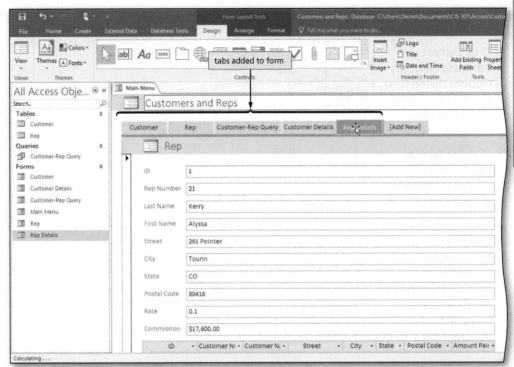

Figure 9–56

To Select a Startup Form

1 CONVERT DATABASE | 2 ANALYZE & DOCUMENT | 3 NAVIGATION PANE | 4 PROPERTIES & INDEXES

5 DATA PART | 6 TEMPLATE | **7 ENCRYPT LOCK & SPLIT** | 8 WEB APP | 9 CUSTOM VIEW

If the database includes a navigation form, it is common to select the navigation form as a **startup form,** which launches when the user opens the database. *Why? Designating the navigation form as a startup form ensures that the form will appear automatically when a user opens the database.* The following steps designate the navigation form as a startup form.

1

- Click File on the ribbon to display the Backstage view (Figure 9–57).

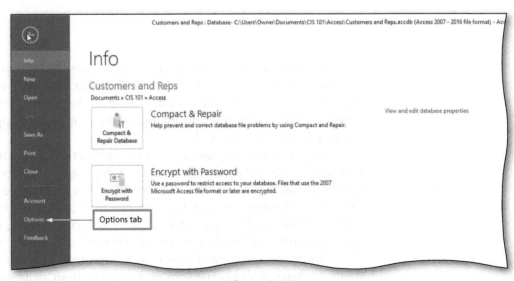

Figure 9–57

2

- Click the Options tab.

- Click Current Database (Access Options dialog box) to select the options for the current database.

- Click the Display Form arrow to display the list of available forms.

- Click Main Menu to select it as the form that will be automatically displayed whenever the database is opened (Figure 9–58).

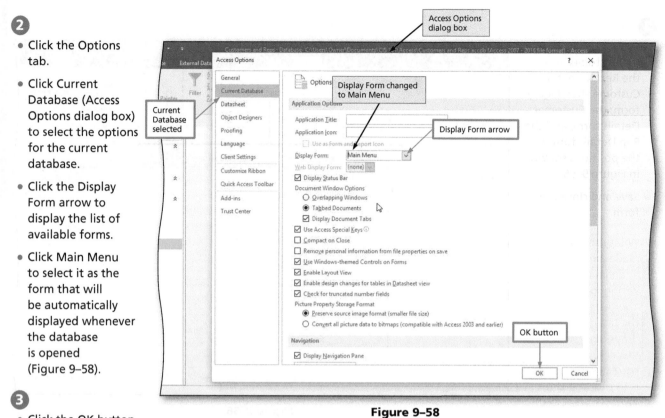

Figure 9–58

3

- Click the OK button (Access Options dialog box) to save your changes.

- Click the OK button (Microsoft Access dialog box) when Access displays a message indicating that you must close and reopen the database for the change to take effect.

- Close the database.

Break Point: If you wish to stop working through the module at this point, you can close Access now. You can resume the project at a later time by running Access, and continuing to follow the steps from this location forward.

Templates

An Access **template** is a file that contains the elements needed to produce a specific type of complete database. You can select a template when you create a database. The resulting database will contain all the tables, queries, forms, reports, and/or macros included in the template. In addition, with some templates, the resulting database might also contain data.

Some templates are also available as **application parts**. Application parts are very similar to templates in that selecting a single application part can create tables, queries, forms, reports, and macros. The difference is you select a template when you first create a database, whereas you select an application part after you have already created a database. The objects (tables, queries, forms, reports, and macros) in the application part will be added to any objects you have already created.

Access provides a number of templates representing a variety of types of databases. You can also create your own template from an existing database. When you create a template, you can choose to create an application part as well. When creating templates and application parts, you can also include data if desired.

To Create a Template and Application Part

The following steps create a template from the Customers and Reps database. *Why? The Customers and Reps database now contains all the tables, queries, and forms you want in the template. You will then be able to use the template when you want to create similar databases.* The steps also create an application part from the database so that you can reuse the parts in other databases.

- Open the Customers and Reps database and enable the content (Figure 9–59).

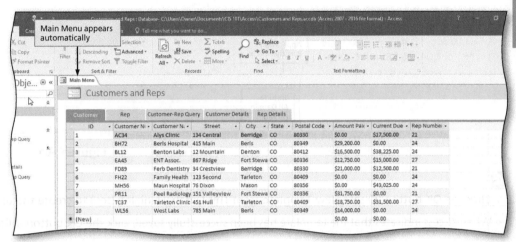

Figure 9–59

- Close the Main Menu form.
- Open the Backstage view.
- Click the Save As tab.
- Click the Template button in the Save Database As area to indicate you are creating a template (Figure 9–60).

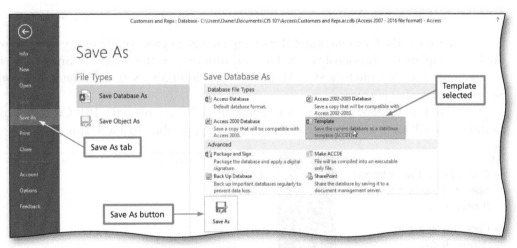

Figure 9–60

3

- Click the Save As button to display the Create New Template from This Database dialog box.
- Type `Customers and Reps` as the name for the new template.
- Type `Database of customers and reps with navigation form menu.` as the description.
- Click the Application Part check box to indicate that you also want to create an application part.

- Click the 'Include All Data in
Package' check box to indicate
you want to include the data
in the database as part of the
template (Figure 9–61).

Why include data?
Anytime a user creates a
database using the template,
the database will automatically
include data. This enables the
users to see what any reports,
forms, or queries look like with
data in them. Once the users
have the reports, forms, and
queries the way they want them,
they can delete all this data. At
that point, they can begin adding
their own data to the database.

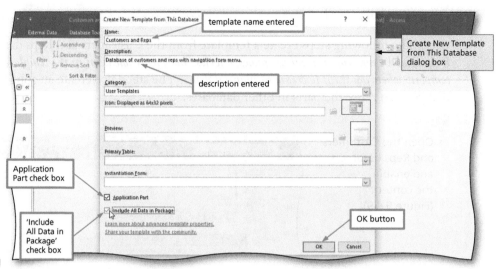

Figure 9–61

4

- Click the OK button (Create New Template from This Database dialog box) to create the template.

- When Access indicates that the template has been successfully saved, click the OK button (Microsoft Access dialog box).

To Use the Template

1 CONVERT DATABASE | 2 ANALYZE & DOCUMENT | 3 NAVIGATION PANE | 4 PROPERTIES & INDEXES
5 DATA PART | 6 TEMPLATE | **7 ENCRYPT LOCK & SPLIT** | 8 WEB APP | 9 CUSTOM VIEW

You can use the Customers and Reps template just as you would use any other template, such as the Blank
database template you previously used. The only difference is that, after clicking the New tab in the Backstage
view, you need to click the PERSONAL link. *Why? The PERSONAL link displays any templates you created and lets
you select the template you want.*

The following steps use the template created earlier to create the PJP Customers database. Later in the
module, you will learn how to use this database to import tables to a web app.

1

- Click File on the ribbon to
open the Backstage view,
if necessary.

- Click the New tab
(Figure 9–62).

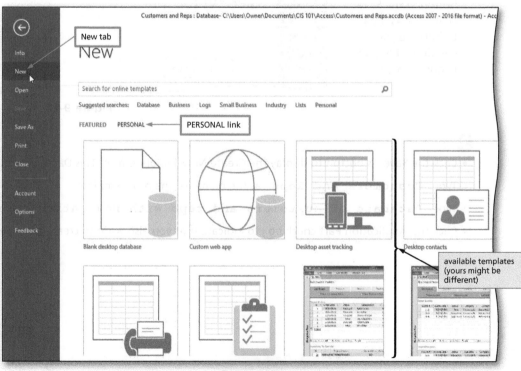

Figure 9–62

2

- Click the PERSONAL link to display the templates you have created (Figure 9–63).

3

- Click the 'Customers and Reps' template that you created earlier.

- Type **PJP Customers** as the name of the database and then navigate to the location where you will store the new database (for example, the Access folder in the CIS 101 folder).

Figure 9–63

- Click the Create button to create the database from the template.

- Close the database.

- If desired, sign out of your Microsoft account.

- Exit Access.

Note: Unless your instructor indicates otherwise, you are strongly encouraged to simply read the material in this module from this point on without carrying out any operations. If you decide to try it for yourself, it is important to make a backup copy of your database and store it in a secure location before performing the operation. That way, if something damages your database or you can no longer access your database, you still can use the backup copy. In addition, for the material on web apps, you must have access to a SharePoint site.

Using an Application Part

To use the application part you created, you first need to create a database. After doing so, you click the Application Parts button (Create tab | Templates group) to display the Application Parts menu (Figure 9–64).

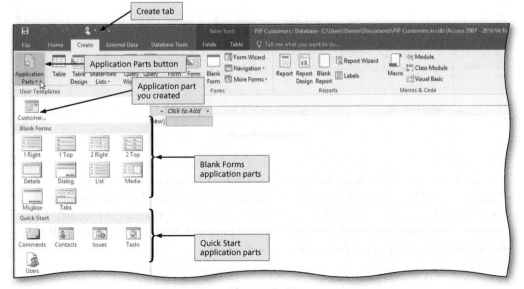

Figure 9–64

You can then click the application part you created, which will be located in the User Templates section of the Application Parts menu. If you have any open objects, Access will indicate that "all open objects must be closed before instantiating this application part" and ask if you want Access to close all open objects. After you click the Yes button, Access will add all the objects in the Application part to the database. If you had already created other objects in the database, they would still be included.

TO USE THE APPLICATION PART

Specifically, to use the application part created earlier, you would use the following steps.

1. Create or open the database in which you want to use the application part.
2. Display the Create tab and then click the Application Parts button (Create tab | Templates group).
3. Click the application part to be added.
4. If Access indicates that open objects must be closed, click the Yes button.

Blank Forms Application Parts

Blank Forms application parts (see Figure 9–64) represent a way to create certain types of forms. To do so, you click the Application Parts button to display the gallery of application part styles, and then click the desired type of form, for example, 1 Right. Access then creates a form with the desired characteristics and assigns it a name. It does not open the form, but you can see the form in the Navigation Pane (Figure 9–65).

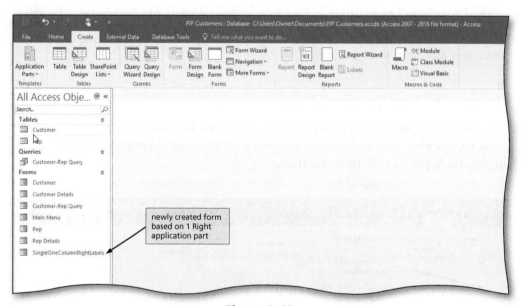

Figure 9–65

You can modify the form by opening the form in Layout or Design view (Figure 9–66). This particular form automatically creates a Save button. Clicking this button when you are using the form will save changes to the current record. The form also automatically includes a Save & Close button. Clicking this button will save changes to the current record and then close the form.

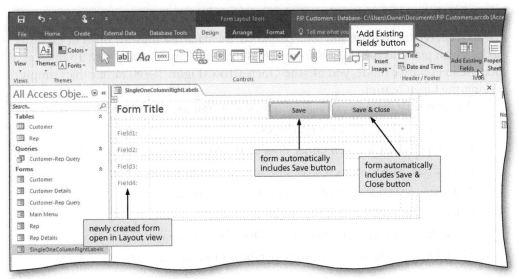

Figure 9–66

To add the specific fields you want to the form, display a field list. You can then drag a field onto the form while holding down the CTRL key (Figure 9–67). Once you have added the field, you can change the corresponding label by clicking the label to select it, clicking the label a second time to produce an insertion point, and then making the desired change.

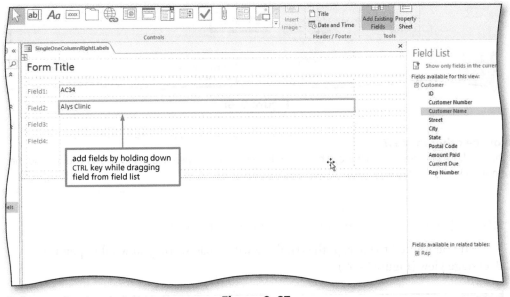

Figure 9–67

Encrypting a Database

Encrypting refers to the storing of data in the database in an encoded, or encrypted, format. Anytime a user stores or modifies data in the encrypted database, the database management system (DBMS) will encode the data before actually updating the database. Before a legitimate user retrieves the data using the DBMS, the data will be decoded. The whole encrypting process is transparent to a legitimate user; that is, he or she is not even aware it is happening. If an unauthorized user attempts to bypass all the controls of the DBMS and get to the database through a utility program or a word processor, however, he or she will only be able to see the encoded, and unreadable, version of the data. In Access, you encrypt a database and set a password as part of the same operation.

BTW
Encryption and Passwords
Encryption helps prevent unauthorized use of an Access database. Consider using encryption when the database contains sensitive data, such as medical records or employee records. Passwords should be eight or more characters in length. The longer the length of the password and the more random the characters, the more difficult it is for someone to determine. Use a combination of uppercase and lowercase letters as well as numbers and special symbols when you create a password. Make sure that you remember your password. If you forget it, there is no method for retrieving it. You will be unable to open the encrypted database.

TO OPEN A DATABASE IN EXCLUSIVE MODE

To encrypt a database and set a password, the database must be open in exclusive mode, which prevents other users from accessing the database in any way. To open a database in exclusive mode, you use the Open arrow (Figure 9–68) rather than simply clicking the Open button.

To open a database in exclusive mode, you would use the following steps.

1. If necessary, close any open databases.
2. Click Open or click 'Open Other Files' in Backstage view to display the Open screen.
3. Click Browse on the Open screen to display the Open dialog box.
4. Navigate to the location of the database to be opened.
5. Click the name of the database to be opened.
6. Click the Open arrow to display the Open button menu.
7. Click Open Exclusive to open the database in exclusive mode.

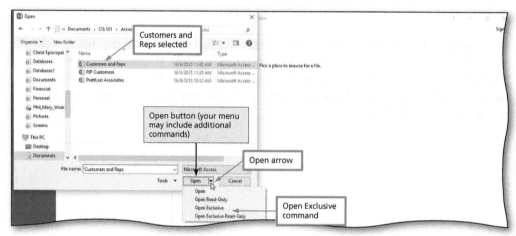

Figure 9–68

What is the purpose of the other modes?

The Open option opens the database in a mode so that it can be shared by other users. Open Read-Only allows you to read the data in the database, but not update the database.

Encrypting a Database with a Password

If you wanted to encrypt the database with a password, you would open the Backstage view (Figure 9–69).

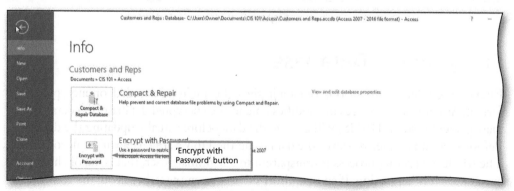

Figure 9–69

You would then select 'Encrypt with Password' and enter the password you have chosen in both the Password text box and Verify text box (Figure 9–70).

'Set Database Password' dialog box

Customers and Reps

Password text box

Verify text box

password appears as asterisks (*)

OK button

Figure 9–70

TO ENCRYPT A DATABASE WITH A PASSWORD

With the database open in exclusive mode, you would use the following steps to encrypt the database with a password.

1. Click File on the ribbon to open the Backstage view and ensure the Info tab is selected.
2. Click the 'Encrypt with Password' button to display the Set Database Password dialog box.
3. Type the desired password in the Password text box in the Set Database Password dialog box.
4. Press the TAB key and then type the password again in the Verify text box.
5. Click the OK button to encrypt the database and set the password.
6. If you get a message indicating that row level locking will be ignored, click the OK button.
7. Close the database.

Is the password case sensitive?

Yes, you must enter the password using the same case you used when you created it.

Opening a Database with a Password

When you open a database that has a password, you will be prompted to enter your password in the Password Required dialog box. Once you have done so, click the OK button. Assuming you have entered your password correctly, Access will then open the database.

Decrypting a Database and Removing a Password

If the encryption and the password are no longer necessary, you can decrypt the database. The database will no longer have a password. If you later found you needed the database to be encrypted, you could repeat the steps to encrypt the database and add a password. The button to encrypt a database with a password has changed to Decrypt Database (Figure 9–71).

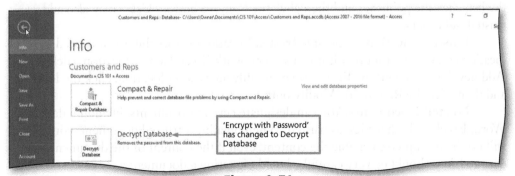

Figure 9–71

To Decrypt the Database and Remove the Password

To decrypt a database that you have previously encrypted and remove the password, you would use the following steps.

1. Open the database to be decrypted in exclusive mode, entering your password when requested.
2. Open the Backstage view and ensure the Info tab is selected.
3. Click the Decrypt Database button to display the Unset Database Password dialog box.
4. Type the password in the Password dialog box.
5. Click the OK button to remove the password and decrypt the database.
6. Close the database.

The Trust Center

The Trust Center is a feature within Access where you can set security options and also find the latest information on technology related to privacy, safety, and security. To use the Trust Center, you click File on the ribbon and then click the Options tab to display the Access Options dialog box. You then click Trust Center to display the Trust Center content (Figure 9–72). You would then click the 'Trust Center Settings' button to display the Trust Center dialog box in which you can make changes in the following categories.

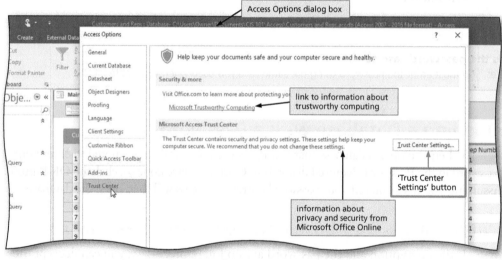

Figure 9–72

Trusted Publishers. Clicking Trusted Publishers in the Trust Center dialog box shows the list of trusted software publishers. To view details about a trusted publisher, click the publisher and then click the View button. To remove a trusted publisher from the list, click the publisher and then click the Remove button. Users may also add trusted publishers.

Trusted Locations. Clicking Trusted Locations shows the list of trusted locations on the Internet or within a user's network. To add a new location, click the 'Add new location' button. To remove or modify an existing location, click the location and then click the Remove or Modify button.

Trusted Documents. You can designate certain documents, including database, Word, Excel, and other files, as trusted. When opening a trusted document, you will not be prompted to enable the content, even if the content of the document has changed. You should be very careful when designating a document as trusted and only do so when you are absolutely sure the document is from a trusted source.

Add-ins. Add-ins are additional programs that you can install and use within Access. Some come with Access and are typically installed using the Access Setup program. Others can be purchased from other vendors. Clicking Add-ins gives you the opportunity to specify restrictions concerning Add-ins.

ActiveX Settings. When you use ActiveX controls within an Office app, Office prompts you to accept the controls. The ActiveX settings allow you to determine the level of prompting from Office.

Macro Settings. Macros written by other users have the potential to harm your computer; for example, a macro could spread a virus. The Trust Center uses special criteria, including valid digital signatures, reputable certificates, and trusted publishers, to determine whether a macro is safe. If the Trust Center discovers a macro that is potentially unsafe, it will take appropriate action. The action the Trust Center takes depends on the Macro Setting you have selected. Clicking Macro Settings enables you to select or change this setting.

Message Bar. Clicking Message Bar lets you choose whether the message bar should appear when content has been blocked.

Privacy Options. Clicking Privacy Options lets you set security settings to protect your personal privacy.

Trusted Add-in Catalogs. Use this option to specify trusted catalogs of web add-ins. You can also indicate whether Access will allow web add-ins to start.

BTW
Active X controls
Active X controls are small programs that can run within an Office app. The calendar control is an example of an Active X control.

Locking a Database

By **locking** a database, you can prevent users from viewing or modifying VBA code in your database or from making changes to the design of forms or reports while still allowing them to update records. When you lock the database, Access changes the file name extension from .accdb to .accde. To do so, you would use the Make ACCDE command shown in Figure 9–3.

BTW
Locked Databases
When you create a locked database, the original database remains unchanged and is still available for use.

TO CREATE A LOCKED DATABASE (ACCDE FILE)

To lock a database, you would use the following steps.

1. With the database open, click File on the ribbon to open the Backstage view.
2. Click the Save As tab.
3. Click Make ACCDE in the Advanced area.
4. Click the Save As button.
5. In the Save As dialog box, indicate a location and name for the ACCDE file.
6. Click the Save button in the Save As dialog box to create the file.

Using the Locked Database

You would use an ACCDE file just as you use the databases with which you are now familiar, with two exceptions. First, you must select ACCDE files in the 'Files of type' box when opening the file. Second, you will not be able to modify any source code or change the design of any forms or reports. If you right-clicked the Customer form, for example, you would find that the Design View command on the shortcut menu is dimmed, as are many other commands (Figure 9–73).

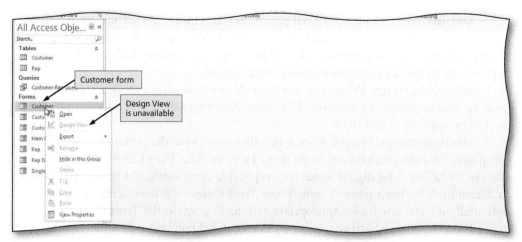

Figure 9–73

It is very important that you save your original database in case you ever need to make changes to VBA code or to the design of a form or report. You cannot use the ACCDE file to make such changes, nor can you convert the ACCDE file back to the ACCDB file format.

Record Locking

You can indicate how records are to be locked when multiple users are using a database at the same time. To do so, click File on the ribbon, click the Options tab, and then click Client Settings. Scroll down so that the Advanced area appears on the screen (Figure 9–74).

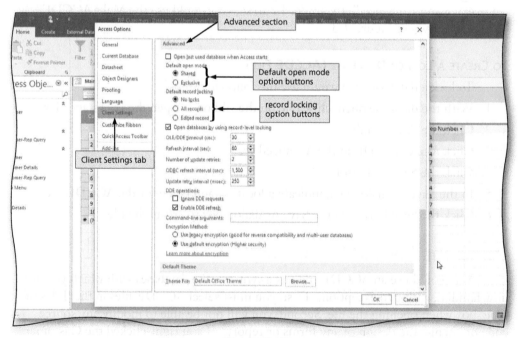

Figure 9–74

If you wanted the default open mode to be exclusive (only one user can use the database at a time) rather than shared (multiple users can simultaneously use the database), you could click the Exclusive option button. You can also select the approach you want for record locking by clicking the appropriate record locking option button. The possible approaches to record locking are shown in Table 9–3.

Table 9–3 Record Locking Approaches	
Locking Type	**Description**
No locks	When you edit a record, Access will not lock the record. Thus, other users also could edit the same record at the same time. When you have finished your changes and attempt to save the record, Access will give you the option of overwriting the other user's changes (not recommended), copying your changes to the clipboard, or canceling your changes.
All records	All records will be locked as long as you have the database open. No other user can edit or lock the records during this time.
Edited record	When you edit a record, Access will lock the record. When other users attempt to edit the same record, they will not be able to do so. Instead, they will see the locked record indicator.

Database Splitting

You can **split** a database into two databases, one called the **back-end database** containing only the table data, and another database called the **front-end database** containing the other objects. Only a single copy of the back-end database can exist, but each user could have his or her own copy of the front-end database. Each user would create the desired custom reports, forms, and other objects in his or her own front-end database, thereby not interfering with any other user.

When splitting a database, the database to be split must be open. In the process, you will identify a name and location for the back-end database that will be created by the Access splitter. In the process, you would display the Database Splitter dialog box (Figure 9–75).

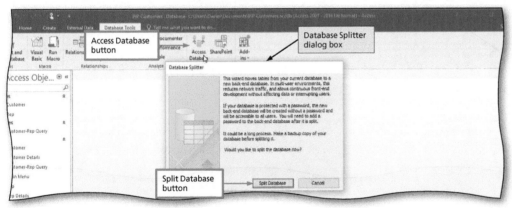

Figure 9–75

You would also have to select a location for the back-end database (Figure 9–76). Access assigns a name to the back-end database that ends with an underscore and the letters, be. You can override this name if you prefer.

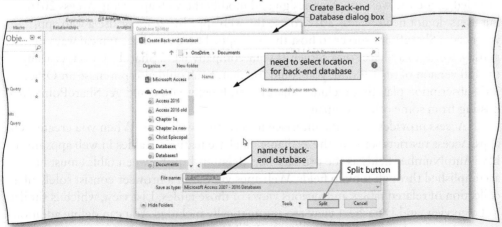

Figure 9–76

TO SPLIT THE DATABASE

To split a database, you would use the following steps.

1. Open the database to be split.
2. Display the Database Tools tab.
3. Click the Access Database button (Database Tools tab | Move Data group) to display the Database Splitter dialog box.
4. Click the Split Database button to display the Create Back-end Database dialog box.
5. Either accept the file name Access suggests or change it to the one you want.
6. Select a location for the back-end database.
7. Click the Split button to split the database.
8. Click the OK button to close the dialog box reporting that the split was successful.

The Front-End and Back-End Databases

The database has now been split into separate front-end and back-end databases. The front-end database is the one that you will use; it contains all the queries, reports, forms, and other components from the original database. The front-end database only contains links to the tables, however, instead of the tables themselves (Figure 9–77). The back-end database contains the actual tables but does not contain any other objects.

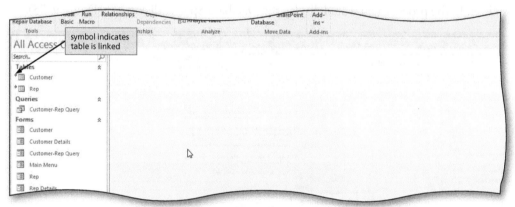

Figure 9–77

Web Apps

A **web app** is a database that you use in a web browser. You do not need to have Access installed to use the web app. You design and modify the web app using Access 2016, but users do not need Access 2016 to use the web app. To create or use a web app, you need a SharePoint server to host the web app. There are three typical ways of getting access to a SharePoint server. If your company has a SharePoint server using the full version of SharePoint, you could use that. You could also purchase an Office 365 subscription plan that includes SharePoint. Finally, you could get SharePoint 2016 hosting from some other company.

Access provides a specific interface for creating web apps. When you create web apps, Access restricts some of the available database features. Tables in web apps must have AutoNumber fields as the primary key. Relationships between tables must be accomplished through lookup fields. Web apps viewed in a browser consist solely of a collection of related tables and various views of those tables. List view, which is similar to Form view, and Datasheet view are automatically included. You can define additional summary views that group data on selected fields.

Creating Web Apps

You can create custom web apps, in which you will indicate the specific tables and fields you want to include. Alternatively, you can select one of the web app templates. In either case, you must enter a name for your app as well as a web location for the app (Figure 9–78).

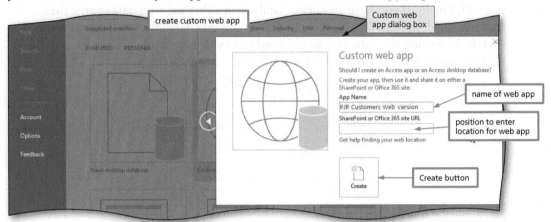

Figure 9–78

To Create a Web App

To create a web app, you would use the following steps.

1. In Backstage view, on the New tab, click either 'Custom web app' to create a web app of your own design or one of the web app templates to create a web app matching the template.

2. Enter a descriptive name for the web app.

3. If you see a list of available locations for the web app, you can select one of the locations. If not, or if none of the available locations is appropriate, enter the URL that points to your SharePoint site.

4. Click the Create button to create the web app.

5. If requested, enter the User ID and password for your SharePoint site and click the Sign In button to finish creating the web app on your SharePoint site.

Figure 9–79 shows the result of creating a custom web app called PJP Customers Web Version.

BTW

SharePoint 2016
SharePoint offers users the ability to store data on the web so that access to that data can be shared across a network. It is essentially a storage location that can be accessed collaboratively. No special software is required on the customer side. SharePoint 2016 allows users to share calendars, blogs, wikis, surveys, document libraries, and task lists.

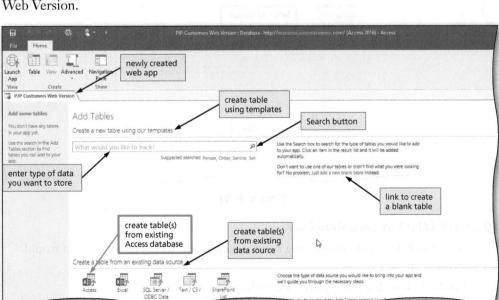

Figure 9–79

Creating Tables for the Web App

There are three ways of creating the tables for the web app. First, you can use a template, in which case Access will determine the fields to be included in the table. Alternatively, you can create a blank table and then enter the fields and data types yourself. Finally, if you have an Access database or other existing data source that contains the desired tables, such as the PJP Customers database, you can import the data. In importing the data, you would need to identify the name and location of the file that contains the desired data (Figure 9–80).

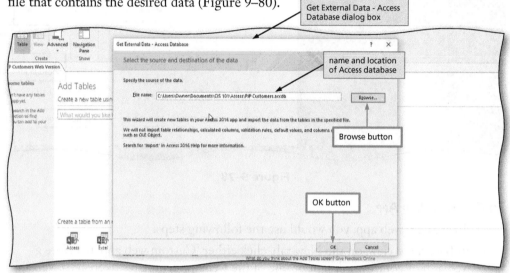

Figure 9–80

After identifying the file containing the tables, you would be presented with a list of tables in that file (Figure 9–81). You could select individual tables in the list or select all the tables by clicking the Select All button. Once you have made your selection, you would click the OK button to import the data.

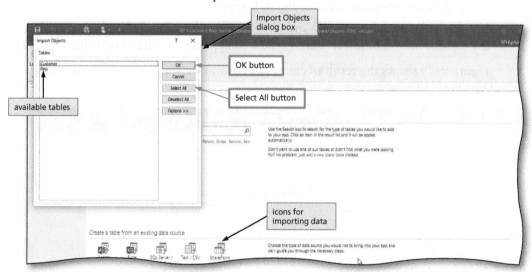

Figure 9–81

TO CREATE TABLES BY IMPORTING DATA

To import data from an existing source such as an Access database, you would use the following steps.

1. Click the icon for the type of data to import.
2. Browse to the location of the data to import and select the file to import.
3. Click the OK button.

4. Select the tables to import. If you want to import all the tables in the data source, click the Select All button.

5. Click the OK button to import the data.

TO CREATE TABLES FROM TEMPLATES

Access provides templates to assist in the creation of tables. To create a table for a web app from a template, you would use the following steps.

1. Enter the type of object for which you will be storing data and click the Search button.

2. When Access presents a list of options, click the option that best fits your needs.

TO CREATE BLANK TABLES

You can create a blank table for the web app and then enter the names, data types, and other characteristics of the fields in Design view just as you have created other tables. To create a blank table, you would use the following step.

1. Click the 'add a new blank table' link to create the table and display the table in Design view.

The Rate field has a special field size, Single, which is necessary to display decimal places. If you create the Rep table as a blank table in a web app, do you still have the option to change the field size to Single?
Not exactly. The possible field sizes for Number fields are slightly different when you create a web app than when you create a desktop database. The possibilities are Whole Number (no decimal places), Fixed-point number (6 decimal places), and Floating-point number (variable decimal places). If you import a table from a desktop database in which you have set the field size to Single, Access will automatically assign the field the Floating-point number field size, which is appropriate.

Using Views

Figure 9–82 shows the web app with the two tables created during the import process. The Customer table is currently selected. The web app offers two views, List view and Datasheet view. List view, in which the data appears as a form, is currently selected. Figure 9–82 shows the appearance of the view, not the actual data. You will see the data when you run the app.

To make changes to the way the table appears in List view, you would click the floating Edit button, which appears in the middle of the list.

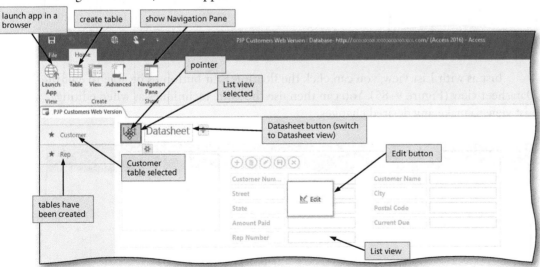

Figure 9–82

If you click the Edit button, you will be able to edit the view (Figure 9–83). Editing the view allows you to change the appearance of the view, not the underlying data. The process is similar to modifying the layout of a form in either Layout or Design view. You can display a field list as shown in the figure by clicking the 'Add Existing Fields' button. You can add a field by dragging it from the field list into the desired location in the view. You can delete an existing field from the view by clicking the field, and then pressing the DELETE key. You can move fields within the list by dragging them to the desired location. You can also click a field and then click the Formatting button to display the FORMATTING menu. Using that menu, you can display a tooltip for the field, choose whether the field is visible, or choose whether the field is enabled.

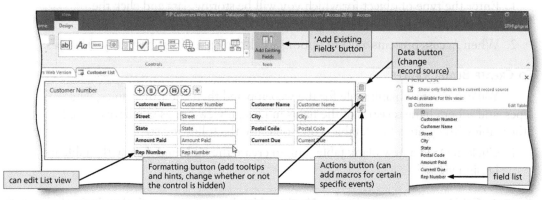

Figure 9–83

Clicking the Datasheet view button for the same table displays the Datasheet view, which is similar to the normal Datasheet view you see when working with a desktop database (Figure 9–84).

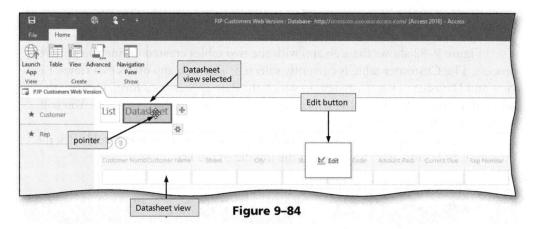

Figure 9–84

Just as with List view, you can click the floating Edit button to be able to edit the Datasheet view (Figure 9–85). You can then use the same techniques as when editing List view to make any desired changes.

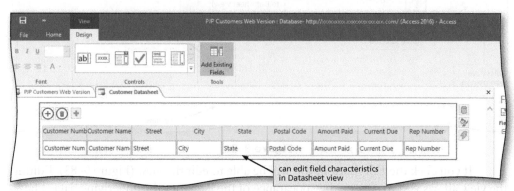

Figure 9–85

TO EDIT VIEWS

To edit a view, you would use the following steps.

1. Click the table whose view you want to edit.
2. Click the view to edit.
3. Click the Edit button.
4. When finished editing, click the Close button for the view you are editing.
5. Click the Yes button to save your changes. Click the No button if you do not want to save your changes.

Viewing Data

When you later run the web app, you will see the actual data in the database. You can view the data in either List or Datasheet view or you can make changes to the data, which are immediately available to other users.

You can also view the data in a typical Access format. To do so, select the table you want to view and click the Settings/Action button, or right-click the table, to display the Settings/Action menu (Figure 9–86).

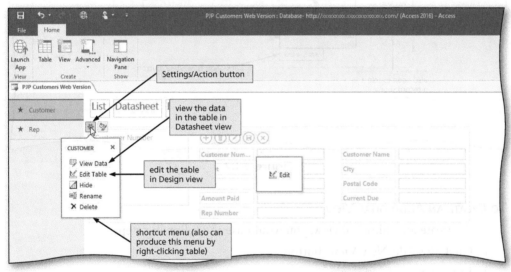

Figure 9–86

If you click View Data on the Settings/Action menu, you will see the data in Datasheet view. You can both view and change the data.

You can also modify the design of a table using the Settings/Action button. To do so, you would click Edit Table rather than View Data. You would then see the table displayed in Design view. You can make changes to the table design similar to how you have updated other tables in Design view.

What is the purpose of the other commands on the Settings/Action menu?
If you select Hide, the selected table will not appear when you run the app. If you hide a table, you can later select Unhide, in which case it will once again appear. You can rename a table by selecting Rename and delete the table by selecting Delete.

Creating an Additional View

You can create additional views that are then included in the app. To do so, click the 'Add New View' button (Figure 9–87) to display the ADD NEW VIEW dialog box. You also can click the View button (Home tab | Create group) to display the dialog box. Figure 9–87 also shows the list of available view types. The available types are List Details (List view), Datasheet, Summary, and Blank. You have already seen List and Datasheet views. You will see how to create a Summary view later in this module. A Blank view allows you to create a view from scratch, similar to using a blank form.

In the ADD NEW VIEW dialog box, you enter a name for the view, select the View Type, and then select the record source. The record source can be either a table or a query.

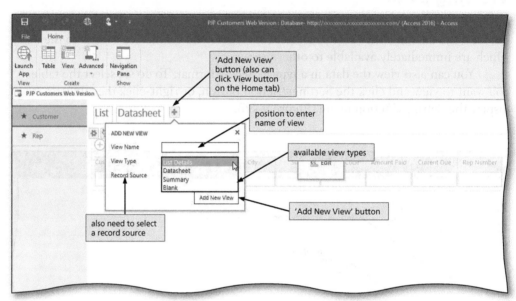

Figure 9–87

TO CREATE AN ADDITIONAL VIEW

To create an additional view, you would use the following steps.

1. Click the 'Add New View' button.
2. Enter a name for the view.
3. Click the View Type arrow to display the menu of available view types.
4. Click the desired view type.
5. Click the Record Source arrow to display a list of the available tables and queries.
6. Click the desired table or query.
7. Click the 'Add New View' button to create the new view.

CONSIDER THIS

How can you delete a view you do not want?
Click the view to select the view. Click the Settings/Action button that will appear near the view to display a shortcut menu. Click Delete on the shortcut menu. Click the OK button to confirm the deletion.

Creating Additional Objects

You can create tables by clicking the Table button (Home tab | Create group). You will then see the same Add Tables screen you saw earlier in Figure 9–79. You then have the same three options for creating tables: You can create the table using a template, create a blank table, or import a table from an existing data source.

You can create other objects, such as queries, by clicking the Advanced button (Home tab | Create group) to produce the Advanced menu (Figure 9–88). The Advanced menu gives you options for creating queries, blank views, blank List views, blank Datasheet views, and various types of macros.

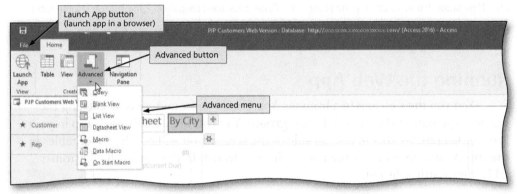

Figure 9–88

To use any of the blank views, you can place fields in the view by dragging the field from a field list, just as you have done in previous modules with forms and reports. Creating macros uses the same process you have seen earlier. However, creating macros in the web app does limit some of the available options for macros. Creating a query in the web app is also similar to the process you used to create queries earlier; the design grid used in the web app is similar to that used in Access (Figure 9–89). As with macros, creating queries in the web app limits some of the options, but the options that are present function in the manner you would expect. Once you have created a query, you can then use it as the record source for a view.

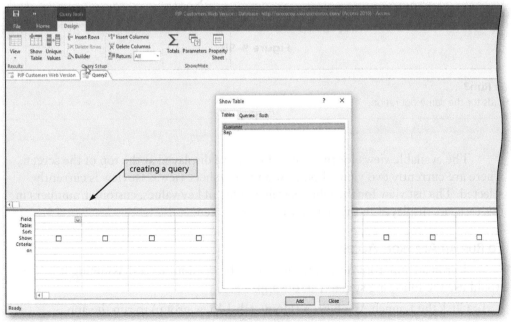

Figure 9–89

TO CREATE ADDITIONAL OBJECTS

To create an additional object, you would use the following steps.

1. To create a table, click the Table button (Home tab | Create group), and then indicate whether you will create the table using a template, create a blank table, or import a table from an existing data source.

2. To create another type of object, click the Advanced button (Home tab | Create group) to display the Advanced menu, and then select the type of object to create.

How can you see the additional objects you have created?
You can only see them in the Navigation Pane. To display the Navigation Pane, click the Navigation Pane button (Home tab | Show group).

Running the Web App

You run the web app in a browser. You can do so from Access by clicking the Launch App button (Home tab | View group). You will then see the web app in your browser (Figure 9–90). On the left side of the screen, you will see the list of tables in the app. At any time, one of the tables will be selected. In the figure, the Customer table is currently selected.

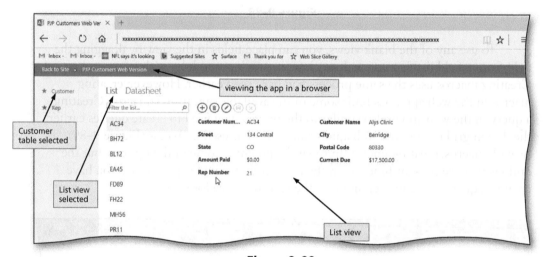

Figure 9–90

Is Launch the same as Run?
Yes. They are different words for the same operation.

The available views for the selected table are displayed at the top of the screen. There are currently two views, List view and Datasheet view. List view is currently selected. The list view for the table as well as a list of key values, customer numbers in this case, are displayed in the center area of the screen.

TO RUN AN APP FROM ACCESS

To run an app from Access, the app must be open in Access. Assuming it is, you would use the following step to run the app.

1. Click the Launch App button (Home tab | View group) to run the app.

To display a table in Datasheet view, first be sure the desired table is selected. Next, click the Datasheet link. The table will appear in Datasheet view (Figure 9–91).

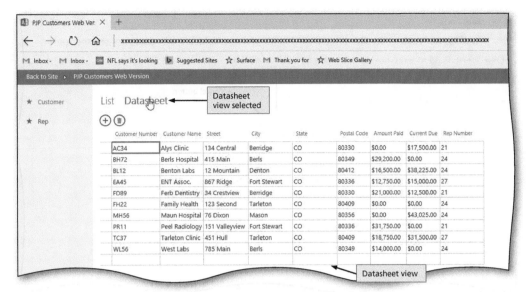

Figure 9–91

If you click the List link, the table will again appear in List view (Figure 9–92). Click one of the customer numbers on the left to display the data for that customer. You can update the data for the customer currently on the screen, add a new customer, or delete a customer. To do so, click the button for the desired action. If you click the Add button, the form will be blank and you can type the data for the new customer. If you click the Delete button, you will be asked to confirm the deletion. If you do, the customer currently on the screen will be deleted.

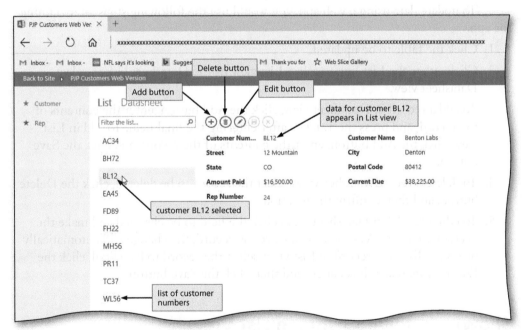

Figure 9–92

If you click the Edit button, the buttons change slightly (Figure 9–93). The Add, Delete, and Edit buttons are dimmed, whereas the Save and Cancel buttons are not. After making a change, such as the change of the state as shown in the figure, you can click the Save button to save the change or the Cancel button to cancel the change.

Figure 9–93

You can also update data in Datasheet view. To add a record, click the Add button and type the contents of the new record. To delete a record, click anywhere in the record, click the Delete button, and then confirm the deletion. To edit a record, click in the field to be changed and make the desired change.

TO UPDATE DATA USING A WEB APP

To update data using a web app, you would use the following steps after running the app.

1. Click the table to be updated.
2. Click either the List link to select List view or the Datasheet link to select Datasheet view.
3. To add a record in Datasheet view, click the Add button, enter the contents of the record, and press the TAB key after entering the final field. To add in List view, click the Add button, enter the contents of the record, and click the Save button.
4. To delete a record in either view, select the record to be deleted, click the Delete button, and then confirm the deletion.
5. To edit a record in Datasheet view, click the field to be changed and make the necessary change. As soon as you leave the record, the change will automatically be saved. To edit a record in List view, select the record to be edited, click the Edit button, make the change, and then click the Save button.

Showing a Relationship in List View

If you view the "one" table in a one-to-many relationship in List view, you will see the corresponding records in the "many" table appear in a datasheet. Figure 9–94 shows the Rep table appearing in List view. The data for the selected rep appears in List view. The customers of the selected rep appear in a datasheet just below the data for the rep. Note that this is the only way to see the relationship. Viewing the "one" table in Datasheet view will not show the relationship, nor will viewing the "many" table in either view.

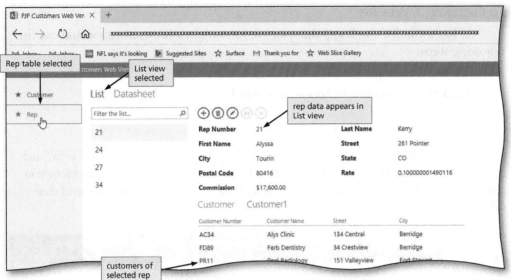

Figure 9–94

Running a Web App from a Browser

To run a web app, you navigate to your SharePoint site and simply run the app. You do not have to run Access, open the app, and then run the app. It is not even necessary to have Access on your computer. You can run the app directly from your browser.

TO RUN A WEB APP FROM A BROWSER

To run a web app from a browser, you would use the following steps.

1. Type the URL for your SharePoint site and press the ENTER key.
2. When requested, type your user name and password.
3. Click the OK button to display the contents of your SharePoint site.
4. Click the desired web app to run the app.

Customizing a Web App

You can customize a web app from within Access. If you are running the app in a browser, you launch Access by clicking the Settings button and then clicking the 'Customize in Access' command (Figure 9–95).

Figure 9–95

To Customize a Web App

To customize a web app that you are running in a browser, you would use the following steps.

1. Click the Settings button.
2. Click the 'Customize in Access' command.

Adding a Summary View

One of the ways you can customize a web app is to add an additional view, such as a Summary view. After selecting the table for which you want to add the view, you would use the 'Add New View' button to select Summary as the view type and then select the record source table (Figure 9–96).

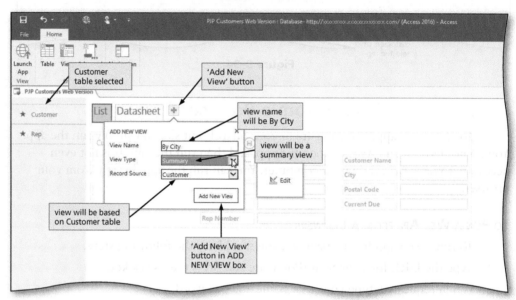

Figure 9–96

Clicking the 'Add New View' button in the ADD NEW VIEW dialog box creates the view. You can edit the view using the EDIT button. Then, you can use the Data button to display the DATA box, where you indicate a Group By field, Sort Order, Calculation Field, and Calculation Type (Figure 9–97).

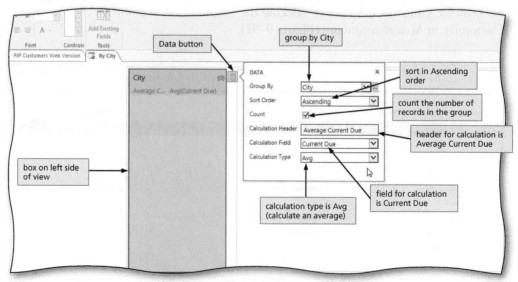

Figure 9–97

By clicking the box on the right and then clicking the Data button, you can enter up to four fields to be displayed and optionally display captions for the fields. Specifying the popup view determines the view that will appear as a popup when the user clicks a specific record and will give additional information about that record. The final step is to enter the sort order (Figure 9–98).

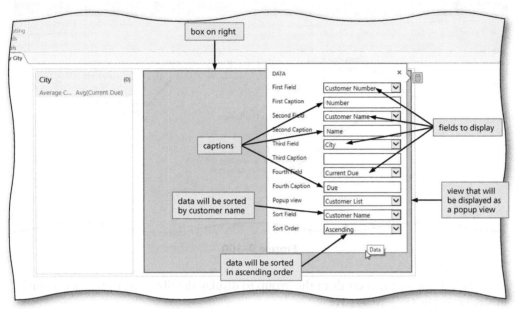

Figure 9–98

After closing the view and saving the changes, you can run the app by clicking the Launch App button, being sure the appropriate table is selected. You click the new view to test the view, and then close the view (Figure 9–99).

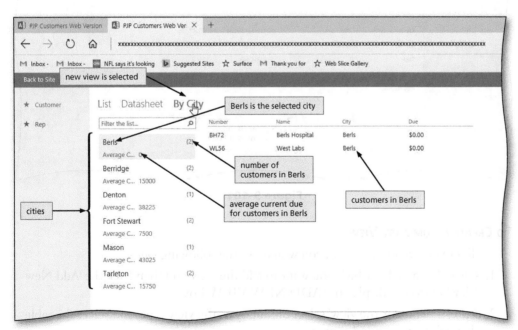

Figure 9–99

If you select another value in the left-hand column, all the corresponding records will now appear in the right-hand column (Figure 9–100).

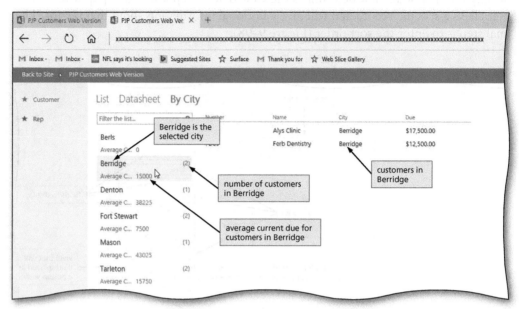

Figure 9–100

Select one of the records in the group to display details concerning that record in a popup view (Figure 9–101).

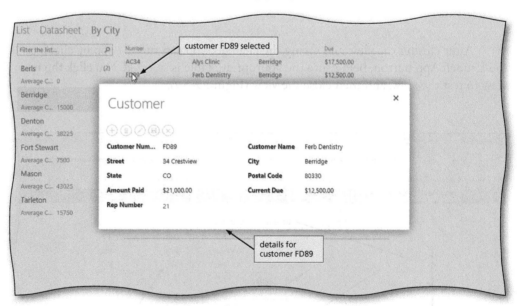

Figure 9–101

TO CREATE A SUMMARY VIEW

To create a Summary view, you would use the following steps.

1. Click the table for which you want to add the view and then click the 'Add New View' button to display the ADD NEW VIEW box.

2. Enter a name for the view, select Summary as the view type, and select the table that will be the record source.

3. Click the 'Add New View' button (ADD NEW VIEW dialog box) to create the view.

4. Click the Edit button to edit the view.

5. Click the box on the left side of the view and then click the Data button to display the DATA box.

6. Enter the Group By field, sort order, whether you want a count displayed, the header for the calculation, the field for the calculation, and the calculation type (average or sum).

7. Close the DATA box, click the box on the right, and then click its Data button.

8. Enter up to four fields to be displayed. You can optionally enter captions for any of the fields.

9. Enter the popup view.

10. Enter the sort order.

11. Close the view and click the Yes button when asked if you want to save your changes.

Summary

In this module you have learned to convert Access databases to and from earlier versions; use Microsoft Access tools to analyze and document an Access database; add custom categories and groups to the Navigation Pane; use table and database properties; use field properties to create a custom input mask; allow zero-length strings; create indexes; use automatic error checking; create custom data parts; create and use templates and application parts; encrypt a database and set a password; understand the Trust Center; lock a database; split a database; create and run a web app; and customize a web app.

CONSIDER THIS: PLAN AHEAD

What decisions will you need to make when administering your own databases?
Use these guidelines as you complete the assignments in this module and administer your own databases outside of this class.

1. Determine whether a database needs to be shared over the web.

    a. Do you have users who would profit from being able to access a database over the web? If so, you will need to create a web app, which requires you to have access to a SharePoint server.

    b. Determine the tables that should be in the web app.

    c. Determine the views of the tables that should be included in the web app.

2. Determine whether you should create any templates, application parts, or data type parts.

    a. Is there a particular combination of tables, queries, forms, reports, and/or macros that you would like to enable users to easily include in their databases? If so, you could create a template and an application part containing the specific objects you want them to be able to include.

    b. Is there a particular collection of fields that you would like to enable users to include in a table with a single click? If so, you could create a data type part containing those fields.

3. Determine whether a database needs to be converted to or from an earlier version.

    a. Do users of a previous version of Access need to be able to use the database? If so, you will need to be sure the database does not contain any features that would prevent it from being converted.

    b. Do you use a database that was created in an earlier version of Access that you would like to use in Access 2016? If so, you can convert the database for use in Access 2016.

4. Determine when to analyze and/or document the database.

    a. Once you create a database, you should use the table and performance analyzers to determine if any changes to the structure are warranted.

    b. You should also document the database.

5. Determine the most useful way to customize the Navigation Pane.

    a. Would it be helpful to have custom categories and groups?

    b. What objects should be in the groups?

    c. Would it be helpful to restrict the objects that appear to only those whose names contain certain characters?

6. Determine any table-wide validation rules.

    a. Are there any validation rules that involve more than a single field?

7. Determine any custom database properties.

    a. Are there properties that would be helpful in documenting the database that are not included in the list of database properties you can use?

8. Determine indexes.

    a. Examine retrieval and sorting requirements to determine possible indexes. Indexes can make both retrieval and sorting more efficient.

9. Determine whether the database should be encrypted.

    a. If you need to protect the security of the database's contents, you should strongly consider encryption.

    b. As part of the process, you will also set a password.

10. Determine whether the database should be locked.

    a. Should users be able to change the design of forms, reports, and/or macros?

11. Determine whether the database should be split.

    a. It is often more efficient to split the database into a back-end database, which contains only the table data, and a front-end database, which contains other objects, such as queries, forms, and reports.

CONSIDER THIS

How should you submit solutions to questions in the assignments identified with a symbol?
Every assignment in this book contains one or more questions identified with a symbol. These questions require you to think beyond the assigned database. Present your solutions to the questions in the format required by your instructor. Possible formats may include one or more of these options: write the answer; create a document that contains the answer; present your answer to the class; discuss your answer in a group; record the answer as audio or video using a webcam, smartphone, or portable media player; or post answers on a blog, wiki, or website.

Apply Your Knowledge

Reinforce the skills and apply the concepts you learned in this module.

Administering the AllAround Services Database

Instructions: Run Access. Open the Apply AllAround Services database that you modified in Module 8. (If you did not complete the exercise, see your instructor for a copy of the modified database.)

Perform the following tasks:

1. Open the Client table in Design view and create an index that allows duplicates on the Client Name field. Zero-length strings should not be allowed in the Client Name field.

2. Create a custom input mask for the Client Number field. The first two characters of the client number must be uppercase letters and the last two characters must be numerical digits.

3. Create an index on the combination of Client Type and Amount Paid. Name the index TypePaid.

4. Save the changes to the Client table.

5. Use the Database Documenter to produce detailed documentation for the Services table. Export the documentation to a Word RTF file. Change the name of the file to LastName _Documentation.rtf where LastName is your last name.

6. Use the Table Analyzer to analyze the table structure of the Client table. Open the Word RTF file that you created in Step 5 and make a note of the results of the analysis at the end of the file.

7. Use the Performance Analyzer to analyze all the tables in the database. Describe the results of your analysis in your RTF file.

8. Populate the Status property for the database with the value Apply AllAround Services.

9. If requested to do so by your instructor, populate the Status property with your first and last name.

10. Create a custom property with the name, Due Date. Use Date as the type and enter the current date as the value.

11. Submit the revised Apply AllAround Services database and the RTF file in the format specified by your instructor.

12. ✹ Can you convert the Apply AllAround Services database to an Access 2002–2003 database? Why or why not?

Extend Your Knowledge

Extend the skills you learned in this module and experiment with new skills. You may need to use Help to complete the assignment.

Note: To complete this assignment, you will be required to use the Data Files. Please contact your instructor for information about accessing the Data Files.

Instructions: Run Access. Open the Extend Paws for a Cause database. The Extend Paws for a Cause database contains information about a thrift store that raises money for a local animal shelter.

Perform the following tasks:
1. Change the Current Database options to ensure that the Main Menu opens automatically.

2. Currently, when you open the Items table in Datasheet view, the table is ordered by Item Number. Change the property for the table so the table is in order by Description.

3. Customize the Navigation Pane by adding a custom category called Thrift Store. Then add two custom groups, Regular and Reduced, to the Thrift Store category.

4. Add the Item Master Form and Available Items Report to the Regular group. Add the Item Sale Report, the Reduced Price Report, and the Seller and Items Query to the Reduced group.

5. Add the Address Quick Start field to the Seller table. Move the Phone Number field so that it follows the Country Region field. Save the changes to the table.

6. If requested to do so by your instructor, add a table description to the Seller table that includes your first and last name.

7. Submit the revised database in the format specified by your instructor.

8. ✹ What advantages are there to listing items by Description rather than by Item Number?

Expand Your World

Create a solution which uses cloud and web technologies by learning and investigating on your own from general guidance.

Problem: There are many ways to share an Access database. Some ways require each user to have Microsoft Access installed on their computer, while others do not. The method you select depends on factors such as need and available resources.

Instructions: Perform the following tasks:

1. Create a blog, a Google document, or a Word document on OneDrive on which to store your findings.

2. Use the web to research different ways to share an Access database such as PrattLast Associates with others. Be sure to note any specific resources needed, such as an Access database or a SharePoint server, any costs involved, and provide examples of different reasons for sharing a database such as PrattLast Associates. Record your findings in your blog, Google document, or Word document, being sure to appropriately reference your sources.

3. Submit the assignment in the format specified by your instructor.

4. ❊ Based on your research, what method would you choose to share your Access databases?

In the Labs

Design, create, modify, and/or use a database following the guidelines, concepts, and skills presented in this module. Labs are listed in order of increasing difficulty. Labs 1 and 2, which increase in difficulty, require you to create solutions based on what you learned in the module; Lab 3 requires you to apply your creative thinking and problem solving skills to design and implement a solution.

Lab 1: Administering the Gardening Supply Database

Problem: Gardening Supply has determined a number of database administration tasks that need to be done. These include creating indexes and custom input masks, adding table and database properties, creating a template, and splitting a database.

Instructions: Perform the following tasks:

1. Run Access and open the Lab 1 Gardening Supply database that you modified in Module 8. (If you did not complete the exercise, see your instructor for a copy of the modified database.)

2. Open the Open Orders table in Datasheet view and add the Quick Start Priority field to the end of the table. In Datasheet view, use a filter to assign the value Normal to all records where the Amount is less than $400.00. Assign the value High to all other orders.

3. Open the Customer table in Design view and create custom input masks for the following fields: Customer Number, State, Postal Code, and Sales Rep Number. The Customer Number field should consist of two uppercase letters followed by two numbers. The State field should contain two uppercase letters. Both the Postal Code and Sales Rep Number fields can only contain numbers.

4. Create an index on the Customer Name field that allows duplicates.

5. Change the options to ensure that the Main Menu form is displayed automatically when a user opens the database.

6. Save the Lab 1 Gardening Supply database as a template with data but not as an application part. Name the template Lab 1 Gardening Supply Template. You do not need a description. Create a new database from the Lab 1 Gardening Supply template. Name the database Lab 1 Gardening Supply New. Split the Lab 1 Gardening Supply New database.

7. If requested to do so by your instructor, open the front-end database, open the Forms List in Layout view, and add a title with your first and last name.

8. Submit the revised databases in the format specified by your instructor.

9. ✳ In this exercise, you split a database into a front-end and a back-end. Why would you split a database?

Lab 2: **Administering the Discover Science Database**

Problem: Discover Science has determined a number of database administration tasks that need to be done. These include creating indexes and custom input masks, adding table and database properties, and creating a locked database.

Instructions: Perform the following tasks:

1. Run Access and open the Lab 2 Discover Science database that you modified in Module 8. (If you did not complete the exercise, see your instructor for a copy of the modified database.)

2. Open the Item table in Design view and add a validation rule that ensures that the wholesale cost is always less than the retail price of an item. Include validation text.

3. Create an index on the combination of item type and description. Name the index TypeDesc.

4. Do not allow zero-length strings for the Description field.

5. Create custom input masks for the Item Number and the Vendor Code fields.

6. Save the changes to the table design.

7. In Datasheet view, add the Address Quick Start field to the Vendor table following the Vendor Name field. Delete the Attachments field.

8. If requested to do so by your instructor, change the Vendor Name for Vendor Code GS to your last name and change the phone to your phone number.

9. Rename the Main Menu form to Discover Science Menu.

10. Change the Current Database options to ensure that the Discover Science Menu opens automatically.

11. Create a locked database for the Lab 2 Discover Science database.

12. Submit the revised database and the locked database in the format specified by your instructor.

13. ✳ Why would you lock a database?

Lab 3: **Consider This: Your Turn**

Administering the Marketing Analytics Database

Part 1:   The management of the Marketing Analytics company has asked you to perform a number of administration tasks. Open the Lab 3 Marketing Analytics database that you modified in Module 8. (If you did not complete the exercise, see your instructor for a copy of the modified database.) Use the concepts and techniques presented in this module to perform each of the following tasks.

Continued >

In the Labs *continued*

a. Change the Current Database options to ensure that the Main Menu form opens automatically when the user opens the database.

b. Open the Client table in Design view and add custom input masks for the Client Number and Postal Code fields. Create an index for the Client Name field that allows duplicates. Do not allow zero-length strings for the Client Name field.

c. Open the Marketing Analyst table in Design view and create an index named LastFirst on the last name and the first name.

d. Open the Seminar Offerings table in Design view and create a validation rule to ensure that Hours Spent are less than or equal to Total Hours. Include validation text.

e. Open the Seminar Offerings table in Datasheet view and add the Quick Start Status field to the table. In Datasheet view, use a filter to assign the value, Not Started, to all offerings where the Hours Spent is 0. Assign the value, In Progress, to all other offerings.

f. Populate the Editor custom database property with your first and last name.

g. Use the 1 Right Blank Forms application part to create a form for the Seminar Offerings table. Include all fields except Status on the form. Change the title and the name of the form to Seminar Offerings.

Submit your assignment in the format specified by your instructor.

Part 2:   You made several decisions while completing this project, including using an application part to create a form. What was the rationale behind your decisions? Would you use an application part to create another form? Why or why not?

0 | Using SQL

Objectives

You will have mastered the material in this module when you can:

- Understand the SQL language and how to use it
- Change the font or font size for queries
- Create SQL queries
- Include fields in SQL queries
- Include simple and compound criteria in SQL queries
- Use computed fields and built-in functions in SQL queries

- Sort the results in SQL queries
- Use aggregate functions in SQL queries
- Group the results in SQL queries
- Join tables in SQL queries
- Use subqueries
- Compare SQL queries with Access-generated SQL
- Use INSERT, UPDATE, and DELETE queries to update a database

Introduction

The language called **SQL (Structured Query Language)** is a very important language for querying and updating databases. It is the closest thing to a universal database language, because the vast majority of database management systems, including Access, use it in some fashion. Although some users will be able to do all their queries through the query features of Access without ever using SQL, those in charge of administering and maintaining the database system should be familiar with this important language. You can also use Access as an interface to other database management systems, such as SQL Server. Using or interfacing with SQL Server requires knowledge of SQL. Virtually every DBMS supports SQL.

Project — Using SQL

PrattLast Associates wants to be able to use the extended data management capabilities available through SQL. As part of becoming familiar with SQL, PrattLast would like to create a wide variety of SQL queries.

Similar to creating queries in Design view, SQL provides a way of querying relational databases. In SQL, however, instead of making entries in the design grid, you type commands into SQL view to obtain the desired results, as shown in Figure 10–1a. You can then click the View button to view the results just as when you are creating queries in Design view. The results for the query in Figure 10–1a are shown in Figure 10–1b.

Figure 10–1 (a) Query in SQL

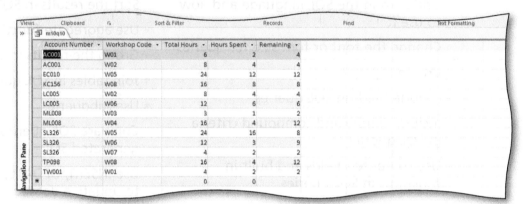

Figure 10–1 (b) Results

In this module, you will learn how to create and use SQL queries like the one shown in Figure 10–1. The following roadmap identifies general activities you will perform as you progress through this module:

1. Create a query in SQL VIEW
2. Use SIMPLE CRITERIA in a query
3. Use COMPOUND CRITERIA in a query
4. SORT RESULTS of a query
5. GROUP RESULTS of a query
6. JOIN TABLES in a query
7. USE a SUBQUERY in a query
8. UPDATE DATA with a query

SQL Background

In this module, you query and update a database using the language called **SQL (Structured Query Language)**. Similar to using the design grid in the Access Query window, SQL provides users with the capability of querying a relational database.

Because SQL is a language, however, you must enter **commands** to obtain the desired results, rather than completing entries in the design grid. SQL uses commands to update tables and to retrieve data from tables. The commands that are used to retrieve data are usually called **queries**.

SQL was developed under the name SEQUEL at the IBM San Jose research facilities as the data manipulation language for IBM's prototype relational model DBMS, System R, in the mid-1970s. In 1980, it was renamed SQL to avoid confusion with an unrelated hardware product called SEQUEL. Most relational DBMSs, including Microsoft Access and Microsoft SQL Server, use a version of SQL as a data manipulation language.

Some people pronounce SQL by pronouncing the three letters, that is, "ess-que-ell." It is very common, however, to pronounce it as the name under which it was developed originally, that is, "sequel."

BTW
Enabling the Content
For each of the databases you use in this module, you will need to enable the content.

To Change the Font Size

1 SQL VIEW | 2 SIMPLE CRITERIA | 3 COMPOUND CRITERIA | 4 SORT RESULTS
5 GROUP RESULTS | 6 JOIN TABLES | 7 USE SUBQUERY | 8 UPDATE DATA

You can change the font and/or the font size for queries using the Options button in the Backstage view and then Object Designers in the list of options in the Access Options dialog box. There is not usually a compelling reason to change the font, unless there is a strong preference for some other font. It often is worthwhile to change the font size, however. *Why? With the default size of 8, the queries can be hard to read. Increasing the font size to 10 can make a big difference.* The following steps change the font size for queries to 10.

- Run Access and open the database named PrattLast Associates from your hard disk, OneDrive, or other storage location.

- Click File on the ribbon to open the Backstage view.

- Click Options to display the Access Options dialog box.

- Click Object Designers to display the Object Designer options.

- In the Query design area, click the Size box arrow, and then click 10 in the list to change the size to 10 (Figure 10–2).

- Click the OK button to close the Access Options dialog box.

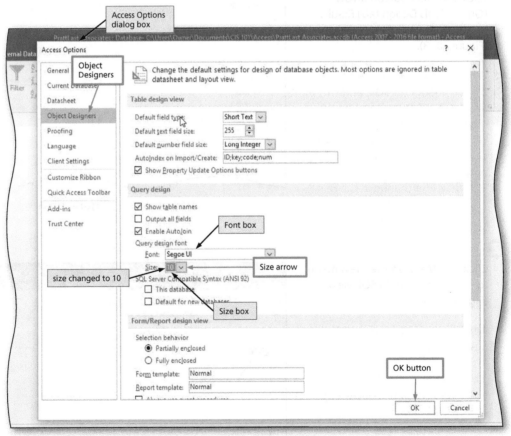

Figure 10–2

SQL Queries

When you query a database using SQL, you type commands in a blank window rather than filling in the design grid. When the command is complete, you can view your results just as you do with queries you create using the design grid.

To Create a New SQL Query

1 SQL VIEW | 2 SIMPLE CRITERIA | 3 COMPOUND CRITERIA | 4 SORT RESULTS
5 GROUP RESULTS | 6 JOIN TABLES | 7 USE SUBQUERY | 8 UPDATE DATA

You begin the creation of a new **SQL query**, which is a query expressed using the SQL language, just as you begin the creation of any other query in Access. The only difference is that you will use SQL view instead of Design view. *Why? SQL view enables you to type SQL commands rather than making entries in the design grid.* The following steps create a new SQL query.

- Close the Navigation Pane.

- Display the Create tab.

- Click the Query Design button (Create tab | Queries group) to create a query.

- Close the Show Table dialog box without adding any tables.

- Click the View button arrow (Query Tools Design tab | Results group) to display the View menu (Figure 10–3).

Q&A

Why did the icon on the View button change to SQL, and why are there only two items on the menu instead of the usual five?
Without any tables selected, you cannot view any results. You can only use the normal Design view or SQL view. The change in the icon indicates that you could simply click the button to transfer to SQL view.

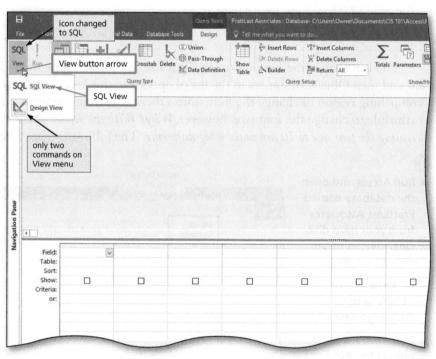

Figure 10–3

- Click SQL View on the View menu to view the query in SQL view (Figure 10–4).

Q&A

What happened to the design grid?
In SQL view, you specify the queries by typing SQL commands rather than making entries in the design grid.

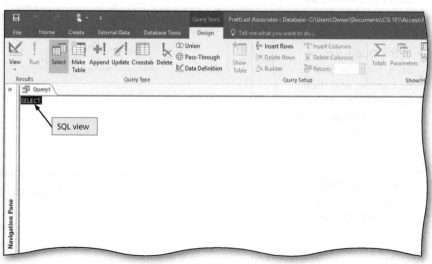

Figure 10–4

SQL Commands

The basic form of SQL expressions is quite simple: SELECT-FROM-WHERE. The command begins with a **SELECT clause**, which consists of the word, SELECT, followed by a list of those fields you want to include. The fields will appear in the results in the order in which they are listed in the expression. Next, the command contains a **FROM clause**, which consists of the word FROM followed by a list of the table or tables involved in the query. Finally, there is an optional **WHERE clause**, which consists of the word WHERE followed by any criteria that the data you want to retrieve must satisfy. The command ends with a semicolon (;), which in this text will appear on a separate line.

SQL has no special format rules for placement of terms, capitalization, and so on. One common style is to place the word FROM on a new line, and then place the word WHERE, when it is used, on the next line. This style makes the commands easier to read. It is also common to show words that are part of the SQL language in uppercase and others in a combination of uppercase and lowercase. This text formats SQL terms in uppercase letters. Because it is a common convention, and necessary in some versions of SQL, you will place a semicolon (;) at the end of each command.

Microsoft Access has its own version of SQL that, unlike some other versions of SQL, allows spaces within field names and table names. There is a restriction, however, to the way such names are used in SQL queries. When a name containing a space appears in SQL, it must be enclosed in square brackets. For example, Account Number must appear as [Account Number] because the name includes a space. On the other hand, City does not need to be enclosed in square brackets because its name does not include a space. For consistency, all names in this text are enclosed in square brackets. Thus, the City field would appear as [City] even though the brackets are not technically required by SQL.

BTW
Touch Screen Differences
The Office and Windows interfaces may vary if you are using a touch screen. For this reason, you might notice that the function or appearance of your touch screen differs slightly from this module's presentation.

BTW
Touch and Pointers
Remember that if you are using your finger on a touch screen, you will not see the pointer.

To Include Only Certain Fields

1 SQL VIEW | 2 SIMPLE CRITERIA | 3 COMPOUND CRITERIA | 4 SORT RESULTS
5 GROUP RESULTS | 6 JOIN TABLES | 7 USE SUBQUERY | 8 UPDATE DATA

To include only certain fields in a query, list them after the word, SELECT. If you want to list all rows in the table, you do not include the word, WHERE. *Why? If there is no WHERE clause, there is no criterion restricting which rows appear in the results. In that case, all rows will appear.* The following steps create a query for PrattLast Associates that will list the number, name, amount paid, and current due amount of all accounts.

1

- Type **SELECT [Account Number],[Account Name],[Amount Paid],[Current Due]** as the first line of the command, and then press the ENTER key.

Q&A What is the purpose of the SELECT clause?
The SELECT clause indicates the fields that are to be included in the query results. This SELECT clause, for example, indicates that the Account Number, Account Name, Amount Paid, and Current Due fields are to be included.

- Type **FROM [Account]** as the second line to specify the source table, press the ENTER key, and then type a semicolon (**;**) on the third line.

Q&A What is the purpose of the FROM clause?
The FROM clause indicates the table or tables that contain the fields used in the query. This FROM clause indicates that all the fields in this query come from the Account table.

- Click the View button (Query Tools Design tab | Results group) to view the results (Figure 10–5).

Q&A My screen displays a dialog box that asks me to enter a parameter value. What did I do wrong?
You typed a field name incorrectly. Click Cancel to close the dialog box and then correct your SQL statement.

Q&A Why does AC # appear as the column heading for the Account Number field?
This is the caption for the field. If the field has a special caption defined, Access will use the caption rather than the field name. You will learn how to change this later in this module.

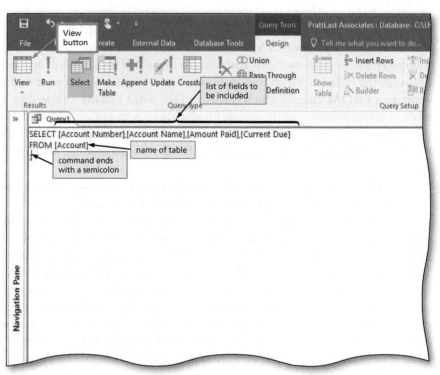

Figure 10–5 (a) Query to List the Account Number, Account Name, Amount Paid, and Current Due for All Accounts

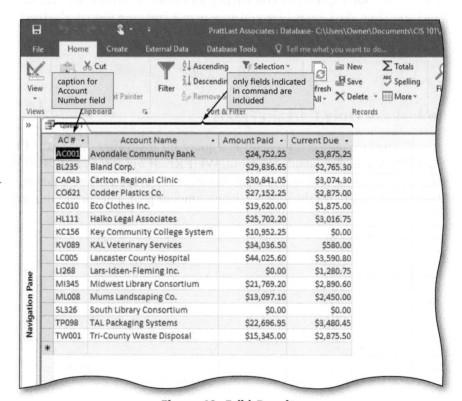

Figure 10–5 (b) Results

2

- Click the Save button on the Quick Access Toolbar, type **m10q01** as the name in the Save As dialog box, and click the OK button to save the query as m10q01.

To Prepare to Enter a New SQL Query

1 SQL VIEW | 2 SIMPLE CRITERIA | 3 COMPOUND CRITERIA | 4 SORT RESULTS
5 GROUP RESULTS | 6 JOIN TABLES | 7 USE SUBQUERY | 8 UPDATE DATA

To enter a new SQL query, you could close the window, click the No button when asked if you want to save your changes, and then begin the process from scratch. A quicker alternative is to use the View menu and then select SQL View. ***Why?*** *You will be returned to SQL view with the current command appearing. At that point, you could erase the current command and then enter a new one. If the next command is similar to the previous one, however, it often is simpler to modify the current command instead of erasing it and starting over.* The following step shows how to prepare to enter a new SQL query.

1

- Click the View button arrow (Home tab | Views group) to display the View menu (Figure 10–6).
- Click SQL View to return to SQL view.

Q&A Could I just click the View button, or do I have to click the arrow?
Because the icon on the button is not the icon for SQL view, you must click the arrow.

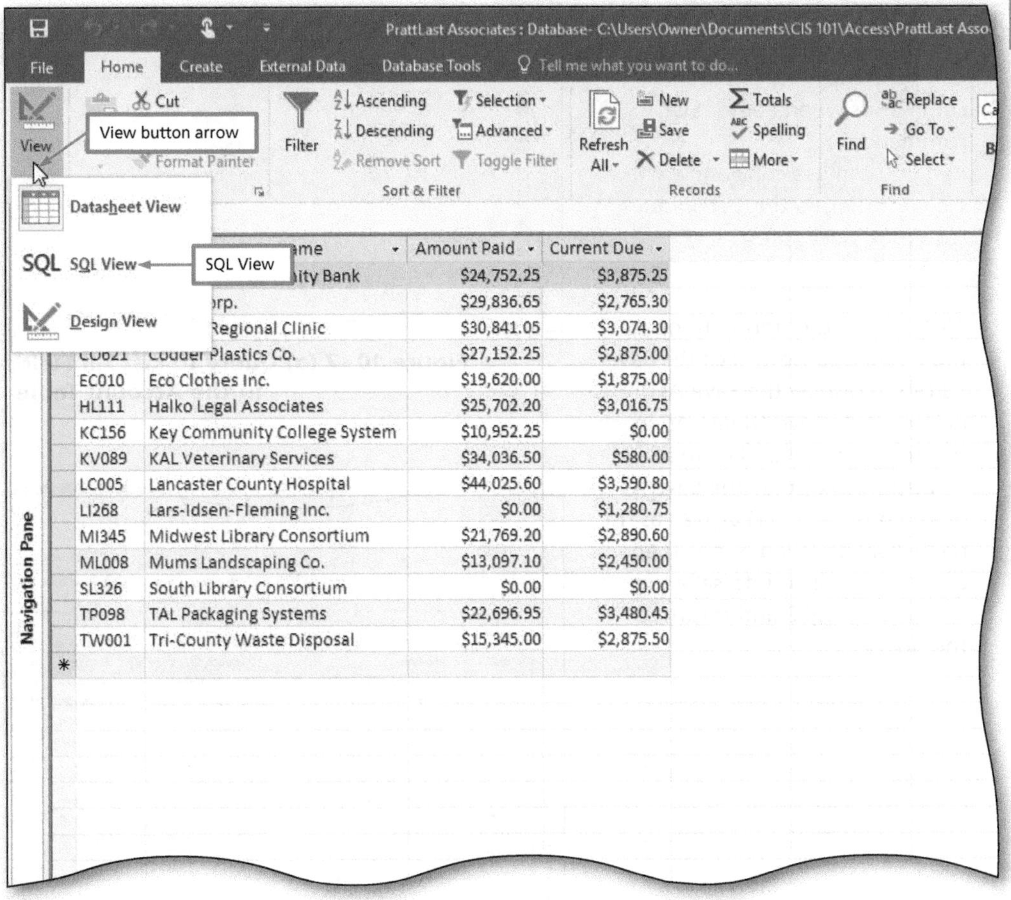

Figure 10–6

To Include All Fields

1 SQL VIEW | 2 SIMPLE CRITERIA | 3 COMPOUND CRITERIA | 4 SORT RESULTS
5 GROUP RESULTS | 6 JOIN TABLES | 7 USE SUBQUERY | 8 UPDATE DATA

To include all fields, you could use the same approach as in the previous steps, that is, list each field in the Account table after the word SELECT. There is a shortcut, however. Instead of listing all the field names after SELECT, you can use the asterisk (*) symbol. ***Why?*** *Just as when working in the design grid, the asterisk symbol represents all fields.* This indicates that you want all fields listed in the order in which you described them to the system during data definition. The following steps list all fields and all records in the Account table.

1

- Delete the current command, type **SELECT *** as the first line of the command, and then press the ENTER key.

- Type **FROM [Account]** as the second line, press the ENTER key, and type a semicolon (**;**) on the third line.

- View the results (Figure 10–7).

Q&A Can I use copy and paste commands when I enter SQL commands?
Yes, you can use copy and paste as well as other editing techniques, such as replacing text.

2

- Click File on the ribbon to open the Backstage view, click the Save As tab to display the Save As gallery, click 'Save Object As' in the File Types area, click the Save As button to display the Save As dialog box, type **m10q02** as the name for the saved query, then click the OK button to save the query as m10q02 and return to the query.

Q&A Can I just click the Save button on the Quick Access Toolbar as I did when I saved the previous query? If you did, you would replace the previous query with the version you just created. Because you want to save both the previous query and the new one, you need to save the new version with a different name. To do so, you must use 'Save Object As', which is available through the Backstage view.

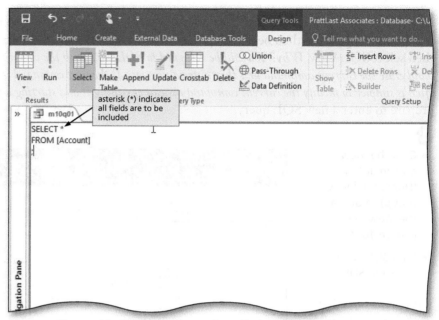

Figure 10–7 (a) Query to List All Fields and All Records in the Account Table

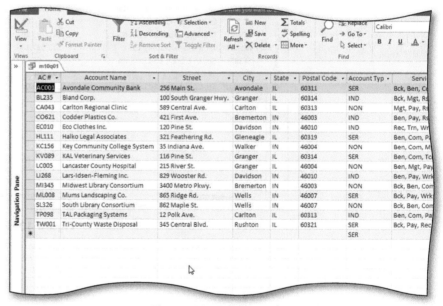

Figure 10–7 (b) Results

To Use a Criterion Involving a Numeric Field

To restrict the records to be displayed, include the word WHERE followed by a criterion as part of the command. If the field involved is a numeric field, you simply type the value. In typing the number, you do not type commas or dollar signs. *Why? If you enter a dollar sign, Access assumes you are entering text. If you enter a comma, Access considers the criterion invalid.* The following steps create a query to list the account number and name of all accounts whose current due amount is $0.00.

1

- Return to SQL view and delete the current command.

- Type **SELECT [Account Number],[Account Name]** as the first line of the command.

- Type **FROM [Account]** as the second line.

- Type **WHERE [Current Due]=0** as the third line, and then type a semicolon (**;**) on the fourth line.

Q&A What is the purpose of the WHERE clause?
The WHERE clause restricts the rows to be included in the results to only those that satisfy the criteria included in the clause. With this WHERE clause, for example, only those rows on which Current Due is equal to 0 will be included.

- View the results (Figure 10–8).

Q&A On my screen, the accounts are listed in a different order. Did I do something wrong?
No. The order in which records appear in a query result is random unless you specifically order the records. You will see how to order records later in this module.

2

- Save the query as m10q03.

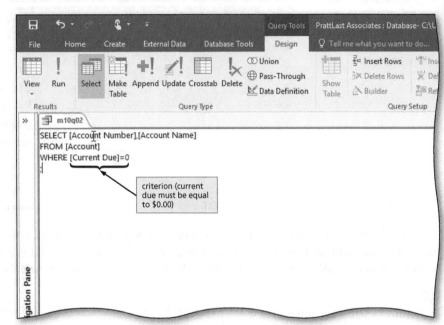

Figure 10–8 (a) Query to List the Account Number and Account Name for Those Accounts Where Current Due Is Equal to 0

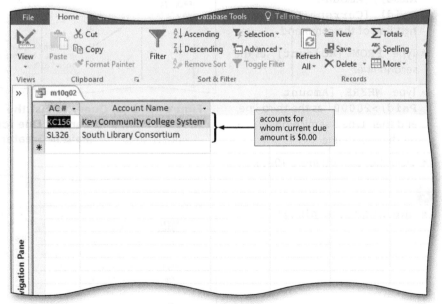

Figure 10–8 (b) Results

BTW
**Context-Sensitive
Help in SQL**
When you are working in
SQL view, you can obtain
context-sensitive help on
any of the keywords in
your query. To do so, click
anywhere in the word about
which you wish to obtain
help and press the F1 key.

Simple Criteria

The criterion following the word WHERE in the preceding query is called a simple criterion. A **simple criterion** has the form: field name, comparison operator, then either another field name or a value. The possible comparison operators are shown in Table 10–1.

Table 10–1 Comparison Operators	
Comparison Operator	**Meaning**
=	equal to
<	less than
>	greater than
<=	less than or equal to
>=	greater than or equal to
<>	not equal to

To Use a Comparison Operator

1 SQL VIEW | 2 SIMPLE CRITERIA | 3 COMPOUND CRITERIA | 4 SORT RESULTS
5 GROUP RESULTS | 6 JOIN TABLES | 7 USE SUBQUERY | 8 UPDATE DATA

In the following steps, PrattLast Associates uses a comparison operator to list the account number, account name, amount paid, and current due for all accounts whose amount paid is greater than $20,000. *Why? A comparison operator allows you to compare the value in a field with a specific value or with the value in another field.*

- Return to SQL view and delete the current command.

- Type **SELECT [Account Number],[Account Name],[Amount Paid],[Current Due]** as the first line of the command.

- Type **FROM [Account]** as the second line.

- Type **WHERE [Amount Paid]>20000** as the third line, and then type a semicolon (**;**) on the fourth line.

- View the results (Figure 10–9).

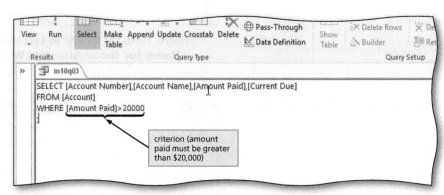

Figure 10–9 (a) Query to List the Account Number, Account Name, Amount Paid, and Current Due for Those Accounts Where Amount Paid Is Greater Than $20,000

- Save the query as m10q04.

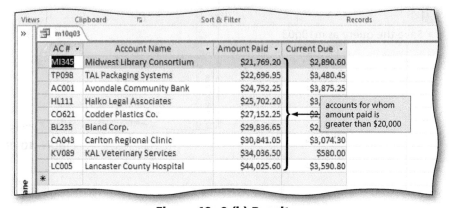

Figure 10–9 (b) Results

To Use a Criterion Involving a Text Field

If the criterion involves a text field, the value must be enclosed in quotation marks. *Why? Unlike when you work in the design grid, Access will not insert the quotation marks around text data for you in SQL view. You need to include them.* The following example lists the account number and name of all of PrattLast Associates' accounts located in Granger, that is, all accounts for whom the value in the City field is Granger.

1

- Return to SQL view, delete the current command, and type **SELECT [Account Number], [Account Name]** as the first line of the command.

- Type **FROM [Account]** as the second line.

- Type **WHERE [City]='Granger'** as the third line and type a semicolon (**;**) on the fourth line.

- View the results (Figure 10–10).

Could I enclose the text field value in double quotation marks instead of single quotation marks?
Yes. It is usually easier, however, to use single quotes when entering SQL commands.

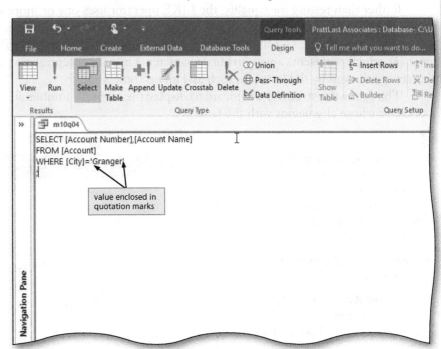

Figure 10–10 (a) Query to List the Account Number and Account Name for Those Accounts Whose City Is Granger

2

- Save the query as m10q05.

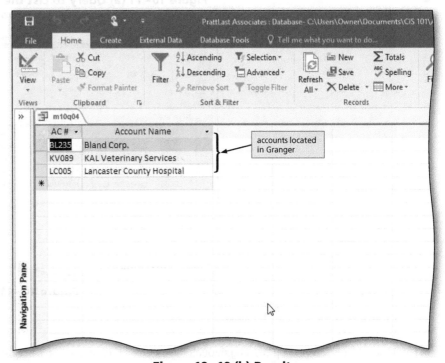

Figure 10–10 (b) Results

To Use a Wildcard

In most cases, the conditions in WHERE clauses involve exact matches, such as retrieving rows for each account located in the city of Granger. In some cases, however, exact matches do not work. *Why? You might only know that the desired value contains a certain collection of characters.* In such cases, you use the LIKE operator with a wildcard symbol.

Rather than testing for equality, the LIKE operator uses one or more wildcard characters to test for a pattern match. One common wildcard in Access, the **asterisk** (*), represents any collection of characters. Thus, G* represents the letter, G, followed by any string of characters. Another wildcard symbol is the question mark (?), which represents any individual character. Thus, T?m represents the letter T, followed by any single character, followed by the letter, m, such as Tim or Tom.

The following steps use a wildcard to display the account number and name for every account of PrattLast Associates whose city begins with the letter, G.

- Return to SQL view, delete the previous query, and type **SELECT [Account Number],[Account Name],[City]** as the first line of the command.

- Type **FROM [Account]** as the second line.

- Type **WHERE [City] LIKE 'G*'** as the third line and type a semicolon (**;**) on the fourth line.

- View the results (Figure 10–11).

2

- Save the query as m10q06.

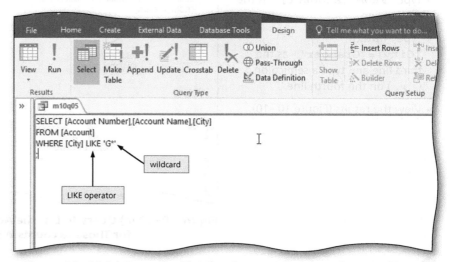

Figure 10–11 (a) Query to List the Account Number, Account Name, and City for Those Accounts Whose City Begins with the Letter G

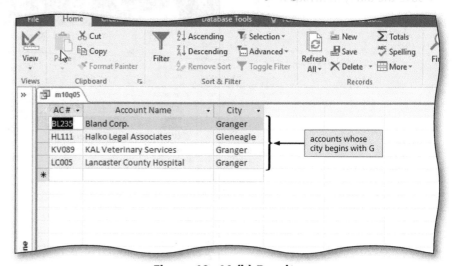

Figure 10–11 (b) Results

Break Point: If you wish to stop working through the module at this point, you can close Access now. You can resume the project later by running Access, opening the database called PrattLast Associates, creating a new query in SQL view, and continuing to follow the steps from this location forward.

Compound Criteria

You are not limited to simple criteria in SQL. You can also use compound criteria. **Compound criteria** are formed by connecting two or more simple criteria using AND, OR, and NOT. When simple criteria are connected by the word AND, all the simple criteria must be true in order for the compound criterion to be true. When simple criteria are connected by the word OR, the compound criterion will be true whenever any of the simple criteria are true. Preceding a criterion by the word NOT reverses the truth or falsity of the original criterion. That is, if the original criterion is true, the new criterion will be false; if the original criterion is false, the new one will be true.

BTW
Entering Field Names
Be sure to enclose field names in square brackets. If you accidentally use parentheses or curly braces, Access will display a syntax error (missing operator) message.

To Use a Compound Criterion Involving AND

1 SQL VIEW | 2 SIMPLE CRITERIA | 3 **COMPOUND CRITERIA** | 4 **SORT RESULTS**
5 **GROUP RESULTS** | 6 **JOIN TABLES** | 7 **USE SUBQUERY** | 8 **UPDATE DATA**

The following steps use a compound criterion. *Why? A compound criterion allows you to impose multiple conditions.* In particular, the steps enable PrattLast to display the number and name of those accounts that are located in Wells and who have a current due amount of $0.00.

- Return to SQL view, delete the previous query, and type **SELECT [Account Number],[Account Name]** as the first line of the command.

- Type **FROM [Account]** as the second line.

- Type **WHERE [City]= 'Wells'** as the third line.

- Type **AND [Current Due]=0** as the fourth line and type a semicolon (**;**) on the fifth line.

Q&A What is the purpose of the AND clause?
The AND clause indicates that there are multiple criteria, all of which must be true. With this AND clause, only rows on which BOTH City is Wells AND Current Due is 0 will be included.

- View the results (Figure 10–12).

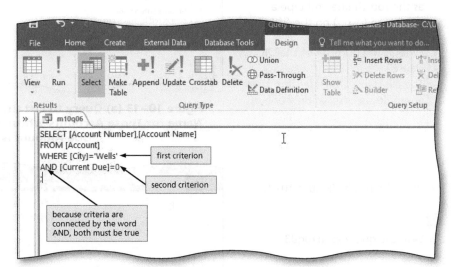

Figure 10–12 (a) Query to List the Account Number and Account Name for Those Accounts Whose City Is Wells and Whose Current Due Amount Is Equal to $0

- Save the query as m10q07.

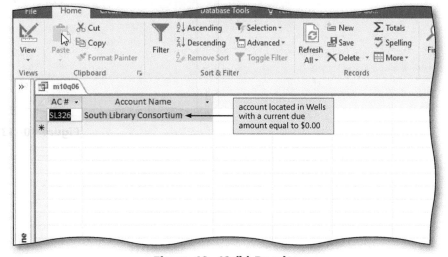

Figure 10–12 (b) Results

To Use a Compound Criterion Involving OR

The following steps use a compound criterion involving OR to enable PrattLast Associates to display the account number and name of those accounts located in Wells or for whom the current due amount is $0.00. *Why? In an OR criterion only one of the individual criteria needs to be true in order for the record to be included in the results.*

- Return to SQL view, delete the previous query, and type **SELECT [Account Number], [Account Name]** as the first line of the command.

- Type **FROM [Account]** as the second line.

- Type **WHERE [City]='Wells'** as the third line.

- Type **OR [Current Due]=0** as the fourth line and type a semicolon (**;**) on the fifth line.

Q&A

What is the purpose of the OR clause?

The OR clause indicates that there are multiple criteria, only one of which needs to be true. With this OR clause, those rows on which EITHER City is Wells OR Current Due is 0 (or both) will be included.

- View the results (Figure 10–13).

- Save the query as m10q08.

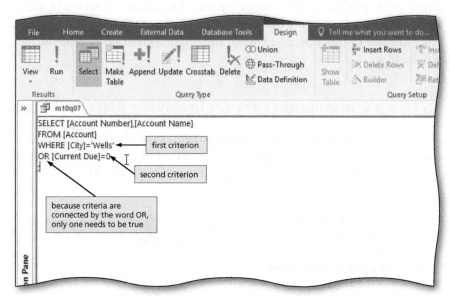

Figure 10–13 (a) Query to List the Account Number and Account Name for Those Accounts Whose City Is Wells or Whose Current Due Amount Is Equal to $0

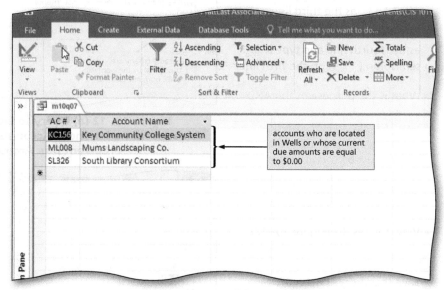

Figure 10–13 (b) Results

To Use NOT in a Criterion

Why? *You can negate any criterion by preceding the criterion with the word NOT.* The following steps use NOT in a criterion to list the numbers and names of the accounts of PrattLast Associates not located in Wells.

- Return to SQL view and delete the previous query.

- Type `SELECT [Account Number],[Account Name],[City]` as the first line of the command.

- Type `FROM [Account]` as the second line.

- Type `WHERE NOT [City]= 'Wells'` as the third line and type a semicolon (`;`) on the fourth line.

- View the results (Figure 10–14).

2

- Save the query as m10q09.

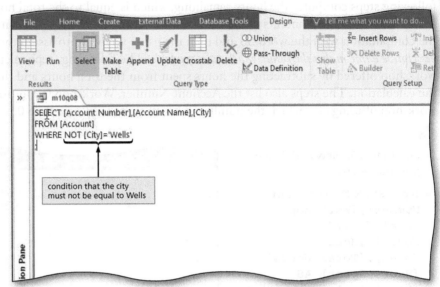

Figure 10–14 (a) Query to List the Account Number, Account Name, and City for Those Accounts Whose City Is Not Wells

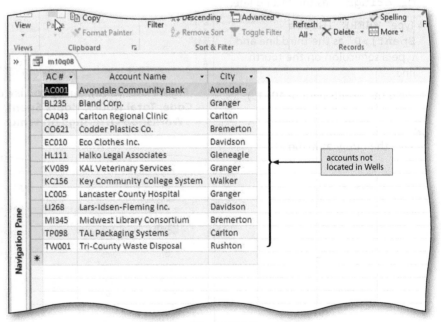

Figure 10–14 (b) Results

To Use a Computed Field

Just as with queries created in Design view, you can include fields in queries that are not in the database, but that can be computed from fields that are. Such a field is called a **computed** or **calculated field**. Computations can involve addition (+), subtraction (-), multiplication (*), or division (/). The query in the following steps computes the hours remaining, which is equal to the total hours minus the hours spent.

To indicate the contents of the new field (the computed field), you can name the field by following the computation with the word AS and then the name you want to assign the field. *Why? Assigning the field a descriptive name makes the results much more readable.* The following steps calculate the hours remaining for each workshop offered by subtracting the hours spent from the total hours and then assigning the name Remaining to the calculation. The steps also list the Account Number, Workshop Code, Total Hours, and Hours Spent for all workshop offerings for which the number of hours spent is greater than 0.

- Return to SQL view and delete the previous query.

- Type `SELECT [Account Number],[Workshop Code],[Total Hours],[Hours Spent],[Total Hours]-[Hours Spent] AS [Remaining]` as the first line of the command.

- Type `FROM [Workshop Offerings]` as the second line.

- Type `WHERE [Hours Spent]>0` as the third line and type a semicolon on the fourth line.

- View the results (Figure 10–15).

2

- Save the query as m10q10.

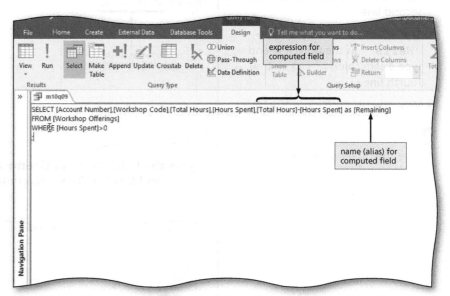

Figure 10–15 (a) Query to List the Account Number, Workshop Code, Total Hours, Hours Spent, and Hours Remaining for Those Workshop Offerings on Which Hours Spent Is Greater Than 0

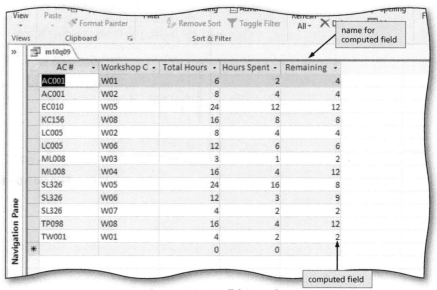

Figure 10–15 (b) Results

Sorting

Sorting in SQL follows the same principles as when using Design view to specify sorted query results, employing a sort key as the field on which data is to be sorted. SQL uses major and minor sort keys when sorting on multiple fields. By following a sort key with the word DESC with no comma in between, you can specify descending sort order. If you do not specify DESC, the data will be sorted in ascending order.

To sort the output, you include an **ORDER BY clause**, which consists of the words ORDER BY followed by the sort key. If there are two sort keys, the major sort key is listed first. Queries that you construct in Design view require that the major sort key is to the left of the minor sort key in the list of fields to be included. In SQL, there is no such restriction. The fields to be included in the query are in the SELECT clause, and the fields to be used for sorting are in the ORDER BY clause. The two clauses are totally independent.

To Sort the Results on a Single Field

1 SQL VIEW | 2 SIMPLE CRITERIA | 3 COMPOUND CRITERIA | **4 SORT RESULTS**
5 GROUP RESULTS | 6 JOIN TABLES | 7 USE SUBQUERY | 8 UPDATE DATA

The following steps list the account number, name, amount paid, and current due for all accounts sorted by account name. ***Why?*** *PrattLast Associates wants this data to appear in alphabetical order by account name.*

- Return to SQL view and delete the previous query.

- Type **SELECT [Account Number],[Account Name],[Amount Paid],[Current Due]** as the first line of the command.

- Type **FROM [Account]** as the second line.

- Type **ORDER BY [Account Name]** as the third line and type a semicolon on the fourth line.

Q&A What is the purpose of the ORDER BY clause?

The ORDER BY clause indicates that the results of the query are to be sorted by the indicated field or fields. This ORDER BY clause, for example, would cause the results to be sorted by Account Name.

- View the results (Figure 10–16).

- Save the query as m10q11.

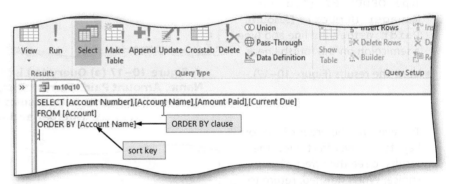

Figure 10–16 (a) Query to List the Account Number, Account Name, Amount Paid, and Current Due for All Accounts with the Results Sorted by Account Name

AC #	Account Name	Amount Paid	Current Due
AC001	Avondale Community Bank	$24,752.25	$3,875.25
BL235	Bland Corp.	$29,836.65	$2,765.30
CA043	Carlton Regional Clinic	$30,841.05	$3,074.30
CO621	Codder Plastics Co.	$27,152.25	$2,875.00
EC010	Eco Clothes Inc.	$19,620.00	$1,875.00
HL111	Halko Legal Associates	$25,702.20	$3,016.75
KV089	KAL Veterinary Services	$34,036.50	$580.00
KC156	Key Community College System	$10,952.25	$0.00
LC005	Lancaster County Hospital	$44,025.60	$3,590.80
LI268	Lars-Idsen-Fleming Inc.	$0.00	$1,280.75
MI345	Midwest Library Consortium	$21,769.20	$2,890.60
ML008	Mums Landscaping Co.	$13,097.10	$2,450.00
SL326	South Library Consortium	$0.00	$0.00
TP098	TAL Packaging Systems	$22,696.95	$3,480.45
TW001	Tri-County Waste Disposal	$15,345.00	$2,875.50

rows sorted by account name

Figure 10–16 (b) Results

To Sort the Results on Multiple Fields

The following steps list the account number, name, amount paid, current due, and account manager number for all accounts. The data is to be sorted on multiple fields. *Why? PrattLast wants the data to be sorted by amount paid within account manager number. That is, the data is to be sorted by account manager number. In addition, within the group of accounts that have the same manager number, the data is to be sorted further by amount paid.* To accomplish this sort, the Account Manager Number field is the major (primary) sort key and the Amount Paid field is the minor (secondary) sort key. Remember that the major sort key must be listed first.

❶

- Return to SQL view and delete the previous query.

- Type **SELECT [Account Number],[Account Name],[Amount Paid],[Current Due],[Account Manager Number]** as the first line of the command.

- Type **FROM [Account]** as the second line.

- Type **ORDER BY [Account Manager Number],[Amount Paid]** as the third line and type a semicolon on the fourth line.

- View the results (Figure 10–17).

 Experiment

- Try reversing the order of the sort keys to see the effect. View the results to see the effect of your choice. When finished, return to the original sorting order for both fields.

❷

- Save the query as m10q12.

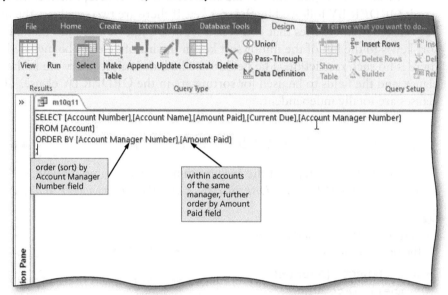

Figure 10–17 (a) Query to List the Account Number, Account Name, Amount Paid, Current Due, and Account Manager Number for All Accounts with Results Sorted by Account Manager Number and Amount Paid

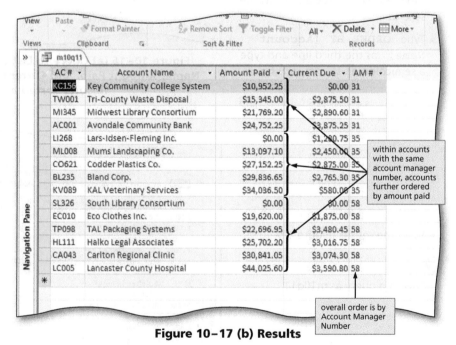

Figure 10–17 (b) Results

Using SQL Access Module 10 **AC 563**

Access Module 10

1 SQL VIEW | 2 SIMPLE CRITERIA | 3 COMPOUND CRITERIA | 4 SORT RESULTS
5 GROUP RESULTS | 6 JOIN TABLES | 7 USE SUBQUERY | 8 UPDATE DATA

To Sort the Results in Descending Order

Why? To show the results in high-to-low rather than low-to-high order, you sort in descending order. To sort in descending order, you follow the name of the sort key with the DESC operator. The following steps list the account number, name, amount paid, current due, and account manager number for all accounts. PrattLast wants the data to be sorted by descending current due within account manager number. That is, within the accounts having the same manager number, the data is to be sorted further by current due in descending order.

1

- Return to SQL view and delete the previous query.

- Type **SELECT [Account Number],[Account Name],[Amount Paid],[Current Due],[Account Manager Number]** as the first line of the command.

- Type **FROM [Account]** as the second line.

- Type **ORDER BY [Account Manager Number],[Current Due] DESC** as the third line and type a semicolon on the fourth line.

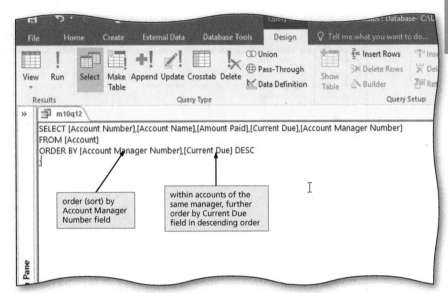

Figure 10–18 (a) Query to List the Account Number, Account Name, Amount Paid, Current Due, and Account Manager Number for All Accounts with Results Sorted by Account Manager Number and Descending Current Due

Q&A

Do I need a comma between [Current Due] and DESC?
No. In fact, you must not use a comma. If you did, SQL would assume that you want a field called DESC. Without the comma, SQL knows that the DESC operator indicates that the sort on the Current Due field is to be in descending order.

- View the results (Figure 10–18).

2

- Save the query as m10q13.

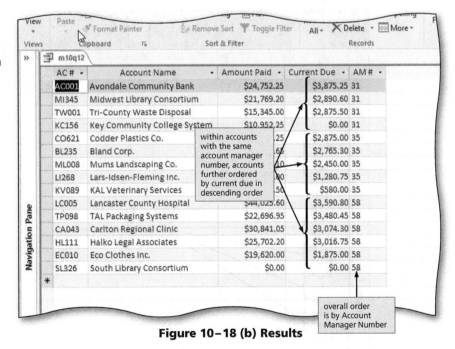

Figure 10–18 (b) Results

To Omit Duplicates When Sorting

When you sort data, duplicates are normally included. For example, the query in Figure 10–19 sorts the account numbers in the Workshop Offerings table. Because any account can be offered many workshops at a time, account numbers can be included more than once. PrattLast does not find this useful and would like to eliminate these duplicate account numbers. To do so, use the DISTINCT operator in the query. *Why? The DISTINCT operator eliminates duplicate values in the results of a query.* To use the operator, you follow the word DISTINCT with the field name in parentheses.

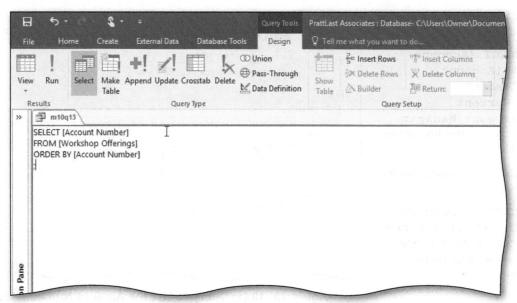

**Figure 10–19 (a) Query to List the Account Numbers in the Workshop
Offerings Table Sorted by Account Number**

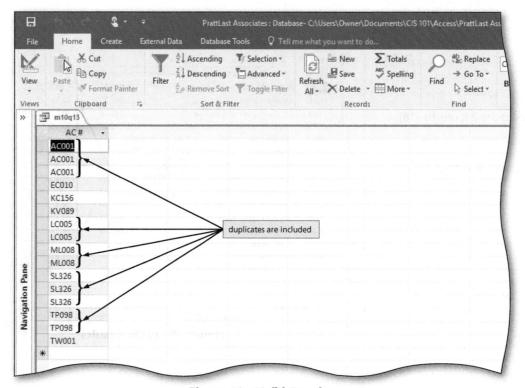

Figure 10–19 (b) Results

The following steps display the account numbers in the Workshop Offerings table in account number order, but with any duplicates removed.

- Return to SQL view and delete the previous query.
- Type **SELECT DISTINCT([Account Number])** as the first line of the command.
- Type **FROM [Workshop Offerings]** as the second line.
- Type **ORDER BY [Account Number]** as the third line and type a semicolon on the fourth line.
- View the results (Figure 10–20).

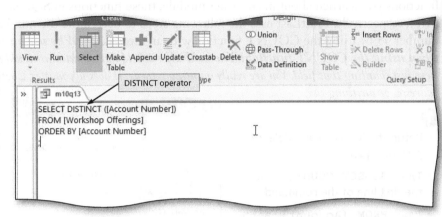

Figure 10–20 (a) Query to List the Account Numbers in the Workshop Offerings Table Sorted by Account Number, Ensuring That No Account Number Is Listed More Than Once

- Save the query as m10q14. Return to the query.

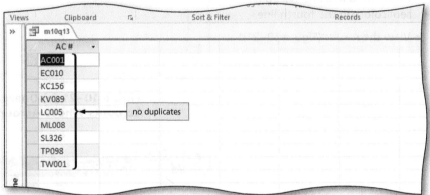

Figure 10–20 (b) Results

How do you determine sorting when creating a query?

Examine the query or request to see if it contains words such as *order* or *sort* that would imply that the order of the query results is important. If so, you need to sort the query.

- **Determine whether data is to be sorted.** Examine the requirements for the query looking for words like *sorted by*, *ordered by*, *arranged by*, and so on.
- **Determine sort keys.** Look for the fields that follow sorted by, ordered by, or any other words that signify sorting. If the requirements for the query include the phrase, ordered by account name, then Account Name is a sort key.
- **If there is more than one sort key, determine which one will be the major sort key and which will be the minor sort key.** Look for words that indicate which field is more important. For example, if the requirements indicate that the results are to be ordered by amount paid within account manager number, Account Manager Number is the more important sort key.

CONSIDER THIS

Break Point: If you wish to stop working through the module at this point, you can close Access now. You can resume the project later by running Access, opening the database called PrattLast Associates, creating a new query in SQL view, and continuing to follow the steps from this location forward.

To Use a Built-In Function

SQL has built-in functions, also called aggregate functions, to perform various calculations. Similar to the functions you learned about in an earlier module, these functions in SQL are COUNT, SUM, AVG, MAX, and MIN, respectively. PrattLast uses the following steps to determine the number of accounts assigned to manager number 35 by using the COUNT function with an asterisk (*). *Why use an asterisk rather than a field name when using the COUNT function? You could select a field name, but that would be cumbersome and imply that you were just counting that field. You are really counting records. It does not matter whether you are counting names or street addresses or anything else.*

1

- Return to SQL view and delete the previous query.

- Type **SELECT COUNT(*)** as the first line of the command.

- Type **FROM [Account]** as the second line.

- Type **WHERE [Account Manager Number]='35'** as the third line and type a semicolon on the fourth line.

- View the results (Figure 10–21).

Why does Expr1000 appear in the column heading of the results? Because the field is a computed field, it does not have a name. Access assigns a generic expression name. You can add a name for the field by including the AS clause in the query, and it is good practice to do so.

2

- Save the query as m10q15.

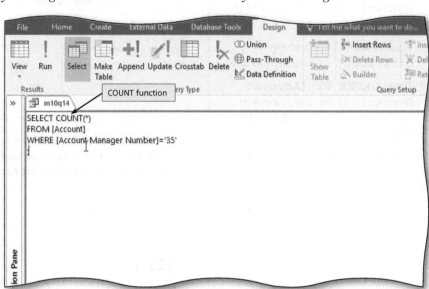

Figure 10–21 (a) Query to Count the Number of Accounts Whose Account Manager Number Is 35

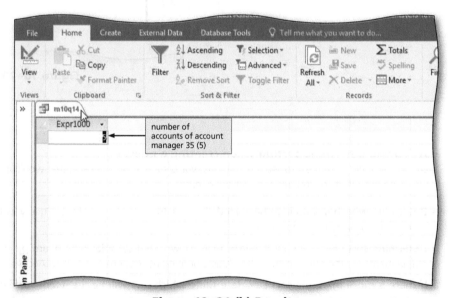

Figure 10–21 (b) Results

To Assign a Name to the Results of a Function

PrattLast Associates would prefer to have a more meaningful name than Expr1000 for the results of counting account numbers. *Why? The default name of Expr1000 does not describe the meaning of the calculation.* Fortunately, just as you can assign a name to a calculation that includes two fields, you can assign a name to the results of a function. To do so, follow the expression for the function with the word AS and then the name to be assigned to the result. The following steps assign the name, Account Count, to the expression in the previous query.

- Return to SQL view and delete the previous query.

- Type **SELECT COUNT(*) AS [Account Count]** as the first line of the command.

- Type **FROM [Account]** as the second line.

- Type **WHERE [Account Manager Number]='35'** as the third line and type a semicolon on the fourth line.

- View the results (Figure 10–22).

❷

- Save the query as m10q16.

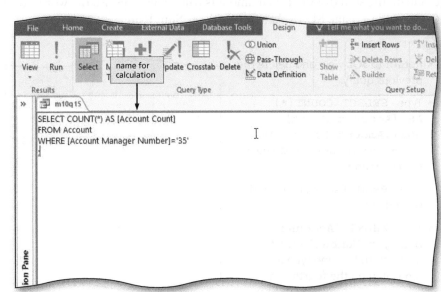

Figure 10–22 (a) Query to Count the Number of Accounts Whose Account Manager Number Is 35 with Results Called Account Count

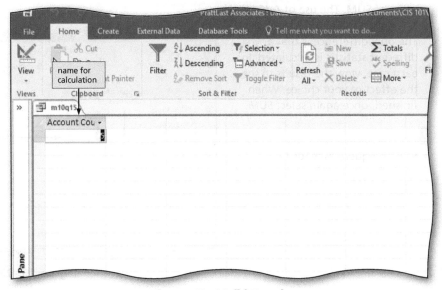

Figure 10–22 (b) Results

To Use Multiple Functions in the Same Command

There are two differences between COUNT and SUM, other than the obvious fact that they are computing different statistics. First, in the case of SUM, you must specify the field for which you want a total, instead of an asterisk (*); second, the field must be numeric. *Why? If the field is not numeric, it does not make sense to calculate a sum. You could not calculate a sum of names or addresses, for example.* The following steps use both the COUNT and SUM functions to count the number of accounts whose account manager number is 35 and calculate the sum (total) of their amounts paid. The steps use the word AS to name COUNT(*) as Account Count and to name SUM([Amount Paid]) as Sum Paid.

- Return to SQL view and delete the previous query.

- Type `SELECT COUNT(*) AS [Account Count], SUM([Amount Paid]) AS [Sum Paid]` as the first line of the command.

- Type `FROM [Account]` as the second line.

- Type `WHERE [Account Manager Number]='35'` as the third line and type a semicolon on the fourth line.

- View the results (Figure 10–23).

Experiment

- Try using the other functions in place of SUM. The use of AVG, MAX, and MIN is similar to SUM. The only difference is that a different statistic is calculated. In each case, view the results to see the effect of your choice. When finished, once again select SUM.

- Save the query as m10q17.

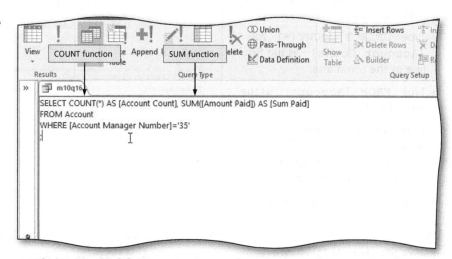

Figure 10–23 (a) Query to Count the Number of Accounts Whose Account Manager Number Is 35 with Results Called Account Count and Calculate the Sum of Amount Paid with Results Called Sum Paid

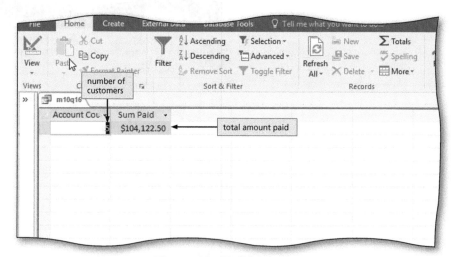

Figure 10–23 (b) Results

Grouping

Recall that grouping means creating groups of records that share some common characteristic. When you group rows, any calculations indicated in the SELECT command are performed for the entire group.

To Use Grouping

1 SQL VIEW | 2 SIMPLE CRITERIA | 3 COMPOUND CRITERIA | 4 SORT RESULTS
5 GROUP RESULTS | 6 JOIN TABLES | 7 USE SUBQUERY | 8 UPDATE DATA

PrattLast Associates wants to calculate the totals of the Amount Paid field, called Sum Paid, and the Current Due field, called Sum Due, for the accounts of each manager. To calculate the totals, the command will include the calculations, SUM([Amount Paid]) and SUM([Current Due]). To get totals for the accounts of each manager, the command will also include a **GROUP BY clause**, which consists of the words, GROUP BY, followed by the field used for grouping, in this case, Account Manager Number. *Why? Including GROUP BY Account Manager Number will cause the accounts for each manager to be grouped together; that is, all accounts with the same account manager number will form a group. Any statistics, such as totals, appearing after the word SELECT will be calculated for each of these groups.* Using GROUP BY does not mean that the information will be sorted.

The following steps use the GROUP BY clause to produce the results PrattLast wants. The steps also rename the total amount paid as Sum Paid and the total current due as Sum Due by including appropriate AS clauses; finally, the steps sort the records by account manager number.

1

- Return to SQL view and delete the previous query.

- Type **SELECT [Account Manager Number], SUM([Amount Paid]) AS [Sum Paid], SUM([Current Due]) AS [Sum Due]** as the first line of the command.

- Type **FROM [Account]** as the second line.

- Type **GROUP BY [Account Manager Number]** as the third line.

Q&A What is the purpose of the GROUP BY clause?

The GROUP BY clause causes the rows to be grouped by the indicated field. With this GROUP BY clause, the rows will be grouped by Account Manager Number.

- Type **ORDER BY [Account Manager Number]** as the fourth line and type a semicolon on the fifth line.

- View the results (Figure 10–24).

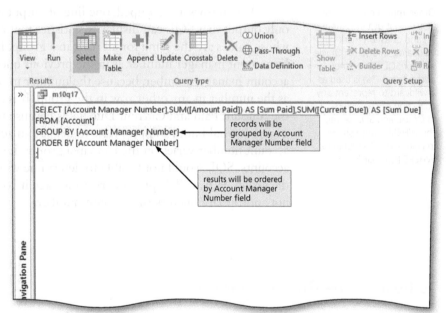

Figure 10–24 (a) Query to Group Records by Account Manager Number and List the Account Manager Number, the Sum of Amount Paid, and the Sum of Current Due

2

- Save the query as m10q18.

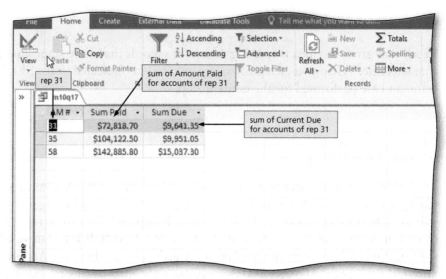

Figure 10–24 (b) Results

BTW
Wildcards
Other implementations of SQL do not use the asterisk (*) and question mark (?) wildcards. In SQL for Oracle and for SQL Server, the percent sign (%) is used as a wildcard to represent any collection of characters. In Oracle and SQL Server, the WHERE clause shown in Figure 10-11a would be WHERE [City] LIKE 'G%'.

Grouping Requirements

When rows are grouped, one line of output is produced for each group. The only output that SQL can display is statistics that are calculated for the group or fields whose values are the same for all rows in a group. For example, when grouping rows by account manager number as in the previous query, it is appropriate to display the account manager number, because the number in one row in a group must be the same as the number in any other row in the group. It is appropriate to display the sum of the Amount Paid and Current Due fields because they are statistics calculated for the group. It would not be appropriate to display an account number, however, because the account number varies on the rows in a group; the manager is associated with many accounts. SQL would not be able to determine which account number to display for the group. SQL will display an error message if you attempt to display a field that is not appropriate, such as the account number.

To Restrict the Groups That Appear

1 SQL VIEW | 2 SIMPLE CRITERIA | 3 COMPOUND CRITERIA | 4 SORT RESULTS
5 GROUP RESULTS | 6 JOIN TABLES | 7 USE SUBQUERY | 8 UPDATE DATA

In some cases, PrattLast Associates may want to display only certain groups. For example, management may want to display only those account managers for whom the sum of the current due amounts are less than $10,000.00. This restriction does not apply to individual rows, but instead to groups. You cannot use a WHERE clause to accomplish this restriction. *Why? WHERE applies only to rows, not groups.*

Fortunately, SQL provides the **HAVING clause**, which functions with groups similarly to the way WHERE functions with rows. The HAVING clause consists of the word HAVING followed by a criterion. It is used in the following steps, which restrict the groups to be included to those for which the sum of the current due is less than $10,000.00.

- Return to SQL view.

- Click the beginning of the fourth line (ORDER BY [Account Manager Number]) and press the ENTER key to insert a new blank line.

- Click the beginning of the new blank line, and then type **HAVING SUM([Current Due])<10000** as the new fourth line.

Q&A What is the purpose of the HAVING clause?
The HAVING clause restricts the groups that will be included to only those satisfying the indicated criteria. With this clause, only groups for which the sum of the current due amount is less than $10,000 will be included.

- View the results (Figure 10–25).

2

- Save the query as m10q19.

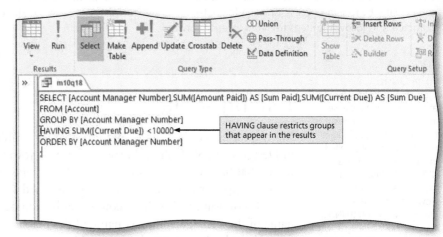

Figure 10–25 (a) Query to Restrict the Results of the Previous Query to Only Those Groups for Which the Sum of Current Due Is Less Than $10,000

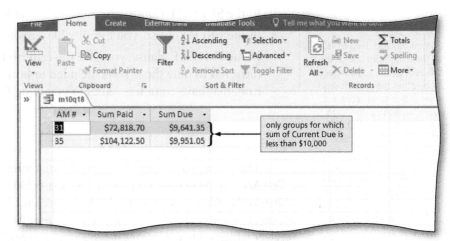

Figure 10–25 (b) Results

How do you determine grouping when creating a query?
Examine the query or request to determine whether records should be organized by some common characteristic.

- **Determine whether data is to be grouped in some fashion.** Examine the requirements for the query to see if they contain individual rows or information about groups of rows.

- **Determine the field or fields on which grouping is to take place.** By which field is the data to be grouped? Look to see if the requirements indicate a field along with several group calculations.

- **Determine which fields or calculations are appropriate to display.** When rows are grouped, one line of output is produced for each group. The only output that can appear are statistics that are calculated for the group or fields whose values are the same for all rows in a group. For example, it would make sense to display the manager number, because all the accounts in the group have the same manager number. It would not make sense to display the account number, because the account number will vary from one row in a group to another. SQL could not determine which account number to display for the group.

Break Point: If you wish to stop working through the module at this point, you can close Access now. You can resume the project later by running Access, opening the database called PrattLast Associates, creating a new query in SQL view, and continuing to follow the steps from this location forward.

BTW
Inner Joins
A join that compares the tables in the FROM clause and lists only those rows that satisfy the condition in the WHERE clause is called an inner join. SQL has an INNER JOIN clause. You could replace the query shown in Figure 10–26a with FROM [Account] INNER JOIN [Account Manager] ON [Account].[Account Manager Number]=[Account Manager]. [Account Manager Number] to get the same results as shown in Figure 10–26b.

BTW
Outer Joins
Sometimes you need to list all the rows from one of the tables in a join, regardless of whether they match any rows in the other table. For example, you can perform a join on the Account and Workshop Offerings table but display all accounts — even the ones without workshop offerings. This type of join is called an outer join. In a left outer join, all rows from the table on the left (the table listed first in the query) will be included regardless of whether they match rows from the table on the right (the table listed second in the query). Rows from the right will be included only if they match. In a right outer join, all rows from the table on the right will be included regardless of whether they match rows from the table on the left. The SQL clause for a left outer join is LEFT JOIN and the SQL clause for a right outer join is RIGHT JOIN.

Joining Tables

Many queries require data from more than one table. Just as with creating queries in Design view, SQL should provide a way to **join** tables, that is, to find rows in two tables that have identical values in matching fields. In SQL, this is accomplished through appropriate criteria following the word WHERE.

If you want to list the account number, name, account manager number, first name of the manager, and last name of the manager for all accounts, you need data from both the Account and Account Manager tables. The Account Manager Number field is in both tables, the Account Number field is only in the Account table, and the First Name and Last Name fields are only in the Account Manager Table. You need to access both tables in your SQL query, as follows:

1. In the SELECT clause, you indicate all fields you want to appear.
2. In the FROM clause, you list all tables involved in the query.
3. In the WHERE clause, you give the criterion that will restrict the data to be retrieved to only those rows included in both of the two tables, that is, to the rows that have common values in matching fields.

Qualifying Fields

There is a problem in indicating the matching fields. The matching fields are both called Account Manager Number. There is a field in the Account table called Account Manager Number, as well as a field in the Account Manager Table called Account Manager Number. In this case, if you only enter Account Manager Number, it will not be clear which table you mean. It is necessary to **qualify** Account Manager Number, that is, to specify to which field in which table you are referring. You do this by preceding the name of the field with the name of the table, followed by a period. The Account Manager Number field in the Account table, for example, is [Account].[Account Manager Number].

Whenever a query is potentially ambiguous, you must qualify the fields involved. It is permissible to qualify other fields as well, even if there is no confusion. For example, instead of [Account Name], you could have typed [Account].[Account Name] to indicate the Account Name field in the Account table. Some people prefer to qualify all fields, and this is not a bad approach. In this text, you will only qualify fields when it is necessary to do so. Each field is qualified individually.

1 SQL VIEW | 2 SIMPLE CRITERIA | 3 COMPOUND CRITERIA | 4 SORT RESULTS
5 GROUP RESULTS | 6 JOIN TABLES | 7 USE SUBQUERY | 8 UPDATE DATA

To Join Tables

PrattLast Associates wants to list the account number, account name, account manager number, first name of the manager, and last name of the manager for all accounts. The following steps create a query to join the tables. **Why?** *The data comes from two tables.* The steps also order the results by account number.

1

- Return to SQL view and delete the previous query.

- Type `SELECT [Account Number],[Account Name],[Account].[Account Manager Number],[First Name],[Last Name]` as the first line of the command.

- Type `FROM [Account], [Account Manager]` as the second line.

Q&A Why does the FROM clause contain more than one table?
The query involves fields from both tables.

- Type `WHERE [Account].[Account Manager Number]=[Account Manager].[Account Manager Number]` as the third line.

Q&A What is the purpose of this WHERE clause?
The WHERE clause specifies that only rows for which the manager numbers match are to be included. In this case, the manager number in the Account table ([Account].[Account Manager Number]) must be equal to the manager number in the Account Manager table ([Account Manager].[Account Manager Number]).

- Type `ORDER BY [Account Number]` as the fourth line and type a semicolon on the fifth line.

- View the results (Figure 10–26).

2

- Save the query as m10q20.

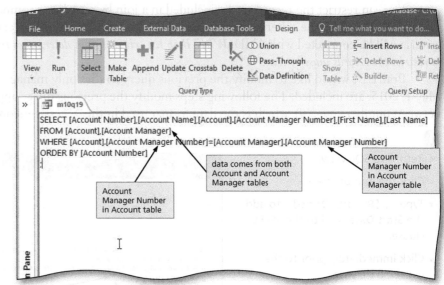

Figure 10–26 (a) Query to List the Account Number, Account Name, Account Manager Number, First Name, and Last Name for All Accounts

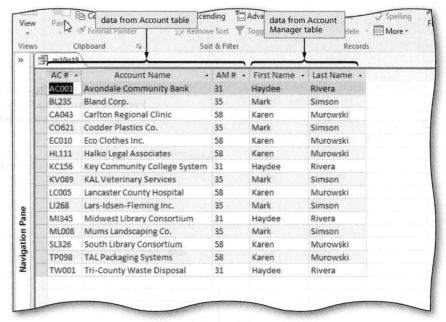

Figure 10–26 (b) Results

To Restrict the Records in a Join

You can restrict the records to be included in a join by creating a compound criterion. The compound criterion will include the criterion necessary to join the tables along with a criterion to restrict the records. The criteria will be connected with AND. *Why? Both the criterion that determines the records to be joined and the criterion to restrict the records must be true.*

PrattLast would like to modify the previous query so that only managers whose start date is prior to May 1, 2015, are included. The following steps modify the previous query appropriately. The date is enclosed between number signs (#), which is the date format used in the Access version of SQL.

1

- Return to SQL view.

- Click the end of line 1.

- Type `, [Start Date]` to add the Start Date field to the SELECT clause.

- Click immediately prior to the ORDER BY clause.

- Type `AND [Start Date]<#5/1/2015#` and press the ENTER key.

Q&A Could I use other formats for the date in the criterion?
Yes. You could type #May 1, 2015# or #1-May-2015#.

- View the results (Figure 10–27).

2

- Save the query as m10q21.

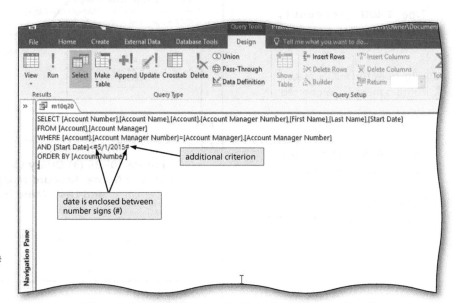

Figure 10–27 (a) Query to Restrict the Results of Previous Query to Only Those Accounts Whose Start Date Is Before 5/1/2015

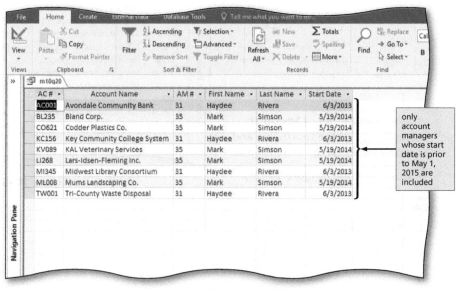

Figure 10–27 (b) Results

Aliases

When tables appear in the FROM clause, you can give each table an **alias**, or an alternative name, that you can use in the rest of the statement. You create an alias by typing the name of the table, pressing the spacebar, and then typing the name of the alias. No commas or periods are necessary to separate the two names.

You can use an alias for two basic reasons: for simplicity or to join a table to itself. Figure 10–28 shows the same query as in Figure 10–27, but with the Account table assigned the letter, A, as an alias and the Account Manager table assigned the letter, M. The query in Figure 10–28 is less complex. Whenever you need to qualify a field name, you can use the alias. Thus, you only need to type M.[Account Manager Number] rather than [Account Manager].[Account Manager Number].

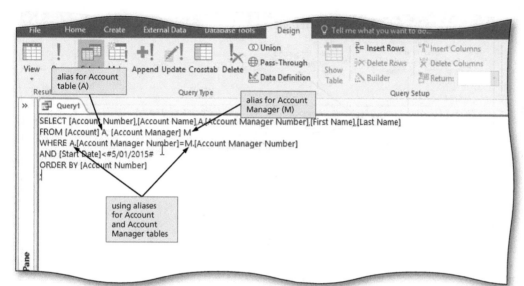

BTW

Qualifying Fields
There is no space on either side of the period that is used to separate the table name from the field name. Adding a space will result in an error message.

Figure 10–28

To Join a Table to Itself

1 SQL VIEW | 2 SIMPLE CRITERIA | 3 COMPOUND CRITERIA | 4 SORT RESULTS
5 GROUP RESULTS | 6 JOIN TABLES | 7 USE SUBQUERY | 8 UPDATE DATA

The other use of aliases is in joining a table to itself. An example of this type of join would enable PrattLast to find account numbers and names for every two accounts located in the same city. One such pair, for example, would be account BL235 (Bland Corp.) and account KV089 (KAL Veterinary Services) because both accounts are located in the same city (Granger). Another example would be account BL235 (Bland Corp.) and account LC005 (Lancaster County Hospital) because both accounts are also located in the same city (Granger). Finally, because both KV089 and LC005 are located in the same city (Granger), there would be a third pair: KV089 (KAL Veterinary Services) and LC005 (Lancaster County Hospital).

If there were two Account tables in the database, PrattLast could obtain the results they want by simply joining the two Account tables and looking for rows where the cities were the same. Even though there is only one Account table, you can actually treat the Account table as two tables in the query by creating two aliases. You would change the FROM clause to:

```
FROM [Account] F, [Account] S
```

SQL treats this clause as a query of two tables. The clause assigns the first Account table the letter, F, as an alias. It also assigns the letter, S, as an alias for the Account table. The fact that both tables are really the single Account table is not a problem. The following steps assign two aliases (F and S) to the Account table and list the account number and account name of both accounts as well as the city in which both are located. The steps also include a criterion to ensure F.[Account Number] < S.[Account Number]. *Why? If you did not include this criterion, the query would contain four times as many results. On the first row in the results, for example, the first account number is BL235 and the second is KV089. Without this criterion, there would be a row on which both the first and second account numbers are BL235, a row on which both are KV089, and a row on which the first is KV089 and the second is BL235. This criterion only selects the one row on which the first account number (BL235) is less than the second account number (KV089).*

❶

- Return to SQL view and delete the previous query.

- Type **SELECT F.[Account Number],F.[Account Name],S.[Account Number],S.[Account Name],F.[City]** as the first line of the command to select the fields to display in the query result.

- Type **FROM [Account] F,[Account] S** as the second line to create the aliases for the first and second Account tables.

- Type **WHERE F.[City]=S.[City]** as the third line to indicate that the cities in each table must match.

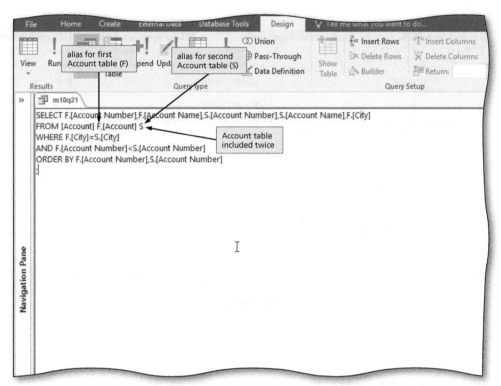

Figure 10–29 (a) Query to List the Account Name and Account Number for Pairs of Accounts Located in the Same City

- Type **AND F.[Account Number]<S.[Account Number]** as the fourth line to indicate that the account number from the first table must be less than the account number from the second table.

- Type **ORDER BY F.[Account Number], S.[Account Number]** as the fifth line to ensure that the results are sorted by the account number from the first table and further sorted by the account number from the second table.

- Type a semicolon on the sixth line.

- View the results (Figure 10–29).

❷

- Save the query as m10q22.

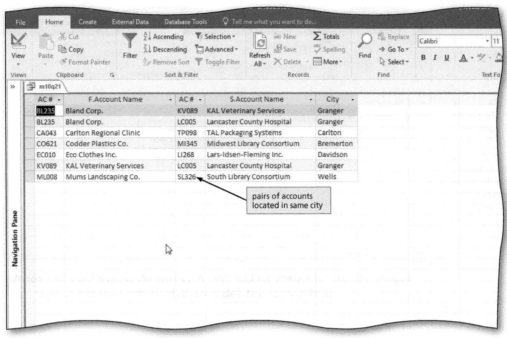

Figure 10–29 (b) Results

CONSIDER THIS

How do you determine criteria when creating a query?

Examine the query or request to determine any restrictions or conditions that records must satisfy to be included in the results.

- **Determine the fields involved in the criteria.** For any criterion, determine the fields that are included. Determine the data types for these fields. If the criterion uses a value that corresponds to a Text field, enclose the value in single quotation marks. If the criterion uses a date, enclose the value between number signs (for example, #4/15/2015#).

- **Determine comparison operators.** When fields are being compared to other fields or to specific values, determine the appropriate comparison operator (equals, less than, greater than, and so on). If a wildcard is involved, then the query will use the LIKE operator.

- **Determine join criteria.** If tables are being joined, determine the fields that must match.

- **Determine compound criteria.** If more than one criterion is involved, determine whether all individual criteria are to be true, in which case you will use the AND operator, or whether only one individual criterion needs to be true, in which case you will use the OR operator.

Subqueries

It is possible to place one query inside another. You will place the query shown in Figure 10–30 inside another query. When you have done so, it will be called a **subquery**, which is an inner query, contained within parentheses, that is evaluated first. Then the outer query can use the results of the subquery to find its results. In some cases, using a subquery can be the simplest way to produce the desired results, as illustrated in the next set of steps.

BTW
SELECT clause
When you enter field names in a SELECT clause, you do not need to enter a space after the comma. Access inserts a space after the comma when you save the query and close it. When you re-open the query in SQL view, a space will appear after each comma that separates fields in the SELECT clause.

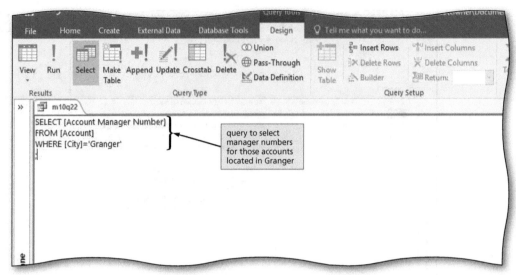

BTW
SQL Standards
The International Standards
Organization (ISO) and the
American National Standards
Institute (ANSI) recognize SQL
as a standardized language.
Different relational database
management systems may
support the entire set of
standardized SQL commands
or only a subset.

**Figure 10–30 (a) Query to List the Account Manager Number for All Records
in the Account Table on Which the City Is Granger**

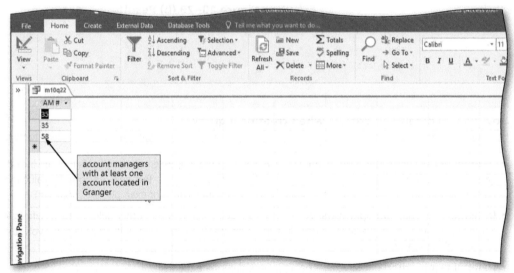

Figure 10–30 (b) Results

CONSIDER THIS

Why does account manager 35 appear twice?

The PrattLast Associates database includes two accounts whose city is Granger and whose account manager number is 35. This is not a problem because in the next query it is only important what numbers are included, not how many times they appear. If you wanted the numbers to only appear once, you would order the results by Account Manager Number and use the DISTINCT operator.

Using SQL **Access Module 10 AC** 579

Access Module 10

1 SQL VIEW | 2 SIMPLE CRITERIA | 3 COMPOUND CRITERIA | 4 SORT RESULTS
5 GROUP RESULTS | 6 JOIN TABLES | 7 USE SUBQUERY | 8 UPDATE DATA

To Use a Subquery

The following steps use the query shown in Figure 10–30 as a subquery. *Why? PrattLast Associates can use this query to select manager numbers for those managers who have at least one account located in Granger.* After the subquery is evaluated, the outer query will select the manager number, first name, and last name for those managers whose manager number is in the list produced by the subquery.

- Return to SQL view and delete the previous query.

- Type **SELECT [Account Manager Number], [First Name], [Last Name]** as the first line of the command.

- Type **FROM [Account Manager]** as the second line.

- Type **WHERE [Account Manager Number] IN** as the third line.

- Type **(SELECT [Account Manager Number]** as the fourth line.

- Type **FROM [Account]** as the fifth line.

- Type **WHERE [City]='Granger')** as the sixth line and type a semicolon on the seventh line.

- View the results (Figure 10–31).

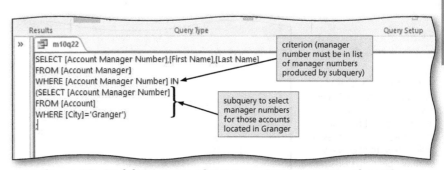

Figure 10–31 (a) Query to List Account Manager Number, First Name, and Last Name for All Account Managers Who Represent at Least One Account Located in Granger

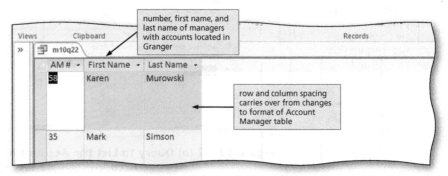

Figure 10–31 (b) Results

- Save the query as m10q23.

Using an IN Clause

The query in Figure 10–31 uses an IN clause with a subquery. You can also use an IN clause with a list as an alternative to an OR criterion when the OR criterion involves a single field. For example, to find accounts whose city is Granger, Rushton, or Wells, the criterion using IN would be City IN ('Granger', 'Rushton', 'Wells'). The corresponding OR criterion would be City='Granger' OR City= 'Rushton' OR City= 'Wells'. The choice of which one to use is a matter of personal preference.

You can also use this type of IN clause when creating queries in Design view. To use the criterion in the previous paragraph, for example, include the City field in the design grid and enter the criterion in the Criteria row.

BTW

BETWEEN Operator
The BETWEEN operator allows you to search for a range of values in one field. For example, to find all accounts whose amount paid is between $10,000.00 and $20,000.00, the WHERE clause would be WHERE [Amount Paid] BETWEEN 10000 AND 20000.

Comparison with Access-Generated SQL

When you create a query in Design view, Access automatically creates a corresponding SQL query that is similar to the queries you have created in this module. The Access query shown in Figure 10–32, for example, was created in Design view and includes the Account Number and Account Name fields. The City field has a criterion (Granger).

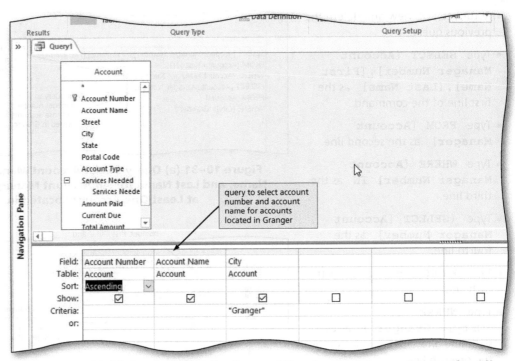

Figure 10–32 (a) Query to List the Account Number and Account Name for All Accounts Whose City Is Granger

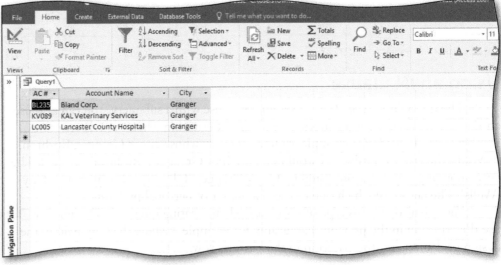

Figure 10–32 (b) Results

The SQL query that Access generates in correspondence to the Design view query is shown in Figure 10–33. The query is very similar to the queries you have entered, but there are three slight differences. First, the Account.[Account Number] and Account.[Account Name] fields are qualified, even though they do not need to be; only one table is involved in the query, so no qualification is necessary. Second, the City field is not enclosed in square brackets. The field is legitimately not enclosed in square brackets because there are no spaces or other special characters in the field name. Finally, there are extra parentheses in the criteria.

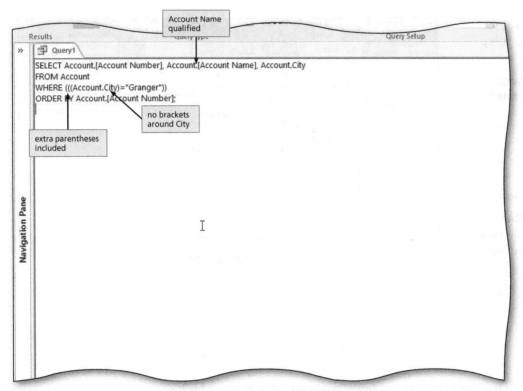

Figure 10–33

Both the style used by Access and the style you have been using are legitimate. The choice of style is a personal preference.

Updating Data Using SQL

Although SQL is often regarded as a language for querying databases, it also contains commands to update databases. You can add new records, update existing records, and delete records. To make the change indicated in the command, you will click the Run button.

BTW
Action Queries
When you use the INSERT, UPDATE, or DELETE commands in SQL, you are creating action queries. The query is making a change to the database. To effect this change, you must click the Run button in the Results group.

To Use an INSERT Command

You can add records to a table using the SQL INSERT command. The command consists of the words INSERT INTO followed by the name of the table into which the record is to be inserted. Next is the word VALUE, followed by the values for the fields in the record. Values for text fields must be enclosed within quotation marks. *Why? Just as you needed to type the quotation marks when you used text data in a criterion, you need to do the same when you use text values in an INSERT INTO command.* The following steps add a record that PrattLast Associates wants to add to the Workshop Offerings table. The record is for account EC010 and Workshop W04, and indicates that the workshop will be offered for a total of 16 hours, of which 0 hours have already been spent.

1

- If necessary, return to SQL view and delete the existing query.

- Type **INSERT INTO [Workshop Offerings]** as the first line of the command.

What is the purpose of the INSERT INTO clause?
The clause indicates the table into which data is to be inserted.

- Type **VALUES** as the second line.

- Type **('EC010','W04' ,16,0)** as the third line and type a semicolon on the fourth line (Figure 10–34).

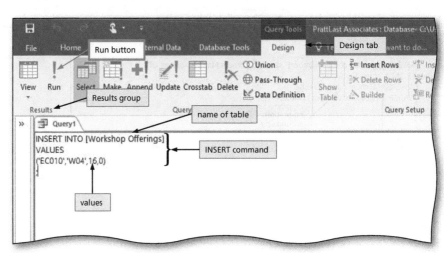

Figure 10–34

What is the purpose of the VALUES clause?
The VALUES clause, which typically extends over two lines, indicates the values that are to be inserted into a new record in the table. For readability, it is common to place the word VALUES on one line and the actual values on a separate line.

2

- Run the query by clicking the Run button (Query Tools Design tab | Results group).

- When Access displays a message indicating the number of records to be inserted (appended), click the Yes button to insert the records.

I clicked the View button and did not get the message. Do I need to click the Run button?
Yes. You are making a change to the database, so you must click the Run button, or the change will not be made.

How can I see if the record was actually inserted?
Use a SELECT query to view the records in the Workshop Offerings table.

3

- Save the query as m10q24.

To Use an UPDATE Command

You can update records in SQL by using the UPDATE command. The command consists of UPDATE, followed by the name of the table in which records are to be updated. Next, the command contains one or more SET clauses, which consist of the word SET, followed by a field to be updated, an equal sign, and the new value. The SET clause indicates the change to be made. Finally, the query includes a WHERE clause. ***Why? When you execute the command, all records in the indicated table that satisfy the criterion will be updated.*** The following steps use the SQL UPDATE command to perform an update requested by PrattLast Associates. Specifically, they change the Hours Spent to 4 on all records in the Workshop Offerings table on which the account number is EC010 and the workshop code is W04. Because the combination of the Account Number and Workshop Code fields is the primary key, only one record will be updated.

1

- Delete the existing query.

- Type **UPDATE [Workshop Offerings]**   as the first line of the command.

 What is the purpose of the UPDATE clause?

The UPDATE clause indicates the table to be updated. This clause indicates that the update is to the Workshop Offerings table.

- Type **SET [Hours Spent]=4**   as the second line.

 What is the purpose of the SET clause?

The SET clause indicates the field to be changed as well as the new value. This SET clause indicates that the hours spent is to be set to 4.

- Type **WHERE [Account Number]='EC010'**   as the third line.

- Type **AND [Workshop Code]='W04'**   as the fourth line and type a semicolon on the fifth line (Figure 10–35).

 Do I need to change a field to a specific value such as 4?

No. You could use an expression. For example, to add $100 to the Current Due amount, the SET clause would be SET [Current Due]=[Current Due]+100.

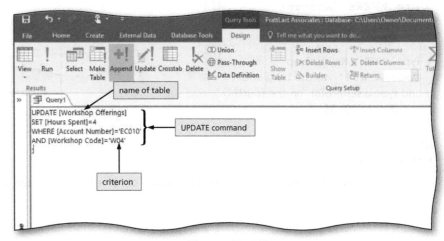

Figure 10–35

2

- Run the query.

- When Access displays a message indicating the number of records to be updated, click the Yes button to update the records.

 How can I see if the update actually occurred?

Use a SELECT query to view the records in the Workshop Offerings table.

3

- Save the query as m10q25.

To Use a DELETE Command

You can delete records in SQL using the DELETE command. The command consists of DELETE FROM, followed by the name of the table from which records are to be deleted. Finally, you include a WHERE clause to specify the criteria. **Why?** *When you execute the command, all records in the indicated table that satisfy the criterion will be deleted.* The following steps use the SQL DELETE command to delete all records in the Workshop Offerings table on which the account number is EC010 and the workshop code is W04, as PrattLast Associates has requested. Because the combination of the Account Number and Workshop Code fields is the primary key, only one record will be deleted.

1

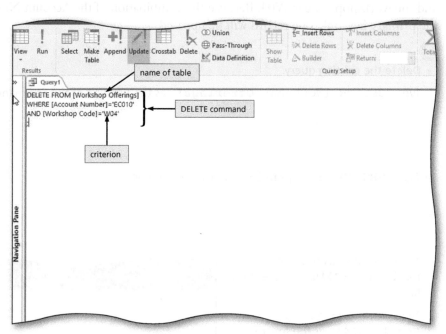

- Delete the existing query.

- Type **DELETE FROM [Workshop Offerings]** as the first line of the command.

Q&A What is the purpose of the DELETE clause?

The DELETE clause indicates the table from which records will be deleted. This DELETE clause indicates that records will be deleted from the Workshop Offerings table.

- Type **WHERE [Account Number] = 'EC010'** as the second line.

- Type **AND [Workshop Code] = 'W04'** as the third line and type a semicolon on the fourth line (Figure 10–36).

Figure 10–36

2

- Run the query.

- When Access displays a message indicating the number of records to be deleted, click the Yes button to delete the records.

Q&A How can I see if the deletion actually occurred?

Use a SELECT query to view the records in the Workshop Offerings table.

3

- Save the query as m10q26.

- Close the query.

How do you determine any update operations to be performed?
Examine the database to determine if records must be added, updated, and/or deleted.

- **Determine INSERT operations.** Determine whether new records need to be added. Determine to which table they should be added.

- **Determine UPDATE operations.** Determine changes that need to be made to existing records. Which fields need to be changed? Which tables contain these fields? What criteria identify the rows that need to be changed?

- **Determine DELETE operations.** Determine which tables contain records that are to be deleted. What criteria identify the rows that need to be deleted?

To Restore the Font Size

Earlier you changed the font size from its default setting of 8 to 10 so the SQL queries would be easier to read. Unless you prefer to retain this new setting, you should change the setting back to the default. The following steps restore the font size to its default setting.

BTW
Datasheet Font Size
You also can use the Access Options dialog box to change the default font and font size for datasheets. To do so, click Datasheet in the Access Options dialog box and make the desired changes in the Default font area.

1. Click File on the ribbon to open the Backstage view.

2. Click Options to display the Access Options dialog box.

3. If necessary, click Object Designers to display the Object Designer options.

4. In the Query design area, click the Size box arrow, and then click 8 in the list that appears to change the size back to 8.

5. Click the OK button to close the Access Options dialog box.

6. If desired, sign out of your Microsoft account.

7. Exit Access.

Summary

In this module you have learned to create SQL queries; include fields in a query; use criteria involving both numeric and text fields as well as use compound criteria; use computed fields and rename the computation; sort the results of a query; use the built-in functions; group records in a query and also restrict the groups that appear in the results; join tables and restrict the records in a join; and use subqueries. You looked at a SQL query that was generated automatically by Access. Finally, you used the INSERT, UPDATE, and DELETE commands to update data.

What decisions will you need to make when creating your own SQL queries?
Use these guidelines as you complete the assignments in this module and create your own queries outside of this class.

1. Select the fields for the query.
   a. Examine the requirements for the query you are constructing to determine which fields are to be included.

2. Determine which table or tables contain these fields.
   a. For each field, determine the table in which it is located.

3. Determine criteria.
   a. Determine any criteria that data must satisfy to be included in the results.
   b. If there are more than two tables in the query, determine the criteria to be used to ensure the data matches correctly.

4. Determine sort order.
   a. Is the data to be sorted in some way?
   b. If so, by what field or fields is it to be sorted?

5. Determine grouping.
   a. Is the data to be grouped in some way?
   b. If so, by what field is it to be grouped?
   c. Identify any calculations to be made for the group.

6. Determine any update operations to be performed.
   a. Determine whether rows need to be inserted, changed, or deleted.
   b. Determine the tables involved.

How should you submit solutions to questions in the assignments identified with a symbol?
Every assignment in this book contains one or more questions identified with a symbol. These questions require you to think beyond the assigned database. Present your solutions to the questions in the format required by your instructor. Possible formats may include one or more of these options: write the answer; create a document that contains the answer; present your answer to the class; discuss your answer in a group; record the answer as audio or video using a webcam, smartphone, or portable media player; or post answers on a blog, wiki, or website.

Apply Your Knowledge

Reinforce the skills and apply the concepts you learned in this module.

Using Criteria, Joining Tables, and Sorting in SQL Queries

Instructions: Run Access. Open the Apply AllAround Services database that you modified in Module 9. (If you did not complete the exercise, see your instructor for a copy of the modified database.) Use SQL to query the Apply AllAround Services database.

Perform the following tasks:
   1. Find all clients whose client type is RET. Display all fields in the query result. Save the query as AYK Step 1 Query.
   2. Find all clients whose amount paid or current due is $0.00. Display the Client Number, Client Name, Amount Paid, and Current Due fields in the query result. Save the query as AYK Step 2 Query.

3. Find all clients in the Client table who are not located in Carlton. Display the Client Number, Client Name, and City in the query results. Save the query as AYK Step 3 Query.

4. Display the Client Number, Client Name, Supervisor Number, First Name, and Last Name for all clients. Sort the records in ascending order by supervisor number and client number. Save the query as AYK Step 4 Query.

5. Display the Supervisor Number, First Name, Last Name, and Hourly Rate for all supervisors whose Hourly Rate is greater than $13.50. Save the query as AYK Step 5 Query.

6. If requested to do so by your instructor, rename the AYK Step 5 Query as Last Name Query where Last Name is your last name.

7. Submit the revised database in the format specified by your instructor.

8. ✹ What WHERE clause would you use if you wanted to find all clients located in cities beginning with the letter K?

Extend Your Knowledge

Extend the skills you learned in this module and experiment with new skills. You may need to use Help to complete the assignment.

Note: To complete this assignment, you will be required to use the Data Files. Please contact your instructor for information about accessing the Data Files.

Instructions: Run Access. Open the Extend Helping Hands database. The Extend Helping Hands database contains information about a local business that provides nonmedical services to adults who need assistance with daily living.

Perform the following tasks:

1. Find all clients where the client's first name is either Tim or Jim. Display the Client Number, First Name, Last Name, and Address fields in the query result. Save the query as EYK Step 1 Query.

2. Find all clients who live in Upper Darby or Drexel Hill. Use the IN operator. Display the Client Number, First Name, Last Name, and City fields in the query result. Save the query as EYK Step 2 Query.

3. Find all clients whose amount paid is greater than or equal to $500.00 and less than or equal to $600.00. Use the BETWEEN operator. Display the Client Number, First Name, Last Name, and Amount Paid fields in the query result. Save the query as EYK Step 3 Query.

4. Use a subquery to find all helpers whose clients are located in Springfield. Display the Helper Number, First Name, and Last Name fields in the query result. Save the query as EYK Step 4 Query.

5. If requested to do so by your instructor, rename the EYK Step 4 Query as First Name City Query where First Name is your first name and City is the city where you currently reside.

6. Submit the revised database in the format specified by your instructor.

7. ✹ What WHERE clause would you use to find the answer to Step 2 without using the IN operator?

Continued >

Expand Your World

Create a solution, which uses cloud and web technologies, by learning and investigating on your own from general guidance.

Problem: Many SQL tutorials are available on the web. One site, www.w3schools.com/sql, has an online SQL editor that allows you to edit SQL commands and then run commands. You will use this editor to create and run queries.

Note: For each SQL statement that you create and run, use the asterisk (*) to select all fields in the table. Copy the SQL statement and the number of results retrieved to your blog, Google document, or Word document.

Perform the following tasks:

1. Create a blog, Google document, or Word document on OneDrive on which to store your SQL statements and the number of results obtained from the query. Include your name and the current date at the beginning of the blog or document.

2. Access the www.w3schools.com/sql website and spend some time becoming familiar with the tutorial and how it works.

3. Using the website, create a query to find all records in the OrderDetails table where the ProductID is 4 and the Quantity is greater than 20.

4. Create a query to find all records in the Customers table where the ContactName begins with the letter P. (*Hint:* Use the percent symbol (%), not the asterisk in this query.)

5. Create a query to find all records in the Employees table where the birth date of the employee is after January 1, 1960. (*Hint:* View all the records in the table first to determine how dates are stored. Enclose the date with single quotes.)

6. Submit the document containing your statements and results in the format specified by your instructor.

7. ✺ What differences did you notice between the online SQL editor and Access SQL? Which one would you prefer to use? Why?

In the Labs

Design, create, modify, and/or use a database following the guidelines, concepts, and skills presented in this module. Labs are listed in order of increasing difficulty. Labs 1 and 2, which increase in difficulty, require you to create solutions based on what you learned in the module; Lab 3 requires you to apply your creative thinking and problem solving skills to design and implement a solution.

Lab 1: Querying the Gardening Supply Database Using SQL

Problem: Gardening Supply wants to learn more about SQL and has determined a number of questions it wants SQL to answer. You must obtain answers to the questions using SQL.

Instructions: Perform the following tasks:

1. Run Access and open the Lab 1 Gardening Supply database that you modified in Module 9. (If you did not complete the exercise, see your instructor for a copy of the modified database.) Create a new query in SQL view.

2. Find all customers who are located in the city of Quaker. Include the Customer Number, Customer Name, and City in the query results. Save the query as ITL 1 Step 2 Query.

3. Find all customers located in New Jersey (NJ) with an amount paid greater than $3,000.00. Include the Customer Number, Customer Name, and Amount Paid fields in the query results. Save the query as ITL 1 Step 3 Query.

4. Find all customers whose names begin with the letter P. Include the Customer Number, Customer Name, and City fields in the query results. Save the query as ITL 1 Step 4 Query.

5. List all states in descending alphabetical order. Each state should appear only once. Save the query as ITL 1 Step 5 Query.

6. Display the customer number, customer name, sales rep number, sales rep first name, and sales rep last name for all customers. Sorts the results in ascending order by sales rep number and customer number. Save the query as ITL 1 Step 6 Query.

7. List the average balance due grouped by sales rep number. Include the sales rep number in the result and name the average balance as Average Balance. Save the query as ITL 1 Step 7 Query.

8. Find the customer numbers, names, and sales rep numbers for all customers that have open orders. Use the alias O for the Open Orders table and C for the Customer table. Each customer should appear only once in the results. Save the query as ITL 1 Step 8 Query.

9. Find the customer number, name, and city for every two customers who are located in the same city. Save the query as ITL 1 Step 9 Query.

10. Find the average amount paid for sales rep 30. Name the average amount paid as Average Paid. Save the query as ITL 1 Step 10 Query.

11. If requested to do so by your instructor, open the Sales Rep table and change the first and last name for sales rep 30 to your first and last name.

12. Submit the revised database in the format specified by your instructor.

13. ✳ What WHERE clause would you use to find all records where one of the Products Needed was MULCH?

Continued >

In the Labs *continued*

Lab 2: **Querying the Discover Science Database Using SQL**

Problem: Discover Science wants to learn more about SQL and has determined a number of questions it wants SQL to answer. You must obtain answers to the questions using SQL.

Instructions: Perform the following tasks:

1. Run Access and open the Lab 2 Discover Science database that you modified in Module 9. (If you did not complete the exercise, see your instructor for a copy of the modified database.) Create a new query in SQL view.

2. Find all records in the Item table where the difference between the retail price and the wholesale cost of an item is less than $5.00. Display the item number, description, wholesale cost, and retail price in the query results. Save the query as ITL 2 Step 2 Query.

3. Display the item number, description, and inventory value for all items. Inventory value is the result of multiplying wholesale cost by the number of items on hand. Name the computed field Inventory Value. Save the query as ITL 2 Step 3 Query.

4. Find all items where the description begins with the letter G. Include the item number and description in the query results. Save the query as ITL 2 Step 4 Query.

5. Display the vendor name, item number, description, retail price, and quantity on hand for all items where the number on hand is greater than 15. Sort the results in ascending order by vendor name and descending order by on hand. Save the query as ITL 2 Step 5 Query.

6. Find the average wholesale cost by vendor. Name the computed field Avg Wholesale. Include the vendor code in the result. Save the query as ITL 2 Step 6 Query.

7. Find the total number of reordered items in the Reorder table. Name the computed field Total Ordered. Save the query as ITL 2 Step 7 Query.

8. Add the following record to the Reorder table. (*Hint:* Use # symbols at the beginning and the end of the date ordered value.)

Item Number	Date Ordered	Number Ordered
9201	9/7/2017	5

Save the query to add the record as ITL 2 Step 8 Query.

9. If requested to do so by your instructor, rename the ITL 2 Step 8 Query as LastName Reorder Query where LastName is your last name.

10. Update the Number Ordered field to 7 for those records where the Item Number is 9201. Save the query to update the records as ITL 2 Step 10 Query.

11. Delete all records from the Reorder table where the Item Number is 9201. Save the query to delete the records as ITL 2 Step 11 Query.

12. Submit the revised database in the format specified by your instructor.

13. ✹ How would you write an SQL query to increment the number ordered by 2 for all items where the Item Number was 8344?

Lab 3: **Consider This: Your Turn**

Querying the Marketing Analytics Database Using SQL

Instructions: Open the Lab 3 Marketing Analytics database that you modified in Module 9. (If you did not complete the exercise, see your instructor for a copy of the modified database.)

Part 1:   Use the concepts and techniques presented in this module to create queries using SQL for the following. Save each query using the format ITL 3 Step x Query where x is the step letter.

  a. Find the names of all clients who have the letters, ion, in their client name.

  b. Find the totals of the amount paid and current due amounts for all clients. Assign the names Total Paid and Total Due.

  c. Find all marketing analysts who started before 1/1/2016. Display the marketing analyst first name, last name, and start date. (*Hint:* Use # symbols at the beginning and the end of the start date value.)

  d. Find the marketing analyst for each client. List the marketing analyst number, first name, last name, client number, and client name. Assign the alias C to the Client table and M to the Marketing Analyst table. Sort the results in ascending order by marketing analyst number and client number.

  e. Restrict the records retrieved in Step d above to only those records where the current due amount is greater than $3,000.00.

  f. Find the average current due amount grouped by marketing analyst number. Include the marketing analyst number in the results and assign the name Average Due to the average current due amount.

  g. Restrict the records retrieved in Step f above to only those groups where the average current due amount is greater than $2,000.00.

  h. List the client number, client name, seminar code, seminar description, and hours spent for all seminar offerings. Sort the results by client number and seminar code.

Submit your assignment in the format specified by your instructor.

Part 2:   You made several decisions while completing this assignment. What was the rationale behind your decisions? How could you modify the query in Step h to find only those clients where hours spent is equal to zero?

11 | Database Design

Objectives

You will have mastered the material in this module when you can:

- Understand the terms entity, attribute, and relationship

- Understand the terms relation and relational database

- Understand functional dependence and identify when one column is functionally dependent on another

- Understand the term primary key and identify primary keys in tables

- Design a database to satisfy a set of requirements

- Convert an unnormalized relation to first normal form

- Convert tables from first normal form to second normal form

- Convert tables from second normal form to third normal form

- Understand how to represent the design of a database using diagrams

Introduction

This module presents a method for determining the tables and fields necessary to satisfy a set of requirements. **Database design** is the process of determining the particular tables and fields that will comprise a database. In designing a database, you must identify the tables in the database, the fields in the tables, the primary keys of the tables, and the relationships between the tables.

The module begins by examining some important concepts concerning relational databases and then presents the design method. To illustrate the process, the module presents the requirements for the PrattLast Associates database. It then applies the design method to those requirements to produce the database design. The module applies the design method to a second set of requirements, which are requirements for a company called TDK Distributors. It next examines normalization, which is a process that you can use to identify and fix potential problems in database designs. The module concludes by explaining how to use a company's policies and objectives — which are typically addressed in existing documentation — to plan and design a database. Finally, you will learn how to represent a database design with a diagram.

Project — Design a Database

This module expands on the database design guidelines presented earlier. Without a good understanding of database design, you cannot use a database management system such as Access effectively. In this module, you will learn how to design two databases by using the database design process shown in Figure 11–1.

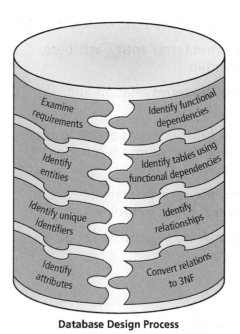

Database Design Process

Figure 11– 1

You will design a database for PrattLast Associates that is similar to the database you have used in the previous modules. You will also design a database for TDK Distributors, a distributor of energy-saving and water-conservation devices.

Entities, Attributes, and Relationships

Working in the database environment requires that you be familiar with some specific terms and concepts. The terms *entity*, *attribute*, and *relationship* are fundamental when discussing databases. An **entity** is like a noun: it is a person, place, thing, or event. The entities of interest to PrattLast Associates, for example, are such things as account managers, accounts, and workshops. The entities that are of interest to a college include students, faculty, and classes; a real estate agency is interested in buyers, sellers, properties, and agents; and a used car dealer is interested in vehicles, accounts, salespeople, and manufacturers. When creating a database, an entity is represented as a table.

An **attribute** is a property of an entity. The term is used here exactly as it is used in everyday English. For the entity *person*, for example, the list of attributes might include such things as eye color and height. For PrattLast Associates, the attributes of interest for the entity *account* are such things as name, address, city, and so on. For the entity *faculty* at a school, the attributes would be such things as faculty number, name, office number, phone, and so on. For the entity *vehicle* at a car dealership, the attributes are such things as the vehicle identification number, model, price, year, and so on. In databases, attributes are represented as the fields in a table or tables.

A **relationship** is an association between entities. There is an association between account managers and accounts, for example, at PrattLast Associates. An account manager is associated with all of his or her accounts, and an account is associated with the one account manager to whom the account is assigned. Technically, you say that an account manager is *related* to all of his or her accounts, and an account is *related* to his or her account manager.

The relationship between account managers and accounts is an example of a one-to-many relationship because one account manager is associated with many accounts, but each account is associated with only one account manager. In this type of relationship, the word *many* is used in a way that is different from everyday English; it might not always mean a large number. In this context, for example, the term *many* means that an account manager might be associated with *any* number of accounts. That is, one account manager can be associated with zero, one, or more accounts.

There is also a relationship between accounts and workshops. Each account can be offered many workshops, and each workshop can be offered to many accounts. This is an example of a many-to-many relationship.

How does a relational database handle entities, attributes of entities, and relationships between entities? Entities and attributes are fairly simple. Each entity has its own table; in the PrattLast Associates database, there is one table for account managers, one table for accounts, and so on. The attributes of an entity become the columns in the table. In the table for accounts, for example, there is a column for the account number, a column for the account name, and so on.

What about relationships? Relationships are implemented through matching fields. One-to-many relationships, for example, are implemented by including matching fields in the related tables. Account managers and accounts are related, for example, by including the Account Manager Number field in both the Account Manager table and the Account table.

Many-to-many relationships are implemented through an additional table that contains matching fields for both of the related tables. Accounts and workshops are related, for example, through the Workshop Offerings table. Both the Account table and the Workshop Offerings table contain Account Number fields. In addition, both the Workshop and the Workshop Offerings table contain Workshop Code fields.

BTW

Entities

PrattLast Associates could include many other entities in a database, such as entities for employees, and for inventories of software and hardware. The decisions on which entities to include are part of the process of determining database requirements based on user needs.

BTW

Relationships

One-to-one relationships also can occur but they are not common. To implement a one-to-one relationship, treat it as a one-to-many relationship. You must determine which table will be the one table and which table will be the many table. To do so, consider what may happen in the future. In the case of one project that has one employee assigned to it, more employees could be added. Therefore, the project table would be the one table and the employee table would be the many table.

Relational Databases

A relational database is a collection of tables similar to the tables for PrattLast Associates that appear in Figure 11–2. In the PrattLast Associates database, the Account table contains information about the accounts to which PrattLast Associates provides human resource services (Figure 11–2a). Note that, for simplification purposes, the tables in the figure do not include all the fields of the final PrattLast database in Module 10.

Account									
Account Number	Account Name	Street	City	State	Postal Code	Amount Paid	Current Due	Account Manager Number
AC001	Avondale Community Bank	256 Main St.	Avondale	IL	60311	$24,752.25	$3,875.25	31
BL235	Bland Corp.	100 South Granger Hwy.	Granger	IL	60314	$29,836.65	$2,765.30	35
CA043	Carlton Regional Clinic	589 Central Ave.	Carlton	IL	60313	$30,841.05	$3,074.30	58
CO621	Codder Plastics Co.	421 First Ave.	Bremerton	IN	46003	$27,152.25	$2,875.00	35
EC010	Eco Clothes Inc.	120 Pine St.	Davidson	IN	46010	$19,620.00	$1,875.00	58
HL111	Halko Legal Associates	321 Feathering Rd.	Gleneagle	IL	60319	$25,702.20	$3,016.75	58
KC156	Key Community College System	35 Indiana Ave.	Walker	IN	46004	$10,952.25	$0.00	31
KV089	KAL Veterinary Services	116 Pine St.	Granger	IL	60314	$34,036.50	$580.00	35
LC005	Lancaster County Hospital	215 River St.	Granger	IL	46004	$44,025.60	$3,590.80	58
LI268	Lars-Idsen-Fleming Inc.	829 Wooster Rd.	Davidson	IN	46010	$ 0.00	$1,280.75	35
MI345	Midwest Library Consortium	3400 Metro Pkwy.	Bremerton	IN	46003	$21,769.20	$2,890.60	31
ML008	Mums Landscaping Co.	865 Ridge Rd.	Wells	IN	46007	$13,097.10	$2,450.00	35
SL326	South Library Consortium	862 Maple St.	Wells	IN	46007	$ 0.00	$0.00	58
TP098	TDK Packaging Systems	12 Polk Ave.	Carlton	IL	60313	$22,696.95	$3,480.45	58
TW001	Tri-County Waste Disposal	345 Central Blvd.	Rushton	IL	60321	$15,345.00	$2,875.50	31

Figure 11–2 (a) Account Table

PrattLast assigns each account to a specific account manager. The Account Manager table contains information about the managers to whom these accounts are assigned (Figure 11–2b).

Account Manager								
Account Manager Number	Last Name	First Name	Street	City	State	Postal Code	Salary	Bonus Rate
31	Rivera	Haydee	325 Twiddy St.	Avondale	IL	60311	$36,750.00	0.15
35	Simson	Mark	1467 Hartwell St.	Walker	IN	46004	$24,000.00	0.12
42	Lu	Peter	5624 Murray Ave.	Davidson	IN	46007	$48,750.00	0.09
58	Murowski	Karen	168 Truesdale Dr.	Carlton	IL	60313	$40,500.00	0.08

Figure 11–2 (b) Account Manager Table

The Workshop table lists the specific workshops that the account managers at PrattLast Associates offer to their accounts (Figure 11–2c). Each workshop has a code and a description. The table also includes the number of hours for which the workshop is usually offered and the workshop's increments, that is, the standard time blocks in which the workshop is usually offered. The first row, for example, indicates that workshop W01 is Dealing with Unacceptable Employee Behavior. The workshop is typically offered in 2-hour increments for a total of 4 hours.

Workshop			
Workshop Code	Workshop Description	Hours	Increments
W01	Dealing with Unacceptable Employee Behavior	4	2
W02	Writing Effective Policies and Procedures	8	4
W03	Payroll Law	3	1
W04	Workplace Safety	16	4
W05	The Recruitment Process	24	4
W06	Diversity in the Workplace	12	3
W07	Americans with Disabilities Act (ADA)	4	2
W08	Workers' Compensation	16	4

Figure 11–2 (c) Workshop Table

The Workshop Offerings table contains an account number, a workshop code, the total number of hours for which the workshop is scheduled, and the number of hours the account has already spent in the workshop (Figure 11–2d). The first record shows that account number AC001 has currently scheduled workshop W01. The workshop is scheduled for 6 hours, of which 2 hours have currently been spent. The total hours are usually the same as the number of hours indicated for the workshop in the Workshop table, but it can differ.

Workshop Offerings			
Account Number	Workshop Code	Total Hours	Hours Spent
AC001	W01	6	2
AC001	W02	8	4
AC001	W03	3	0
EC010	W05	24	12
KC156	W08	16	8
KV089	W07	4	0
LC005	W02	8	4
LC005	W06	12	6
ML008	W03	3	1
ML008	W04	16	4
SL326	W05	24	16
SL326	W06	12	3
SL326	W07	4	2
TP098	W03	3	0
TP098	W08	16	4
TW001	W01	4	2

Figure 11–2 (d) Workshop Offerings Table

The formal term for a table is relation. If you study the tables shown in Figure 11–2, you might see that there are certain restrictions you should place on relations. Each column in a table should have a unique name, and entries in each column should match this column name. For example, in the Postal Code column, all entries should in fact *be* postal codes. In addition, each row should be unique. After all, if two rows in a table contain identical data, the second row does not provide any information that you do not already have. In addition, for maximum flexibility, the order in which columns and rows appear in a table should be immaterial. Finally, a table's design is less complex if you restrict each position in the table to a single entry, that is, you do not permit multiple entries, often called **repeating groups,** in the table. These restrictions lead to the following definition:

A **relation** is a two-dimensional table in which:

1. The entries in the table are single-valued; that is, each location in the table contains a single entry.
2. Each column has a distinct name, technically called the *attribute name*.
3. All values in a column are values of the same attribute; that is, all entries must correspond to the column name.
4. Each row is distinct; that is, no two rows are identical.

Figure 11–3a shows a table with repeating groups, which violates Rule 1. Figure 11–3b shows a table in which two columns have the same name, which violates Rule 2. Figure 11–3c shows a table in which one of the entries in the Workshop Description column is not a workshop description, which violates Rule 3. Figure 11–3d shows a table with two identical rows, which violates Rule 4.

Figure 11–3 (a) Workshop Offerings Table Violation of Rule 1 — Table Contains Repeating Groups

Figure 11–3 (b) Workshop Table Violation of Rule 2 — Each Column Should Have a Distinct Name

Workshop			
Workshop Code	**Workshop Description**	**Hours**	**Increments**
W01	Dealing with Unacceptable Employee Behavior	4	2
W02	Writing Effective Policies and Procedures	8	4
W03	?@!	3	1
W04	Workplace Safety	16	4
W05	The Recruitment Process	24	4
W06	Diversity in the Workplace	12	3
W07	Americans with Disabilities Act (ADA)	4	2
W08	Workers' Compensation	16	4

value does not correspond to column name; that is, it is not a workshop description

Figure 11–3 (c) Workshop Table Violation of Rule 3 — All Entries in a Column Must Correspond to the Column Name

Workshop			
Workshop Code	**Workshop Description**	**Hours**	**Increments**
W01	Dealing with Unacceptable Employee Behavior	4	2
W02	Writing Effective Policies and Procedures	8	4
W03	Payroll Law	3	1
W03	Payroll Law	3	1
W04	Workplace Safety	16	4
W05	The Recruitment Process	24	4
W06	Diversity in the Workplace	12	3
W07	Americans with Disabilities Act (ADA)	4	2
W08	Workers' Compensation	16	4

identical rows

Figure 11–3 (d) Workshop Table Violation of Rule 4 — Each Row Should Be Distinct

In addition, in a relation, the order of columns is immaterial. The order of rows is also immaterial. You can view the columns or rows in any order you want.

A **relational database** is a collection of relations. Rows in a table (relation) are often called **records** or **tuples**. Columns in a table (relation) are often called **fields** or **attributes**. Typically, the terms *record* and *field* are used in Access.

To depict the structure of a relational database, you can use a commonly accepted shorthand representation: you write the name of the table and then within parentheses list all of the fields in the table. Each table should begin on a new line. If the entries in the table occupy more than one line, the entries that appear on the next line should be indented so it is clear that they do not constitute another table. Using this method, you would represent the PrattLast Associates database as shown in Figure 11–4.

Account (Account Number, Account Name, Street, City, State, Postal Code, Amount Paid, Current Due, Account Manager Number)

Account Manager (Account Manager Number, Last Name, First Name, Street, City, State, Postal Code, Salary, Bonus Rate)

Workshop (Workshop Code, Workshop Description, Hours, Increments)

Workshop Offerings (Account Number, Workshop Code, Total Hours, Hours Spent)

Figure 11–4

The PrattLast Associates database contains some duplicate field names. For example, the Account Manager Number field appears in *both* the Account Manager table *and* the Account table. This duplication of names can lead to possible confusion. If you write Account Manager Number, it is not clear to which Account Manager Number field you are referring.

When duplicate field names exist in a database, you need to indicate the field to which you are referring. You do so by writing both the table name and the field name, separated by a period. You would write the Account Manager Number field in the Account table as Account.Account Manager Number and the Account Manager Number field in the Account Manager table as Account Manager.Account Manager Number. As you learned previously, when you combine a field name with a table name, you say that you **qualify** the field names. It is *always* acceptable to qualify field names, even if there is no possibility of confusion. If confusion may arise, however, it is *essential* to qualify field names.

Functional Dependence

In the PrattLast Associates database (Figure 11–2), a given account number in the database will correspond to a single account because account numbers are unique. Thus, if you are given an account number in the database, you could find a single name that corresponds to it. No ambiguity exists. The database terminology for this relationship between account numbers and names is that Account Number determines Account Name, or, equivalently, that Account Name is functionally dependent on Account Number. Specifically, if you know that whenever you are given a value for one field, you will be able to determine a single value for a second field, the first field is said to **determine** the second field. In addition, the second field is said to be **functionally dependent** on the first.

There is a shorthand notation that represents functional dependencies using an arrow. To indicate that Account Number determines Account Name, or, equivalently, that Account Name is functionally dependent on Account Number, you would write Account Number → Account Name. The field that precedes the arrow determines the field that follows the arrow.

If you were given a city and asked to find a single account's name, you could not do it. Given Granger as the city, for example, you would find two account names, Bland Corp. and KAL Veterinary Services (Figure 11–5). Formally, you would say the City does *not* determine Account Name, or that Account Name is *not* functionally dependent on City.

In the Account Manager table, is Last Name functionally dependent on Account Manager Number?
Yes. If you are given a value for Account Manager Number, for example 42, you will always find a *single* last name, in this case Lu, associated with it.

In the Account table, is Account Name functionally dependent on Account Manager Number?
No. A given Account Manager Number occurs on multiple rows. Account Manager Number 35, for example, occurs on a row in which the Account Name is Bland Corp. It also occurs on a row in which the Account Name is KAL Veterinary Services. Thus, rep number 35 is associated with more than one account name.

Account								
Account Number	Account Name	Street	City	State	Postal Code	Amount Paid	Current Due	Account Manager Number
AC001	Avondale Community Bank	256 Main St.	Avondale	IL	60311	$24,752.25	$3,875.25	31
BL235	Bland Corp.	100 South Granger Hwy.	Granger	IL	60314	$29,836.65	$2,765.30	35
CA043	Carlton Regional Clinic	589 Central Ave.	Carlton	IL	60313	$30,841.05	$3,074.30	58
CO621	Codder Plastics Co.	421 First Ave.	Bremerton	IN	46003	$27,152.25	$2,875.00	35
EC010	Eco Clothes Inc.	120 Pine St.	Davidson	IN	46010	$19,620.00	$1,875.00	58
HL111	Halko Legal Associates	321 Feathering Rd.	Gleneagle	IL	60319	$25,702.20	$3,016.75	58
KC156	Key Community College System	35 Indiana Ave.	Walker	IN	46004	$10,952.25	$0.00	31
KV089	KAL Veterinary Services	116 Pine St.	Granger	IL	60314	$34,036.50	$580.00	35
LC005	Lancaster County Hospital	215 River St.	Granger	IL	46004	$44,025.60	$3,590.80	58
LI268	Lars-Idsen-Fleming Inc.	829 Wooster Rd.	Davidson	IN	46010	$0.00	$1,280.75	35
MI345	Midwest Library Consortium	3400 Metro Pkwy.	Bremerton	IN	46003	$21,769.20	$2,890.60	31
ML008	Mums Landscaping Co.			IN	46007	$13,097.10	$2,450.00	35
SL326	South Library Consortium	862 Maple St.	Wells	IN	46007	$0.00	$0.00	58
TP098	TDK Packaging Systems	12 Polk Ave.	Carlton	IL	60313	$22,696.95	$3,480.45	58
TW001	Tri-County Waste Disposal	345 Central Blvd.	Rushton	IL	60321	$15,345.00	$2,875.50	31

(Callout: city is Granger; name is Bland Corp.)

(Callout: city is also Granger, but name is KAL Veterinary Services (same city, but different account name))

Figure 11–5

In the Workshop Offerings table, is Hours Spent functionally dependent on Account Number?
No. There is a row, for example, in which the Account Number is AC001 and the Hours Spent is 2. There is another row in which the Account Number is AC001 but the Hours Spent is 4, a different number.

In the Workshop Offerings table, is Hours Spent functionally dependent on Workshop Code?
No. There is a row, for example, in which the Workshop Code is WO3 and the Hours Spent is 0. There is another row in which the Workshop Code is W03 but the Hours Spent is 1, a different number.

On which fields is Hours Spent functionally dependent?
To determine a value for Hours Spent, you need both an Account Number and a Workshop Code. In other words, Hours Spent is functionally dependent on the combination, formally called the **concatenation**, of Account Number and Workshop Code. That is, given an Account Number *and* a Workshop Code, you can find a single value for Hours Spent.

On which fields is Total Hours functionally dependent?
Because the Total Hours field for a given workshop can vary from one account to another, Total Hours is also functionally dependent on the combination of Account Number and Workshop Code.

On which fields would Total Hours be functionally dependent if every time a workshop was scheduled, Total Hours had to be the same as the number of hours given in the Workshop table?
In that case, to determine Total Hours, you would only need to know the Workshop Code. Thus, Total Hours would be functionally dependent on Workshop Code.

Primary Key

The **primary key** of a table is the field or minimum collection of fields — the fewest number of fields possible — that uniquely identifies a given row in that table. In the Account Manager table, the account manager's number uniquely identifies a given row. Any account manager number appears on only one row of the table. Thus, Account Manager Number is the primary key. Similarly, Account Number is the primary key of the Account table, and Workshop Code is the primary key of the Workshop table.

CONSIDER THIS

Is the Account Number field the primary key for the Workshop Offerings table?
No, because it does not functionally determine either Total Hours or Hours Spent.

Is the Workshop Code field the primary key for the Workshop Offerings table?
No, because, like Account Number, it does not functionally determine either Total Hours or Hours Spent.

What is the primary key of the Workshop Offerings table?
The primary key is the combination of the Account Number and Workshop Code fields. You can determine all other fields from this combination. Further, neither the Account Number nor the Workshop Code alone has this property.

Is the combination of the Workshop Code and Workshop Description fields the primary key for the Workshop table?
No. Although it is true that you can determine all fields in the Workshop table by this combination, Workshop Code alone also has this property. The Workshop Code field is the primary key.

BTW

Candidate Keys
According to the definition of a candidate key, a Social Security number is a legitimate primary key. Many databases use a person's Social Security number as a primary key. However, many institutions and organizations are moving away from using Social Security numbers because of privacy issues. Instead, many institutions and organizations use unique student numbers or employee numbers as primary keys.

The primary key provides an important way of distinguishing one row in a table from another. In the shorthand representation, you underline the field or collection of fields that comprise the primary key for each table in the database. Thus, the complete shorthand representation for the PrattLast Associates database is shown in Figure 11–6.

Account (<u>Account Number</u>, Account Name, Street, City, State, Postal Code, Amount Paid, Current Due, Account Manager Number)

Account Manager (<u>Account Manager Number</u>, Last Name, First Name, Street, City, State, Postal Code, Salary, Bonus Rate)

Workshop (<u>Workshop Code</u>, Workshop Description, Hours, Increments)

Workshop Offerings (<u>Account Number</u>, <u>Workshop Code</u>, Total Hours, Hours Spent)

Figure 11–6

Occasionally, but not often, there might be more than one possibility for the primary key. For example, if the PrattLast Associates database included the account manager's Social Security number in the Account Manager table, either the account manager number or the Social Security number could serve as the primary key. In this case, both fields are referred to as candidate keys. Similar to a primary key, a **candidate key** is a field or combination of fields on which all fields in the table are functionally dependent. Thus, the definition for primary key really defines candidate key as well. There can be many candidate keys, although having more than one is very rare. By contrast, there is only one primary key. The remaining candidate keys are called **alternate keys**.

Database Design

This section presents a specific database design method, based on a set of requirements that the database must support. The section then presents a sample of such requirements and illustrates the design method by designing a database to satisfy these requirements.

Design Process

The following is a method for designing a database for a set of requirements.

1. Examine the requirements and identify the entities, or objects, involved. Assign names to the entities. The entities will become tables. If, for example, the design involves the entities departments and employees, you could assign the names, Department and Employee. If the design involves the entities accounts, orders, and parts, you could assign the names, Account, Orders, and Part.

NOTE: The word, Order, has special meaning in SQL. If you use it for the name of a table, you will not be able to use SQL to query that table. A common approach to avoid this problem is to make the name plural. That is the reason for choosing Orders rather than Order as the name of the table.

2. Assign a unique identifier to each entity. For example, if one of the entities is "item," you would determine what it takes to uniquely identify each individual item. In other words, what enables the organization to distinguish one item from another? For an item entity, it may be Item Number. For an account entity, it may be Account Number. If there is no such unique identifier, it is a good idea to add one. Perhaps the previous system was a manual one where accounts were not assigned numbers, in which case this would be a good time to add Account Numbers to the system. If there is no natural candidate for a primary key, you can add an AutoNumber field, which is similar to the ID field that Access adds automatically when you create a new table.

3. Identify the attributes for all the entities. These attributes will become the fields in the tables. It is possible that more than one entity has the same attribute. At PrattLast Associates, for example, accounts and account managers both have the attributes of street address, city, state, and postal code. To address this duplication, you can follow the name of the attribute with the corresponding entity in parentheses. Thus, Street (Account) would be the street address of an account, whereas Street (Account Manager) would be the street address of an account manager.

4. Identify the functional dependencies that exist among the attributes.

5. Use the functional dependencies to identify the tables. You do this by placing each attribute with the attribute or minimum combination of attributes on which it is functionally dependent. The attribute or attributes on which all other attributes in the table are dependent will be the primary key of the table. The remaining attributes will be the other fields in the table. Once you have determined all the fields in the table, you can assign an appropriate name to the table.

6. Determine and implement relationships among the entities. The basic relationships are one-to-many and many-to-many.

One-to-many. You implement a one-to-many relationship by including the primary key of the "one" table as a foreign key in the "many" table. A **foreign key** is a field in one table whose values are required to match the *primary key* of another table. In the one-to-many relationship between account managers and accounts, for example, you include the primary key of the Account Manager Table, which is Account Manager Number, as a foreign key in the Account table. You may have already included this field in the earlier steps. If so, you would simply designate it as a foreign key. If you had not already added it, you would need to add it at this point, designating it as a foreign key.

Many-to-many. A many-to-many relationship is implemented by creating a new table whose primary key is the combination of the keys of the original tables. To implement the many-to-many relationship between accounts and workshops, for example, you would create a table whose primary key is the combination of Account Number and Workshop Code, which are the primary keys of the original tables. Both of the fields that make up the primary key of the new table will also be foreign keys. The Account Number field, for example, will be a foreign key required to match the primary key of the Account table. Similarly, the Workshop Code field will be a foreign key required to match the primary key of the Workshop table.

You may have already identified such a table in the earlier steps, in which case, all you need to do is to be sure you have designated each portion of the primary key as a foreign key that is required to match the primary key of the appropriate table. If you have not, you would add the table at this point. The primary key will consist of the primary keys from each of the tables to be related. If there are any attributes that depend on the combination of fields that make up the primary key, you need to include them in this table. (*Note:* There may not be any other fields that are dependent on this combination. In that case, there will be no fields besides the fields that make up the primary key.)

The following sections illustrate the design process by designing the database for PrattLast Associates. The next section gives the requirements that this database must support, and the last section creates a database design based on those requirements.

Requirements for the PrattLast Associates Database

Systems analysts have examined the needs and organizational policies at PrattLast Associates and have determined that the PrattLast Associates database must support the following requirements:

1. For an account, PrattLast needs to maintain the account number, name, street address, city, state, postal code, amount paid, and the amount that is currently due. They also need the total amount, which is the sum of the amount already paid and the current amount due.

2. For an account manager, store the account manager number, last name, first name, street address, city, state, postal code, salary paid, and bonus rate.

3. For a workshop, store the workshop code, workshop description, hours, and increments. In addition, for each offering of the workshop, store the number of the account for whom the workshop is offered, the total number of hours planned for the offering of the workshop, and the number of hours already spent in the workshop. The total hours spent may be the same as the normal total number of hours for the workshop, but it need not be. This gives PrattLast the flexibility of tailoring the offering of the workshop to the specific needs of the account.

4. Each account has a single account manager to which the account is assigned. Each account manager may be assigned many accounts.

5. An account may be offered many workshops and a workshop may be offered to many accounts.

Design of the PrattLast Associates Database

The following represents the application of the design method for the PrattLast Associates requirements.

1. There appear to be three entities: accounts, account managers, and workshops. Reasonable names for the corresponding tables are Account, Account Manager, and Workshop, respectively.

2. The unique identifier for accounts is the account number. The unique identifier for account managers is the account manager number. The unique identifier for workshops is the workshop code. Reasonable names for the unique identifiers are Account Number, Account Manager Number, and Workshop Code, respectively.

3. The attributes are:

Account Number

Account Name

Street (Account)

City (Account)

State (Account)

Postal Code (Account)

Amount Paid

Current Due

Account Manager Number

Last Name

First Name

Street (Account Manager)

City (Account Manager)

State (Account Manager)

Postal Code (Account Manager)

Salary

Bonus Rate

Workshop Code

Workshop Description

Hours

Increments

Total Hours

Hours Spent

Remember that parentheses after an attribute indicate the entity to which the attribute corresponds. Thus, Street (Account) represents the street address of an account in a way that distinguishes it from Street (Account Manager), which represents the street address of an account manager.

CONSIDER THIS

Why is Total Amount not included?
Total Amount, which is Amount Paid plus Current Due, can be calculated from other fields. You can perform this calculation in queries, forms, and reports. Thus, there is no need to include it as a field in the Account table. Further, by including it, you introduce the possibility of errors in the database. For example, if Amount Paid is $5,000, Current Due is $2,000, yet you set Total Amount equal to $8,000, you have an error. You would also need to be sure to change Total Amount appropriately whenever you change either Amount Paid or Current Due. If it is not stored, but rather calculated when needed, you avoid all these problems.

If including the Total Amount field is not appropriate, why did we include the Total Amount field in the Account table in earlier modules?
Access allows calculated fields. Rather than storing a value, you simply indicate the calculation. Access will calculate the value when needed. This approach avoids the above problems, so you actually could include the field. Often, however, you will still decide to not include a calculated field. If you plan to use another database management system, for example, an earlier version of Access, you should not include it. In addition, if you are using Access but plan to use the database with SQL Server, you should not include it.

4. The functional dependencies among the attributes are:

   Account Number → Account Name, Street (Account), City (Account),
      State (Account), Postal Code (Account), Amount Paid,
      Current Due, Account Manager Number

   Account Manager Number → Last Name, First Name, Street (Account
      Manager), City (Account Manager), State (Account Manager),
      Postal Code (Account Manager), Salary, Bonus Rate

   Workshop Code → Workshop Description, Hours, Increments

   Account Number, Workshop Code → Total Hours, Hours Spent

CONSIDER THIS

Why is Total Hours listed with Account Number and Workshop Code rather than just with Workshop Code?
If the total hours were required to be the same as the number of hours for the workshop, then it would indeed be listed with Workshop Code because it would not vary from one account to another. Because PrattLast wants the flexibility of tailoring the number of hours for which a particular workshop is offered to the specific needs of the account, Total Hours is also dependent on Account Number.

The account's name, street address, city, state, postal code, amount paid, and current due are dependent only on account number. Because an account has a single account manager, the account manager number is dependent on account number as well. The account manager's last name, first name, street address, city, state, postal code, salary, and bonus rate are dependent only on account manager number. A workshop description, the number of hours for the workshop, and the increments in which the workshop is offered are dependent only on workshop code. The total hours for a particular workshop offering as well as the hours already spent are dependent on the combination of account number and workshop code.

5. The shorthand representation for the tables is shown in Figure 11–7.

Account (<u>Account Number</u>, Account Name, Street, City, State, Postal Code, Amount Paid, Current Due, Account Manager Number)

Account Manager (<u>Account Manager Number</u>, Last Name, First Name, Street, City, State, Postal Code, Salary, Bonus Rate)

Workshop (<u>Workshop Code</u>, Workshop Description, Hours, Increments)

Workshop Offerings (<u>Account Number</u>, <u>Workshop Code</u>, Total Hours, Hours Spent)

Figure 11–7

6. The following are the relationships between the tables:

a. The Account and Account Manager tables are related using the Account Manager Number fields, which is the primary key of the Account Manager table. The Account Manager Number field in the Account table is a foreign key.

b. The Account and Workshop Offerings tables are related using the Account Number field, which is the primary key of the Account table. The Account Number field in the Workshop Offerings table is a foreign key.

c. The Workshop and Workshop Offerings tables are related using the Workshop Code field, which is the primary key of the Workshop table. The Workshop Code field in the Workshop Offerings table is a foreign key.

Does a many-to-many relationship exist between accounts and workshops?
Yes. The Workshop Offerings table will implement a many-to-many relationship between accounts and workshops. You identified this table as part of the database design process. If you had not, you would need to add it at this point.

In the Workshop Offerings table, the primary key consists of two fields, Account Number and Workshop Code. There are two additional fields, Total Hours and Hours Spent. What if the design requirements did not require these additional fields? Would we still need the Workshop Offerings table?
Yes, because this table implements the many-to-many relationship between accounts and workshops. It is perfectly legitimate for the table that implements a many-to-many relationship to contain no columns except the two columns that constitute the primary key.

In the Workshop Offerings table, the primary key consists of two fields, Account Number and Workshop Code. Does the Account Number field have to come first?
No. The Workshop Code could have come first just as well.

CONSIDER THIS

NOTE: In the shorthand representation for a table containing a foreign key, you would represent the foreign key by using the letters FK, followed by an arrow, followed by the name of the table in which that field is the primary key. For example, to indicate that the Account Manager Number in the Account table is a foreign key that must match the primary key of the Account Manager table, you would write FK Account Manager Number → Account Manager.

The shorthand representation for the tables and foreign keys is shown in Figure 11–8. It is common to list a table containing a foreign key after the table that contains the corresponding primary key, when possible. Thus, in the figure, the Account Manager table has been moved so that it comes before the Account table.

Account Manager (<u>Account Manager Number</u>, Last Name, First Name, Street, City, State, Postal Code, Salary, Bonus Rate)

Account (<u>Account Number</u>, Account Name, Street, City, State, Postal Code, Amount Paid, Current Due, Account Manager Number)
FK Account Manager Number → Account Manager

Workshop (<u>Workshop Code</u>, Workshop Description, Hours, Increments)

Workshop Offerings (<u>Account Number</u>, <u>Workshop Code</u>, Total Hours, Hours Spent)
FK Account Number → Account
FK Workshop Code → Workshop

Figure 11–8

TDK Distributors

The management of TDK Distributors, a distributor of energy-saving and water-conservation items, has determined that the company's rapid growth requires a database to maintain customer, order, and inventory data. With the data stored in a database, management will be able to ensure that the data is current and more accurate. In addition, managers will be able to obtain answers to their questions concerning the data in the database quickly and easily, with the option of producing a variety of reports.

Requirements for the TDK Distributors Database

A system analyst has interviewed users and examined documents at TDK Distributors, and has determined that the company needs a database that will support the following requirements:

1. For a sales rep, store the rep's number, last name, first name, street address, city, state, postal code, total commission, and commission rate.

2. For a customer, store the customer's number, name, street address, city, state, postal code, balance owed, and credit limit. These customers are businesses, so it is appropriate to store a single name, rather than first name and last name as you would if the customers were individuals. Additional fields you need to store are the number, last name, and first name of the sales rep representing this customer. The analyst has also determined that a sales rep can represent many customers, but a customer must have exactly one sales rep. In other words, one sales rep must represent each customer; a customer cannot be represented by zero or more than one sales rep.

3. For an item, store the item's number, description, units on hand, the category the item is in, and the price.

4. For an order, store the order number, order date, the number and name of the customer placing the order, and the number of the sales rep representing that customer. For each line item within an order, store the item's number and description, the number ordered, and the quoted price. The analyst also obtained the following information concerning orders:

a. There is only one customer per order.

b. On a given order, each item is listed as a single line. For example, item DR93 cannot appear on multiple lines within the same order.

c. The quoted price might differ from the actual price in cases in which the sales rep offers a discount for a certain item on a specific order.

Design of the TDK Distributors Database

The following steps apply the design process to the requirements for TDK Distributors to produce the appropriate database design:

1. Assign entity names. There appear to be four entities: reps, customers, items, and orders. The names assigned to these entities are Rep, Customer, Item, and Orders, respectively.

2. Determine unique identifiers. From the collection of entities, review the data and determine the unique identifier for each entity. For the Rep, Customer, Item, and Orders entities, the unique identifiers are the rep number, the customer number, the item number, and the order number, respectively. These unique identifiers are named Rep Number, Customer Number, Item Number, and Order Number, respectively.

3. Assign attribute names. The attributes mentioned in the first requirement all refer to sales reps. The specific attributes mentioned in the requirement are the sales rep's number, last name, first name, street address, city, state, postal code, total commission, and commission rate. Assigning appropriate names to these attributes produces the following list:

> **Rep Number**
>
> **Last Name**
>
> **First Name**
>
> **Street**
>
> **City**
>
> **State**
>
> **Postal Code**
>
> **Commission**
>
> **Rate**

The attributes mentioned in the second requirement refer to customers. The specific attributes are the customer's number, name, street address, city, state, postal code, balance, and credit limit. The requirement also mentions the number, first name, and last name of the sales rep representing this customer. Assigning appropriate names to these attributes produces the following list:

> **Customer Number**
>
> **Customer Name**
>
> **Street**
>
> **City**
>
> **State**

BTW
Line Items
A line item is a unit of information that appears on its own line. For example, when you purchase groceries, each grocery item appears on its own line. Line items also can be referred to as order line items or item detail lines.

Postal Code

Balance

Credit Limit

Rep Number

Last Name

First Name

CONSIDER THIS

Do you need to include the last name and first name of a sales rep in the list of attributes for the second requirement?
There is no need to include them in this list, because they can both be determined from the sales rep number and are already included in the list of attributes determined by Rep Number. They will be removed in a later step.

There are attributes named Street, City, State, and Postal Code for sales reps as well as attributes named Street, City, State, and Postal Code for customers. To distinguish these attributes in the final collection, the name of the attribute is followed by the name of the corresponding entity. For example, the street for a sales rep is Street (Rep) and the street for a customer is Street (Customer).

The attributes mentioned in the third requirement refer to items. The specific attributes are the item's number, description, units on hand, category, and price. Assigning appropriate names to these attributes produces the following list:

Item Number

Description

On Hand

Category

Price

The attributes mentioned in the fourth requirement refer to orders. The specific attributes include the order number, order date, the number and name of the customer placing the order, and the number of the sales rep representing the customer. Assigning appropriate names to these attributes produces the following list:

Order Number

Order Date

Customer Number

Customer Name

Rep Number

The statement concerning orders indicates that there are specific attributes to be stored for each line item within the order. These attributes are the item number, description, the number ordered, and the quoted price. If the quoted price must be the same as the price in the Item table, you could simply call it Price. According to requirement 4c, however, the quoted price might differ from the item price. Thus, you must add the quoted price to the list. Assigning appropriate names to these attributes produces the following list:

Item Number

Description

Number Ordered

Quoted Price

The complete list grouped by entity is as follows:

Rep

    Rep Number

    Last Name

    First Name

    Street (Rep)

    City (Rep)

    State (Rep)

    Postal Code (Rep)

    Commission

    Rate

Customer

    Customer Number

    Customer Name

    Street (Customer)

    City (Customer)

    State (Customer)

    Postal Code (Customer)

    Balance

    Credit Limit

    Rep Number

    Last Name

    First Name

Item

    Item Number

    Description

    On Hand

    Category

    Price

Orders

    Order Number

    Order Date

    Customer Number

    Customer Name

    Rep Number

For line items within an order:

    Order Number

    Item Number

    Description

    Number Ordered

    Quoted Price

4. Identify functional dependencies. The fact that the unique identifier for sales reps is the Rep Number gives the following functional dependencies:

Rep Number → Last Name, First Name, Street (Rep), City (Rep), State (Rep), Postal Code (Rep), Commission, Rate

The fact that the unique identifier for customers is the Customer Number gives the following preliminary list of functional dependencies:

Customer Number → Customer Name, Street (Customer), City (Customer), State (Customer), Postal Code (Customer), Balance, Credit Limit, Rep Number, Last Name, First Name

The fact that the unique identifier for items is the Item Number gives the following functional dependencies:

Item Number → Description, On Hand, Category, Price

The fact that the unique identifier for orders is the Order Number gives the following functional dependencies:

Order Number → Order Date, Customer Number, Customer Name, Rep Number

---

Do you need to include the name of a customer and the number of the customer's rep in the list of attributes determined by the order number?

There is no need to include the customer name and the rep number in this list because you can determine them from the customer number, and they are already included in the list of attributes determined by customer number. They will be removed in the next step.

The final attributes to be examined are those associated with the line items within the order: Item Number, Description, Number Ordered, and Quoted Price.

Why are Number Ordered and Quoted Price not included in the list of attributes determined by the Order Number?

To uniquely identify a particular value for Number Ordered or Quoted Price, Order Number alone is not sufficient. It requires the combination of Order Number and Item Number.

The following shorthand representation indicates that the combination of Order Number and Item Number functionally determines Number Ordered and Quoted Price:

Order Number, Item Number → Number Ordered, Quoted Price

Does Description need to be included in this list?

No, because Description can be determined by the Item Number alone, and it already appears in the list of attributes dependent on the Item Number.

The complete list of functional dependencies with appropriate revisions is as follows:

Rep Number → Last Name, First Name, Street (Rep), City (Rep), State (Rep), Postal Code (Rep), Commission, Rate

Customer Number → **Customer Name, Street (Customer), City (Customer), State (Customer), Postal Code (Customer), Balance, Credit Limit, Rep Number**

Item Number → **Description, On Hand, Category, Price**

Order Number → **Order Date, Customer Number**

Order Number, Item Number → **Number Ordered, Quoted Price**

5. Create the tables. Using the functional dependencies, you can create tables with the attribute(s) to the left of the arrow being the primary key and the items to the right of the arrow being the other fields. For tables corresponding to those entities identified in Step 1, you can simply use the name you already determined. Because you did not identify any entity that had a unique identifier that was the combination of Order Number and Item Number, you need to assign a name to the table whose primary key consists of these two fields. Because this table represents the individual line items within an order, the name Line Item is a good choice. The final collection of tables for TDK Distributors is shown in Figure 11–9.

Rep (<u>Rep Number</u>, Last Name, First Name, Street,
   City, State, Postal Code, Commission, Rate)

Customer (<u>Customer Number</u>, Customer Name, Street,
   City, State, Postal Code, Balance, Credit Limit,
   Rep Number)

Item (<u>Item Number</u>, Description, On Hand, Category, Price)

Orders (<u>Order Number</u>, Order Date, Customer Number)

Line Item (<u>Order Number</u>, <u>Item Number</u>, Number Ordered,
   Quoted Price)

Figure 11–9

6. Identify relationships.

   a. The Customer and Rep tables are related using the Rep Number fields. The Rep Number field in the Rep table is the primary key. The Rep Number field in the Customer table is a foreign key.

   b. The Orders and Customer tables are related using the Customer Number fields. The Customer Number field in the Customer table is the primary key. The Customer Number field in the Orders table is a foreign key.

   c. The Line Item and Orders tables are related using the Order Number fields. The Order Number field in the Orders table is the primary key. The Order Number field in the Line Item table is a foreign key.

   d. The Line Item and Item tables are related using the Item Number fields. The Item Number field in the Item table is the primary key. The Item Number field in the Line Item table is a foreign key.

Does a many-to-many relationship exist between orders and items?
Yes. The Line Item table will implement a many-to-many relationship between orders and items. You identified this table as Line Item in the database design process. If you had not, you would need to add it at this point.

CONSIDER THIS

CONSIDER THIS

In the Line Item table, the primary key consists of two fields, Order Number and Item Number. There are two additional fields, Number Ordered and Quoted Price. What if the design requirements did not require these additional fields? Would we still need the Line Item table?
Yes, because this table implements the many-to-many relationship between orders and items. It is perfectly legitimate for the table that implements a many-to-many relationship to contain only the two columns that constitute the primary key.

The shorthand representation for the tables and foreign keys is shown in Figure 11–10.

Rep (<u>Rep Number</u>, Last Name, First Name, Street,
    City, State, Postal Code, Commission, Rate)

Customer (<u>Customer Number</u>, Customer Name, Street,
    City, State, Postal Code, Balance, Credit Limit,
    Rep Number)
    FK Rep Number → Rep

Item (<u>Item Number</u>, Description, On Hand, Category, Price)

Orders (<u>Order Number</u>, Order Date, Customer Number)
    FK Customer Number → Customer

Line Item (<u>Order Number</u>, <u>Item Number</u>, Number Ordered,
    Quoted Price)
    FK Order Number → Orders
    FK Item Number → Item

Figure 11–10

Sample data for the TDK Distributors database is shown in Figure 11–11.

Rep

Rep Number	Last Name	First Name	Street	City	State	Postal Code	Commission	Rate
20	Kaiser	Valerie	624 Randall	Georgetown	NC	28794	$2,542.50	0.05
35	Hull	Richard	532 Jackson	Kyle	SC	28797	$3,216.00	0.07
65	Perez	Juan	1626 Taylor	Byron	SC	28795	$2,487.00	0.05

Customer

Customer Number	Customer Name	Street	City	State	Postal Code	Balance	Credit Limit	Rep Number
148	Al's Hardware Store	2837 Greenway	Oxford	TN	37021	$2,550.00	$7,500.00	20
282	Brookings Direct	3827 Devon	Ashton	VA	20123	$431.50	$2,500.00	35
356	Ferguson's	382 Wildwood	Georgetown	NC	28794	$2,785.00	$7,500.00	65
408	The Energy Shop	1828 Raven	Granger	NC	27036	$1,285.25	$5,000.00	35
462	Walburg Energy Alternatives	12 Polk	Walburg	NC	28819	$1,412.00	$2,500.00	65
524	Kline's	838 Ridgeland	Oxford	TN	37021	$3,762.00	$7,500.00	20
608	Conservation Foundation	372 Oxford	Ashton	VA	20123	$106.00	$5,000.00	65
687	CleanPlanet	282 Evergreen	Lowton	TN	37084	$2,851.00	$5,000.00	35
725	Patricia Jean's Home Center	282 Columbia	Walburg	NC	28819	$248.00	$7,500.00	35
842	The Efficient Home	28 Lakeview	Pineville	VA	22503	$4,221.00	$7,500.00	20

Figure 11–11 (Continued)

Orders

Order Number	Order Date	Customer Number
12608	4/5/2018	148
12610	4/5/2018	356
12613	4/6/2018	408
12614	4/6/2018	282
12617	4/8/2018	608
12619	4/8/2018	148
12623	4/8/2018	608

Item

Item Number	Description	On Hand	Category	Price
AT94	Air Deflector	50	General	$5.45
BV06	Energy Saving Kit	45	Energy	$42.75
CD52	Fluorescent Light Bulb	65	Energy	$4.75
DL71	Low Flow Shower Head	21	Water	$8.75
DR93	Smoke Detector	38	General	$6.10
DW11	Retractable Clothesline	12	General	$13.25
FD21	Water Conservation Kit	22	Water	$13.45
KL62	Toilet Tank Water Saver	32	Water	$3.35
KT03	Programmable Thermostat	8	Energy	$34.25
KV29	Windows Insulator Kit	19	Energy	$4.95

Line Item

Order Number	Item Number	Number Ordered	Quoted Price
12608	AT94	11	$5.45
12610	DR93	5	$6.10
12610	DW11	3	$12.50
12613	KL62	10	$3.35
12614	KT03	6	$33.00
12617	BV06	2	$40.25
12617	CD52	20	$4.25
12619	DR93	12	$6.00
12623	KV29	8	$4.95

Figure 11–11

Normalization

After you create your database design, you should analyze it using a process called **normalization** to make sure the design is free of potential update, redundancy, and consistency problems. This process also supplies methods for correcting these problems.

The normalization process involves converting tables into various types of **normal forms**. A table in a particular normal form possesses a certain desirable set of properties. Several normal forms exist, the most common being first normal form (1NF), second normal form (2NF), and third normal form (3NF). The forms create a progression in which a table that is in 1NF is better than a table that is not in 1NF;

a table that is in 2NF is better than one that is in 1NF; and so on. The goal of normalization is to take a table or collection of tables and produce a new collection of tables that represents the same information but is free of problems.

First Normal Form

A table that contains a **repeating group**, or multiple entries for a single row, is called an **unnormalized table**. Recall from the definition of relation that an unnormalized table actually violates the definition of relation.

Removal of repeating groups is the starting point in the goal of having tables that are as free of problems as possible. In fact, in most database management systems, tables cannot contain repeating groups. A table (relation) is in **first normal form (1NF)** if it does not contain repeating groups.

In designing a database, you may have created a table with a repeating group. For example, you might have created a Workshop Offerings table in which the primary key is the Account Number and there is a repeating group consisting of Workshop Code, Total Hours, and Hours Spent. In the example, each account appears on a single row and Workshop Code, Total Hours, and Hours Spent are repeated as many times as necessary for each account (Figure 11–12).

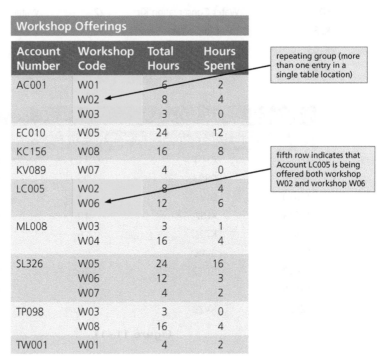

Figure 11–12

In the shorthand representation, you represent a repeating group by enclosing the repeating group within parentheses. The shorthand representation for the Workshop Offerings table from Figure 11–12 is shown in Figure 11–13.

Workshop Offerings (<u>Account Number</u>, (Workshop Code, Total Hours, Hours Spent))

Figure 11–13

Conversion to First Normal Form

Figure 11–14 shows the normalized version of the table. Note that the fifth row of the unnormalized table (Figure 11–12) indicates that account LC005 is currently being offered both workshop W02 and workshop W06. In the normalized table, this information is represented by *two* rows, the seventh and the eighth. The primary key for the unnormalized Workshop Offerings table was the Account Number only. The primary key for the normalized table is now the combination of Account Number and Workshop Code.

Workshop Offerings			
Account Number	Workshop Code	Total Hours	Hours Spent
AC001	W01	6	2
AC001	W02	8	4
AC001	W03	3	0
EC010	W05	24	12
KC156	W08	16	8
KV089	W07	4	0
LC005	W02	8	4
LC005	W06	12	6
ML008	W03	3	1
ML008	W04	16	4
SL326	W05	24	16
SL326	W06	12	3
SL326	W07	4	2
TP098	W03	3	0
TP098	W08	16	4
TW001	W01	4	2

seventh row indicates that Account LC005 is being offered workshop W02

eighth row indicates that Account LC005 is being offered workshop W06

Figure 11–14

In general, when converting a non-1NF table to 1NF, the primary key will typically include the original primary key concatenated with the key of the repeating group, that is, the field that distinguishes one occurrence of the repeating group from another within a given row in the table. In this case, Workshop Code is the key to the repeating group and thus becomes part of the primary key of the 1NF table.

To convert the table to 1NF, remove the parentheses enclosing the repeating group and expand the primary key to include the key to the repeating group. The shorthand representation for the resulting table is shown in Figure 11–15. Notice that the primary key is now the combination of the Account Number field and the Workshop Code field.

Workshop Offerings (<u>Account Number</u>, <u>Workshop Code</u>, Total Hours, Hours Spent)

Figure 11–15

Second Normal Form

Even though the following table is in 1NF, problems may exist that will cause you to want to restructure the table. In the database design process, for example, you might have created the Workshop Offerings table shown in Figure 11–16.

Workshop Offerings (<u>Account Number</u>, Account Name, <u>Workshop Code</u>, Workshop Description, Total Hours, Hours Spent)

Figure 11–16

This table contains the following functional dependencies:

Account Number → Account Name

Workshop Code → Workshop Description

Account Number, Workshop Code → Total Hours, Hours Spent

This notation indicates that Account Number alone determines Account Name, and Workshop Code alone determines Workshop Description, but it requires *both* an Account Number *and* a Workshop Code to determine either Total Hours or Hours Spent. Figure 11–17 shows a sample of this table.

description of workshop W06 occurs more than once

Account					
Account Number	**Account Name**	**Workshop Code**	**Workshop Description**	**Total Hours**	**Hours Spent**
AC001	Avondale Community Bank	W01	Dealing with Unacceptable Employee Behavior	6	2
AC001	Avondale Community Bank	W02	Writing Effective Policies and Procedures	8	4
AC001	Avondale Community Bank	W03	Payroll Law	3	0
EC010	Eco Clothes Inc.	W05	The Recruitment Process	24	12
KC156	Key Community College System	W08	Workers' Compensation	16	8
KV089	KAL Veterinary Services	W07	Americans with Disabilities Act (ADA)	4	0
LC005	Lancaster County Hospital	W02	Writing Effective Policies and Procedures	8	4
LC005	Lancaster County Hospital	W06	Diversity in the Workplace	12	6
ML008	Mums Landscaping Co.	W03	Payroll Law	3	1
ML008	Mums Landscaping Co.	W04	Workplace Safety	16	4
SL326	South Library Consortium	W05	The Recruitment Process	24	16
SL326	South Library Consortium	W06	Diversity in the Workplace	12	3
SL326	South Library Consortium	W07	Americans with Disabilities Act (ADA)	4	2
TP098	TDK Packaging Systems	W03	Payroll Law	3	0
TP098	TDK Packaging Systems	W08	Workers' Compensation	16	4
TW001	Tri-County Waste Disposal	W01	Dealing with Unacceptable Employee Behavior	4	2

name of Account LC005 occurs more than once

Figure 11–17

The name of a specific account, LC005 for example, occurs multiple times in the table, as does the description of a workshop. This redundancy causes several problems. It is certainly wasteful of space, but that is not nearly as serious as some of the other problems. These other problems are called **update anomalies**, and they fall into four categories:

1. **Update.** A change to the name of account LC005 requires not one change to the table, but several: you must change each row in which LC005 appears. This certainly makes the update process much more cumbersome; it is logically more complicated and takes longer to update.

2. **Inconsistent data.** There is nothing about the design that would prohibit account LC005 from having two or more different names in the database. The first row, for example, might have Lancaster County Hospital as the name, whereas the second row might have Lancaster Community Hospital.

3. **Additions.** There is a real problem when you try to add a new workshop and its description to the database. Because the primary key for the table consists of both Account Number and Workshop Code, you need values for both of these to add a new row. If you have an account to add but there are so far no workshops scheduled for it, what do you use for a Workshop Code? The only solution would be to make up a placeholder Workshop Code and then replace it with a real Workshop Code once the account requests a workshop. This is certainly not an acceptable solution.

4. **Deletions.** In Figure 11–17, if you delete workshop W01 from the database, you would need to delete all rows on which the Workshop Code is W01. In the process, you will delete the only row on which account TW001 appears, so you would also *lose* all the information about account TW001. You would no longer know that the name of account TW001 is Tri-County Waste Disposal.

These problems occur because there is a field, Account Name, that is dependent only on an Account Number, which is just a portion of the primary key. There is a similar problem with Workshop Description, which depends only on the Workshop Code, not the complete primary key. This leads to the definition of second normal form. Second normal form represents an improvement over first normal form because it eliminates update anomalies in these situations. In order to understand second normal form, you need to understand the term, nonkey field.

A field is a **nonkey field**, also called a **nonkey attribute**, if it is not a part of the primary key. A table (relation) is in **second normal form (2NF)** if it is in first normal form and no nonkey field is dependent on only a portion of the primary key.

Note that if the primary key of a table contains only a single field, the table is automatically in second normal form. In that case, there could not be any field dependent on only a portion of the primary key.

Conversion to Second Normal Form

To correct the problems, convert the table to a collection of tables in second normal form. Then name the new tables. The following is a method for performing this conversion.

1. Take each subset of the set of fields that make up the primary key and begin a new table with this subset as its primary key. The result of applying this step to the Workshop Offerings table is shown in Figure 11–18.

(Account Number,
(Workshop Code,
(Account Number, Workshop Code,

Figure 11–18

2. Place each of the other fields with the appropriate primary key; that is, place each one with the minimal collection of fields on which it depends. The result of applying this step to the Workshop Offerings table is shown in Figure 11–19.

(<u>Account Number</u>, Account Name)

(<u>Workshop Code</u>, Workshop Description)

(<u>Account Number</u>, <u>Workshop Code</u>, Total Hours, Hours Spent)

Figure 11–19

3. Give each of these new tables a name that is descriptive of the meaning of the table, such as Account, Workshop, and Workshop Offerings.

   Figure 11–20 shows samples of the tables.

Account	
AC #	**Account Name**
AC001	Avondale Community Bank
BL235	Bland Corp.
CA043	Carlton Regional Clinic
CO621	Codder Plastics Co.
EC010	Eco Clothes Inc.
HL111	Halko Legal Associates
KC156	Key Community College System
KV089	KAL Veterinary Services
LC005	Lancaster County Hospital
LI268	Lars-Idsen-Fleming Inc.
MI345	Midwest Library Consortium
ML008	Mums Landscaping Co.
SL326	South Library Consortium
TP098	TDK Packaging Systems
TW001	Tri-County Waste Disposal

name of Account LC005 occurs only once

Workshop	
Workshop Code	**Workshop Description**
W01	Dealing with Unacceptable Employee Behavior
W02	Writing Effective Policies and Procedures
W03	Payroll Law
W04	Workplace Safety
W05	The Recruitment Process
W06	Diversity in the Workplace
W07	Americans with Disabilities Act (ADA)
W08	Workers' Compensation

description of workshop W06 occurs only once

Figure 11–20 (Continued)

Workshop Offerings			
Account Number	Workshop Code	Total Hours	Hours Spent
AC001	W01	6	2
AC001	W02	8	4
AC001	W03	3	0
EC010	W05	24	12
KC156	W08	16	8
KV089	W07	4	0
LC005	W02	8	4
LC005	W06	12	6
ML008	W03	3	1
ML008	W04	16	4
SL326	W05	24	16
SL326	W06	12	3
SL326	W07	4	2
TP098	W03	3	0
TP098	W08	16	4
TW001	W01	4	2

Figure 11–20

The new design eliminates the update anomalies. An account name occurs only once for each account, so you do not have the redundancy that you did in the earlier design. Changing the name of an account is now a simple process involving a single change. Because the name of an account occurs in a single place, it is not possible to have multiple names for the same account in the database at the same time.

To add a new account, you create a new row in the Account table, and thus there is no need to have a workshop offering already scheduled for that account. In addition, deleting workshop W01 has nothing to do with the Account table and, consequently, does not cause account TW001 to be deleted. Thus, you still have its name, Tri-County Waste Disposal, in the database. Finally, you have not lost any information in the process.

CONSIDER THIS

Can I reconstruct the data in the original design from the data in the new design?
Yes, and SQL is the best way to accomplish this. The following SQL query would produce the data in the form shown in Figure 11–17:

```
SELECT [Account].[Account Number], [Account Name],
   [Workshop].[Workshop Code], [Workshop Description],
   [Total Hours], [Hours Spent]
FROM [Account],[Workshop],[Workshop Offerings]
WHERE [Account].[Account Number]=
   [Workshop Offerings].[Account Number]
AND [Workshop].[Workshop Code]=
   [Workshop Offerings].[Workshop Code];
```

BTW
3NF
The definition given for third normal form is not the original definition. This more recent definition, which is preferable to the original, is often referred to as Boyce-Codd normal form (BCNF) when it is important to make a distinction between this definition and the original definition. This text does not make such a distinction but will take this to be the definition of third normal form.

Third Normal Form

Problems can still exist with tables that are in 2NF, as illustrated in the Account table whose shorthand representation is shown in Figure 11–21.

Account (<u>Account Number</u>, Account Name, Street, City, State, Postal Code, Amount Paid, Current Due, Account Manager Number, Last Name, First Name)

Figure 11–21

The functional dependencies in this table are:

Account Number → Account Name, Street, City, State, Postal Code, Amount Paid, Current Due, Account Manager Number, Last Name, First Name

Account Manager Number → Last Name, First Name

As these dependencies indicate, Account Number determines all the other fields. In addition, Account Manager Number determines Last Name and First Name.

Because the primary key of the table is a single field, the table is automatically in second normal form. As the sample of the table shown in Figure 11–22 demonstrates, however, this table has problems similar to those encountered earlier, even though it is in 2NF. In this case, it is the last name and first name of a manager that can occur many times in the table; see manager 31, Haydee Rivera, for example. (Note that the three dots represent fields that do not appear due to space limitations.)

Account

Account Number	Account Name	...	Amount Paid	Current Due	Account Manager Number	Last Name	First Name
AC001	Avondale Community Bank	...	$24,752.25	$3,875.25	31	Rivera	Haydee
BL235	Bland Corp.	...	$29,836.65	$2,765.30	35	Simson	Mark
CA043	Carlton Regional Clinic	...	$30,841.05	$3,074.30	58	Murowski	Karen
CO621	Codder Plastics Co.	...	$27,152.25	$2,875.00	35	Simson	Mark
EC010	Eco Clothes Inc.	...	$19,620.00	$1,875.00	58	Murowski	Karen
HL111	Halko Legal Associates	...	$25,702.20	$3,016.75	58	Murowski	Karen
KC156	Key Community College System	...	$10,952.25	$0.00	31	Rivera	Haydee
KV089	KAL Veterinary Services	...	$34,036.50	$580.00	35	Simson	Mark
LC005	Lancaster County Hospital	...	$44,025.60	$3,590.80	58	Murowski	Karen
LI268	Lars-Idsen-Fleming Inc.	...	$0.00	$1,280.75	35	Simson	Mark
MI345	Midwest Library Consortium	...	$21,769.20	$2,890.60	31	Rivera	Haydee
ML008	Mums Landscaping Co.	...	$13,097.10	$2,450.00	35	Simson	Mark
SL326	South Library Consortium	...	$0.00	$0.00	58	Murowski	Karen
TP098	TDK Packaging Systems	...	$22,696.95	$3,480.45	58	Murowski	Karen
TW001	Tri-County Waste Disposal	...	$15,345.00	$2,875.50	31	Rivera	Haydee

Figure 11–22

name of manager 31 occurs more than once

This redundancy results in the same set of problems described previously with the Workshop Offerings table. In addition to the problem of wasted space, you have similar update anomalies, as follows:

1. **Updates.** A change to the name of a manager requires not one change to the table, but several changes. Again, the update process becomes very cumbersome.

2. **Inconsistent data.** There is nothing about the design that would prohibit a manager from having two different names in the database. On the first row, for example, the name for manager 31 might read Haydee Rivera, whereas on the third row (another row on which the manager number is 31), the name might be Haydee Muniz.

3. **Additions.** In order to add rep 71, whose name is Marilyn Webb, to the database, she must have at least one account. If she has not yet been assigned any accounts, either you cannot record the fact that her name is Marilyn Webb, or you have to create a fictitious account for her to represent. Again, this is not a desirable solution to the problem.

4. **Deletions.** If you were to delete all the accounts of manager 31 from the database, then you would also lose all information concerning manager 31.

These update anomalies are due to the fact that Account Manager Number determines Last Name and First Name, but Account Manager Number is not the primary key. As a result, the same Account Manager Number and consequently the same Last Name and First Name can appear on many different rows.

You have seen that 2NF is an improvement over 1NF, but to eliminate 2NF problems, you need an even better strategy for creating tables in the database. Third normal form provides that strategy.

Before looking at third normal form, you need to become familiar with the special name that is given to any field that determines another field, like Account Manager Number in the Account table. Any field or collection of fields that determines another field is called a **determinant**. Certainly the primary key in a table is a determinant. Any candidate key is a determinant as well. (Remember that a candidate key is a field or collection of fields that could function as the primary key.) In this case, Account Manager Number is a determinant, but because several rows in the Account table could have the same Account Manager Number, that field is not a candidate key for the Account table shown in Figure 11–22, and that is the problem.

A table is in **third normal form** (3NF) if it is in second normal form and if the only determinants it contains are candidate keys.

Conversion to Third Normal Form

You have now identified the problem with the Account table: it is not in 3NF. You need a way to correct the deficiency in the Account table and in all tables having similar deficiencies. Such a method follows.

First, for each determinant that is not a candidate key, remove from the table the fields that depend on this determinant, but do not remove the determinant. Next, create a new table containing all the fields from the original table that depend on this determinant. Finally, make the determinant the primary key of this new table.

In the Account table, for example, Last Name and First Name are removed because they depend on the determinant Account Manager Number, which is not a candidate key. A new table is formed, consisting of Account Manager Number as the primary key, Last Name, and First Name. Specifically, you would replace the Account table in Figure 11–22 with the two tables shown in Figure 11–23.

Account (<u>Account Number</u>, Account Name, Street, City, State, Postal Code,
Amount Paid, Current Due, Account Manager Number)

Account Manager (<u>Account Manager Number</u>, Last Name, First Name)

Figure 11–23

Figure 11–24 shows samples of the tables.

Account					
Account Number	**Account Name**	**...**	**Amount Paid**	**Current Due**	**Account Manager Number**
AC001	Avondale Community Bank	...	$24,752.25	$3,875.25	31
BL235	Bland Corp.	...	$29,836.65	$2,765.30	35
CA043	Carlton Regional Clinic	...	$30,841.05	$3,074.30	58
CO621	Codder Plastics Co.	...	$27,152.25	$2,875.00	35
EC010	Eco Clothes Inc.	...	$19,620.00	$1,875.00	58
HL111	Halko Legal Associates	...	$25,702.20	$3,016.75	58
KC156	Key Community College System	...	$10,952.25	$0.00	31
KV089	KAL Veterinary Services	...	$34,036.50	$580.00	35
LC005	Lancaster County Hospital	...	$44,025.60	$3,590.80	58
LI268	Lars-Idsen-Fleming Inc.	...	$0.00	$1,280.75	35
MI345	Midwest Library Consortium	...	$21,769.20	$2,890.60	31
ML008	Mums Landscaping Co.	...	$13,097.10	$2,450.00	35
SL326	South Library Consortium	...	$0.00	$0.00	58
TP098	TDK Packaging Systems	...	$22,696.95	$3,480.45	58
TW001	Tri-County Waste Disposal	...	$15,345.00	$2,875.50	31

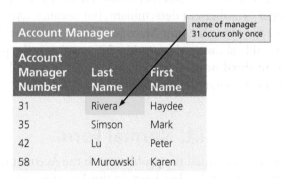

name of manager
31 occurs only once

Account Manager		
Account Manager Number	**Last Name**	**First Name**
31	Rivera	Haydee
35	Simson	Mark
42	Lu	Peter
58	Murowski	Karen

Figure 11–24

This design corrects the previously identified problems. A manager's name appears only once, thus avoiding redundancy and making the process of changing a manager's name a very simple one. With this design, it is not possible for a manager to have two different names in the database. To add a new account manager to the database, you add a row in the Account Manager table; it is not necessary to have a pre-existing account for the manager. Finally, deleting all the accounts of a given manager will not remove the manager's record from the Account Manager table, so you retain the manager's name; all the data in the original table can be reconstructed from the data in the new collection of tables. All previously mentioned problems have indeed been solved.

Can I reconstruct the data in the original design from the data in the new design?
Yes. The following SQL query would produce the data in the form shown in Figure 11–22:

```
SELECT [Account Number], [Account Name], [Street],
  [City], [State], [Postal Code], [Amount Paid],
  [Current Due], [Account].[Account Manager Number],
  [Last Name], [First Name]
FROM [Account],[Account Manager]
WHERE [Account].[Account Manager Number]=
  [Account Manager].[Account Manager Number];
```

Special Topics

In addition to knowing how to design a database and how to normalize tables, there are two other topics with which you should be familiar. First, you may be given a requirement for a database in the form of a document that the database must be capable of producing; for example, an invoice. In addition, you should know how to represent your design with a diagram.

BTW
Existing Documents
Other examples of existing documents would be purchase orders, procedure manuals, organizational policy manuals, inventory lists, and so on.

Obtaining Information from Existing Documents

Existing documents can often furnish helpful information concerning the database design. You need to know how to obtain information from the document that you will then use in the design process. An existing document, like the invoice for the company named TDK Distributors shown in Figure 11–25, will often provide the details that determine the tables and fields required to produce the document.

The first step in obtaining information from an existing document is to identify and list all fields and give them appropriate names. You also need to understand the business policies of the organization. For example, in the order shown in Figure 11–25, the information on TDK Distributors is preprinted on the form, and it is not necessary to describe the company. The following is a list of the fields you can determine from the invoice shown in Figure 11–25.

> **Order Number**
> **Order Date**
> **Customer Number**
> **Customer Name**
> **Street (Customer)**
> **City (Customer)**
> **State (Customer)**
> **Postal Code (Customer)**
> **Rep Number**
> **Last Name (Rep)**
> **First Name (Rep)**
> **Item Number**
> **Description**
> **Number Ordered**
> **Price**
> Total
> **Order Total**

INVOICE

TDK Distributors

543 Main Street
Kyle, SC 28797
Phone (803)-555-0190 Fax (803)-555-0191

ORDER: 12617
DATE: APRIL 8, 2018

TO:
Customer: 462
Walburg Energy Alternatives
12 Polk
Walburg, NC 28819

SALES REP: 65
Juan Perez

ITEM NUMBER	DESCRIPTION	NUMBER ORDERED	PRICE	TOTAL
BV06	Energy Saving Kit	2	40.25	80.50
CD52	Fluorescent Light Bulb	20	4.25	85.00
		TOTAL		165.50

Make all checks payable to TDK Distributors
Total due in 15 days. Overdue accounts subject to a service charge of 1% per month.

Thank you for your business!

Figure 11–25

Next, you need to identify functional dependencies. If the document you are examining is unfamiliar to you, you may have difficulty determining the dependencies and may need to get all the information directly from the user. On the other hand, you can often make intelligent guesses based on your general knowledge of the type of document you are studying. You may make mistakes, of course, and these should be corrected when you interact with the user. After initially determining the functional dependencies, you may discover additional information. The following are possible initial functional dependencies:

Customer Number → Customer Name, Street (Customer), City (Customer), State (Customer), Postal Code (Customer), Rep Number, Last Name (Rep), First Name (Rep)

Item Number → Description, Price

Order Number → Order Date, Customer Number, Order Total

Order Number, Item Number → Number Ordered, Price, Total

You may find, for example, that the price for a particular item on an order need not be the same as the standard price for the item. If that is the case, Price and Total are functionally dependent on the combination of Order Number and Item Number, not just Item Number alone. You may also decide to change the field name to Quoted Price to indicate the fact that it can vary from one order to another.

For the same reasons that you did not include Total Amount in the PrattLast Associates database, you would probably not want to include either Total or Order Total. Both can be computed from other data. The other correction that you should make to the functional dependencies is to realize that the last name and first name of a rep depend on the data in the Rep Number field.

Given these corrections, a revised list of functional dependencies might look like the following:

Rep Number → Last Name, First Name

Customer Number → Customer Name, Street (Customer), City (Customer), State (Customer), Postal Code (Customer), Rep Number

Item Number → Description, Price

Order Number → Order Date, Customer Number

Order Number, Item Number → Number Ordered, Quoted Price

After you have determined the preliminary functional dependencies, you can begin determining the tables and assigning fields. You could create tables with the determinant – the field or fields to the left of the arrow – as the primary key and with the fields to the right of the arrow as the remaining fields. This would lead to the following initial collection of tables shown in Figure 11–26.

Rep (Rep Number, Last Name, First Name)

Customer (Customer Number, Customer Name, Street, City, State, Postal Code, Rep Number)

Item (Item Number, Description, Price)

Orders (Order Number, Order Date, Customer Number)

OrderLine (Order Number, Item Number, Number Ordered, Quoted Price)

Figure 11–26

Adding the foreign key information produces the shorthand representation shown in Figure 11–27.

Rep (<u>Rep Number</u>, Last Name, First Name)

Customer (<u>Customer Number</u>, Customer Name, Street, City, State, Postal Code,
  Rep Number)
  FK Rep Number → Rep

Item (<u>Item Number</u>, Description, Price)

Orders (<u>Order Number</u>, Order Date, Customer Number)
  FK Account Number → Customer

OrderLine (<u>Order Number</u>, <u>Item Number</u>, Number Ordered, Quoted Price)
  FK Order Number → Orders
  FK Item Number → Item

Figure 11–27

BTW
Merging Entities
When you merge entities, do not assume that the merged entities will be in 3NF. Apply normalization techniques to convert all entities to 3NF.

At this point, you would need to verify that all the tables are in third normal form. If any are not in 3NF, you need to convert them. If you had not determined the functional dependency of Last Name and First Name on Rep Number earlier, for example, you would have had Last Name and First Name as fields in the Account table. These fields are dependent on Rep Number, making Rep Number a determinant that is not a primary key, which would violate third normal form. Once you converted that table to 3NF, you would have the tables shown in Figure 11–27.

You may have already created some tables in your database design. For example, you may have obtained financial data on customers from the Accounting department. If so, you would need to merge the tables in Figure 11–27 with those tables you already created. To merge tables, you combine tables that have the same primary key. The new table contains all the fields in either individual table and does not repeat fields that are present in both tables. Figure 11–28, for example, illustrates the merging of two tables that both have the Customer Number field as the primary key. In addition to the primary key, the result contains the Customer Name and Rep Number fields, which are included in both of the original tables; the Street, City, State, and Postal Code fields, which are only in the first table; and the Balance and Credit Limit fields, which are only in the second table. The order in which you decide to list the fields is immaterial.

Merging

Customer (<u>Customer Number</u>, Account Name, Street, City, State, Postal Code,
  Rep Number)

and

Customer (<u>Customer Number</u>, Customer Name, Balance, Credit Limit, Rep Number)

gives

Customer (<u>Customer Number</u>, Customer Name, Street, City, State, Postal Code,
  Balance, Credit Limit, Rep Number)

Figure 11–28

Diagrams for Database Design

You have now seen how to represent a database design as a list of tables, fields, primary keys, and foreign keys. It is often helpful to also be able to represent a database design with a diagram. If you have already created the database and relationships in Access, the Relationships window and Relationships report provide a helpful diagram of the design. Figure 11–29 shows the Access Relationship diagram and report for the PrattLast Associates database. In these diagrams, rectangles represent tables. The fields in the table are listed in the corresponding rectangle with a key symbol appearing in front of the primary key. Relationships are represented by lines with the "one" end of the relationship represented by the number, 1, and the "many" end represented by the infinity symbol (∞).

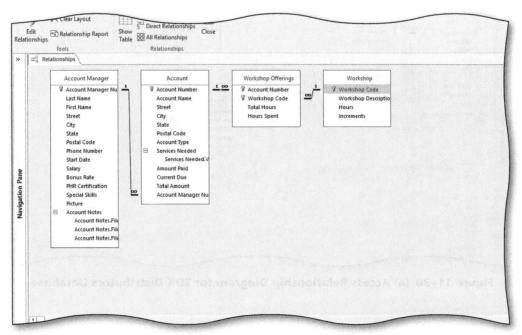

Figure 11–29 (a) Access Relationship Diagram for PrattLast Associates Database

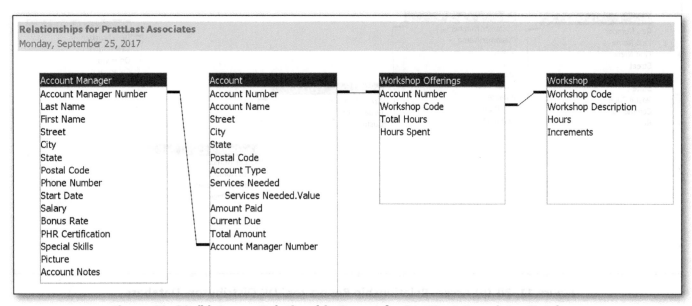

Figure 11–29 (b) Access Relationship Report for PrattLast Associates Database

Figure 11–30 shows the Access Relationship diagram and report for the TDK Distributors database.

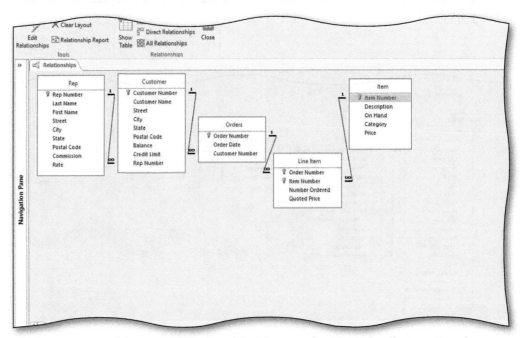

Figure 11–30 (a) Access Relationship Diagram for TDK Distributors Database

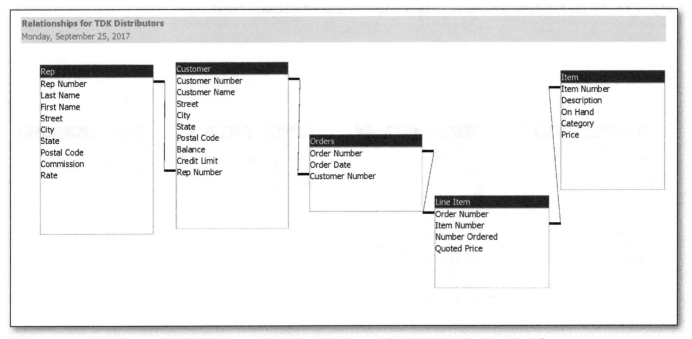

Figure 11–30 (b) Access Relationship Report for TDK Distributors Database

Another popular option for diagramming a database design is the **entity-relationship diagram (ERD)**. Figure 11–31 shows a sample ERD for the PrattLast Associates database. In this type of diagram, rectangles represent the tables. The primary key is listed within the table above a line. Below the line are the other fields in the table. The arrow goes from the rectangle that represents the many part of the relationship to the one part of the relationship.

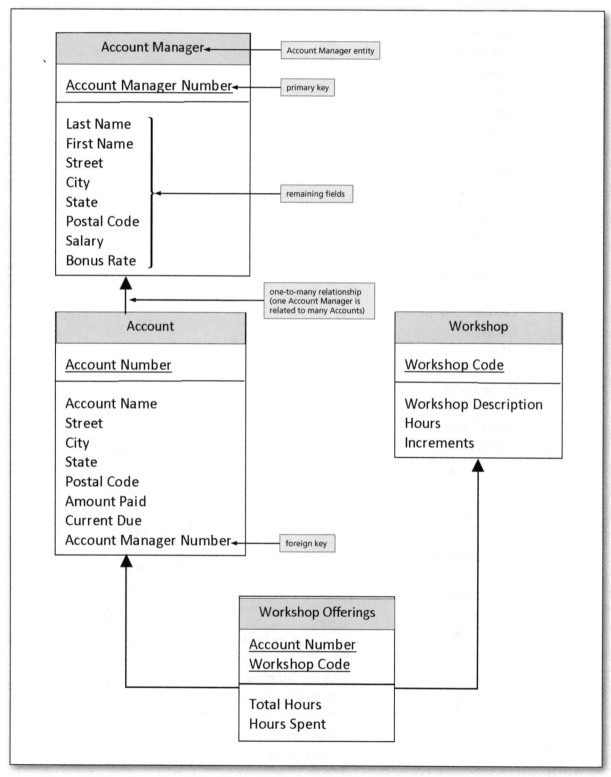

Figure 11–31

Figure 11–32 shows a similar diagram for the TDK Distributors database.

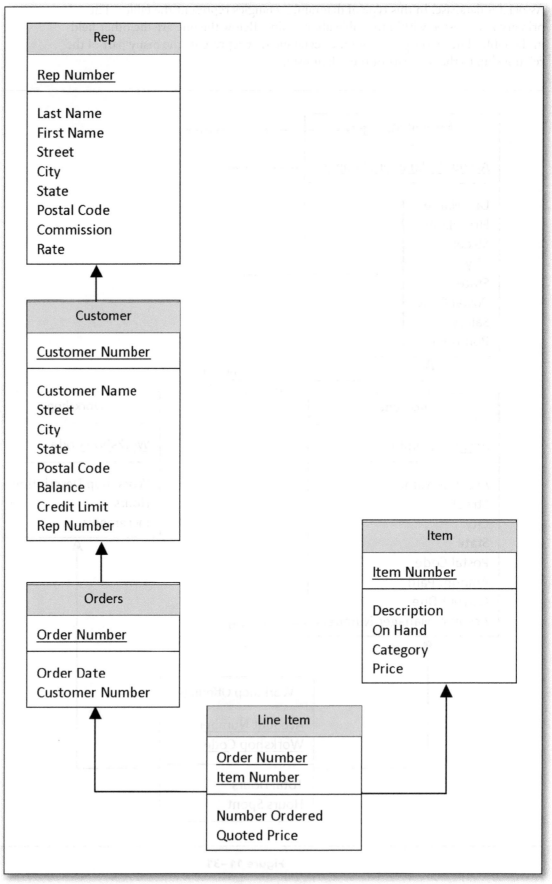

Figure 11–32

There are many options for such diagrams. Some options include more detail than shown in the figure. You can include, for example, such details as data types and indexes. Other options have less detail, showing only the name of the table in the rectangle, for example. There are also other options for the appearance of the lines representing relationships.

Summary

In this module, you have learned the following concepts.

1. An entity is a person, place, thing, or event. An attribute is a property of an entity. A relationship is an association between entities.

2. A relation is a two-dimensional table in which the entries in the table are single-valued, each column has a distinct name, all values in a column are values of the same attribute (that is, all entries must correspond to the column name), and each row is distinct.

3. In a relation, the order of columns is immaterial. You can view the columns in any order you want. The order of rows is also immaterial. You can view the rows in any order you want.

4. A relational database is a collection of relations.

5. Rows in a table (relation) are often called records or tuples. Columns in a table (relation) are often called fields or attributes. Typically, the terms *record* and *field* are used in Access.

6. If you know that whenever you are given a value for one field, you will be able to determine a single value for a second field, then the first field is said to determine the second field. In addition, the second field is said to be functionally dependent on the first.

7. The primary key of a table is the field or minimum collection of fields that uniquely identifies a given row in that table.

8. The following is a method for designing a database for a set of requirements.

   a. Examine the requirements and identify the entities (objects) involved. Assign names to the entities.
   b. Identify a unique identifier for each entity.
   c. Identify the attributes for all the entities. These attributes will become the fields in the tables.
   d. Identify the functional dependencies that exist among the attributes.
   e. Use the functional dependencies to identify the tables.
   f. Identify any relationships between tables by looking for matching fields where one of the fields is a primary key. The other field will then be a foreign key. In the shorthand representation for the table containing the primary key, represent the foreign key by using the letters FK, followed by an arrow, followed by the name of the table containing the primary key.

9. A table (relation) is in first normal form (1NF) if it does not contain repeating groups.

10. To convert a table to 1NF, remove the parentheses enclosing the repeating group and expand the primary key to include the key to the repeating group.

11. A field is a nonkey field (also called a nonkey attribute) if it is not a part of the primary key. A table (relation) is in second normal form (2NF) if it is in first normal form and no nonkey field is dependent on only a portion of the primary key.

12. To convert a table to 2NF, take each subset of the set of fields that make up the primary key and begin a new table with this subset as its primary key. Place each of the other fields with the appropriate primary key; that is, place each one with the minimal collection of fields on which it depends. Give each of these new tables a name that is descriptive of the meaning of the table.

13. Any field (or collection of fields) that determines another field is called a determinant. A table is in third normal form (3NF) if it is in second normal form and if the only determinants it contains are candidate keys.

14. To convert a table to 3NF, for each determinant that is not a candidate key, remove from the table the fields that depend on this determinant, but do not remove the determinant. Create a new table containing all the fields from the original table that depend on this determinant and make the determinant the primary key of this new table.

15. An entity-relationship diagram (ERD) is a diagram used to represent database designs. In ERDs, rectangles represent tables and lines between rectangles represent one-to-many relationships between the corresponding tables. You can also diagram a database design by using the Access relationship window.

CONSIDER THIS

How should you submit solutions to questions in the assignments identified with a symbol?

Every assignment in this book contains one or more questions identified with a symbol. These questions require you to think beyond the assigned database. Present your solutions to the questions in the format required by your instructor. Possible formats may include one or more of these options: write the answer; create a document that contains the answer; present your answer to the class; discuss your answer in a group; record the answer as audio or video using a webcam, smartphone, or portable media player; or post answers on a blog, wiki, or website.

Apply Your Knowledge

Reinforce the skills and apply the concepts you learned in this module.

Understanding Keys and Normalization

Instructions: Answer the following questions in the format specified by your instructor.

1. Figure 11–33 contains sample data for a Student table. Use this figure to answer the following:
   a. Is the table in first normal form (1NF)? Why or why not?
   b. Is the table in second normal form (2NF)? Why or why not?
   c. Is the table in third normal form (3NF)? Why or why not?
   d. Identify candidate keys for the table.

Student

SSN	Student_ID	Name	Major Department Code	Major Department Name
1111	123-6788	Theresa	CS	Computer Science
2222	346-8809	Juan	IT	Information Technology
3333	433-7676	Lee	CS	Computer Science
4444	654-4312	Barbara	ACC	Accounting

Figure 11–33

2. Figure 11–34 contains sample data for items and vendors who supply these items. In discussing the data with users, you find that item numbers – but not descriptions – uniquely identify items, and that vendor names uniquely identify vendors. Multiple vendors can supply the same item. For example, agate bookends can be purchased from either Atherton Group or Gift Specialties.

   a. Convert the data in Figure 11–34 into a relation in first normal form (1NF) using the shorthand representation used in this module.

   b. Identify all functional dependencies using the notation demonstrated in the module.

Item

Item Number	Description	Vendor Name	City	Wholesale Cost
3663	Agate Bookends	Atherton Group	Rock Hill	16.25
		Gift Specialties	Indian Land	16.20
4573	Crystal Growing Kit	Atherton Group	Rock Hill	6.75
		Gift Specialties	Indian Land	6.80
		Smith Distributors	Ballantyne	6.70

Figure 11–34

3. ✸ Using only the data in Figure 11–33, how could you identify the entities and attributes that would be the starting point for a database design?

Extend Your Knowledge

Extend the skills you learned in this module and experiment with new skills. You may need to use Help to complete the assignment.

Modifying a Database Design and Understanding Diagrams

Instructions: Answer the following questions in the format specified by your instructor.

1. Using the shorthand representation illustrated in this module, indicate the changes you would need to make to the PrattLast Associates database design shown in Figure 11–8 in order to support the following requirements:

   a. An account may not necessarily work with one account manager; it can work with several account managers.

   b. Hours and Total Hours do not vary based on account.

Continued >

Extend Your Knowledge *continued*

2. Using the shorthand representation illustrated in this module, indicate the changes you would need to make to the TDK Distributors data design shown in Figure 11–10 to support the following requirements:

   a. The price for an item does not change; it is the same for all customers.

   b. TDK also needs to keep track of the wholesale cost of an item.

3. Use the Access Relationships Report for the Marketing Analytics database shown in Figure 11–35 to answer the following:

   a. Identify the foreign keys in the Seminar Offerings table.

   b. What is the purpose of the Seminar Offerings table?

   c. What is the primary key of the Seminar Offerings table?

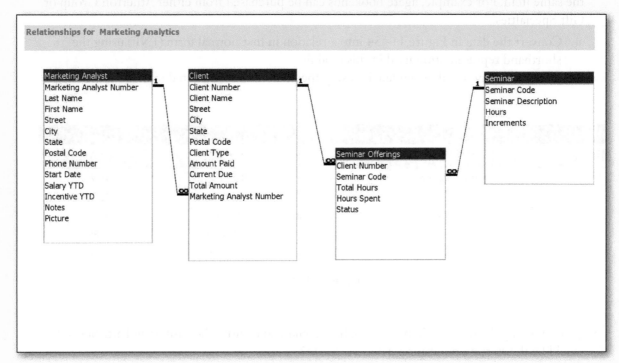

Figure 11–35

4. ✷ TDK Distributors has decided to add its suppliers to the database. One supplier can supply many items but an item has only one supplier. What changes would you need to make to the database design for TDK Distributors?

Expand Your World

Create a solution which uses cloud and web technologies, by learning and investigating on your own from general guidance.

Instructions: There are several websites that provide examples of database models, such as www.databaseanswers.org/data_models/index.htm. These models provide a good starting point for creating your own database design.

1. Create a blog, a Google document, or a Word document on OneDrive on which to store your assignment. Include your name and the current date at the beginning of the blog or document.

2. Access the www.databaseanswers.org/data_models/index.htm website or another website of your choice that provides data models.

3. Browse the different database models and select one in which you have an interest.

4. In your own words, create a scenario for which the database model would work. Study the model to see if you need to modify it to make it applicable to your scenario. If changes are necessary, document the required modifications.

5. ✸ Why did you select the model that you did? How easy was it to understand the entities, attributes, and relationships? Were the relations in 3NF?

In the Labs

Design, create, modify, and/or use a database following the guidelines, concepts, and skills presented in this module. Labs are listed in order of increasing difficulty. Labs 1 and 2, which increase in difficulty, require you to create solutions based on what you learned in the module; Lab 3 requires you to apply your creative thinking and problem solving skills to design and implement a solution.

Lab 1: Designing a Database for Sports Leagues

Instructions: Answer the following questions in the format specified by your instructor.

1. A database for a local community center that offers multiple sports leagues for adults must support the following requirements:

   a. For a league, store its number and name, for example, 072, Basketball. Each league has a participant cost associated with it, a start date for the league, and a maximum number of participants.

   b. For a participant, store his or her number, first name, last name, home telephone number, and mobile telephone number.

   One participant can enroll in many sports leagues, and one league can include many participants.

2. Based on these requirements:

   a. Identify and list the entities and attributes of those entities.

   b. Identify and list the functional dependencies.

   c. Create a set of third normal form (3NF) relations using the shorthand notation given in the module. Be sure to identify all primary keys and foreign keys appropriately.

   Submit your database design in the format specified by your instructor.

Continued >

STUDENT ASSIGNMENTS

In the Labs *continued*

3. ✳ Because each league plays at a different location, the community center director would like to add locations to the database. He would also like to include the participant's birth date. In which table(s) would you place these attributes?

Lab 2: **Normalizing a Client Relation**

Instructions: Answer the following questions in the format specified by your instructor.

Consider the following relation:

Client (Client#, ClientName, Balance Due, TherapistID, TherapistName, ServiceCode, ServiceDesc, ServiceFee, ServiceDate)

This is a relation concerning data about clients of physical therapy practice and the services the therapists perform for their clients. The following dependencies exist in Client:

Client# → ClientName, BalanceDue

TherapistID → TherapistName

ServiceCode → ServiceDesc, ServiceFee

Client#, TherapistID, ServiceCode → ServiceDate

1. Convert Client to 1NF based on the functional dependencies given.
2. Convert to a set of relations in 3NF.
3. ✳ The database design needs to include an attribute for the date of the client's last visit. In what table would you place this attribute?

Lab 3: **Consider This: Your Turn**

Designing a Database for Outdoor Adventure

Instructions: Outdoor Adventures is a small business that organizes day-long guided trips of New England. You have been asked to create a database to keep track of the trips and the guides who lead these trips as well as customers who reserve these trips. Use the concepts and techniques presented in this module to design a database to meet the following requirements:

Part 1:   The Outdoor Adventure database must support the following requirements:

   a.   For each guide, store his or her guide number, last name, first name, street address, city, state, postal code, telephone number, and date hired.
   b.   For each trip, store the trip ID number, the trip name, the location from which the trip starts, the state in which the trip originates, the trip distance, the maximum group size, the type of trip (hiking, biking, or paddling), and the guide number, first name, and last name of each guide. A guide may lead many trips and a trip may be led by many different guides.
   c.   For each customer, store the customer number, last name, first name, street address, city, state, postal code, and telephone number.
   d.   For each reservation, store the reservation number, the trip ID number, the trip date, the number of persons included in the reservation, and the customer number, first name, and last name of the customer who made the reservation.

Based on these requirements:

a. Identify and list the entities and attributes of those entities.
b. Identify and list the functional dependencies.
c. Create a set of third normal form (3NF) relations using the shorthand notation given in this module. Be sure to identify all primary keys and foreign keys appropriately.

Submit your database design in the format specified by your instructor.

Part 2: You made several decisions while designing this database. What was the rationale behind these decisions? Are there other requirements that would have been helpful to you in the design process?

Index

Note: **Bold** page numbers refer to pages where key terms are defined.

Index